French Poetry: The Renaissance through 1915

THE CRITICAL COSMOS SERIES

French Poetry: The Renaissance through 1915

Edited and with an introduction
by *HAROLD BLOOM*
Sterling Professor of the Humanities
Yale University

CHELSEA HOUSE PUBLISHERS
New York ◇ Philadelphia

© 1990 by Chelsea House Publishers, a division of
Main Line Book Co.

Introduction © 1990 by Harold Bloom

Printed and bound in the United States of America

10 9 8 7 6 5 4 3 2 1

Library of Congress Cataloging-in-Publication Data

French poetry: the Renaissance through 1915/edited with an
introduction by Harold Bloom.
    p. cm.—(The Critical cosmos series)
    Includes index.
    Summary: A collection of critical essays examining French
poetry from the Renaissance through 1915.
ISBN 0-87754-997-4
    1. French poetry—History and criticism. [1. French
poetry—History and criticism.] I. Bloom, Harold. II.
Series.
PQ405.F74 1987   87-11767
841'.009—dc19   CIP
                                               AC

Contents

Editor's Note

This volume brings together the best critical essays available in English upon French poetry (except for drama) from its true beginnings with Villon and Marguerite de Navarre through Apollinaire, who died fighting for France in World War I. I am grateful to Karin Cope and Chantal McCoy for their erudition and judgment in helping me to edit this volume.

My introduction studies the sequence of Hugo, Baudelaire, Mallarmé, and Rimbaud, emphasizing the role of Hugo as the inevitable point of departure for all who came after him.

The historic sequence begins with Jefferson Humphries' Gnostic interpretation of François Villon, emphasizing the psychic and sexual anarchy in Villon's violent vision. Robert D. Cottrell follows with his reading of Marguerite de Navarre's poetry, centering upon her rhetoric of tears, the falling cadence of her grief.

A very different rhetorical world opens in Maurice Scève's *Délie*, studied here by Elisabeth Guild, who deconstructs the sequence into "frames," with all their signs of fragmentation, plurality, and mobility. Ann Rosalind Jones sets forth the differences in the relation to male poetic tradition of the Renaissance women poets Louise Labé and Pernette du Guillet, who attempt to change the rules of the game of poetic influence.

Joachim Du Bellay's *Antiquités de Rome* is seen by Daniel Russell as a reconstruction of the cultural continuity of Rome by means of emblematic images. Ronsard's sonnets are analyzed by Terence C. Cave in terms of the poet's intelligent awareness of the incompatibility of poetry and experience. La Fontaine is celebrated in Ross Chambers's exposition on the delicious fable "Les Femmes et le secret."

We move to the Romantics with a meditation upon the consciousness of Lamartine by Georges Poulet, who finds in this poet without external forms an achieved impotence (as it were) not wholly unlike the celebrated "sterility" of Mallarmé. Alfred de Vigny is viewed by Martha Noel Evans as a dismantler of the mirror of life and so as akin to Poulet's Lamartine, each blanched by the "purity" of his poetic language.

The titanic Victor Hugo, strongest poet of his nation's tradition, is first introduced by Joan C. Kessler, who centers upon his problematic image of the Tower of Babel. Margery Sabin traces the difference between Hugo's assertions of the poet's spiritual power, and the more ambitious visions of the English High Romantic poets.

The *Gaspard de la nuit* of Aloysius Bertrand is analyzed by Richard Sieburth as a sequence of paratexts. Gérard de Nerval, purest of visionary poets, is first seen by Shoshana Felman as a transformer of hallucination into the narrative of *Aurélia*, and then is deconstructed in his *Sylvie* by Rodolphe Gasché.

Georges Poulet returns in a mapping of Musset's consciousness of the immortal moment of love. High priest of art for art's sake, Gautier is analyzed in his fantastic writings by Albert B. Smith, who finds in them the quest for an ideal beauty.

Baudelaire receives two sharply distinct homages, the first from the late Paul de Man, most distinguished of deconstructors, the second from the Marxist Fredric Jameson. De Man shows the negating effects of figurative language in Baudelaire, while Jameson sees the poet as a postmodernist of a transfigured Sublime that affirms what crushes the self.

Barbara Johnson reflects upon Mallarmé's intertextual struggles with his prime precursor, Baudelaire, while James Lawler explicates Mallarmé's "Toast funèbre." Verlaine's poetic diction is examined by Carol de Dobay Rifelj, who finds in his use of slang and familiar language a more innovative poet than the lover of Rimbaud generally is taken to be.

Corbière's parodistic relation to the great Hugo is studied by Robert L. Mitchell, after which the reader's share in Lautréamont's *Maldoror* is set forth by Robin Lydenberg. Three of Rimbaud's verse poems are read by Marshall Lindsay as instances of the poetics of the seer of *Une Saison en enfer* and the *Illuminations*. Karin J. Dillman follows with an analysis of Rimbaud's profound questioning of the subject, his dark insight that the I is always an other.

Jules Laforgue's ironic balance is praised by Warren Ramsey. In this book's final essay, Dennis G. Sullivan reads Apollinaire's poetry as an intuition that denies the efficacy of all ontological claims.

Introduction

In his *William Shakespeare* (1864), Hugo attempted to proclaim his own radical originality, as the prophet of French Romanticism:

> The Nineteenth century springs only from itself; it does not receive an impulse from any ancestor; it is the child of an idea . . . but the Nineteenth century has an august mother, the French Revolution.

Even as Shakespeare had no poetic father (though one might argue for Chaucer, noting the link between the Wife of Bath and Falstaff), so Hugo, the nineteenth century incarnate, denied any precursor except the Revolution. It is true that the Bible and Shakespeare counted for more in Hugo's poetry than any French forerunners, at least once the early effect of Chateaubriand rapidly wore away. Blake, Wordsworth, Coleridge, Shelley, and Keats, turning themselves away from Pope, had the native tradition of Spenser, Shakespeare, and Milton to sustain them, but Hugo and his contemporaries could not see themselves similarly as a renaissance of the Renaissance. Boileau could be defied by Keats, charmingly and convincingly, but French literary culture can no more eliminate the influence of Boileau than French thought can cease to be Cartesian, despite the tyranny of German philosophy in France since the student upheavals of the later 1960s.

I myself always recall, with amiable zest, a train ride back from Princeton to Yale that I enjoyed a decade or so ago with the leading theoretician of Gallic deconstruction. We were recent friends, had encountered one another while lecturing separately at Princeton, and fell into cultural debate on the train. Deploring a belated French modernism that wholly absorbed my friend, I urged the poetic strength of Victor Hugo as against that of the more fashionable Mallarmé. In honest amazement, my philosophic companion burst forth: "But, Harold, in France Victor Hugo is a poet read only by schoolchildren!"

It seems safe enough to prophesy that Hugo, like Shelley, always will bury his undertakers. He goes into English about as well as Shelley goes into French, so that there are no adequate translations of Hugo's poetry and there are not likely to be any. Yet curiously enough, Hugo is a poet who in some ways fits better into Anglo-American than into French literary tradition. He is, at his strongest, a mythopoeic or visionary poet akin to Blake and Shelley, as Swinburne first saw. Unfortunately, Hugo has nothing like Blake's conceptual powers and also he does not approximate the subtle, skeptical intellect of Shelley. Since he also lacked epic precursors in his own language, Hugo had the advantage neither of Blake's and Shelley's gifts, nor of their agonistic relationship to that mortal god, John Milton. Hugo had to become his own Milton, with rather mixed results, one must sadly admit, thinking of *La Fin de Satan* and *Dieu*. Astonishing as those curious epics are, they lack the authority of Hugo at his strongest, in "A Albert Dürer" and "Tristesse d'Olympio," "Sonnez, sonnez toujours" and "Booz endormi," "A Théophile Gautier" and "Orphée," and so many others. This is the authority of a Sublime directness: "Qu'il m'exauce. Je suis l'âme humaine chantant,/Et j'aime."

Whether or not table-rappings with assorted spooks sometimes helped to sabotage Hugo's eloquent directness, after 1853, is not clear to me. Seances seem to have been more benign for W. B. Yeats and James Merrill than they were for the already dangerously theomorphic Hugo. The spirits were tricky with Yeats, and are sometimes wicked with the urbane and kindly Merrill, but they seem to have been so thoroughly cowed by the overbearing Hugo as nearly everyone else was. Apocalyptic poetry is a dangerous genre, particularly if attempted at some length. Yeats shrewdly developed the dialectics of his eschatology in the two versions (1925, 1937) of his prose tract, *A Vision*, and then based apocalyptic lyrics like "The Second Coming" and "Leda and the Swan" upon the more sequestered exegetical work. Merrill, with insouciant audacity, follows Dante and Blake by incorporating his doctrinal speculations directly into *The Changing Light at Sandover*. Hugo is more puzzling, in that he never worked his preternatural revelations into a system, whether in prose or verse. Instead, he wrote titanic, fragmentary poems, that both expound and refuse to expound his cosmological imaginings. *La Fin de Satan*, *Dieu*, and much of *La Légende des siècles* form together the closest French equivalent to that great mode of English poetry of which *Paradise Lost* is the masterpiece, and Blake's *The Four Zoas*, *Milton*, and *Jerusalem*, Shelley's *Prometheus Unbound*, and Keats's two *Hyperion* fragments are the grand second wave.

La Fin de Satan began under the title of *Satan pardonné*, which is an oxymoron, since a pardoned Satan hardly could be Satan. But there is much that is oxymoronic in the design and the rhetoric of Hugo's epic fragments. This is accompanied by a consistent parataxis, doubtless biblical in its stylistic origins, but beautifully subversive in Hugo's later rhetoric, since his syntax thus refuses traditional distinctions between higher and lower orders, up and down, heaven and the abyss. Here is Satan in the night, limning his best night-piece in *La Fin de Satan:*

> Jadis, ce jour levant, cette lueur candide,
> C'était moi.—Moi!—J'étais l'archange au front splendide,
> La prunelle de feu de l'azur rayonnant.
> Durant le ciel, la vie et l'homme; maintenant
> Je suis l'astre hideux qui blanchit l'ossuaire.
> Je portais le flambeau, je traine le suaire;
> J'arrive avec la nuit dans ma main; et partout
> Où je vais, surgissant derrière moi, debout,
> L'hydre immense de l'ombre ouvre ses ailes noires.

The cunning power of this is that Hugo's Satan, unlike Milton's, is no different in value before and after his fall. The syntax and the tropological pattern combine to make equal the rising light with its white glow and the supposedly hideous star that casts a white glow upon the boneyard. Satan as torchbearer or Lucifer is one with Satan trailing the winding sheet and arriving with night in his hand. An archangel making all things golden is neither better nor worse than the being behind whom the great hydra of darkness opens its black wings. This Satan hardly requires pardon. It is as though, for the later Hugo, there are no opposites, provided that the Sublime be intense enough.

Texture rather than architectonics is the strength of the later Hugo in verse. The lack of an epic precursor in French, or at least one that he could recognize, cost him a great deal. I remember his apocalyptic poems as individual passages or moments, not as fully achieved designs. If he was not Blake or Shelley or Keats, he remains their peer in great, isolated fragments, visions of an abyss that he had found for himself. He wrote his own elegy partly in his lament for Gautier, where he hymns the departure (though in 1872) of his own century, the Romantic nineteenth:

> Passons; car c'est la loi; nul ne peut s'y soustraire;
> Tout penche; et ce grand siècle avec tous ses rayons
> Entre en cette ombre immense où pâles nous fuyons.
> Oh! quel farouche bruit font dans le crépuscule
> Les chênes qu'on abat pour le bûcher d'Hercule!
> Les chevaux de la mort se mettent à hennir,
> Et sont joyeux, car l'âge éclatant va finir;
> Ce siècle altier qui sut dompter le vent contraire,
> Expire . . . —Ô Gautier! toi, leur égal et leur frère,
> Tu pars après Dumas, Lamartine et Musset.

> L'onde antique est tarie où l'on rajeunissait;
> Comme il n'est plus de Styx il n'est plus de Jouvence.
> Le dur faucheur avec sa large lame avance
> Pensif et pas à pas vers le reste du blé;
> C'est mon tour; et la nuit emplit mon œil troublé
> Qui, devinant, hélas, l'avenir des colombes,
> Pleure sur des berceaux et sourit à des tombes.

The Hercules for whose pyre the great oaks are being filled so noisily is hardly Gautier, but is rather Booz (Boaz), whose eyes held light and grandeur, and who turned to God as naturally as he turned to himself, because the timelessness was already his own:

> Le vieillard, qui revient vers la source première,
> Entre aux jours éternels et sort des jours changeants;
> Et l'on voit de la flamme aux yeux des jeunes gens,
> Mais dans l'oeil du vieillard on voit de la lumière.

II

Sartre ended his book on Baudelaire by insisting that this poet, like Emerson's ideal being, made his own circumstances:

> But we should look in vain for a single circumstance for which he was not fully and consciously responsible. Every event was a reflection of that indecomposable totality which he was from the first to the last day of his life. He refused experience. Nothing came from outside to change him and he learned nothing.

Could there have been such a person? Can any poet refuse the experience of reading his precursors? Was Victor Hugo a circumstance for which Baudelaire was fully and consciously responsible? Valéry, who was (unlike Sartre) a theorist of poetic influence, thought otherwise:

> Thus Baudelaire regarded Victor Hugo, and it is not impossible to conjecture what he thought of him. Hugo reigned; he had acquired over Lamartine the advantage of infinitely more powerful and more precise *working materials*. The vast range of his diction, the diversity of his rhythms, the superabundance of his images, crushed all rival poetry. But his work sometimes made concessions to the vulgar, lost itself in prophetic eloquence and infinite apostrophes. He flirted with the crowd, he indulged in dialogues with God. The simplicity of his philosophy, the disproportion and incoherence of the developments, the frequent contrasts between the marvels of detail and the fragility of the subject, the inconsistency of the whole—everything, in a word, which could shock and thus instruct and orientate a pitiless young observer toward

his future personal art—all these things Baudelaire was to note in himself and separate from the admiration forced upon him by the magic gifts of Hugo, the impurities, the imprudences, the vulnerable points in his work—that is to say, the possibilities of life and the opportunities for fame which so great an artist left to be gleaned.

With some malice and a little more ingenuity than is called for, it would be only too tempting to compare Victor Hugo's poetry with Baudelaire's, with the object of showing how exactly *complementary* the latter is to the former. I shall say no more. It is evident that Baudelaire sought to do what Victor Hugo had not done; that he refrained from all the effects in which Victor Hugo was invincible; that he returned to a prosody less free and scrupulously removed from prose; that he pursued and almost always captured the production of *unbroken charm*, the inappreciable and quasi-transcendent quality of certain poems—but a quality seldom encountered, and rarely in its pure state, in the immense work of Victor Hugo. . . .

Hugo never ceased to learn by practice; Baudelaire, the span of whose life scarcely exceeded the *half* of Hugo's, developed in quite another manner. One would say he had to compensate for the probable brevity and foreshadowed insufficiency of the short space of time he had to live, by the employment of that critical intelligence of which I spoke above. A score of years were vouchsafed him to attain the peak of his own perfection, to discover his personal field and to define a specific form and attitude which would carry and preserve his name. Time was lacking to realize his literary ambitions by numerous experiments and an extensive output of works. He had to choose the shortest road, to limit himself in his gropings, to be sparing of repetitions and divergences. He had therefore to seek by means of analysis what he was, what he could do, and what he wished to do; and to unite, in himself, with the spontaneous virtues of a poet, the sagacity, the skepticism, the attention and reasoning faculty of a critic.

One can transpose this simply enough into very nearly any of the major instances of poetic influence in English. Attempt Wallace Stevens, a true peer of Valéry, but with a more repressed or disguised relation to Whitman than Baudelaire manifested towards Hugo:

> It is evident that Wallace Stevens sought to do what Walt Whitman had not done; that he refrained from all the effects in which Walt Whitman was invincible; that he returned to a prosody less free and scrupulously removed from prose; that he pursued and almost always captured the production of *unbroken charm*, the inappreciable and quasi-transcendent quality of certain poems—but a qual-

ity seldom encountered, and rarely in its pure state, in the immense work of Walt Whitman.

Valéry, unlike both Formalist and Post-Structuralist critics, understood that Hugo was to French poetry what Whitman was to American poetry and Wordsworth was to all British poetry after him: the inescapable precursor. Baudelaire's Hugo problem was enhanced because the already legendary poetic father was scarcely twenty years older than the gatherer of *Les Fleurs de mal*. All French literary movements are curiously belated in relation to Anglo-American literature. Current French sensibility of the school of Derrida is merely a revival of the Anglo-American literary Modernism of which Hugh Kenner remains the antiquarian celebrant. "Post-Structuralist Joyce" is simply Joyce as we read and discussed him when I was a graduate student, thirty-five years ago. In the same manner, the French Romanticism of Hugo in 1830 repeated (somewhat unknowingly) the movement of British sensibility that produced Wordsworth and Coleridge, Byron and Shelley and Keats, of whom the first two were poetically dead, and the younger three long deceased, well before Hugo made his revolution.

Baudelaire started with the declaration that the Romanticism of 1830 could not be the Romanticism (or anything else) of 1845. T. S. Eliot, as was inevitable, cleansed Baudelaire of Romanticism, baptized the poet an Original Sinner and a Neo-Classicist, and even went so far as to declare the bard of Lesbos a second Goethe. A rugged and powerful literary thinker, Baudelaire doubtless would have accepted these amiable distortions as compliments, but they do not help much in reading him now.

His attitude towards Hugo, always tinged with ambivalence, became at times savage, but a student of poetic influence learns to regard such a pattern as one of the major modes of misprision, of that strong misreading of strong poets that permits other strong poets to be born. *The Salon of 1845* blames the painter Boulanger on poor Hugo:

> Here we have the last ruins of the old romanticism—this is what it means to come at a time when it is the accepted belief that inspiration is enough and takes the place of everything else; this is the abyss to which the unbridled course of Mazeppa has led. It is M. Victor Hugo that has destroyed M. Boulanger—after having destroyed so many others; it is the poet that has tumbled the painter into the ditch. And yet M. Boulanger can paint decently enough—look at his portraits. But where on earth did he win his diploma as history-painter and inspired artist? Can it have been in the prefaces and odes of his illustrious friend?

That Baudelaire was determined not to be destroyed by Hugo was clear enough, a determination confirmed by the rather invidious comparison of Delacroix to Hugo in *The Salon of 1846:*

Up to the present, Eugène Delacroix has met with injustice. Criticism, for him, has been bitter and ignorant; with one or two noble exceptions, even the praises of his admirers must often have seemed offensive to him. Generally speaking, and for most people, to mention Eugène Delacroix is to throw into their minds goodness knows what vague ideas of ill-directed fire, of turbulence, of hazardous inspiration, of confusion, even; and for those gentlemen who form the majority of the public, pure chance, that loyal and obliging servant of genius, plays an important part in his happiest compositions. In that unhappy period of revolution of which I was speaking a moment ago and whose numerous errors I have recorded, people used often to compare Eugène Delacroix to Victor Hugo. They had their romantic poet; they needed their painter. This necessity of going to any length to find counterparts and analogues in the different arts often results in strange blunders; and this one proves once again how little people knew what they were about. Without any doubt the comparison must have seemed a painful one to Eugène Delacroix, if not to both of them; for if my definition of romanticism (intimacy, spirituality and the rest) places Delacroix at its head, it naturally excludes M. Victor Hugo. The parallel has endured in the banal realm of accepted ideas, and these two preconceptions still encumber many feeble brains. Let us be done with these rhetorical ineptitudes once and for all. I beg all those who have felt the need to create some kind of aesthetic for their own use and to deduce causes from their results, to make a careful comparison between the productions of these two artists.

M. Victor Hugo, whose nobility and majesty I certainly have no wish to belittle, is a workman far more adroit than inventive, a labourer much more correct than *creative*. Delacroix is sometimes clumsy, but he is essentially creative. In all his pictures, both lyric and dramatic, M. Victor Hugo lets one see a system of uniform alignment and contrasts. With him even eccentricity takes symmetrical forms. He is in complete possession of, and coldly employs, all the modulations of rhyme, all the resources of antithesis and all the tricks of apposition. He is a composer of the decadence or transition, who handles his tools with a truly admirable and curious dexterity. M. Hugo was by nature an academician even before he was born, and if we were still living in the time of fabulous marvels, I would be prepared to believe that often, as he passed before their wrathful sanctuary, the green lions of the Institut would murmur to him in prophetic tones, "Thou shalt enter these portals."

For Delacroix justice is more sluggish. His works, on the contrary, are poems—and great poems, *naïvely* conceived and executed with the usual insolence of genius. In the works of the former there is nothing left to guess at, for he takes so much pleasure in exhibiting his skill that he omits not one blade of grass nor even the reflection of a street-lamp. The latter in his works throws open immense vistas to the most adventurous imaginations. The first enjoys a certain calmness, let us rather say a certain detached egoism, which causes an unusual coldness and moderation to hover above his poetry—qualities which the dogged and melancholy passion of the second, at grips with the obstinacies of his craft, does not always permit him to retain. One starts with detail, the other with an intimate understanding of his subject; from which it follows that one only captures the skin, while the other tears out the entrails. Too earthbound, too attentive to the superficies of nature, M. Victor Hugo has become a painter in poetry; Delacroix, always respectful of his ideal, is often, without knowing it, a poet in painting.

This is grand polemical criticism, deliciously unfair to the greatest French poet ever. Hugo is now adroit, but not inventive; a correct laborer, but not creative. Few critical remarks are as effectively destructive as "with him even eccentricity takes symmetrical forms." Hugo is somehow a mere, earthbound painter of nature and an academic impostor doomed from birth to be an institutional pillar. Baudelaire's stance towards Hugo over the next decade became yet more negative, so that it is at first something of a surprise to read his letters to the exiled Hugo in 1859. Yet the complex rhetoric of the letters is again wholly human, all-too-human, in the agon of poetic influence:

> So now I owe you some explanations. I know your works by heart and your prefaces show me that I've overstepped the theory you generally put forward on the alliance of morality and poetry. But at a time when society turns away from art with such disgust, when men allow themselves to be debased by purely utilitarian concerns, I think there's no great harm in exaggerating a little in the other direction. It's possible that I've protested too much. But that was in order to obtain what was needed. Finally, even if there were a little Asiatic fatalism mixed up in my reflections I think that would be pardonable. The terrible world in which we live gives one a taste for isolation and fatality.
>
> What I wanted to do above all was to bring the reader's thoughts back to that wonderful little age whose true king you were, and which lives on in my mind like a delicious memory of childhood. . . .
>
> The lines I enclose with this letter have been knocking around in my brain for a long time. The second piece was written with the *aim of imitating you* (laugh at my absurdity, it makes me laugh myself) after I'd reread some poems in your collections, in which

such magnificent charity blends with such touching familiarity. In art galleries I've sometimes seen wretched art students copying the works of the masters. Well done or botched, these imitations sometimes contained, unbeknownst to the students, something of their own character, be it great or common. Perhaps (perhaps!) that will excuse my boldness. When *The Flowers of Evil* reappears, swollen with three times as much material as the Court suppressed, I'll have the pleasure of inscribing at the head of these poems the name of the poet whose works have taught me so much and brought such pleasure to my youth.

"That wonderful little age" doubtless referred to the Romanticism of the Revolution of 1830, that enchanted moment when Victor Hugo was king. But the true reference is to the nine-year-old Baudelaire, who found in his precursor "a delicious memory of childhood," and no mere likeness. When Baudelaire goes on to speak of imitation he cannot forbear the qualification "something of their own character, great or common." A few months later, sending his poem "The Swan" to Hugo, he asked that the poem be judged "with your paternal eyes." But, a year later, Baudelaire again condemned Hugo for "his concern with contemporary events . . . the belief in progress, the salvation of mankind by the use of balloons, etc."

The whip of ambivalence lashed back and forth in Baudelaire. Though a believer in salvation through balloons, the bardic Hugo was also, in his bad son's estimate, a force of nature: "No other artist is so universal in scope, more adept at coming into contact with the forces of the universe, more disposed to immerse himself in nature." That might seem definitive, but later Baudelaire allowed himself this diatribe, which hardly dents the divine precursor:

> Hugo thinks a great deal about Prometheus. He has placed an imaginary vulture on a breast that is never lacerated by anything more than the flea-bites of his own vanity. . . .
>
> Hugo-the-Almighty always has his head bowed in thought; no wonder he never sees anything except his own navel.

It is painful to read this; more painful still to read the references to Hugo in Baudelaire's letters of 1865–66. One moment, in its flash of a healthier humor, renders a grand, partly involuntary tribute to the normative visionary who both inspired and distressed Baudelaire:

> It appears that he and the Ocean have quarreled! Either he has not the strength to bear the Ocean longer, or the Ocean has grown weary of his presence.

To confront, thus again, the rock-like ego of that force of nature, your poetic father, is to admit implicitly that he returns in his own colors, and not in your own.

Proust, in a letter to Jacques Rivière, compared Baudelaire to Hugo and clearly gave the preference to Baudelaire. What Wallace Stevens, following Baudelaire, called the profound poetry of the poor and of the dead, seemed to Proust wholly Baudelaire's, and not Hugo's. But as love poets, Hugo and Baudelaire seemed more equal, even perhaps with Hugo the superior. Proust said he preferred Hugo to Baudelaire in a great common trope:

> Elle me regarda de ce regard suprême
> Qui reste à la beauté quand nous en triômphons.

> She gazed at me with that supreme look
> Which endures in beauty even while it is vanquished.
> > (Hugo)

> Et cette gratitude infinie et sublime
> Qui sort de la paupière ainsi qu'un long soupir

> And that sublime and infinite gratitude
> which glistens under the eyelids like a sigh.
> > (Baudelaire)

Both tropes are superb; I too prefer Hugo's, but why did Proust have that preference, or pretend to have it? Both beauties have been vanquished, but Hugo's by the potent Victor himself, while Baudelaire's Hippolyta reflects the triumph of Delphine, who stares at her victim with the shining eyes of a lioness. Proust, perhaps rather slyly, says he prefers the heterosexual trope to the Lesbian one, but does not say why. Yet, superb critic that he was, he helps us to expand Valéry's insight. Resolving to do precisely what Hugo had not done, Baudelaire became the modern poet of Lesbos, achieving so complex a vision of that alternative convention of Eros as to usurp forever anyone else's representation of it:

> Comme un bétail pensif sur le sable couchées,
> Elles tournent leurs yeux vers l'horizon des mers,
> Et leurs pieds se cherchant et leurs mains rapprochées
> Ont de douces langueurs et des frissons amers.

> Les unes, cœurs épris de longues confidences,
> Dans le fond des bosquets où jasent les ruisseaux,
> Vont épelant l'amour des craintives enfances
> Et creusent le bois vert des jeunes arbrisseaux;

> D'autres, comme des sœurs, marchent lentes et graves
> A travers les rochers pleins d'apparitions,
> Où saint Antoine a vu surgir comme des laves
> Les seins nus et pourprés de ses tentations;

Il en est, aux lueurs des résines croulantes,
Qui dans le creux muet des vieux antres païens
T'appellent au secours de leurs fièvres hurlantes,
O Bacchus, endormeur des remords anciens!

Et d'autres, dont la gorge aime les scapulaires,
Qui, recélant un fouet sous leurs longs vêtements,
Mêlent, dans le bois sombre et les nuits solitaires,
L'écume du plaisir aux larmes des tourments.

O vierges, ô démons, ô monstres, ô martyres,
De la réalité grands esprits contempteurs,
Chercheuses d'infini, dévotes et satyres,
Tantôt pleines de cris, tantôt pleines de pleurs,

Vous que dans votre enfer mon âme a poursuivies,
Pauvres sœurs, je vous aime autant que je vous plains,
Pour vos mornes douleurs, vos soifs inassouvies,
Et les urnes d'amour dont vos grands cœurs sont pleins!

> Pensive as cattle resting on the beach,
> they are staring out to sea; their hands and feet
> creep toward each other imperceptibly
> and touch at last, hesitant then fierce.
>
> How eagerly some, beguiled by secrets shared,
> follow a talkative stream among the trees,
> spelling out their timid childhood's love
> and carving initials in the tender wood;
>
> others pace as slow and grave as nuns
> among the rocks where Anthony beheld
> the purple breasts of his temptations rise
> like lava from the visionary earth;
>
> some by torchlight in the silent caves
> consecrated once to pagan rites
> invoke—to quench their fever's holocaust—
> Bacchus, healer of the old regrets;
>
> others still, beneath their scapulars,
> conceal a whip that in the solitude
> and darkness of the forest reconciles
> tears of pleasure with the tears of pain.
>
> Virgins, demons, monsters, martyrs, all
> great spirits scornful of reality,
> saints and satyrs in search of the infinite,
> racked with sobs or loud in ecstasy,

you whom my soul has followed to your hell,
Sisters! I love you as I pity you
for your bleak sorrows, for your unslaked thirsts,
and for the love that gorges your great hearts!

Richard Howard's superb translation greatly assists my inner ear, in-adequate for the nuances of Baudelaire's French, in the labor of appre-hending what Erich Auerbach memorably spoke of as Baudelaire's aesthetic dignity, that all-but-unique fusion of Romantic pathos and classical irony, so clearly dominant in these immense quatrains. Yet I would place the emphasis elsewhere, upon that psychological acuity in which Baudelaire surpasses nearly all poets, Shakespeare excepted. Freud, speculating upon female homosexuality, uttered the grand and plaintive cry, "we find mas-culinity vanishing into activity and femininity into passivity, and that does not tell us enough." Baudelaire does tell us enough, almost more than enough, even as Melanie Klein came after Freud and Karl Abraham to tell us much more than enough. The "damned women," really little children, play at being masculine and feminine, for Baudelaire's great insight is that Lesbianism transforms the erotic into the aesthetic, transforms compulsion into a vain play that remains compulsive. "Scornful of reality" and so of the reality principle that is our consciousness of mortality, Baudelaire's great spirits search out the infinite and discover that the only infinity is the hell of repetition. One thinks back to Delphine and Hippolyta; Baudelaire sees and shows that Delphine is the daughter revenging herself upon the mother, even as Hippolyta revenges herself upon the mother in quite an-other way. When Hippolyta cries out, "Let me annihilate myself upon/ your breast and find the solace of a grave!" then we feel that Baudelaire has made Melanie Klein redundant, perhaps superfluous. The revenge upon the mother is doubtless Baudelaire's revenge upon his own mother, but more profoundly it is the aesthetic revenge upon nature. In Baudelaire's own case, was it not also the revenge upon that force of nature, too con-versant with ocean, that victorious poetic father, the so-often reviled but never forgotten Victor Hugo?

III

Like all true poets, Verlaine is a poet of death, but death for Mallarmé
means precisely the discontinuity between the personal self and the voice
that speaks in the poetry from the other bank of the river, beyond death.
—PAUL DE MAN

How much discontinuity can there be between a poet's personal self and the voice that goes on speaking in her poetry after she herself is dead? The question is itself figurative, since discontinuity, in this context, is pro-fessedly a trope for death, an irony or allegory rather than a synecdoche or symbol. Poet's elegies, frequently for other poets, notoriously are elegies for the later poet's own poetic self. Spenser for Sidney; Milton for the minor versifier Edward King; Shelley for Keats; Arnold for Clough; Swinburne for Baudelaire—these follow a common pattern, in which the elegist's concern has little to do with the dead poet. Whitman lamenting Lincoln; Wallace Stevens meditating upon his friend Henry Church; Hart Crane praising the urn of the painter Ernest Nelson—these depart from the pattern, because of the American difference, first established by Emerson in his essays and addresses.

The grandest elegy of poet for poet in the French tradition is Hugo's farewell to Gautier, but Mallarmé is generally taken as the central elegist because of his Homages and Tombs: for Poe, Baudelaire, Verlaine, and Wagner. One might propose Paul Valéry for the distinction, not in his verse, but in his copious prose memorializations of his crucial precursor. In his "Note and Digression" (1919) written a quarter century after his study of Leonardo, Valéry set forth his vision of writing with exemplary clarity:

> In the case of writing, however, the author feels himself to be at once the *source* of energy, the *engineer*, and the *restraints*. One part of him is impulsion; another foresees, organizes, moderates, suppresses; a third part (logic and memory) maintains the conditions, preserves the connections, and assures some fixity to the *calculated* design. *To write* should mean to construct, as precisely and solidly as possible, a machine of language in which the released energy of the mind is used in overcoming *real* obstacles; hence the writer must be divided against himself. That is the only respect in which, strictly speaking, the whole man acts as *author*. Everything else is not *his*, but belongs to a part of him that has escaped. Between the emotion or initial intention and its natural ending, which is disorder, vagueness, and forgetting—the destiny of all thinking— it is his task to introduce obstacles created by himself, so that, being interposed, they may struggle with the purely transitory nature of psychic phenomena to win a measure of renewable action, a share of independent existence.

Is the presence of the precursor in one's own work also an obstacle created by oneself? Is the writer divided against herself in a wholly autonomous way? Valéry, beautifully consistent, persuaded himself of this, but should he persuade us? "Opposites are born from opposites," he observes in his remarkably influential "Letter about Mallarmé," where he even introduces (without developing) the evasive notions of "the influence of a mind on itself and of a work on its author." If we substitute "Valéry" for "Mallarmé," and add "Mallarmé" to "the Romantic poets and Baudelaire," then this famous paragraph of Valéry ostensibly on Mallarmé becomes a self-analysis:

So it was that Mallarmé, developing in himself a few qualities of the Romantic poets and Baudelaire—selecting whatever they offered that was most exquisitely finished, making it his constant rule to obtain at every point the sort of results that in them were rare, exceptional, and produced as if purely by chance—little by little wrought out a highly individual *manner* from this obstinacy in choosing the best and this rigor in exclusion; and then went on to deduce from them a doctrine and problems that, in addition *to being completely novel, were prodigiously foreign to the modes of thinking and feeling known to his fathers and brothers in poetry.* For the direct desire, the instinctive or traditional (and in either case unreflecting) activity of his predecessors, he substituted an artificial conception, minutely reasoned and obtained by a certain sort of analysis.

In his Notebooks, Valéry insisted that "I was struck by Mallarmé. I admired—from a distance. I loved him. I rethought him. I felt and developed my difference." Yet in a letter to Albert Thibaudet, Valéry wrote, "I knew Mallarmé, *after* having undergone his influence to the limit, and at the very moment when in my own mind I wanted to guillotine all literature." The statements are subtly irreconcilable, even by the subtlest of minds, Valéry's. In a further letter to Thibaudet, rather less interestingly, Valéry says, "as to Mallarmé's influence, my view briefly is that it was almost nonexistent."

Concerning Mallarmé's *Un Coup de dés,* Valéry extravagantly observed, "He has undertaken finally to raise a printed page to the power of the midnight sky." Were this remarked of *Hamlet* or of *Paradise Lost,* it would be hyperbolic, but it helped set the standard for Mallarmé's critical admirers, who lead me to expect such astonishing displays of unprecedented poetic power that the actual pages of Mallarmé are liable to be somewhat disappointing. Since such luminaries as Lacan and Derrida seem to me closer to Mallarmé than they are to Nietzsche or Freud, it becomes difficult not to read Mallarmé through Hegelian lenses or even as so many Heideggerian vistas. None of this is fair to Mallarmé or to the American reader who is not a faithful follower of Gallic deconstruction. *Hérodiade* seems to me to find its authentic equivalents in Tennyson, Mallarmé's older contemporary, particularly in his great monologues "Tithonus" and "Lucretius." The poetic metaphysics of solipsism, might, and death are curiously compounded by both visionaries, as they are by Walt Whitman in America. That peculiar anguish of poetic creation, more striking in Mallarmé than in Baudelaire, finds its strong analogue in the horror of self-consciousness in Tennyson's "Lucretius" and in Whitman as he ebbs with the ocean of life.

Several of the critics collected in my *Modern Critical Views: Mallarmé* present Mallarmé as the unique poet of discontinuity, negativity, and a lyricism released both from subjectivity and from referentiality. Sometimes I reflect that what we now call symbolist or modernist poetry in France is what we still call Victorian poetry in Great Britain and the work of the American Renaissance here. Much of what Leo Bersani locates in Rimbaud and Mallarmé, or Paul de Man in Mallarmé alone, is precisely akin to what perceptive readers find in Browning, Tennyson, and Whitman. They, rather than the dreadful Poe, are the original and vital continuators of Blake and Wordsworth, Shelley and Keats, even as Baudelaire, Rimbaud, and Mallarmé were the crucial continuators of Hugo and French Romanticism. The blinkers of Anglo-American literary modernism, of the Eliot-Pound era, do not afflict our critical vision now in America, but they order these matters differently in literary France, where everything has been belated at least from Romanticism on and where they still discover *Finnegans Wake* daily.

IV

Rimbaud, heir of both Hugo and Baudelaire, potentially was a stronger poet than either, just as Hart Crane, influenced by Eliot and Stevens, possessed poetic gifts that could have transcended the work of both precursors. Crane's identification with Rimbaud takes on a particular poignancy in this context, reminding us of imaginative losses as great as those involved in the early deaths of Shelley and of Keats. The scandal of Rimbaud, which would have been considerable in any nation's poetic tradition, was magnified because of the relative decorum, in terms of form and rhetoric, of French Romantic poetry, let alone of the entire course of French poetic tradition. A crisis in French poetry would seem a ripple in the Anglo-American tradition, which is endlessly varied and heterodox.

Except for Rimbaud and a few more recent figures, French poetry does not have titanic eccentrics who establish entirely new norms. Rimbaud was a great innovator within French poetry, but would have seemed less so had he written in the language of William Blake and William Wordsworth, Robert Browning and Walt Whitman. *A Season in Hell* comes more than eighty years after *The Marriage of Heaven and Hell*, and the *Illuminations* does not deconstruct the poetic self any more radically than do the Browning monologues and *Song of Myself*. One must be absolutely modern, yes, and a century after Rimbaud it is clear that no one ever is going to be more absolutely modern than the poet of *The Prelude* and the crisis lyrics of 1802. I once believed that the true difference between English and French poetry was the absence of French equivalents of Chaucer and Spenser, Shakespeare and Milton. A larger difference, I now believe, is Wordsworth, whose astonishing originality ended a continuous tradition that had gone unbroken between Homer and Goethe.

Rimbaud had strong precursors in the later Hugo and in Baudelaire, but so great was Rimbaud's potential that he would have benefited by an even fiercer agon, like the one Wordsworth conducted with Milton and to a lesser extent with Shakespeare. The strongest French poets, down to Valéry, finally seem to confront a composite precursor, Boileau-Descartes, part classical critic, part philosopher. That develops very different urgencies from those ensuing when you must wrest your literary space from Milton or Wordsworth. The difference, even in the outcast Rimbaud, sets certain limits both to rhetoric and to vision.

Those limits, critics agree, come closest to being transcended, in very different ways, in *Une Saison en enfer* and *Les Illuminations.* Leo Bersani, impressively arguing for the "simplicity" of the *Illuminations,* affirms that Rimbaud's greatness is in his negations. Making poetry mean as little as possible is thus seen as Rimbaud's true ambition. If Rimbaud's "The I is another" is the central formula, then the *Illuminations* becomes the crucial work. But since poetry, like belief, takes place between truth and meaning, the Rimbaldian-Bersanian dream of literary negation may be only a dream. What would a poem be if it were, as Bersani hopes, "non-referential, non-relational, and devoid of attitudes, feelings and tones"? Bersani is the first to admit that the *Saison* is anything but that; it overwhelmingly reveals a coherent self, though hardly one of durable subjectivity. The trope and topos we call "voice" is so strong in *Saison* that we must judge it to be a High Romantic prose poem, whatever we take the *Illuminations* to be.

Saison, far more than Blake's *Marriage,* is always in danger of falling back into the normative Christianity that Rimbaud wants to deny, and that he evidently ceased to deny only upon his death bed. Kristin Ross, in a brilliant exegesis, reads *Saison* as opening out onto a sociohistorical field of which presumably Marcuse, in the name of Freud, was a prophet. I hear *Eros and Civilization* in Ross's eloquent summation of Rimbaud's stance as, "I *will be* a worker—but only at the moment when work, as we know it, has come to an end." If Bersani beautifully idealizes Rimbaud's aesthetic ambition, then Ross nobly idealizes his supposed socialization, though in a post-apocalyptic beyond. I am condemned to read Rimbaud from the perspective of Romanticism, as does John Porter Houston, and the poet I read has all the disorders of romantic vision, but much of the meanings as well, and they hardly seem to me social meanings.

So much the worse for the wood that finds it is a violin, or the brass that finds it is a bugle, or the French boy of yeoman stock who at sixteen could write "Le Bateau ivre," transuming Baudelaire's "Le Voyage." Rimbaud's violent originality, from "Le Bateau ivre" on, drives not against meaning but against anyone whatsoever, even Baudelaire, bequeathing Rimbaud any meaning that is not already his own. More even than the later Victor Hugo, to whom he grudgingly granted the poetic faculty of Vision, Rimbaud could tolerate no literary authority. Perhaps if you could combine the visionary Hugo and Baudelaire into a single poet, Rimbaud would have had a precursor who might have induced in him some useful anxiety, but the Anglo-American poetic habit of creating for oneself an imaginary, composite poetic forerunner was not available to Rimbaud.

Barely two years after "Le Bateau ivre," Rimbaud had finished *Une Saison en enfer.* Blake is supposed to have written "How Sweet I Roam'd from Field to Field" before he was fourteen, but except for Blake there is no great poet as precocious as Rimbaud in all of Western literary history. Like Blake a poet of extraordinary power at fourteen, Rimbaud quite unlike Blake abandoned poetry at nineteen. A trader and gunrunner in Africa, dead at thirty-seven, having written no poetry in the second half of his life, Rimbaud necessarily became and remains the mythical instance of the modern poet as the image of alienation. The myth obscures the deeper traditionalism of *Saison* in particular. Despite the difference implicit in the belated Romanticism of France, Rimbaud is as High Romantic as Blake or Shelley, or as Victor Hugo.

Une Saison en enfer has been called either a prose poem or a *récit*; it could also be named a miniature "anatomy" in Northrop Frye's sense of that genre. Perhaps it ought to be regarded as a belated Gnostic Gospel, like its hidden model, the canonical Gospel of John, a work which I suspect was revised away from its original form, one where the Word became, not flesh, but *pneuma,* and dwelt among us. Of all Rimbaud's writings, the *Saison* is most like a Hermetic Scripture. Rimbaud had never heard of Blake, who had promised the world his Bible of Hell, but *Saison* in its form always reminds me of *The Marriage of Heaven and Hell,* though it is very different in spirit from that curiously genial instance of apocalyptic satire.

In no way is it condescending to call *Saison* also the Gospel of Adolescence, particularly when we remember that Rousseau had invented that interesting transition, since literature affords no traces of it before him. To think of Rousseau reading *Saison* is grotesque, but in a clear sense Rimbaud indeed is one of Rousseau's direct descendants. Rimbaud doubtless attempted to negate every inheritance, but how could Rimbaud negate Romanticism? His negation of Catholicism is nothing but Romantic, particularly in its ambivalences.

The pattern unfolded in the nine sections of *Saison* would have been familiar to any Alexandrian Gnostic of the second century A.D. Rimbaud begins with a Fall that is also a catastrophic Creation, abandoning behind him the feast of life and yet remembering "la clef du festin ancien," the key of charity. The feast must therefore be a communion table, the pleroma or fullness from which Rimbaud has fallen away into the Gnostic kenoma, or emptiness of Hell that is simple, everyday bodily existence. Satan, in *Saison,* is the Gnostic Demiurge rather than the Catholic Devil, but then it is soon clear enough that Rimbaud himself, insofar as there is "himself," is a Demiurge also, a peasant or serf Demiurge, as it were. Perhaps Rimbaud's largest irony is his "Je ne puis comprendre la révolte," since the serfs rose up only to plunder. The medieval yearnings of the "Mauvais sang" section all resemble the rapaciousness of wolves against an animal they have not killed, and so the wolf Rimbaud, his pagan blood returning, is now passed by:

Le sang païen revient! L'Esprit est proche, pourquoi Christ ne m'aide-t-il pas, en donnant à mon âme noblesse et liberté. Hélas! l'Evangile a passé! l'Evangile! l'Evangile.

J'attends Dieu avec gourmandise. Je suis de race inférieure de toute éternité.

The Holy Ghost is near, but the gluttonous waiting-for-God only guarantees Christ's withholding of charity. Nobility and freedom do not come to the serf lusting for a preternatural salvation. A riot of barbarism is therefore preferable to a supposed civilization in a world bereft of revelation. This is the dialectic of libertine Gnosticism, and reminds me that the American work closest to Rimbaud in spirit is Nathanael West's *Miss Lonelyhearts*, with its superbly squalid version of the ancient Gnostic doctrine that Gershom Scholem grimly called "Redemption through Sin." Rimbaud peals throughout the rest of his "Bad Blood" section the iron music of atavism, in a full-scale justification of his own systematic derangement of the senses, only to collapse afterwards into the night of a real hell. Rimbaud's Hell is shot through with glimpses of divinity and seems to be married to Heaven in a literal way very different from Blake's ironic dialectic. God and Satan appear to be different names for one and the same spirit of lassitude, and Rimbaud thus prepares himself for his deepest descent, into delirium and its memories of his life of intimacy with Verlaine.

When I think of *Saison* I remember first the sick brilliance of Verlaine, the Foolish Virgin, addressing Rimbaud, the Infernal Bridegroom. If *Saison* has any common readers, in the Johnsonian sense, what else would they remember? Rimbaud, had he wished to, could have been the most consistently savage humorist in the French language. Poor Verlaine is permanently impaled as that masochistic trimmer, the Foolish Virgin, unworthy either of salvation or damnation. The authority of this impaling is augmented by the portrait of the Infernal Bridegroom's forays into poetic alchemy, which are surely to be read as being just as ridiculous as the Foolish Virgin's posturings. So strong is the Rimbaud myth that his own repudiations of divinity and magic do not altogether persuade us. Thinking back to *Saison*, we all grimace wryly at Verlaine as Foolish Virgin, while remembering with aesthetic respect those verbal experiments that Rimbaud renounces so robustly.

To climb out of Hell, Rimbaud discovers that he must cast off his own Gnostic dualism, which means his not wholly un-Johannine Gnostic Christianity. Much of the sections "L'Impossible" and "L'Eclair" are given to the quest away from Christianity, or rather the only Christianity that seems available. But since the quest involves those two great beasts of nineteenth-century Europe, Transcendental Idealism and the Religion of Science, Rimbaud discovers that neither God nor Rimbaud is safely mocked. "Matin," following these dismissed absurdities, first restores Rimbaud's Gnosticism, his sense that what is best and oldest in him goes back to before the Creation-Fall. Hailing the birth of the new labor, the new wisdom, Rimbaud moves into his remarkable "Adieu," with its notorious motto: "Il faut être absolument moderne," the epigraph to the life's work of Rimbaud's Gnostic heir, Hart Crane. No longer a magus or an angel, Rimbaud is given back to the earth, a peasant again, like his ancestors. To think of the earth hardly seems a Gnostic formulation, and the famous closing passage of *Saison* abandons Gnosticism once and for all in an extraordinary breakthrough into visionary monism:

> "—j'ai vu l'enfer des femmes là-bas;—et il me sera loisible de *posséder la verité dans une âme et un corps.*"

I take it that Rimbaud saw *down there*—in his relation with Verlaine—"the hell of women," precisely the Oedipal romance that he sought to flee. Possessing the truth in a single mind and a single body—one's own—is a narcissistic revelation akin to that of Walt Whitman's at the close of *Song of Myself.* Christianity *and* Gnosticism alike are rejected, and so are both heterosexuality and homosexuality. *Saison* ends with an inward turning closer to Whitman than to Hugo or to Baudelaire:

> Cependant c'est la veille. Recevons tous les influx de vigueur et de tendresse réelle. Et à l'aurore, armés d'une ardente patience, nous entrerons aux splendides villes.

It is a passage worthy of the poet whom the late James Wright called "our father, Walt Whitman." We can hardly murmur "our father, Arthur Rimbaud," but we can remember Hart Crane's equal devotion to Whitman and to Rimbaud, and we can be grateful again to Crane for teaching us something about our ancestry.

François Villon, the Misfit

Jefferson Humphries

Nous cognoissons que ce monde est prison
(We know this world to be a prison)
—VILLON, translated by Galway Kinnell

THE GENRE OF *LE LAIS*

Villon is best known for two long poems, *Le Lais* and *Le Testament*, in both of which a dying narrator makes bequests to friends and enemies. The latter poem is larger, more mature, and therefore richer, but the *Lais* contains all of Villon's obsessions in a limited volume of words, and for that reason I will use a close reading of it to gain entry to the other works. Mock testaments were a literary commonplace of the time. The form reflects the fusion which medieval theology had effected of the moment of death and the moment of judgment, death as the moment at which the good and evil of a lifetime were tallied up, weighed in the balance. In the fifteenth century, it was believed that an individual's destiny in the afterlife depended on his state of mind at the time of this inventory. The drama of salvation or perdition was concurrent with the individual's shedding his possessions, singling out others for reward or retribution, his last look back at his life, works, and goods.

> God and his court are there to observe how the dying man conducts himself during this trial—a trial he must endure before he breathes his last and which will determine his fate in eternity. This test consists of a final temptation. The dying man will see his entire life as it is contained in the book, and he will be tempted either by despair over his sins, by the vainglory of his good deeds, or by the passionate love for things and persons. His attitude during this fleeting moment will erase at once all the sins of his life if he wards off temptation or, on the contrary, will cancel out all his

From *The Otherness Within: Gnostic Readings in Marcel Proust, Flannery O'Connor, and François Villon.* © 1983 by Louisiana State University Press.

good deeds if he gives way. The final test has replaced the Last Judgment.

(Philippe Ariès, *Western Attitudes toward Death from the Middle Ages to the Present*)

A will, as a record of a man's reflections on his goods, friends, enemies, the accumulated detritus of a life, became a highly significant document, in a spiritual sense, one notarized by death itself.

The usual testament-poem was satirical and obscene. The anonymous "Pig's Testament" bequeaths the porker's "bones to the dicemaker, his feet to the errand runner, and his penis to the priest" (G. Kinnell, *The Poems of François Villon*). Villon's tone, however, is one of both pathos and fierce sarcasm. All in all, he takes the form very seriously and in a manner consistent with the popular idea that the moment of death gave meaning to an individual's life, that death shaped life into a clear, complete narration, with beginning, middle, and end. Death revealed the sense, the form which life had obscured. In all his poetry, Villon seeks to make sense of himself, to puzzle out his life, using the authority of death. Of course, he was not really dying when he wrote them. It is virtually certain, however, that he was, when he wrote the longer *Testament*, all the things he says he was— sick, impotent, in pain, hoarse, prematurely old. In the *Lais*, dying is rather a metaphor for having been spurned in love, for loss, then, and the ensuing work of mourning, detachment of libido from the lost love object. The poem is a legal metaphor for a psychic process.

STANZA ONE: "IN HARNESS"

> L'an quatre cens cinquante six
> Je Françoys Villon escollier
> Considerant, de sens rassis
> Le frain aux dens, franc au collier
> Qu'on doit ses oeuvres conseillier
> Comme Vegece le raconte
> Sage Rommain, grant conseillier
> Ou autrement on se mesconte.

> [In the year fourteen fifty-six
> I the scholar François Villon
> Sound of mind, in harness
> Champing the bit, believing
> As Vegetius the wise Roman
> And great counselor advises
> We must think out our works
> Or else miscalculate.]

The first figure of the *Lais* compares the narrator to a beast of burden. As David Kuhn has demonstrated, Villon characteristically deals not in metaphor or simile—both "integrating" sorts of figure—so much as in *équivoques*, descriptive evasions of figurative language which point to a property or properties common to two or several things, in this case the *frain* and the *collier* common to the narrator and a prototypical workhorse or ox. We might suppose this to be an exception to Villon's usual practice, for the speaker does not actually sport bridle or harness. But there is really no periphrastic simile here at all; the equivocation, "doubling" of sense is simply linguistic rather than physical, having to do with actual shared physical properties. Such a linguistic "scattering" of meaning is most characteristic of Villon, most evidently in his jargon poems but throughout all his work.

The word *frain* comes from the Latin *frenum*, meaning bridle, reins, bit, curb, that which restrains, a restraining object or force. No less a rhetorician than Cicero uses the expression *frenum mordere* just as Villon does, as meaning, "to chafe against restraint." Two closely related words are the verb *frenare*, to hold in, and *frendare*, to gnash the teeth or simply to crush. Phonemically, all these are related to *fremere*, which may mean to grumble or complain, something done with the mouth and which might be accompanied by a gnashing of teeth. *Fremere* in French becomes *frémir:* "to be agitated by a slight movement of oscillation or vibration, producing a slight, obscure sound." All of these evoke another French word of fairly recent coinage in Villon's time: *frénésie*, "a violent delirium brought on by acute cerebral ailment." In this one word, there is layer upon layer of "sense," a discomposure and perturbation of sense suggested by all its phonic and epigrammatic strata: restraint, containment, crushing, *repression*, madness, trembling, vibration, productive of a low sound, a tremor which might be a plaint, a groaning.

All of which jars with *de sens rassis*, the legalistic statement of mental competency. *Rassis* itself adds interesting connotations. Its first known use was to describe lead which had cooled and hardened, resolidified, returned to a physical equilibrium. *Frain, rassis:* there is a tension drawn by both words, within and between them, a movement of pacification, which is a movement towards solidness, heaviness, weightiness, a stolid and palpable equipoise, containment, restraint, but the restraint is producing a tension, an audible vibration, a low tremor which might well be madness.

Franc au collier evokes the same tension, within itself and in contrast with *de sens rassis* and *le frain aux dens*. A horse which is *franc du collier* is one which works well in harness, pulls with great energy. We may suppose that the substitution of *au* for *du* is not intended to change the meaning. The expression *franc du collier* means, by figurative extension, "to act freely and boldly." The expression is severely oxymoronic due to an ambiguity immanent in the word *franc*. What began as meaning a good, strong, energetic beast of burden, one which pulls in the harness as if free of it, as if the harness were not there, winds up meaning simply, to act boldly and freely. "Free in the collar" has become "free of the collar." But it is crucial that the latter meaning is the metaphorical one. *Franc du collier*, in its met-aphorical sense (as applied to men), really means "acting as though free when in fact not free at all but strapped in, encumbered."

Franc comes from the Germanic tribe which gave France its name. Metonymically, it came to refer to the "free" status of the members of that tribe. Later it comes to mean "metaphysically, morally free," "honest, open," "simple, pure," and finally, "of unmistakable authenticity"—"that which is truly such." It is the antonym of *douteux, équivoque*. The word also, by metonymic derivation from the Frankish people, means a unit of mon-etary exchange originally equal to a pound. Freedom is allied with economy, exchange, and these are always for Villon code words for sexuality. In the fourth stanza for instance he will speak of the necessity of *"autres complans,"* "new fields to plow," *"et frapper en ung autre coing,"* "and a new die for striking coins." These expressions are literal *équivoques*, pointing to physical properties in which several acts overlap: breaking earth, pouring molten metal into a mold to form a coin, and coitus. Remember that *rassis* originally meant "hardened," lead which had been cooled and solidified. The expres-sion *franc au collier*, signifying free and yet not free, encircled, bound, evokes the image of a piece of money in a necklace, or any setting, a band around its circumference or even a die. A bit of liquid gold, *lapis philosophorum*, poured and set, trapped in a shape.

Villon would be identifying himself as the coin then, but he must also be the one who pours it—sexually, it is the male who plows, strikes the coin. He is coin and coiner, act and actor, dance and dancer, written and writer. The gold in the die is solid, but in its molecular structure liquefaction is latent, immanent. And though occulted in the iron or sand of the die, it is still gold, gold though coated with base metal, liquid though solid, free though bound. It will not declare itself "purely, simply," yet it is pure and simple, the purest and simplest of substances. It cannot be named, described; it is none of the things it has been, and all of them. The only container, "die," which may give it "free rein"—contain it and liberate it at once—is language. So there is great irony in saying that "We must think out our works/Or else miscalculate." We may think them out all we please; when it comes to what truly matters, we are "bound" to miscalculate any-way. Thinking out, indeed, is a protracted miscalculation, a failure to re-duce, contain. It is, or should be, an uncalculation, an unraveling. If coin and coiner are the same, neither can contemplate the other as a totalized thing. A thing cannot calculate itself when it is not itself, but both itself and something else, always becoming something else.

It is also worthy of note that after giving the date, the first stanza brings up the matter of identity: *"Je Françoys Villon escollier."* *Escollier*, in the con-text, is equivocal indeed, containing "collar" and the contraction *es, en + les*—in harness or collar. The harness is allied with the egoistic *Je*, then, which is identified as the learned, the writerly *ego faber*, the plodding, careful thinker-out of things. The first stanza rhymes *escollier, collier*, and *conseillier*, the latter occurring twice. *Conseillier* splits the two syllables of *collier* and interjects a third. *Seille* means simply bucket, a wooden hollow receptacle for water. *Con* is a vulgar name for the female sexual organ, Villon's "die" for coining, also a hollow, for containing, receiving, and shaping the male essence. *Ciller*, which can be phonetically obtained by dropping one letter (an orthographic liberty which medieval scribes would have thought quite negligible and minor), means to blink, to close the eyes quickly, conjuring the image of a cavity by turns open and closed. The irony of the stanza's last line is again underscored: *conseillier ses oeuvres* implies an oscillating movement, a closing which immediately comes undone, reopens. It implies an always incomplete movement towards closure. Short of closure, of course, we always must miscalculate. There are too many variables for the equation to admit a solution.

STANZA TWO: "THE PRISON OF GREAT LOVE"

> En ce temps que j'ay dit devant
> Sur le Noel, morte saison
> Que les loups se vivent du vent
> Et qu'on se tient en sa maison
> Pour le frimas, pres du tison
> Me vint ung vouloir de brisier
> La tres amoureuse prison
> Qui souloit mon cuer debrisier.

> [In the year above mentioned
> Near Christmas, the dead time
> When wolves live on the wind
> And men stick to their houses
> Against the frost, close by the blaze
> A desire came to me to break out
> Of the prison of great love
> That was breaking my heart.]

Christmas time, "the dead season," the season of death, when "wolves live on the wind," "and men stick to their houses/Against the frost, close by the blaze." *Devant*, in the first line, becomes *du vent* in the third, a word connoting time and space metamorphosed into a meteorological phenomenon. Again, rather than the obvious conclusion, that here is a periphrastic statement that the wolves are starving, it is true to the spirit of Villon to wonder what more equivocal figuration might be occurring. Wind is displaced air; it often implies noise, vibration of air concurrent with displacement, as in wind instruments. Again the motif of vibration is visible, a low noise, perhaps a plaintive one. The noise made by wind is often characterized as whining or groaning, and the image of a man at home by the fire in the dead of winter calls up memories of such sounds.

Vivre, in the meantime (*"se vivent du vent"*), can have a transitive meaning. To "live" something is to experience it deeply, intimately, as in Proust's saying, "My loves, I have lived them, I have felt them [*Mes amours, je les ai vécus, je les ai sentis*]," or Sartre's, "A feeling is a defined way of living our connection with the world around us [*Un sentiment est une manière définie de vivre notre rapport au monde qui nous entoure*]." So the vibration, grinding of the teeth on the bit, the *frénésie* of the *frain aux dens* is partly a phenomenon of wind (inhaling/exhaling). In the season of death, survival, for *les loups*, is a matter of perceiving the wind's music very acutely, feeling and hearing the *va-et-vient* of air very carefully. That music is the play of ambiguity itself, the uncertainty of direction and identity, and language, already introduced in the first stanza.

The most interesting word here, though, is *loup*. An archaic meaning of it is a lesion, a wound, by metonymic connection with the wolf who would make it with his teeth—biting the flesh as if it were a bit. Add a mute "e" and *loupe* is obtained, from the Frankish *luppa*, "large unformed mass of a clotted matter." More specifically, it refers to a pearl or precious stone with an imperfection. So that the motif of a "hollow," a cavity, is repeated, this time with the connotation of pain, an emptiness made by the violent removal of flesh, and consequent clotting, the formation of an imperfection, a scar, such as that in an "imperfectly crystallized stone," which keeps it from being transparent, causes it to refract or reflect or obstruct the passage of light. There is also the common adjectival use of the word *wolf* in French to mean extreme, as in *une faim de loup* or *un froid de loup* (wolfishly hungry, wolfishly cold). An open wound feels extremes of cold and wind more acutely than whole flesh. It "lives" it more vividly.

This fourth line throws the second two into relief: "And men stick to their houses/Against the frost, close by the blaze." Men protect their wounds from the searing of the wind; men hide from the howling elements and stay close to the fire so that they don't "live" the cold, so that the wind doesn't score their wounds and make them groan and howl. A *tison* is the remains of a log, most of which has been burnt up. The contrast drawn is between an enveloping, vast, windy, noisy cold, inhabited by animals, or, more abstractly, brutish beings, the brutish aspect of life, and the enclosed, narrow space of the house, lit and warmed by the tiny, expiring flames.

This tableau gives a specific topography of the figure which follows, of breaking out "Of the prison of great love." A prison is an enclosure like a house, offers a small space in which warmth and light may survive in an atmosphere of cold and dark, in which the howling of the wind may be more or less ignored. But it also implies forced confinement, "collaring." Breaking out of the prison means freedom, unbinding, release of the repressed, but also madness, frenzy, the screaming, biting cold wind. It means that the wound, filling like a die with blood, will harden, the blood dry, set (*rassis*) in the cavity and in so doing feel the blows of the elements. Freedom means pain. It also means revelation, the emergence from concealment of the flaws which make the living matter distort, twist light—cavities in which the wind makes odd, "unnatural" noises. The prison is the house of *great* love, and the confinement it imposed "Was breaking my heart." The heart of the prison, of course, is the *tison*, and in this sense the breaking heart is the prison's own. The prison, its warmth and light, feed on their own heart, gradually consume and "break" it. So life feeds on itself, "breaks" itself, in its subservience to death, its dependence on death.

Villon's desire, in writing this poem, is to break out of the prison of love, which is the prison of life, with all that implies. He wants to break out in order to escape death—the core/*cuer* of the prison which feeds it and drags it down. His project is to escape love, life, and thereby death as well.

> STANZA THREE: "CELLE DEVANT MES YEULX / CONSENTANT
> À MA DESFAÇON"

> Je le feis en telle façon
> Voyant celle devant mes yeulx
> Consentant à ma desfaçon
> Sans que ja luy en fust mieulx
> Dont je me dueil et plains aux cieulx
> En requerant d'elle venjance
> A tous les dieux venerieux
> Et du grief d'amours allejance.

> [I came to this point
> By watching her before my eyes
> Agreeing to my undoing
> Without even profiting from it
> Which is why I groan and cry to heaven
> And ask every god of love
> To give me revenge upon her
> And ease from love's pain.]

Death was in the fifteenth century a conventional metaphor for lost love, and here Villon introduces, without naming her or giving any particulars as to her identity, the author of his unhappiness, the one who consents to his "undoing" (*desfaçon*) apparently out of sheer malice, without "gaining" anything from it. As David Kuhn has pointed out, woman is like snow ("*Mais où sont les neiges d'antan?*") in Villon's work, an emblem and an agent of the instability and ambiguousness of the self and its world. For the poet, "she," abstract woman, is a living *équivoque*, a winking wound, blinking cavity, the undoing (death) immanent in life. *Celle* has no clear antecedent and there is no development of the character forthcoming. "She" remains pronominal, hypothetical, unnamed and unnameable. The poem circles her, this blank center, like an empty harness or an unfilled die, a house whose embers have expired or a prison with no prisoners inside, a wound without blood; one long circumlocutionary lament of its absent locus.

There are three feminine nouns in the preceding stanza: *maison, saison,* and *prison.* All have to do with physical and temporal limitation, confinement and duration, the passage of time, parameters enforced by laws and men or the elements of the physical world (and, any good gnostic would add, its gods, the evil archons, the shock troops of time and space). The desire to escape these confinements, to break out of the prison of love and life, has come from the spectacle of "her" rejection of the narrator. Yet she is life, love, the house, the prison, the season of love. Love's, life's treachery have made Villon want to break out of them. They are melting him down, un-making (*des-façon*) him, consuming the ember of his heart "without even profiting from it." Finally, the motif of groaning, the almost inaudible lament, breaks through the surface of the language and becomes overt: "Which is why I groan and cry to heaven [Dont je me dueil et plains aux cieulx]. He is not mourning "her" but what she has agreed to, *his* unmaking, his own self. Tautologically, he calls on all the gods "of Venus" to avenge this, his loss of himself, on "her," who is love, his prisonkeeper, who in his pantheon is Venus. He wants to turn the goddess' own dogs on her.

Venereus in Latin often refers specifically to sexual love, as in *res Venereae,* when it doesn't mean simply, "of Venus." But does Villon mean the gods subservient to Venus or the gods superior to her? He is not clear, and perhaps it doesn't matter. What would seem to matter very much is the contrast drawn between these gods of *sexual* desire (venereal gods) and the poet's *grief d'amours, amor* being desire in its more emotional, less physical aspect, personified not as Venus but as Cupid. But "Cupid" in Villon's pantheon is feminine, "celle." Villon's project then would be to set sex against love. Love (*amor*) is his prison (*celle/cellule*) and he is calling on lust to loose him from the grip of more emotional attachment.

The most significant word in this stanza, for me, is *dueil*—it appears in the fifth line. This is from the Latin *dolere,* to suffer pain, mentally or bodily. In French, the noun *deuil* has always had the specific connotation of loss by death of a loved one. Villon is mourning his loss of himself. His use of the word is reflexive. His grief emanates from his "coming undone." The hole at the center of this poem, "*celle*," the absence unnameable, is himself. The love he is talking about is, in one sense at least, self-love. The love object he has lost personifies this emptiness inside him, the death immanent in all life, and which is the principle of life, the possibility of it. The negativity of death is always at the heart of life, precedes life, fuels it and gradually extinguishes it just as combustion causes wood to give off warmth and light and to reduce itself to its chemical origins, to undo. The harness begins empty and ends empty, plenitude is temporary and illusory, a "miscalculation." Death (*La Morte Saison/Saison de la Mort/Saison de la*

Celle-ule) is the prison and the guard, life and love. How can we break out of "her" harness? Of course, we might have guessed that the unspecified center of a poem written as a will would be death.

Villon, like Freud much later, sees death as *desfaçon*. This allies it with his favorite figure, the *équivoque,* which scatters, dissembles, and disassembles, deconstructs its own pretense to sense, or in the case of Villon's poems in jargon, which appear willfully nonsensical, act like palimpsests, meanings layered as richly and carefully as the multicolored strata of some fantastic torte, creating fault lines on the surface: one layer's ambiguity causes the whole to quiver, symptom of a poetic schizophrenia. This immanent negativity is death, scatterer, undoer, but also revealer of secrets, Proserpine. When Villon implores the *dieux venerieux* to avenge the perfidy of love, he is calling on the deities of flesh, of *carrion,* to overthrow the supposed gods of love, those hypocrites and deceivers. Cupid's arrows drug humans into ignorance of the nature of their own flesh, let them see beauty in (soon-to-be) rotting flesh, *including their own.* Here is a testimonial from *Le Testament.*

> C'est d'umaine beaulté l'issue
> Les bras cours et les mains contraites
> Les espaulles toutes bossues
> Mamelles, quoy? toutes retraites
> Telles les hanches que les tetes
> Du sadinet, fy! quant des cuisses
> Cuisses ne sont plus mais cuissetes
> Grivelees comme saulcisses.
> Ainsi le bon temps regretons
> Entre nous, povres vielles sotes
> Assises bas a croupetons
> Tout en ung tas comme pelotes
> A petit feu de chenevotes
> Tost allumees, tost estaintes
> Et jadis fusmes si mignotes
> Ainsi en prent a mains et maintes.

> [This is what human beauty comes to
> The arms short, the hands shriveled
> The shoulders all hunched up
> The breasts? Shrunk in again
> The buttocks gone the way of the tits
> The quim? aagh! As for the thighs
> They aren't thighs now but sticks
> Speckled all over like sausages.

This is how we lament the good old days
Among ourselves, poor silly crones
Dumped down on our hunkers
In little heaps like so many skeins
Around a tiny hempstalk fire
That's soon lit and soon gone out
And once we were so adorable
So it goes for men and women.]

We need to keep in mind the hypothetical situation of a dying man who, by his attitude at the moment of death, will either save or damn his soul. He is faced with the problem of how to confront the loss of all he never really owned at all, the loss which is always implicit in possession (an illusion created by the "vapours" of amour) and precedes it. His body, his loved one(s), his possessions, his identity. This is a constant theme in all of Villon's work, reflected in his fondness for acrostics spelling out his name, but perhaps most visible in the ballade every line of which contains the words *"je congnois,"* I know.

Prince, je congnois tout en somme
Je congnois coulourez et blesmes
Je congnois Mort quit tout consomme
Je congnois tout fors que moy mesmes.

[Prince, I know all things
I know the rosy-cheeked and the pale
I know Death who devours all
I know everything but myself.]

He cannot concretize himself, totalize himself. Only death can do this. The problem is first a psychological one. Freud tells us that the self is constituted through its first love objects, usually parents. The ego comes into being to cathect and to emulate these object-choices, to internalize them as the superego. Objects might be projected or internalized—it is impossible to know which comes first—but suffice to say that the investment of libido in the self and investment of libido in objects are both necessary to what Freud called "love-attachment."

In cases of melancholia, when the ego perceives that it has lost something dear, whether the loss is real or whether the object was ever in any sense "possessed," the loss is felt as a real deficit of the ego's own substance, of libido; the ego makes no distinction between self-love and object-love. What it loves in others is projected; what it loves in itself are the introjected features of others. No distinction between the two is possible. If the object of love turns out to be death, a synecdochal figure of death, carrion, the self turns out to be the very same thing.

The ego cannot love carrion, death, once it recognizes them, once it is no longer so drugged by desire. It can love neither itself nor anyone else.

Freud makes a distinction between simple mourning and melancholia, which he expressed as the difference between perceiving the world as empty and perceiving the self (and the world) as empty. Mourning is the "normal" process. In it the self remains in love with itself; its structure, subtended by libido (self-love), is not threatened. The melancholic, however, is afflicted by a pathological clarity. He sees his own shortcomings with a brutal lucidity. This is Villon's state. He has realized the immanence of death in himself, in his lover, in love, in life. How can he love, others or himself, without loving death? His inability to love himself turns the scaffolding of the self to jelly, scatters sense, meaning, the normative structure which is the self's constitution, the psychic *modus operandi* of every human, soldered with libido. Like Proust, like O'Connor, Villon cannot bring himself to kiss life because it looks to him like a rotting corpse. This means he cannot bear to see himself in the mirror. Jean Laplanche has shown that this same notion, this inkling that Thanatos and Eros might be one and the same, is implicit, present but repressed, in Freud's own work.

Villon expresses the anxiety of this knowledge in his fondness for equivocal figurations and for antiphrasis. The best example of the latter is the famous ballade which begins with a line from Charles d'Orléans, "I die of thirst beside the fountain":

> Je meurs de seuf aupres de la fontaine
> Chault comme feu et tremble dent a dent . . .
>
> D'ung cigne blanc que c'est ung corbeau noir
> Et qui me nuyst croy qu'il m'ayde a povoir
> Bourde, verté, au jour d'uy m'est tout un
> Je retiens tout, rien ne sçay concepvoir
> Bien recueully, debouté de chascun.
>
> [I'm hot as fire, I'm shaking tooth on tooth . . .
>
> A white swan is a black crow
> The people who harm me think they help
> Lies and truth today I see they're one
> I remember everything, my mind's a blank
> Warmly welcomed, always turned away.]

A more overtly psychological instance is *Le Debat de Villon et Son Cuer*. This poem is a dialogue between ego and superego, which can find no suitable milieu in which to meet. Like a homonymic *équivoque,* they are confined to one self, and yet desire and spiritual love, the lust of the id and the constraints of the superego, find no room to overlap in the ego, and the latter must swing wildly back and forth, in schizophrenic fashion, from the one to the other. One voice of the poem laments the sins of the flesh, while the other bewails the failure of the flesh, its aging. Each bemoans its incapacity to prevail over the other. Purely carnal love, embodied in *la grosse*

Margot ("On filth we dote, filth is our lot") is opposed to the pure love of his mother, of his benefactor Guillaume de Villon, of the pure, "chaste" woman, always the one who rejects Villon, whom he loses before he has ever possessed her. In the self, as in the poem, layers of meaning are superimposed, various codes membraneously laminated on each other, creating oozing fissures, fault lines in the surface.

> Rien ne congnois—Si fais—Quoy?—Mouche en let
> L'ung est blanc, l'autre est noir, c'est la distance—
> Est ce donc tout?—Que veulx tu que je tance?
> Se n'est assez je recommenceray—
> Tu es perdu—J'y mettray resistance—
> Plus ne t'en dis—Et je m'en passeray—

> [You don't know a thing—Yes I do—What?—Flies in milk
> One's white, one's black, they're opposites—
> That's all?—How can I say it better?
> If that doesn't suit you I'll start over—
> You're lost—Well I'll go down fighting—
> I've nothing more to tell you—I'll survive without it—]

"I can't love, and I can't be loved," "I can't love myself, and I can't love anyone else," these formulas paraphrase the broken economy of libido suggested by the use of coinage and the casting of coins as figures of desire, libidinal transaction: "I can't get back in circulation/No more than cried-down money [je ne me puis mettre/Ne que monnoye qu'on descrie]."

In one passage of the *Testament*, Villon compares Narcissus' fate to Orpheus', concluding that they are the same.

> Orpheüs le doux menestrier
> Jouant de fleustes et musetes
> En fut en dangier d'un murtrier
> Chien Cerberus a quatre testes
> Et Narcisus le bel honnestes
> En ung parfont puis se noya
> Pour l'amour de ses amouretes
> Bien est eureux qui riens n'y a

> [Love made the sweet minstrel Orpheus
> Playing his flutes and bagpipes
> Risk death from the murderous
> Dog four-headed Cerberus
> It made the fair-haired boy Narcissus
> Drown himself down in a well
> For love of his lovelies
> Lucky the man who has no part in it.]

Narcissus, of course, never knew he was in love with himself. It is impossible to separate love from self-love. Any kind of love is a descent into hell, is to die and be buried *without knowing it.* Both Orpheus and Narcissus went to their ends without any idea that that was what they were doing, drugged by love, hallucinating life where there was only death, Venus where was Proserpine.

Villon, however, is no longer deceived. He has realized the emptiness of his self, and his world. Where once he "took encouragement/From those sweet looks and winning ways/That seemed so sincere [prins en ma faveur/ Ces doulx regars et beaux semblans/De tres decevante saveur]"(his own and others'), he now sees betrayal and destruction. He proposes to replace the old deities of love, redefine love itelf: "I need fresh fields to plough/ And another die for coining in [Planter me fault autres complans/Et frapper en ung autre coing]." To avoid the prison of life ("She" who "took me prisoner" and "wills and orders that I suffer/Death and cease to live [Veult et ordonne que j'endure/La mort et que plus je ne dure]"), he proposes to embrace death, the immanence of death in every thing: "*Sound of limb I die* . . . And become a martyred lover/One of the saints of love [Par elle meurs les membres sains/Au fort je suis amant martir/Du nombre des amoureux sains]."

What he means to "take leave of" and "put from himself" in the seventh stanza are the hallucinations which normal investment of libido makes possible. He is committing himself to a state of permanent melancholia, the pathological state of mourning occasioned, according to Freud, by the "narcissistic" sort of object-choice, by a confusion of object-love and self-love, and by a powerful ambivalence in the relation to the lost object.

In melancholia the relation to the object is no simple one; it is complicated by the conflict of ambivalence. The latter is either constitutional, i.e. it is an element of every love-relation formed by this particular ego, or else it proceeds from precisely those experiences that involved a threat of losing the object. For this reason the exciting causes of melancholia are of a much wider range than those of grief, which is for the most part occasioned only by a real loss of the object, by its death. In melancholia, that is, countless single conflicts in which love and hate wrestle together are fought for the object; the one seeks to detach the libido from the object, the other to uphold this libido-position against assault. These single conflicts cannot be located in any system but the Ucs, the region of memory-traces of things (as contrasted with word-cathexes). The efforts to detach the libido are made in this system also during mourning; but in the latter nothing hinders these processes from proceeding in the normal way through the Pcs to consciousness. For the work of melancholia this way is blocked, owing perhaps to a number of causes or to their combined operation. Constitutional ambivalence belongs by nature to what is repressed, while traumatic experiences with the object may have stirred to activity something else that has been repressed. Thus everything to do with these conflicts of ambivalence remains excluded from consciousness, until the outcome characteristic of melancholia sets in. This, as we know, consists in the libidinal cathexis that is being menaced at last abandoning the object, only, however, to resume its occupation of that place in the ego whence it came. So by taking flight into the ego love escapes annihilation. After this regression of the libido the process can become conscious; it appears in consciousness as a conflict between one part of the ego and its self-criticizing faculty.

("Mourning and Melancholia")

Of course, it is just such ambivalence that conditions Villon's view of everything, himself as well as the object, an ambiguity which must finally be that of life and death, the one within the other.

This is a confusion which Freud himself, and indeed, Western culture, have never resolved. As Laplanche has made clear, Freud struggled in vain to make an effective distinction between Thanatos and Eros. For Villon, of course, this ambivalence is not the exception at all but the rule, not, as Freud has it, a neurotic symptom. Rather, melancholia is the only possible result of realizing the intrinsic perfidy of any love object, internal or external, melancholia as a sense of loss of self and loved one(s). Freud himself comes very near to admitting that the melancholic is more lucid than his mentally healthy brethren: "We only wonder why a man must become ill before he can discover truth of this kind." Villon would doubtless reply that, naturally, if health is defined as a blindness to the horror of life and love, to the death within them, then clarity of vision must be considered "sick."

THE STRATEGY: PSYCHIC AND SEXUAL ANARCHY

First the narrator proposes to call "her," the female locus of his poetical universe, by a more appropriate name or names than the innocent sounding "Venus" or "love"—Proserpine, or death, or prison, or prison-keeper, or perhaps most ominous and fitting of all, the transparent pronoun *she*, for she is nothing but flux. Why Villon chooses to characterize the force of death-in-life as female is a complicated issue, rendered largely moot by what "she" emblemizes: the equivocal nature of reality which obscures as well the distinction between man and woman. It undoubtedly owes something to contemporary poetic convention, which made lost love a commonplace for death, and to Villon's own personal psychic history. Her equivocal sexuality, however, is suggested by the very terms in which he takes his leave of her: "I'm sure it's best that I leave (*fouïr*)/So Goodbye I'm off to Angers." Kuhn has shown that *fouïr* plays upon the two meanings of *foutre* and *fouiller*, while *aller a Angiers* is synonymic with *ongier, foutre,* and *aller a Bourges*, which means "to become a pederast." Mightn't we surmise, then, that to avoid "such danger," he means to give himself up to a homosexual ardor? "Since she won't let me have/Her favors. . . ." There are broad hints in his other works that Villon suffered from venereal disease, and this might be one sense in which he refers to "danger," the sense in which love, sex, literally attack the body's tissues. Evoking homosexuality, the narrator gives a clear signal as to the meaning of what he is really proposing: a permanent melancholia, sense of loss, and the clarity of vision, knowledge, implicit therein. He means to ignore apparent distinctions, to see through the hallucinatory conventions of "normal" behavior. He will escape danger by identifying with it, becoming indistinguishable from it.

This is of course no real escape, and he is not proposing real escape. There can be no exit from one's own self, substance. What he means to do is to join in the dance of death (sex, life) in full knowledge of what it is, to lie with death while seeing it for what it is, to infect himself deliberately, pervert himself willfully, wreak violence, above all sexual/psychic violence, which to Villon is not distinguishable from poetic violence, deliberately. He means to adapt the Misfit's (note the overlapping terminology of the two writers: Mis-fit, *des-façon*) strategy of random physical violence to sexuality and therefore, necessarily, to psychology as well; he intends to combine the doctrines of Marcel and the Misfit. His violence will be sexual, psychic and therefore literary, and physical.

"SOUND OF LIMB I DIE"

This strategy is to act as if dead while still living, to possess nothing, have no center, no heart, to participate in and be part of the forces of corruption and decay. To enact it, he must strip himself of every supposed possession, as a dying man would, starting with his own body. This is precisely what he intends to do: "there's no way-station after you die/And I go into a distant land/So I draw up this present legacy." He leaves his heart—"pale, pitiful, dead and gone"—to "her." He disowns his fame, his cutlass, a pair of pants, a hauberk, books, various items of clothing, comestibles, properties which he never really owned but which are part of his memory's domain. All of these are equivocal figurations of the basic sexual theme: "tools, purses, and coins, for example, serving as symbols for the penis, and gardens, houses, shoes, hats, stockings, and so on, representing the vagina" (Kinnell).

"LASTLY AS I SAT WRITING"

The great bell of the Sorbonne interrupts the inventory of dispossession, tolling nine o'clock, 3 × 3, the number of the Trinity, the hour of Angelus, prayer in remembrance of the Annunciation. The bell, metal cast in a "die," hollow itself like a die, containing a bit of metal which causes it, and the air, to vibrate, make a sound—this to recall to all who hear the resurrection of the body, defiance of death, of Jesus Christ. Villon, too, tries to believe this and take comfort from it. "I stopped and wrote no further," as if writing and prayer were antithetical, or as if one were a substitute for the other, or both. The antithesis is strongly suggested by the sudden reappearance of the heart he is supposed to have given away: "In order to pray as the heart bid," *cuer* being the locus, the centrum of which he supposedly stripped himself. The tolling of Angelus is a sound very different from a low, sad, whistling wind, or a groan—the voice of orthodox religion, as opposed to the voice of the poet/poem; the latter more subtle, more a rustling than a tolling. This moment is one of nostalgia for the heart, for the certainties, illusions of normalcy.

But in taking up his *cuer* again, the poet grows "muddled/Not from any wine I'd taken/But as if my spirit were bound," which is just what he ought to feel, putting on the *collier* of faith, restoring his "heart." Though a part of him yearns to go back, to leave the cold and go back inside by the dying fire, the aging heart, to go on loving "her," to take back what it has lost, it knows that this is not really possible. Whereupon *La Dame Mémoire*, Lady Memory, another avatar of "her," the lost lady, the prison-keeper, "takes up" all the intellectual faculties, defenses, structures of normality, distinction, order, the scaffolding of the well-adjusted self. These are described as her "collateral specie, currency," "species," that is, those faculties akin to her, to memory, and which are the means of exchange, the *modus operandi*, the lubrication in the intellect's economy: the "opinionative," the "intellectual," the "estimative," the "similitative," and the "formative." The "lost one" collects these in her *aulmoire*, the drawer where *aumones*, religious or charitable donations, would be kept, and takes them with her. They are part of her, of what is lost, abolished by the knowledge that they were makeshift, fictive. Without them, "you can go/Mad and lunatic."

The moment of nostalgia for sanity is quickly over, though it appears in other places in Villon's work, and indeed, is an integral part of the sense of lack and loss which is melancholia. It is not, as many critics have maintained, evidence of a fidelity to Catholicism. Rather, his inability to sustain these moments, when they occur, is evidence of his distance from Catholicism. *Oubliance*, a richer word than *forgetfulness*, connoting oblivion, nothingness, non-remembrance and non-sense, is placed on the emptied throne of memory, and the sensory (*le sensitif*), the sensual, the "organs," are brought to power. The sensual and the sexual are the "currency" of *oubliance*, its "collateral species."

Of course, this is no proper ending at all. No real conclusion, closure, is possible. Death is everywhere in the poem, immanent, and cannot mean closure any more. The ink (the intellectual faculties) is frozen and the fire (the *cuer*, locus of things, distinctions) has gone out ("I couldn't have found any fire . . ."). Villon is "Unable to give it another ending." The final stanza, however, does suggest the poet's "diseased" state, the sickness of knowing what he knows and the pain which his loss, his lack, his perpetual melancholia/mourning, cause him: he "doesn't eat, shit or piss/Dry and black like a furnace mop. . . ." In knowledge of death, in cheating death by unmasking it, seeing through its disguises and rending them, doing violence to them, exaggerating its own *danse macabre,* there is no real pleasure, no peace in this world, death's world. As O'Connor's Misfit says, "Shut up Bobby Lee, it's no real pleasure in life." And yet, in that knowledge, in that unpleasure, Villon knew there was a cruel, searing joy: "Verity, are you ready to hear it?/In sickness alone is there joy."

Perhaps that joy amounts to this, the true divine paradox: if death is not only process but, as the Middle Ages saw it, passage as well, then living so close to it would bring us into proximity with the real life to come, as close as we in this world can be—not to hell, which only prolongs death eternally, but to the crumb of gold always absent from the alchemist's alembic, the elemental distillate of uncreated life.

Descartes: an intellectual biography

nonfiction

194 .B4268

Gaukroger, Stephen

Bloomfield,
841.09 F88

s

books
uals?

orld

ook clubs
ibrary.

Marguerite de Navarre:
The Rhetoric of Tears

Robert D. Cottrell

FALLING CADENCE

Francis I became ill in mid-February 1547 and died several weeks later on March 31. During Francis' illness, Marguerite wrote several short poems, a few of which were included among the thirty-three poems that appeared at the end of the *Marguerites* (published later in 1547) under the title of *Chansons spirituelles*. In all, Marguerite wrote some forty-seven *chansons*. The fact that she included only thirty-three of them in the *Marguerites* suggests that the number thirty-three is intended to allude to Jesus' age at the time of His crucifixion. The most quintessential, or "musical," of Marguerite's works, the *Chansons* were in many cases written to be sung to well-known hymns. Within the economy of the *Marguerites*, the *Chansons spirituelles* form a single poem only slightly longer than several other poems in the volume. Concerned with death, they account for the falling cadence that marks the conclusion of the *Marguerites*. Indeed, the last word of the thirty-third *chanson*, which concludes the volume, is "deffait [undone]."

The first of the *Chansons spirituelles* is entitled *Pensees de la Royne de Navarre, estant dens sa Litiere, durant la maladie du Roy. Sur le chant de, Ce qui m'est due et ordonné* [Thoughts of the Queen of Navarre, being in her carriage, during the King's illness. To the tune of "What is required and commanded of me"]. In the opening three stanzas, Marguerite returns to a double-edged theme that runs through her poetry: although she recognizes the utter inadequacy of fallen language, she cannot remain silent; she is compelled by inner necessity to go on writing. Whereas for Humanists copiousness was a sign of man's fertile mind and inexhaustible creative

From *The Grammar of Silence: A Reading of Marguerite de Navarre's Poetry.* © 1986 by the Catholic University of America Press.

energy, for Marguerite it signals an ontological flaw. Since the Fall, man has been condemned to language. Marguerite continues to speak, although she knows (or at least claims to know) that words are useless:

> Si la douleur de mon esprit
> Je povois monstrer par parole
> Ou la déclarer par escrit,
> Onque ne feut sy triste rolle;
> Car le mal qui plus fort m'affole
> Je le cache et couvre plus fort;
> Par-quoy n'ay rien qui me console,
> Fors l'espoir de la douce mort.
>
> Je sçay que je ne dois celer
> Mon ennuy, plus que raisonnable;
> Mais si ne sçauroit mon parler
> Atteindre à mon dueil importable:
> A l'escriture véritable
> Defaudroit la force à ma main,
> Le taire me seroit louable,
> S'il ne m'estoit tant inhumain.
>
> (ll. 1–16)

[If I could show by word the sorrow of my spirit, or state it in writing, never would there be such a sad account; for the more forcefully misfortune wounds me, the more forcefully I hide and conceal it. So I have nothing that consoles me except the hope of sweet death. I know that I ought not conceal my grief more than is reasonable; however, my speech would fall short of my intolerable sorrow; the strength in my hand is not sufficient for a true written account; it would be laudable of me to remain silent if that did not seem to me to be so inhuman.]

Declaring that she finds no solace in language, Marguerite asserts that her *chansons* are not linguistic structures at all. They rely not on the artificial code of language and textuality but on the natural code of tears, sighs, and sobs. Weeping is the non-linguistic discourse of the heart.

> Mes larmes, mes souspirs, mes criz,
> Dont tant bien je sçay la pratique,
> Sont mon parler et mes escritz,
> Car je n'ay autre rhétorique.
>
> (17–20)

[My tears, my sighs, my cries, of which I know so well the experience, are my speech and my writing, for I have no other rhetoric.]

The poems in which Marguerite expresses the grief provoked by Francis' illness and death are informed by what we may call the rhetoric of tears.

Marguerite was not with Francis when he died. She was in the monastery at Tusson (in the province of Poitou), where she remained in seclusion for four months following his death. Most of the *Chansons spirituelles* are prayers or *complaintes* composed during Marguerite's stay at Tusson. Whereas the first *chanson*, written before the King's death, sounds the note of impending disaster, the second, which is entitled *Autres Pensees, faites un mois apres la mort du Roy. Sur le chant de, Jouyssance vous donneray* [Other thoughts, written a month after the King's death. To the tune of "I shall give you joy"], demonstrates Marguerite's reaction to the death of her brother:

> Las, tant malheureuse je suis
> Que mon malheur dire ne puys,
> Sinon qu'il est sans espérance:
> Désespoir est desjà à l'huys,
> Pour me jetter au fond du puits
> Où n'a d'en saillir apparence.
>
> Tant de larmes jettent mes yeux
> Qu'ilz ne voyent terre ne cieux:
> Telle est de leur pleur l'abondance.
> Ma bouche se plaint en tous lieux,
> De mon cœur ne peult saillir mieux
> Que souspirs, sans nulle allegeance.
>   (1–12)

[Alas, so unhappy am I that I cannot express my unhappiness except to say that it is without hope. Despair is already at the door to throw me to the bottom of the pit, where there is no way to escape. My eyes are so filled with tears that they see neither earth nor heaven; such is the quantity of their tears. My mouth utters lamentations in every place; nothing better can come from my heart than sighs, without any relief.]

Introducing a theme that will be developed in the longer poems she began to write during the spring and summer of 1547, Marguerite reflects on the utter difference between "absence" and "presence":

> Je n'ay plus que la triste voix,
> De laquelle crier m'en vois
> En lamentant la dure absence.
> Las, de celuy pour qui je vivois,
> Que de si bon coeur je voyois,
> J'ay perdu l'heureuse présence.
>   (19–24)

[I no longer have any voice but a sad one; I see myself crying out, lamenting the cruel absence. Alas, him for whom I lived and whom I saw with such a light heart, I have lost his happy presence.]

Feeling irreparably separated from him whom she considers part of herself (". . . mon corps est banny/Du sien, auquel il feut uny/Depuis le temps de nostre enfance, [my body is banished from his, to which it has been united since the time of our childhood]") (37–39), she responds first by weeping:

> Je crie par bois et par plains,
> Au ciel et terre me complains;
> A rien fors à mon dueil ne pense.
> (46–48)

[I cry out through the woods and through the plains; I mourn to heaven and to earth; I think about nothing except my sorrow.]

The last four stanzas of the poem are an apostrophe to death, which Marguerite calls "tout mon refuge et ma défense" (51). With increasing urgency ("O mort, . . . /Vien donc [O death, come then]"(61–62); "Viens donques, ne retarde pas;/Non: cours la poste à bien grands pas [Come then, do not delay; no; run the course with haste]") (67–68), Marguerite entreats death to "transpercer la Soeur de ta lance [pierce the sister with your lance]" (63).

Seeking to resolve the absence/presence dilemma, she wishes to join Francis in a present that can be attained only by means of the absence provided by death. Claiming that her own death will signal the death of absence and the reign of presence, Marguerite invokes death in the third *chanson*, called *Rondeau fait au mesme temps* [rondeau written at the same time]. She seeks to render present that whose essence is absence by appealing to the most primitive and visceral of our senses, i.e., taste and smell:

> L'odeur de mort est de telle vigueur,
> Que désirer doit faire la liqueur
> De ce morceau, que ne veult avaller
> L'homme ignorant, lequel ne peut aller
> Que par la Mort au lieu de tout honneur.
>
> La mort du Frère a changé dens la Soeur
> (En grand désir de mort) la crainte et peur,
> Et la rend prompte avec luy d'avaller
>   L'odeur de mort.
> (1–9)

[The savor of death is of such vigor that it ought to arouse desire for the juice of this morsel, which the foolish man does not want to swallow, he who can go only by death to the place of all honor.

The death of the brother has changed the sister's anxiety and fear, and makes her (who greatly desires death) ready to swallow with him the savor of death.]

Realizing, however, that she has not yet "swallowed" death, Marguerite says that while waiting to die she will continue to talk about death ("En attendant, de la mort veut parler [While waiting, she (the sister) wishes to talk about death]") (13). The linguistic constructs she now fashions reflect a reality that is non-verbal, for, as an event, death puts an end to speech. The paradox, of course—and Marguerite was aware of it—is that for the reader of her texts the non-verbal reality she seeks to communicate is real only in language. She says that she wishes to attain presence (with Francis) by absenting herself from the body. What she actually does, though, is make her desire for absence present to the reader by embodying it in texts. We are thus dealing with ironic texts, that is to say, with texts that say what they mean through language that does not mean what it says.

During the period immediately following Francis' death, Marguerite wrote not only the *Chansons spirituelles* but also three long poems, the last two of which must be counted among her major poetic works: *La Comédie sur le trépas du roy* [The Play on the death of the king], *La Navire* [The Ship], and *Les Prisons*. All three are conspicuously allegorical. Furthermore, all three are deeply ironic. It is not surprising that irony permeates these texts, for, as theoreticians from Quintilian on have noted, allegory and irony are linked. In the rhetorical tradition, both allegory and irony are defined as saying one thing and meaning another. Discussing the relationship between allegory and ironic language, modern theorist Paul de Man comments that "this definition points to a structure shared by irony and allegory in that, in both cases, the relationship between sign and meaning is discontinuous. . . . In both cases, the sign points to something that differs from its literal meaning and has for its function the thematization of this difference." Each of the three poems Marguerite wrote during the period of grief that followed Francis' death thematizes difference. Each is the product of Marguerite's meditation on the mystery of presence and absence (she lives on, Francis is dead) and, further, on the ability (or inability) of language to express and even alter the nature of this mystery. In a sense, this is true for most of Marguerite's poems. They thematize Marguerite's relationship with Christ in terms of presence and absence. Most of them are allegorical and ironic in the sense in which Quintilian used the word when he said that Socrates' whole life was ironic. In *La Comédie sur le trépas du roy*, *La Navire*, and *Les Prisons*, however, the thematization of difference in terms of presence and absence is given new impetus and greater specificity by Francis' death.

Owing much to medieval tradition, *La Comédie sur le trépas du roy* has many of the formal features of the pastoral elegy as practiced by a number of *grands rhétoriqueurs*. It is composed of monologues and dialogues by four

characters: Amarissime, i.e., Marguerite herself, Securus, i.e., Henri d'Albret, Agapy, i.e., Henri II, and Paraclesis, i.e., a feminine figure representing Christian consolation. (Paraclete, in English, or *Paraclet*, in French
[derived from the Greek *Parakletos*, meaning one who is invoked] was often
used in ecclesiastical works to identify the Holy Spirit as an intercessor
who comforts man.) All express grief and various degrees of consolation
on the occasion of the death of Pan, i.e., Francis I. (Marot had already
called Francis I "Pan" in his *Eglogue au roy sous les noms de Pan et Robin*.)
Consistent with the bucolic setting of *Le Trépas*, Pan is represented as a
shepherd. Because Christ was often thought of as a shepherd (Briçonnet
repeatedly called Christ "Le Berger"), there are instances in *Le Trépas* in
which Francis seems to be identified with Christ. At the center of *Le Trépas*
is Amarissime, whose opening monologue is a series of questions. Like so
many of Marguerite's poems, *Le Trépas du roy* begins on a note of doubt
and confusion:

> Mais est-il vray, est-ce chose assurée
> Que Pan nous est osté de ces bas lieux?
> O la douleur voyre desmesurée!
> Mais est-il vray, est-il ravy aux cieulx?
> C'est vérité.
>
> (1–5)

[But is it true? Is it certain that Pan has been taken away from us
and from these low places? O truly boundless grief! But is it true,
has he been taken away to the heavens? It is true.]

Elaborating on the immeasurability of her grief, Amarissime declares that
she wishes to find a solitary place "Où ma douleur. . . /Puisse chanter
[where my grief . . . can sing]" (20–21). Like the Marguerite of the first
chanson spirituelle, Amarissime announces that she has no rhetoric except
that of grief and tears: "Chantez des vers de douleur seullement,/Qui com-
posez sont sans entendement [Sing only verses of sorrow, which are composed without understanding]" (44–45). Seeking to compensate for the
inability of discourse to contain her pain, she begins to sing. Her song,
which she sings to the tune of the hymn "Jouyssance vous donneray [Joy
I will give you]," is identical to the first stanza of the second *chanson spirituelle*. Throughout the course of the second scene (with Securus) and the
third (with Securus and Agapy), Amarissime alternates spoken discourse
with song, passing freely back and forth from speech, which incarnates
ratio, to music, which embodies the absence of *ratio*. By the end of the third
scene, Amarissime has in fact sung the first ten stanzas of the second *chanson
spirituelle* (she does not sing the last two stanzas) as well as several other
songs in which she is joined by Securus and Agapy.

In the fourth and final scene of the *Comédie*, Paraclesis informs the
others that "Pan est vivant [Pan is alive]" (410). "Pan n'est poinct mort,"

she announces, "mais plus que jamais vit [Pan is not dead, but is more alive than ever]" (404). Expressing the Evangelical notion that the death of the body does not merit tears because it is the passageway to eternal life, Paraclesis exhorts Amarissime, Securus, and Agapy to be joyful:

> Pan est, quoy qu'on die,
> Sain, sans maladie,
> Vif et immortel,
> Contant, satisfaict:
> (Comme esprit parfaict)
> Croiez qu'il est tel.
> Or, soiez contens.
> (470–75)

[Pan is, whatever they say, healthy, without sickness, alive and immortal, content, satisfied; (like the perfect spirit). Believe that this is how he is. Therefore, be content.]

Accepting intellectually Paraclesis' argument, Amarissime cannot, however, experience Francis' absence as a joyful occasion. When Securus and Agapy suggest that they all three sing a song of praise to God, "le grand Pasteur" (535), Amarissime replies:

> Ma pauvre voix vous accompaignera
> En ceste joye, ainsi qu'en la tristesse.
> Mais toutesfois mon oeil se baignera.
> (541–43)

[My poor voice will accompany you in this joy as in sadness. Nevertheless, my eyes will weep.]

The disjunctive "mais" qualifies Amarissime's assent. When Paraclesis says near the end of the *Comédie*, "Or, chantons donc tout d'un accord,/Puisque Pan est vivant, non mort [So, let us sing, all in harmony since Pan is alive, not dead]" (549–50), Amarissime sings along with the others; but she remains unreconciled to the absence of Pan.

The song that concludes *Le Trépas* is in Latin. As at the end of the *Petit Oeuvre*, French gives way to Latin, which, like music, is a paradigmatic or apocalyptic language that transcends *parole* and attains the status of *langue*. The transcendent nature of their song is further emphasized by the fact that the words are those of Job. Singing in unison, all four characters praise God: "Si bona suscepimus de manu Domini, mala autem quare non sustineamus, sicut Domino placuit? Ita factum est. Sit nomen Dei benedictium [If we take happiness from God's hand, must we not take sorrow too? So it has come to pass. Blessed be the name of God]" (Job 2:10 and 1:21). That Amarissime-Marguerite is unable to accept fully the point of view of Paraclesis is proved by the fact that the dilemma she sought to resolve in *Le Trépas* is expressed with even greater intensity in *La Navire*.

CLOSED SYSTEMS

Not until Abel Lefranc published *Les Dernières Poésies de Marguerite de Navarre* (1896) did *La Navire* appear in print. In the manuscript copy, the poem is untitled; nevertheless, the entire packet of manuscripts has an inscription that identifies the first work in the collection as *La Navire:* "Les dernières oeuvres de la Royne de Navar [re]/lesquelles n'ont este imprimees/Premierement le livre que ladicte dame [the word *dame* is added between the lines by another hand] composa en/l'abbaye de Tusson dict le [sic] Navire [The last works of the Queen of Navarre, which have not been printed. First, the book the aforesaid lady wrote in the monastery at Tusson, called "The Ship"]." Following common practice when dealing with an untitled work, the scribe who wrote this inscription no doubt took the first word of Marguerite's poem, which is "navire," and used it as the title.

Shortly after the publication of *Les Dernières Poésies*, Gaston Paris suggested that a suitable title for *La Navire* would be "Consolation de François Ier à sa soeur Marguerite." The title proposed by Paris is not inappropriate. Marguerite's poem conforms to the general format of the *consolatio*, or consolatory poem, which was practiced both by pagan and Christian writers. Like most *consolationes*, *La Navire*, on one level at least, seeks to console the bereaved and to extol the greatness of the departed. Recognizing the descriptive value of the title put forward by Paris, Robert Marichal, whose 1956 critical edition of the poem is the basis of all modern readings of the text, retained the title suggested on the manuscript copy but added Paris' proposed title as a subtitle. Thus, for the modern reader the title of Marguerite's poem as it is printed on the title page of Marichal's edition is *La Navire, ou Consolation du roy François Ier à sa soeur Marguerite.*

There are numerous similarities between *La Navire* and *Le Dialogue en forme de vision nocturne,* the poem Marguerite wrote more than twenty years earlier on the occasion of the death of her niece Charlotte. Less explicitly doctrinal than the *Dialogue*, *La Navire* illuminates the problematics of conversing with the dead and so sheds light on the early work, which comments far less self-consciously than does *La Navire* on the textual problems that inform both poems. Like the *Dialogue*, *La Navire* is a dream vision, or a *visio*, a genre that had special appeal to Marguerite for it allowed her to stress the importance of submission, self-effacement, and receptivity in the life of a Christian. In a *visio*, the dreamer is merely the vehicle of the experience he recalls; he is not the author of his dream. The fiction of a *visio* is that while the dreamer's rational faculties are asleep he becomes the passive page on which an Other writes. Such was the case in the *Comédie du désert*. While Mary slept, God sent her an apocalyptic vision that filled her with joy. In both the *Dialogue* and *La Navire*, the narrator, i.e., Marguerite, falls asleep. The text not only records Marguerite's words but also the words of an Other who speaks a language radically different from hers.

La Navire begins with an unidentified voice that comes out of the undifferentiated linguistic void that surrounds the text:

> Navire loing du vray port assablee,
> Feuille agitee de l'impetueux vent,
> Ame qui est de douleur accablee,
>
> Tire toy hors de ton corps non sçavant,
> Monte a l'espoir, laisse ta vielle masse,
> Sans regarder derriere viens avant.
>
> (1–6)

[Ship grounded far from the true port, leaf blown by the impetuous wind, soul that is overcome with sorrow, wrest yourself from your body, which has no understanding, rise up to hope, abandon your old mass; without looking behind, advance forward.]

For five more stanzas, the voice speaks—now imploringly, now commandingly—to someone identified simply as "aveuglee [the blind woman]" (13). In line 22, the "aveuglee" begins to stir, speaking timidly and hesitatingly at first and then with increasing firmness.

> Que je devins, quant ceste voix j'ouys,
> Je ne le sçay, car soubdain de mon corps
> Furent mes sens d'estonnement fouys!
>
> (22–24)

[What I became when I heard this voice I do not know, for suddenly my senses had fled in astonishment from my body!]

Soon the first-person narrator, the "aveuglee," recognizes the voice as that of her dead brother Francis. A conversation between the grieving Marguerite and the dead Francis ensues and continues for some 1400 lines, after which the sun comes up and Francis announces that he must leave. After a few parting words of advice, he vanishes, leaving Marguerite with the memory of his unexpected appearance. Bearing in mind the general configuration of the poem, we shall now take a closer look at the text.

In the opening lines of the poem, Francis compares Marguerite to a ship tossed about on a stormy sea and declares his intent to console her. A conventional image, the metaphor of a ship assumes richer significance when we realize that the most primitive emblem of Christian faith was not the cross or the ichthyograph but the anchor. Inspired perhaps by Paul's epistle to the Hebrews 6.19 ("Here we have an anchor for our soul, as sure as it is firm"), the anchor appears on the earliest Christian funerary monuments as a symbol of consolation and hope of God's promise of immortality in Christ. Seeing Marguerite buffeted by the turbulent sea of despair, Francis speaks to her, hoping that his words will comfort her. His message is simple. "Quicte ton corps, et lors, spirituelle,/Pourras sçavoir plus que n'as merité [Leave your body and then, spiritual, you will be able to understand more than you have merited]," he says as early as lines 38–39. He repeats this message throughout the poem. As dawn appears, he speaks for the last time: "Tue ta chair, afin que, simple et vuide,/Du vray amour de Dieu tu soyes pleine [Kill your flesh so that, simple and empty, you will be full of the true love of God]" (1393–94). Marguerite knows that Francis is right; but she cannot literally abandon her body. Ostensibly the bearer of consolation, Francis fails to comfort Marguerite. In other words, *La Navire* does not do what it sets out to do, i.e., console.

The most obvious formal feature of the text is also the most important one: the poem is a dialogue between the dead Francis and the living Marguerite. The text is grounded on the premise that language can serve as a mode of exchange between the living and the dead. But the reader, interpreting the text in terms of his ordinary coded knowledge of the world, surely rejects the notion that the text is a mimetic representation of a "real" dialogue between Marguerite and Francis. Language, he knows, cannot extend beyond the realm of time, with which it is consubstantial. Being outside time, the dead cannot communicate with the living through words. The reader tends, therefore, to look for clues that will permit him to give a metaphorical reading to the text, which, claiming the impossible, purports to be a record of an unmediated dialogue between the living and the dead.

By drawing attention to its dialogic form, the text itself, however, seems to resist being metaphorized in this way. *La Navire* consists of alternating speeches by Marguerite and Francis. Every time one of the two speakers begins to talk, the text pointedly identifies him even though the context makes it clear who is speaking. At the end of a speech, the speaker is often identified once again. Each speech is introduced (and often concluded) with an expression such as "Encores dict [again he said]" (31), "Ainsi luy dis [Thus I said to him]" (62), "Il respondict [He answered]" (63), "Lors il me dict [Then he said to me]" (73), "Luy respondis [I answered him]" (116), "Cest voix . . . me dict [This voice said to me]" (175–76). The apparatus of attributive discourse keeps the reader conscious of the fact that he is reading what professes to be a genuine dialogue between the living (if sleeping) Marguerite and the dead (but speaking) Francis. But as he progresses through the poem, the reader senses increasingly that no real exchange occurs between Marguerite and Francis. Language simply does not function as a circuit of communication or as a cognitive channel between the two. Speech fails to facilitate communication. Neither speaker moves from his original position: Marguerite continues to mourn her loss and Francis continues to upbraid her for grieving. Thus the claim of dialogism, which is made by the *form* of the text, is undermined throughout the poem by the absence of exchange between the two speakers, each of whom seems to be locked within a closed system.

Although they use the same words, Marguerite and Francis do not really speak the same language. This point is made early in the poem when Francis rebukes Marguerite for misusing the word "love." Throughout the poem, Marguerite speaks of her "love" for Francis. Each time, Francis interrupts her angrily, telling her that what she calls love is a "faux amour, qui le mal nomme bien,/Et le bien mal [false love, which evil calls good and the good, evil]" (94–95). Her "love" for him, Francis tells her, is nothing but a stubborn, odious attachment to carnal forms. "Love," as he uses the word, is synonymous with *caritas*. It "defait et deforme [undoes and deforms]" (88) man, transforming him into Christ (89–90). Marguerite agrees and says that Francis is no doubt correct. She does not, however, adopt his definition of the word and cotinues to speak of her "love" for him. Whenever Francis tells her that she must overcome her attachment to material forms, Marguerite answers, "Je crois, mais . . . [I believe you, but . . .]" (705). If Marguerite and Charlotte spoke at cross purposes in the *Dialogue*, so do Marguerite and Francis in *La Navire*. Although the poem is formally a dialogue, the text denies that any exchange or intersubjective communication occurs between the two speakers; that is to say, it denies the reality of dialogue. In *La Navire*, attributive discourse is an ironic device that underscores the discontinuous frame of reference within which each speaker is enclosed. Francis and Marguerite cannot speak to each other, for he moves outside time, she, within.

At first, the poem seems to suggest the unfolding of narrative (Francis appears to Marguerite in a dream and tells her to . . .). Narrative is also suggested by the poem's metrical form, the *terza rima*, which *La Navire* shares with the *Dialogue* and the *Petit Oeuvre*. The *terza rima* establishes a forward, linear motion that, in the case of the *Divine Comedy* and the *Petit Oeuvre*, is reinforced by a firm narrative line in the poem itself. In *La Navire*, however, Marguerite rejects narrative because it moves forward in time and so reminds her of her future, which will be marked by the continued absence of her dead brother. Seeking to deny time, she excludes narrative as much as possible from the text. Instead of supporting narrative, the metrical form of the poem becomes an ironic statement on the absence of sustained narrative.

The two most obvious formal tendencies in the text—to be dialogic and to progress narratively along a temporal axis—are conspicuously frustrated. The discontinuity between form and content expresses at the level of discourse the irreconcilable difference between the living Marguerite and the dead Francis, between presence and absence.

Unwilling to move toward the future, which she envisions as a void that everywhere proclaims the absence of her brother, Marguerite rejects the apocalyptic vision, which is the consolation provided by religion. Francis in fact reformulates the Christian apocalypse. In his attempt to draw Marguerite away from her preoccupation with the world of the flesh, he describes the joys he experiences in paradise: "Icy d'amour est la vraye clarté,/Icy se faict de charité le feu,/ . . . [Here is the true light of love; here does fire turn itself into love]" (421–22). "Icy . . . " is repeated four more times within the next few lines. Using anaphora, the main rhetorical figure by which Marguerite expresses the Christian paradigm throughout her poetry, Francis relies heavily on the repertory of images that we have noted in Marguerite's other representations of the apocalypse. Saying "heureux je suis [happy I am]" (472), Francis repeats the word "plaisir." "Ce plaisant jardin/Où il y a plaisir surnaturel [This pleasant garden where there is supernatural pleasure]" (557–58) is the *locus amoenus* where all desires are satisfied. Marguerite, however, rejects the paradise Francis describes. She tells Francis that she, too, seeks pleasure. But sorrow, she adds, resorting to oxymoronic formulation, is her pleasure: "Ma douleur m'est ung savoureux pain . . . larmes, souspirs et cris/Seront mon boire et agreables mectz [My sorrow is for me a savory bread; tears, sighs, and sobs will be my drink and my delicious food]" (247–49). Saying that her sole pleasure is to scratch her wound (334–36), she refuses to transcend concern for the body. As she did in the *Dialogue*, Marguerite, overcome with personal grief, rebels momentarily against the inhuman doctrine of the disembodied spirit that appears to her from the incorporeal world. Indeed, the text owes its existence to the fact that Marguerite refuses to abandon the body.

Hoping to "[la] destourner de la chair [turn her away from the flesh]" (104), Francis admonishes Marguerite to remember their past conversations in which they talked about the happiness of those whom "Charité" (109) burned and annihilated. Francis directs Marguerite's attention toward the past in the hope that it will serve as a springboard to propel her thought toward the future. But Francis's words have an unexpected effect. Unwilling to accept the future, Marguerite seizes upon the opportunity to embrace the past. Her immediate response to her brother is:

> "Las! maintefoy il m'en est souvenu,
> Luy respondis, mais j'ay perdu ce bien
> Que plus tu n'es de moy entretenu.
>
> O la presence a tous yeulx agreable,
> La plus parfaicte et la meilleure grace
> Qui fut jamais et la plus amyable!
> (115–23)

[Alas! often I have remembered it, I answered him, but I have lost this treasure since I cannot converse with you any longer. O presence, agreeable to all eyes, the most perfect and the best grace that ever was, and the most lovable!]

Throughout the rest of the poem, Marguerite, hearing but not heeding her brother's injunction to think about the future, resurrects little by little the past. To escape an intolerable present, she fixes her attention on the past. Memory is the tool she will use to re-experience her absent brother's presence. In her memory he lives not as a disembodied, scolding shade but as she knew him when he was alive. "Amour le veult tousjours tenir," Marguerite exclaims, "non comme mort, mais comme plain de vie,/ *Au temple heureux d'eternal souvenir* [Love wants to hold him always, not as dead but as full of life, in the happy temple of eternal memory]" (163–65, my emphasis). Comparing her heart, the *locus* of memory, to a written record of Francis's deeds and virtues, Marguerite declares:

> J'ay faict mon cueur ung pappier d'inventaire
> Depuis le temps de nostre jeune enfance
> Jusqu'a la fin de luy et son histoire.
>
> (169–71)

[I made my heart an inventory sheet since the time of our early childhood until the end of him and of his story.]

Fashioning her text, Marguerite consciously constructs a monument, a pantheon designed to "contain" Francis. What the reader witnesses throughout the course of the poem is the embodiment of Marguerite's memory, or heart, in language. The absent Francis is encoded into language, and thus becomes present to the reader. In much the same way that the spirit becomes manifest in flesh, Marguerite's memory becomes manifest in a linguistic construct that has the structure of a temple, fixing or containing time.

Concretizing her memory in language, Marguerite elaborates a text that is analogous to a fleshy body. Her concern from now on in the poem is with things fleshy and corporeal, as Francis immediately senses. "O vain et nul ton charnel pensement/Que tient ton cueur a la terre lié [O empty and worthless your carnal thinking, which keeps your heart bound to the earth]" (217–18), Francis exclaims, trying to divert Marguerite's attention away from the past and from language, the medium that structures memory. Polite but indifferent to his comments, Marguerite reaffirms her duty as she sees it: to erect a linguistic structure that will be an incarnation of her memory:

> Tous les plaisirs du monde sont prescriptz
> Dedans mon cueur, ou tourmens et ennuys
> Sont paintz au vif, engravez et escriptz;
>
> Cours sont les jours, courtes me sont les nuictz
> Pour y penser et pour ramentevoir
> Ce que oublier je ne veulx ny ne puis.
>
> Privee suis de l'ouyr et du veoir,
> Ou je trouvois toute felicité;
> Mais vraye amour n'en faict moings son debvoir,
>
> Car elle croist en ma necessité,
> En reveillant sans cesse ma memoire
> Du tempz passé, tant loing d'adversité.
>
> (250–61)

[All the pleasures of the world are rejected in my heart, where torments and sorrows are painted from life, engraved and written; short are the days, short are my nights, to think about them and to remember what I cannot and do not wish to forget. Deprived am I of the sound and the sight of that in which I used to find all my happiness; but true love does not do its duty any the less because of that, for it grows in my need, awakening without ceasing my memory of past time, so far from adversity.]

Because her memory cannot do justice to Francis, the text itself will become a new memory, richer and more vibrantly faithful than the old. Not only does Marguerite incarnate her memory in a text, but the text, in an act of perfect consubstantiality, re-creates her memory in a form that can be transmitted to a reader. For Marguerite, as for Augustine, writing and reading are essentially the same activity. The reader "rewrites," or translates, the text before him, seeing through the literal context to the significance it acquires in the light of a larger perspective. Marguerite's intent in *La Navire* is both to "read" the text engraved in her memory and to fashion a linguistic monument that will serve to commemorate Francis and to "translate" her memory of him into a structure that can be "read" by others.

With a persistence that exasperates Francis, Marguerite dwells on physicality. Declaring that she wishes to portray Francis as love painted him in the portrait she carries in her heart, Marguerite says:

> Je voy tousjours ton visage et beau taint,
> Ton oeil joieulx, qui a tristesse ou joye,
> A tes amis ne pouvoit estre fainct.
>
> (766–68)

[I see always your face and fine coloring, your joyful eyes, which express sadness or joy, which could not be counterfeited for your friends.]

Obsessively, Marguerite repeats words like "corps," "chair," "visage," "face," "bras," "piedz," "mains," "chef," "oz," "voix," and "yeux." Francis tries in vain to obstruct this flow of words that evoke the flesh. "Laisse de moy tous ses charnelz recordz [Set aside all these carnal testimonies]," he says; "recorde toy de Celluy qui l'ouvrage/Faisoit en moy par ses divins accordz [bear testimony of Him who completed the work in me through His divine decrees]" (814–16). But just as Francis' allusion to memory had produced an effect contrary to his intent (later Marguerite ironically accuses *him* of not remembering), so his admonition to think about Christ prompts Marguerite to contemplate Christ's crucified body. Instead of concentrating on Christ's spiritual message, she focuses on the suffering body, on what she calls, in a phrase that retains an echo of the medieval *danse macabre*, "la dance/Du grand Helas [the dance of the great Alas]" (940–41).

Marguerite insists on the body not merely because she rebels against the effacement of her brother's physical presence. The textual enterprise she has set for herself is to construct an *embodiment* of Francis. Her project is to create the *literal* context, the pantheon that readers will translate back into spiritual significance. This point is illustrated graphically in the final third or so of the poem. Having erected a linguistic mausoleum in honor of Francis ("Je te vouldrois par escript honorer, [I would like to honor you through writing]" (446), Marguerite invites, one after the other, three distinguished contemporaries to enter the edifice-text and pay their respects to the dead king. First, Eleonor, Francis' widow, is ushered in: "Eleonor, o noble Royne, approche,/Viens de tes yeulx son sepulcre honorer [Eleonor, O noble queen, approach; come honor with your eyes his sepulcher]" (988–89). Throughout eight stanzas, Marguerite speaks to Eleonor. She then turns to Catherine, who, weeping, is led in. Finally, Henri II, "Roy, filz de Roy [King, son of a King]" (1091), enters and listens to Marguerite as she speaks to him about his father. The presence of Eleonor, Catherine, and Henri gives a public and ceremonial dimension to the text. Ceremony is reflected, too, at the level of discourse, for the three apostrophes are rhetorical exercises that obey the rules laid down for epideictic eloquence by classical and medieval rhetoricians. Public pomp is increased when Marguerite recites Francis' most memorable deeds, fashioning linguistic frescoes (1170-1209) designed to decorate the walls of the mausoleum and to depict Francis' glory.

Beginning as a *complainte*, La Navire modulates into eulogistic discourse. Curtius tells us that "for eulogies of rulers epideixis had developed fixed schemata in Hellenistic times." These schemata were adopted by medieval writers. "Physical and moral excellences," Curtius notes, "were arranged in series—for example, beauty, nobility, manliness (*forma, genus, virtus*)." Physical beauty was particularly important, for it was interpreted as a sign of Nature's favor. By presenting Francis as an exemplary work of Nature, handsome, noble, and manly, Marguerite seeks both to embody her memory in panegyrical language and to fashion a text that, displaying the formal features of epideictic oratory, will have, perhaps, the durability of a classical eulogy. Manipulating the *topoi* of epideixis, Marguerite constructs within the broader framework of her poem a series of set-pieces in which her memory of Francis is transposed from a private into a public register. Designed to serve as public monuments, they have, however, the remoteness, the inertness, the *irrelevance* of an ancient tomb, and so underscore the discontinuity between the living Marguerite and the dead Francis. Formal eulogy fails to translate the "pappier d'inventaire" engraved in Marguerite's heart.

This failure is symptomatic of the text's inability to do what Marguerite would like it to do, i.e., resurrect the past and obliterate absence. Furthermore, the text comments repeatedly on the impossibility of accomplishing the task set for it. The central problem lies in the very structure of memory and language. Early in the poem Marguerite discusses the essential role that absence plays in memory:

> Je n'avois sceu ne bien penser ne croire
> Qu'amour eust sceu par mort prandre accroissance,
> Mais maintenant la chose m'est notoire:
>
> Ainsi que l'oeil a parfaicte plaisance,
> Voiant le bien ou son desir repose,
> Amour le faict vivre par congnoissance,
>
> Rementevant jusqu'a la moindre chose
> Le temps passé de ce roy sans nul vice,
> Au cueur duquel vertu fut tout enclose.
>
> (262–70)

[I had not known, not really thought or believed, that love was able to grow greater by death; but now this is obvious to me. As the eye has perfect pleasure in seeing the good on which its desire has settled, so love makes him live through awareness, recalling in minute detail the past of this king, who had not the slightest vice, whose heart was completely enclosed in virtue.]

Memory depends on absence, for we remember only what is past, other, not present. Without absence, or alterity, there is no memory. This point is illustrated at the beginning of the poem when Francis' voice comes to Marguerite as something Other, something absent from herself. Marguerite discovers that consciousness of Francis' absence permits her love for him to increase. Furthermore, absence plays the same role in language that it plays in memory. Language comes into being only when we are conscious of something Other, which we then designate with a word. The referent, or thing designated, is not contained in the word; it is absent. As Lacan observed, "the word is a presence made of absence." Language, like memory, contains an absence that is immanent in it.

In *La Navire*, Marguerite fashions a linguistic construct by means of which she tries to place herself in a past that is alive in her memory, a past in which Francis still moves and talks. She discovers, however, that language is irremediably temporal. Every speech act is an affirmation of existence in the present. Seeking to deny the present through language, Marguerite succeeds only in situating her own existence in the hateful now. At the same time, the real absence of the referent (Francis) calls into the discourse the things this absence stands for: death, emptiness, silence.

Francis' absence from the text is expressed forcefully at the end of the poem. At the break of dawn, Francis announces that he must leave ("Voicy le jour, il m'en convient aller) [Here is dawn; I must depart]" (1399). Suddenly, Marguerite cries out in language we have not heard since the beginning of the poem:

> "O monseigneur, pas ainsy n'adviendra
> Te departir sy promptement d'icy,
> Dis je en criant, *ma main te retiendra!*"
> (1411–13, my emphasis)

[O my lord, not so will it happen that you depart so promptly from here, I said crying out, my hand will hold you back!]

These are the last words she addresses to Francis. As she speaks, he vanishes, seemingly disproving her claim that "ma main te retiendra!" Marguerite does, however, hold something in her hands: a linguistic cenotaph (*kenos*, empty, + *taphos*, tomb) that contains, or circumscribes, Francis' absence. The ending of the poem, with its overtones of an *aubade*, provides powerful poetic closure because it confirms the Otherness of Marguerite's relation to the text. *La Navire* set out to do what it cannot do (cannot be a consolation, cannot be a dialogue). The fact that the consolatory poem that ought to follow the title (*La Navire, ou Consolation du roy François Ier à sa soeur Marguerite*) is *not there* creates a gap or a silence in the text that duplicates with mimetic exactness the void in Marguerite's life.

We must now account for the last nine stanzas (1414–40) of the poem. As Francis vanishes, Marguerite feels her heart pierced with love ("[le] cueur d'amour transy," 1414). Suddenly—and indeed for the first time in the poem—she is overcome with joy:

> Je n'uz sur moy os, chair, veine ny nerf,
> Qui ne sentist une joye amirable,
> Chassant dehors ennuy pesant et grief;
> (1432–34)

[I did not have any bone, flesh, vein, or nerve that did not feel a wonderful joy, chasing away heavy sorrow and pain.]

Looking at the rising sun, which often represents God in the mystical tradition, Marguerite, dazzled by its beauty, closes her eyes:

> Mais, regardant ce hault ciel desirable,
> L'ardant soleil vint esbloir ma vue,
> Me fermant l'eul par lumiere importable.
> (1435–37)

[But, while I looked at this high, worthy sky, the burning sun dazzled my sight, making me close my eyes because of unbearable light.]

Sight gives way to insight, light to a darkness that, as the Pseudo-Dionysius said of Divine Darkness, "is dark through excess of light" (*Div. Names* 32). Cessation of language at the end of the poem signals Marguerite's return to the undifferentiated state of unconsciousness—or, at least, unawareness of self—from which she was called in the first line of the poem by Francis' voice. Silence and Divine Darkness precede and follow the text, marking the unitive stage in which the Subject fuses with the All. In terms of the Saussurian distinction between *langue* and *parole,* the unitive stage is of the order of *langue.* The text, on the other hand, is always of the order of *parole* and so illustrates (in the classical sense of *illustratio*) the alterity inherent in language itself. *La Navire* demonstrates, above all, the relationship of Otherness.

Marguerite and Francis represent two distinct closed systems. A closed system is one that is independent of its context or that is defined as such (e.g., the solar system); an open system, on the other hand, is one that depends on its environment for its continuing existence and survival (e.g., an organism). For the living Marguerite, Francis, who is dead, is the Other. Similarly, for Francis, Marguerite is the Other. Within the economy of the text, each "system" (Marguerite and Francis) is the "environment" or "context" of the other. Rejecting its "context," each system confirms its boundaries and remains closed. Each defines itself negatively by rejecting the injunctions of the other. Marguerite refuses to obey Francis, who says over and over: "*quicte ton corps, tue ta chair* [abandon your body, kill your flesh]." Francis' commands are paradoxical injunctions. Exhorting Marguerite to mortify the flesh, Francis would have her reject *la parole,* which, embodied in the text, is the means by which she mortifies the flesh. She must, in fact, resist his injunctions in order to obey them. Moreover, the reader shares in Marguerite's dilemma. Francis' injunctions have the pointedness of moral imperatives directed to him as well as to Marguerite. If he obeys them, he will cease attending to the text (flesh). Only by refusing to do what Francis commands can the reader continue to hear (read) the injunctions that he must disobey. Francis, too, disregards the injunction of the Other, for he rejects Marguerite's entreaties to remember their shared past. The lack of positive response on the part of both Marguerite and Francis to each other's appeals underscores (as does, for example, the music with which the *Ravie* answers the three uncomprehending ladies in *Mont-de-Marsan*) the monologism of a closed system.

The final irony of the text is that Marguerite can obey Francis' injunctions only when he ceases to make them. At the level of discourse, Francis' command that Marguerite abandon her body is tantamount to demanding that the text (*corpus verborum*) stop. However, Francis cannot make this injunction outside the textual body he would annihilate. His demands sustain and enflesh the body his injunctions seek to suppress. Only the *deus ex machina* at the end of the poem (*deus,* literally, for the sun represents God) can resolve the dilemma in which Marguerite finds herself. By compelling Francis to vanish from the text, by drying up his injunctions, the sun alters the "context" in which Marguerite operates. As the sun rises, Marguerite's heart is pierced with love. God's presence radiates throughout her being. The system represented by Marguerite, the only remaining system in the text, becomes (or, in Augustinian terms, is now rightly perceived as being) the ultimate closed system—ultimate because there is no "context" or "environment" beyond it.

The model for this kind of system is Cusanus' *machina mundi.* In a celebrated passage from *De Doçta Ignorantia,* Cusanus restates a medieval commonplace and defines the cosmos as "a *machina mundi* whose center, so to speak, is everywhere and whose circumference is nowhere, for God is its circumference and its center, and He is everywhere and nowhere." Since the *machina mundi* comprises everything, there can be no "environment" that transcends its boundaries. It cannot open onto something else, for it is all (*Tout* is Marguerite's word). Because nothing (Marguerite's *Rien*) exists outside it, it is inexorably closed. Being *Tout,* God is the locus where there is coincidence of antitheses, concordance of differences.

Although within the economy of the text Francis represents the Other for Marguerite and Marguerite the Other for Francis, the text in its totality represents the Other for the reader. For him, Marguerite and Francis are sub-systems within the larger system that is the whole text. He sees in Francis and Marguerite symbols of a conflict between desire (for enclosure within Christ, for atemporality) and experience (of doubt, despair, time), between what Marguerite (the author, not the "I" of the poem) *believes* and what she *knows* experientially. In other words, the author's ideology of self (Marguerite's view that the *moi* is infused with the presence of Christ) is in conflict with the actual phenomenology of the self represented in *La Navire,* indeed, in all her poetry. In a sense, each of Marguerite's poems could bear the title of the second poem in the *Marguerites: Discord estant en l'homme par la contrarieté de l'Esprit et de la Chair, et paix par vie spirituelle* [The Discord that is in man because of the opposition of spirit and flesh, and peace through spiritual life].

Writing and Drawing in Scève's *Délie*

Elisabeth Guild

PRELIMINARIES

Readings of the role of the emblems in the *Délie* figure frequently in the body of critical discourse on that text. In what follows, the attempt is to move (from) the established commonplaces and, within the broad problematic of the textual limits of the *Délie,* to reflect on the emblems' *uncommon* place in the text, and less by rereading than by reviewing their topography, to reconsider broadly three topics. Namely, the articulation and disarticulation of movements within these places; the punctual movements between them and the writing of the *dizains;* and how the lover's subject, and the subject of writing, figure in, are figured and disfigured by, the emblems.

"Souffrir non souffrir" is inscribed between the dedicatory *huitain,* "A sa Délie," and the first *dizain,* and then reinscribed after the last *dizain,* even after the word *Fin.* The end is not the end: the (re)inscription follows. And the initial inscription is not initiatory: the dedicatory *huitain* precedes it, in turn already preceded by a name.

Nor is it simply a name: the (not innocent) use of the possessive pronoun "*sa* Délie" already both proposes and presupposes an originary, absent object, who prefigures the writing, even opens up the possibility of its presence—and also (perhaps, undecidably, before the object) the unnamed writing subject. The prior presence of object and subject is therefore inscribed within the initial inscription, and situates that inscription within the space of narrative possibility, between subject and object. Four hundred and forty-nine *dizains* follow, followed in turn by the (re)inscription.

It is tempting to read the (re)inscription as the echo, or the simple repetition of the words "Souffrir non souffrir"; this would imply cyclic

---

From *Paragraph* 6 (October 1985). © 1985 by the Modern Critical Theory Group.

return, perhaps, or a final closing of the text. However, "Souffrir non souffrir" follows "Fin," so seems to be beyond the limits of the writing of the *Délie*, and has no determinable subject, object, or temporality. Here, subject, object, and temporality, writing and reading are suspended; so here, the closure of the *Délie* is indefinitely suspended too, insofar as the time and space of the (re)inscription—which still seems to demand to be read within the limits of the *Délie*, insofar as it *does* play on the initial inscription, and insofar as, retrospectively, the movement between the two plays over the text—are indefinitely open.

The outer limits of the *Délie* seems indeterminable; moreover, even obviously within its apparent circumscription, there are already apparent limits to writing and reading, apparently marginal and exorbitant spaces: that is, the emblems, densely framed, their space not that of writing (or "reading").

In what follows, the question whether the emblems are "intrinsic" or "extrinsic" has no place. Nor will there be any move towards assigning them particular, stable significance as a principle of textual organization or coherence. What is in question is how the presence of the fifty emblems, and the trace of their inscriptions through the *dizains,* as a supplementary presence (used in the sense elaborated by J. Derrida), affects the space of the *dizains'* writing.

But who is the writing subject? And is the term "emblem"—hitherto used only provisionally—appropriate?

JE (SUIS)

The *Délie* has been seen as an intellectually subtle and erotically intense exploration of the themes of love and death. Those themes are disseminated—and therefore are no longer (strictly speaking) themes in the traditional sense—by the voice of the subject, in its passage between the "je" and its object. This passage is oriented by and towards the loved object, although the object is silent, and the subject solitary.

The object is the other, therefore always absent; but this absence makes possible the presence in the *dizains* of different refractions of the other. For instance, a name: "comme Lune infuse dans mes veines/Celle tu fus, es & seras DELIE" (D 22, 7–8); an unnamed addressee: "Te voyant rire auecques si grand grace" (D 96,1); a metonymic fragment of the other—hand, neck, eye, eyes; a metaphor, presenting a difference within the other, the other as different to any prior self; or a space of reflexion, an other self of the subject: "Miroir meurdrier de ma vie mourant" (D 307, 2), often potentially deadly.

The transformations of the object, and the other's difference, seem evident; but it remains to question the nature of the subject. As "je" throughout the *dizains,* its unity and permanence might seem self-evident. But any such identity derives from the first vision of the other, who will orient the previously volatile, aleatory, disoriented subject (D 1). Thus, the subject's voice in the *dizains* depends on the prior presence of the object, prior to the subject's pretence of priority: "Ie t'ay voulu en cest Oeuure descrire" (A sa Délie, 4); and moreover will continue to derive from the other throughout, not fully present, not present to himself: "Vers toy suis vif, & ver moy ie suis mort" (D 100, 10). As can be traced throughout the *Délie*, in the turns and returns of the subject's voice, the identity of the subject is undecidable; beyond his being as fragments and traces of *science* and culture, gathered up and reproduced, he seems to be constituted by *following* the mobile and often contrary being of the object:

> Mais de cestuy la pointe inexorable
> M'incite, & poinct au tourment, ou ie suis
> Par un desir sans fin insatiable
> Tout aueuglé au bien, que ie poursuis,
> (D 217, 6–10)

or losing his being by fleeing what it should follow:

> Pourquoy fuys ainsi vainement celle
> Qui de mon ame à eu le meilleur part?
> Quand m'esloingnant, tant a moy suis rebelle,
> Que de moy fais, & non d'elle, depart,
> (D 263, 1–4)

and also, conversely, through his desire, to be constitutive of the other's textual presence. There is no fixed centre; the subject is only virtual, and should not necessarily be positioned univocally as the "conscience unifiante du recueil" (F. Hallyn).

Critical instances of this lack of continuity of identity are figured by the different positionings of the subject in the inscriptions of the emblems, where the *pointes*, or more precisely fragments of, or resemblances of, the *pointes* of particular *dizains* are presented. The subject in the inscription will tend to be identified with the subject of the visual image presented by the emblem in question; moreover, the movement of identification and interpretation is double: the visual subject is a metaphor for the subject in the inscription, who, as, for instance, succory plant (Emblem XVI), deer (Emblem XVIII), Acteon (Emblem XIX), viper (Emblem XXVII), or butterfly (Emblem XXXI) will therefore both differ from the pronominal subject of the relevant *dizain*, and also, on each occasion, present another different, provisional identity of that subject. The profusion of different provenances of the emblem images—nature, Classical mythology, Christian mythology, the everyday—further militates against the drive to integrate these fragmentary, momentary subjects into a single continuity, and an identifiable totality. To point up the impossibility of integration, one need perhaps only instance one case of what seem to be two incongruous subjects: "Pour le veoir ie pers la vie" (Emblem I) and "Pour te adorer ie vis" (Emblem III).

Although the selection of the instance of a female subject, and of the apparent contradiction between a subject who loses life, and a subject who lives, in no way does justice to the complexity of the issues involved—the relation between the different inscriptions, their trajectories through the text, the orientation of the subject in the inscriptions—to which I shall return, it is a simple device, and does, simply, illustrate the point immediately in question.

EMBLEMATIC DEVICES

Are the emblems of the *Délie emblesmes* or *devises*? Although the sixteenth-century and seventeenth-century Italian and French theoretical discourses on *emblesmes* and *devises* seem to propose repeatedly the same criteria, in fact their terms tend to be ill-defined, and individual variations on the basic received wisdom can cause much confusion, to the extent that what theoretically differentiated *emblesme* from *devise* often seems either obscure, or superficial. The intricacies of the issue are peripheral to the present project, but it is significant that, against a background of theoretical indeterminacy, critical definitions of the iconographic elements of the *Délie* have differed. In the sixteenth century, there is reference to the *dizains'* being accompanied by paradigmatic emblems: "mieux appropriés et plus spirituels que ceux d'Alciat" (I refer to a letter from Jean de Vauzelles to Aretino (1551), as cited by Coleman in *Maurice Scève, Poet of Love* [1975], 55), and in recent critical studies, the term emblem tends to have been used, untheorized; on the other hand, in Menestrier, *La Philosophie des images*, they figure as *devises*, and Coleman has persuasively argued the case for their being considered *imprese amorose*, or *devises* ("Les Emblesmes dans la *Délie* de Maurice Scève," 6–15).

They seem to be emblems, insofar as they are constituted by an image, an inscription, a frame, and a title; but insofar as they are neither didactic nor immediately intelligible and universally significant, being, rather, mysterious and specific, they are *devises*. On the other hand, they can only be included in this category at the price of accepting the attribution of that problematic quality, intention (the notion of intention is inscribed in the term *impresa*, i.e. the Italian name for *devise: impresa*, from *imprendre*, to undertake, intend), and in any case, must be excluded, because human figures, theoretically prohibited in *devise*, are presented by many of the images. More crucially, they are not *devises*, because, as was suggested above, the subject has no stable identity, and therefore no one, no essence, exists as their necessary source.

Furthermore, since the topography and performance of the emblems/*devises* in the *Délie* is not simply assimilable to either any near contemporary theory or practice—for instance, Alciati, *Emblematum Libellus* (1534), La Perrière, *Le Theatre des bons engins* (1539), or Aneau, *Picta Poesis: Ut Pictura Poesis Erit* (1552)—and since, common to all the theorists of both emblems and *devises* is a concern with the relation between, on the one hand, image and inscription, and on the other, between their framed space and their textual context, it may (at the expense of differentiation) be more productive provisionally to keep both terms in play, in the designation, *emblematic devices.*

As a means of approach to the textual problems posed by the emblematic devices in the *Délie*, aspects of the etymology of the term emblem will be more significant than would be any form of description of the emblem as textual phenomenon. The connotations of the term, deriving from ἔμβλημα, through the Latin *emblema*, have already been explored by Hessel Miedema, with reference to Alciati, and by Daniel Russell, in the context of sixteenth-century French usage in general. But their presentation needs to be supplemented here, not least because, in its drifting between ἔμβλημα, *emblema*, and *emblème*, the term has generated so many ex-centric possibilities. Already between the primary Greek definition, as an insertion (either functional—the shaft fitting into the spearhead, an insole—or decorative—a chased or embossed ornament used in the decoration of plates, etc.), and the Latin, primarily aesthetic orientation of the term, as mosaic, inlaid pavement, the problem of the supplement arises. The inlaid pavement as a whole may clearly constitute a decorative insertion into a larger space; the relation between inserted part, and whole, seems unproblematic. But the internal composition of the pavement is uniformly one of insertion; and unlike the Greek ornamental "supplement"—that is, distinctive, extractable, addition—its "supplements," the indiviudal inserted fragments, intractably constitute the totality of the work, simultaneously substance and its decoration, containing, undifferentiated, the difference. If the problem is reformulated in terms of distribution, then its relevance to the *Délie* becomes apparent. The emblem books of the period, for instance Alciati, *Emblematum Libellus,* or Aneau, *Picta Poesis,* are, like the Latin inlaid pavement, composed of emblems, of an even distribution of visual images and written text, whereas in the *Délie,* the distribution is 50:449. Clearly, the insertions must have a different status; but to conclude that the insertions in the *Délie* are additional, incidental, and accidental—although decorative—would be inaccurate. They may form a supplement, but not in any simple sense. They may be as necessary to the *Délie* as an insole (ἔμβλημα/*emblema*) to an ill fitting shoe, or as a grafted cultivated branch (ἔμβλημα/*emblema*) to a wild tree, that is, as a means to its productive cultivation. However restricted their presence in the text (in relation to the volume of *dizains*), they are not simply marginal.

And precisely because they are not simply marginal, the problem of their integration must arise. The grafted branch will, over time, through natural growth, be absorbed by the tree, and its energy transferred; but the relation between textual emblem and context is not analogous. These textual grafts may equally be a potent source of textual productivity; but that potential cannot be gradually absorbed by the text in the manner of a natural organism, and thus their potential may be as much a threat to the integrality of the text as a transforming source of fruitfulness. Furthermore, if their supplementary presence is necessary to textual productivity (as is the cultivated branch to the uncultivated tree), the supplement will potentially destabilize the text, and displace its centre. But wherever the textual margins and centre(s) may be provisionally located, what will be in question is the sort of supplementary textual energy released by the relation between them.

This relation may also be approached through the term *devise*; it is less the etymology of the term than its polysemia and its aleatory associations which are significant as a means to figuring the different possibilities of discourse between the emblematic devices and their context. *Devise*, device: stratagem, contrivance, from *dividere*: to divide—a divisive, disruptive device? But also, *devise*, *deviser*: "s'entretenir familièrement" (*Robert*), to talk, to chat—are *devise* and context, on the contrary, engaged in open, productive dialogue? This function of the term implies a logic of exchange, which extends into the field of economy, both financial and textual: "valeur commerciale sur l'étranger, servant de moyen de transfert des capitaux d'un pays dans un autre." In terms of negotiation and transaction between apparently different systems, the visual and the verbal, between image and inscription, and between emblematic device and *dizain(s)*, in terms of the textual economy of the *Délie*, these connotations of the term *devise* seem more useful than traditional definitions of the relation of the emblem or the *devise* to its context as being that of metaphor to literal context, although the significance of the connotations of that model—illustration and condensation, and the paradigmatic value of the emblematic device as the materialization of verbal metaphor's visual orientation—are valuable.

At this point, by aleatory (visual) association with *devise*, *dévisser*: "défaire (ce qui est vissé)," may be brought into circulation. *Dévisser* gestures towards *délier*, and towards the possibility of seeing the emblematic devices' untying of the text, the *Délie*, and deferring of its closure.

THE TOPOGRAPHY OF THE EMBLEMATIC DEVICE

The theoretical constraints on the relation, within the frame of the emblematic device, between image and inscription, as *corps* to *âme* should also be loosened (*dévissé, délié*). The metaphor is only useful, here, insofar as it is a traditional hierarchy's figure, and can prompt review of writing's apparent privilege over drawing (drawing used loosely here to designate the traces on the face of the woodcut) when both derive from *graphô*. In the exploration of the relations between image and inscription, frame, and title, and of how these elements figure in the *Délie*, and in the move to trace the nature of, and limits to, *reading* them, the terms drawing and writing will be more productive than any figurative equivalent.

The Disentitled Title

The title figures first, here, in a list—title, image, inscription, frame—in which it has no proper place. In the recent editions of the *Délie* by McFarlane and Charpentier, the text of the title falls between and outside both emblematic device proper, and *dizain*. But in the original editions of the *Délie*, the titles only figure as items in a contextual list, in the *Table* at the end, thus at the typographical limits, of the text. So, the title should not strictly be included under each emblematic device, because of all that its presence excludes. (In order clearly to review the place of the emblematic device in the *Délie*, the discussion will be based only on the 1544 and 1564 editions [i.e., the first edition and, with reference to the emblematic devices, the first significantly different edition], neither of which gives titles, except in their *Table*.)

It appears simply to describe the image. But it is selective, and thereby circumscribes it. There is a wide variety of types of title: designating the image as a whole—for instance, "La Femme qui desuuyde" (Emblem VIII), or "L'Alembic" (Emblem XXIII); designating a part or parts—for instance, "La Girouette" (Emblem XV), or "La Cycoree" (Emblem XVIII); proffering common nouns ["La Girouette," "Le Cerf," "Le Chat et la ratiere" (Emblems XV, XVIII, and XXXIII)]; proper names ["Acteon," "Orpheus" (Emblems XIX and XX)]; or a combination of the two ["Cleopatre et ses serpentz" (Emblem XXX)]; describing a state—for instance, "La Lune en tenebres" (Emblem XXXVII), or signalling the possibility of a narrative—for instance, "Leda et le cygne" (Emblem XLI), or "Le Mort ressuscitant" (Emblem XLIV), etc. Nonetheless, common to all types is the fact that they only designate the iconic aspect of the image, and not its (more significant) symbolic possibilities. Whether the presence of the title is read as an indication of the inscrutability of the image without writing's support or grounding, or of its ambiguity, the further, undesignated, fruitful interpretative possibilities of the image, as presented in the earliest editions, without the overprivileged and arresting presence of the title, should be recognized.

Moreover, the title's presence occludes the movement between the emblematic device and the contextual *dizain(s)*, in that it interposes a description of a different order. And yet, on another level, its presence—a linear, verbal message, outside the frame, designating (an aspect of) the visual image within the frame—apparently mediating visual and verbal systems, seems to reduce the difference between the process of reading the verbal text, the *dizains*, and that of "reading" within the space of the frame, where the organization and orientation of graphic traces differs from that of writing, as do the time and space of their aleatory "reading."

"L'Image N'a Pas de Sens Propre"

It would seem that reading writing's trace differs from "reading"—viewing—images in that it is a question of reading beyond the materiality of that trace, and, ideally, comprehending a signified which the signifier exists only to convey in its purity; whereas on the other hand, "reading"—"viewing" the image implies no such immediate transcendence towards a signified: the immediate materiality of the trace obtrudes. But whether so clear a difference can be traced in the *Délie*, is still in question.

The pictorial aspect of the emblematic devices seems relatively simple: graphic traces appear to represent in (albeit often rudimentary) three-dimensional form, the objects, figures, and situations in question, although nothing that is proper to those objects of representation is present. But as aspects of emblematic devices, the case is less simple, for the pictorial images cannot be separated from their function in terms of the poetics of the *Délie*. Their provenance, status, and relation to writing are all problematic.

"L'image n'a pas de sens propre" (Antoine Compagnon, *La Seconde Main*): that is, with reference to emblems and *devises* in general, it itself has no predetermined, fixed, defining meaning. However, this indeterminacy is only provisional; the image is present in function of the emblem or *devise*, and its significance circumscribed accordingly. In the specific context of the *Délie*, the potential significance of the image is plural only to the extent that its emblematic function allows, and moreover, insofar as the poetics of this text determines.

According to some theorists (for instance, Aneau and Menestrier), the pictorial image's very possibility of meaning is dependent on, subsequent to, its incorporation within an emblem or *devise*. Until then, it seems to be either dumb—"une Poësie muette" (Menestrier, *L'Art des emblemes*)—or even dead: "Praemortua, semisepultaque," *vitally* dependent on the verbal: "ibi ego tales eiconas non temere effictas esse ratus, recepi me ex mutis, & mortuis, vocales, viuas effecturum: inspirata viuacis Poëseos velut anima quod quam alacriter recepi" (Aneau, *Picta poesis* [Lyon, Bonhomme]).

Thus, if the "meaning" or "significance" of the pictorial image is to be defined in terms of the verbal rather than the visual, it seems that its meaning or significance cannot be proper, but must be improper, derivative. Writing, the verbal, assumes the privileged voice—although this maybe an improper assumption, for writing itself is traditionally only the dumb, arbitrary trace of speech.

All of the above assumes that "image" is the proper term for the type of pictorial representation in question. But these representations are not immediate reproductions of the objects represented: the images on which emblems and *devises* in general seem to centre—and this is particularly true of the specific emblematic devices on the *Délie*—are already less pictorial representations than icons, and less icons than symbols. They have a coded and conventional (verbal) basis: they derive from Classical myth and legend—Narcissus, Dido, Leda, Acteon, etc.; Christian myth—Lazarus, Babel, for example; proverbs; existing poetry; prior emblems; they are culturally determined, exist within writing's space, and seem most immediately dependent on the writing of the *Délie* itself.

There they offer visual metaphors which correspond to, or *devisent* with, the *pointes* of the relevant *dizains*, in a variety of ways; they are not simply derivative, or amplificatory devices, but authentification of, and supplement to, the related verbal structure's proper sense(s).

But if the "readability" of the images (retaining this term in order to avoid the specificities of "icon" and "symbol") seems to derive primarily from their dependence on prior texts, their potential readings—as "texts" within texts—may, however, exceed those texts. Moreover, the emblematic devices' inclusion of prior texts not necessarily traced by the *dizains* of the *Délie* may, to some extent, be read as a sign of their exceeding the *dizains* which seem to frame their reading: instead of being framed by their writing, they partly frame *their* reading.

It seems, in general, that as parts of emblematic devices the images are already dependent on writing, and therefore cannot offer more authentic representations of their objects than writing can, but the theoretical possibility of the pictorial image's priority over writing may be admitted. For instance: "la peinture, dont . . . la Poësie imite l'artifice" (Menestrier, *L'Art des emblemes*); this priority would derive from its status as a more "natural" language than writing, and also, its (dangerous) charm, and its potentially more potent voice than writing's, in terms of both pleasure and instruction: "l'esprit est bien plus vivement touché par ces images, qu'il ne seroit par un simple discours, & l'impression que ces figures font sur l'ame est bien plus efficace que celle des paroles" (Menestrier, *L'Art des emblemes*).

This therefore admits the possibility if not of a "sens propre" of the image then of a *sens* which is *propre* to the image, beyond assimilation to writing, *propre* as writing's other. The image offers an ambiguously direct *and* indirect representation of its object—with all the seduction of the veil. The possibility of this *sens propre,* a potentially disruptive force in the text— if by text is understood a totally coherent, unified whole—may perhaps, in part, explain the critical tendency anxiously to privilege the writing of the *Délie*, and to insist on the incorporation of the emblematic devices, undervaluing their difference, overlooking the displacement, dislocations, and evasions of textual coherence their presence produces, concentrating more on how they *devisent* with the *dizains* than on how they *dévissent*, or *délient* the text.

There is a conventional alternative to the interpretative incorporation of the emblematic devices: that is, strategically to relegate them to the margins of the text's significance, thus to acknowledge their occlusion by their dense material frames. To occlude: "to close (a vessel or opening); to prevent the passage of a thing by placing something in the way," *and:* "of certain metals, etc., to *absorb and retain . . . within their substance*" (SOED, my emphasis). In the context of a discussion of the emblematic devices' frames, the double action of that verb will prove significant. But first, before (although within) the frame, the place of the inscription should not be overlooked.

Tracing the Inscription

The images and frames of the 1544 and 1564 editions of the *Délie* differ; but in both cases the inscriptions are inscribed around the image, in the margin between image and frame. In the 1544 edition they describe (not always completely) the form suggested by the image and delineated by the inner edge of the frame: (1) rectangle, (2) circle, (3) lozenge, (4) ellipse, (5) triangle, or (6) oval. In the later edition, all the inner edges form rectangles, and already, an unbroken single line forms a rectangular frame around the image. Thus the inscription seems to fall within the outer frame, and seems to share the space of the image, to be simultaneously present (Once within the frame, within the space of the image, writing begins to lose transparency, and seems to be assimilated by drawing. It is symptomatic of this loss that modern editions of the *Délie* reset the *dizains'* writing in modern typography, but not that of the inscriptions); and although, particularly in the later edition, its location in the margin seems to suggest the priority of the image: "les mots separez de la figure ne signifient rien de complet, mais . . . s'unifient avec la figure pour signifier quelque chose" (Menestrier, *La Philosophie des images*), it may initially be encountered as a means to organizing the pictorial space: "sans que pourtant on puisse dire que ces paroles soient l'Ame de la Devise, mais seulement le mot qui en exprime la proprieté" (Menestrier, paraphrasing Lucarini, *Imprese dell'Officioso Academei Intronato*).

But beyond its function both as an interpretative and (to some extent) a material frame, the inscription also relates the emblematic device to the *pointe* of the related *dizain*(s) in a variety of ways.

The images, and the formation and production of the emblematic devices, seem strictly to have been materially subsequent to the writing of the *dizains*. But this is immaterial: each of the fifty emblematic devices' images and inscriptions is encountered prior to its *dizain*(s), and thus variations between inscription and *pointe* will seem to be located not in the (provisionally more forceful) former, but in the latter. And moreover, there will always be difference, between supplement and *pointe*; even when the words of the inscription and the *pointe* seem to be identical (as in Emblem III and D 24, Emblem V and D 42, Emblem XXXII and D 285, for instance), because the inscription falls within the frame of the emblematic device, as a nonlinear trace, there is not strict identity.

However, before tracing the difference in writing and reading within the frame, and before further exploring different possibilities (beyond the traditional) for writing's presence and potential functions there, it is necessary to interpose some discussion of the frame—an interposition symptomatic of its operation in the *Délie*.

"Ca Boite et Ça Ferme Mal"

Already, what has been called the "question . . . abyssale" is already in the air (J. Derrida, "Parergon," in *La Vérité en peinture*); fragments of figurative "frames" already scattered through the discussion have pointed the difficulty of locating the "frame," beyond its simply material presence. And despite the three-dimensional density of the material frames—whose cornucopian aspect is possibly more spectacularly disruptive of textual continuity than the images' presence, an effect in no way diminished by the fact that there are only six different, and therefore repeated designs—even the nature of that material presence in the text is difficult to determine. "Ni oeuvre, ni hors d'oeuvre . . . Le cadre parergonal se détache, lui, sur deux fonds, mais par rapport à chacun de ces deux fonds, il se fond dans l'autre" (Derrida, "Parergon"); this, in conjunction with the general instability of the term "frame" itself, may frame up (falsify, falsely fix), unnecessarily limit possible readings of the *Délie*.

Stated simply, the function of the frame is to demarcate, to surround, and include all those elements necessary to, or which adhere to, the work in question, and to exclude everything beyond; thus, to define what it circumscribes in relation to a given context. In the *Délie* specifically, the density of the frame may further serve to point up the three-dimensional aspect of the space it surrounds.

There, the frames of the emblematic devices appear to be those elaborate structures that include image and inscription, create an "entité" (Hallyn) and exclude as contextual the rest of the *Délie*, the *dizains*—or conversely, exclude the emblematic devices from the *dizains'* space, thereby defining their marginality.

The problem of inclusion and exclusion does not end there—because the frame cannot simply be located there. It has already been suggested that the provenances of the images "frame" the *dizains* with prior texts, and that the inscriptions, being textually precedent, "frame" the related *pointes*. But on the other hand, the inscription's trace around the image already also inscribes a sort of frame, within the (framing) margin. Moreover, the 1544 and 1564 "frames" differ. The frames of the emblematic devices of the 1564 edition are not air-tight, and thus seem materially to allow writing freely to enter the device's space—but to make only one step, into the margin, because drawing's space is already closed, framed. But in the 1544 edition, the frames do materially seal off the emblematic device, and whilst that space, that of drawing, writing's other, is open to displaced writing (insofar as an inscription is present within the frame), so that drawing and writing *devisent*, the completely included writing of the inscription is now completely excluded (within the frame) from the rest of the text, its provenance.

Thus there is no simple frame, and no simple textual economy. The possibility of exchange (*devise*) between the different systems and fields, drawing and writing, visual and verbal, is indefinitely deferred, due to the different editions' different frames. And as a corollary, no single centre to the *Délie* can be traced. The presence of the different systems or fields produces plural forces and moves: writing either seeks violently to enter the space of drawing, or else seeks to relegate it to the margins of the text; but drawing, from the margins, violently draws writing in. Writing and drawing double the movement of desire between writing subject and loved object: "Lors estant creu en desir effrené/Plus le l'attire et plus a soy m'en-traine" (D 33, 9–10). Writing is drawn towards a different centre, and although it does not yet arrive: "ie ne puis desirant arriuer" (D 320, 10), its centre is displaced, and there is a centrifugal dissemination of writing and writing subject.

The agonistics of these textual moves can perhaps begin to be eluci-dated by a provisional rhetorical description of the performance of the emblematic device. According to Fontanier's definitions, whilst it seems perhaps to function as a *parenthèse*, bracketed off by its frame, its textual energy is, rather, at least that of an *epiphonème*, or even, most accurately, an *hypotypose*—and of an *hypotypose* which demands priority that would potentially violently dislocate its context, precipitate textual disintegration.

But even *hypotypose* is not an adequate term; although it suggests the visual, it is still primarily verbal in connotation, and—like any provisional rhetorical description of the textual relation in question—must be supple-mented by a term which offers clearer associations with the visual: *ana-morphosis*. That is, the relation of emblematic device to context may be characterized as follows: its presence entails an ambiguous perspective, demands of the reader/viewer double, or ambiguous vision; it acts as a "mise en pointe" of its context, exposing, calling into question the accepted relations and values inscribed there—for instance, writing's privilege, the unity of the text, textual intelligibility; and, as Hallyn observes of the an-amorphic skull in Holbein's *Ambassadors:* "l'anamorphose est à la repré-sentation en perspective 'légitime' ce que la mort est à la vie: un principe de décomposition" ("Holbein: La Mort en abyme"). This is not to confuse the different perspectives of drawing and writing—but to suggest that in the *Délie*, where writing claims legitimacy and priority, the punctual pres-ence of drawing, unless somehow circumscribed (whether by material frames, or by interpretative frame-ups), may indeed threaten writing (the "legitimate" body of the text) with decomposition.

The anamorphic emblematic device in the *Délie* may elude specific rhetorical classification; but its textual presence may be comparable to that of the rhetorical figure in general: that is, as the place of passion and desire, and therefore of potentially disruptive energy, a place of resistance to tex-tual incorporation. But it may also present the possibility of a more im-mediate representation of its object than writing's, and thus of achieving what writing desires. Also, in achieving what writing desires, it would also figure the death of writing.

The images that figure in the emblematic devices apparently depend, of course, on prior discourse—writing('s). On the other hand, their pres-ence cannot be fully accounted for, or made intelligible by, that discourse. There remain traces which have an immediacy prior to, or more potent than, the written text. Hence writing's double strategy: both circumscrip-tion (a move doubled by interpretative dismissal of the emblematic devices to the margins), and insistent repetition, in the form of inscription, of the move to enter and finally to appropriate what is proper to the image, its space, as a means to authenticate its own discourse.

Neither device succeeds, either in the economy of the 1544 or of the 1564 text. As inscription, within the frame, in drawing's space, writing both fails to attain drawing's propriety, and also, through its improper attempt on drawing's property, loses its own propriety: "ie scay bien, que pour estre forclos/De ta mercy, de mon bien tu me priues" (D 192, 7–8). For, as inscription, writing becomes an emphatically material presence, with no possibility of an ideal transparency, or of immediacy of representation. Moreover, as inscription, writing's trace in the margin between drawing and frame is predominantly *graphic*, that is, not properly writing or drawing, but tending towards an undifferentiated *graphô*.

In such a state of decomposition, dispossession, and disfigurement, writing differs from itself, and is no longer properly readable. It figures its own death: "Fuyant ma mort i'haste ma fin" (Emblem XVIII), or: "en ce poinct (a parler rondement)/Fuyant ma mort, i'accelere ma fin" as the *pointe* (D 159, 9–10) repeats the inscription, with some difference.

"EN TOUS LIEUX IE TE SUIS"

But what place have decomposition and death in a text in which *themes* of decomposition and death seem to figure less than themes of death's defeat, or indefinite deferral—as in, for instance, D 378: "Tu me sera la Myrrhe incorruptible/Contre les vers de ma mortalité' (9–10), or as implied by the suspension of time and of the contingencies of subject and object achieved by the initial inscription's different (re)inscription? And furthermore (combining the domains of themes and textuality) when, beyond any "frame" that might be perceived in the representation of a coffin in the final emblematic device, as its inscription, "Apres la mort ma guerre encore me suyt," suggests, writing, the text, continues:

> Aussi ie voy bien peu de difference
> Entre l'ardeur, qui noz coeurs poursuyura,
> Et la vertu, qui viue nous suyura
> Outre le Ciel amplement long, & large.
> Nostre Geneure ainsi doncques viura
> Non offensé d'aulcun mortel Letharge?
> (D 449, 4–10)

It is a question of the text's plural logics and possibilities, and above all, of the productive tensions between them—so that the place of death and decomposition is, in the end, everywhere in the text (see, for instance, D 167, or Emblem XXVII: "Pour te donner vie ie me donne mort," or Emblem XXXVI: "Dedens ie me consume"). From any one of its plural centres, to its (unlocatable) limits, wherever their location, the presence of the emblematic devices ensures the openness of the text, of its possibilities of meaning.

Plurality of themes—emphatically not that of positive plenitude—is doubled by textual plurality: the emblematic devices neither decidably destructively fragment, nor cause to disintegrate the text (*dévisser*)—nor offer a means to total integrality or sense of integration (*deviser*). The unstable relation between emblematic device and context, writing and writing's other, drawing, ghosts the moves interminably played out between plural subject and object. They figure the desire of the discontinous self to find fullness and completion in the other—a desire in which a sense of precariousness, fragmentation, and self-destruction is always already present: "maulgré moy, trop vouluntairement/le me meurs pris es rhetz, que i'ay tendu" (D 411, 9–10); a grammar of desire whose subject and object are indeterminate, whose conjugations are deponent, whose conjunctions are unreliable, whose ellipses are hiatus, whose verbs are intransitive, or frequently reflexive (of an untraceable subject)—for instance: "De moy ie m'espou(u)ante" (Emblem XXVI), or: "Pour te donner vie ie me donne mort" (Emblem XXVII). Subject and object even seem reversible, or interchangeable: they figure the tension between the desire to discover the self in the other and the awareness of the impossibility of its fulfilment, and of the realization that such an impulse must prefigure a loss of self to other:

> . . . ta vertu aux Graces non diforme
> Te rend en moy si representatiue,
> Et en mon coeur si bien a toy conforme
> Que plus, que moy, tu t'y trouuerois viue.
> (D 229, 7–10)

That loss is thematized in many *dizains* in terms of absence and presence (see for instance D 264), and also, crucially, in terms of *s'abymer* and *se dissoudre*:

> Le hault penser de mes frailes desirs
> Me chatouilloit a plus haulte entreprise,
> Me desrobant moymesme a mes plaisirs,
> Pour destourner a la memoire surprise
> Du bien, auquel l'Ame demoura prise:
> Dont, comme neige au Soleil, ie me fondz
> Et mes souspirs dès leurs centres profondz
> Si haultement esleuent leurs voix viues,
> Que plongeant l'Ame, et la memoire au fondz,
> Tout ie m'abysme aux oblieuses riues.
> (D 118)

But perhaps the most intense and dramatic configurations of the development of the theme of the heliotropic movement of subject towards object, towards the discovery of the only possibility of being, as following the other, or being in the other's being—thematic doubling of the writing-drawing agonistics—are the *momentary* elisions of self and other in the ambiguity of *je suis:* être, suivre, "En tous lieux iete suis" (Emblem 16):

> Comme des raiz du Soleil gracieux
> Se paissent fleurs durant le Primeuere,
> Ie me recrée aux rayons de ses yeulx,
> Et loing, & près autour d'eulx perseuere.
> Si que le Coeur, qui en moy le reuere,
> La me feit veoir en celle mesme essence,
> Que feroit l'Oeil par sa belle presence,
> Que tant ie honnore, & que tant ie poursuys:
> Parquoy de rien ne me nuyt son absence,
> Veu que'en tous lieux, maulgré moy, ie la suys,
>
> (D 141)

and:

> En toy ie vis, ou que tu sois absente:
> En moy ie meurs, ou que soye present.
> Tant loing sois tu, tousiours tu es presente:
> Pour pres que soye, encores suis ie absent.
>
> (D 144, 1–4)

"L'EXTERNE NE RESTE JAMAIS DEHORS"

The fragmentation, plurality, and mobility of "frames" displaces the logic of the frame (of the emblematic device), and the agonistics of drawing and writing, writing and drawing, continues, ghosted by the moves of the subject.

The coffin in the final emblem provisionally puts in perspective, "frames," these potentially endless textual displacements and decompositions. Only to have been already displaced by Titus-Carmel, *The Pocket Sized Tlingit Coffin*—model and 127 drawings—, as written about by Derrida in "Cartouches": "un coffin sans core, sans noyau central et organisateur."

Louise Labé and Pernette du Guillet: Assimilation with a Difference: Renaissance Women Poets and Literary Influence

Ann Rosalind Jones

The two main currents of love poetry in the Renaissance are named after men: Neoplatonism recalls the author of the *Symposium*, Petrarchism the composer of the *Canzoniere*. And besides having its sources in male figures, the poetry they engendered was practiced overwhelmingly by male poets. What makes these apparently self-evident statements interesting to feminist critics is the fact that women were also part of these traditions: the objects of love in male-authored poetry spoke as the lovers of men in female-authored texts. But this shift in role from the inspirers of men's poetry to the performers of their own did not lead women to invent new feminine discourses. The women poets, rather, wrote within but against the center of the traditions that surrounded them, using Neoplatonic and Petrarchan discourse in revisionary and interrogatory ways.

I will be concerned here with the reception of lyric conventions in the poetry of two women members of the Ecole lyonnaise, Pernette du Guillet and Louise Labé. Pernette, the daughter and wife of aristocrats, died at twenty-five; her *Rymes* (1545) were published late in the year of her death. Louise Labé, the daughter and wife of rich ropemakers, published her twenty-four *Sonnets* (1555) at thirty-five. Both wrote in clearly recognizable modes (du Guillet as a Neoplatonist, Labé as a Petrarchan) and in response to specific men: du Guillet to Maurice Scève, Labé to an unnamed but evidently Petrarchan lover/poet, often identified as Olivier de Magny. Both *Les Rymes* and the *Sonnets* reflect earlier traditions in refractive ways, bringing new emphasis and fundamental questioning to the modes in which they are written.

From the start, this inside-outside position was inevitable for women love poets. Male poets questioned the conventions they had taken over

From *Yale French Studies* no. 62 (1981). © 1981 by *Yale French Studies*.

from classical and Italian poetry; indeed, mockery of the clichés of Neoplatonic and Petrarchan poetry soon became a convention itself. Ronsard,
for example, rejects conventional astrological metaphors in *Sonnets pour
Hélène* because they are inadequate (Hélène is more stable than the moon,
rarer than the light of the sun); Du Bellay advises his lady in "Contre les
Pétrarquistes" to resist the fantastic praises of Petrarchans and Neoplatonists alike. But neither poet challenges the basic rhetorical situation of such
poetry: a man speaking to gain a woman's love. The logic of their dissection
of other poets lies precisely in the fact that they themselves are speaking
from the same position, only better—so more deservingly. Women poets,
however, write from a position outside the convention altogether, from a
new and marginal space that calls into question the polarities implicit in
such poetry. If a woman poet expresses her love for a man in the Neoplatonic mode, she ceases to be the transcendent ideal called upon in Scève's
Délie, for example. Likewise, a woman who analyzes her suffering in the
absence of her lover, in the Petrarchan mode, reverses the relationship on
which Petrarchan poetry depends: the distance and silence of the lady
versus the pain and longing, hence the speech, of the lover. To speak as
a woman in either of these discourses (most poets, in fact, combined them)
is to contradict the role they assign to women: the opaque target of the
masculine gaze, of male desire, of male praise and persuasion. By virtue
of their sex, early women poets challenged the rhetorical and symbolic
order on which love poetry was based.

French feminist critics have argued recently that all women, as a result
of their exclusion from phallocentric discourse, challenge that discourse
whenever they speak or write. Julia Kristeva argues for this cultural marginality as an advantage, while Luce Irigaray celebrates women's innate
resistance to the "ready-made grids" of men's linguistic codes. Seen from
such perspectives, Pernette and Labé's use of a feminine voice in poetry
previously limited to male speakers presents a significant test case for
theories of literary influence. For one thing, the identification of "borrow-
ings" from male-authored poetry becomes problematic in the analysis of
poetry by women. If a male poet speaks of "un beau sein," for example,
he may well be citing his predecessors; his conventionally gendered voice
calls up a conventional referent. But if a woman writes in praise of a male
"beau sein," she changes the referent of the male-voiced phrase by virtue
of the voice she gives the poem: speaking as a woman, she calls up a
different image. Women poets also quote male poets ironically—parodic
praises insincerely delivered—and thus call into question the precision of
claims that a woman is "citing" her male predecessors. Most important,
psychoanalytic theories such as Harold Bloom's of individual relationships
between master poets and their ephebes fail to account for a situation in
which the poets are not men and men but men and women.

Pernette du Guillet never earned the notoriety that Labé did, and
modern critics have treated her as a more or less unproblematic case of

assimilation to Neoplatonism. I would argue, however, that she reveals the contradictions inherent in writing as a woman within that convention. Rather than effacing the tensions raised by an idealized figure who begins to declare her subjectivity in terms taken from the idealizing vocabulary, her poems call into question the role postulated for her in Scève's *Délie* even while she seems to be cooperating in a lyrical dialogue with him. One reason why she is less read than Labé may be that her entry into the public world was orchestrated to be such a quiet one. Her editor, Antoine du Moulin, presented *Les Rymes* with a preface in which he praised Pernette as a "virtuous, noble, and highly spiritual Lady." (Quotations of *Les Rymes* are from Victor Graham's edition [Geneva: Droz, 1968]. All translations from the French are my own.) He claimed to be making her poems public only in response to the "loving insistence of her grieving husband," and he wrote a huitain emphasizing that the love depicted in the poems to follow was so pure that it could leave no room for critical gossip. In an era when women were only beginning to be published—and often, as had been the case with Christine de Pisan, finding themselves at the center of controversy when they did—du Moulin's caution is understandable. And in a social climate in which chastity and silence were enjoined upon women, his defense of Pernette makes even more sense. One example of the link imagined between women's chastity and their silence is Francesco Barbaro's advice, from his influential conduct book *De Re Uxoria* (Paris, 1513, 1553). Praising a woman of exemplary modesty who withdrew her bare arm from the sight of a male admirer, he goes on to say, "It is proper, however, that not only arms but indeed also the speech of women never be made public; for the speech of a noble woman can be no less dangerous than the nakedness of her limbs." Pernette was spared such dangers. For one thing, she was dead, a subject for eulogy rather than a target for temptation. Praised in epitaphs for her "chaste body, where Virtue had its seat," published with her husband's blessing and vouched for by a respectful editor, she was introduced as an honorably modest figure even though a woman poet.

Les Rymes, like their author, offered little ammunition to detractors. Throughout her eight or so poems, du Guillet uses an elevated Neoplatonic vocabulary and tone; she envisions "an awakened spirit" and "holy affection" as the endpoints of their spiritual ascent. Two stanzas of her Chanson 7 reveal her sensitivity to possible suspicions about her chastity:

> Qui dira que, d'ardeur commune
> Qui les Jeunes gentz importune
> De toy je veulx, et puis holà:
> Je ne sçay rien moins, que cela. . . .
> Mais qui dira que d'amour saincte
> Chastement au cueur suis attaincte,
> Qui mon honneur onc ne foula:
> Je ne sçay rien mieulx, que cela.

[Whoever says that I desire you with the common passion that drives the young, and then that's all!—I know nothing less than that. But whoever says that my heart is touched with holy love, which never did my honor harm, I know nothing better than that.]

As well as disarming the judgments likely to be passed on the morality of a woman love poet, du Guillet emphasizes the reciprocity—even the identity—between the lovers. One formula for this reciprocity in the Scève-du Guillet exchange is their interlocking scheme of poetic naming. Scève assigns the name Délie (the Delian, Diana of Delos, goddess of the moon) to his lady; she refers to her beloved as "mon Jour" and "mon Soleil." She compares him to Apollo in her fourth epigram, claiming twinship with him, and in Epigram 5 she declares that she hopes to become his *semblable*: "Je tascheray faire enmoy ce bien croistre,/Qui seul en toy me pourra transmuer [I will try to increase in myself this good, which alone can transform me into you]." She further assumes identical loyalties as a consequence of their union. Love, having assigned them equal happiness, assigns them equal duties as well (Epigram 26):

> Prenez le cas que, comme je suis vostre
> (Et estre veulx) vous soyez tout à moy:
> Certainement par ce commun bien nostre
> Vous me debvriez tel droict, que je vous doy.

[Take it as given that as I am yours (and want to be), you are entirely mine. Certainly, according to our shared good, you would owe me the same right I owe you.]

A relationship conceived in this way presents a striking contrast to the seductive casuistry in much male-authored poetry and to the realities of marriage in the tightly controlled patriarchal families of the Renaissance. The Neoplatonic ideal may have had a good deal to offer women on the imaginative, if not the practical social plane. Du Guillet seems to fit smoothly into a metaphorical and ethical system that assigns her as active and visible role as her *Soleil*'s.

Yet the exchange between *Les Rymes* and *Délie* actually runs less smoothly than these poems suggest. Du Guillet's ideas of love are different, even opposed to Scève's. In spite of her claim to write only in reverent imitation of her "*maistre*," she diverges from his sequence in ways that can best be understood as evidence of the problematic interplay between the woman poet and the male-centered tradition to which she was responding. A first contradiction between the role Scève assigns Délie and the role Pernette acts out in her own sequence arises from the contrasting connotations they give their meteorological imagery. To Scève, Délie as moon is distant and dreadful. The lunar metaphor carries on earlier traditions in which the lady is *dompna* or *dea,* and it allows Scève to darken the atmosphere of her supremacy over him. He attributes to her the fatal powers of

Hecate and Proserpina as well as Diana (D 22), and his awestruck attempts to interpret the lunar cycle dramatize how her phases—"maculé," "pallissant," "rougissant en Martial visage" [spotted, turning pale, reddening with a face like Mars's]—terrify him (D 193). Out of step with the cycle of night and day, he claims that her every appearance at moonrise triggers off his struggle between terror and desire: "Toutes les foys, que sa lueur sur Terre/Iecte sur moy un, ou deux de ses raiz,/En ma pensee esmeult l'obscure guerre [D 358: Every time her light on earth casts one or two rays upon me, it stirs up the dark war in my thoughts]." The symbol of lady moon has instability and mystery built into it; the poet of *Délie* presents Délie/Diana as a mythical Other.

Pernette writes in a totally different vein. The central element in her love is *contentement,* the satisfaction of all needs, and most of her poems are variations on the theme of calm joy. In her description of her enamorment (Epigram 2), she uses night and day as metaphors for her spiritual states, ending with the enduring illumination brought her by her Sun:

> La nuict estoit pour moy si tresobscure
> Que Terre, et Ciel elle obscurissoit,
> Tant qu'à Midy de discerner figure
> N'avois pouvoir, qui fort me marrissoit.
>   Mais quand je vis que l'aulbe apparoissoit
> En couleurs mille et diverse, et seraine,
> Je me trouvay de liesse si pleine
> (Voyant desjà la clarté à la ronde)
> Que commençay louer à voix haultaine
> Celuy que feit pour moy ce Jour au Monde.

[To me the night was so very dark that it blotted out earth and sky, so that even at mid-day I could not make out any shape, which alarmed me very much. But when I saw that dawn was appearing, in a thousand hues, various and serene, I was so full of delight, seeing light all around, that I started to praise in uplifted voice him who brings this daylight into the world for me.]

While Scève insists in his enamorment poem on the fatality of Délie's effects, recalling her piercing glance and power as "Basilisque," giver of life in death (D 1), or confesses that he spends his nights awake in the grip of obsessive longing, du Guillet rejects both paradox and reversed pathetic fallacy: "Jà n'est besoing que plus je me soucie/Si le jour fault, ou que vienne la nuict,/. . . Puis que mon Jour par clarté adoulcie/M'esclaire toute [Epigram 8: I no longer need be concerned whether daylight goes or night comes, . . . because my Day, with tender brilliance, enlightens me through and through]. Standing outside any system of symbols for the traditionally female beloved, she asserts the constancy of love against the vicissitudes of literal and metaphoric nights.

Like Scève, she sometimes uses Petrarchan oxymoron, basing a poem on the joy-in-suffering of love—one instance of the mixture of conventions in most Renaissance love lyric. But her emphasis usually falls on the positive side of *le doux mal d'aimer*. She treats the theme of Epigram 15, for example—that each lover's pain, since it is a proof of love, causes the other lover's happiness—playfully, with epigrammatic point, repeating "content" so often that it overwhelms the other side of the conventional opposition:

> Pour contenter celuy qui me tourmente,
> Chercher ne veulx remede à mon tourment:
> Car, en mon mal voyant qu'il se contente,
> Contente suis de son contentement.

[To content him who torments me, I seek no remedy for my torment, for seeing that he's contented by my woe, I am contented by his contentment.]

The voice in this poem has nothing about it of the shifting mystery that Scève attributes to his female partner.

Another thematic center of *Les Rymes* is the intellectual respect du Guillet gives her Sun, whose "esprit" benefits not only her but all those who come under his influence. Chanson 9 is a lilting statement of the idea:

> O heureux jour, bien te doit estimer
> Celle qu'ainsi as voulu allumer,
> > Prenant tousjours cure
> > Reduire à clarté
> > Ceulx que nuict obscure
> > Avoit escartés!
> > > Ainsi esclairée
> > > De si heureux jour,
> > > Seray asseurée
> > > De plaisant sejour.

[O blessed Day, she whom you deigned to set afire must value you highly, always careful as you are to bring back to the light those whom dark night has led astray! Thus enlightened, I will be certain of a happy life.]

Here, as elsewhere, Pernette suppresses sexual union as a step on the ladder of love. In other contexts, *"allumer"* (l. 36) could have an erotic meaning, but Pernette uses it to describe her beloved's effect on a plural and mixed-sex public (*"ceulx,"* l. 39), thus enlarging her theme of the lasting happiness based on wisdom. Such an assertion of tranquil security would come as a shock in *Délie*. Scève projects an eternal union for his lovers, but only in a conjectural afterlife. He is far from claiming it as a steady certainty in the tormented present of his sequence.

All these differences stand out in a pair of poems critics have typically used to illustrate the similarities between du Guillet and Scève. Her Epigram 13 and his Dizain 136 both celebrate the unity of the lovers, but the emphasis is different. Scève asserts the erotic power of the force that makes them one, while du Guillet looks to its honorable and lasting consequences:

EPIGRAM 13

L'heur de *mon mal,* enflammant le desir,
Feit distiller deux cueurs en un *debvoir*:
Dont *l'un* est vif pour le doulx desplaisir,
Qui faict que Mort tient l'autre en son pouvoir.
     Dieu aveuglé, tu nous a faict avoir
Du bien le mal en effect *honnorable*:
Fais donc aussi, que nous puissions avoir
En nos espritz contentement durable!

[The happy outcome of my woe, enflaming desire, distills two hearts into one duty: one of them lives on the sweet suffering that gives death power over the other. Blind god, you have given us the ill of good that's honorable in its results: let us also be able to keep lasting contentment in our spirits.]

DÉLIE 136

L'heur de *nostre heur* enflambant le desir
Vnit *double ame* en vn mesme *pouoir*:
L'vne mourante vit du doulx desplaisir
Qui l'autre viue à fait mort receuoir.
     Dieu aveuglé tu nous a fait auoir
Sans autrement ensemble consentir,
Et posseder, *sans nous en repentir,*
Le bien du mal en effect *desirable:*
Fais que puissions aussi long *sentir*
Si doulx mourir en vie respirable.

(Italics mine)

[The happy outcome of our happiness, enflaming desire, unites a double soul in a shared power: one, dying, lives in the sweet suffering that has brought the other, living, to death. Blind god, you have let us possess, without otherwise feeling the same, and have, without repentance, the good of ill that is desirable in its results: let us also feel such sweet dying as long as we have the breath of life.]

Neither poem can be interpreted as referring unambiguously to a sexual encounter: in the Neoplatonic lexicon, both "*le mal du bien*" and "*le bien du mal*" more likely refer to the lovers' transcendence through suffering. But du Guillet's poem is explicitly less erotic than Scève's, oriented as she is toward honor, spirit and stability rather than present bliss. In spite of his protestations of innocence, Scève's dying souls and sweet death belong to a register of involuntary pleasure quite different from the dutiful consciousness of Pernette's hearts. Most commentators have assumed that Scève rewrote Pernette's poem for the better. Certainly, as Jacqueline Risset shows, his version is semantically and sonorously more unified than hers: she maintains her separation in the "mon mal" of l. 1, while he makes the lovers one through the "nostre heur," "double ame," and the ellisions and alliteration of his first two lines (*L'Anagramme du désir: essai sur la* Délie *de Maurice Scève*). But the sensuous fusion in Scève's poem is appropriate because he is saying something different from Pernette. She is insisting on the *équité* and propriety of her love, speaking not as the Délie of *Délie* but as the chaste and future-minded narrator of the relationship as she defines it. The demands of her social role and her interpretation of love as shared knowledge distinguish her poem sharply from Scève's.

A deep contradiction would confront the poets, moreover, were they to bring the theoretical basis of their Neoplatonism into a shared discourse. As long as only one partner engages in Neoplatonic speech, his desire to become his own best self by taking on the superior virtues of his beloved presents no problems. But an impasse results from the identical claims of two such lovers: if man and woman alike assert their inferiority to the ideal other, how is either one to satisfy the other's adoration? It is misleading to speak, as critics have done, of a dialogue between Scève and du Guillet. They circle, rather, in separate orbits defined by the fact that the mode in which they write has developed in an androcentric literary universe. Even more striking is the contradiction between the serene voice in which Pernette addresses her sun and the terrifying silence and inconsistency Scève attributes to Délie. Were he to represent her as speaking out of the reciprocity on which both sets of poems are ostensibly based, the mystery and struggle that generate his sequence would vanish. His speech depends on the severity of his lunar beloved; confronted with Pernette's poetic voice, the male poet's productive anxiety would founder in a rhetorical absurdity. *Délie* needs Délie's silence.

One strange, short poem in *Les Rymes,* Epigram 28, foregrounds the contradictions between Pernette's claims of obedience to her Sun and her actual poetic practice. V.-L. Saulnier conjectures that the poem was a rationalization of her marriage (c. 1538). Whatever its occasion, she rejects her lover's power over her in a blunt style that is also a rejection of the diction of Neoplatonic compliment:

> Si je ne suis telle que soulois estre,
> Prenez vous en au temps, qui m'a appris
> Qu'en me traictant rudement, comme maistre,
> Jamais sur moy ne gaignerez le prys.

The struggle and rupture suggested in these lines intrude sharply upon the lasting contentment predicated elsewhere in *Les Rymes,* as does the reference to domination rather than shared duty. And yet it is not surprising that Pernette returns to the fold in the second quatrain. But she does so on her own condition: having judged from her sun's actions that his claims to loyalty are sincere, she accepts again the relationship and the vocabulary she has learned from him:

> Et toutefois, vous voyant tousjours pris
> En mon endroit, vostre ardeur me convye
> Par ce hault bien, que de vous j'ay compris
> A demeurer vostre toute ma vie.

[If I am not longer as I used to be, blame time for it, which has taught me that by treating me harshly, as a master, you will never win the upper hand over me. Nonetheless, seeing you still captive in my vicinity, your ardor, in the name of that lofty good I have understood through you, convinces me to remain yours all my life.]

Pernette insists on a new basis for her role as Neoplatonic disciple: her sun's humble behavior under fire. The abrupt declaration of independence in the first quatrain and the delicate balance worked out in the second typify the ways she uses convention throughout her poems. In her celebrations of reciprocity, she refuses the position of all-powerful celestial lady, as she refuses any authority on the part of her spiritual mentor if it involves a lapse from the discourse of equals. And even when she uses forms and ideas close to Scève's, the sound of her voice within his amatory scheme calls Délie/*Délie* into question. Pernette's relationship to the social and literary expectations within which she maneuvers might best be described as critical participation. She remains obedient to the norms of Neoplatonism; indeed, her emphasis on the symmetry of her love makes her a purer practitioner of the theory than the dark Petrarchan paradoxes of *Délie* make of Scève. Rhetorically, however, her poems contradict his: silent and alarming as object of love, she is contented and fluent as lover/poet herself.

Du Guillet's representations of her particular interests through the gridwork of Neoplatonism are less radical than revisionary. Next to them, the direct challenge Louise Labé offers Petrarchism stands out more clearly. The central fact in the relationship between a Petrarchan lover/poet and his beloved is that it is not centrally a relationship at all, but a creative projection on the part of the male poet. Petrarch's fascination with Laura is fed by her indifference and her absence. He lives on memory and longing, and he can continue writing for her after her death because her death changes none of the conditions on which his writing depends. Although most of his followers preferred to keep their Dianas and Phyllises alive, they nonetheless held onto the theme of feminine inaccessibility that had motivated the hope and despair of the *Canzoniere*. Into such a convention the voice of a woman Petrarchan must be a startling intrusion. A beloved who says, "I am here; I, too, burn and freeze; I am yours" would put a sudden stop to any poetry of deprivation and fantasy.

Labé broke the rules of Petrarchan discourse and other rules as well. She published her poems herself (she, not her printer Jean de Tournes, applied for the *privilège du roy*), addressed them to a man who was not her husband and who inspired a love far less chaste than fiery, and wrote an introductory epistle to a woman friend in which she attacked the monopoly men had over education and culture: "Mademoiselle, the harsh laws of men no longer prevent women from applying themselves to the arts and sciences: I think that those who are able should take advantage of this honorable freedom . . . and show men the wrong they used to do us by depriving us of the pleasure and fame that learning could have brought us." If she had designed the topic and the presentation of her sonnets to provoke her readers, she could hardly have done better. Before and after her death she was attacked as a "common prostitute" or defended on the basis of her "chaste spirit"; whether she was blamed or praised, the terms of the debate remained the decency or indecency of her private life. Natalie Davis, in her study of Lyon, sums up the attitudes according to which she was condemned: "The public and independent identity of Louise Labé was based on behavior that was unacceptable in a modest . . . woman. The books Louise read and wrote were lascivious; her salons an impure gathering of the sexes; and her literary feminism impudent" (*Society and Culture in Early Modern France*). Her *Sonnets* make it easy to understand how her writing contributed to her notoriety. Although she says in several poems that her lover is gone, their separation as a backdrop for the sequence pales next to the exclamatory eroticism of some of the poems and the unrepentant facing up to the consequences of love in others. Even if she had limited herself to the oxymoronic melancholy of Petrarchism, her woman's voice would have shattered its rhetorical underpinning. But she goes further, adding Ovidian sensuality and a defiant persona to a tradition that had a genteel propriety among most of her predecessors.

Labé also interrogates one Petrarchan convention from within: the *blason*. Lists of praises for feminine beauty were such a commonplace by the sixteenth century that a set of norms and nomative similes was in place: hair like golden wires, skin like ivory or alabaster, eyes like stars. By considering what form such analytic evaluation of a man might take, Labé reverses the roles of observer and observed that underlie poetry in praise of women; and she is led by the absence of a standard for masculine beauty to interrogate any poetic system for defining beauty.

She raises the issue for the first time in Sonnet 2, built on a series of apostrophes to her beloved's eyes and to the hopeless passion they set off in her. Using the *blason* details (ll. 1, 7–8) to frame her list of the man's effects on her life, she imitates structurally the inescapable intensity of her response:

> O beaus yeus bruns, ô regars destournez,
>   O chaus soupirs, ô larmes espandues,
>   O noires nuits vainement atendues,
>   O jours luisans vainement retournez:
> O tristes pleins, ô desirs obstinez,
>   O tems perdu, ô peines despendues,
>   O mile morts en mile rets tendues,
>   O pires maus contre moy destinez.

In the first tercet she returns to her beloved's attractions, but her final exclamation has an edge of irony, of mock astonishment, as though his charms were out of proportion to her mere woman's resistance:

> O ris, ô front, cheveus, bras, mains et doits:
>   O lut pleintif, viole, archet et vois:
>   Tant de flambeaus pour ardre une femelle!

She accounts for her sense of disproportion in the last tercet, which depends for its pathos on the assumptions underlying the male-authored *blason*. When a male poet praises his lady, the poem has strategic purposes: his enthusiasm is designed at least partly to win her favor. But Labé's beloved, though he is as irresistible as any woman, is impervious to her praise:

> De toy me plein, que tant de feus portant,
>   En tant d'endrois d'iceus mon coeur tatant
>   N'en est sur toy volé quelque estincelle.

[O beautiful brown eyes, o glances turned aside, o hot sighs, o poured out tears, o dark night awaited in vain, o bright days in vain to come back: o sad laments, o stubborn desires, o misspent time, o wasted pains, o thousand deaths laid in a thousand nets, o fiercest ills aimed against me. O laughter, forehead, hair, arms, hands and fingers, o plaintive lute, viol, bow and voice: so many torches to set a woman on fire! I reproach you because, although you bear so many fires, feeling out my heart with them in so many places, not a single spark has flown onto you.]

Labé is expressing wonder at the failure, in her case, of the conventions of praise and response. A woman's beauty inspires her lover to poetic virtuosity, which he turns back toward her in hope of reward. The system circles around neatly, and although it may be halted temporarily by the lady's chaste refusal, it can incorporate her chastity as yet another reason to praise her. When a woman speaks the praises, however, there is no equivalent explanation to console her for the man's failure to respond. Labé's beloved is simply not interested; his beauty is inexplicably self-enclosed. The sonnet is an exploration of dead-ended convention, of non-reciprocal roles.

Labé's poem contrasts strongly to Sonnet 55 of Olivier de Magny's *Souspirs* (1556), although they share the first eight lines. While Labé sharpens the focus of her list by returning to the man's charms and summing up their effect in the ironic "tant de flambeaus!" of l. 11, de Magny multiplies his apostrophes in his first tercet, calling on a mix of actions and motives and adding a line that emphasizes the confusion of the ongoing list:

> O pas epars, ô trop ardente flame,
> > O douce erreur, ô pensers de mon ame,
> > Qui ça, qui lá, me tournez nuict et jour,

And while Labé closes in on a lucid concluding statement of her disappointment, expanding the metaphor of seductiveness as fire to question the man's lack of response, de Magny expands his appeals, first to his own eyes, then to observers as varied as gods, heavens, and—anti-climactically—unspecified human beings:

> O vous mes yeux, non plus yeux mais fonteines,
> > O dieux, ô cieux, et personnes humaines,
> > Soyez pour dieu tesmoins de mon amour.

[O wandering steps, o too ardent flame, o sweet wandering, o thoughts of my soul, which turn me here and there, night and day, o you, my eyes, no longer eyes but fountains, o gods, o heavens, be for god's sake witnesses to my love] (*Les Souspirs*, ed. David Wilkins [Geneva: Droz, 1978]).

The diffuseness of this conclusion results partly from de Magny's incorporation of phrases translated from the opening and closing of Petrarch's Sonnet 161 ("O passi sparsi, o pensier' vaghi e pronti"). But the significant distinction is that de Magny's poem lacks the coherent self-consciousness of Labé's. Confronted with the lack of fit between her beloved's imperviousness and the smoother-running *topos* of praise for a lady's resistance, she makes a witty, rueful drama out of her puzzlement. De Magny, by contrast, seems to be afloat in a sea of undifferentiated citation. His combination of Petrarch and Labé is so decentered that he joins the "regards destournez" of his first line illogically to his closing call for witnesses: how can an averted gaze attest to his suffering? Set against de Magny's sonnet, Labé's demonstrates the clarity a woman poet could gain by dealing as an outsider with formulas de Magny cites and combines without question. He assembles a rambling mosaic; she undergoes a process of discovery.

Labé abandons praise of male beauty altogether in Sonnet 21, after a second *blason* has likewise failed to impress her beloved (Sonnet 10). Instead, she questions the basis on which *blasons* are built. By asking what perfection for a man would be, listing empty categories, she calls attention to the absence of any feminine consensus about masculine beauty:

> Quelle grandeur rend l'homme venerable?
>> Quelle grosseur? quel poil? quelle couleur?
>> Qui est des yeus le plus emmieleur? . . .
>> Quel naturel est le plus amiable?

Her response is a refusal to set up criteria:

> Je ne voudrois le dire assurément,
>> Ayant Amour forcé mon jugement:
>> Mais je say bien et de tant je m'assure,
> Que tout le beau que l'on pourroit choisir,
>> Et que tout l'art qui ayde la Nature,
>> Ne me sauraient acroitre mon desir.

[What height makes a man worthy of admiration? What breadth? what hair? what coloring? Whose eyes are most beguiling? What innate manner is most endearing? I wouldn't like to say for certain, for love has forced my judgment. But I know and am certain of this much: that all the beauty one could choose, and all the art that improves nature, could not increase my desire.]

By opposing this confession of her passionate subjectivity to any rational assessment of how well her beloved conforms to an ideal, Labé attacks the credibility of conventionally detailed *blasons*. Her critique goes further than Ronsard or Du Bellay's revision of inadequate and exaggerated praise; standing outside the norms evolved in male poets' depictions of women, she dismantles the claim to truth of any compliment based on pre-set standards.

In her next to last poem, Sonnet 23, Labé offers a final explanation for her mistrust of the *blason*: the compliments her lover gave her are now suspect because he has abandoned her. She builds both quatrains on citation, but it is parodic citation. Throwing the Petrarchan clichés back at the man who used them, she repeats them verbatim as evidence of his falsity:

> Las! que me sert, que si parfaitement
>> Louas jadis et ma tresse doree,
>> Et de mes yeus la beaute comparée
>> A deus soleils, dont Amout finement
> Tira les trets causes de ton tourment?

The sonnet is written *ad hominem*, like Pernette's Epigram 28. An overbearing Neoplatonist, a hypocritical Petrarchan: rejecting their behavior as lovers, the women poets reject their habits of language as well. Like Pernette, Labé returns to a conventional attitude and vocabulary at the end of the poem, affirming her faith in her faraway lover and using the Petrarchan "martyrdom" to refer to the misery of separation:

> Pardonne moy, Amy, à cette fois,
> Estant outree et de despit et d'ire:
> Mais je m'assure, quelque part que tu sois,
> Qu'autant que moy tu soufres de martire.

[Alas! what good is it to me that you once praised my golden hair so perfectly, and the beauty of my eyes, compared to two suns from which love craftily drew the arrows that caused your suffering? . . . Forgive me, love, this time, for I was beside myself with spite and rage: But I am certain, wherever you may be, that you suffer martyrdom as much as I.]

The turnabout, however, is not entirely reassuring. After such a forceful enactment of anger, her claim to renewed faith is hard to believe, and her last sentence has something of the power play about it: "I will go on playing the game," she implies, "as long as I can believe in you—but you see what I am capable of if you give me reason to doubt you." Like Pernette in her reacceptance of the "hault bien" of Neoplatonism, Labé returns to Petrarchism only after she has convinced herself that her Petrarchan deserves her love. Both women arrive at this position only after rejecting lovers whose actions belie thier claims as poets: masculine literary stance is put through feminine ethical interrogation. But Labé is more explicit and more sarcastic in her denunciation than Pernette, and the poem sums up her relationship to Petrarchism as a whole: explosive assimilation. She appears to accept the dramatic situation and vocabulary of the convention, but her self-examining, combative voice actually pulls the props out from underneath it.

Taken together, then, what do du Guillet and Labé show about sixteenth-century women's responses to their social and literary context? That they wrote and were published at all suggests the importance of their historical situation in Lyon—a city, a generation, and perhaps most important, a mixed-sex group open to experimentation. The Ecole lyonnaise obviously provided a more encouraging environment than those that have silenced women in other times and places. Another idiosyncrasy is that both poets present themselves in direct personal relationship to a model: Pernette identifies her poetic partner as her lover, and Labé links her questioning of Petrarchism to one of its practitioners. Yet the shock of the women's voices, like their critical sifting through of the conventions represented by each man, are best understood as reactions to male-authored love poetry in general. In a curious way, the Renaissance moralists' assessments of both women pinpoint a perculiarity that a modern Bloomian focus on interacting poets is likely to overlook: Pernette and Labé were remarkable, for good or ill, because they wrote as members of the female sex. (Bloom admits the historical if not the gender limitation of his theory in *The Anxiety of Influence* [New York: Oxford University Press, 1973].) The requirements of her role as aristocratic wife were certainly one influence on Pernette's adoption of a Neoplatonism less intersected with Petrarchan longing than Scève's, while Labé's exploration of the sexual irreversibility of the *blason* arose from her outsider's view of male habits of praise.

That outsider's view is a necessity for feminist critics as we move beyond the habit of assuming gender neutrality in literature—in practice, the notion that all literature is produced by men responding to men (or by women responding to men as men do). The poems of du Guillet and Labé need to be interpreted with an awareness of their authors' specificity as women, a historical specificity shaped by sexual ideologies and the exclusion of women from the world of letters. Pernette, speaking of men's infidelities in her Fifth Song, playfully suggests one form of imitation to the "Dames" she is addressing: "Faisons pareil office [Let's do the same]." But this study has shown that women's poetry does not—in fact, cannot—reproduce men's. Speaking out of silence, entering the terrain of male discourse from the margins, Pernette and Labé take over its central position as speakers and appropriate its rituals for their own ends. Their women's situations and women's voices do more than modify poetic style. They rewrite the rules of the game.

Du Bellay's Emblematic Vision of Rome

Daniel Russell

M. A. Screech has recently claimed that in the *Antiquitéz de Rome,* Du Bellay pays little attention to things seen, and that the imagery in these sonnets is of no visual interest. Henri Chamard must have felt much the same way when he noted that the poet of the *Antiquitéz* disregarded details in favor of a general impression. Such judgements are fairly accurate in some respects, for it is indeed quite impossible to find any precise descriptions of particular Roman monuments in the *Antiquitéz de Rome.* In spite of the word "description" in Du Bellay's full title (*Le premier livre des Antiquitéz de Rome contenant une générale déscription de sa grandeur, et comme une deploration de sa ruine plus un songe ou vision sur le mesme subject.*), nothing is described in the modern sense of the word, as it has been defined by nineteenth-century positivism and realism. But in the light of such statements, the prominence of verbs of visual perception in the sonnets of this *recueil* is disconcerting. One encounters verbs like *voir, apercevoir,* and *regarder* in key positions in over three-fourths of the forty-seven sonnets.

An awareness of the way Du Bellay intended such verbs to function is essential to an understanding of the poet's strategy, and the structure of his imagery in this *recueil.* The problem here obviously involves definitions and usage. Since the details of realistic, particularized description have little place in these poems, the verbs of visual perception in them must then be understood figuratively as indicating suppositions, imaginary pictures, or visions.

The role of these figurative uses of the verb *voir* and its synonyms in Renaissance poetry can best be summed up in the poetry-as-painting metaphor which the Renaissance derived—at least in part—from a slight misunderstanding of the phrase *ut pictura poesis* in Horace's *Ars Poetica.* Du

From *Yale French Studies* no. 47 (1972). © 1972 by *Yale French Studies.*

Bellay set his *Antiquitéz de Rome* squarely within the context of this Neo-Horatian metaphor when he described his undertaking for Henri II in the dedicatory sonnet as ". . . ce petit tableau/Peint, le mieux que j'ay peu, de couleurs poëtiques [. . . this little picture/Painted as well as I could with poetic colors]." And Du Bellay would come back to this metaphor on occasion, as in the twenty-fifth sonnet of the collection where he made the following wish:

> Peusse-je aumoins d'un pinceau plus agile
> Sur le patron de quelque grand Virgile
> De ces palais les portraits façonner . . .

> [If only I could, with a more agile brush
> After the model of some great Virgil
> Fashion portraits of these palaces . . .]

Such poetic "portraits" were probably intended in some sense to resemble the "talking pictures" described by Simonides. But in order to understand the fascination exerted by the *ut pictura poesis* metaphor throughout the Renaissance, one must ask what it tells us about the structure and effect of poems composed with reference to this metaphorical *rapprochement* of painting and poetry.

The emblem, and variations on the emblematic structure, formed the most extensive experiment with the metaphorical suggestion that a formal union of poetry and painting was possible. An emblem was imagined to be an ideogrammatic presentation in which the interpretation or reading of a picture, real or imagined, was suggested in a written text. Either the picture or the text could be absent from the actual presentation of the emblem, but this absence did not change the reader's understanding of the emblem as an essentially double text, the absent text being implicit in the text which was present.

By presenting the emblem as a double "text," and the emblem's audience as "readers," I have wished to stress that, contrary to the belief held by most students of the emblem (until quite recently), the emblem is primarily a literary phenomenon. This becomes clear if the emblem is considered as a double method or mode of apprehension and communication rather than as the "Doppelform" implied by certain German critical and historical studies of the emblem.

This double text was composed of a discursive (written) and an ideogrammatic (pictorial) transcription of a message. While there was a tendency to exalt the intuitive approaches to meaning and understanding which the emblem theoretically made accessible, it seems more likely that the emblem actually translated the ambivalent Renaissance attitude toward the written text. On the one hand, it was still considered a transcription of oral language, but the text was also beginning to generate a different kind of language with a spatial dimension generally made possible by the standardization of print. It was especially this aspect of the emblematic concept of literature, with the attendant possibility of play between the visual and the oral, which was exploited by poets like Scève, Du Bellay, and Agrippa d'Aubigné. They would occasionally use this kind of double language to stylize and complicate their imagery into little enigmas with surprise endings. From the reader's point of view, such imagery was tolerable and perhaps even pleasing, only if he had easy and almost simultaneous access to all parts of the text. Such access became increasingly possible with print.

It is not unlikely that Du Bellay knew the first book of emblems composed by the Italian jurist Andrea Alciati, and he must certainly have known the work of the emblematist Gilles Corrozet, who published his *Olive*. Du Bellay's affinities with emblem literature have been noticed, but never analyzed to any great extent. V.-L. Saulnier has found some of the sonnets in the *Olive* comparable to the emblematic glosses in Maurice Scève's *Délie*. And A.-M. Schmidt has chosen the adjective "emblématique," appropriately I think, to characterize the sonnets of the *Songe*. These last fifteen sonnets of the *Antiquitéz* must indeed have been read as emblems or potential emblems in the sixteenth century since Jan van der Noodt, a Dutch humanist engaged in Protestant polemic, chose to make them into a series of apocalyptic emblems by presenting their imagery mirrored in a series of ideogrammatic illustrations. He published these emblems in 1568 in his *Theatre for Worldlings,* which probably circulated rather widely in its English, French, and Dutch editions.

The sonnets of the *Songe* are visual in the sense that they record and describe the author's visions; elsewhere in the *Antiquitéz de Rome,* the sonnets either present visual suppositions and imaginary scenes (e.g. "Comme on void la fureur par l'Aquilon chassee . . . [As one sees the fury chased by the North wind]" Sonnet 16, ll 5ff.) or evoke impressions resulting from a tourist-like encounter with the monumental ruins of Rome. In deciding whether some or all of these poems are emblematic, it is not enough to ask if they could be illustrated. The emblem is not simply an illustrated poem. In an emblematic image, the poet seems to be striving consciously for intensity by creating an illusion of the simultaneous presentation of all the elements of the image. He creates this effect of simultaneity by presenting all the elements of the image in such a way that the reader is supposed to be unaware of the exact metaphorical thrust until he has reached the end of the development. Then the pleasurable sensation of discovery can be likened to the immediate, "visual" intuition of an idea. Therefore, such an image can be profitably reinforced by a picture which permits every element of the image to be grasped at once, thus reinforcing the illusion of Neo-Platonic intuition. The picture permits the reader to apprehend the image as a global entity. It serves as an intermediary and point of reference in the actual explorations undertaken back and forth throughout the text, in an effort to solve the riddle by investigating the possible metaphorical relationships between the various parts of the image.

Images situated and delimited in chronological time, like Ronsard's "Comme on voit sur la branche, au mois de mai, la rose . . . [As one sees, on a branch, in the month of May, a rose]," could be illustrated; but the illustration would not greatly enhance or clarify the narrative, linear exposition of the image. Furthermore, Ronsard's image only asks the reader to recall a scene he could easily situate in his own remembered past, whereas the more demanding emblematic image often tends to make the reader construct an imaginary picture in which there must be selection, stylization, and stress of certain details, often under the influence of iconographical techniques and commonplaces.

Those sonnets containing the invocations and incantations at the beginning of the *Antiquitéz*, as well as the lists of wonders of the world and the like, are not particularly emblematic. But they do prepare a ritual, almost obsessive atmosphere in which other images may be presented in such a way as to stop any discursive or narrative flow for a moment, and fix the poetic meditation emblematically upon some aspect of the general theme. This intensification often seems to be accomplished in part through a kind of pictorial presentation of the image. The description of a dead oak in the twenty-eighth sonnet is a fairly typical example. The picture is framed by the first line "Qui a veu quelquefois un grand chesne asseiché . . . [Whoever perchance has seen a great dead oak]," and the twelfth line which begins "Qui tel chesne a peu voir . . . [He who may have seen such an oak]." This frame breaks any possible narrative progression, sets the image apart from the surrounding text (in the sense that the *recueil* is a single text), and signals its importance. Like plants in many emblem book wood-cuts, the tree also stands completely detached from the physical world around it. The only other objects in the image are the trophies hanging on the tree. They constitute an element of decorative iconographical stylization also found in emblem wood-cuts. Furthermore, the oak itself was one of the commonplaces of emblem literature, and Du Bellay used it in this sonnet just as Claude Mignault prescribed in his commentaries on Alciati's emblems: "Il [the oak] se peust aussi accommoder ou à un homme, ou à quelque autre chose, qui jadis a esté en grande reputation, mais maintenant ne porte que l'ombre d'un grand nom, comme Lucain parle de Pompee mort. [It (the oak) can also be accommodated either to a man or to some other thing which once possessed a great reputation but now bears only the shadow of a great name as Lucan speaks of the dead Pompey.]" Du Bellay used Lucan as his model, and in his comparison he writes:

> Qui tel chesne a peu voir, qu'il imagine encores
> Comme entre les citez, qui plus florissent ores,
> Ce vieil honneur poudreux est le plus honnoré.

> [He who may have seen such an oak, may he imagine further
> How among the cities which are most flourishing today,
> This old dusty honor is the most honored.]

He associates or "accommodates" the oak with "quelque autre chose, qui jadis a esté en grande reputation . . . [some other thing which once possessed a great reputation]."

In sonnet 12, Du Bellay described the Giants' ascent toward heaven and their repulsion by Jupiter hurling lightning bolts. The various elements of this image were presented simultaneously in emblem illustrations, from Bartelémy Aneau's *Picta Poesis* (1552) to Otto van Veen's *Horatii Emblemata* (1607). Such illustrations emphasize the effect of simultaneity, which Du Bellay was apparently trying to capture in his description. In the first quatrain, for example, everything seems to be happening at once, outside time and the causal flow of events:

> Telz que lon vid jadis les enfans de la Terre
> Plantez dessus les monts pour escheller les cieux,
> Combattre main à main la puissance des Dieux,
> Et Juppiter contre eux, qui ses fouldres desserre . . .

> [Just as people long ago saw the children of the Earth
> Braced upon mountains to climb to the heavens,
> Fight hand to hand the power of the Gods,
> And Jupiter loose his thunderbolts against them . . .]

With the exception of a rather weak *puis* in the second quatrain, the various parts of the description are related only by coordinate conjunctions.

Du Bellay used the verb *voir* to introduce three different pictures in this sonnet. After the mythological scene, the reader is asked to imagine the parallel historical scene of the Roman monuments rising above the seven hills in a new challenge to the gods. The final scene seems to bring the reader and the poet/tourist together, looking at "ces champs deshonorez/ Regretter leur ruine . . . [those dishonored fields lamenting their ruin]." The repetition of "tel" at the beginning of each pictorial description not only serves to separate and frame the scenes, but also suggests that each scene repeats the previous scene. This sense of repetition, coupled with the absence of conjunctions and prepositions indicating hypotactic causal relationships, tends to stop any narrative flow and concentrate the reader's attention on this aspect of the poetic meditation.

The word "emblem" originally referred to some sort of ornamental inlay such as *marqueterie* and mosaic, or an appliquéed overlay which could be detached easily. The verb in classical Greek which is the ultimate source of the word "emblem" could also refer to the grafting of a cultivated branch onto a wild tree. The first two images in this sonnet could be understood as this kind of addition; additions which specify and emphasize the importance of the basic scene by pointing to some aspect of it, or by forcing a certain perception of the scene which will articulate or single out some particular meaning which could be read into the scene. They bring certain implications of the scene into sharper relief; they inform a shapeless perception with meaning.

Sonnet 16 ("Comme lon void de loing sur la mer courroucee") shows several apparently unrelated scenes being brought to bear in much the same way upon one aspect of the general theme. In this sonnet, one finds a ship breaking up on a rock, the wind dying down, and a flame dying out. Pictorial immobility and iconographical influence are reflected in expressions like "une montagne d'eau [a mountain of water]" and "la flamme ondoyante [the undulating flame]." Since each picture can conceivably be interpreted allegorically in many different ways, no logical progression is possible until the poet has solved the enigma of their relationship to each other. He perceives it by bringing them all into focus upon a single aspect of his general theme in the last tercet where he explains:

> ainsi parmy le monde
> Erra la Monarchie: & croissant tout ainsi
> Qu'un flot, qu'un vent, qu'un feu, sa course vagabonde
> Par un arrest fatal s'est venuë perdre icy.

> [thus throughout the world
> Wandered Monarchy: and growing just like
> A wave, a wind, a fire, its vagabond course
> By a fatal decree came to die out here.]

Since the relationship between the three images remains problematic until the last tercet, the reader finds himself constantly referring back and forth from one scene to another in an effort to determine their collective thrust. This process of comparison produces a magnifying, mirror reverberation among the images, which in turn produces the intensification I would characterize as emblematic.

Actually, the picture-images in either of these sonnets could easily be thought of as a series of mirror images, all being brought to bear upon a single theme, intensifying the reader's preoccupation with it much as mirrors intensify light by focusing scattered rays upon a single point. A sort of metaphorical reverberation, therefore, tends to magnify the subject under consideration. Such a combination of images also articulates and stresses variations on the subject, just as the positioning and nature of the mirrors varies the focal point of the light reflected.

In sonnet 16, it is evident that the effect of immobility and magnification is achieved not only through the repetition of certain paratactic structures (as in sonnet 12) or the verbal translation of pictorial techniques and iconographical motifs (as in sonnet 28), but also through the major emblematic strategy of the enigma. Du Bellay often tends to arrange his imagery so that the meaning or moral becomes clear in a surprise ending which may take the form of a sententious statement. The image is consciously structured this way in sonnet 6 ("Telle que dans son char la Berecynthienne"), where Du Bellay reversed the terms of the metaphorical comparison which he had borrowed from Virgil. Instead of talking of Rome first, and then, almost as an ornamental afterthought, adding the comparison to Cybele as Virgil had done, Du Bellay abruptly introduced the Cybele image in the first lines with no real indication of its eventual relation to the general theme. His intention is doubly obscured since Cybele is identified only by the epithet "Berecynthienne."

When Du Bellay says in sonnet nine, "Je ne dy plus la sentence commune . . . [I no longer say the common proverb"; l. 9], he is clearly indicating how seriously he took the Renaissance emblematist's theoretical belief in the importance of obscurity in enhancing and preserving the message of his presentation. Unlike many emblematists, however, Du Bellay is not often content to deal with commonplace proverbs. And this further effort for obscurity contributes to the magnifying immobility of the image by forcing the reader to hold all the components in mind while searching for the solution to the enigma instead of moving rapidly from one point to the next, as in the linear and causal progression of a narrative exposition where he could easily leap ahead to the impending conclusion if it took the form of a common proverb.

In an emblem, the riddle element is often closely linked to a tri-partite form consisting of a title or epigram, an illustration, and a longer explanatory text. The combination of an illustration and its title propose the enigma which will be solved in the main textual exposition. To see the tripartite enigmatic structure which governs the metaphorical strategy in many of the sonnets of the *Antiquitéz*, the *recueil* must be considered in its entirety. In the full title, and in the first four or five sonnets, Du Bellay set forth, in the manner of a ritual invocation, his main theme of the grandeur and decadence of imperial Rome. This dominant theme, in confrontation with the image or images proposed in the quatrains of a sonnet, poses a riddle to be solved by the explanation concentrated toward the end of the poem. The solution of the riddle images in Du Bellay's poetry is often further complicated as in emblems, by the use of erudite periphrasis (e.g. "le brave filz d'Aeson," sonnet 10, l. 1), puns like the shepherd-pastor/pastor-of-men image designed to summarize the rise and fall of the Roman empire in sonnet 18, and rebus-like constructions like the *corneille* (symbol of brutish stupidity) disguised as an eagle in sonnet 17 to satirize the attempts of the Germanic barbarians to infiltrate the Roman empire.

The advantage of such enigmatic structures can be mainly didactic; the moderately difficult access to the meaning of an emblem was designed to excite enough curiosity to stimulate interest in, and memory of, a didactic message. The apparently random grouping of metaphorical components reminded the Renaissance reader of the hieroglyphics he supposed were ideogrammatic. The concentration and immobility of the elements of the pictorial image led to the magnification which the Renaissance reader tended to mistake for the kind of visual intuition Renaissance occultists and Neoplatonists prized so highly in their quest for ultimate truth.

It is unlikely that Du Bellay was attracted to the occult or quasi-magical qualities of the emblematic image. And its didactic capabilities were of limited interest to him here. Du Bellay's goal in the *Antiquitéz de Rome* seems rather to have been a subjective reconciliation of his humanistic conception and knowledge of ancient Rome with the disconcerting discovery of modern Rome as he found it in the 1550s. The emblematic image provided a means for bringing these two clashing impressions close enough together to yield the unified "general description" of Rome promised in the title. The emblematic accommodates unusual, personal, and untraditional *rapprochements* in its symbolism; and the pictorial spatialism of its structure helps hold the components of such *rapprochements* together. In the immobility of each image, the *signifiant* and *signifié* seem to fuse, forming icons which unite history and mythology with Du Bellay's pessimistic message of the transience of all things of this world. By being pictorial, and consequently isolated from any surrounding context, the emblematic image tends to abolish time by shifting the components from a space that could be translated into chronology, to a space which is purely conventional and, therefore, allegorical. It links or reunites two situations which have been separated by time. In the emblematic image, Du Bellay reconstructed the cultural and historical continuity of Rome which he had not found as a humanist-tourist.

Ronsard as Apollo: Myth, Poetry and Experience in a Renaissance Sonnet-Cycle

Terence C. Cave

Ronsard's first cycle of love-poetry (*Les Amours*, 1552) (sonnet-numbers and quotations are given throughout according to the 1552 text as reproduced in P. Laumonier's edition of the *Œuvres complètes* [in the *Société des textes français modernes* series], vol. IV. Translations from both Ronsard and Petrarch are my own.) opens with a sonnet ("Vœu") in which the notion of the poet's vocation predominates, encompassing the love-experience itself. The book of poems is presented, together with the poet's heart, as a votive offering to the Muses, and the image ("idole") which the poet adores is placed in their temple. In the second quatrain Ronsard inserts himself specifically into a myth of poetic activity: directed by celestial influence ("ung astre fatal"), he has been received into the dance of the Muses. When Ronsard revised the poem later in his career, he modified this passage, casting himself in a quasi-Apolline role as leader of the dance; he thus confirmed retrospectively the destiny foreshadowed in 1552, asserting his supremacy and independence in the domain of poetic creation.

There is little doubt that the "Vœu" mirrors Ronsard's own order of priorities in the composition of the sequence: unlike Scève, or Petrarch himself, he is concerned far more with the exploration of a mode of poetic expression than with the documentation of an amorous experience, whether "real" or "imaginary." Yet there is a sense in which his assumption of the traditional pose of the unrequited lover proves to be central to his self-consciousness as a poet: a tension is set up between the two roles, defining a new variant of the dialogue between poetry and experience. The tension is clearly visible in a sonnet which—explicitly this time, and in the 1552 version—draws a parallel between Ronsard and Apollo: not Apollo Musagetes, but Apollo enamoured of the Trojan Cassandra. This sonnet

From *Yale French Studies* no. 47 (1972). © 1972 by *Yale French Studies*.

(no. 36) is one of those which play on the legendary and mythical associations of the beloved's name; and since name imagery is used within the Petrarchan tradition to explore and connect central preoccupations of the poet, it has a *prima facie* claim to the reader's attention. It alludes to the myth according to which Apollo offers to confer on Cassandra the gift of prophecy if she will make love to him; she agrees and receives the gift, but then withholds her favours. Ronsard's exploitation of the myth stresses the irony of Apollo's situation: although he is the god of music, he plucks his lyre "in vain," for his song can charm only the landscape and not Cassandra; likewise, the fact that he is "sick" ("mal sain") belies his powers as physician-god. He is a divinity exiled from heaven ("loing du ciel": "bany du ciel" according to a later variant), subjected to human limitations at the hands of a mortal woman. The tercets dwell upon the sympathy of flowers and river with both Apollo's plight and Ronsard's, expanding the notion of a landscape charmed by a divine music: thus the effectiveness of poetry is reaffirmed, though always within the limits defined by the second quatrain.

As a variation on the theme of Apollo, this sonnet stands in contrast to the celebrated central section of the "Ode à Michel de l'Hospital," published in the same year, where the Apolline force, in association with the Muses, is presented as the means of transmission from heaven to earth of divine inspiration in accordance with the Neoplatonist allegorisation of the *furor pœticus*. Apollo is here a mediator, harmoniously linking the divine with the human; he represents both spiritual energy and metaphysical equilibrium. But the "Ode" is at this point schematic and theoretical, treating the notion of poetry in isolation from emotional experience; while the irony of the sonnet is directed precisely at such a separation of the poetic activity—however potent in itself—from the fulfilment of extra-poetic needs.

Within the sonnet-sequence itself, the Neoplatonist *furor* reappears from time to time, connected now with love rather than poetry. Indeed, the opening poems of the sequence sketch out an interpretation of love which is at certain points analogous to Neoplatonism: the notion of a wise folly ("Vœu," l. 11), the possession by a divine, nonrational force (sonnet I), the celestial origin of Cassandra's beauty (sonnet II). The structure of experience implied here, superimposed on the Petrarchan notion of spiritual elevation through love, would theoretically allow inward fulfilment regardless of whether the love is physically or even emotionally requited. But once again, the Apollo-Cassandra sonnet undermines the ideal: far from seeking perfection through his love for a quasidivine woman, Ronsard identifies himself now with a divinity crippled by the refusal of a mortal woman to give him physical fulfilment. An analogous pattern appears in the well-known sonnet "Je vouldroy bien richement jaunissant . . . " (no. XX), where the poet is reduced to the role of witness: Jupiter's potent metamorphoses embody that release of emotional and physical energies which he cannot himself achieve. Similarly, in "Or que Juppin . . ." (no. CXXVII), the poet's unrequited love excludes him from the dynamic creativity of the natural world, which is shown to proceed from the supernatural powers of Jupiter. In all these instances, a divine principle must become incarnate and realise itself at the human and physical level if it is to be effective. Sonnet XXXVI remains particularly important because it shows that this "divine principle" may sometimes be equated with poetic activity; hence what is implied, once again, is a conscious failure on the part of the poet to find a counterpart in his own experience for the manifestations of his poetic creativity.

The spring imagery of sonnet CXXXVII centres first on potency (in the quatrains), then on abundance:

> Or que les prez, et ore que les fleurs,
> De mille et mille et de mille couleurs,
> Peignent le sein de la terre si gaye . . .

[Now that the meadows, and now that the flowers paint the bosom of the joyful earth with thousand upon thousand of colours . . .]

An echo of this image occurs in sonnet CIII, which compares Cassandre's beauty with that of the spring: "Il peint les champs de dix mille couleurs, / Tu peins mes vers d'un long esmail de fleurs. [He (April) paints the fields with ten thousand colours; you (Cassandre) paint my verses with a profusion of brightly-coloured flowers]." (Cf. also no. 25, second tercet.) But in this instance, the allusion to poetry itself adds a further dimension of significance, for the analogy between a cornucopian nature and the poetic creativity stimulated by Cassandre reflects a major aspect of Ronsard's aesthetic. In the 1550 preface to the *Odes* he had connected the need for "copious diversity" in the ode with the multiplicity of nature; and elsewhere, both in his theoretical writings and the poems themselves, the same pattern reappears, often accompanied by flower imagery like that of *Amours* CIII: Apollo's magic effect on nature in sonnet XXXVI is a case in point. These metaphors of creativity imply a certain confidence in the poet's activity, even where it is forced to operate in a void: in one sense, the poet can reduplicate nature, creating a universe in which he can move freely, without reference to the constraints of "reality." A similar process obtains in the many poems of this cycle which evoke the enactment of physical passion, normally through the medium of dream, fantasy, or metamorphosis. Sonnet XX ("Je vouldroy . . .") is one such poem, in that the metamorphosis imagery, although distanced from the poet's experience, nevertheless embodies for the duration of the poem the sensual liberation which Cassandre denies. The imagery of gold and flowers exploited in the quatrains evokes a characteristic sense of richness, fertility, abundance; likewise in sonnets CI and CII, where the realisation of desire takes place amid the perfume of innumerable flowers ("Parmy l'odeur de tes [= de

Vénus] plus belles fleurs"; "Parmy l'odeur de mile et mile roses"). These imaginative explorations are not simply the expression of a sensual disposition at odds with the spiritualising tendencies of Petrarch and of Neoplatonism. Reflecting the "aesthetic of abundance," they move quite explicitly out of "reality" into that realm of inexhaustible possibilities provided by poetic creation itself; and the physical fulfilment which they so often depict acquires, through the identification of erotic fantasy with aesthetic fantasy, a symbolic sense. Poetry can at times mediate a metamorphosis of the self, an extension or redemption of emotional experience:

> Mon Dieu, quel heur, et quel contentement,
> M'a fait sentir ce faux recollement,
> Changeant ma vie en cent metamorphoses.

[Ah God, what joy and what satisfaction this false embrace has made me feel, changing my life in (into?) a hundred metamorphoses.] (No. CI.)

Such poems thus have an affinity with Ronsard's Utopian preoccupations as represented by the *Isles fortunées* of 1553, by his recurrent use of the myth of the Golden Age: what is central here is the power of poetry to create myth, or rather the status of poetry as a mythical extension of experience. Yet at this point one must return to the tensions of the Apollo-Cassandra sonnet. The "fantasy" poems themselves stress, in most instances, the fragility—if not the falseness—of the experience they bring into being; Apollo's frustration expresses still more clearly and forcefully the irony of a situation in which the virtually superhuman power of the poet to conjure with experience is rendered gratuitous by a failure to make contact with "reality." Once again, this failure is not—or at least not only—the inability of the historical Ronsard to achieve physical fulfilment in love. It is rather the expression of an unresolved aesthetic problem: that of relating poetic creation to a human centre, of establishing an authentic continuity between art and experience. The Neoplatonist theory of inspiration supplied Ronsard with a ready-made framework within which poetry itself could ostensibly be given a supernatural status and hence an unassailable seriousness; he also had access to the inexhaustible supply of poetic materials opened up by Dorat's instruction and his own reading. But the way in which the divine principle might be given a living shape and his materials meaningfully activated had still to be discovered. It was easy enough for Ronsard to speak of the *fureur* of love or poetry, and to exploit a poetic language hallowed by tradition; it was less easy to provide a human correlative for poetic experiment. In the *Deffence et illustration*, Du Bellay had defined theoretically the link between imitation (as opposed to translation) and feeling, the need for the model to be projected through the "naturel" of the individual poet; *Amours* XXXVI suggests that Ronsard was aware of this problem, but had not yet found a way of relating his poetic powers to an intrinsically fulfilling experience. Hence the fragmentary nature of the Neoplatonist references in this sequence; hence also the somewhat bewildering diversity of tone and the open-ended structure of the cycle as a whole. The Apollo-Cassandra sonnet betrays a void which could not be filled by a purely aesthetic abundance, however cornucopian.

This interpretation of Ronsard's first sonnet-cycle can be restated in terms of the function and status of image. At the level of rhetoric imagery is fundamental to the "long esmail de fleurs," the rich poetic ornamentation symbolised by the ideal landscape. Furthermore, myth and other forms of image had been consecrated—by Neoplatonist theory, emblem-theory, and the whole allegorising tradition—as a means of insight into both moral and metaphysical experience; hence they seemed to provide Ronsard with a vehicle for the exploration of such experience. Yet he was ill-adapted to the elaboration of allegorical schemas, while on the other hand he was not always able to anchor individual images in a significant intuitive insight. Thus he found himself with a wealth of imagery at his disposal, but without the means fully to exploit its potency: the flowers proliferate, but remain gratuitously decorative.

In sonnet XXXVI itself, the mythological situation and its attendant imagery constitute a conceit, an elegant gesture operating in an enclosed aesthetic world. Yet it also implies a conscious reflection on the status of such gestures. It follows from this that the 1552 *Amours* focus on a problem posed by artistic creation rather than by love, although the "unrequited love" situation provides a perfect means of exploring the problem. This interpretation, while it presupposes a correct identification of "symptomatic" poems or lines within the sequence, also takes into account the whole experiment in Petrarchan style which the sequence constitutes; for it establishes a relationship between Ronsard's exploitation of derived material and his awareness of the need to move beyond the derivative and the gratuitously aesthetic.

Ronsard's preoccupations in the 1552 *Amours* are brought into sharper focus if they are compared with those of Petrarch himself in the *Canzoniere*. Petrarch exploits name-imagery on many more different levels than Ronsard, whose "Cassandre" references operate within two or three closely related areas of legend or myth (the Trojan war, prophecy, the Apollo-Cassandra situation). The name of Laura affords a range of symbolism covering the whole spectrum from the ideal landscape centred on the tree ("il lauro") and the breeze ("l'aura"), via myth (Apollo and Daphne), to the moral connotations of the laurel-crown (honour and fame), and thence to the laurel-tree as a symbol of spiritual nourishment and protection, reaching out—sometimes explicitly—towards the Christian symbol of the tree of life. This imagery is central to the *Canzoniere* as a sequence in that it forms a *leitmotif* of considerable fertility, marking out both the explicit and the implicit structures of the work as a whole. Prior to the 1347–8 version, the cycle opened with a sonnet based on the myth of Apollo and

Daphne (34); in a later version (1356–8) a *sestina* on the ultimate rejection of the "laurel tree" as a means to moral elevation (142) was the last poem of the *in vita* section; while later still (1366–7), the *Canzoniere* itself closed with a sonnet (318) in which a double laurel image summarises the two phases *(in vita, in morte)* of the whole love-experience. The laurel motif was thus a focal point throughout in the shaping of the *Canzoniere*; at the same time, it appears that the mythological preoccupations of the early "Apollo, s'ancor vive . . . " (34) tended to be progressively replaced, as the cycle evolved, by the explicity moral and religious statement of the definitive opening and closing poems.

These aspects of the sequential arrangement of the poems reflect an internal structure—that of the experience embodied in the cycle—which operates on two levels. The obsessive love documented by Petrarch constitutes its own moral and spiritual domain, symbolised by the recurrent laurel image; but the image, like the love itself, also points towards a higher level of experience. Viewed from within, the love for Laura appears to be spiritually enriching, however anguished, while in retrospect it is simply a youthful delusion, the "giovenile errore" of the opening sonnet. Laura is finally replaced by the Virgin Mary, who alone can procure peace for the soul. Hence the two levels of experience are shown to be analogous, though ultimately incompatible; and in so far as the laurel mediates between them, incarnating the analogy, it comes to symbolise the focal point of a quest for valid spiritual experience.

In the *sestina* "Giovene donna . . ." (30), the image of Laura sitting beneath the laurel (as in 34) becomes the obsessive object of a pursuit which will never be resolved, prompting an awareness of the passage of time and the brevity of life. A similar pattern appears in the *sestina* "A la dolce ombra . . ." (142) where, threatened by the perilous influence of Venus ("dal terzo cielo"), the lover seeks refuge in the shade of the laurel and constantly returns to it ("tornai sempre devoto a i primi rami"), finding nothing elsewhere to equal its perfection; yet in this instance the passage of time ultimately leads him to abandon it for the more fruitful 'tree' of the love of God:

> ora la vita breve, e 'l loco, e 'l tempo
> mostranmi altro sentier di gire al cielo,
> e di far frutto non pur fior e frondi.
>   Altr'amor, altre frondi, et altro lume,
> altro salir al ciel per altri poggi
> cerco, ché n'è ben tempo, et altri rami.

[Now the brevity of life, and the place, and the time, show me another way of reaching heaven, and of bringing forth fruit, not merely flowers and leaves. I seek—for it is none too soon—another love, other leaves, and another light, another path upward to heaven by other heights, and other branches.]

Laura's laurel seems to transcend the limitations of time (stanzas 3 and 4); but since it bears no fruit, the transcendence is illusory. Hence the poem centres on the substitution of a true object of aspiration for a false one, rendered by a modulation of the focal image.

The sonnet "Non veggio . . ." (107) picks up once again the theme of obsession, translated in the second tercet into an admirable image of the expanding ramifications of the love-experience: the single laurel here becomes a whole forest amid which his adversary Love artfully ("con mirabil arte") leads him astray. At this point, the external object of pursuit (represented in the earlier part of the sonnet by Laura's eyes) becomes wholly identified with inward experience. The image of the forest suggests a labyrinthine wandering within the self, an interior exploration which is no longer controllable. Once again, this situation may be redeemed elsewhere by a schematic moral allegorisation of the tree planted in the lover's heart (228) or—as in 142 and 318—by the image of a second tree replacing the first. It is clear nevertheless that through its many variants the laurel-tree comes to represent an inward, meditative centre upon which all the preoccupations of the poet—psychological, moral and religious—converge in the search for authenticity of experience.

The relationship of this inward centre to poetry itself is characteristically defined in the *canzone* "In quella parte . . ." (127). Although the expression of love may relieve suffering (stanza 1), it has only an ancillary function; beside the meditation on love which takes place in the secrecy of thought, words are of no value:

> Ben sai, canzon, che quant'io parlo è nulla
> al celato amoroso mio pensero,
> che dì e notte ne la mente porto.

[Well you know, my song, that whatever I say is nothing beside my hidden amorous thought which day and night I carry in my mind.] (Cf. also "Così potess'io . . ."[95].)

Elsewhere, the tension between poetry and experience takes a different form: Laura has deflected him from the path which leads to fame as Latin poet and scholar, so that one 'laurel' is in opposition to the other (24, 60); likewise, in 166, Petrarch's "Apolline" gifts, his Parnassian inspiration, have been abandoned in favour of a humbler vernacular poetry. It is evident that, whichever side is stressed in this conflict of values, the independently creative function of poetry—that is to say of the poems of the *Canzoniere* itself—is never asserted. Although the poet speaks occasionally of conferring immortality on Laura, or the love-experience, or himself, by the excellence of his writing, the experience always remains the centre of attention. Ronsard's self-identification with an Apollo whose music gratuitously animates the landscape has no equivalent in Petrarch; in the *Canzoniere*, love-poetry is produced in the shadow of the ubiquitous laurel-tree:

> Cosí cresca il bel lauro in fresca riva,
> e chi 'l piantò pensier leggiadri et alti
> ne la dolce ombra al suon de l'acque scriva.

[Thus may the beautiful laurel continue to grow on a cool bank, and may he who planted it write down his graceful and lofty thoughts in its sweet shade, to the sound of the waters.] ("Non Tesin . . . " [148], second tercet.)

Conversely, although the theme of amorous obsession is present in Ronsard, it is not related to a meditative centre, to an inward experience which remains constant while yielding an ever richer network of meaning. The tree, with its structure of roots, branches, leaves, flowers and—ultimately—fruit, is replaced in Ronsard by an endless abundance of flowers. Petrarch's ideal landscape is a closed configuration of physical and spiritual beauties at the centre of which Laura sits beneath the laurel; Ronsard's is centrifugal and cornucopian, reflecting the creative energies of the natural world or of the poet.

A similar contrast is perceptible in the two poets' handling of the metamorphosis motif. The reflexive, self-mirroring nature of Petrarch's meditation is indicated by the *canzone* "Nel dolce tempo . . . " (23), where each of the lover's successive transformations represents a quintessential aspect of the love-experience. All revolve around a predetermined situation, and all are subordinated to the first metamorphosis—recalled at the conclusion—in which the lover becomes the laurel tree: hence he himself becomes, in a sense, the object of meditation, the incarnation of his own obsession. Metamorphosis as imagined by Ronsard, on the other hand, is most often a means of liberation from a sterile situation, and is characteristically linked with fantasy, dreams, and wish-fulfilment.

The universe of Petrarch's *Canzoniere* has a closed structure, offering an exhaustive interpretation of an experience ostensibly fundamental to the life of the poet. It is diachronic, in that it documents the evolution of the *innamoramento*; but it is also synchronic. The whole sequence, with its recurrent themes and images and its fluctuating psychological states, revolves around the meditative centre expressed at the literal level as the "celato amoroso pensero" and at the figurative level by the polyvalent name-imagery. It is this imagery above all which defines, and points to a resolution of, the love-experience, making manifest in the symbol of the two trees both an antithesis and an analogy, in a manner reminiscent of the corresponding symbol in Biblical typology. Hence the function of the *Canzoniere* as a poetic structure is to present an interpretative model of experience. Whether it is wholly successful in this respect is a question which cannot be pursued within the limits of this article; the contrast with Ronsard's *Amours*, however, could hardly be more marked. Ronsard's universe, in the 1552 cycle at least, is fragmented and open-ended: the moral and intellectual structures which are sketched out here and there are torn apart by the self-generating force of the poetic imagination, so that it is frequently difficult for the reader to decide whether a notion or image derived from an intellectual system is being used "seriously" or "decoratively." There is no Christian framework to stabilise and resolve the fluctuations of tone: the one prevailing power is that of poetry, extending experience beyond the point at which it can be authenticated by reference to an extra-poetic criterion.

In 1569—two years after the first "Apollo" variant of the "Vœu"—Ronsard published a poem which he later entitled "La Lyre." It contains a detailed description of mythological scenes depicted on a lyre which had ostensibly been presented to him by his patron Monsieur de Belot. In these scenes, Apollo plays the leading role; indeed, the lyre is dedicated to "le Gaulois Apollon," and Laumonier adduces evidence to suggest that this Gallic Apollo is identifiable with Ronsard himself. Furthermore, certain of the scenes on the lyre are analogous with central aspects of Ronsard's poetic activity. In the first, for example, Apollo appears at the feast of the gods, harmonising with his music the "ancient discord" between Pallas and Neptune: this passage echoes the first song of the Muses in the "Ode à Michel de l'Hospital" and recalls Ronsard's early ambition to inaugurate in France an age of peace and cultural splendour after the Italian wars. Other episodes seem to recall his triumph, as court poet, over his rivals; his claims for the power and permanence of poetry; his shift of style from the "Pindaric" manner to amorous themes and more specifically the "beau stile bas" of the 1555–56 love-cycles; the tension in his personal life between a taste for pastoral solitude and the pursuit of advancement at court; and his "committed" poetry of the 1560s. The myths of Apollo thus allow Ronsard in this instance to sketch out a synchronistic interpretation of his own career, universalising it and transposing it into the Utopian framework of the decorative fresco. Into this schema is inserted an image of Bacchus, pouring forth from his cornucopia a rich profusion of fruits: hence, once again, a motif suggesting creative abundance appears at the centre of a representation of Ronsard's poetic activity; and the connection is endorsed by a Bacchic passage earlier in the poem, where Ronsard depicts himself cultivating the vine and being rewarded by the gift of Bacchic *fureur*.

As in the "Vœu," so too in "La Lyre," Ronsard identifies himself with Apollo in order to affirm and indeed to enhance his own poetic destiny. Yet the beginning of the poem stresses the periodicity of inspiration, and the sense of sterility which arises when it is absent; and the lyre itself clearly inhabits its own aesthetic world remote from immediate realities. Poetry, then, is still for Ronsard a Utopian activity which can never be fully integrated into experience, even where, as in the allegorisation of the poet's career, it exploits biographical data. It is true there is in this poem, which emerged from the contemplative atmosphere of the priory of Saint-Cosme, less exasperation than in the 1552 *Amours*. The world of poetry, if not all-embracing, is seen at least as being self-sufficient: the finely decorated lyre, the votive offering to Apollo, requires no justification beyond its own harmony and beauty. Thus the activity of the poet is seen as itself constituting, within certain limits, an authentic experience. This is perhaps the sense of the allegory: equilibrium has been reached, for the moment, in the dialogue between Apollo Musagetes and Apollo lover of Cassandre.

Nevertheless the discontinuity revealed by the earlier poem retains its significance. For much of Ronsard's major work evokes a sense of deficiency, of a sterility which the richness and abundance of his poetic creation could only partially redeem. It is apparent in the poems of his "middle years," in the elegies, in the seasonal hymns and other mythological poems; in the constant struggle to secure adequate patronage; in the *Sonets pour Hélène*; and above all in the failed ambition to write an epic poem which would immortalise both himself and the hoped-for age of Augustan glory in France. Ronsard's intelligent awareness of this duality and his resulting concern with the status of what the poet creates constitute a principal focus of his poetic *œuvre* and of its significance for the reader. By exploiting the self-generating power of poetry as myth, Ronsard revealed the incompatibility of poetry and experience, the intransigeance of reality, and hence, ultimately, the fragility of all Utopias.

Histoire d'oeuf: Secrets and Secrecy in a La Fontaine Fable

Ross Chambers

"LES FEMMES ET LE SECRET"

Rien ne pèse tant qu'un secret;
Le porter loin est difficile aux Dames:
    Et je sais même sur ce fait
    Bon nombre d'hommes qui sont femmes.
Pour éprouver la sienne un mari s'écria
La nuit étant près d'elle: "O dieux! qu'est-ce cela?
    Je n'en puis plus; on me déchire;
Quoi! j'accouche d'un oeuf !—D'un oeuf !—Oui, le voilà
Frais et nouveau pondu: gardez bien de le dire:
On m'appellerait poule. Enfin n'en parlez pas."
    La femme neuve sur ce cas,
    Ainsi que sur mainte autre affaire,
Crut la chose, et promit ses grands dieux de se taire.
    Mais ce serment s'évanouit
    Avec les ombres de la nuit.
    L'épouse indiscrete et peu fine,
Sort du lit quand le jour fut à peine levé:
    Et de courir chez sa voisine.
"Ma commère, dit-elle, un cas est arrivé:
N'en dites rien surtout, car vous me feriez battre.
Mon mari vient de pondre un oeuf gros comme quatre.
    Au nom de Dieu gardez-vous bien
    D'aller publier ce mystère.
—Vous moquez-vous? dit l'autre. Ah, vous ne savez guère

From *Sub-Stance* 32 (1981). © 1981 by *Sub-Stance*.

Quelle je suis. Allez, ne craignez rien."
La femme du pondeur s'en retourne chez elle.
L'autre grille déjà de conter la nouvelle:
Elle va la répandre en plus de dix endroits.
    Au lieu d'un oeuf elle en dit trois.
Ce n'est pas encor tout, car une autre commère
En dit quatre, et raconte à l'oreille le fait,
    Précaution peu nécessaire,
    Car ce n'était plus un secret.
Comme le nombre d'oeufs, grâce à la renommée,
    De bouche en bouche allait croissant,
    Avant la fin de la journée
    Ils se montaient à plus d'un cent.

             (La Fontaine, *Fables* VIII.6)

"Women and Secrecy"

Nothing weighs so heavy as a secret; to carry one far is a difficult feat for Ladies: and indeed in this connection I know of quite a few men who are women.

To test his wife a husband cried out one night, lying at her side: "Ye Gods! What is this? I cannot endure it; I am being torn apart; What! I am giving birth to an egg!"—"An egg?"—"Yes, here it is, fresh and new laid: take care not to talk of it: I would be called a hen. In short, not a word." The wife, new to this kind of thing, as to many another affair, believed it, and swore to the gods to keep silence. But her oath vanished with the shades of night. The indiscreet and none too bright spouse leaves her bed when day had scarce dawned: and makes haste to her neighbor's house. "Gossip dear," says she, "a strange thing has happened: whatever you do say nothing about it, or you would get me beaten. My husband has just laid an egg as big as four eggs put together. In God's name take care not to be publishing this mystery."—"Are you joking?" says the other. "Ah, you have not much of an idea of the kind of person I am. Go, and fear not." The egg-layer's wife returns home. The other is already burning to tell the news: she spreads it in more than ten places. Instead of one egg she says three. And that is not all, for another gossip says four, whispering the tale in people's ears, an unnecessary precaution, for by now it was no secret. As the number of eggs, through the operation of fame, got increasingly larger from mouth to mouth, by the end of the day the total had reached five score and more.

             (Literal translation by Ross Chambers)

Only divulgence makes a secret. Obviously, it need not be *actually* divulged; but I cannot say "I have a secret, I won't tell it to anyone," unless

I have previously thought "I *could* tell it to someone." However, only the shared secret achieves full reality and performs the true function of secrecy, which is not private and personal, but public and social. The sharing of a secret defines social groups by the simple criterion of inclusion or exclusion: there are those who are "in on" the secret and those who aren't, or to complexify, those who know the secret, those who know there is a secret but are not permitted to share it, and those who are ignorant both of the existence of the secret and its content. In this way, secrecy has obvious links with the distribution of power, since those who are *in possession* (of the secret, and of power) are in a position to use for their own purposes the desire to know (in those who know they are excluded from the secret) or else (in the case of the ignorant) to perpetrate all kinds of mystifications.

But the secret of secrets, the secret which it is most vital to know, is that there are no secrets. In initiation rites, the candidates frequently discover the triviality of the alleged mysteries they are being inducted into, and sometimes they learn that the mysteries are more accurately a mystification, the point being to exclude women and children and hence define the "men" rather than to make available information of a transcendent or even indispensable kind. But initiation is only a special case. Generally speaking, there are no secrets because a secret exists only as discourse, and the discourse which "realizes" the secret is that which destroys it as a "secret" (as something unspoken). In this sense I spoke of secrecy as a language which constitutes and defines, by inclusion, the "in" group while identifying by exclusion those "others" who do not belong. This means that, being a public phenomenon, a secret is the opposite of what one imagines. It is not a blank or a zero (zero information, zero communication) unavailable for investigation; it is an *egg*, a palpable object which can be examined and studied. But it follows, as in La Fontaine's fable, that there are those who are in the secret about secrecy and who know that there are no secrets that are not eggs, and others for whom the egg is a deceptive object, since they see it as the true secret.

But—still according to La Fontaine—the secret is an egg also because, as speech, it contains within itself a certain power of growth: since it exists only through being communicated to others, it is capable of initiating an infinitely expanding communication process, and thus of giving rise to a whole community of sharers of the secret, grouped around a nucleus (the "secret") which, as such, has no existence whatsoever. Word spreads "de bouche en bouche" (l. 35) and, independently of truth or falsity, the original egg becomes "plus d'un cent" (l. 37). But falsity, as we know, is of the essence, both for those who, being aware of the nature of secrecy, know that a secret is not a secret but an egg (the opposite of itself), and (more especially) for those who mistake the egg for the true secret. This fact— that falsity is consequently a characteristic of all exchanges of "secret" information—is what the fable indicates by the process of exaggeration which accompanies the spread of the story: the original egg is soon "gros comme quatre" (l. 21), then it is three (l. 29), then four eggs (l. 31) before becoming "plus d'un cent." In short, the multiplication of the number of people who are in on the secret produces a corresponding degree of falsity in the information involved, so that the people are less and less the sharers of the "same" secret; and the egg thus comes to figure the galloping fictionality of all language.

For this reason there is a close kinship between secrecy on the one hand and, on the other, that discursive and social phenomenon *par excellence*, that feast of fictionality which is called gossip. I am not sure that the functionality of gossip, as a means of testing circuits of communication and maintaining group structures, has been fully recognized. Its informational unreliability being commonly acknowledged, it serves of course as a scapegoating mechanism (the object of gossip being by definition excluded from the discourse group, and such an object of scandal being necessary, as René Girard has abundantly demonstrated, to the health of social groups), but it serves also to activate and employ—*à vide*, so to speak, or at least in a non-tragic way—the channels of circulation which ensure the cohesion and identity of a given group. Through gossip, the scapegoat is expelled, not only in an eminently symbolic way but in a way which is recognized as such; however the unity of the group is nevertheless confirmed and strengthened. Is there a social group in which gossip does not occur, and in which the practice is not at the same time condemned? This universality suggests the usefulness of the phenomenon, but our uneasiness over the uncontrolled propagation of false information is a sign that we are vaguely aware of the symbolic function it performs. Why would one promise to keep a supposed scandal to oneself, unless one was aware that in spreading it one was committing an injustice? But why should one spread it, then, unless it be that such an act of injustice is required by some social necessity? In La Fontaine's village, it is clear in any case that the group of "commères" is formed, not simply around the shared secret of the egg, but also, per medium of gossip, around the scandalous object that is the monster, half man and half hen, excluded as the referent of female speech from their community.

At this point, however, it becomes necessary to ask who is the real victim here. Reading the fable as an exemplification of the shared secret as discourse, we entered the text via its conclusion (informational falsity as the means whereby gossip constitutes a community through inclusion and exclusion). If one enters via the beginning, as the hen-man invites us to (as a manifestation of the theme stated in the moral of "hommes qui sont femmes," l. 4), then it is not so much the secret as discourse which engages our attention as the performative aspects of secrecy as a social "pact." A secret is a performative in the sense that only the act of telling it turns the content of the words into a "mystère" (l. 24), and this by virtue of a set of shared conventions between teller and tellee which produce a relationship of complicity. La Fontaine's narrative twice shifts into the mode of the "scene" so as to show the characters specifying the conventions of secrecy:

> "Enfin n'en parlez pas."
> La femme
>
> . . . . .
>
> Crut la chose, et promit ses grands dieux de se taire;

and:

> "N'en dites rien surtout, car vous me feriez battre.
>
> . . . .
>
> —Vous moquez-vous? dit l'autre. Ah! vous ne savez guère
> Quelle je suis. Allez, ne craignez rien."

However, what gives point to these exchanges is one's contextual knowledge that the vows of silence will be broken: these people are women, and the rules of gossip determine their treatment of secrets. This implies that although a promise is made to keep the secret, it is nevertheless understood that the secret is unlikely to be kept. In short there is second-degree complicity resulting from the fact that in addition to the promise to keep the secret there is a convention concerning the probability of its being divulged. This rule is known to the husband, who otherwise would have no reason to test ("éprouver," l. 5) his wife; and it is formulated at the outset by the fabulist:

> Rien ne pèse tant qu'un secret;
> Le porter loin est difficile aux Dames.

As for the women, who do not acknowledge the rule explicitly in their speech, they put it into practice by their actions.

However, there is a third and final convention which the fable does not formulate as a moral (like the second) or illustrate in specific dialogue (like the first); one just sees the women applying it automatically. This convention, which brings us to the deepest level of convention (since it goes completely unspoken), is embodied in the rule that, whereas a secret may well be repeated, it is not repeated indiscriminately. The news of the egg travels "de bouche en bouche," each woman as she hears it "grille déjà" (l. 28) to spread it; but the story travels only from woman to woman, "commère" to "commère," and no woman repeats it, for example, to her son or her husband. Among the conventions governing secrecy as a performative, there is a rule of repeatability, then (necessary, as stated, for the social functioning of the secret), but also a rule limiting this repeatability to appropriate hearers. This is of course an exclusion rule, defining *a contrario* the group which is positively defined by application of the repeatability rule. But this does not exhaust the social consequences of the discretion rule.

For, although in the fable men are excluded from the women's secret, the secret in question is a harmless one, and indeed it is a pure mystification invented by a man to test out ("éprouver"), or verify, a social phenomenon. And the moral makes it clear that in general terms discretion with respect to secrets is not a quality of women but an aspect of male superiority. For women, it is "difficult" to carry a secret far without divulging it (that is, there is no woman who does not experience this difficulty, even though some women are able to surmount it), whereas

> je sais même sur ce fait
> Bon nombre d'hommes qui sont femmes

(some men, a majority perhaps, have no trouble in keeping secrets, even though exceptions exist in the shape of men-who-are-women). The text is ironic, of course, and the euphemistic humor functions to imply that, in fact, telling secrets is a universal phenomenon—which, as we have seen, is the prime lesson of the fable. But a further implication is that, within the context of universal divulgence, the concept of "keeping a secret" does not lose its meaning—it is synonymous with the practice of a certain discretion. In short, there are no secrets but there *is* secrecy—and it is in the art of discretion (of knowing when to speak and when not to speak) that "les Dames" are said to be deficient.

This means that the fact that the women in the fable do not tell the secret of the egg to their husbands or children does not count as discretion on their part, even though for us it may illustrate the rule limiting the repeatability of secrets. Their treatment of the story of the egg is accountable for in other terms and by virtue of another phenomenon: I mean the fact that in society dominated groups may well have, and keep, certain secrets— but secrets which are of derisory significance, since they have no impact on the distribution of power. The women are the victims of a mystification perpetrated by a man who does know how to keep a secret (the secret of the mystification)—or who, at least, keeps it for a time (since it is evident that at some point he must have gotten around to telling it to someone— but to whom?). This suggests clearly that the question of discretion, of discernment in the divulging of secrets, has to do with the larger question of the way power is exercised in society; and it requires us to take a closer look at the curious tripartite division—indiscreet women versus "hommes qui sont femmes" versus men capable of exercising discretion—indicated in the moral. For, following the logic of our analysis, male discretion in the end can only consist of that form of discernment which involves identifying those dangerous men who are women so as not to entrust secrets to them, thus ensuring that they are not improperly divulged. And the fault attributed to women is not that they only tell secrets among themselves, but that they tell one another their secrets without restraint.

But the fable implies that the alleged character-weakness of women, who cannot "carry far" a secret, is in fact the consequence of ignorance and the sign of their dominated position within society. For the wife of the fable is not just naïve,

> neuve sur ce cas,
> Ainsi que sur mainte autre affaire,

she is kept in a state of naïveté by a husband who, far from wishing to enlighten her, is more concerned to *test* his "épouse indiscrète et peu fine" (l. 16), that is, to confirm her simple-mindedness and thus justify his own superiority. To this end, he stoops to a quite grotesque deception. The text stresses the spontaneity of women's behavior: the wife

> promit ses grands dieux de se taire.
> Mais ce serment s'évanouit
> Avec les ombres de la nuit;

and:

> L'autre grille déjà de raconter la nouvelle:
> Elle va la répandre en plus de dix endroits.
> Au lieu d'un oeuf elle en dit trois.

The unmotivated way they run about telling secrets contrasts with the husband whose behavior is directed by precise intentions ("pour éprouver la sienne"). Perhaps this proves that it is difficult for them to carry a secret far without telling it; but it also suggests that if they were better informed they would be more cautious in their actions. For the secret which is carefully kept from them is precisely this, that secrecy is closely bound up with the maintenance of power.

What then of the husband? Is he a man or a man-woman? His abrupt, peremptory style of speech in addressing his wife (ll. 8–10) suggests a man who is not in the habit of communicating with his spouse other than by assertions and orders (and one might conclude that it is because the wife is not encouraged to communicate with her husband that she is so ready to hasten, when she has something to share, "chez la voisine," l. 18). The strange experiment he mounts does not simply reveal his contempt for the spouse whom he so coldly deceives; it reposes on the telling of a false secret, to be sure, but also on the maintenance of a true secret—the secret of the falsity of the first secret. In all this, it is easy to recognize the reserved behavior of a man concerned to maintain his position of mastery. And yet, to do this, he runs the risk of being thought a "poule" (l. 10), a "pondeur" (l. 27); and this is precisely the reputation ("renommée," l. 34) he does finally acquire. However, reputation does not make him *genuinely* a man-woman; rather what one sees here is the importance of the stakes, and the extent of the husband's cleverness. Ready as he is to risk his manly reputation and become a man-woman in public repute so as to confirm and maintain his conjugal superiority, he does not hesitate, as a means to that end, to play the role of an egg-layer ("pondeur") by indiscriminately revealing his male secret to his wife, who will proceed (as he knows and intends) to spread it throughout the village. In this sense, the content of his secret (the laying of an egg) is redundant with its performative effect.

However, let us not lose track of the vital point: the secret is false, the egg-laying a simulation. The husband can run the risk of acquiring the reputation of a man-woman among the women because (1) they are only women, (2) he himself knows the "renommée" to be false, and (3) he can always, if need be, tell the true secret to those who will appreciate it, that is, the men. Indeed it seems that this latter course is actually the one he has taken since *we* know the secret from reading the fable: like the story of the egg, it can be said of the secret of the mystification that "ce n'[est] plus un secret" (l. 33). And of course it was necessary for this secret to come to light, not only to protect the husband's reputation but also so that the naïveté of the women, their lack of discretion, their inability to carry a secret far, in short all the female faults which are confirmed by the story, can be brought to general notice. As an "histoire gauloise," the fable has a clear function: to tell the husband's male secret so as to enhance the prestige of men by confirming the poor reputation of women and exposing them to mockery.

But storytelling, as Louis Marin has pointed out, is not without its traps. It seems that in this case, by pretending to be a hen-man, the husband has set off a mechanism of divulgence which, as its end-result, turns him retrospectively into a real man-woman. "De bouche en bouche," the story told with a view to preserving male prestige (by countering the reputation of hen-man the husband has acquired among women) appears to have reached the ear, then the mouth (or pen) of a storyteller—the author of the fable—who spreads it *indiscriminately*, in violation of the rules of male discretion. "Publishing the mystery" (cf. l. 23) so that it now reaches an unrestricted audience, the fable makes its information available, not only to "appropriate" hearers, but also to those men and women who have the greatest stake in knowing it, the victims of male discretion. For there is no way to tell the story of "Les Femmes et le secret" without laying bare the inner workings of the trick played on the wife, that is, the true secret which ought to have remained the property of men alone; and when these inner workings are revealed to those who ought not to be "in on the secret," then the "histoire gauloise" ceases to play its traditional role and becomes something else again, let us say a "fable"—a form of discourse from which a lesson can be learned.

Storytelling is indeed traditionally conceived as a means of communicating knowledge, and the etymology of the word "narrator" (one who knows) links it to the family of the verb *cognoscere*. If a secret is necessarily a secret divulged, then narrative is the reverse of the coin, the necessary corollary of the notion of "secret." Hence the great interest displayed by La Fontaine's text in the act of narration, which it twice displays in a narrative "scene," and each time in paradigmatic form. The husband relates to his wife his fictional misadventure as it is supposed to be occurring, and he gives it the canonical tripartite structure recognized by narrative grammar: (1) "O dieux! qu'est-ce cela?" (2) "Quoi! J'accouche d'un oeuf!" (3) "D'un oeuf?—Oui, le voilà/Frais et nouveau pondu . . ." The wife in turn uses the phrase now standard for describing narrative as a performative:

"Ma commère, dit-elle, un cas est arrivé . . ."

And twice more narrative becomes the object of the narrative in the fable: one woman "grille déjà de raconter la nouvelle: / Elle va la répandre en plus de dix endroits" (ll. 28–29); and another "raconte à l'oreille le fait,"

> Précaution peu nécessaire,
> Car ce n'était plus un secret.

In all these cases, the act of narration constituted by the fable itself is being mirrored (or embedded, *mis en abyme*) within the narration; and one notes that the fact of storytelling itself is *common* to both the man and the women characters, independently of the different value attached to male and female divulgence of secrets. In Lucien Dällenbach's terms, "Les Femmes et le secret" is a quite spectacularly "specular" text (*Le Récit spéculaire*).

If so, then the fact that its subject matter concerns the manner in which a secret comes to be "no longer a secret" (cf. l. 33) is significant. The subject reproduces the process of transformation, from secrecy to non-secrecy, by which the text itself has come into being, since it repeats the characters' secrets and divulges their knowledge, but in such a way as to radically alter the rules. For whereas the repeatability of male secrets is determined by the rule of discretion, and that of female secrets conforms to the conventions of gossip, narrative is subject to a quite different repeatability rule. The addressee of a story neither commits him/herself to repeat a story nor not to repeat it, since it is understood that a narrative not governed by the rules of secrecy is repeatable at will. But one does not repeat just any story to just any person; what determines the "tellability" of a story, and hence its repeatability, is the "interest" it has in the illocutory circumstances of the moment, an interest which is determined by the relationship between teller and tellee in their own particular historical context. William Labov has pointed out that every narrator takes great care to establish the interest of what he is recounting, the reason behind his narration—in short, its "point" (*Language in the Inner City: Studies in the Black English Vernacular*). As a literary text and "opera aperta," the fable must presuppose this type of repeatability (as a function of interest), and that is why it can be said that, although it repeats secrets, it is no longer subject to the rules of secrecy.

This means, of course, that the narrator of "Les Femmes et le secret," judged from the male point of view, is behaving like a woman, that is without discretion—but the secret he is divulging is *not* a female secret (which would have little importance); it is, quite to the contrary, the major male secret. This is what makes him the true man-woman, or egg-layer of the fable. The husband is only apparently a man-woman, as a result of his lie; and he becomes a real man-woman more or less accidentally, having been sufficiently indiscreet as to reveal his secret to an informer who passed it on to the narrator. But the narrator, who is in on the male secret yet feels free to tell it like a woman, in such a way that it ceases to be a secret, is the genuine man-woman. The egg he lays shares with the husband's egg its fictionality; but the difference lies in the fact that whereas the husband's egg is a mystification, the narrator's egg-laying is a *demystifying*—and hence, scandalous—act.

For the great male secret, the secret of secrets which ought not to have been divulged, is a double secret. It is first of all the secret of the mystification perpetrated by men on women; but it is also the secret of the reasons behind this mystification. Men exercise power by means of deception because their power has no natural basis: men are not a separate, radically different species, and the power they claim is consequently obtained only by virtue of a deception *concerning this very fact*, a deception calculated to prove, and perpetuate, women's "difference." But what the fabulist does is to tear aside the veil and reveal the essential secret, the secret which in fact comprises all the "knowledge" he lays claim to as narrator:

> Et je sais même sur ce fait
> Bon nombre d'hommes qui sont femmes.

If "quite a number" of men are women, the social division on which male power reposes is a false division, which is maintained only through the operation of male secrecy. And to declare, as the fabulist does, that there are "men who are women" is *automatically* to claim for oneself the status of man-woman, while declaring oneself the ally of women.

So the "interest" of the fable—its point—is of a pedagogical kind; but its pedagogy is liberationist. The text addresses itself to all those whose interest it is to learn what is being kept from them (what the narrator "knows" and communicates). "To lay an egg," in English, suggests error and miscalculation; and in this English sense the true "pondeur" is the husband. For the narrator makes no error and displays no deficiency in discernment (but only in male "discretion"). And the egg he lays is a truly fertile one, since the secret brought to light so long ago is still being learned, and its consequences realized, today. Perhaps by now it is time the word was spread.

Lamartine

Georges Poulet

Not a mental tension, not an expectation, not a concentration of vigilant thought, but simply the initial inertia of a soul absorbing nothing, in which nothing lives, from which, it would seem, all withdraws in order to leave it to its vacuity, as a sail that, in turning, discloses the expanse:

> My heart rests, my soul lies in silence;
> The world's distant noise dies as it comes,
> As a far sound is enfeebled by distance,
> Brought by the wind to an uncertain ear.

Without a doubt, in this constantly recurring moment in Lamartian poetry, the soul's vacuity is not total. Something resounds with it, a murmur is heard which a breeze has carried to the threshold of consciousness. But one would be wrong to imagine that here there is a true motion overtaking the mind, similar to a wave running toward the shore to pour onto it its rich weight of water. There is nothing here of the immediate profusion that one finds in the great singers of sensibility, a Shakespeare, a Keats, a Rimbaud. On the contrary, if any distant sound reaches the ear, it is less to recall the existence of the exterior reality, than to announce its retreat. The outside murmur arrives attenuated, half emptied of its substance; and as soon as it comes it expires; it only manifests itself to betray the immateriality of its non-presence:

> Here the last sounds of the world come to die . . .

As in Josephine Soulary's sonnet, one may distinguish in Lamartine's poetry two intersecting processions. Living and dying touch each other,

---

going in their opposite directions. On one side, there is that which is arriving, but what almost no longer exists; it fades at the instant it touches our senses; on the other, there is life that continues to resound, but farther and farther into the distance: flight of external reality, carrying its presence—less and less perceptible—elsewhere, while what flows back to the abandoned soul is like an insubstantial shadow left by the vanishing thought in the mind.

> And the evening breeze, dying along the beach,
> Brought back to me thy songs prolonged on the waves.

Does what is felt here, only if the song is prolonged, have an essentially excentric movement? The vibration of sound propagates itself, but in withdrawing from the auditor. Nevertheless, the breeze brings back the echo of the fading song. It is as if there were two voices, of which one was sustained in the distance, and the other came to die with the wind in the center of the perceptive field. Such is the curious scission that one notices in Lamartine's poetry. One might say that in it, the human being is condemned to separate himself in two distinct ways from ambient reality; in one way, in allowing himself to flee to the horizon; and on the other hand in seeing die at his feet the forms he has abandoned in his flight. Extinction of sound, retreat of sonorous life, a farewell mingling with the silence, and, at the same time, a corresponding diminution of light, a fading of light:

> The sun of our days fades from its first dawn;
> On our languid foreheads it barely still sends out
> A few trembling rays to combat the night . . .

Very often the paling and the deafening combine:

> To the soft clarity of the serene arch
> We will sing together seated under the jasmine,
> Until the time when the moon, gliding toward Misena,
> Loses itself, paling in the morning fires.

> She sings, and her voice dies at intervals,
> And, the chords of the lute more lightly struck,
> The subsiding echoes give to the zephyr
> Only dying sighs, broken by the silence.

> Half of the sky paled, and the breeze
> Weakened in the sails, immobile and without voice,
> The shadows ran, and under their grey shade
> All on the sea and sky was at once effaced;
> And in my soul, paling and measured,
> All sounds here below fell with the day . . .

What pales, what falls silent, what fails with the day, is every minute of existence. No one experiences as does Lamartine, in the often-repeated manner, the sense of duration as a running flood: "Time escapes me, and flies!"—But, in escaping me, where does it fly to? It flies far from the present, far from me, into the past, into space. Universal phenomenon! A great poetical meeting ground! Who has not sung of his effacement accomplished in the soul and in space, at one and the same time? But no one, unless it be Lamartine, had *begun* by being a poet of effacement. Ordinarily, one begins by singing of that which lies around one and beyond, which, in appearing, causes a similar life to appear in the soul. The theme of disappearance comes later. But, with Lamartine, it seems to have been there from the beginning; it is the great original theme. For Lamartine, to think and to sing, is to think and sing a reality which, *already* given, *begins at once* to be withdrawn. In other words, it is only when that which one enjoys is protected in one's grasp that Lamartine shakes off the kind of happy stupor in which he would willingly spend the rest of his days, to take consciousness of a world which exists for him only from that moment when it is in danger of no longer existing.

Lamartine is, par excellence, the poet of a dissolving reality. This dissolution of the real manifests itself in the first place by what one could call cloudiness.

This cloudiness is the metamorphosis of the world into clouds. As soon as things appear with Lamartine, they mist over:

> Already I see life, through a cloud
> Fade for me into the shadow of the past . . .

As the cause precedes the consequence, cloudiness precedes fading. Seen through a cloud, life itself becomes a cloud. It loses its solidity. It changes itself into a species of cotton. Nothing in Lamartine is more striking than this lack of consistence, revealed by the objects of the exterior world. At the instant when the poet discovers them, it would seem that they had already undergone a first process of disintegration which causes them to pass into a liquid state. Now they are ready to change into vapor. This incessant renewed vaporization of the Lamartian universe, and of all he comprehends, could make one think of the no less famous Baudelairean vaporization. But the two phenomena possess only superficial similarities. With Baudelaire, the vaporization is caused by the transformation of perceptible forms into an infinity of droplets of which each one is a mirror and a prism; in such a way that the melting of things accomplishes itself in the magical intensification of the light, the multiplication of colors and the powdering of a thousand iridescent particles. But it is quite different with Lamartine. The vaporization with him is rather a gaseousness than a pulverization. Or rather, if there is a pulverization, it is less crystalline and mirroring than flaky. It is not a state, even though transitory. It is a movement by which things hasten to their dissolution; comparable to a wave whose crumbling dust

In flakes of light
Rolls and disperses in the distance all these fragments of the
    day.

Fragmentation, therefore, with Lamartine, does not have the effect of
the substitution of a multitude of distinct fragments for the shattered entity.
The primary substance does not disintegrate in sharp and sudden bursts.
Quite on the contrary, one has the impression of an almost imperceptible
disintegration similar to the ravelling of clouds. Every form, less and less
precise, seems to have been given over to an element which wears or gnaws
at it, which tears it shred by shred, obliterating the details of its contours
and leaving it without recognizable characteristics. Speaking of the Ossian
world, to which his own has such a strong resemblance, Lamartine writes:
"I involuntarily assimilated into myself the indeterminate, the revery, the
oblivion in contemplation, the look fixed on confused apparitions in the
distance. For me it was sea after shipwreck on which floated by moonlight
patches of debris; in which one saw a few faces of young girls lifting their
white arms, loosing their damp hair onto the spume of the waves; on which
one could distinguish plaintive voices broken by the roar of the surf against
the reef." And he adds, speaking now more particularly of his own thought:
"This is the unwritten book of reverie whose pages are covered with enigmatic characters, in which the floating imagination makes and unmakes its
own poems, as the dreaming eye in the clouds makes and unmakes its
countrysides."

Like the mythical book of reverie, the Lamartian poem is made up of
clouds and debris, vague faces given over to the fluctuations of an aquatic
and misty world. A world rapidly unravelling itself, even though it is
covered over by a liquid element, or a mist, even though in withdrawing,
the fogs or the waters take with them the forms that seemed to float therein.
Thus, with Lamartine, everything softens and weakens, brings itself to an
end, or enters into the element enveloping it. Everything unravels under
the thickness of the veils or in the absence of forms. Above all, everything
is confounded. Far from ending at the multiplication of the real, the dissolution of things has for effect the reduction of them to unity. A unity,
naturally, as different as possible from the Neoplatonic unity, and which
has, as principle, not as with Amiel the concentration of all the virtualities
in the monad, but on the contrary, the absorption of these in the universal
mass, absolutely undifferentiated. Also, no matter how distinct the visual
or auditory phenomena by which Lamartine begins making a minute description, almost at once we see them lose their true identity to participate
in a sonorous and luminous movement infinitely vaster and more imprecise
than themselves, in which they are soon diluted as a drop of wine in the
sea.—Here are two examples:
The first, concerning light, describes a sunrise:

In proportion to the lifting day, the distinct brilliance of the azure
or flame color of the luminous bars *diminish and melt* in the *general*

gleaming of the atmosphere; and the moon which had been suspended over our heads, rosy and the color of fire, *dims*, takes on
a mother of pearl tint and *sinks into the depths of the sky*, as a silver
disc whose color *pales* in proportion to its penetration into deep
water.

The second is relative to sound and reproduces the murmur of a town:

All these sounds, already *weakened* by the advanced hour, . . . *melt
instant by instant into one voiceless and indecisive humming*, forming
a harmonious music in which human sounds, the stifled respi-
ration of a great dozing city, *mingle, so that one can no longer distinguish them* from the sounds of nature, the distant reverberations
of the waves and gusts of wind that bend the sharp crests of the
cypresses.

General atmospheric gleam, the humming of a whole town—almost
always one sees appear with Lamartine some vast confused entity, that,
surging above the multiple manifestations of perceptive phenomena, opens
its broad breast to make them welcome, to make room for them, and to
unify them while transforming them into the same substance as itself.
Everything mingles and is confounded into a single mass, everything rapidly permits itself to be identified with a whole, at once both homogenous
and indistinct. A moment before they disappear, one can still see the condemned forms detaching themselves from the depths in which they will
be lost. Some final characteristic permits of their recognition, such as the
debris which Lamartine saw floating on the water. For it is in effect a species
of supreme floating, so to speak, at which we are assisting:

> And before my eyes floating at random
> With pieces of sky, and shreds of nature!

Detached, in shreds, already inconsistent and changing face, the floating
forms have the appearance of being supported in space as petals glide on
the surface of the water. But a breath draws them, their aerial navigation
takes them farther and farther from the gaze, until their contours end by
blurring in some grisaille, to mingle with the ambient immensity of the
very horizon's line.

Suppressed at the horizon, the forms let nothing subsist except the
horizon. Never, with Lamartine, does the gaze fix itself before they have
attained this absorbing mist in which they are consumed and which constitutes the border of the unique countryside the poet describes. If, in the
first place, quite near one, it would be possible to make out a host of precise
details which would swell the description, it would suffice on the contrary,
as it invariably does with Lamartine, that the eye be carried farther and
farther away, so that it should perceive less and less of things and see the
last of those subsisting, melt at the horizon line. Of this centrifugal and
purely negative movement, where it is a question of ridding oneself of all
forms along the way, one can find dozens of such examples in Lamartine.

In the evening, the moon floated with its flecks of light on the tepid tides of the river. The dreaming astral body opened, at the extremity of the Seine's bed, luminous avenues and fantastic perspectives *in which the eye lost itself in vaporous and shadowy views.*

At my left, the valley, in dropping toward the shores of the sea, widens and presents to the gaze its hilly flanks, more and more wooded and cultivated; its serpentine river between the breasts of the hills crowned with monasteries and with villages. *Farther away,* the palm trees of the plain lift up, behind the low hills of olive trees, their plumage of a yellow green, intersecting the long golden line of sand bordering the sea. *The gaze loses itself at last in an indefinite distance,* between the sky and the waves.

But the most beautiful sentence perhaps, is this, on the temples of Baalbek:

The great temples were before us like statues on their pedestals; the sun struck them with a last ray that withdrew slowly from one column to another, like the shadows of a lamp which the priest carries to the depth of the sanctuary.

Admirable image, one of the purest that one can find from Lamartine's pen, and which very exactly expresses what is essential in him, the movement by which every image drifts toward absence, as the day glides toward nightfall. Such is really the thought or, if that word is too strong, the fundamental experience of the poet, retreat, the gradual engulfment of all that which is and has forms in the immense negative entity of formlessness. An invariable scheme presides at these descriptions. First, in a light essay, the glance of the poet goes from form to form. But nowhere is it gratified nor does it linger. The impetus by which it carries itself forward to meet the exterior world is less the radiantly regular and progressive movement of a conquest, than an effusion similar to a movement of flight. There is nothing here resembling the action of a center taking possession of the expanse. In proportion as it excentrically displaces itself toward the periphery of the horizon, the attention of the poet completely turns away from the place from which it has emanated, so that contemplation with him is not so much an aggrandizement of the zone embraced by the glance, as an evacuation of the territories which he has successively seized and abandoned. So that the field of vision is comparable to a circle of which the circumference ceaselessly augments, but in such a way that a kind of vaster and more visible *no man's land* separates it from the center. In this indefinite retreat of vague thought there is no more striking example than the following text, taken from the *Voyage en Orient.* One distinguishes in it with particular clarity the different stages followed by the Lamartian glance, before ending in the final vaporization of all forms in the absolute centrifugality of a horizon, beyond which it seems that the universe is in flight:

> At my feet, the valley of Jehoshaphat stretched out like a vast sepulcher; the dry Cedron furrowed a whitish cleft . . . ; somewhat to the right, the Mount of Olives hid itself, letting, between the sparse links of the volcanic cones and the naked mountains of Jericho and Saint-Saba, the horizon *extend and prolong itself* like a luminous avenue between the tops of the unequal cypresses; the gaze sent itself out, drawn by the azure brilliance and the lead-enness of the Dead Sea, which shone at the feet of rising moun-tains, and, behind, the blue chain of mountains of Arabia Petraea bounded the horizon. Yet *bounded* is not the word, for the moun-tains seemed transparent as crystal, and one saw or thought one saw *extend far off a vague and indefinite horizon swimming in ambient vapors* of an air colored purple and ceruse.

How can one speak here, still, of the *line* of a horizon? In the same way that at the interior of this line all things have the tendency to lose their contours and to merge one with the other, now even the trace of the line of the horizon shivers and one no longer knows if what one glimpses beyond still belongs to the world of the earth, or to that of space.

II

> Nevertheless the falling evening holds serene languors
> Which the end gives to all, to joys as to sorrows
>
> . . . .
>
> For our senses, this hour offers gentle impressions
> *Like muffled steps on mosses:*
> The bitter-sweet kiss of farewells.
> The crystalline and transparent air is limpid,
> Mountains of vaporized azure drift, liquid,
> Melting into the azure of the skies.

From the muffling of sounds to the unification of colors, everything participates here in the same phenomena of identification with vaporiza-tion. It would be an error, however, to imagine that the mountains mingle with the sky for the simple reason that they become the same color. First of all, something which seems to be vaguely suggested by the text is that the distant mountains, situated at the very back of the perspective, are like a last vestige of the world, progressively engulfed in shadow, so that it is the earth itself, or rather what remains of it, that goes into the distance to unify itself with the azure air. But this is not enough to say, and the identity of colors should be taken here as an indication of a more general identity, which is an identity of substance. If the earth is indistinguishable finally, from the sky, if, like the sky, it takes on a truly celestial and aerial tint, that is because, at the very farthest reach, it has become something aerial and celestial. Thus there clearly appears the decisive reason for the phenomena of vaporization in Lamartine. His express goal is to spiritualize the ambient world. The vaporized world is a world dematerialized. When the operation has succeeded, when the alchemy of the poet has sufficiently etherealized the forms and blended the colors, nothing is left to oppose the identification of visible reality with the infinite extent in whose chasm it lies. From one end to the other, from the point of departure from which radiates the gaze of the spectator, to the indecisive zone it reaches, where the earth becomes sky and the sky vapor, all is now of the same nature. Earth and sky, and all they support and contain, with the prodigious variety of the objects of creation, seem to be mingled into a homogenous continuity, like the surface of a lake or an atmosphere cleared of all exhalations. In the same way as there is in Lamartine an initial, but still terrestrial, point of repose which is the languor of a soul letting the trouble caused by pleasures of sense be lulled, there is also in him, but more tardily, a second point of rest, more exalted, more serene, which is the quietude of a soul liberated from the senses, liberated from forms, attaining, by a stripping down, realized with a strange facility, to the consciousness of a world so purged of all matter that it differs in no respect from the purity of space. With Lamartine, the vaporization has no other goal: it reduces the world to space. Space which appears finally as the unique reality, omnipresent, omniform, and omnisubstantial, in which end, as rivers in the sea, the thousand cogitations of poetry. Poetry discovers space; even more, it transforms everything into space. Everything it feels, everything it thinks, everything it imagines, all that it sings, becomes space.

The Lamartian volatilization does not only operate on the concrete forms of creation. It is, at base, so efficacious, so universal, and so contagious that it even infects the words which are the equivalent of it. When Maurice Blanchot, for example, asserts that all language replaces presence by absence in substituting the abstraction for the reality, he does not consider the extreme case of Lamartine. In fact, with Lamartine the transformation of the real into the unreal does not stop there. The abatement of sounds, the fading of light, the retreat of things, the growing indistinctness of contours, all these phenomena by which, as we have seen, the concrete realities metamorphose themselves in Lamartine into their ideal reflections, into their verbal images, all this pursues to the very heart of the images, and the verbal flux which expresses them, its insensible work of deteriorization. In such a way that one can say that, with Lamartine, not only the world of real things is abolished by the negative magic of writing, but also the world of the word, this too, is gravely affected. The deafening, the paling, become a deafening and a paling of the language itself. What is now blurred is not simply the universe imagined by Lamartine, it is the universe of Lamartine's word. Speech, which little by little is divested of everything it could conserve that still might be distinct, becomes in the final accounting the vaguest language there could be: a sort of long modulation, of which the harmony is not made up of independent elements linked to one another by a measure, but the unrolling of one sonorous web which, like the general background of certain pictures, spreads and stretches out on all sides to give the most smooth and indefinite surface possible to the continuity of the verbal space.

Lamartine, poet of pure space; or, even more exactly, poet whose words, verses, stanzas, poems, seem less to succeed one another than to continue indefinitely, one into the other, as those undifferentiated parts, without substance and always similar, which altogether form pure space.

But is this to say that Lamartine is the poet of *empty* space?

It would certainly seem so. In fact, has not all this poetry for its final goal to efface the universe, to make space appear? Consequently, is this not a poetry of a deprived universal space, deprived of things, of a space haunted, like that of Mallarmé's poems, by the disappearance of the vivacious and the *bel aujourd'hui*? A space without life, similar to those of the ice fields or sidereal expanses?—Is it really this, however? In contrast to the Mallarméan extents, one feels certain that, in spite of their denuding, the expanses sung by Lamartine are not frozen or uninhabitable. On the contrary, a warm breath moves over them. A temperate climate favors them, and, even more than climate, an atmosphere, tenuous, it is true, but dense enough so that the winged creatures can breathe and fly in it. Far from being a vacuum, the Lamartian space seems to be occupied by a quintessential matter, uniformly distributed, which could well be the residue of the volatilization of the real. By an imaginative process whose chemistry is far from clear, it appears that the world, in vanishing, has become truly divine. As solids become liquid in order to next become gases, this dematerializing matter becomes soul, to push on its substantial refinement to a state similar and perhaps identical with that of divinity. This, naturally enough, does not present itself as a definition of the system of beliefs formulated by Lamartine, always supposing there is one. The famous pantheism of the poet, denounced by his critics, is only a rather clumsy idea, proposed *a posteriori* by the author of *La Chute d'un ange*, to explain a phenomenon, for him, indubitable, and perhaps more exalted than any other, which is the *universal diffusion of the spirit in space*. Lamartian space is only initially and imperfectly the place of material and concrete things. After that, it is definitively, substantially, naturally, thanks to a dematerialization process of matter, the place where the divine life of the spirit is spread and animated.

It is not otherwise, in what is *reasoned* but in what is *imagined* in one of the most faithful of the Lamartian dreams, the Socrates of the *Meditations:*

> Perhaps really, in the immense expanse,
> In everything mingling, *a soul is poured out;*
> And these brilliant heavenly bodies sown above our heads,

Are living suns and living fires;
And the Ocean, striking its frightened shores,
With its growling waves rolls an angered soul;
So our fragrant air flying in a pure air
Is a spirit floating on azure wings;
So the day is an eye distributing light,
The night, a beauty veiling her eyelid;
And at last in the sky, on the earth, in every place,
Everything is intelligent, all lives, all is a god.

Animism, panpsychism, it is easy to give a name to the system of ideas which these lines express—moreover, with an uneven merit—representative of the Lamartian genius. Yet if one compares them to other verses which translate the same animism, for example to such poets of the Renaissance as Du Bellay, Belleau, du Bartas, and above all, Ronsard, one can see the difference. The animism of Ronsard is before all else a vivifying principle, a quasi-animal energy working in the interior of stones, of trees, of men, to make them exist and realize themselves. The world is the result of its efficacy, the living witness of its virtue. Neither Ronsard nor his friends would have dared, even in thought, to detach such an animal force from the terrestrial or cosmic flesh it animated.—But take Lamartine. From the brilliant heavenly bodies, already so little material in their aerial and distant perfection, thought glides to the ocean, to fragrant air, to the light. It seems that the soul pours itself out more with more ease when its habitation is more spiritual; until the moment when it finds its perfect situation, far from bodies, even though celestial, in space.

If the Lamartian space is animated, it is, therefore, by a life reserved by preference to spirits or the spirit. Space is the ideal place for the existence of discarnate entities. It is not without reason that Lamartine's imagination has turned toward angelology. Apart from the souls of the dead, of which he makes frequent use, and apart from, naturally, God Himself, soul of souls, king of angels, immanent in space, he has only the birds and the angels with which to enliven space; and even the Lamartian birds are submitted, like all the rest, to the process of dematerialization, resembling angels, rather than birds in flesh and in bone. Lamartian space is also filled with angels; and one could even say that, the better to people it, all the world is angelicized. The famous title, *La Chute d'un ange*, is the reversing of the process familiar in the Lamartian universe: the movement by which the fallen being rediscovers its wings, becomes once more an angel, and thus repairing the effect of its fall, ascends again into its ancient spatial territory.

But since space now appears as the natural place for liberated minds, there is no further reason for the poet to remain on earth and to look *from afar* into space. If Lamartine's poetry is in the first instance poetry of the progress of things, of the flight of forms, of an ascension of all the objects of contemplation, it becomes in the second place a poetry of the very mounting of the poet himself, rejoining, so to speak, everything he has caused to precede him. Perhaps there is nothing more moving in this poetry than the moment when he places himself between the lifting of the image and the more tardy ascension of the being who at first had been content to see them rise. A moment of pause and silence, a moment when the being, at last understanding that he has exchanged the world of things for a world deserted by things, begins to love this beautiful aerial desert that things, in withdrawing themselves, have disclosed to him:—"*Come, the enamoured silence occupies distant space. . . .*"—The invitation of space has, for Lamartine, the accent and the voice of sirens. In his universe, the angels are like sirens of the sky: sirens whispering in the ear not voluptuous submarine promises, but the pleasures of souls without bodies, the pleasures of space:

> Lift yourself up, voice of my soul,
> With the dawn, with the night!
> Spring forth like the flame,
> Spread yourself out like sound!

In the main, the pleasures of space for Lamartine are no different than those tasted today by the amateurs of skiing. Altitude, the virginity of the situations and the matter, the exquisite abolition of the body consumed by the facility with which it can move, as if it floated in a pure expanse: in a certain sense, certainly, skiers are souls or are angels. Not being able to glide on snowfields, Lamartine has done what, imaginatively, comes closest to this exercise; he is transported into the beyond. There is no dream more often taken up again, more intensely lived by Lamartine, than his dream in which he finds himself dead and liberated from his body:

> I love to let myself be rocked in this silence,
> To feel myself no longer living or thinking,
> To believe that the mind, which in vain the body recalls,
> Has quit beyond return its mortal husk
> And forever swims in the rays of the sky.
>
> Thus when our soul, to its source flown,
> Leaves its terrestrial valley forever,
> Every beat of its wings lifting it to the skies,
> It enlarges the horizon which spreads beneath its eyes.
>
> On the rays of the evening, on the wings of the wind,
> It rises to God like a living fragrance.

Here, therefore, at last, is the soul of the poet emplaning in space.— But what is it to emplane in space? For Baudelaire, for example, it is to continue to vibrate. To fly, swim, roll, all these terms serve him to express a sort of *Cogito* of the dilation of the senses. Like a tightened cord which prolongs waves of sound while amplifying them, Baudelaire is conscious of the sensation which swells, which propagates itself, which fills environing space; and, at the same time, he feels the sensation which lifts and transports him, so that on the crest of his wave he follows the same course and participates in the same swelling forth. This invasion of space is therefore entirely determined by the intensity of sensation. The more acute the sensation, the more inhabited space is enlarged.—Now it is not the same with Lamartine. His poetry has as principle, as one knows, obliteration, fading, which is to say not a *crescendo*, but a *diminuendo*, and even finally, the extinguishing of sensation. Also, with Lamartine the expansion of the spirit does not depend on something positive, but, quite the contrary, on a negation and an abnegation. It is, in fact, as we have seen, in ridding itself of its forms, in lightening itself of the weight of matter, that this poetry succeeds in elevating and dilating itself. Its expansion follows an *unballasting*. He who takes clear orders wins the field of play. Space is an opening plain for the gambolling of the spirit. "I soar in freedom in the fields of the possible," cries Lamartine. If the fields of the possible are much more spacious than those of the real, it is precisely for the reason that they are cleared of all reality. They are pure vacancy. Nothing in them is in opposition to the infinite progression of the spirit:

> He mounts up, and the horizon grows with every instant,
> He mounts, and before him the immensity is spread
> As if under the gaze of a new dawn;
> At every step a world seems to germinate under his eyes,
> Up to the supreme summit where his enchanted eye
> *Takes hold of space and soars in liberty.*

Elsewhere Lamartine says:

> Spreads into all of space and lives in all of time.

When all is said and done, as in Newton's hypothesis on the irradiation of light, the movement of growth which is the question here, does not proceed by translation into fullness, but by diffusion in an ethereal milieu. The soul overflows itself. To grow is for it a thing as natural as for water to pour. Give it immensity, and it becomes immensity:

> It seems to me, my God, that my oppressed soul,
> Before immensity, grew great in me . . .

> Already, already, I swim in waves of light;
> Space grows before me . . .

Growing space, and I grow in space. External space? interior space? Who could tell! Does it have to do with the *sensorium* of God, of the habitation of elected souls, or again of this sort of expanse which is the profundity and the duration and in which simultaneously are all remembrances refound? Perhaps of these three kinds of space at once. In that case, they form an uninterrupted medium in which thought freely extends itself in the manner of circles:

> As for us, we are not astonished at this power of repercussion of the human soul sounding across all souls and all ages; there are in the heart of the hero, the poet or the saint, impulses of force that break the sepulcher, the firmament, time and *that travel, like the eccentric circles of the pebble thrown into the sea,* slowly to die on the farthest shores of the ocean bed. The heart of man, when it is moved by the idea of God, *carries its emotions as far as the ocean* carries the undulations of its margins.

The lake, the beautiful ideal lake of Lamartine and Elvire, has therefore become an ocean, along whose immense surface, in circles, human emotion develops. It develops itself in tending toward a distant periphery, which is called God.

III

Thus Lamartine refinds or conserves something of the great theological symbol of the infinite circle. For him, too, God is

> *The limitless circle in which all is written.*

One could even say that this boundlessness particularly suits the poet's conception of divinity. There is in fact nothing more natural to Lamartine's effusive thought than a peripheric God; nothing is more natural to him, too, than to conceive this periphery under the least determined form possible. In a word, Lamartine interprets the definition of God, namely, God is an infinite circle, in the following manner: God has indefinite contours, God is a Being infinitely vague. Even more: for Lamartine, God is that which is at the extremity of a thought which in dilating itself dilutes itself in such a way that God is perhaps this final dilution of thought or of its disappearance when it has expended its expansive force. Now in this extreme place, where the first impetus "comes to die on the last beaches," in this most peripheral of all places, what is left? There remains a thought which vanishes in the very feeling of its weakness, and an object which is still withdrawing, which is retiring beyond the circle, which proves itself unseizable. In the final reckoning, as with how many other poets, there is the experience with Lamartine of an overtaking and abandonment. That is to say, no matter how great the force of the expanding spirit, it is always surpassed by the power of evasion of the object he covets. Lamartine is one who goes on to the pursuit of that of which he dreams, knowing already from the moment of departure that no matter how long the course, he is beaten from the beginning, and, as we say, *laissé au poteau* [left at the post]:

> How could I not, carried by Aurora's chariot,
> Vague objects of my desires, leap as far as thee!

Is it a matter here only of Elvire, or a higher object, with whom, by fleeing and being lifted in flight, she ends by confounding herself? Be that as it may, there is in Lamartine not simply a flight of things, a flight of beings, but a very flight of God. It could not be otherwise. Since on the one hand all this poetry stems from a movement engendered by the retreat of the being, and not by its presence, and as on the other hand it is not possible to assign any limit to this retreat, the result is that Lamartine's poetry can only be that of an infinite flight, not alone a flight *to* God, but a flight *of* God. It has been held to be a poetry of divine immanence. This is perfectly true, but it is of a flowing immanence, fleeing, as water disappears through the fingers. Certainly, it is not amiss to say that God is everywhere present in the Lamartian universe; but He is present as mountains that rise up, yet that, at the same time, merge and are lost. God is immanent, but His immanence never ceases to fade away in its transcendence.

It is true that, tired of imagining this eternally peripheric God, Lamartine tried to conceive a God-center. Let us push aside, he says, the thought of a God entirely diluted in the infinity of His creation:

> Not that second chaos which a pantheist adores,
> *Where in the immensity even God evaporates.*
> Made of brutally confused elements, pell-mell,
> In which good is no longer good, and evil is no longer evil;
> But this whole, *God-center of the universal soul,*
> Subsisting in Its work, and subsisting without it.

A very rare apparition with this poet is the word *center*. For the whole movement of his poetry is accomplished in the form of a continual flight toward an ever-fleeing circumference. One barely has the right to consider it as a movement emanating from a center. Rather one should understand it under the aspect of a radically excentric movement, a movement that does not in the least try to establish a coherent coming-and-going between the center and the periphery, but which *forgets* the center, that without respite diffuses itself toward a singularly decentered God. In several other passages, as well, Lamartine rejects the anarchic cosmos which is his, as he also rejects the orientation toward a peripheral God, which was that of his poetry. Now, like Dante, he reverses the perspective, transforming the excentricity of his essential approach into an unexpected concentricity.

Already, in the *Meditations,* he asks if the "divine ray" of the soul should revivify itself in a series of reincarnations on earth,

> Or whether, seven times changing destiny and sphere,
> And mounting from star to star toward its *divine center,*
> An *ever fleeing goal which it endlessly approaches.*

Historically this is the question that divided Pierre Leroux and Jean Reynaud. But what matters to us is that, of these two hypotheses, it is manifestly the second that Lamartine prefers and that he is to develop elsewhere throughout his great unfinished epic poem. In the Foreword to *La Chute d'un ange* he writes: "I believe that the sole work of humanity, as a collective being and as an individual being, is to gravitate toward God, *approaching Him always.*"

One doubtful point is that Lamartine's poetry pretends in these instances to become the contrary to what it is. It is a poetry of amortization, in brief, of *withdrawing*. Now here it wishes to become a poetry of *approaching*. But in the lines just cited, one expression reveals to us that Lamartine is incapable of frankly exchanging vaporization for centralization. If the soul approaches the center, he says, it is by an endless movement in the direction of "an ever-fleeing goal." The divine center, therefore, is behaving like the divine periphery. One must consider not Dante, but Pascal here. Periphery and center flee in an eternal flight. And in flying, they do what all objects of thought do in the Lamartine universe: they pass from presence to absence.

An absence that now seems a goal of all poetic movement. Absence of things, absence of the world, absence of words, absence of God. And completing this series of absences, there is the absence of the very one who had gone in pursuit of those absent; for, at the limit, losing turn by turn every one of the objects of grace to which he still held with some firmness, it is the poet himself who dissolves in his own absence:

> . . . .
> The remains of my soul *evaporate*
> In accents *lost* upon the airs . . .

> The more I sound the abyss, alas! the
> more I *am lost therein!*

Such, to put it rigorously, is Lamartine's final experience. After the loss of all objects comes the loss of the self-subject. The vanishing of the soul is, in fact, the consequence of the vanishing of things. It becomes as impossible to hold any possible distinction between self and non-self, as between the world and the world beyond. Nothing is no longer separated from nothing. Everything being merged with everything, all is at one and the same time full and void. There is a general flight of the being, and in a vague movement of flux and reflux, a no less total absence of forms.

Here, in a sense, is an extraordinary success. Poetry has never been so completely removed from the Cartesian spirit that makes of the clear and the distinct not only a principle of truth but a principle of beauty: "Poetry," Lamartine says magnificently, "has stripped itself more and more of its artificial form; *it has no other form than itself.*"

Therefore, with Lamartine, one comes to this new, disconcerting, perhaps contradictory, thing, a poetry almost without external forms, *a poetry,* in consequence, *of the inform.*

But a poetry that sinks into the inform rapidly becomes inexpressible. By dint of diluting his song, Lamartine can no longer sing anything, can no longer sing:

> *My soul searches in vain for the words with which*
> *to pour itself out . . .*

> *All words expire in impotent efforts.*

Lamartine's impotence is not so different as it seems at first sight from the sterility of Mallarmé. Their torment is the same. The poetry of the inform becomes a sort of glib discharge, no less futile and substanceless than the mute contemplation of a blank page. And Lamartine prolongs even longer than Mallarmé, his poetical aphasia, broken at long intervals by this temporary resuscitation of forms which one calls memory.

Alfred de Vigny: Mirror Images in "La Maison du berger"

Martha Noel Evans

That homely object the mirror has played over the centuries an extraordinarily rich metaphoric role. At various times a figure of human vanity, an image of the mimetic function of art, or a mythic emblem of self-consciousness, it has lately been elaborated and enriched as a metaphor of human consciousness by psychoanalysts like Jacques Lacan and Luce Irigaray. In his essay "Le Stade du miroir" Lacan brilliantly condenses Hegel's description of self-consciousness and Freud's formulation of narcissism into a new mythic figure: the child before the mirror. In Lacan's view the process by which the child reaches self-consciousness always includes the splitting and projection of the self into an external image so that the self is first perceived as being *out there, in the mirror*. The formation of the Ego, one of the products of this defensive strategy, thus inextricably links visual processes with aggressive impulses.

In *Speculum de l'autre femme* (Paris: Editions de Minuit, 1974), Luce Irigaray develops further the meaning of this myth by asserting that the child before the mirror must of necessity be a male. His otherness, i.e., his femaleness, is aggressively split off and projected into the inverted image of the mirror self. While Irigaray insists that the predominance of vision in the formation of identity is a peculiarly male characteristic, she does share two assumptions with Lacan: first, that the processes of vision are linked with aggressivity; and second, that the phenomenology of sight will yield a general logic and geometry defining the subject's relationship to space and finally to the outside world.

Lacan says in "Le Stade du miroir," "l'image spéculaire semble être le seuil du monde visible." As "the threshold of the visible world," the mirror

From *The French Review* 56, no. 3 (February 1983). © 1983 by the American Association of Teachers of French.

takes on, then, a central hermeneutic role in the meaning of seeing. The ancient *vanitas* and *speculum mundi* have evolved into a *psyché*, a looking glass, in which we simultaneously look *out* and *into* ourselves. The mirror has become the image of the sighted psyche.

All of this seems a long way from Romantic poetry, but the psychoanalytic mirror will serve us well as we look at Alfred de Vigny's poem "La Maison du berger" (1844). The very lexicon of the poem, studded as it is with mirrors and sight imagery, seems to make an appeal to the reader to see the seeing in this poem. Vigny's belief in the Romantic notions of poetry as a concentrating mirror and in the poet as Seer is well known. I would like to go beyond these beliefs in order to examine, in the light of Lacan's and Irigaray's myths, what this poetry reflects and how the Seer sees.

"La Maison du berger" is in the form of a letter addressed by the poet to his mistress, Eva, pressing her to flee the city with him. But Vigny immediately introduces a new and curious modification of the traditional ethics of Romantic pastoralism. As the poet presents it, the corruption and moral decay attendant on urban life do not depend, as one might expect, on the superficiality and dishonesty of city dwellers, but rather on the inevitable and unavoidable visibility of the individual to the gaze of anonymous lookers:

> Si ton corps, frémissant des passions secrètes,
> S'indigne des regards, timide et palpitant;
> S'il cherche à sa beauté de profondes retraites
> Pour la mieux dérober au profane insultant,
>
> . . . .
> Pars courageusement, laisse toutes les villes.
> (ll. 15–18, 22)

In this passage, it seems to be the very visibility of his mistress that makes her morally vulnerable, as if she could be penetrated and possessed by these insulting looks. The poet paradoxically reveals the sadistic component of his own visual imagination and at the same time imagines the woman timidly palpitating under the powerful and oppressive gaze of the multitude. Vigny has supplanted the traditional ethics of pastoralism by another ethics inherent in what he conceives to be the power politics of vision. Eva's passion, for instance, is no more pure than the villainous desires of the city dwellers. What gives it its particular taint is its public visibility. The poet can therefore protect and purify his mistress by taking her away into hiding: "Viens y cacher l'amour et ta divine faute" (l. 47).

In this initial section of the poem, vision creates its own moral dynamics: it is a closed system, defined by extreme polarities and by either/or oppositions. To be seen is to be blinded and made powerless by the look of the other in a visual process of pre-emption and sexual debasement. The moral polarities set up here by Vigny promote *prostitution*, in its original etymological sense, to the position of major crime in urban social life: Eva is shamed by *standing forth* in the other's field of vision.

The logic and tone of the opening section lead us to expect that the proposed pastoral retreat will serve the purpose of establishing a form of interaction superior to the prostitution of city life. We expect Vigny to erect a third observation post from which he can watch both the seers and the seen. But although his physical retreat from society seems to propose this new triangular geometry to us, emotionally the poet remains within the dyadic struggle for visual mastery. His removal from society is not so much a liberation as a strategic retreat meant to enhance his position on the battlefield. Vigny does not spurn society's duel of looks but rather maneuvers in order to win it by reversing the direction of forces. He flees the self-alienation of visibility in order to achieve mastery as the Seer.

The poet's pastoral retreat is a feint, then, meant to enslave the multitudes who have enslaved him: "Du haut de nos pensers vois les cités serviles/Comme les rocs fatals de l'esclavage humain" (ll. 24–25). From his elevated position, the poet establishes his power by looking down on the multitudes, both physically and morally. He becomes "un roi de la Pensée [a king of Thought]" (*The Journal of a Poet*), and his gift of poetic vision is defined in this moral scheme precisely by the dominance he achieves by being able to see without being seen.

The poet must thus be concealed, and the landscape he describes as his asylum is seen as a function of this need. By a process of emotional projection onto the visible world, Nature is turned into a reflection of the poet's desires. The place of hiding becomes itself a process of self-concealment: "La forêt a voilé ses colonnes profondes/La montagne se cache" (ll. 33–34).

The poet hides himself in the hiding of Nature. He takes refuge in the mobile shepherd's hut. But eventually he finds his surest asylum in an unexpected place, the gaze of his mistress:

> Je verrai si tu veux, les pays de la neige,
> Ceux où l'astre amoureux dévore et resplendit,
>
> . . . .
> Que m'importe le jour? Que m'importe le monde?
> Je dirai qu'ils sont beaux quand tes yeux l'auront dit.
>> (ll. 57–58, 62–63)

The poetic process is here expressed entirely in terms of sight and vision. It is, in fact, a strangely *silent* process, promoted only by Eva's will to see. In a wordless exchange, Eva provides the will to see while the poet furnishes the power of vision. By means of this symbiosis the poet becomes a passive instrument while maintaining his power of sight through the will of a blind other. The poet is thus safely shielded by Eva from the dangers of visibility. Her gaze becomes a mask for the poet to hide behind. And this mask has a double function: it protects the poet both from the hostile looks of others and from the responsibility of his own desire to be a Seer.

This desire, which appears here as a gift of love, reveals its root in the soil of aggressivity, affirming Lacan's assertion that altruism is always the product of a deeper wish to destroy: "le sentiment altruiste est sans promesse pour nous, qui perçons à jour l'aggressivité qui sous-tend l'action du philanthrope, de l'idéaliste . . . voire du réformateur."

The aggressivity underlying the will of this poetic idealist and pastoral reformer becomes extraordinarily clear in the following section of the poem. Having secured Eva as a mask, as the source of his sight, the poet unleashes a series of angry imprecations whose aggressive power produces images of hallucinatory brilliance. Vigny's poetry, which he calls elsewhere "le miroir magique de la vie," seems rather here to turn into a carnival gallery of distorting mirrors, for everything the poet looks at becomes twisted into the grotesque shapes of corruption.

Seeing, here, is a process of laying bare, of penetrating and possessing, just as previously the gazes of the "profane insultant" violated Eva. Politicians, statesmen, even the Muse, appear to the poet as actors in the debasing drama of prostitution described earlier. As before, Vigny translates relationships of power inherent in social visibility into the language of promiscuous and sadistic sexuality. Even the virgin Muse is transformed by the poet's angry gaze into "une fille sans pudeur" singing like a streetwalker "aux carrefours impurs de la cité" (ll. 155, 158). And what corrupted her, what made her bad, was precisely her solicitation, not of sex, but of the other's look: "Dès que son œil chercha le regard des satyrs/Sa parole trembla, son serment fut suspect" (ll. 150–51).

What the poet's second look at society reveals is that things are exactly the opposite of what they first seemed to be. As in the opening section of the poem, all reality is divided into a closed system of polar opposites; gradations are banished; hierarchies denied. All aspects of human life thus fall into mutually exclusive categories; love or hate, master or slave, virgin or prostitute. Looking at the world is like looking at a mirror where every image is reversed, turned around. Vigny literalizes this process of reversal and betrayal in an image of sexual inversion. As the final instance of the debauchery of the Muse, the poet pictures her in ancient Greece, perched happily in the midst of a pederastic festival: "Un vieillard t'enivrant de son baiser jaloux/. . . parmi les garçons t'assit sur ses genoux" (ll. 163, 165).

What is most interesting about this economy of projection, reversal, and inversion is that the poet participates blindly in his own process of vision. While presenting himself as the pastoral poet who is "above it all," he is actually the occasion for the very depravity he reviles. His own look prostitutes the object of his gaze. So while he thought to hide from the capricious and hostile power of the other's look, he has, in fact, hidden from his own aggression. Although the angry and debasing thrusts of his look are concealed from the poet's consciousness, they become paradoxically visible everywhere in the spectacle of the outside world. The poet's anger, which he does not acknowledge as his own, seems therefore to be coming at him *from the outside*.

This blind spot, the focus of the poet's denied aggression, becomes particularly visible in Vigny's dazzling diatribe against the railroad. The railroad appears first of all as the corrupt and sexually inverted counterpart of the shepherd's hut. While the rolling hut wanders free like the "mobile pensée" (l. 251) of the female mind, the phallic railroad reduces space into a network of constricting straight lines. This coldly predictable machine re-emerges, however, in the contradictory guise of a fiery bull that eats up men and boys. In the poet's double vision the steam engine is at once a scientific apparatus and a dangerous, perverse monster:

> Sur le taureau de fer qui fume, souffle et beugle,
> L'homme a monté trop tôt. Nul ne connaît encor
> Quels orages en lui porte ce rude aveugle.
>
> . . . .
>
> Son vieux père et ses fils, il les jette en otage
> Dans le ventre brûlant du taureau de Carthage.
> (ll. 78–80, 82–83)

While the presentation of the railroad as a "chemin triste et droit" (l. 121) logically furthers the pastoral thematics of the poem, the ambivalence of Vigny's vision is overwhelmed by its own wildness. The mythical "dragon mugissant" (l. 90) devours its own impotent apparition as cold machinery, just as the monster's unseeing eye stares down the poet with the blindness of his own rage.

The poet's helplessness in the face of his own anger finally structures all knowledge in a paranoid mode. Vigny views the truth as a hostile force whose main property is to victimize him. This anguished sense of victimization, of undeserved betrayal, takes shape in the second apparition of Nature. The poet's aggression finally breaks out of its silent hiding place in Eva's gaze and speaks in the voice of a proud and punishing woman:

> "Je n'entends ni vos cris ni vos soupirs; à peine
> Je sens passer sur moi la comédie humaine
> Qui cherche en vain au ciel ses muets spectateurs,
> Je roule avec dédain sans voir et sans entendre."
> (ll. 285–88)

The split of the poet's consciousness is reified in this hallucinatory image of Nature where the actual relationship of self and other is at once proposed and denied. To the poet's bitter disappointment, Nature does not recognize him as her own; but, on the other hand, neither does the poet recognize her as his double. The poet's own blindness has made him invisible. The unseeing stare of his own image looks through him as if he were not there. The nightmare of reflexivity has been accomplished; the impalpable figure in the mirror has become the source of vision, while the Ego has dissolved into nothingness.

Significantly, this I/eye, this distanced self whom he does not recognize, is envisaged by the poet not as a "he" but as a "she," *la marâtre Nature,* an unnatural and perverse mother. What the poet has cut off from consciousness and rejected as a debasing component of his identity is therefore not only his aggression but also the female part of himself. The poet as "she" appears in two images in the poem: in the punishing but eloquent figure of Nature and in the passive, silent figure of Eva. In the last section of the poem, following the song of Nature, the themes of narcissism and split consciousness finally become explicit in the metaphor of the mirror.

Eva is described as a reflecting pool where God has forever fated narcissistic man to contemplate himself, "tourmenté de s'aimer, tourmenté de se voir" (l. 231). She thus becomes simultaneously a passive instrument of reflection and the place where the poet will inscribe his self-knowledge. Poetry, "ce fin miroir solide, étincelant et dur" (l. 200), and woman, "ce miroir d'une autre âme" (l. 234), merge in a bivalent symbol where love and vision blend in the single process of producing self-conscious poetic language. In his effort to forestall the dizzying process of self-contradiction and reversal, the poet here seeks unity as poetry looking at itself. Doubleness of vision seems at last evaded; subject and object, reflection and mirror, appear to fuse in the shining diamond of poetry's song.

But like someone trying in a quick turn to catch a glimpse of his own back, poetry's look at itself must of necessity be fleeting and oblique. In order to see as One, in order to see the One, the poet must try to immobilize this evanescent moment of first sight: "Aimez ce que jamais on ne verra deux fois" (l. 308). What one sees only once is "true" because it does not change: it is forever fixed in its initial appearance. The truth is made One, is made pure, only by its disappearance.

Once again, the poet's effort to escape the tormenting vision of his own Otherness is not achieved through synthesis and integration but rather by a repetition of the same denial that was the original source of his alienation. The poet can no more recuperate the denied part of himself by visualizing it *out there* in a female reflection than Narcissus could be requited by his own image in a pool. Eva's very function as reflection disables her as a healer of the poet's narcissistic wound; immobilized by her imagined passivity, she is powerless to desire. Her love therefore can find expression only in regret, in mourning:

> appuyée aux branches incertaines
> Pleurant comme Diane au bord de ses fontaines
> Son amour taciturne et toujours menacé.
>
> (ll. 334–36)

At the end of "La Maison du berger," the image of the mirror is itself split as it becomes the figure of an irreversibly divided consciousness. The aggression and dissolution inherent in self-enunciation splinter Vigny's mirror of poetry into two component parts. On the one hand, the quicksilver reflecting surface embodied in Eva, the moon-maiden, is the projection of the poet's passive femininity, of the silence and dissolution that threaten him, of the death that inhabits him. On the other hand, the poet isolates himself within the crystal covering of the mirror to become the pure, preserving Word, self-present and diamond-hard, never menaced by change or dissolution.

As a result of this final splitting, the poet remains an everlasting "pur esprit, roi du monde//visible Saint-Esprit," while his Other, woman, becomes the pool of banishment where the poet's frailty, his mortality, shimmers palely in the light reflected from the sun of his intellect. The female part of the mirror becomes the mercurial image of fleeting time while the male part represents the imperishable diamond of thought. He is the One, and she is the process of self-destruction that sustains his unity.

The two parts are contiguous without ever being joined, since fusion with his Other represents for Vigny a horrifying and repugnant union with his own death, with his own putrefaction. The preserving crystal and the quick-silver of mortality are separated by an infinitesimal space, the pressurized domain of fear and hostility whose purpose it is to keep death at a safe distance, *out there*.

But by exteriorizing his own death, Vigny has paradoxically and tragically cut himself off from his own vitality. In his attempt to localize his fear and anger in the outside world, he has, in fact, rendered himself defenseless against them. These feelings that threaten from within become hauntingly omnipresent without; they color all that the poet sees with a somber and heavily charged light. The triumphant figures of life and independence in "La Maison du berger" are persistently overshadowed by the specters of death and dependence. All expressions of love in this poem have, if I may use the term, a necrophilic halo. Nature, that sweet refuge, is also a tomb; the shepherd's hut, the symbol of Romantic revery, is called a "char nocturne" (l. 53); and the nuptial bed, erotic bower of pleasure, turns into a coffin-like "lit silencieux" (l. 56). The diamond of poetry itself becomes a dazzling and sadistic evil eye whose aggressive rays flutter fatally around the image of the mourning mistress, forever weeping, forever silent, forever dying.

Vigny experiences his relationship with the world as a duel with a persecuting Other. As the place where he can be most intensely alone and therefore most significantly in control of this duel, poetry becomes for Vigny a kind of therapeutic process of self-domination by dominating others. But this poetry, which represents for Vigny the gift of sight, is also a focus of his own blindness. The mimetic function of poetry, this "miroir magique de la vie," is thus fragmented and undermined by its function as *psyché*, the narcissistic looking-glass. The mirror of life is dismantled in "La Maison du berger" in a personal mythology that will persist in Vigny's poetry. The reflecting quick-silver of the world, at once beautiful and menacing, is separated from the crystal protective surface, the diamond of poetry, which will sing its invulnerability in a language blanched by its own purity and impoverished by its very unity.

Babelic Ruin, Babelic "Ebauche":
An Introduction
to a Hugolian Problematic

Joan C. Kessler

The Tower of Babel is, for Victor Hugo, the paradigm of the incomplete construction, and as such is the sometimes explicit but often implicit symbolic center around which revolve the complex Hugolian thematics of fragmentation. There is a deeply significant ambivalence in the fragmented Tower, an image of disintegration and ruin which at the same time suggests the rough rudimentary stages of construction. As a ruin, Babel attests to the mortality of its builders, the vanity of their attempt to achieve divinity and their dismal failure to escape the realm of the finite. Yet the Tower as "ébauche" points to rather different patterns of meaning. While Hugo's poetic articulation of the "ébauche" does often tend to suggest human limitation and finitude, which could only be transcended in the act of completion, from another perspective it is precisely the fragment, the incomplete construction which is valorized as a manifestation of the infinite. The obsessive elaboration of the images of ruin and "ébauche" in a striking multiplicity of contexts suggests their extraordinary richness as guides to the decipherment of Hugo's text.

"Rien ne ressemble à une ruine comme une ébauche," Hugo remarks in *Le Rhin,* on the occasion of his visit to the unfinished Cologne Cathedral. In the mysterious light of a "ciel crépusculaire" (readers of *Les Chants du crépuscule* are familiar with the particular overtones of ambivalence which enrich this traditionally romantic topos) the poet observes the two separate structures of apse and bell tower, which, standing each in isolation from the other, are the components of the incomplete masterpiece. It is revealing that Hugo employs the noun "tronçon"—connoting that which has been cut down or fragmented—to describe the as yet unjoined parts of the cathedral ("ce tronçon de clocher et ce tronçon d'église"). By the use of the

From *Stanford French Review* 7, no. 3 (Winter 1983). © 1983 by ANMA Libri & Co.

verb "rejoindre" (as opposed to "joindre" or the like) to convey the projected union of the fragments, Hugo continues the subtle suggestion of a life-restoring return to some mysterious original unity: "séparés à cette heure par un si vaste espace, [les deux tronçons] se rejoindront un jour et vivront d'une vie commune." Present amid the fragments is the very tool of construction, an immense crane which appears to the observer as a "plume gigantesque posée comme sur un casque." What appears to be a slightly frivolous image of a feather protruding from a helmet takes on significance in the light of the double meaning of "plume" (pen), and the equally ambivalent descriptive adjective "posée," which suggests a setting down (of a gigantic instrument) by some unearthly hand. It is important to note that, although the display of the uncompleted fragments is in itself aesthetically compelling, the entire tone of the passage is pervasively future-directed, envisioning the joining of the "tronçons" in a not too remote future ("dans un siècle ou deux") to form "la plus grande cathédrale du monde." The result of this is obviously the overwhelming valorization of the completed structure.

This entire passage calls for an intertextual reading. The prisoner-hero of *Le Dernier Jour d'un condamné*, condemned to die by the guillotine, is faced with the prospect of literal truncation. The horrible fragmentation of a vital, living unity is for the condemned man the very essence of the awesome enigma, death—just as, conversely, the joining together of the disconnected church and tower (body and head, so to speak) of the Cologne Cathedral is conceived in terms of a restitution of spiritual vitality to the waiting, lifeless "tronçons."

The essential figurative value of the Hugolian "tronçon" reveals itself most vividly in chapter 11 of *Le Dernier Jour d'un condamné*, in which the prisoner discovers the inscriptions on the wall of his cell. As he gazes at the partially effaced text, he is obsessed by the desire to reconstruct the whole, the meaning which the inscriptions' fragmented condition necessarily obscures. "J'aimerais à recomposer un tout de ces fragments de pensée, épars sur la dalle; à retrouver chaque homme sous chaque nom; à rendre le sens et la vie à ces inscriptions mutilées, à ces phrases démembrées, à ces mots tronqués, corps cans tête comme ceux qui les ont écrits." The desire for completion is thus, very significantly, a desire for fully revealed meaning, and the revelation of meaning is equated here with the renewal of life itself ("rendre le sens et la vie").

Once again it is illuminating to consider one of Hugo's transcribed observations, in *Le Rhin*, of an actual ruin along the banks of the Rhine (Lettre XX: De Lorch à Bingen). "Derrière la colline où j'étais assis . . . j'apercevais une sombre ruine, colossal monceau de basalte brun." This ruin of an old chateau is at the same time, in a very real sense, an "ébauche," for it provokes in the observer an attempt at completion—that is, a reconstruction of *meaning*. Hugo literally interrogates the ruined structure: "J'allais et je venais dans ces décombres, cherchant, furetant, interrogeant. . . ."

It is thus in the deepest sense of the word—and by a strange process of metaphorical equivalence—that Hugo is able to affirm, "Ce chateau était une énigme." Moreover, the tombstone which Hugo discovers within the ruin reveals a parallel mode of fragmentation. Sculpted on the stone is a horseman lacking a head, accompanied by an inscription containing the large capital letter X. (X is the letter, as Hugo goes on to explain, which designates the inaccessible and the unknown.) The symbolic identity of the undeciphered inscription and headless body is emphasized by the repetitive structure of the terse description which fuses the two representations into one: "Le mot de cette énigme, c'était une inscription sans date, une épitaphe sans nom, un homme sans tête." Hugo reflects that "cette façon de voiler, tout en la signalant, la tombe et la mémoire de l'homme décapité est propre à toutes les époques et à tous les peuples." The process of communicating while at the same time concealing, of hinting at a sense which is never fully unmasked, is particularly intriguing to Hugo. The special complexity of this passage arises in part from the fact that the "homme décapité" is at once signified and signifier. The deceased man's "memory" is veiled by the obscurity which surrounds the realm of the dead—yet the body without a head is itself the very figure of the enigma, the fragment which must be reconstituted into a whole in order to yield meaning.

In a striking gothic legend recounted in *Promontorium Somnii*, an ominous spider ("la tarentule") forces her victims to dance endlessly in a circle. In the fatal course of the dance, the victims lose their original wholeness to become a grotesque collection of fragments: "les pieds s'y usent . . . les tibias s'usent . . . les genous s'usent . . . les femurs s'usent, on danse sur le torse devenu moignon; le torse s'use, et let danseurs finissent par n'être plus que des têtes sautelant et se tenant par les mains, avec des tronçons de côtes autour du cou imitant des pattes, et l'on dirait d'énormes tarentules; de sorte que l'araignée les a faits araignées." In Hugo's work, the spider characteristically suggests the capricious dictates of chance, the opacity of fate, indeed an entire realm of darkness and materiality—a metaphysical underworld. In *L'Homme qui rit*, inscrutable Chance is in turn explicitly equated with the concept of the fragment: "Les choses déconcertantes que nous nommons, dans la nature, caprice, et dans la destinée, hasard, sont des tronçons de loi entrevus." What is more, in this passage in *Promontorium Somnii*, the victims, now spiders themselves, burrow into the earth in a process of "creusement" which results in the formation of a "cercle horrible," a mysterious natural amphitheatre. "Dans les Pyrénées, ces cercles s'appellent oules . . . Gavarnie est une oule." The very word "Gavarnie" functions as an intertextual signal, as this natural geological phenomenon is for Hugo rich with figurative import. In his travel notes *Alpes et Pyrénées*, as well as in the lengthy metaphysical poem *Dieu*, Gavarnie is evoked as nothing less than a superhuman Babel, constructed by the architect of the abyss.

While the particular tale of the spider contributes to certain important patterns of meaning in the Hugolian text, it is also significant that the entire realm of gothic legend, of which it is a part, occupies a privileged position in *Promontorium Somnii*. For Hugo, an essential feature of this medieval mythology, the gothic age's legacy from pagan polytheism, is the materiality of its images, its evocation of supernatural forces within chthonic nature. "Ce va et vient imperturbable du surnaturel dans le naturel" both fascinates and troubles Hugo. "Dieu ne gagne pas grand'chose à la fantasmagorie gothique," he explains with apparent condescension and complacency in *Promontorium Somnii*, "L'homme ne sera adulte que le jour où son cerveau pourra contenir dans sa plénitude et dans sa simplicité la notion divine. *Le Dieu morcelé* de l'antiquité est encore le seul que puisse comprendre le moyen-âge" (italics mine). Once more the concept of the fragment takes on special significance. In pagan and gothic legend, Hugo suggests, the unity and totality of the divine *idea* is splintered into a multiplicity of *images* of the divine. This proliferation of material forms is thus an inadequate first stage in the process of apprehending the essence of God as pure, simple, immaterial spirit. Yet the ideal of divine wholeness and unity becomes problematic when viewed in the context of the essay as a whole. *Promontorium Somnii* is in fact a celebration of the grotesque, the excessive nightmarish configurations of the dream (*le rêve*) which form the very substance of the poetic, visionary imagination. The world of the monstrous and distorted is the pathway to the realm of the abyss—and in the darkness of the abyss our limited human modes of understanding are expanded to envelop the infinite. Moreover, it is the "fragmented" realm of polytheistic thought, with its manifold material incarnations of the divine, which is the paradigm of metaphoric language. "Qu'est ceci? c'est une pierre; non, c'est le dieu Lapis. . . . Qu'est ceci? c'est un arbre; non, c'est Priape." In his cumulative, proliferating, almost vertiginous transcription of these "rêveries," Hugo yields to their seductive power. It is revealing that the crescendo reaches its height with the striking transition from the realm of popular superstition to the figurative language of Dante: "Tout le monde sait qu'on voit dans la lune un homme suivi d'un chien et portant un fagot. Qui ne voit pas cet homme sera changé en loup-garou. Pourquoi? C'est que cet homme est Caïn. Dante ne dit pas: la lune décline; il dit [*Enfer*, chant 20]: 'Déjà Caïn avec son fardeau d'épines touche la mer sous Séville.' " The idea of the fragmentation of the divinity ("le Dieu morcelé") has a parallel in the process by which the original, almost divine unity of the human tongue was splintered into an obscure, chaotic multiplicity (Babel). (It was this fragmentation of language, of course, which condemned the Tower itself to the state of a perpetual fragment.) The problem remains: although the fall from original wholeness and unity is a fall from the divine ideal (and idea), the recapturing of this ideal would necessitate the disappearance of language as Hugo knew it—the opaque, earthly language of metaphor. For to "complete" the language of fragmentation, to make it whole again, implies its destruction—as surely as the "completion" of the enigma implies the disappearance of the opaque entity that was its very being. This is a tragic paradox, and one which is central to the entire Hugolian oeuvre.

A similar problem is articulated by one of the "voices" whose supernatural insights compose the first half of *Dieu*. After having evoked the mysterious powers of the poet and his familiarity with the secrets of the tomb and eternity, the voice indicates the sole limit to the poet's power: "il peut tout. Hors ceci: nommer Dieu." This inability is paralleled, in the text, by man's inability to comprehend the mysterious "nom" as it is given continuous, infinite expression by the whole of creation.

> L'homme à saisir ce mot s'est parfois occupé;
> Mais en vain, car ce nom ineffable est coupé
> En autant de tronçons qu'il est de créatures;
> Il est épars au loin dans les autres natures;
> Personne n'a l'alpha, personne l'oméga;
> Ce nom, qu'en expirant le passé nous légua,
> Sera continué par ceux qui cont à naître;
> Et tout l'univers n'a qu'un objet: nommer l'être!

Hugo's use of the noun "tronçons" is particularly suggestive in this context. Once again it is a question of the fragmentation of an ineffable spiritual unity into a multiplicity of material "créatures," who in turn give the divine "nom" multiple and concerted utterance. The divine essence has been translated into temporality, and thus the expression given to it by creation must be a temporal expression of the infinite—namely, a poem without end. The idea of "naming God," which at first suggests the evocation of the divinity in one unified notion (that which the mortal, limited poet strives for but is incapable of) gradually takes on the sense of a continuous articulation, the work of the universal poet. This universal poet is explicitly, of course, Nature, but implicitly the more-than-human genius-creator whose work is modeled on the universal poem. This never-ending poem is the epitome of the incomplete construction, which can have no conclusion until all temporal language is abolished—that is to say, condensed into a purely spiritual, all-encompassing word. Meanwhile, it is the fragmentation of this divine entity which gives rise to the mysterious rhythms of nature and indeed of all poetic creation:

> Et l'ombre épouvantable en ses aveugles ondes
> Roule des millions de millions de mondes,
> Et le sillon engendre et la fosse enfouit
> Et tout se développe et tout s'évanouit,
>
> . . . .
>
> Et toujours, à jamais, sans qu'il cesse un moment
> D'emplir le jour, la nuit, l'éther, le firmament,
> Sans qu'aucun autre bruit l'intérrompe et s'y mêle,
> Le nom infini sort de la bouche éternelle.

As is evident in these lines, the idea of the never-ending poem is linked to a cyclical pattern of construction and destruction. In *Philosophie: Commencement d'un livre*, Hugo meditates upon the paradox which is the law of the universe:

> Des commencements de fonctions se mêlent à des achèvements de destinées; tout crépuscule est double; aurore est soir. Cette formidable crysalide qu'on appelle l'univers tressaille éternellement de sentir à la fois agoniser la chenille et s'éveiller le papillon.
>
> Rien ne s'achève à pic; tout ce qui finit une chose en ébauche une autre.

In his novel, *Les Travailleurs de la mer*, Hugo evokes the ceaseless, hollowing toil of the sea by means of an elaborate architectural metaphor:

> Les écueils . . . appartiennent à un art mystérieux que l'auteur de ce livre a nommé quelque part l'Art de la Nature. . . . Ces constructions sont multiformes. Elles ont l'enchevêtrement du polypier, la sublimité de la cathédrale, l'extravagance de la pagode, l'amplitude du mont. . . . Elles ont des alvéoles comme un guêpier, des tanières comme une taupinière, des cachots comme une bastille, des embuscades comme un camp. . . . Leur figure architecturale se transforme, se déconcerte, affirme la statique, la nie, se brise, s'arrête court, commence en archivolte, finit en architrave; bloc sur bloc.

No single architectural form can itself convey the vertiginous formations of the ocean-artist; rather, the endless metamorphosis of one into another is finally resolved into a gigantesque architectural paradigm: "la loi de ce babélisme échappe." Here Hugo's text spawns an expression which insists on the paradoxical equivalence between a constructed work (the implicit Babel) and an ongoing process. Hugo hints at an essential feature of this architecture of the abyss: "Rien de plus émouvante pour l'esprit que cette farouche architecture, toujours croulante, toujours debout." This vast construction of nature, like the fragmented Babel, is neither entirely completed nor entirely demolished, but rather exists perpetually at a point of equilibrium between the forces of construction and destruction. Babel becomes in Hugo's text the mysterious locus of intersection between two fiercely contending universal imperatives.

The very first glimpse, in *Les Travailleurs de la mer*, of the proliferating life of the abyss is afforded by Hugo's evocation of the monstrous creatures which swarm in and about the Rochers Douvres. It is telling that the text conveys this vision through the image of a chaotic aggregate of fragments:

> De vagues linéaments de gueules, d'antennes, de tentacules, de nageoires, d'ailerons, de machoires ouvertes, d'écailles, de griffes, de pinces, y flottent, y tremblent, y grossissent, s'y décomposent, et s'y effacent dans la transparence sinistre.

As is frequent in Hugo's work, the monstrous Babelic agglomeration takes the form of a swarming hive: "D'effroyables essaims nageants rodent, faisant ce qu'ils ont à faire. C'est une ruche d'hydres." Significantly, not only does the text render these monstrous forms through the mode of fragmentation, but the sea creatures themselves are "fragments" in a more profound sense; they are explicitly "ébauches" of the life process: "[D]ans une paix affreuse, les ébauches de la vie vacquent aux farouches occupations de l'ombre." Here the "ébauche" suggests a state of chaotic, primordial, incipient form—that which is at once amorphous and deeply mysterious. According to the text, a glimpse into this realm of monstrous forms constitutes a plunge into the workings of a vast imagination: "Voir le dedans de la mer, c'est voir l'imagination de l'Inconnu." This observation calls for an intertextual reading; in a revealing passage in *Promontorium Somnii*, Hugo dilates the notion of visionary reverie to cosmic proportions:

> La nature n'a-t-elle pas rêvé aussi? le monde ne s'est-il pas ébauché par un songe? . . . Dans le mastodonte, dans le mammon, . . . dans le ptérodactyle, n'y a-t-il pas toute l'incohérence du rêve? . . . Oui, sans que cela puisse en rien détruire et amoindrir l'idée de perfection attachée aux évolutions successives des lois naturelles, . . . le tâtonnement terrible du rêve est mêlé au commencement des choses.
>
> Tu rêves donc aussi, ô Toi! Pardonne-nous nos songes alors.

In the same essay, Hugo had stated laconically but tellingly, "La rêverie est un creusement." In such poems as "La Pente de la rêverie" (*Les Feuilles d'automne*) and "Au statuaire David" (*Les Rayons et les ombres*), vertiginous visionary reverie assumes the form of a Babelic spiral; it is thus only fitting that the monstrous cosmic imagination of the Creator should manifest the structure of Babel.

In *Les Travailleurs de la mer*, Babelic Nature is, in the deepest sense, "Dieu morcelé"—that which by definition involves the fragmentation of the divine unity into the realm of proliferating materiality. Indeed this Babel is in its very essence a construction of darkness and chaos; the multiplicity of nature's phenomena is conceived in the text as diabolic: "Si le démon Légion existe, c'est lui, à coup sûr, qui est le Vent." Another important Hugolian text, the poem "Ce que dit la bouche d'ombre" (*Les Contemplations*), explicitly depicts creation as a fall from an ideal unity and harmony:

> Dieu n'a créé que l'être impondérable.
> Il le fit radieux, beau, candide, adorable,
> Mais imparfait; sans quoi . . .
>
> . . . .
>
> Cette perfection, dans l'infini perdue,
> Se serait avec Dieu mêlée et confondue,
> Et la création, à force de clarté,

> En lui serait rentré et n'aurait pas été.
> La création sainte où rêve le prophète,
> Pour être, ô profondeur, devait être imparfaite.

Original clarity and wholeness give way to the realm of the incomplete, the dark enigma of materiality. It is striking that in the same poem the hierarchy of creation from darkness to still greater darkness is rendered through the image of a spiraling Babel:

> Etages effrayantes! cavernes sur cavernes.
> Ruche obscure du mal, du crime et du remord!
>
> ·
>
> O châtiment! dédale aux spirales funèbres!
> Construction d'en bas qui cherche les ténèbres,
> Plonge au-dessous du monde et descend dans la nuit,
> Et, Babel renversée, au fond de l'ombre fuit!

Yet the conclusion of this poem envisages the final, triumphant transfiguration of matter into spirituality, darkness into light, the monstrous into the angelic. Thus just as Nature, with its cycles of fecundation and decay, is at any given moment both "ébauche" and ruin, so too the whole of Creation, viewed in relation to the beginning and end of time, is at once a lapse from celestial harmony and "ébauche" of the millenial perfection to come.

   In Hugo's novel, *L'Homme qui rit*, the mutilation of the child Gwynplaine by the child-trafficking "comprachicos" is a powerful metaphor of the degradation of the masses by society's injustice. In the description of the comprachicos' procedure, Hugo gives the word "ébauche" its full symbolic resonance: "On prenait un homme et l'on faisait un avorton; . . . Là où Dieu a mis l'harmonie, on mettait la difformité. Lá où Dieu a mis la perfection, on rétablissait l'ébauche." Yet this "progrès en arrière" is the reverse of the true progress which will lead from slavery to liberation, which will start with the mutilated, fragmented form and transform it into a perfected whole. The liberation of the people from the tyranny of worldly oppressors parallels the liberation of humanity as a whole from imprisoning matter and blind fate. Ursus' theatrical interlude, "Chaos vaincu," dramatizes this redemptive process: "Comment la divinité adhère à l'ébauche, de quelle façon s'accomplit la pénétration de l'âme dans la matière, . . . comment le défiguré se transfigure, comment l'informe devient paradisiaque." This is the significance of the mysterious "transformation de la foule en peuple," the great utopian task which, in the modern age, is left to none other than the "génie." Hugo proclaims in *William Shakespeare*, "Nous concluons à une littérature ayant ce but: le peuple." Literature will be the agency of humanity's ascent from its tragically benighted condition to the light of the Ideal.

   Yet to effect this completion of the "ébauche" (the populace), literature itself must evolve from an inaccessible and obscure entity—a "monologue littéraire . . . [où] on n'entre pas"—to a popular, transparent form: " . . . nous ne figurons la poésie que les portes toutes grandes ouvertes." Hugo had already dealt with such a process of artistic evolution in *Notre-Dame de Paris*. In the chapter "Ceci tuera cela," he describes the transition from "theocratic" (Romanesque) architecture, "livres ténébreux que les initiés seuls savent déchiffrer," to the more secularized Gothic constructions which are "pénétrables à toute âme, à toute intelligence, symboliques encore, mais faciles à comprendre comme la nature. Entre l'architecture théocratique et celle-ci, il y a la différence d'une langue sacrée à une langue vulgaire." Yet, significantly, the cathedral of Notre-Dame, the very paradigm of Hugo's novel, has not undergone a total transformation. While the gothic aspects of the edifice testify to its "popular" evolution, it has not abandoned the mystery and opacity of its "theocratic" romanesque roots. Such a hybrid construction embodies for Hugo the idea of process and continual development. Architecture itself as the premodern language of humanity is supplanted by the printed word. The final, climactic paragraph of "Ceci tuera cela," in which the colossal edifice of print appears as a prodigious Tower of Babel, stresses above all that this construction is truly without end. Apparently sympathetic to basic Enlightenment goals, Hugo glorifies the heroic efforts of a humanity dedicated to the cause of progress ("concours acharné de l'humanité tout entière, refuge promis à l'intelligence contre un nouveau déluge, contre une submersion de barbares"), but refuses to grant the possibility of completion, the actual attainment of the goal: "Du reste le prodigieux édifice demeure toujours inachevé."

In "La Vision d'où est sorti ce livre," the poetic vision which introduces *La Légende des siècles*, Hugo evokes a giant architectural construction, the "mur des siècles," which appears with the force of a revelation. This endlessly rising edifice, the accumulation of centuries of human history, is a dark and chaotic pile in which good and evil are linked as inseparably as vertebrae and from which Satan himself stands out conspicuously. Although this great mass is clearly the product of the whole of humanity, of "tout le prodige humain, noir, vague, illimité," it is simultaneously the work of one colossal being who has used the crimes and sorrows of the human race as mere elements of construction:

> Quel titan avait peint cette chose inouïe?
> Sur la paroi sans fond de l'ombre épanouie
> Qui donc avait sculpté ce rêve ou j'étouffais?
> Quel bras avait construit avec tous les forfaits,
> Tous les deuils, tous les pleurs, toutes les épouvantes,
> Ce vaste enchaînement de ténèbres vivantes?

This tenebrous edifice rises into the light of a new dawn: "Et, commencée en nuit, finissait en lueur." Yet presently Hugo will bear witness to the devastation of the gigantic edifice of history following the climactic ap-

pearance of the spirits of the *Oresteia* and the Apocalypse, who pronounce
the words "Fatalité!" and "Dieu!" What remains in the wake of this revelation is a total ruin; the "mur prodigieux, complet" has become a cemetery
filled with the debris of "siècles tronqués." Each age stands in isolation,
devoid of the connections with past and future time which alone had given
it meaning ("plus de lien;/Chaque époque pendait démantelée"). The truncation of the centuries is in a very real sense the destruction of signification.
In a telling simile, the architectural ruin is compared to an eternally unfinished sentence:

> Ressemblant à la phrase interrompue et sombre
> Que l'ouragan, ce bègue errant sur les sommets,
> Recommence toujours sans l'achever jamais.

It is this ruin which Hugo will evoke as the paradigm of his own *Légende*.
The final lines of "La Vision . . . " express this clearly, and make explicit
that which had been implicit since the beginning, the metaphor of Babel.

> Ce livre, c'est le reste effrayant de Babel;
> C'est la lugubre Tour des Choses, l'édifice
> Du bien, du mal, des pleurs, du deuil, du sacrifice,
> Fier jadis, dominant les lointains horizons,
> Aujourd'hui n'ayant plus que de hideux tronçons,
> Epars, couchés, perdus dans l'obscure vallée;
> C'est l'épopée humaine, âpre, immense—écroulée.

Yet the significance of this vast and monumental ruin is precisely that it
offers itself simultaneously as an "ébauche." These remains are in their
very essence oxymoronic, for mingled indissociably with them is the light
of a future dawn ("Décembre où l'avenir, vague aurore, est mêlé"). The
original chaotic construction—history developing on its own, without the
guidance of spiritual revelation—is not destined to be consummated in
completion. The advent of the visionary texts of Aeschylus and John, the
revolutionary shattering of history, makes it possible for a new and literary
construction—namely *La Légende des siècles*—to rise out of the ruins of the
old. A new construction which is also a reconstruction, inasmuch as Hugo's
vision seems to proclaim that the elaboration of the poetic text and the
elaboration of history are now one and the same. In a deeply mystical
sense, history is accomplished in and through Hugo's Babelic poem.

The production of the text is thus predicated on the fragmentation of
meaning, but the implications of this metaphorical structure still remain
somewhat elusive. Is it merely a question of an old world-meaning, so to
speak, which is destined to be at once replaced and revitalized? Will Hugo's
Babel achieve a veritable reconstruction of "sens," or will it remain a perpetual ruin—"ébauche"? It is significant that in the preface to *La Légende
des siècles*, which immediately precedes "La Vision . . . " and by which the
reading of this poem is inevitably colored, Hugo presents his volume si-

multaneously as a "commencement"—that which will be given meaning by the later volumes of a projected trilogy—and as a complete entity in itself. "Il existe solitairement et forme un tout; il existe solidairement et fait partie d'une ensemble." Hugo explains that his poem will be followed and completed by *La Fin de Satan* and *Dieu*; the finite and fragmented shall be completed by the infinite. The suggestive language of the preface expresses, however, more than just a plan for the future development of the author's oeuvre. The statement that seems an expression of modesty—"nul ne peut répondre d'achever ce qu'il a commencé, pas une minute de continuation certaine n'est assurée à l'oeuvre ébauchée"—takes on a deeper, ironic significance when read in the light of Hugo's insistence in *Notre-Dame de Paris* that the Great Work, the "prodigieux édifice," will always remain incomplete. In fact, *Dieu*, which was intended to be the final "couronnement" of the poetic cycle, was destined to remain unfinished. The oxymoronic ambiguity of the Preface, in which the poetic text is envisaged as that which aspires toward completion but does not require completion (indeed, continually defers it), proclaims the truly "Babelic" nature of the work.

Indeed, there are instances in Hugo's oeuvre in which the "ébauche" is represented explicitly and unambiguously as the true manifestation of the infinite. From this perspective, its "completion" would imply not its spiritual perfection, but its demotion to a less mysterious, earthly plane. In the preface to *Cromwell*, Hugo characterizes the "beau" as an "ensemble complet mais restreint comme nous." It is finite precisely because it is *able* to be completed. On the other hand, the grotesque and the monstrous constitute the "détail d'un grand ensemble qui nous échappe, et qui s'harmonise, non pas avec l'homme, mais avec la création toute entière. Voilà pourquoi il nous présente sans cesse des aspects nouveaux, mais incomplets." In an interestingly ambivalent verse in "Le Satyre" (*La Légende des siècles*), Hugo reveals the divine identity of the fragment; chaos itself is a god: "Le chaos est un dieu; son geste est l'élément/Et lui seul a ce nom sacré: Commencement."

In a suggestive passage in *Le Rhin*, Hugo contrasts the dark and immoral character of history with the virtuous nature of the "conte," and explains the darkness of history by referring both to the *divine* and the *incomplete*. It is because of man's own limitation that he strives to complete and conclude: "[L'homme] tâtonne dans l'ombre, il n'est sûr de rien, il a besoin de tout borner par un enseignement, un conseil et une leçon; et il n'oserait pas inventer des événements sans conclusion immédiate." God alone is master of the incomplete construction, which is dark and inscrutable precisely because it belongs to the realm of the infinite: "Dieu, qui fait l'histoire, montre ce qu'il veut et sait le reste."

An essential problem within the Hugolian text remains: What is the true nature of the divine? Is it the meaning which at the end of time will "complete" and thus destroy the monstrous, obscure constructions of history?—or do the concepts of clarity, order, and even "meaning" threaten the very existence of that which is most sacred because it is most mysterious? In one sense the enigma is the human condition—the chaos into which man has fallen and out of which the text of history and simultaneously Hugo's text seem inexorably to be leading. Yet at the same time, it is the enigma rather than its solution, obscurity rather than illumination, that Hugo persists in identifying with the divine mystery. The artist's supernal task is to complete the human "ébauche," to effect man's spiritual transfiguration—yet the opacity of the "incomplete" Babelic text is the very condition of its existence as art, and perhaps its truest link to the realm of the divine.

Victor Hugo:
From Spectacle to Symbol

Margery Sabin

Hugo's frequently declamatory tone may mislead us to expect a boldness not really asserted by either his poetry or criticism. In comparison to the English Romantics, Hugo proposes only a modest conception of the poet's spiritual power. In the Preface to the volume *Les Voix intérieures* (1837), Hugo's image of the poet as "echo" implies even more humility than he seems to realize:

> La Porcia de Shakespeare parle quelque part de cette *musique que tout homme a en soi.*—Malheur, dit-elle, à qui ne l'entend pas!— Cette musique, la nature aussi l'a en elle. Si le livre qu'on va lire est quelque chose, il est l'écho, bien confus et bien affaibli sans doute, mais fidèle, l'auteur le croit, de ce chant qui répond en nous au chant que nous entendons hors de nous.

> [Shakespeare's Portia speaks somewhere of that *music which every man has in himself*. Woe, she says, to the man who does not hear it! This music, nature too possesses. If the book you are about to read is anything at all, it is the echo, no doubt confused and weakened, but faithful, the author believes, to that song which answers within us to the song which we hear outside of ourselves.]

It is hard to know from Hugo's language in what sense poetry is to echo nature's voice, or whether there is an important distinction in his mind between echoing nature and echoing human response to nature. But the very image of an echo differs fundamentally from the central image of the poet's music in English Romanticism, the Aeolian harp.

From *English Romanticism and the French Tradition.* © 1976 by the President and Fellows of Harvard College. Harvard University Press, 1976.

The touch of the breeze moves the Aeolian harp to music. The harp does not merely echo the breeze which may, indeed, be inaudible until received by the instrument and transformed to music. Poetic genius is a special fitness to receive the motions of life in the natural universe and out of them to generate music or a new order of meaning. The making of an echo is less mysterious. It does not invite the same reverent or speculative attention. In comparison to the Aeolian harp, an echo is objective, impersonal. It reproduces a sound that has a distinct, prior existence of its own.

According to Hugo in the Preface to *Les Voix intérieures*, the poet performs at once as an echo of the voices of man, of nature, and of "les événements," the public world of circumstance:

> Si l'homme a sa voix, si la nature a la sienne, les événements ont aussi la leur. L'auteur a toujours pensé que la mission du poète était de fondre dans un même groupe de chants cette triple parole qui renferme un triple enseignement, car la première s'adresse plus particulièrement au coeur, la seconde à l'âme, la troisième à l'esprit. *Tres radios.*

> [If man has his voice, and nature has hers, then events have theirs too. The author has always thought that the poet's mission was to cast into a single group of songs this triple voice which yields a triple lesson: the first speaks most particularly to the heart, the second to the soul, the third to the mind. *Tres radios.*]

Although Hugo distinguishes different voices and different human faculties, his rhetorical flourishes gloss over the crucial relationships: between man and nature, between heart and soul and intellect. Hugo's tone of public proclamation does not encourage us to speculate about the basic nature of the poetic process. As in "Ce qu'on entend sur la montagne," Hugo calls attention to the importance of the sounds echoed by the poet rather than to the process of their becoming poetic speech. He summons the reader to heed the diverse voices of the universe audible in his poems. We are not invited to contemplate the mysterious workings of the poet's instrument, nor do we think of him as the single maker of the song he sings. The position of the poet as echo is more grandiose, yet more self-effacing at the same time.

The relatively successful poem, "Spectacle rassurant," shows the poet perform as echo of a more delicate music than in "Ce qu'on entend sur la montagne." The very range of tones in Hugo's poetry is worth remarking, for the poet as echo hardly possesses a distinctive voice of his own:

> Tout est lumière, tout est joie.
> L'araignée au pied diligent
> Attache aux tulipes de soie
> Ses rondes dentelles d'argent.

La frissonnante libellule
Mire les globes de ses yeux
Dans l'étang splendide où pullule
Tout un monde mystérieux!

La rose semble, rajeunie,
S'accoupler au bouton vermeil;
L'oiseau chante plein d'harmonie
Dans les rameaux pleins de soleil.

Sa voix bénit le Dieu de l'âme
Qui, toujours visible au coeur pur,
Fait l'aube, paupière de flamme,
Pour le ciel, prunelle d'azur!

Sous les bois, où tout bruit s'émousse,
Le faon craintif joue en rêvant;
Dans les verts écrins de la mousse
Luit le scarabée, or vivant.

La lune au jour est tiède et pâle
Comme un joyeux convalescent;
Tendre, elle ouvre ses yeux d'opale
D'où la douceur du ciel descend!

La giroflée avec l'abeille
Folâtre en baisant le vieux mur;
Le chaud sillon gaîment s'éveille,
Remué par le germe obscur.

Tout vit, et se pose avec grâce,
Le rayon sur le seuil ouvert,
L'ombre qui fuit sur l'eau qui passe,
Le ciel bleu sur le coteau vert!

La plaine brille, heureuse et pure;
Le bois jase; l'herbe fleurit . . . —
Homme! ne crains rien! la nature
Sait le grand secret, et sourit.

[All is light, all is joy. The busy-footed spider hangs his rings of silver lace on the silky tulips. The shivering dragonfly mirrors the globes of his eyes in the splendid pool, swarming with a whole mysterious world. The rose, in her new youth, seems to mate with the scarlet bud; the bird sings, full of harmony, in the boughs full of sun. His voice blesses the God of the soul who, always visible to the pure in heart, makes the dawn, that fiery lid, for the sky, that clear blue eye. In the woods, where all noises soften, the timid fawn plays and dreams; in the green casing of the moss shines the beetle, living gold. The moon at dawn is warm and pale, like a joyful convalescent; tenderly she opens her eyes of opal, pouring down the sweetness of the sky! The gillyflower and the bee frolic together, kissing the old wall. The warm furrow merrily awakens, stirred by the hidden seed. Everything is alive, and alights with grace: the ray of sun on the open threshold, the fleeting shadow on the running stream, the blue sky on the green hillside! The plain shines, happy and pure; the woods twitter, the grass blossoms . . . —Man! have no fear! Nature knows the great secret, and smiles.]

The graceful varied rhythms and sound patterns of "Spectacle rassurant" make audible the delicate awakening of spring, while the imagery of the poem records the visual spectacle. As in "Ce qu'on entend sur la montagne," there is little sense of specific occasion in the poem, but the absence of personal drama seems appropriate here, effectively placing the poet as spectator of a scene that is complete in itself and separate from him. Hugo holds only a transparent lens to the scene, the visual counterpart of an echo. He may enlarge the tiny creatures of nature—the spider, the dragonfly, the beetle—or he may focus on the large masses of shape and color, "le ciel bleu sur le coteau vert." But the lively serenity of the scene is made to seem autonomous; it owes nothing, apparently, to the modifying power of the poet's eye. Hugo's tone is matter-of-fact, even when he attributes emotions to the landscape: "Tout est lumière, tout est joie," "La plaine brille, heureuse et pure;/Le bois jase; l'herbe fleurit." The simple declarative renders the feelings of nature as unmistakable as color or light.

Hugo's attentiveness to spring in "Spectacle rassurant" seems to suspend or discipline the poet's inner life, in accord more with the aim of an Imagist description than a Wordsworthian meditation. Daffodils become a spectacle or "show" in "I Wandered Lonely as a Cloud" because of the poet's response to them, even more so since the poem presents the memory of an experience rather than the direct perception of a scene. Similarly, in the simple lyric, "Lines Written in Early Spring," Wordsworth interposes his experience on a particular remembered occasion between the reader and the scene. He does not echo spring; he is the instrument that composes the scene into "a thousand blended notes":

> I heard a thousand blended notes
> While in a grove I sate reclined,
> In that sweet mood when pleasant thoughts
> Bring sad thoughts to the mind.
>
> (ll. 1–4)

Wordsworth's originality (and his perversity) in a poem such as "Lines Written in Early Spring" comes from his refusal to accept, merely as a matter of course, the pleasure generally and conventionally associated with nature. To find "pleasure" in a scene of playful birds and budding trees does not indicate an extraordinary personal response. Wordsworth's simplicity of diction, rhythm, and stanza in part acknowledges the normality of the scene and of his feeling. Yet the poem also has a more assertive undertone. Wordsworth insists that we make more of his experience of this ordinary event. He presents his perception as though it were remarkable, even preposterous:

> The budding twigs spread out their fan,
> To catch the breezy air;
> And I must think, do all I can,
> That there was pleasure there.
>
> (ll. 17–20)

This scene, Wordsworth tells us, composed itself in his mind in terms of metaphors: the budding twigs, to his perception, were like a fan, spread purposefully to catch the breeze and also graciously, as if to refresh the birds and even the speaker himself. His metaphoric perception was so complete that he cannot help but believe a sentient power was present in the motion. Pleasure was in the scene, a feeling akin to human emotion, though significantly purer than the feelings of the happy-sad human observer.

Wordsworth objected to the personifications of eighteenth-century descriptive poetry partly because, as a rhetorical convention, personification in itself expressed no special passion, while he regarded with religious reverence his moments of seeing life and feeling in natural forms. Metaphors which animate natural objects must dramatize the responsiveness of the mind to the hidden life of the universe. In "Lines Written in Early Spring," imaginative perception generates religious emotion. Wordsworth protests that his feeling of belief is involuntary, unarguable, for it inheres in the very activity of his perception—in the laws which govern his mode of seeing, hearing, and remembering. The early lyric already illustrates the laws of Imagination invoked in the "Preface of 1815": "Imagination . . . has no reference to images that are merely a faithful copy, existing in the mind, of absent external objects; but is a word of higher import, denoting operations of the mind upon those objects, and processes of creation or of composition governed by certain fixed laws."

The style of "Spectacle rassurant" is not mechanical, yet neither is it "imaginative," in Wordsworth's sense. Hugo makes the blessedness of spring objective rather than the inward persuasion of the observer. The tone is closer to a Blake song, like "The Ecchoing Green," than to Wordsworth:

> The Sun does arise,
> And make happy the skies;
> The merry bells ring

> To welcome the Spring;
> The skylark and thrush,
> The birds of the bush,
> Sing louder around
> To the bells' chearful sound,
> While our sports shall be seen
> On the Ecchoing Green.
>
> (ll. 1–10)

Like "Spectacle rassurant," Blake's song simply declares the presence of feeling in the landscape. But in "The Ecchoing Green," Blake compares the earth to an echo, not the poet. The landscape echoes the jubilance of the children who sing the song. It is the gift of innocence, in Blake's view, to extend human happiness to all objects in the universe. The declarative assurance of the poem expresses the certitude of innocence. To the children the happiness of nature is literal.

Hugo's matter-of-fact tone is more puzzling, for the landscape of "Spectacle rassurant" does not seem to echo any person's inner state. At the end of the poem, a reassuring lesson for men is announced: "Homme! ne crains rien! la nature/Sait le grand secret, et sourit." The ending turns the poem public and didactic—having recorded the state of nature, the poet draws the lesson for the congregation of readers. There is no sense that this poet, this human observer, has shared in Nature's secret, nor is his lack of participation made to seem noteworthy. The poem ends on a note of achievement rather than disappointment, even though from the perspective of English Romanticism, little of what a poet might be expected to want from a springtime scene has been achieved.

Hugo's apparent indifference to his individual inner life in "Spectacle rassurant" sets him apart from English poets in the Romantic period and also later. He does not question his exclusion from Nature's secret, nor does he measure his lack of feeling against the richer inward experience of other poets, as Hardy, for example, does so suggestively in "The Darkling Thrush."

> I leant upon a coppice gate
>   When Frost was spectre-gray,
> And Winter's dregs made desolate
>   The weakening eye of day.
> The tangled bine-stems scored the sky
>   Like strings of broken lyres,
> And all mankind that haunted nigh
>   Had sought their household fires.
>
> The land's sharp features seemed to be
>   The Century's corpse outleant;
> His crypt the cloudy canopy,

The wind his death-lament.
The ancient pulse of germ and birth
  Was shrunken hard and dry,
And every spirit upon earth
  Seemed fervourless as I.

At once a voice arose among
  The bleak twigs overhead
In a full-hearted evensong
  Of joy illimited;
An aged thrush, frail, gaunt, and small,
  In blast-beruffled plume,
Had chosen thus to fling his soul
  Upon the growing gloom.

So little cause for carollings
  Of such ecstatic sound
Was written on terrestrial things
  Afar or nigh around,
That I could think there trembled through
  His happy good-night air
Some blessed Hope, whereof he knew
  And I was unaware.

The English poet, standing at the demise of the nineteenth century, takes his bearings in relation to the poetry of the century gone by. His concern is with the limits of his perception—what he sees and hears and what he can or cannot make of it. Lingering past dusk in the shrunken winter scene, Hardy perceives the decay of the Romantic landscape. The lyre is broken and only a death-lament can be heard in the wind. For this poet, "terrestrial things" mainly confirm the hard and dry reality of his own desolation. The English poet, however, even when surrounded by a scene as "fervourless" as his own spirit, is still attuned to any remaining sign of mysterious vitality. And the sound of joy still does come to him suddenly in the song of the thrush, even though this bird has almost human pathos and bravery rather than the mysterious blessedness of the Romantic bird. Hearing the aged thrush, the poet does not easily nor altogether disbelieve that a secret does still tremble through Nature's voice.

Whereas Hugo, in "Spectacle rassurant," is content to report that Nature has and knows a secret, "The Darkling Thrush" expresses Hardy's rather different concern with his individual responsiveness to reassuring natural signs. The fact that the bird sings matters to Hardy, but it matters most in relation to what he thinks, feels, believes in response to hearing that song. The subtlety of Hardy's last two stanzas is in their understatement of response. The poet can still hear birdsong as "ecstatic sound"; he can still regard that sound as spiritually significant, but his own voice does not burst forth in joy. For a moment, in stanza three, a new tone begins, "At once a voice arose among. . . ." But the lyricism quickly descends to the more sober narrative tone, "An aged thrush, frail, gaunt, and small." In the last stanza, the poet's voice sounds more puzzled than thrilled. The act of perception for Hardy no longer has the persuasiveness asserted by Wordsworth, "And I must think, do all I can/That there was pleasure there." Instead, a bare possibility of faith comes out of the incongruity between the poet's different perceptions. There is so little visible cause for happiness in the scene, and yet the bird sounds so happy—out of this incongruity, the poet "could think" there is some secret cause for the bird's ecstatic sound.

"The Darkling Thrush" records both an achievement and a disappointment, to be measured in relation to all those famous other English poems where cuckoos, thrushes, nightingales, and skylarks aroused poets to rich experiences of feeling and belief. Hardy reconsiders the possibility of moving from perception to faith. To discern blessed hope in the song of a bird involves a sequence of mental acts—a sequence that he can still perform, but only tentatively and with new uncertainty about its significance. In "The Darkling Thrush," Hardy (like Stevens, Frost, and many other twentieth-century poets in English) is as interested in reevaluating his psychological sequence as he is in any more personal or more general subject.

The bird in "Spectacle rassurant" stays apart from the famous birds in English poetry since Wordsworth, for Hugo's bird articulates a blessing independent of the poet's response or lack of response:

> L'oiseau chante plein d'harmonie
> Dans les rameaux pleins de soleil.
>
> Sa voix bénit le Dieu de l'âme
> Qui, toujours visible au coeur pur,
> Fait l'aube, paupière de flamme,
> Pour le ciel, prunelle d'azur!

[The bird sings, full of harmony, in the boughs full of sun. His voice blesses the God of the soul who, always visible to the pure in heart, makes the dawn, that fiery lid, for the sky, that clear blue eye.]

Hugo simply echoes the clear blessing to be heard in the bird's song, without questioning the extent of his response or the psychological origin of his sense of blessing. The bird's song does not seem to arouse his memory, as in Wordsworth's "To the Cuckoo"; he does not imagine himself joining the bird in song or flight, like Keats in "Ode to a Nightingale." He expresses no yearning, or hope, or illusion of being with a bird or like a bird. Nor does he show a more characteristically modern questioning of the fictive character of his poetic bird. Its blessing seems clear beyond question, apart from the poet's mental experience on this or another occasion.

The bird in "Spectacle rassurant" declares the presence and power of God to be manifest in the dawn and in the sky. But how does the poet (or the bird) come to compare the sky to the pupil of an eye? and what exactly does it mean for the natural sky to be the opening through which divine light enters the world? God, says the bird, is always visible to the pure heart. Some mode of cognition other than natural perception is implied—intuition or faith, perhaps only doctrinal teaching. The bird's song has the tone of a creed to be learned by heart. The cryptic brevity of the images recalls the peculiar combination of reticence and presumption in "Ce qu'on entend sur la montagne." Hugo simply lists the spiritual meanings of nature; he names the true and permanent spiritual identity of things, without claiming his experience of perception as the authority for what he announces.

Metaphors that start in perception tend to characterize the appearances of things at some particular time. Daffodils do not always appear to dance, nor do branches always move like fans. Wordsworth may take inward possession of a spectacle and thus seem to release it from time, but his metaphors originate in his mind's encounter with the changing world of appearances, just as the whole imaginative experience begins in a particular place at a particular time. Thus, Wordsworth's metaphors and similes characteristically refer to actions; in rhetorical terms, the metaphor centers on verbs and verbal forms of speech. Even similes which start by comparing substantives go on to disclose the action of things as the point of comparison: "I wandered lonely as a cloud/That floats on high . . . ," "She shall be sportive as the fawn/That wild with glee across the lawn/Or up the mountain springs." In the "Preface of 1815," Wordsworth's examples of imaginative language are all metaphors in the verbs of sentences: three metaphoric uses of "hang" (from Virgil, Shakespeare, and Milton); from Wordsworth's own poetry, the nightingale's voice "buried" among trees, and the leechgatherer; "Motionless as a cloud the old man stood," like "a sea-beast crawled forth, which on a shelf/Of rock or sand reposeth." Images of stillness are still perceptions of a thing's action—what it does rather than what it is. The imagination, in Wordsworth's view, perceives the hidden meaning of motions, or discovers action, volition, spirit even in the appearance of total stillness.

Hugo's figurative language makes natural things represent timeless spiritual truths more conclusively. Instead of Wordsworth's verbs, Hugo's metaphors are often substantives in apposition to a noun; they confer new, more exalted names on natural things. To call the sky the pupil of an eye, for example, implies no particular encounter of the mind with an object. Hugo does not brood over the glimpses of eternity shadowed forth in his response to temporal appearances. The symbolic meaning of natural things is as securely attached to them as their color or shape or name. The spiritualizing metaphors are no more contingent on acts of perception than is a royal title.

Hugo's brief poem "Unité," from *Les Contemplations*, shows how the kind of symbolic identification implicit in Hugo's individual metaphors can govern the structure of a whole poem:

> Par-dessus l'horizon aux collines brunies,
> Le soleil, cette fleur des splendeurs infinies,
> Se penchait sur la terre à l'heure du couchant;
> Une humble marguerite, éclose au bord d'un champ,
> Sur un mur gris, croulant parmi l'avoine folle,
> Blanche, épanouissait sa candide auréole;
> Et la petite fleur, par-dessus le vieux mur,
> Regardait fixement, dans l'éternel azur,
> Le grand astre épanchant sa lumière immortelle.
> —Et moi, j'ai des rayons aussi!—lui disait-elle.

[Above the tawny hills on the horizon, the sun, that flower of all infinite splendor, was looking down on earth at the end of day. A humble daisy, blooming at the edge of a field, on top of a gray wall crumbling among wild oats, was spreading her pure white halo. And the little flower above the old wall was gazing in the eternal blue toward the great star pouring forth its immortal light: "I too have beams," she said.]

"Unité" appears in the first section of *Les Contemplations*, entitled "Aurore." The two volumes of *Les Contemplations* form an autobiographical record of the poet's development from 1830 to 1855. Symbolic interpretation of nature belongs, by the design of the volume, to the period of the poet's early maturity. But "Unité" is not itself an autobiographical poem. There is no individual voice in the poem, nor any record of feelings or experience. The poet is unindividualized except for his power to register the symbols offered by nature. At the end, he only echoes the flower's assertion of its own symbolic status.

The poem ends rather flatly; the interesting part comes earlier. After the neutral description of the first line, "Unité" opens into a tribute to the sun, "Le soleil, cette fleur des splendeurs infinies." The metaphor stands in apposition to the noun. The sun is given the new title of flower, and the title is simply declared. At first, the metaphor here may not seem to spiritualize the object, since the sun already has more traditional spiritual dignity than a flower. But it is symptomatic of Hugo's metaphoric practice that the flower in line two is less an object in nature than a figure of speech, part of a rhetorical formula of praise that does, after all, exalt the sun. The sun is the flower of creation, the finest part of the universe, the most splendid of splendors. Although Hugo hints some visual analogy between sun and flower as he pictures the sun bending over the hills at dusk, the metaphor announces the sun's permanent value rather than its impressiveness at a particular time. The suggestion of flowerlike grace in the movement of the sun at twilight is not elaborated. Instead, Hugo turns to identify the flower, the main object of his attention.

The humble white daisy illuminates the dreary wall as the sun gives radiance to the brown earth. Two actions are compared, but there is no development of movement in the metaphor. The daisy does not act notably like the sun; it unfolds its petals in the way that flowers do. Curiously Hugo does not take advantage of the natural fact that daisies close their petals at night, a fact registered in the very name of the English flower, "days-eye." Hugo's daisy is fully open at twilight. Moreover, the placement of words in the lines (their displacement even from ordinary usage) diverts attention from the verbs to the nouns and adjectives, especially to the isolated adjective, "Blanche." The metaphor depends on the color and form of the petals, their halo of white, not on the impression made by this flower's behavior at a particular time.

Hugo reinforces the permanent spiritual meaning of the flower by taking advantage of the symbols fixed in language, partly from etymology. "Candide" comes from the Latin *candidus* and designates both the color white and its traditional figurative meaning. The white daisy represents humble but radiant purity, as the very name of the flower in French, "marguerite," signifies purity and preciousness, through its derivation from the Latin, *margarita* or pearl. The association with the name of an early Christian saint, the virgin and martyr, Marguerite, and also the Biblical allusion to "the pearl" in Matthew (13:45-46) are more pertinent to the resonance of the symbol than any naturalistic fact.

Like the halo of a saint, the white circle of petals on the flower represents symbolically the purity of the object and its relationship to the light of God. Like other emblems of divinity—the pearl, a halo, the sun itself—the flower embodies divine light in material form. The analogy between flower and sun discloses the unity of nature from high to low and also the repetition of divine symbols: in nature, history, the Bible, and even in the forms of language.

Natural things in Wordsworth's poetry never acquire such clear and permanent symbolic identity. Chance encounters in the world of time—hearing the song of a solitary reaper, coming upon a leechgatherer or an old blind beggar—yield only glimpses of symbolic meaning. Terrestrial things do not articulate their own symbolic meanings, especially since Wordsworth's imagination tends to discover spirituality in the least articulate things. The poet's mind creates the symbol in our presence; sometimes he even unmakes it again before the end of the poem. In "To a Butterfly," for instance, Wordsworth broods upon the symbolic implications of a butterfly he has been watching, only to turn away in the second stanza of the poem from the symbol he has begun to create:

I've watched you now a full half-hour,
Self-poised upon that yellow flower;
And, little Butterfly! indeed
I know not if you sleep or feed.
How motionless!—not frozen seas
More motionless! and then
What joy awaits you, when the breeze
Hath found you out among the trees,
And calls you forth again!

This plot of orchard-ground is ours;
My trees they are, my Sister's flowers;
Here rest your wings when they are weary;
Here lodge as in a sanctuary!
Come often to us, fear no wrong;
Sit near us on the bough!
We'll talk of sunshine and of song,
And summer days, when we were young;
Sweet childish days, that were as long
As twenty days are now.

    The poet has been watching the butterfly for a "full half-hour" without being able to discern exactly what it is doing. Out of his very uncertainty, hints of symbolic meaning begin to arise. The butterfly seems to exemplify the "self-poise" of objects in nature, a serene self-absorption remarkable and strange to the self-conscious and restless observer. The poet holds the mystery of the creature in awe. His mind works upon what he sees, moving from simple exclamation—"How motionless!"—to the surprising metaphor of "frozen seas." The stillness of the small creature brings to the poet's mind an image of the vast, impenetrable forces of nature. As his mind continues its movement, imagining the joy that awaits the butterfly at the call of the breeze, the significance of the creature becomes more complex. By the end of the stanza, the butterfly may be tentatively understood as an emblem of Nature's mystery and remoteness. It also exemplifies the strange harmony of natural life, where the will of the breeze and the joy of the creature are the same, where sleeping and feeding are indistinguishable, where playful gaiety may be preceded by deathlike stillness.

    Wordsworth only intimates the larger meaning of the butterfly in the terms of his response. But there is also a melancholy, even slightly impatient undertone to his meditation. The butterfly is indifferent to the speaker's attention and, perhaps for that very reason, seems to embody a poise forever denied to man. Before the subtle hint of envy or longing on the speaker's part becomes explicit, however, he turns abruptly away from the symbolic implications of the spectacle. In the second stanza, the speaker becomes suddenly assertive, patronizing, eager to hold the butterfly back from its impending flight by inviting it to share an intimacy inconceivable in the terms of the earlier symbol. The butterfly changes its meaning to the speaker or, rather, he reduces it to a particular, fragile creature come to rest on his property. The natural world of trees, flowers, earth now appears subject to human ownership. The butterfly may be safe there because of the speaker's gentleness. At the very end, he begins to entertain a new image of the butterfly as a possible companion for nostalgic musing. The essential strangeness of the butterfly is put out of mind as if the creature could be imagined to have the same inner experience as the man and his sister.

In Wordsworth's poetry, the unstable symbolic meaning of natural objects is often both a strength and a problem for the poem. The process of making and sometimes undoing or withdrawing from a symbol gives dramatic movement and complexity to the poem, but we are often unsure how much the poet is in control of these effects. The sense of ironic reversal in the second stanza of "To a Butterfly" may be more vivid to the reader than to the poet; in Wordsworth there is rarely the clear distinction between speaker and poet upon which this kind of irony depends. Even so, we can feel sure that Wordsworth does mean to show how the symbolic meaning of a butterfly is contingent upon the observer. The things of nature assert no fixed meaning apart from one's power to see with the eye of imagination. Hugo's metaphors, in contast, grant permanent validity to the symbolic terms, in the way that the bread and wine of the Eucharist have permanent symbolic meaning apart from any individual act of Communion. Recognition of the divinity symbolically present in nature does not, for Hugo, in itself signify communion. Hugo's figurative style gives natural symbols a dogmatic, almost ecclesiastical authority rather than the force of inward persuasion.

It is therefore appropriate that in one of Hugo's most explicit statements of faith, Nature appears to enact a version of the Catholic Mass. In "Relligio," the poet answers the question, "quelle est ta bible?" (what is your Bible?) by pointing to the sky:

> La lune à l'horizon montait, hostie énorme;
> Tout avait le frisson, le pin, le cèdre et l'orme,
>   Le loup, et l'aigle, et l'alcyon;
> Lui montrant l'astre d'or sur la terre obscurcie,
> Je lui dis:—Courbe-toi. Dieu lui-même office,
>   Et voici l'élévation.

[On the horizon the moon was rising, enormous wafer; everything was shivering, the pine, the cedar, and the elm, the wolf, the eagle, and the halcyon; pointing to the golden star on the darkened earth, I said: "Kneel down. God himself is officiating, and this is the elevation of the Host."]

The poet boldly leaves the Church to worship in the temple of Nature. But the service there is still a form of the Mass. The moon, in a rather grotesque metaphor, symbolically represents an enormous wafer of Communion. Hugo is initiated into all the details of the natural Mass but even here he does not seem moved to take Communion, nor does he intimate how one may actually partake of the divinity embodied in natural forms.

In the absence of the poet's direct experience of communion, Hugo's poetry of nature tends toward one or another form of creed or sermon. In "Relligio," the poet preaches to a companion. In other poems, the reader, or Man generally, is lectured. Hugo characteristically establishes an initiated commentator in the poem who instructs an ignorant, perhaps skeptical, sometimes even recalcitrant audience. When Hugo used the fiction of talking birds or flowers, he divides his voice into both commentator and audience, but with a clear distinction between the voices sustained. One voice, often the main voice in the poem, affirms the divinity symbolically present in nature. The purpose is reassurance, but the tone is often reproachful, as if the other figure were holding stubbornly to gloom. Occasionally, the resistance becomes active, and the poem approaches the form and tone of debate. The voices of nature tediously insist upon their reassuring secrets but, despite a show of patient attention, the human figure within the poem seems as unmoved as the reader.

Hugo's poetry of nature sometimes seems on the verge of acknowledging its own dullness. In "Je lisais . . . ," for example, the human voice within the poem unambiguously announces the hollowness of nature's sermon, yet Hugo nevertheless allows a black martin to preach his unpersuasive doctrine at length: "Tout est plein de jour, même la nuit;/Et tout ce qui travaille, éclaire, aime ou détruit,/A des rayons. [Everything is full of light, even the night; and everything that works, gives light, loves, or destroys, has beams]."

The poet shows himself dutifully attentive to the bird's pieties, but he is like an unpromising novice in an alien religious order. He never swerves from his own conviction that the essential facts of human life are sinfulness and death:

> Je répondis:—Hélas! tu te trompes, oiseau.
> Ma chair, faite de cendre, à chaque instant succombe;
> Mon âme ne sera blanche que dans la tombe;
> Car l'homme, quoiqu'il fasse, est aveugle ou méchant.—
> Et je continuai la lecture du champ.

> [I answered: "—Alas! bird, you are wrong. My flesh, made of ashes, yields at every instant; my soul will not be white until the grave. For man, whatever he does, is blind or wicked.—" And I went on reading the book of the field.]

The debate seems pointless, for the man states his conviction decisively. His generalizations and paradoxes have the same authoritative tone as the bird's. There is no movement toward conversion intimated in the poem, nor even any real debate, for the bird and the man have really nothing to say to each other. Continuing reverence for the Book of Nature in the face of the man's own contrary certainty seems merely perfunctory. Nature's lesson in the poem is as pedantic and doctrinaire as a Sunday School lesson, but with even less relevance than orthodox Christian doctrine to the man's simply stated consciousness of his destiny: "Mon âme ne sera blanche que dans la tombe."

Hugo's pitting of Nature's dogma against human feeling differs from the ambivalence of feeling often expressed by Wordsworth. Different attitudes toward death, for example, do not oppose each other in doctrinal debate in Wordsworth's poetry, where the grounding of the poem in perception avoids both the didacticism and the artificiality of Hugo's talking birds and flowers. Wordsworth shows human feeling open to Nature's influence—literally, a flowing in of experience. Indeed, the experience of perception in Wordsworth's poetry is what finally distinguishes the living from the dead. The dead neither see nor hear. The living do, and this essential fact of life generates ambivalent feelings: fear, joy, sorrow, awe, reconciliation. In Wordsworth's elegiac poetry, from the Lucy sequence to the sonnet, "Surprised by Joy," the poet's perception of the still living earth variously complicates his grief for a dead person and his attitude toward his own mortality. Imaginative perception comes to seem intrinsic to mourning and also to whatever reconciliation to death may follow.

There is no counterpart to Wordsworthian elegy in the poetry of Victor Hugo. Never "surprised by joy" in a landscape, Hugo has no basis for Wordsworth's rich and ambiguous interplay of feeling and perception. Hugo seems cut off from the main sources of richness in the Wordsworthian mode by his unyielding conviction that the deepest human feelings are untouched by natural appearances. Yet by preserving the separateness of human consciousness, Hugo also avoids certain constraints of the Wordsworthian tradition. He seems freer than the English poet to turn away, simply and decisively, from spectacles which have nothing to do with him. In some of Hugo's most interesting poems after 1843 (beginning with the elegies for his daughter), Hugo abandons the effort to be either the priest or the obedient parishioner in Nature's temple. The unpersuasiveness of Nature's blessing, implicit in the style of the earlier poetry, becomes more explicit. The poet's sense of his separate consciousness either becomes the poetic subject or else frees the poet to consider other subjects. Sorrow, mourning, consciousness of sin, longing for another person or for death— these distinctively human feelings are made to overshadow all that the nonhuman world may show or signify. In the poem, "La clarté du dehors . . . ," for example, to disregard nature comes to seem like fortitude and integrity, a refusal to be distracted from the distinctively human experience of spiritual hope or despair:

Moi, je laisse voler les senteurs et les baumes,
Je laisse chuchoter les fleurs, ces doux fantômes,
   Et l'aube dire: Vous vivrez!
Je regarde en moi-même, et, seul, oubliant l'heure,
L'oeil plein des visions de l'ombre intérieure,
   Je songe aux morts, ces délivrés!

[As for me, I let the balmy scents waft through the air; I let the flowers—those sweet ghosts—whisper, and let the dawn say: "You shall live!" I look into myself, and, alone, oblivious of time, my eye full of visions of the inner shadows, I think of the dead, the liberated!]

In Hugo's late poems, the word "vision," instead of referring to the poet's knowledge of nature's hidden spirituality, comes to mean the vivid consciousness of inner states of mind and feeling: "L'oeil plein des visions de l'ombre intérieure." This idea of "vision" returns Hugo to the record of "des états d'âme," in Rousseau's sense, but with a difference, for Hugo regards the inner world itself as if it were a spectacle. He need not rely on the direct statement of feeling, as Rousseau did, for all the reservoirs of image and metaphor which he opened for the description of nature are also available for the symbolic landscape of the inner life. Through the traditional religious associations of the imagery, Hugo's symbols of feeling can seem like "visions" of objective spiritual truth, but the poet's visionary power does not sustain itself on the "quickening impulse" of "sensible impressions," in the Wordsworthian way. His inward eye does not dwell on even the memory of nature's spectacle, for his sense of spiritual reassurance or despair has its own rhythm, separate from nature and untouched by its apparent life.

      II

The nonperceptual character of Hugo's figurative language acquires new value in poems that emphasize the separate and inward origin of human spirituality. When Hugo was ostensibly studying the Bible of Nature, the uncertain grounding of his imagery in perception was confusing. But the same kind of imagery strengthens the impressions of the poet's deliberate turning away from the visible light: "La clarté du dehors ne distrait pas mon âme. [Outer brightness does not distract my soul.]" The surreal landscape of the mind is bright or dark irrespective of Nature's appearance:

On croit être à cette heure où la terre éveillée
Entend le bruit que fait l'ouverture du jour,
Le premier pas du vent, du travail, de l'amour,
De l'homme, et le verrou de la porte sonore,
Et le hennissement du blanc cheval aurore.
                  ("Eclaircie")

[It feels like the hour when the awakened earth hears the sound of opening day: the first step of the wind, of labor, of love, of man, and the lock of the sonorous door, and the neighing of the white horse dawn.]

A state of spiritual illumination feels like dawn, but no natural dawn brings joy, as Wordsworth's sunrise does in Book IV of *The Prelude*. Hugo's nonperceptual imagery enforces the idea that Grace does not, cannot, originate in perception. His image of the white horse dawn positively flouts naturalistic fact. Dawn does not sound at all like the neighing of a white horse. This dawn exists in the mind, not in nature; it is a symbol of spiritual illumination in a private mythology with traditional supernatural associations—here, to Apollo and also to the white horse in the Book of Revelation.

"Le Pont," the poem that opens Hugo's last, visionary book of *Les Contemplations*, altogether separates spiritual darkness and illumination from the common light of day:

> J'avais devant les yeux les ténèbres. L'abîme
> Qui n'a pas de rivage et qui n'a pas de cime
> Etait là, morne, immense; et rien n'y remuait.
> Je me sentais perdu dans l'infini muet.
> Au fond, à travers l'ombre, impénétrable voile,
> On apercevait Dieu comme une sombre étoile.
> Je m'écriai:—Mon âme, ô mon âme! il faudrait,
> Pour traverser ce gouffre où nul bord n'apparaît,
> Et pour qu'en cette nuit jusqu'à ton Dieu tu marches,
> Bâtir un pont géant sur des millions d'arches.
> Qui le pourra jamais? Personne! ô deuil! effroi!
> Pleure!—Un fantôme blanc se dressa devant moi
> Pendant que je jetais sur l'ombre un oeil d'alarme,
> Et ce fantôme avait la forme d'une larme;
> C'était un front de vierge avec des mains d'enfant;
> Il ressemblait au lys que la blancheur défend;
> Ses mains en se joignant faisaient de la lumière.
> Il me montra l'abîme où va toute poussière,
> Si profond, que jamais un écho n'y répond,
> Et me dit:—Si tu veux, je bâtirai le pont.
> Vers ce pâle inconnu je levai ma paupière.
> —Quel est ton nom? lui dis-je. Il me dit:—La prière.

[Dark shadows were before my eyes. The abyss which has no shore and no summit was there, dismal, immense; and nothing was stirring in it. I felt lost in the voiceless infinite. In the depths, through the impenetrable shade, God was discernible, like a somber star. I cried out: "My soul, o my soul! To cross over this chasm which seems boundless, and to walk up to your God in this night, you would have to build a bridge on a million arches. Who could

ever do it? No one! O grief! O terror! Weep!" A pale ghost rose
before me as I glanced in fear into the darkness, and this ghost
had the form of a tear, the forehead of a virgin, and the hands of
a child. It looked like the lily whose whiteness is its defense. Its
hands drawn together emanated light. It showed me the abyss
into which all dust goes, so deep that it never sends back any
echo, and it said: "If you wish, I shall build the bridge." I raised
my eyes toward this pale stranger. "What is your name?" I asked.
It told me: "Prayer."]

The abyss in "Le Pont" is a symbolic landscape that reappears, more
memorably, in the poetry of Baudelaire. . . . Baudelaire's landscape of despair is more interesting than Hugo's; it is more complex and elusive in its
significance. Yet Baudelaire's originality, as well as his continuity with other
French poetry in the nineteenth century, stands out more clearly when we
realize that his symbolic landscape of the mind is also fully visible in poems
by Victor Hugo.

Spiritual darkness is all the eye can see in "Le Pont." We are not
tempted to mistake the scene for an actual place in nature—its shape, or
rather its shapelessness—is as evidently symbolic as the image of Chaos
in *Paradise Lost* (which Hugo probably had in mind for his own image):

> a dark
> Illimitable Ocean, without bound,
> Without dimension; where length, breadth and highth
> And time and place are lost.

Milton paradoxically uses the essence of physical definition—the very
idea of "dimension"—to designate a place apart from any place, "The womb
of Nature, and perhaps her grave." In Book X of *Paradise Lost*, Sin and
Death build a bridge across this abyss for easier passage between Hell and
Earth. As Anne Ferry has argued, the allegorical character of Milton's language in this part of the poem separates Sin, Death, and the bridge across
Chaos from other characters and places in Milton's myth. Eden, or even
the region where Satan and his troops reign, are "real" places in Milton's
story, though their physical character also has metaphoric significance. The
bridge across Chaos, in contrast, seems to have only symbolic existence.
It is an emblem of the moral and spiritual condition created by Satan, born
of his mind like his offspring, Sin and Death. Hugo's abyss in "Le Pont"
is also a projected image. The landscape of the mind becomes visible, as
in a dream or hallucination. The poet recognizes the abyss; he is not en-
countering it for the first time. Whether a recurrent vision of his own has
returned or whether he recognizes the universal and traditional landscape
of spiritual despair—*that* abyss, the one without boundary, was there.

No suggestion appears in "Le Pont" that the abyss may be illuminated
by the light of nature: "On apercevait Dieu comme une sombre étoile."
The dark star is not an emblem of divinity discovered in nature. The verb

"apercevoir" defines an awakening of consciousness, different from natural perception. A peculiarly unnatural star figuratively expresses the poet's awareness that God is present, though infinitely remote, as alien and unwelcoming as a dark star. Natural stars in themselves play no role in the spiritual drama.

In *Paradise Lost* the bridge to boundless darkness was built for all men by Sin and Death at the time of the Fall. By imagining a bridge to God built by Prayer, Hugo tries to revise Milton's story, eliminating the figure of Christ. Natural perception cannot bridge the abyss separating man from the divine; but neither is Christ necessary. Hugo seems to argue that man has within him the power to create the exit from despair by envisioning it, just as he creates the abyss through inner vision. Prayer appears first in the form of a tear, as if to signify the power of human suffering by itself to generate its own release. The poet cries, or commands himself to cry; immediately the white phantom in the form of a tear appears.

The weakness of Hugo's argument, however, becomes apparent in his own failure to make the vision of spiritual hope strong enough to stand against the vision of despair earlier in the poem. The first six lines are the vivid part of the poem. Hugo's figure of Prayer never becomes more than a phantom patched out of Christian remnants: the face of a virgin, the hands of a child, the whiteness of a lily. The attributes of Prayer are doctrinaire, yet without living connection to the doctrine they evoke. Nor can we translate the Christian fragments into symbols of purely personal feeling, for their meaning is rooted in a definite theology. In the first part of "Le Pont," a symbolic landscape with traditional religious overtones effectively represents feelings of despair and fear. Prayer also seems to represent a state of feeling, but the poetic form for that emotion never becomes more than an awkward contrivance. The language is dull in comparison to the beginning of the poem, and the speaker remains peculiarly dissociated from his own vision.

Hugo introduces traditional religious symbols to carry spiritual promises into the void, almost as if he were anticipating T. S. Eliot: "These fragments I have shored against my ruins." But Eliot's fragments are incomparably richer than Hugo's brief and lifeless lily, child, and tear, and Eliot also expects less of them. Hugo's Prayer is supposed to build a powerful structure, "Bâtir un pont géant sur des millions d'arches," yet the poem neither affirms a theology nor creates the impression of an emotion which could support the effort. As in his earlier poems of natural theology, the reassurance seems arbitrary and contrived. An optimistic voice speaks with confidence but with no accountable source of authority. The phantom Prayer in "Le Pont" is therefore no more persuasive than the pedantic black martin in "Je lisais. . . . " Hugo wants to show the human spirit capable of generating its own vision of salvation. But the reassurances in Hugo's poetry of vision can seem as remote from inward conviction as the sermons of birds and flowers.

Baudelaire, in "De Profundis clamavi" (among other poems), avoids

Hugo's weakness by directly confronting the mind's incapacity to transcend its own vision of despair. As if to expose Hugo's ineffectual resolution in "Le Pont," Baudelaire actually begins his poem in prayer, but no promise of redemption ensues. The inwardness of vision in Baudelaire's poetry tends to mean that the poet is constrained to hear only his own voice and he has nothing new to tell himself. Thus, instead of Hugo's vague spiritual optimism, Baudelaire challenges the very idea of redemption through poetic vision. The challenge is profound in implication, for if the act of vision is not redemptive, the poet has no special spiritual authority and poetry must relinquish the presumption to spiritual guidance.

> J'implore ta pitié, Toi, l'unique que j'aime,
> Du fond du gouffre obscur où mon coeur est tombé.
> C'est un univers morne à l'horizon plombé,
> Où nagent dans la nuit l'horreur et le blasphème;
>
> Un soleil sans chaleur plane au-dessus six mois,
> Et les six autres mois la nuit couvre la terre;
> C'est un pays plus nu que la terre polaire;
> —Ni bêtes, ni ruisseaux, ni verdure, ni bois!
>
> Or il n'est pas d'horreur au monde qui surpasse
> La froide cruauté de ce soleil de glace
> Et cette immense nuit semblable au vieux Chaos;
>
> Je jalouse le sort des plus vils animaux
> Qui peuvent se plonger dans un sommeil stupide,
> Tant l'écheveau du temps lentement se dévide!

[I implore your pity from the depths of the dark abyss where my heart is fallen, Thou, the only one I love. It is a bleak world, with a low leaden sky, where horror and blasphemy swim in the night. A sun without warmth hovers for six months, and the other six months night covers the earth; it is a land more barren than the polar wastes—no beasts, nor brooks, nor grass, nor woods! There surely is no horror in the world greater than the cold cruelty of this icy sun and this vast night, like old Chaos. I envy the fate of the lowest animals who can sink into dumb sleep, so slowly does the skein of time unwind!]

Echoes of Hugo's vocabulary—"gouffre obscur," "un univers morne," "immense nuit"—identify the same abyss evoked in "Le Pont." (Although Baudelaire seems to have written "De Profundis clamavi" a few years before Hugo's "Le Pont," Baudelaire's poem need not be taken as a direct reply to this poem by Hugo for my comparison of the poets. Forms of "des visions de l'ombre intérieure" appear in poems by Hugo written through the 1840s.) The image of Chaos, suggested by Hugo's description, is explicit in "De Profundis clamavi." The dissociation of this landscape from nature is explicit too, in the paradoxically frozen sun and in the dark, cold barrenness of the scene, empty of all natural life.

In "De Profundis clamavi," however, Baudelaire uses the traditional overtones of his imagery to quite different effect than Hugo. Whereas Hugo wants to generalize the character of his despair so that his redeeming vision will also have public authority, Baudelaire manipulates the impression of familiarity to suggest the common tedium of his condition. His sense of the abyss may represent the universal plight of the fallen spirit, but Baudelaire's speaker seems more concerned with how his commonness shades into cliché. He seems to regard even his own despair as a cliché, if only because he has known it so long. There is a peculiar flatness to the poetic voice, as if, to him, even horror had become mundane: "Or il n'est pas d'horreur au monde qui surpasse/La froide cruauté de ce soleil de glace." He seems too much the connoisseur of horror to be aroused by talking about it.

In its most straightforward form, in the form most often attempted by Hugo, the symbolic representation of feeling works by objectification. Instead of stating feeling directly ("I feel horror, dread, hopelessness"), the poet shows us a world of objects. The symbolic objects represent feeling; we infer from the poet's descriptive language what feelings govern his experience. Symbolic vision thus releases the poet from the banality of a direct vocabulary of emotion. A limitless reservoir of things—from nature, from other literature, from the Bible—becomes available to express the inner life, to give it variety and significance.

Baudelaire, however, makes the relationship of feeling to symbolic vision less straightforward, even paradoxical. In his language, feelings often become so objectified that they no longer even seem to belong to the poetic voice. The sense of dissociation between feeling and vision that is confusing at the end of "Le Pont" becomes a device for irony in "De Profundis clamavi." The vision of the abyss represents horror, but the feeling of horror no longer dominates the poet's tone, as it does in Hugo's direct exclamation, "ô deuil! effroi!" In "De Profundis clamavi," horror becomes an object, out there, in the symbolic landscape: "Où nagent dans la nuit l'horreur et le blasphème." Baudelaire treats the name of his feeling as though it were a thing, separate from him, and, in a sense, it is separate, for the voice in the poem seems devoid of horror. The poet sounds more bored than afraid; or, if afraid, then only of his own tedium.

Baudelaire thus uses symbolic vision to distance his voice from the monotony of his emotions. The symbol of feeling becomes, at least in part, ironic, for it registers the absence rather than the presence of lively feeling in the poet. Baudelaire plays the monotonous rhythm of his voice against the extremity of his symbols. Whereas Rousseau used the rhythms of his prose to suggest more intensity, more immediacy of emotion than his words of feeling could contain, Baudelaire turns his more varied metaphoric language to the reverse effect of exposing how dull even his extremity of feeling is. He dramatizes the peculiar horror of coming to feel less not more than the content of his language states.

Yet the Baudelaire poem still records "un état d'âme." The drama in "De Profundis clamavi" is totally inward; as in Rousseau, the important relationship is between the poet's feeling (or lack of feeling) and his language, rather than between the mind and any external reality. That the poet is confined to his exclusively inner world is, indeed, the essence of his monotonous plight, for despite the initial form of prayer, the poem intimates no possibility that any presence from outside the mind could penetrate this abyss. Nor can his mind alone create even the illusion of other forms. From Baudelaire's point of view, Hugo is naïve to grant suffering the power to generate a phantom visitor to the abyss. Baudelaire insists instead upon the sterile repetitiveness of spiritual despair. As in many other poems by Baudelaire, the tedium rather than the intensity of the inner life becomes Baudelaire's main theme in "De Profundis clamavi"—indirectly through the style of the entire poem, and then, explicitly, in the lament of the final stanza:

> Je jalouse le sort des plus vils animaux
> Qui peuvent se plonger dans un sommeil stupide,
> Tant l'écheveau du temps lentement se dévide!

[I envy the fate of the lowest animals who can sink into dumb sleep, so slowly does the skein of time unwind!]

No Wordsworthian perception of nature's mysterious "self-poise" complicates Baudelaire's envy of beasts. His image of dumb sleep represents only his desire to escape consciousness of monotony. He can imagine no release other than bestial oblivion, for by the end of the poem, even the act of envisioning the abyss seems part of the monotony of being there. The skein of time continues its slow unwinding, whether or not the poet busies himself with futile descriptions of his plight.

Instead of moving toward some moral or religious resolution, in the manner of Hugo, Baudelaire turns the act of symbolic vision self-consciously against itself. The "état d'âme" in the poem seems utterly hopeless, yet there is an odd tone of triumph at the end. Though the image of the skein offers no promise of escape, the image itself is new in the poem and it has a satisfying decisiveness. The unexpected grammatical turn of the last sentence suggests a play of mind at odds with the yearning for oblivion. As the formal design of the sonnet comes neatly to completion, one is drawn to separate the satisfaction of the poetic form from the hopelessness of statement within the poem. Regardless of what Baudelaire says about endless monotony, the poem itself does finally manage to interrupt, if not actually halt, the dull unraveling of time.

In "De Profundis clamavi," the sonnet itself is the one object to appear in the abyss. This object is not a bridge to salvation. Yet Baudelaire's design gives the aesthetic gesture a symbolic importance it does not have for Victor Hugo. The completed form of the poem in itself becomes a symbol of human freedom and inventiveness. Though the poet envisions no escape from the abyss, in the end he unexpectedly does succeed in forming his inner emptiness into a definite shape. He contrives the decisive ending by himself, with no aid from external impressions. No new experience has changed or even touched his mind. His consciousness is not penetrated even by any outside measure of time. Yet though he remains as deep in the abyss as before, the gesture of the poem also represents the unpredictable and subtle power of the poet's spirit to rescue itself from oblivion by the very way he expresses his yearning for it. Through a surprising turn of image and phrase, the poet shapes his formless despair into the strict form of the sonnet. He asserts control, if not mastery, over his inner void by containing it in the clear forms of his art.

Aloysius Bertrand:
Gaspard de la nuit:
Prefacing Genre

Richard Sieburth

Baudelaire writes in the dedication to Arsène Houssaye which prefaces his *Petits Poèmes en prose:*

> J'ai une petite confession à vous faire. C'est en feuilletant, pour
> la vingtième fois au moins, le fameux *Gaspard de la nuit* d'Aloysius
> Bertrand . . . que l'idée m'est venue de tenter quelque chose d'ana-
> logue. . . . Mais, pour dire le vrai, je crains que ma jalousie ne
> m'ait pas porté bonheur. Sitôt que j'eus commencé le travail, je
> m'aperçus que non seulement je restais bien loin de mon mystér-
> ieux et brilliant modèle, mais encore que je faisais quelque chose
> (si cela peut s'appeler *quelque chose*) de singulièrement différent,
> accident dont tout autre que moi s'enorgueillerait sans doute, mais
> qui ne peut qu'humilier profondément un esprit qui regarde
> comme le plus grand honneur du poète d'accomplir *juste* ce qu'il
> avait projeté de faire.

Baudelaire's attempt to provide an origin for his *Petits Poèmes en prose*, as
Barbara Johnson has elegantly argued in *Défigurations du langage poétique*,
involves far more than a simple act of homage to "le fameux *Gaspard de la
nuit*" or a coy confession of failure. By referring to *Gaspard* as his "mysterious and brilliant model" while at the same time underscoring his "accidental" deviation and distance from that model, Baudelaire in effect
deconstructs the distinction between imitation and originality, thereby subverting the relation of model to copy, source to derivation into one of sheer,
irreducible *difference.* Johnson maintains (quite persuasively) that this kind
of deconstructive strategem is a characteristic feature of the Baudelairean

From *Studies in Romanticism* 24, no. 2 (Summer 1985). © 1985 by the Trustees of Boston
University.

(and Mallarméan) prose poem. Far from constituting a clear-cut manifesto of the *poème en prose*, Baudelaire's *dédicace* to Houssaye in fact involves us in a number of rhetorical riddles which serve to problematize both the boundaries of genre and the genre of those boundaries which define and delimit oppositions between originality and imitation, lyric and narrative, poetry and prose, literal and figurative language—while at the same time undercutting the traditional hierarchical relation of the preface to the "body" of the work. For if, as Baudelaire himself claims in the very first sentence of this dedication, his volume of prose poems has "ni queue ni tête, puisque tout, au contraire, y est à la fois tête et queue, alternativement et réciproquement," then we are left to infer that this preface is perhaps best anatomized as both head *and* tail, that is, as something situated at once above and behind, at once before and after, at once inside and outside the work it introduces. Indeed, Johnson observes, there is little to stop us from reading Baudelaire's preface itself as a prose poem. Conversely, it would be entirely possible to read the prose poems that follow as kinds of prefaces.

As Jacques Derrida remarks in his essay "Hors livre" (which may or may not be a preface to *La Dissémination*), prefaces tend to be written *after* the texts which they precede or pre-dict, yet they often also mask this temporal dislocation:

> [Une préface] énoncerait au futur ("vous allez lire ceci,") le sens ou le continu conceptuels . . . de ce qui aurait *déjà été écrit*. . . . Pour l'avant-propos, reformant un vouloir-dire après le coup, le texte est un écrit—un passé—que, dans une fausse apparence de présent, un auteur caché et tout-puissant, en pleine maîtrise de son produit, présente au lecteur comme son avenir. . . . Le *pré* de la préface rend présent l'avenir, le représente, le rapproche, l'aspire et en le devançant le met en devant. Il le réduit à la forme de présence manifeste.

"Opération essentielle et dérisoire," Derrida concludes, habitually suspicious of any textual strategy that would pretend to conflate before and after, inside and outside, head and tail into an illusory totality or presence. The full ramifications of Derrida's playful defacing or effacing of the preface in "Hors livre" lie well beyond my scope here (his intention is nothing less than to make us "perdre la tête, ne plus savoir où donner de la tête"). I would simply like to follow up on a few (perhaps rhetorical) questions he poses at the outset of *La Dissémination:*

> Mais que font les préfaces? La logique n'en est-elle pas plus surprenante? Ne faudra-t-il pas en reconstituer un jour l'histoire et la typologie? Forment-elles un genre? S'y regroupent-elles selon la nécessité de tel prédicat commun ou bien sont-elles autrement et en elles-mêmes partagées?

These questions are relevant not only to Baudelaire's preface to his *Petits Poèmes en prose*, but also further illuminate the paradoxical relation of his prose poems to those of "le fameux *Gaspard de la nuit*," this "mysterious and brilliant model" which serves as a preface or "point de départ" (Baudelaire's term) for his own undertaking and which, according to most literary historians, decisively announces the entire tradition of the modern French *poème en prose*. *Gaspard de la nuit*, this inaugural work, is itself preceded by a preface (or, more precisely, by several prefaces) whose logic and whose implications are no less disconcerting than Baudelaire's dedication to Houssaye, and which rehearse very much the same kinds of issues raised by the preface to the *Petits Poèmes en prose*—issues involving the genesis and genealogy of the prose poems which follow, their derivativeness or originality, the relation of reading to their writing, the nature of their authorship or authority, and above all, the perplexing question of their generic indeterminacy, particularly as reflected by their narrative discontinuity or fragmentation.

One could, following Derrida's lead, attempt to situate both Baudelaire's dedication and the prefatory matter of Bertrand's *Gaspard de la nuit* within a broader history and/or typology of the preface, and perhaps sketch out a few provisional definitions of the preface as a (literary) genre—a genre, one might add, particularly rich in a period which, like the late 18th or 19th century, is so crucially concerned with the nature of origins or beginnings or *incipits*. Derrida devotes himself primarily to the discussion of Hegel's various prefaces and introductions, but one need only cite a few more or less random instances from French literature to evoke the varieties and complexities of the *discours préfaciel* during this period: the two prefaces to Rousseau's *La Nouvelle Hélöise*, Chateaubriand's prefaces to *Atala* and *René*, Hugo's prefaces to his *Odes et ballades*, to *Les Orientales* and, of course, to *Cromwell*, Sainte-Beuve's pseudo-biographical introduction to the *Vie, poésies et pensées de Joseph Delorme*, Gautier's prefaces to "Albertus" or *Mademoiselle de Maupin*, Balzac's "Avant-Propos" to the *Comédie humaine* . . . the list is virtually endless.

As this small sample already indicates, however, any history or typology of the preface immediately tends to shade into that larger grey area which Gérard Genette has marked out as the domain of the *paratext* and which he defines as including:

> titre, sous-titre, intertitres; préfaces, postfaces, avertissements, avant-propos, etc.; notes marginales, infra-paginales, terminales; épigraphes, illustrations; prière d'insérer, bande, jaquette, et bien d'autres types de signaux accessoires, autographes ou allographes, qui procurent au texte un entourage (variable) et parfois un commentaire, officiel ou officieux, dont le lecteur le plus puriste et le moins porté à l'érudition externe ne peut pas toujours disposer aussi facilement qu'il le voudrait et le prétend.
>
> (*Palimpsestes*)

Without venturing very far into the vast territory Genette opens up here, and without attempting to define the preface as a (literary) genre, I would simply like to explore some of the ways in which the various prefaces or paratexts of *Gaspard de la nuit* address themselves to the problem of genre, and more specifically, how they dramatize those fundamental paradoxes and perplexities which the prose poem—this misborn, hybrid, "accidental" genre—proposes both to its author and reader.

Title, subtitle, epigraph, preface, etc.—all these dimensions of the paratext provide, as Genette points out, "un des lieux privilégiés de la dimension pragmatique de l'oeuvre, c'est-á-dire de son action sur le lecteur—lieu en particulier de ce qu'on nomme volontiers, depuis les études de Philippe Lejeune sur l'autobiographie, le *contrat* (ou *pacte*) générique." What the paratext rehearses or orients, then, is a certain activity or protocol of reading. Baudelaire's dedication to Houssaye, as we have seen, not only speaks of how the book was generated by his reading of *Gaspard* but also proposes a model of reading to its eventual public: "Nous pouvons couper où nous voulons, moi ma rêverie, vous le manuscrit, le lecteur sa lecture; car je ne suspends pas la volonté rétive de celui-ci au fil interminable d'une intrigue superflue." The discontinuous mode of reading authorized by this preface inevitably problematizes any received notion of poetic or narrative genre. If (to follow Baudelaire's metaphors) we can pick up or leave off our perusal at any point, if we can hack up the work into autonomous fragments or stumps, if we can eliminate vertebrae and fuse the spine into new postures, what kind of textual body are we dealing with? Where does this ouroboros-like serpent begin or end? At what point do we read it as prose? At what points as poetry? At what points as both? Or neither? And since the author of this book describes himself as a reader (or dreamer), at what point does *his* restive reader in turn crisscross over into authorship, decomposing and recomposing the work at whim? In short, what horizons of expectation are we to bring to a work which declares its boundaries to be forever shifting?

Something of the same rich predicament faces the reader and/or author of *Gaspard de la nuit*. And at issue, here too, is the placement (or displacement) of a number of boundaries or margins which throw into question just where a text (or its reading) may be said to begin or end, and which in turn ask us to continually readjust our expectations as to where the line might fall between poetry and prose, lyric and narrative, metaphor and metonymy, poiesis and mimesis. It is enough to pick up any edition of *Gaspard de la nuit* to be immediately struck by the elaborate paratextual apparatus that bounds, surrounds, and zones the work, demarcating its various openings and closures with a multiplicity of mobile frontiers and borders. Let me quickly recall the overall architectonics of the volume, for it provides a virtuoso example of a book constructed on the principle of liminality.

A governing title: *Gaspard de la nuit* (a title, it turns out, which is actually the name of the book's putative author). A subtitle: *Fantaisies à la manière de Rembrandt et de Callot* (a direct intertextual lift, or plagiarism, of an E. T. A.

Hoffmann title). An author's name: Aloysius Bertrand (actually something of an editorial invention: the first [posthumous] edition of *Gaspard* appeared under the more prosaic name Louis Bertrand; the more poetic "Aloysius" is a bit of romantic onomastics popularized by Baudelaire and Mallarmé). Following the title page, two verse epigraphs evoking Dijon—one by Sainte-Beuve, the other anonymous (although written by Bertrand himself)—open the volume, inscribing it under the sign of poetry while situating its major geographical and historical locus. There follows a long prose introduction or prologue entitled "Gaspard de la nuit" and signed Louis Bertrand, which formulates (without resolving) the paradoxes and indeterminacies which govern the entire volume. Something of a shaggy dog story, it is a preface that, significantly enough, never quite manages to get going or (to use a Bertrandian metaphor akin to Baudelaire's thyrsis) that never quite spools its narrative thread around a bobbin.

Things start to unravel in the very first paragraphs of the story. The narrative begins conventionally enough—"J'étais un jour assis à l'écart dans le jardin de l'Arquebuse"—but the narrator immediately (and uncannily) goes on to suggest that he might have easily been confused with one of the statues in the park: "Immobile sur un banc, on eût pu me comparer à la statue du bastion Bazire. Ce chef d'oeuvre du figuriste Sévallée et du peintre Guillot représentait un abbé assis et lisant. Rien ne manquait à son costume. De loin, on le prenait pour un personnage; de près, on voyait que c'était un plâtre." Right at the outset, then, attention is called to the uncertain boundary separating the world of artistic representation from the real. The fact that the statue in question depicts a reader (and—shades of *Madame Bovary*—"un abbé assis et lisant") in turn links the issue of representationality directly to those conventions of reading which will be tested—and subverted—by the diabolic prose poems that follow.

The narrator, however, is rudely jolted out of his statuesque immobility: "Le toux d'un promeneur dissipa l'essaim de mes rêves." This is merely the first in a series of disruptions that break the tenuous narrative thread of the preface (such abrupt intrusions of discordance on harmonious revery will also play an important role in many of the following prose poems, many of which are constructed on the principle of an equilibrium that is suddenly—and often comically—disrupted). The disruptive stranger is referred to by the narrator as "un pauvre diable dont l'extérieur n'annonçait que misères et souffrances." It is only some twenty pages later, upon learning his true identity at the end of the preface, that we realize that the phrase "un pauvre diable" which we had initially assumed to be metaphorical should in fact have been read literally, since the narrator's interlocutor turns out to be none other than the devil himself, alias Gaspard de la nuit.

The mysterious stranger also plays something of a *Doppelgänger* role vis-a-vis the narrator. Described as one of "ces artists au petit pied, joueurs de violon et peintres de portraits, qu'un faim irrassasiable et une soif inextinguible condamnent à courir le monde sur la trace du juiferrant," the musical and pictorial analogies announce the dual emphasis on painterly description and melodic sonority one finds in the following prose poems, while the stranger's nomadic desire in turn prefigures the ever-shifting, mobile boundaries of the subsequent *Fantaisies*. No wonder that the pair, seated on the park bench like two Bouvard et Pécuchets *avant la lettre*, should immediately recognize their profound twinship:

> —"Vous êtes poète!" me répondit-il en souriant.
> —"Poète, si c'est être poète que d'avoir cherché l'art"
> —"Vous avez cherché l'art! et l'avez-vous trouvé?"
> —"Plût au ciel que l'art ne fût pas une chimère"
> —"Une chimère! . . . Et moi aussi je l'ai cherché!" s'écria-t-il
> avec l'enthousiasme du génie, et l'amphase du triomphe.

Though this may seem a rather trivial example of doubling, the specular identity of narrator and interlocutor (or of poet and devil, author and reader) bears directly on the uncertain status of narrative and poetic authority within the work as a whole and, more specifically, serves to dramatize the difficulties of distinguishing the simulacrum from the real, the derivation from the original. Indeed, Gaspard addresses himself precisely to the issue of originality toward the end of the preface, situating the relation of model to copy in a theological context:

> —"Nous ne sommes, nous, monsieur, que les copistes du créateur. La plus magnifique, la plus triomphante, la plus glorieuse de nos oeuvres éphémères n'est jamais que l'indigne contrefaçon, que le rayonnement éteint de la moindre de ses oeuvres immortelles. Toute originalité est un aiglon qui ne brise la coquille de son oeuf que dans les aires sublimes et foudroyantes du Sinai.—Oui, monsieur, j'ai longtemps cherché l'art absolu! O délire! O folie!"

Although this passage has occasionally been interpreted as a renunciation of the poet's demiurgic or alchemical pursuit of an *art absolu* that would rival the work of the creator, these words are after all spoken by the devil and may therefore simply constitute another rhetorical ruse on his part. Indeed, Gaspard's humble disclaimer of originality curiously prefigures Baudelaire's own diabolically double-edged confession in the preface to his *Petits Poèmes en prose* of his failure to faithfully imitate *Gaspard de la nuit*.

But to return to our two protagonists on their park bench in Dijon: "Le fil de la conversation était noué. Maintenant sur quelle bobine allait-il s'envider?" As it so happens, the bobbin around which the following twenty pages will turn is the question, "Qu'est-ce l'art?" Over the course of this inquiry into the chimera of art, however, the narrative thread of the encounter progressively veers off into a bewildering tangle of ellipses and discontinuities. The initial narratorial "je" of Bertrand is virtually displaced (and effaced) by the "je" of Gaspard who from this point onward dominates the remainder of the preface with a rambling monologue only periodically punctuated by Bertrand's impatient repetition of the same question ("Et l'art?") as he vainly tries to get his interlocutor back on track. Gaspard's devilish refusal to spool his divagations around any central axis clearly parodies those techniques of deferred or frustrated narrative perfected by Sterne, Diderot, and Nodier.

Although Gaspard's monologue is organized by the most rudimentary of plots—it may be read as a quest romance recounting the various stages in his *Bildung* as a poet and the various spiritual transformations he has undergone in the course of his alchemical search for "l'art, cette pierre philosophale du XIXe siècle"—this simple framework is atomized into a series of virtually autonomous segments, each of which tends to problematize the very possibility of narrative (and mimesis), and each of which prefigures both the stylistic and thematic features of the following *Fantaisies*. The fact that Gaspard's meandering monologue is distributed into a discontinuous series of rhetorical set pieces may in fact throw light on the emergence of the modern prose poem out of precisely those elements of narrative prose which are, as it were, least essential or most marginal to its *diegesis:* descriptions, anecdotes, vignettes, in short, those elements which are often construed as superfluous or merely ornamental *digressions* from the forward thrust of narrative.

Gaspard's first digression is a *Märchen*-like fable of his love for—and loss of—an enigmatic young maiden who may or may not have come to life out of the pages of "un petit livre en langue baroque et inintelligible" which he had been reading. Both the indeterminacies of this story (was the girl real or merely a readerly fantasy?) as well as its mysterious and utterly inexplicable chain of events are a model of the highly telescoped plots of many of Bertrand's prose poems, crafted by an aesthetic which deliberately deploys ellipses in order to open breaches or blanks within narrative sequence. Gaspard's second digression is a pastiche of romantic purple prose, a *pittoresque* evocation of Nature such as one might find in Chateaubriand's *Atala* or *Les Martyrs* and which clearly indicates the intertextual filiation of early 19th century *prose poétique* and the descriptive base of many of Bertrand's *poèmes en prose:*

> Tantôt je frayais à mes rêveries un sentier de mousse et de rosée, de silence et de quiétude, loin de la ville. Que de fois j'ai ravi leurs quenouilles de fruits rouges et acides aux halliers mal hantés de la fontaine de Jouvence et de l'hermitage de Notre-Dame-D'Etang, la fontaine des esprits et des fées, l'hermitage du diable! Que de fois j'ai ramassé le buccin pétrifié, et le corail fossile sur les hauteurs pierreuses de Saint-Joseph, ravinées par l'orage! Que de fois j'ai pêché l'écrevisse dans les gués échevelés des Tilles, parmi les cressons qui abritent la salamandre glacée, et parmi les nénuphars dont bâillent les fleurs indolentes!

As Phillipe Hamon has shown, the effect of this kind of descriptive set piece—characterized by a predominance of parallelisms, anaphora, and the lexical saturation of a specialized taxonomic or classificatory system—is profoundly anti-narrative, given its rigorous organization along paradigmatic as opposed to syntagmatic lines.

This displacement of metonymic sequentiality by metaphoric equivalence, or to put it slightly differently, this fragmenting of narrative into discontinuous inventory, catalogue, or list, is well-illustrated by the following segment of Gaspard's monologue (again introduced by the disruptive "Et l'art?"). Having studied Nature, Gaspard (echoing *René*) moves on to the study of "les monuments des hommes," that is, to History. But despite the fact that he initially defines History as a possible source or model of narrative (Dijon, he notes, "aurait de merveilleuses histoires de guerre à vous raconter"), the same process of denarrativization sets in as he pursues the topic. Instead of telling a story, History is reduced to a sheer paratactic list of names and events; its temporal axis is spatialized into the topography of a tableau or stage where past and present coexist simultaneously in the form of a great static cavalcade of historical sites and figures magically resurrected by the power of naming and by the sorcery of a syntax perforated by dashes and ecstatic marks of exclamation:

> Dijon se lève; il se lève, il marche, il court!—trente *dindelles* carillonnent dans un ciel bleu d'outremer, comme en peignait le vieil Albert Dürer. La foule se presse aux hôtelleries de la rue Bouchepot, aux étuves de la porte aux Chanoines, au mail de la rue Saint-Guillaume, au change de la rue Notre-Dame, aux fabriques d'armes de la rue des Forges, à la fontaine de la place des Cordeliers, au four banal de la rue de Bèze, aux halles de la place Champeaux, au gibet de la place Morimont;—bourgeois, nobles, vilains, soudrilles, prêtres, moines, clercs, marchands, varlets, juifs, lombards, pèlerins, ménestrels, officiers du parlement et de la Chambre des comptes, officiers des gabelles, officiers de la monnaie, officiers de la gruerie, officiers de la maison du duc;—qui clament, qui sifflent, qui chantent, qui geignent, qui prient, qui maugréent;—dans des basternes, dans des litières, à cheval, sur des mules, sur la haquenée de saint François.—Et comment douter de cette résurrection?

Despite its exuberance, however, this *simultanéiste* presentation of History as spectacle or tableau translates a radical sense of historical dispossession: History (as the prose poems included in the section "Le Vieux Paris" or "Les Chroniques" will further demonstrate) can no longer be seized as a coherent, totalizing narrative, but only as an anachronistic fantasy generated by the gaps and absences articulated by its ruins.

The final segment of Gaspard's soliloquy completes the account of the genesis of his *Fantaisies* and offers yet another possible ancestor of the prose poem. Having presented us first with a sample of an elliptical *Märchen*-like fable or ballad, then with a swatch of Chateaubriandesque *prose poétique*, followed by a Hugolian exercise in the oneirics of History, Gaspard now moves us into the register of the *fantastique* à la Hoffmann or Nodier. This episode, which involves a series of sculpted figures coming to life in the cathedral of Dijon—a gargoyle breaks into laughter, the Black Virgin cavorts in the nave, the cast-iron bellringer Jacquemart and his wife take on human guises—possesses a certain degree of narrative continuity (unlike the paratactic inventories of the previous segments), but by bewildering the boundaries between literal and figurative, natural and supernatural, waking and dream, this final fragment creates something akin to the "hesitation" Todorov speaks of in relation to the fantastic and thereby tends to erode the epistemological ground of narrativity and representationality altogether (as do many of the "fantastic" prose poems included in the section of *Gaspard* entitled "La Nuit et ses prestiges").

So *unheimlich* is this episode that Bertrand, who has been tolerant enough of his interlocutor so far, now suspects he is dealing with a mad monomaniac—only to discover on the final page of the preface that all the while he has been discoursing with the devil (who, it seems, may also be a hermaphrodite.) Having vainly searched for M. Gaspard de la Nuit all over Dijon in order to return the manuscript that has been left in his keeping, Bertrand finally decides to exercise his own authority (if not authorship) over the work: "Si Gaspard de la Nuit est en enfer, qu'il rôtisse, J'imprime son livre." The relation of original to copy remains equivocal to the very end, for if these *Fantaisies* are indeed the productions of the mysterious Gaspard, their *re*production nonetheless lies in the hands of Bertrand—or any other poor devil who happens to read them. The situation again recalls Baudelaire's *dédicace* to Houssaye: this preface to what are commonly considered the founding examples of the modern *poème en prose* in French concludes with the very impossibility of ascribing any clear origin or authorship to this diabolic genre.

This lengthy prologue is followed by a text labelled "Preface," signed not by Bertrand this time, but by his double, Gaspard de la Nuit, author of the book we are about to read. This preface addresses itself, appropriately enough, to the two faces of art: "L'art a toujours deux faces antithétiques, médaille dont, par exemple, un côté accuserait la ressemblance de Paul Rembrandt, et le revers, celle de Jacques Callot." Gaspard, one gathers, is rewriting the *Préface de Cromwell*, for the head of his coin, art in the noble meditative manner of Rembrandt, resembles the Hugolian sublime, while its tail, the extroverted caricature of Callot, is more akin to the Hugolian grotesque. Gaspard, however, gives little currency to this "double personnification" of art. Heads or tails, it is all the same to him: instead of parading "en tête de son livre quelque belle théorie littéraire," he will simply "se contente[r] de signer son oeuvre—Gaspard de la Nuit." By preferring to let his *name* speak in the place of literary *theory*, Gaspard calls attention to the devilish implications of all this playful *Doppelgängerei:* authorship (and its authority) is no more than a signature on a page; to ask who is the true originator of these *Fantaisies* (Bertrand or Gaspard?) is as futile as trying to decide which way they face (toward the poetic sublime or toward the prosaic grotesque?).

Gaspard's "Preface" is followed by a two-page dedication to Victor Hugo, preceded by two epigraphs. Dated Paris, 20 September 1836, it is unsigned, as if to further confuse (or diminish) the identity of its author: the only name that counts here after all is Hugo's, for the mere display of his "nom illustre" at the head of the page (so the dedication runs) may some day encourage a future bibliophile to exhume the corpse of "cette oeuvre moisie et vermoulue," to resurrect this *mort-né* from its tomb, thereby releasing (in a metaphor certainly not lost on Mallarmé) "le frêle essaim de mes esprits qu'auront emprisonnés si longtemps des fermaux de vermeil dans une geôle de parchemin." To borrow a neologism from Genette, this dedication plays at being at once *posthume* and *antéthume.*

If the reader has managed to keep his head throughout all this prefatory matter, he may now proceed to the body of the book—whose title, as he learns on the next page, has now slightly shifted to read "Les Fantaisies de Gaspard de la nuit," followed by the somewhat redundant indication, "Ici Commence le premier livre des Fantaisies de Gaspard de la nuit." Each of the work's six books—entitled respectively "Ecole Flamande," "Le Vieux Paris," "La Nuit et ses prestiges," "Les Chroniques," "Espagne et Italie," and "Silves"—is framed by the notations "Ici Commence . . . " or "Ici Finit . . . ," anachronistic recalls of the scribal "Incipits" or "Explicits" found on medieval manuscripts, and which serve (like the closing dedication to Charles Nodier) to further zone the work into a series of discrete fragments or segments, each one carefully delimited by its own frontiers or margins.

The paratextual paraphernalia which punctuates the entire volume is also at work in each of the individual prose poems which compose it. Each piece, without exception, is prefaced by a roman numeral, a title, and one or more epigraphs. This barrage of epigraphs no doubt follows the vogue for *exergues* in French writing of the twenties and thirties. Lucienne Frappier-Mazur, for example, has examined Balzac's epigraphic strategies, and Stendhal's epigraphs in *Le Rouge et le noir* have also come in for analysis, but there is, as far as I know, still no systematic study of this particular aspect of romantic paratextuality. In Bertrand's case, he seems primarily to be imitating Hugo's consistent use of epigraph in *Odes et ballades* and *Les Orientales,* as well as the kind of elaborate paratextual performances of his other great mentor, Charles Nodier. Indeed, the paratexts of a work like Nodier's *Smarra* (1821)—which involve a title, a subtitle, a sub-subtitle, a fictional author's name, a translator's name, two prefaces, and a panoply of epigraphic citations—provide a clear analogue to *Gaspard* and suggest the following hypothesis. Since *Smarra* raises many of the same questions as *Gaspard* (is it to be read as a poem or as prose narrative? is it an original work or a translation? is it a transcription of dream or a *conte fantastique?*), one can perhaps assume that the greater the generic indeterminacy or unconventionality of the work, the more elaborate or more pertinent its paratextual apparatus tends to become. (Further examples might be Wordsworth's preface to the *Lyrical Ballads* or Coleridge's prose introduction to "Kubla Khan," and in the French domain, Mallarmé's preface to *Un Coup de dés* or the first five books of the *Chants de Maldoror* which, according to Lautréamont, serve as a "frontispiece" or "hybrid preface" to the "novel" that follows in Book 6.)

But to return to the epigraphs which precede each of Bertrand's prose poems. On the one hand, these *exergues* serve to close the texts in on themselves by establishing their outer margin and by permitting a kind of internal *mise en abyme* between the body of the poem and its various headings. At the same time, however, these preliminary citations also place into question the very possibility of reading the text as a bounded, self-enclosed, self-referential artifact. By weaving it into a larger web of intertextuality, by opening it out beyond its typographic borders, these epigraphs would seem to demand that the prose poem be read not in isolation but dialogically, that is, in relation to the kinds of authors or genres or modes of discourse which preface it in quotation. The provenance of these epigraphs is various, and reveals the variety of contexts and/or conventions against which the prose poems of *Gaspard de la nuit* invite reading. Some are drawn from ancient proverbs, the Bible, medieval songs or ballads, or obscure alchemical texts of the Renaissance—and in these cases the archaism of the epigraph provides an original sample, as it were, of the anachronistically displaced idiom which Bertrand's prose poems deliberately simulate. Other epigraphs are drawn from the works of contemporary poets as various as Hugo, Lamartine, Vigny, Byron, and Coleridge, as if to call the reader's attention to the fact that the texts which these citations introduce are at once *like* contemporary poems and yet utterly dissimilar. Finally, and perhaps most significantly, a number of epigraphs are drawn from narrative genres and suggest further models (or dialogical counterparts) for "Les Fantaisies de Gaspard de la Nuit"—the historical novel (Scott, Cooper, Chateaubriand, Hugo), the fantastic tale (Nodier, Hoffmann), and the ballad.

The epigraphs of *Gaspard de la nuit*, then, make possible an elaborate game with boundaries, since they function simultaneously as enclosing frames and as intertextual relays designed to open the text out onto other modes of discourse whose generic or stylistic features provide the originals or constants against which Bertrand's texts situate themselves as copies or variants—Hermine Riffaterre has recently examined one of Bertrand's prose poems from precisely this intertextual perspective, insisting that it is the "epigraph that gives the text its constants and turns it into a poem" ("Reading Constants"). But whereas Riffaterre emphasizes the perception of (semantic) constants as that which makes a prose poem a *poem*, I would rather underline the inconstancy or indeterminacy that characterizes the interplay of text and paratext in *Gaspard*. Although title and epigraph are (in order of reading) anterior to the poem they head, does this necessarily imply a hierarchical relation? In other words, do the poems illustrate their titles and/or epigraphs (i.e. by dramatizing or narrativizing or simply expanding some initial seme or "kernel word" they contain)? Or do the titles and epigraphs instead illustrate the poems (that is, come *after* them, resume them)?

I use the term illustration because the very subtitle of *Gaspard—Fantaisies à la manière de Rembrandt et de Callot*—suggest that the texts gathered in the volume are to be construed as literary illustrations (or translations) of pictorial models—a lengthy note by Bertrand to his publisher concerning the illustrations he hoped would decorate the book further corroborates his fascination with the interaction of text and illustrative paratext (which he terms "encadrement"). The problematic phrase is of course "à la manière de," for what does it mean exactly for a literary text to be "in the manner of" graphic art? How do we go about reading words on the page *as if* they were engravings or Dutch genre paintings? Or: how read a text typographically set as prose *as if* it were a poem? Clearly the subtitle of *Gaspard* asks us to consider these *Fantaisies* as analogous to something or somebody else—Rembrandt, Callot, Hoffmann—but it is an analogy whose terms and whose ground remain as indeterminate as the literary genre of the work itself. Bertrand, then, places us in the grip of the same demon of analogy as Baudelaire or, later, Mallarmé. Like (yet unlike) the art of Rembrandt and Callot, like (yet unlike) their various prefaces and epigraphs, like (yet unlike) poetry and/or prose, like (yet unlike) the "art absolu" of the Creator, these fantasies seem to refuse any proper identity or origin of their own in order to situate themselves on boundaries which are constantly shifting, constantly effaced, mere points of transition from place to place.

One last preface in conclusion. In his preface to *Le Cornet à dés*, Max Jacob remarks that a prose poem is above all defined by the manner in which it is *situated*, in other words, by the kinds of margins it generates. And if he praises Bertrand as "l'inventeur du genre tel que je le conçois," it is precisely because he finds in *Gaspard de la nuit* the two major criteria of the prose poem, that is, "du style et de la marge" or, as he also terms it, "composition" and "situation." The particular site or situation occupied by the prose poems of *Gaspard de la nuit*, as I have tried to show, is in large measure given by their surroundings, by the textual space (be it defined by preface, title, or epigraph) on which they border, by their dialogue with margins.

And one final paratext of sorts: a note by Bertrand to "M. Le Metteur en pages" in which he insists that as much white space as possible be "thrown" around and in between the various portions of his text ("Il jettera de *larges blancs* entre ces couplets . . . "). These instructions to the printer are prefaced as follows:

Règle generale.—Blanchir comme si le texte était de la poésie.

Comme si. As if poetry. As if *Gaspard* might also be a preface to the margins, the intervals, the whiteness of Mallarmé's *Un Coup de dés:*

COMME SI

> Une insinuation   simple
>   au silence   enroulée avec ironie
>
>   ou
>
>   le mystère
>
>   précipité
>
>   hurlé
>
> dans quelque proche   tourbillon d'hilarité et d'horreur
>   voltige   autour du gouffre
>
>   sans le joncher
>   ni fuir
>   et en berce le vierge indice
>
>   COMME SI

As if. As if this dice-throw were somehow prefigured by the young Mallarmé's homage to Bertrand: "Un anachronisme a causé son oubli. Cette adorable bague jetée, comme celle des doges, à la mer, pendant la furie des vagues romantiques, et engouffrée, apparaît maintenant rapportée par les lames limpides de la marée."

Gérard de Nerval: Writing Living, or Madness as Autobiography

Shoshana Felman

Nerval:

> I am *madde* (letter to Houssaye).

> I agree officially that I was ill. I cannot agree that I was mad or even hallucinating (letter to A. Deschamps).

> I am afraid I am in a house of wise men and the madmen are on the outside (letter to Mme E. de Girardin).

Rimbaud:

> My turn now. The story of one of my insanities . . . I began it as an investigation. I turned silences and nights into words. What was unutterable, I wrote down. I made the whirling world stand still. . . .

> Not a single one of the brilliant arguments of madness—the madness that gets locked up—did I forget: I could go through them all again, I've got the system down by heart ("Second Delirium: The Alchemy of Words").

Breton:

> Where does the mind's stability cease? For the mind, is the possibility of erring not rather the contingency of good? There remains madness, "the madness that gets locked up," as has been aptly described. That madness or another (*Manifestoes of Surrealism*).

From *Writing and Madness (Literature/Philosophy/Psychoanalysis)*. © 1985 by Cornell University. Cornell University Press, 1985.

They came to tell me that Nadja was mad, confined in the Vau-cluse asylum. . . . But to my mind, all confinements are arbitrary. I still don't see why a human being should be deprived of his freedom. They locked up Sade, they locked up Nietzsche, they locked up Baudelaire (*Nadja*).

Artaud:

But all the same, too many signs show us that what kept us alive isn't working anymore, that we are all madmen, desperate and sick. And I invite *us* to react (*The Theater and Its Double*).

I am suffering from a terrible illness of the mind. . . . I am a man whose mind has made him suffer greatly, and by virtue of that, I have the right to speak. . . . I have accepted once and for all to submit to my inferiority ("Correspondance avec Jacques Rivière").

I would like to write a book that would disturb people, that would be like an open door leading them where they never would have agreed to go, a door opening quite simply onto reality (*Ibid.*).

Foucault:

One could write a history of *limits*—of those obscure gestures, forgotten as soon as they take place, by which a culture rejects something that henceforth will be outside it. . . . Western man's perception of space and time reveals a structure of rejection by which a word can be denounced as not belonging to language, a gesture as not being a meaningful act, and a figure as having no right to take a place in history. This structure is constitutive of both sense and non-sense, or rather, of the reciprocity which links them to each other; it alone can account for the general fact that in our culture there can be no reason without madness, even when the rational knowledge one has of madness subjugates and dis-arms it by according it the fragile status of a pathological anomaly (Préface, *Folie et déraison, histoire de la folie à l'Age Classique*).

Rimbaud: the story of one of my insanities; Nerval: the story of *my* madness; Breton: the madness of *our* history; Artaud: the history of *our* madness; Foucault: the history of *madness*.

In grouping these authors together, I intend neither to map out an itinerary nor to trace a chronology, but rather to suggest a circuit of texts, the possible trajectory of a reading, and to establish—in texts as disparate as they are diverse and across clearly irreducible historic differences—the permanence of a certain discourse: a Romantic discourse, if ever there was one. The word "Romantic" is here used in a sense that still seeks us out, to the extent that it is not so much an answer as a question, not so much an object of knowledge as a sign; to the extent that it remains, indeed, to be defined through the singular adventure of the text.

"THE DOUBLY IMPOSSIBLE TASK"

If Michel Foucault appears today to be something like the "last" Romantic, it is because he marks, in modern discourse, the moment of emergence of a new awareness, whereby a philosophic enterprise complements and takes the place of a poetic one. *Madness and Civilization: A History of Insanity in the Age of Reason* is, in fact, the theoretical outcome of a certain praxis of romantic language.

Foucault's aim . . . is to define the relationship between reason and madness at a point prior to their separation. But since the language of psychiatry is based precisely *on* that separation, since it is a unilateral monologue of reason *about* madness, Foucault must avoid that language to be able to listen to the silence to which madness has been reduced, and to make that silence speak.

Aware, however, of the contradictory tensions involved in the task of *saying a silence*, Foucault himself recognizes that his project of saying madness by circumventing reason is, in fact, an impossible undertaking:

> But the task is no doubt doubly impossible. . . . It was essential at all costs to preserve the *relative*, and to be *absolutely* understood.
>
> There, hidden and expressed in a simple *problem of elocution*, lay the major difficulty of the enterprise: I had to bring to the surface of the language of reason a division and a debate which of necessity remain below it, since this language becomes intelligible only well beyond that division.

"But the task is no doubt doubly impossible." All the same, that impossible book had somehow to be written. And the question can be asked whether every great book is not fundamentally impossible (and as such, all the more necessary).

"THE UNWRITABLE BOOK"

Isn't it remarkable that Gérard de Nerval's *Aurélia* was likewise pronounced by its author to be an impossible book?

In the eyes of Nerval's friends, moreover, *any* book had become impossible for him after his second attack of madness. Alexandre Dumas wrote on that occasion a sort of funeral oration for Nerval's mind:

> It is a charming mind . . . in which, from time to time, a certain phenomenon occurs. . . . Imagination, that resident lunatic, momentarily evicts reason . . . and impels him toward *impossible theories* and *unwritable books*.

Nerval responds to Dumas in his preface to *Les Filles du feu*:

> I dedicate this book to you, *cher maître*, as I dedicated *Lorely* to
> Jules Janin. Several days ago everyone thought I was mad, and
> you devoted some of your most charming lines to the epitaph of
> my mind. . . . Now that I have recovered what is vulgarly called
> reason, let us reason together. . . .
>
> I am going to try to explain to you, my dear Dumas, the phe-
> nomenon about which you spoke.

Nerval's request to Dumas is the same Artaud will make to Rivière a
century later: *"Deign to accept me,"* implores Nerval pathetically, "at least
in the capacity of a monster." "For I cannot hope"—Artaud will echo later—
"that time or work will remedy these absurdities or these failings, and so
much disquiet. . . . Nothing less is at stake for me than knowing whether
or not I will have the right to think, in poetry or in prose." The issue is
just as serious for Nerval, and involves nothing less than the very meaning
of his existence. For behind the apparent sympathy in Dumas's discourse,
as later in Rivière's, there lies a gesture of rejection and exclusion:

> The letter I have just gotten from the Cavern . . . advises me to
> give up "an art which doesn't suit me and for which I have no
> need . . . " Alas! This is a bitter joke, for I have never had more
> need, if not for producing art, at least for its brilliant products.
> This is what you haven't understood.

Nerval's intention is henceforth to annul—by means of writing—this verdict
of exclusion and, without rejecting any part of himself, to make the other
acknowledge him. That is why, without *disavowing* his madness, Nerval
nonetheless undertakes to *deny* it, to contest the reductionist definition
given it by the language of reason. I am no more *mad* today, says Nerval,
than I was *dead* several years ago. Your language, he implies to Dumas,
cancels me out as a subject, reduces me to silence. Now listen to
me, because, contrary to what you may think, I have some things to say,
to say *to you*. "Now that I have recovered what is vulgarly called reason,
let us reason together." Let us reason, that is to say, let us communicate,
even if I must, in order to do that (to make myself heard, to be acknowledged, to continue to talk, to live), pass back through your norms: articulate
a "reasonable" discourse. Nerval's dedication to Dumas thus becomes an
appeal, an entreaty, a recourse to the other, and its irony barely hides the
vehemence, the violence, and the urgency through which Nerval desper-
ately poses as one who is at once mad and not mad, one whose only truth
is to be found in the enigma of the madman he is—and is not.

> I am going to try to explain to you, my dear Dumas, the phenom-
> enon about which you spoke. . . . There are, as you know, certain
> storytellers who cannot make up a story without identifying them-

selves with the characters of their imagination. . . . Well now, can you believe that a story could sweep one so entirely away that one becomes incarnate, as it were, in the hero of one's imagination. . . ! What could have been only a game for you, *maître*, had become for me an obsession, an intoxication.

Every reading, says Nerval, is a kind of madness since it is based on illusion and induces us to identify with imaginary heroes. Madness is nothing other than an intoxicating reading: a madman is one who is drawn into the dizzying whirl of his own reading. Dementia is, above all, the madness of books; delirium, an adventure of the text.

The role of madness in books will be a direct consequence of the role of books in life:

The chain was broken and the hours were marked as minutes. It would have been the Dream of Scipio, the Vision of Tasso, the *Divine Comedy* if I had succeeded in concentrating my memories in a masterpiece. Resigning henceforth the renown of the inspired, the illumined, and the prophetic, I have to offer you only what you so justly call impossible theories, *an unwritable book*.

In point of fact, Nerval's poetic enterprise resembles to an astonishing degree the philosophic enterprise of Foucault. In much the same way as Foucault, Nerval attempts to *say* madness *itself*, to write a history of madness while trying to avoid the trap of "what is vulgarly called reason." Is it a triumph of Unreason or the refusal to believe that "unreason" exists, that there can exist, even in madness, something radically foreign to the reasonableness of things? Like Foucault, Nerval seeks to return to that zero point where Madness and Reason have not yet become mutually exclusive, but are rather conjoined in an enigmatic union:

Someday I will write the story of this descent to the underworld, and you will see that *it was not entirely deprived of reasoning even though it always lacked reason.*

I cannot agree that I was mad or even hallucinating. If I am insulting Medicine, I will be at her feet when she acquires the features of a deity.

Like Foucault, Nerval wishes above all to escape clinical diagnostics, that monologue of reason *about* madness. Like Foucault, he makes every effort to remain outside of the health-sickness opposition in order to reach a truth which lies beyond their contradiction.

Let it be well understood: this reading of one text as it echoes in another, this referring of one text to another is meant here to imply neither an historical relationship nor a literary influence. Foucault has been cited only to provide a modern reference point, allowing us to locate our own discourse in that of Nerval. My aim is not to show in what way Foucault may have read Nerval, but rather, in what way Nerval's text understands— rejoins—Foucault. I read Nerval in an attempt to understand how, in Nerval, today, we are *already read*.

To read *Aurélia* would mean then, here, to follow the trace of the impossible task as it is accomplished in the text: to see in what respect the impossible is necessary and the necessary is impossible; to see how this relationship of the impossible and the necessary is transmuted into a line of force in Romantic discourse—and writing—and why it still continues to challenge us even today.

The problem here again is one of *elocution:* Who speaks in the narrative of *Aurélia* and from what place, from what discursive position does he speak? Since Nerval rejects the medical language and point of view, how can his own mode of discourse be defined? How does he succeed in saying madness? How can madness, in itself, survive translation into language? "What then, in its most general but most concrete form, is madness," writes Foucault, "for those who from the outset reject any sort of mastery knowledge might have over it? Nothing else, doubtless, than the *absence of production* [*l'absence d'oeuvre*]."

How then can Nerval hope to *produce* a literary work out of this very *absence of production*?

THE PLURAL OF "I": THE TENSIONS OF THE NARRATIVE

On the very first page of *Aurélia,* the narrator makes the following statement:

> I am going to attempt to transcribe the impressions of a long illness which took place entirely within the confines of my mind; and I do not know why I use the term "illness," for as far as I myself was concerned, I had never felt better in my life.

This *myself* who *never felt better* does not coincide exactly with the one who says *I* at the beginning of the sentence: "I am going to attempt to transcribe the impression of a long *illness* . . . " It is through this uneasiness of feeling double, through this very division of the self, that the speaker here affirms the (impossible) necessity of overcoming, by the very practice of his discourse, the linguistic separation between health and illness, between reason and madness. The use of the pronoun *I* consequently becomes very complex in the narrative of *Aurélia:* in a process of constant splitting, the *I* stands for two distinct characters: the hero—and the narrator. The hero is a "madman"; the narrator, a man who has recovered his "reason." The hero is given over to sleep and its apparitions; the narrator is wide awake and alert. The hero lives madness in the present; the narrator reports it after the fact: he is out of synchrony with the hero. The hero often describes himself as possessing a supernatural power, a super-strength: "I thought my strength and energy were doubled." "Possessed of electrical forces, I was going to overthrow all who approached me." The narrator's mode of being is defined, on the contrary, as impotence: "*I cannot* give here anything but a rather odd idea of the result of this strife in my mind."

The hero believes he has absolute knowledge: "I seemed to know everything, understand everything." The narrator professes ignorance and doubt: "It was one of those strange relationships which I do not understand myself, and which it is easier to hint at than define"; "These were approximately the words which were either spoken to me or whose meaning I thought I could feel." The hero introduces a visionary, dream-like mode of discourse which constantly moves toward hyperbole or overstatement: "My friend . . . grew larger in my eyes and took on the aspect of an Apostle"; "Immediately one of the stars I could see in the sky began to grow larger." By contrast, the narrator initiates a *critical* mode of discourse which constantly tends toward litotes, understatement, reduction, reserve: "if I had not in view to be useful, *I would stop here*, and make no attempt to describe my later experiences in a series of visions which were either insane, or, vulgarly, diseased."

The structure of *Aurélia* is based, then, upon an unresolvable tension between these two contradictory discursive tendencies in the narrative: the mode of hallucinatory inflation and the mode of critical deflation.

"I IS AN OTHER": THE DOUBLE

The split inherent in the "I" in *Aurélia* determines not just the formal structure of the narrative, but its subject-matter as well. Not only is the narrator distinct from the hero, the hero himself is split and is unable to rejoin himself. This internal division takes concrete form in the hallucination of the *double*. Within the dream discourse, the hero's "I" is constantly dispossessed by the so-called *other*:

> Someone of my build, whose face I could not see, went with my friends. . . . "But there's some mistake!" I cried. "They came for *me* and *another* has gone out!"

> To my terror and fury—it was my own face, my whole form magnified and idealized. . . . I thought I heard talk of a mystical marriage—my own—in which the *other* was to profit from the mistakes of my friends and of Aurélia herself.

> I imagined that the man they were waiting for was my *double*, and that he was going to marry Aurélia.

> The Beloved Bridegroom, the King of Glory, it is He who has judged and condemned me, and taken to His own Heaven the woman He gave me and of whom I am now forever unworthy!

On the one hand, the double is the materialization of the subject's narcissistic preoccupations; on the other, this projected image of likeness dramatizes the impossible, incarnates the sign of a prohibition. For it is precisely as other, as not-I, that the double *can*—and *may*—marry Aurélia; it is by virtue of his otherness that he succeeds in removing the prohibition, in making himself recognized so as to penetrate the space of love. As the "King of Glory," the "Beloved Bridegroom," he usurps the place of the "I" and castrates him. What this means is that the "I" is excluded, exiled from the kingdom of pleasure; and that he realizes that he is and will always be secondary, ex-centric to himself. If his place—as he envisions it—is forever missing, it is because his movements are inscribed within a radical dimension of castration.

LOSS: THE NAME OF THE OTHER

Castration is, in fact, the constituent, constitutive experience of *Aurélia*. If Nerval examines himself and his madness under a feminized title, it is because "woman" symbolizes that locus of lack around which his delirium crystallizes. "Aurélia" is not, in reality, a female character in the narrative, but the nominal force of an absence, a signifier of loss. From the outset, and at the very sources of the story, she is *named* precisely as what is *lost:*

> A woman whom I had loved for a long while and whom I shall call Aurélia, was *lost* to me.

> *Eurydice! Eurydice!* Lost once more!
> All is *finished*, all is *past*. Now I must die and die without hope. What then is death? Nothingness? . . . Would to God it were! But God himself cannot make death a nothingness.

Our past is not what is past. It is something that never stops coming to pass, and to pass us by; it is what never ceases to be repeated as a vanished Present. Time lost is time endlessly recaptured as lost, found once again in the image of loss. Death, then, is not nothingness, but the death-in-life that one must *live*. Loss is the repetition of loss: "twice lost"; "the chain was broken and the hours were marked as minutes" (Preface, *Les Filles du feu*).

> The Thirteenth returns. . . . Once more she is the first;
> And she is still the only one, or is this the only moment;
> For you are surely queen, first and last?
> For you are surely king, o first and last lover? . . .

> Love the one who loved you from cradle to the grave;
> The one alone I love loves me dearly still:
> She is death—or the dead one. . . . Delight or torment!
> ("Artemis" in *Chimeras*)

She is death—or the dead one: this is the supreme image, ultimately anonymous, of woman. That is why Aurélia, *named* as one *lost* at the outset, in the end *loses her name* as well:

> Oh, how beautiful is my dear friend. . . . That night Saturnius came to my assistance and my dear friend took her place at his side. . . . I recognized the beloved features of * * *.

At the height of her femininity, in her final apparition, Aurélia returns to anonymity. Or rather, the text, for the last time, designates her as a blank: at the dream's moment of fulfillment, absence itself is named by a name that is only a gap.

Nameless, her only name the name of absence, woman is no more than the trace of a passing, the illusion of an identity:

> I am the same as Mary, the same as your mother, the same being also whom you have always loved under every form. At each of your ordeals I have dropped one of the masks with which I hide my features and soon you shall see me as I really am.

You shall see me: in the future. For in the present I am precisely what is invisible. "I am the same" means, therefore: I am she who is not; death— or the dead one.

It is in this way that desire is transformed, by a chain of infinite substitutions, into a frantic metonymy: Aurélia's death repeats and consecrates the lovers' separation, which was itself grafted upon the original loss of the mother:

> I never knew my mother, who had insisted on following my father on one of his campaigns. . . . She died of fever and exhaustion in a cold province of Germany.

Repeated frustration becomes the dizzying contemplation of an eternal death, a sickness unto death: "Everywhere the suffering image of the eternal Mother was dying, weeping or languishing."

"THE OUTPOURING OF DREAM"

"Madness," said Schopenhauer before Freud, "is nature's last resort against anxiety." It is because "real life" is nothing other than a gaping hole that Dream, little by little, pours into it. Loss becomes a doorway opening onto the "invisible world." In the hollow of the real grows a compensatory delirium, made through a reversal of signs; born of loss and separation, hallucination endlessly strives to reunite the lovers, to recapture the lost object, to re-establish a cosmic harmony.

> My own role seemed to be to re-establish universal harmony.

One evening, at about midnight . . . I noticed the number on a
house, lit by a street-lamp. The number was that of my own age.
As I looked down I saw in front of me a woman with hollow eyes,
whose features seemed to me like Aurélia's. I said to myself: "I
am being warned either of *her death* or of mine!" . . . I began
searching the sky for a star I thought I knew . . . , walking, as it
were, toward my destiny, anxious to see the star up to the moment
when death would strike me down. . . . It seemed to me that my
friend was employing super-human strength to make me move.
. . . "No," I cried, "I don't belong to your Heaven. Those in that
star are waiting for me. . . . Let me go to them, for the one I love
belongs to them, and it is there we are to meet again."

The number on a house, a figure illuminated by chance, sets off a whole
scene of delirium. Hallucination begins by a reading of signs. Madness is,
before all else, an intuition about the functioning of the symbol, a blind
and total faith in the revelation of a sign which, although spawned by
chance, harkens to a necessity, a fatality: "But what if this grotesque symbol
were something else, what if it were . . . the fatal truth under the mask of
madness?"

The symbol simultaneously conceals and reveals. That is, the symbolic
revelation solicits the interpreter, but also resists him; truth only travels
under a mask. It takes on its full significance only by being *unreadable:*

Then I saw plastic images of antiquity vaguely take form before
me . . . they seemed to represent symbols whose meaning I
grasped only with difficulty. Yet I think what it meant was: "All
this was to teach you the secret of life and you have not understood
it. Religions and legends, saints and poets, all concurred in explaining the fatal enigma, and you have interpreted it wrongly."

THE MAGIC ALPHABET

The entire world is from then on a symbolic discourse, which the hero
interprets according to his desires and fears. His delirious faith in the sign
has as its only goal to conjure away—by magic—the curse of castration, to
regain a lost potency, a potency seen as fundamentally erotic, which will
allow the hero to affirm himself and vanquish the other:

I shouted out: "I know he has struck me once with his weapon,
but I am not afraid and await him, knowing *the sign* with which
to defeat." . . . I stepped back to the throne then, my soul filled
with unutterable pride, and raised my arm to *make a sign* which
to me appeared to have *magical potency.* A woman's cry, vibrant
and clear, and filled with excruciating agony, woke me with a
start. The syllables of the *unknown word* I had been about to utter
died on my lips.

The sign clearly becomes here the symbol of phallic power. That is why madness is conceived all along as a mode of transgressive knowledge; transgression, a breaching of the mystery beyond the limits of what is known or allowed, is also expressed by an erotic metaphor:

> I have never been able to *penetrate* without a *shudder* those ivory or horned *gates* which separate us from the invisible world.

> I used all my willpower to *penetrate further* that mystery whose veils I had partly lifted.

Transgression, however, is only possible through the medium of the symbol: the phallic omnipotence invoked by the magic sign mimics "the syllables of an *unknown world*" which, when the hero awakens, "*die* on his lips." Madness will then set off in quest of this unknown language, this mysterious code of potency—a code which would have no place for lack, a language in which plenitude would become possible:

> The *magic alphabet*, the mysterious hieroglyphs have only come down to us incomplete and falsified, either by time or by men who have an interest in remaining ignorant. *Let us rediscover the lost letter*, the effaced sign, let us recompose the dissonant scale, and *we shall gain power* in the world of the spirits.

The delirious quest for the magic language, however, leads in reality only to the abandonment of human language. The madman no longer uses speech to communicate with those around him. In order to communicate with the spirits, Nerval renounces the world of men. To reach for the star, he takes leave of his friend. Though its goal is to rejoin the other, his delirium in fact only widens the gap that separates him from others. Nerval's tragedy is precisely this loss of the other: this vicious circle of the imaginary—a narcissistic entrapment—is what constitutes the core of his madness.

THE SPHINX

It is in the insane asylum that the circle of narcissism is broken for the first time.

> At last I was torn from these macabre reflections. . . . Among the patients was a young man, once a soldier in Africa, who had refused to take food for six weeks. . . . Moreover, he could neither see nor speak.
>
> This sight made a deep impression on me. Until then I had been given up to the monotonous circle of my own sensations or moral sufferings, and here I met an unaccountable creature, patient and *taciturn*, seated *like a sphinx* at the last gates of existence. I began

to love him because of his misfortune and abandonment, and I felt uplifted by this sympathy and pity.

"This figure in distress," notes Roger Dragonetti, "is again the *double*, but one that reveals to Nerval the image of his own impoverishment: the true likeness of a peer." *I* is no longer so much an *other*, since the other has become an other *self*. "I spent hours examining myself mentally, my head bowed over his, and holding his hands." Recovery thus begins with the discovery of the other.

His mirror image, this living dead man, reveals to Nerval not only the spectacle of his own madness, but also an image of destiny: destiny is silence. "Seated like a *sphinx* at the last gates of existence," this mute creature poses for Nerval the *question of silence,* and reveals at the same time the price of human language—the place of encounter with the other. We then witness an initiation into speech: an initiation that takes the form of a teaching process. The hero himself relearns speech while teaching his pathetic companion to talk:

> I was delighted the first time a word came from his mouth. No one would believe me, but I attributed this commencement of cure in him to my ardent will-power.

> I spent whole hours singing him old village songs. . . . I had the happiness of seeing that he heard them, and he opened his eyes for a second, and I saw that they were blue. . . . Then he began to speak . . . and he recognized me and addressed me in a familiar way, calling me brother.

From the muteness of the poor madman, Nerval derives not only the power to recommence speaking himself, but also the power to become a donor, a dispenser of speech. The communication involved is the reciprocal gift of what one does not have: "Saturnus" restores to Nerval what he himself has lost, what he is deprived of—speech. In the void of mutual privation, there is established in this way an exchange that leads to a double miracle, a double recovery: for Nerval, and for the soldier from Africa, a rebirth into language, and into the Other.

ARIADNE'S THREAD

This rebirth into human language necessarily entails, for Nerval, the abandonment of the magic language:

> I was overjoyed to rediscover these humble relics of those years alternating in fortune and misery. . . . My books, an odd assortment of the knowledge of all ages . . . —they had left me all that! *Those books were enough to drive a wise man mad. Let me try to see to it that they will also be enough to drive a madman wise.* With what

delight have I been able to file away in my drawers the mass of my notes and letters . . . ! Oh joy! Oh mortal sorrow! These yellowed characters, these faded drafts, half-crumpled letters, these are the treasures of my only love. . . . Let me read them again. . . . Many of them are missing, others torn or crossed out; here is what I re-discover.

Madness swings over into a kind of wisdom we now see dawning. If insanity is best described as an intoxication of reading, that which is written in books, then "wisdom" is precisely what has *yet to be written*. Filing one's notes is already a move in the direction of textual production (*l'oeuvre*): it is a rediscovery of the cache of "faded drafts." "Many letters are missing," it is true, and "others torn or crossed out." But human language, in contrast to the "magic alphabet," necessarily implies an acceptance of rupture, of tearing. "These yellowed characters" speak out of the very lack that founds them.

It is noteworthy that at this point the narrative, up to here written in the past tense, suddenly switches to the present tense. "Let me read them again. . . . Many of them are missing . . . here is what I re-discover." Recovery is also a discovery of the present. And the present is a re-reading: a new attitude toward the past. (The first sentence in the present tense occurs several lines earlier, and introduces the passage just quoted; in it, the breach of the present is marked—in both form and content—by a kind of promise of admirable poetic simplicity: "My room lies at the end of the corridor, on the one side of which live the insane, and on the other the asylum servants. It has only the privilege of one window, opening toward the courtyard.")

Writing, the inheritance of the disinherited, now becomes the only consolation for the "disconsolate":

The divinity of my dreams appeared smiling. . . . She said to me: "The ordeal you have undergone is coming to an end. . . ." I wanted some *material sign* of the vision which had consoled me, so *I wrote* these words on the wall: "This night you came to me."

In this sublime night, Nerval stakes claim—on the basis of a doubt—to a drop of ink: "Some sort of duty to recreate everything with recollections" (Mallarmé, "Conférence sur Villiers de l'Isle-Adam"). But here recollection turns toward the future, not the past; it is the promise of an end, which is in fact a re-beginning: "The ordeal you have undergone is coming to an end." The written sign commemorates a meaning. But the memory kept is a memory of language, the trace of a nocturnal visit whose illumination makes *sense* only in that it makes one *wait*. The letter at once promises and defers. The "material sign" marks therefore the juncture at which the past meets the future: at which the past is *yet to be*. Whereas the past is the impossible, that which *did not come to pass*—the impossible love for an "apparition," for a Star—the future, paradoxically enough, is this memory—belonging to no one—of desire, a memory which transforms recollection into waiting: the impossible becomes a hope.

Once again, it is recourse to the symbol that allows one to live, to bear and transcend the real frustration. Writing will, however, bring about a reversal of Nerval's relationship to signs. While the hallucination had been a reading of signs, a deciphering of one's reality, writing will attempt, in contrast, to decipher one's own *dream*. The writer thus becomes the reader, the interpreter, of his own madness:

> I resolved to *fix* my dream-state and learn its secrets. "Why should I not," I asked myself, "at last force those mystic gates, armed with all my will-power, and *dominate* my sensations instead of being *subject* to them? Is it not possible to *control* this fascinating, dread chimera, to *rule* the spirits of the night which play with our reason?"

It is thus that the hero is transformed into a narrator. The critical movement of the narrative has succeeded in fixing, dominating, controlling the movement of the dream. At least for a moment, Nerval rules over those spirits of the night that were playing with his reason; he *dominates* the sign instead of being *subject* to it:

> Surrounded by monsters against which I struggled obscurely, I seized *Ariadne's thread*. . . . One day I will write the story of this descent to the underworld, and you will see that it was not entirely deprived of reasoning even though it always lacked reason.

To *produce a work* out of the very "*absence of production*" [*l'absence d'oeuvre*] meant, thus, to produce a work in which speech is not an already acquired knowledge, but an initiation; to write a book in which writing is, precisely, its own search and its own rite of passage. "To seize Ariadne's thread" was, for Nerval, to recognize that the lost letter will never be refound. It was to be content with a "dissonant scale," an incomplete, deficient alphabet with which to say the unsayable, and nevertheless to attempt to inscribe silence, to arrest the intoxicating swirl of madness. It was to write *Aurélia*.

The Mixture of Genres, the Mixture of Styles, and Figural Interpretation: *Sylvie*, by Gérard de Nerval

Rodolphe Gasché

Chemistry, or rather chemism, simultaneously the art of separating and mixing, became the scientific model for burgeoning Romanticism, that of Iena. It provided the model for its double project: to work out, or rather finish, a theory of literary genres; and, to conceive of their intermixing in a work where universality would proceed from its organic individuality. Claiming that the two Schlegel brothers shared this task may be somewhat arbitrary. Roughly speaking, however, A. W. Schlegel, who as a historian and literary critic was more interested in analyzing and dissecting works of art than in developing a theory of the mixing of their elements, did conclude a movement initiated in the sixteenth and seventeenth centuries by the followers of a rigorous imitation of ancient literature. This task consisted in erroneously founding, as G. Genette has shown, a three-genre theory based upon the poetics of Plato and Aristotle. According to this plan, F. Schlegel would then be at the origin of the idea of a fusion of genres into what Jean-Luc Nancy and Philippe Lacoue-Labarthe have called the Genre or the *Absolu littéraire*. My attention here is to analyse a particular case of such a mixing. But in so doing, my goal is not to show that such a fusion could again be separated into its inassimilable elements. Such a maneuver would be pointless, for the precise reason that genres have already been predetermined in the perspective of their subsequent sublation. I am interested rather in trying to determine the *particular figure* such a mixing assumes. For the uniqueness of mixing, as well as its inevitable facticity, seems to transport the work to the very edge of its individuality.

The text I will examine is Nerval's *Sylvie*. The whole of *Les Filles du feu* would of course have to be considered in order to treat the problem of

From *Glyph: Textual Studies* 7 (1980). © 1980 by The Johns Hopkins University Press, Baltimore/London.

genre mixing; it would not suffice to deal only with this one novella whose author, by the way, was rather familiar with the German Romantics. One would also have to consider the dedication *To Alexandre Dumas;* there the motif of the *unwritable* book should not only guide the reading of the ensemble, but the (Romantic) topos of the *work's absence (absence d'oeuvre)* should as well preside over any analysis of Nervalian madness, as I will try to envisage it later. The novel serves as the paradigm for the mixture of genres, while the novella is at most one of its elements. If it is true that "mixture" must not be confused with a simple association of elements each conserving its unalterable property, but instead, according to its strict meaning within the field of chemistry, must lead to the production of a new chemical body with unique properties, then the novella can be seen simultaneously as a part of the ensemble of *Les Filles du feu* and as a representative part of this ensemble. In a letter to George Sand, Nerval will say that it is "a short novel which is not quite a tale." Even if it is difficult to consider the whole of *Les Filles du feu* as an organic whole, *Sylvie* can still be analyzed as the outcome of a mixing of genres by looking at a good number of distinctions which are intimately intermixed within it.

Sylvie, indeed, proves to be a mixture of old and new, of real and representation, of autobiography and fiction, of Christianity and paganism, of folk poetry and philosophy, of lyricism and drama, etc. As I have said, such a mixture is always unique and tends to inhibit the mediation between singular and universal. In trying to analyse such a mixture now, I would hope to pinpoint that which hinders this mixture from being a true synthesis (*relève*) of each of the elements combined in this chemical mixture. Beyond this, such an analysis should also invalidate not only the reassuring image of a Nerval asserting his Valois roots, but also that other image, hardly more complex, of a Nerval preserving in *Sylvie* the balance between the simple charms of real life and the fascination exerted by the dream. This balance is not upset by what some call Nerval's madness. What does upset this balance (and here madness does have a goodly share) is rather on the order of the supplement, without which the image of such a world, of such a wholeness, could not be born.

The double determination of burgeoning Romanticism as I exemplified it through the two Schlegel brothers is considerably complicated by the fact that the individual and organic unity aimed for by genre mixing is always thought of as being in excess with relation to literature, as its beyond. Now the construction of such a work is seen as something like the complex return of an essential Classicity. It is a complex return, for if it is true that the novel as a mixed poem finds its partner in the Greek *epos,* the Romantic return nevertheless cannot be confused with a return to a natural past situation. Indeed, since the Greeks themselves by rigorously separating the genres (separating the philosophic from the poetic) turned away from the mythical past, such a natural situation could not possibly return. For Romanticism the continuous history of art is fulfilled and completed. But this completion was to issue forth into a totally different art, into an art which would itself necessarily recognize its essence, if one may apply to art what Hegel expected from philosophical reflection. Yet, even so, this completion is never concluded and will continue to give rise to works of art that pertain to that completed art. Thus two similar movements occur. Hegel, by determining, in the *Aesthetics*, the transitory form characterizing the end of Romanticism as a *"Verinnigung in dem Gegenstande,"* showed this end-phase of art to be a return to symbolism. The ancient Persians and Arabs excelled in the production of this form. In the same way, the mixture of genres, *before* poetic dissolution has completed its task, can only be conceived as a return to the original sources and archetypes (*Urbilder*) of the "first ensemble of Greek poetic art" (F. Schlegel). Before achieving the individual, organic and unique work which would be beyond all used past forms and figures, in truth impossible, Romanticism could neither avoid being a (regressive) return to what it conceived as poetry of nature, to a state of undifferentiated expression before any separation into genres has occurred, and ultimately to an original language where images and figures would reign supreme. A. W. Schlegel called this the "original figural quality of languages." In other words, the search for the Romantic work beyond all division (and of which the novel [as *Mischgedicht*] is the model) is inseparable from its thematic realization through the singularity of a former figure.

But this is not yet everything. Even though the novel is created in the image of the former epic genre, it also has a privileged relationship to another genre, or rather, mode of enunciation, namely mimetic drama. As we shall see, this privileged place granted to this particular genre by the novel (because mixed), as well as by the Romantic work in its becoming, will curiously affect the expected dissolution. Hegel then sees the end of Romantic art in terms of prose and subjective virtuosity. He stresses the fact that the modern artist, because he has completely lost the immediate relation of natural interiority to given forms and figures, is necessarily the creator of mixtures which he directs as does the playwright his characters. And in fact, Romanticism (F. Schlegel in particular) considered drama as the true foundation of the novel. Thus, for the Romantics, only ancient drama serves as the ultimate model for the "complete work of art." But then why is there this return to a mode of mimetic representation so severely criticized by Plato in the *Republic?* In a certain way, it is the very absence of lyricism in the Romanticism of Iena which signals the answer to this query. In fact, the criterion for this total work of art resides essentially in the relationship that such a work has with itself. Now the construction of such a self-engendering work which contains its own theory can be imagined only in terms of a self-staging or self-production [*auto-mise-en-scène*]. The relationship the Romantic work entertains with itself, its self-reflexivity (F. Schlegel's *Gespräche über die Poesie* are a beautiful example of this), is not created from a diegetic mode, but on the contrary according to a mode of mediation: the mimetic mode. It seems to me that this is the reason for romanticism's privileging the particular genre of drama in the construction of a mixed work.

I

I will thus be concerned with two things in my reading of *Sylvie*: first, with the particular figure that the mixing of genres and styles provides in Nerval, and second, with the work of staging which must assure the text's relationship with itself. Let me begin by mentioning that, in order to work out their project for a work going beyond all generic differences, the Romantics did not rely solely on the ideal contained in the *poetry of nature*, but also on its decadent repetition manifested, for example, by the Alexandrian poets: a period of dissolution and effervescence. Thus, characterizing the "strange" period (both renovating and decadent) surrounding the tale of *Sylvie*, Nerval writes:

> It was an age in which activity, hesitation, and indolence were mixed up, together with dazzling Utopias, philosophies, and religious aspirations, vague enthusiasms, mild ideas of a Renaissance, weariness with past struggles; insecure optimisms—somewhat like the period of Peregrinus and Apullius.

> [c'était un mélange d'activité, d'hésitation et de paresse, d'utopies brillantes, d'aspirations philosophiques ou religieuses, d'enthousiasmes vagues, mêlés de certains instincts de renaissance; d'ennui des discordes passées, d'espoirs incertains, quelque chose comme l'époque de Pérégrinus et d'Apulée.]

And as one might expect after such a description, the action in *Sylvie* starts where the narrator—whom I shall call Nerval simply for convenience sake—during an outing at the theater, evokes his love for a star named Aurélia. If the space of *Sylvie* opens with this theatrical outing, it is because the narrative unfolds in a theatrical space. I will clarify the different scenes and the scenic levels of this space. In fact, already with the second chapter, "Adrienne," it is discovered that this love for an actress and the repeated frequentation of a theater are the function of a memory, of a forgotten scene from childhood. The fact that this memory is "half-dreamed," "represented" in a state of "half-sleep," only increases its *tableau*-like quality. Here is the memory itself: a large square of green in the courtyard of a castle where Adrienne, "the grandchild of one of the descendants of a family related to the ancient kings of France," in a voice imitating the "quavering tones of ancestors," sings an old ballad to her listeners, believing themselves "in paradise," while the light from the rising moon was falling on her alone, "isolated . . . (from) our attentive circle." The description has all the attributes of a theatrical stage (*scène*). When Nerval finally places a crown of "glistening leaves" on Adrienne's head, and then compares her to Dante's Beatrice, this early scene increasingly appears as the image of a literary scenario, of which it is the representation.

Articulating a double memory—on the one hand of Genre and of generics, and on the other, of the irruption of the difference in genres—the invocation of a celebration where social and temporal differences are abolished ("for this one day of festival she had been allowed to mix in our games" and "the young voices . . . imitate . . . the quavering tones of ancestors"), no doubt has a sense of reconciliation of differences in view. But, at the same time, this scene represents the origin of differences, and primarily, that of sexual difference. Indeed, when Adrienne and Nerval exchange a kiss, "an inexplicable confusion" takes hold of him. With this difference also emerges the *"double image"* between the ideal woman, the nun, and the real woman, Sylvie, between "Death—or the Dead Woman," as Nerval will say in "Artémis," and life, but also between social classes, places (city and country) and times (past and present).

Through this dual determination as a scene of reconciliation and of opening to all differences, this scene functions as the matrix for the play on the same and the other, on identity and difference, on the innumerable doubles which haunt this narrative.

Additional features of this original scene, or rather those relating to the textual matrix, can be gleaned from the other chapters of *Sylvie* concerning Adrienne. The ruins of the Abbey of Châalis, which, as Nerval tells us in *Angélique*, are situated above graves, and where, he says in *Sylvie*, "you (still) breathe a perfume of the Renaissance" as well as "an air of pagan allegory," set the background in chapter VII for the "countryside's solemnity." Having traversed the woods on "unfrequented roads," their pony flying "as if to some witches' Sabbath," Nerval and Sylvie's brother enter on St. Bartholomew's Eve into this "private festival" where "a sort of allegorical representation, in which some of the pupils of the neighboring convent are to participate," will take place. The play is thus performed during a celebration which is somewhat different from the Rousseauist and popular celebration common in Nerval. Our characters watch it in a no less allegorical setting. It is "a mystery play of ancient times" on the destruction of the world and spiritual rebirth. Now, the spirit armed with a flaming sword (the angel of death) who, after the destruction of the world rises up from the abyss to sing the glory of Christ, vanquisher of hell, is none other than Adrienne. Her family had devoted her to a religious life, and she now is reborn doubly transfigured through her costume and vocation. Thus, Adrienne, whose apparition is always dependent on the existence of a scene or stage, on a theatrical system, is transfigured, here among the ruins constructed above funerary monuments, into a pure spirit, an ideal woman. The original scene, therefore, is the place where one is put to death (burial in a convent, allegorical destruction of the world, etc.). The real character is put to death in order to allow her rebirth as an ideal. Before trying to answer the question of the relationship between this double operation of the scene and of the allegory, recall that Nerval, while retracing the details of this memory, wonders if they are actually real, or if he dreamed them. Necessarily, this scene thus takes on an ideal quality. And so does everything which comes from the matrix I have been trying to elucidate. In fact, everything that Nerval now uses to prove the truth of the event in question is but another memory of an allegorical nature:

> Sylvie's brother was a little drunk that evening. For a while we stopped at the keeper's house where I was greatly struck to see a swan with spread wings displayed above the door, and inside some tall cupboards of carved walnut, a large clock in its case, and trophies of bows and arrows of honor . . . But is the apparition of Adrienne as real as these details, as real as the indisputable existence of the Abbey of Châalis? Yet I am certain it was the keeper's son who took us into the hall where the play took place.

> [Le frère de Sylvie était un peu gris ce soir-là. Nous nous étions arrêtés quelques instants dans la maison du garde, où, ce qui m'a frappé beaucoup, il y avait un cygne éployé sur la porte, puis, au dedans, de hautes armoires en noyer sculpté, une grande horloge dans sa gaine, et des trophées d'arcs et de flèches d'honneur . . . Mais l'apparition d'Adrienne est-elle aussi vraie que ces détails et que l'existence incontestable de l'abbaye de Châalis? Pourtant c'est bien le fils du garde qui nous avait introduit dans la salle où avait lieu la représentation.]

Although this setting (anticipating the allegory) combined with the image of the flying swan tends to throw a cloud of doubt over the real existence of Adrienne, the spiritual meaning of the allegory is no less exact. "Perhaps this memory is an obsession!" Nerval explains, indicating that Adrienne may very well have been absent from the scene. But this absence guarantees all the better the spiritual meaning of the allegory. For this mechanism of putting to death in order to be reborn as idea clearly demonstrates that the spiritual meaning of the allegory is a function of the ruin of the original. In order to better illustrate this aspect of the scene, I would like to analyse the beginning of chapter V entitled "The Village."

During the festival, one evening after bringing Sylvie back to her village, Nerval wanders off into the forest where the scene becomes a sort of prehistoric landscape badly illuminated by the moon which hides the clouds from time to time. Nerval falls into a slumber in this landscape of "Druidical rocks" "which still hold the memory of the sons of Armen whom the Romans put to death." He is in the near vicinity of the convent of Saint-S . . . where he believes Adrienne to be, and has a dream which was eliminated from the final version of the tale. Where there is now just a simple dash, one formerly read the following:

> Two beloved figures were battling in my mind: the one seemed to come down from the stars, the other to rise from the earth. The

latter was saying, "I am simple and fresh as the flower from the fields," the other, "I am noble and pure like the immortal beauties conceived in the bosom of God."

[Deux figures aimées se combattaient dans mon esprit: l'une semblait descendre des étoiles et l'autre monter de la terre. La dernière disait: Je suis simple et fraîche comme les fleurs des champs; l'autre: Je suis noble et pure comme les beautés immortelles conçues dans le sein de Dieu.]

Finally, when he awakens, this landscape which retained him during the night by triggering a distant past (Nerval, from the sublime height represented by the Druidical boulders, is unable to distinguish the pond where he had met Sylvie the previous night), fully reveals its allegorical nature:

When I woke up, I gradually recognized the points near the spot where I had lost my way in the night. To my left, I saw the long line of the walls of the convent of Saint-S . . . , the Gens d'Armes hills, with the shattered ruins of the old Carolingian palace. Near it, above the tops of the trees, the tall ruins of the Abbey of Thiers outlined against the horizon its broken walls pierced with trefoils and ogives. Further on, the manorhouse of Pontarmé, still surrounded by its moat, began to reflect the first light of day, while to the south the tall keep of La Tournelle and the four towers of Bertrand-Fosse rose up on the first slopes of Montméliant.

[En me réveillant, je reconnus peu à peu les points voisins du lieu où je m'étais égaré dans la nuit. A ma gauche, je vis se dessiner la longue ligne des murs du couvent de Saint-S . . . , puis de l'autre côté de la vallée la butte aux Gens-d'Armes, avec les ruines ébréchées de l'antique résidence carlovingienne. Près de là, au-dessus des toffes de bois, les hautes masures de l'abbaye de Thiers découpaient sur l'horizon leurs pans de muraille percés de trèfles et d'ogives. Au delà, le manoir gothique de Pontarmé, entouré d'eau comme autrefois, refléta bientôt les premiers feux du jour, tandis qu'on voyait se dresser au midi le haut donjon de la Tournelle et les quatre tours de Bertrand-Fosse sur les premiers coteaux de Montméliant.]

The convent of Saint-S . . . which dominates this semiimaginary geography, and which Nerval believed for an instant to be "the one where Adrienne was," is situated in a mnemonic landscape whose traces bear witness to an irremediably lost past. The convent where Nerval presumes Adrienne to be, because of the nearby megalithic tombs, is a crypt for the ideal, an ideal that already presupposes the death of the original. This is what we learn in the last lines of the narrative from Sylvie:

Poor Adrienne! She died in the convent of Saint-S . . . about 1832.

[Pauvre Adrienne! elle est morte au couvent de Saint-S . . . , vers 1832.]

Let me thus clarify the nature of this scenic mechanism. It doesn't only demand the death of the original in order to prepare its resurrection as an ideal; the ideal itself is perceived as irretrievable. It belongs incontestably to the past. This means at least two things: the scenic matrix does not only assure the repeatability of the ideal through the death of the original, but is also constitutive of the allegory through the ruin of this same ideal. Now, this *double death,* being the condition of possibility of the allegorical meaning, cannot exist without a *third death* which destroys the allegorical meaning itself. This is confirmed in chapter VI, entitled "Othys."

This chapter relating the early morning visit by Sylvie and Nerval to her great-aunt is a veritable return to sources. Sylvie and Nerval, first of all, follow the Thève, "narrowing as it nears its source." Secondly, the aunt's home itself becomes, through the fire which Sylvie carries with her, the place for a reconciliation of elements. ("Upon the arrival of her niece, the house was ablaze. [*Sa nièce arrivant, c'était la feu dans la maison.*]" The house itself was constructed "of unequal blocks of sandstone covered with vines of hops and of Virginia creeper [. . . en pierre de grès inégales que revêtaient des treillages de houblon et de vigne vierge]." Let me recall, as Jean-Pierre Richard does, that sandstone is a mixture of petrified mud, a mixture of earth and humidity [Jean-Pierre Richard, *Poésie et profondeur* (Paris: Seuil, 1955)].) She thus declares her love for the little Parisian here. This return to the origin is at first a search for models, in this case models of lace. Sylvie: "Oh, yes, Aunt . . . if you have any old pieces, I could use them as patterns. [Ah! oui, la tante! . . . Dites donc, si vous en avez des morceaux de l'ancienne, cela me fera des modèles.]"

Quickly going up the stairs which lead to the aunt's bedroom, Sylvie and Nerval enter into a veritable sanctuary of memories from days past:

> In an oval gilt frame, hung at the head of the rustic bed, the portrait of a young man of the good old times smiled . . . his young bride, who could be seen from another medallion, attractive and mischievous-looking, lissom in her open corset laced with ribbons.

> [Le portrait d'un jeune homme du bon vieux temps souriait . . . dans un ovale au cadre doré, suspendu à la tête du lit rustique . . . sa jeune épouse, qu'on voyait dans un autre médaillon, attrayante, maligne, élancée dans son corsage ouvert à échelle de rubans.]

In this sanctuary the two lovers find the earlier model for first love in the form of a *double image.* Now with this discovery the idyllic reconciliation and return to origins start to take on a fantastic (*funambulesque*) quality.

Indeed, this love to which the aunt has remained faithful makes her seem like "the Funambules fairies who put wrinkled masks over their own charming faces, which they uncover at the end of the piece when the Temple of Love appears with its whirling sun shining with magic fires." Modeling themselves after this first love, Sylvie and Nerval themselves will not be able to escape the logic of representation, nor the loss of origin it implies. The transformation of the original model into a lowly street-play, certainly not lacking in charm, begins as soon as Sylvie and Nerval begin slipping on the wedding clothes of the aunt and her defunct husband. In the image of this couple from the past, in the image of the *double image*, they are transformed into the image of eternal youth which the old aunt's wrinkled mask hides. Doubles then appear in this *tableau vivant*, Sylvie being the same as the other, as the aunt, and, of course, conversely. The two lovers thus seem to challenge old age, death and the aunt's evocation of passing time. Now this synthesis of past and present, which, as theatrical synthesis, allows for the play of the same and the other, requires the death of the original in the double way I have shown. But it does so in an even more dramatic way than I have been able to demonstrate until now. When Nerval compares the production (through repetition) of the original model to a pictorial model, a painting by Greuze, the earlier model is consequently radically affected. Similarly, when their meal is transformed into a simulated wedding feast (Sylvie and Nerval become "bride and bridegroom for a whole summer morning") through the repetition of the naive wedding song of yesteryear, this scene is not the simple actualization of the aunt's memories. Instead, these memories mediating the love between Sylvie and Nerval are eclipsed, as if by the shadow of death, when the nuptial song, flowery and loving, is compared to the "Song of Songs" from Ecclesiastes. But isn't it the enormous bouquet of digitalis offered by Sylvie to her aunt which all the more eerily shrouds this scene, in that it announces the approaching death of the aunt? Although no repetition of an original model is possible without such a death, this tragic side of the tale does not hinder the repetition from taking on a carnavalesque appearance. On the contrary, when we learn of the aunt's death in chapter X, Nerval discovers what has happened to the wedding clothes of the old aunt:

> "Ah! Dear Aunty," says Sylvie, "she lent me the dress for the dance at Dammartin carnival two years ago. Poor Aunt, the next year she died!"
>
> She sighed and wept so that I could not ask her how she happened to go to a fancy-dress ball.

> ["Ah! la bonne tante," dit Sylvie, "elle m'avait prêté sa robe pour aller danser au carnaval à Dammartin, il y a de cela deux ans. L'année d'après, elle est morte, la pauvre tante!"
>
> Elle soupirait et pleurait, si bien que je ne pus lui demander par quelle circonstance elle était allée à un bal masqué.]

So the scene of a return to the origins, a return and repetition which are not accomplished without the death of that to which one returns, through the grotesque nature which they cannot avoid assuming, also represents the ruin of the eventual meaning of such an operation. The matrix I have tried to construct out of this memory concerning Adrienne is thus a scenic mechanism. This process of allowing allegorical meaning, and I would add, meaning itself, simultaneously invalidates it because it transforms its operation into a sort of theatrical farce, one not devoid of charm, be it tragic or not, but farce nonetheless. The mechanism in question is thus to be understood as insuring its own exposition (*mise-en-scène*), or rather its own mockery, a reflexive operation by which the *output* of the matrix is disappropriated, incomplete and unaccomplished. This machine, as we have seen, not only engenders difference, but also organizes the whole play between the same and the other which haunts our narrative. Let me now go on to the analysis of these effects.

II

It is in a semidream state that Nerval finds "the memory of Adrienne, a flower of the night efflorescent in the moon's glimmer, flesh-colored and fair phantom gliding over the green grasses half-bathed in white vapors." It resembles a "pencil drawing blurred by time that had been converted into a picture, like those old sketches of the masters you admire in some museum and then you find, somewhere else, the dazzling original." It can be seen to represent the bud, as Nerval says, of this love for a woman of the theater which overcame him every evening during the performance. Thus, the image-bud, the figure which cannot be born without the death of the original, engenders a new original which comes after, and which is derivative of the former image. Being no more than a blurred drawing or sketch in relation to a stunning original to come, the image of Adrienne engenders the original of Aurélia. For her, Nerval appears every evening "in the proscenium boxes in the role of an ardent wooer." The apparition of this theatrical star illuminates the empty space of the stage and gives life to a performance in a theater where Nerval himself, in the role of the suitor, lines up with the actors. "In her I felt myself alive, and she seemed to live for me alone." Now, Aurélia, her natural beauty and the life she incarnates are but a function of the stage lights and of the artificial light of the chandelier. With all of its properties, the stage serves as a "magic mirror" which beautifies and idealizes what it reflects. But the memory of Adrienne reveals to Nerval that Aurélia is but a derived original of the image-bud, and that she is thus, as he was able to say of himself, but "a living tomb." The ideal of Aurélia is not only its own tomb; to the image of Adrienne it is also the crypt of this latter, as dead. This inspires Nerval with the following thought:

To love a nun in the form of an actress! . . . but what if they were one and the same!—

[Aimer une religieuse sous la forme d'une actrice! . . . et si c'était la même!—]

Indeed, if the ideal is *per se* exchangeable (contrary to the real woman), the substitution of an actress for a nun would imply that the difference between the same and the other is without difference. Because of the repetition without difference, the actress could well be the same as the nun. But didn't we see that the function of the matrix was to make possible the repetition of the same by the simultaneous production of the differential other? If the other is the same, where then is the difference? Before picking up on this question a bit later, let me continue the analysis of this original which is the substitute for an "empty image," for an early image which Nerval pursues.

In chapter XIII Nerval returns to Paris and runs to the theater to succumb, once again, to the charms of his actress. He abruptly leaves Paris for Germany to "try and get (his) feelings into order." For this, he undertakes "to put into poetic action the love of the painter Colonna for the fair Laura, whom her parents made a nun, and whom he loved until death." This scenario is to put the theatrical ideal into a play to be performed in "the purgatorial space" theater represents for Nerval. Aurélia accepts the starring role in this play. At this moment Nerval lets it be known that he was the stranger who sent her the adulatory letters. The test fails, for Adrienne isn't the same as the nun, and she does not recognize Nerval as being the little Parisian of before. When another chance comes he makes another effort to clarify his love for Aurélia, and once again in juxtaposing several scenes, Nerval suffers defeat one more time. When Nerval convinces the company he is accompanying as "gentleman poet" to give a performance in Senlis and Dammartin, Nerval tries yet once again to verify that the actress and the nun are one and the same (and, I might add, to reassure himself that he is also one and the same).

I had planned to take Aurélia to the château near Orry to the same square of green where for the first time I saw Adrienne.—She showed no emotion.

[J'avais projeté de conduire Aurélie au château, près d'Orry, sur la même place verte où pour la première fois j'avais vu Adrienne. Nulle émotion ne parut en elle.]

Since Aurélia didn't seem to recognize the area, Nerval reveals his plan to her, and the actress clearly admits that she is not the same person.

You expect me to say, "The actress is the same person as the nun; you are simply looking for drama, that's all, and the end eludes you."

[Vous attendez que je vous dise: "La comédienne est la même que
la religieuse; vous cherchez un drame, voilà tout, et le dénoûement
vous échappe."]

That evening Nerval notices that Aurélia has a liking for the stage-
manager. It is then that he must accept the fact that his love is for another,
that she is not the same, just as the one that Aurélia loves is other than
he. Thus, this scenario in the image of the memory of Adrienne, instead
of engendering the same, only produces the other. Instead of insuring a
repetition without difference, it creates difference. It gives birth to the other
in the scenario of the same.

The day Aurélia performs at Dammartin, Nerval brings Sylvie to the
performance. Sylvie has met Adrienne, and Nerval encourages her to tell
him

> if she did not think the actress like someone she knew.
> "Whom do you mean?"
> "Do you remember Adrienne?"
> She burst out laughing and said, "What an idea!" Then, as if
> reproving herself, she sighed and added, "Poor Adrienne! She
> died in the convent of Saint-S . . . about 1832."

[si elle ne trouvait pas que l'actrice ressemblait à une personne
qu'elle avait connue déjà. "A qui donc?—Vous souvenez-vous
d'Adrienne?"

Elle partit d'un grand éclat de rire en disant: "Quelle idée!" Puis,
comme se le reprochant, elle reprit en soupirant: "Pauvre
Adrienne! elle est morte au couvent de Saint-S . . . , vers 1832."]

Thus the hope that another, here Sylvie, would recognize Aurélia as being
the same fails and seems to put an end to any chance for a possible identity.
Sylvie's burst of laughter implies that Aurélia cannot be the same person.
With this failure, will the narrative then open up into what is called the
recognition of the other and of the real? Far from that, because the very
death of the model will keep the narrative within the framework of the
specular of the same and the other, within the framework of a difference
of the same.

III

Thus leaving this theater where he appeared every evening, Nerval does
not get back to reality. On the contrary, he joins a circle of friends from
whom he also departs, but first by way of a reading room. Mechanically
leafing through a paper, he discovers that on that very day the *Fête du
Bouquet provincial* was taking place in Senlis. This bit of news awakens in
him the memory of a childhood scene: the performance of a provincial
festival which is but the repetition "from age to age of a Druid festival that

had survived the new monarchies and novel religions." This final memory leads to the memory of Adrienne, which makes him realize that he loved a nun in the form of an actress. "But let us get back to reality," as Nerval says.

> Why have I for three years forgotten Sylvie, whom I loved so much? She is waiting for me. Who would marry Sylvie? She is so poor!

> [Et Sylvie que j'aimais tant, pourquoi l'ai-je oubliée depuis trois ans . . . Elle m'attend encore . . . Qui l'aurait épousée? elle est si pauvre!]

Parenthesizing his love for Aurélia, who is but the derived original of an earlier image and who is part of a series of substitutions, Nerval turns toward the other one he had forgotten and who probably must have remained the same. Not being the original in a chain of substitutions, Sylvie is to be unique and should not have changed. Yet, if she remained the same, she remained identical with herself. Thus at the outset this presumed identity equally opens into the logic of substitutions so that the question will not only concern whether she has been able to stay the same, but also whether she ever was identical to herself. Adrienne and the actress are a pair, but they are principally the same, while Sylvie who is unique constitutes a pair when she differs from herself.

> What is she doing at this moment? Is she asleep? . . . No, she is not asleep; today is the festival of the bow, the only celebration of the year when you dance all night. —She's there . . .
>> What time is it?
>> I had no watch.

> [A cette heure, que fait-elle? Elle dort . . . Non, elle ne dort pas; c'est aujourd'hui la fête de l'arc, la seule de l'année où l'on danse toute la nuit. —Elle est à la fête . . .
>> Quelle heure est-il?
>> Je n'avais pas de montre.]

Musing about Sylvie has stopped time. She has become a nocturnal figure during a festival which could well be the same festival where he met Adrienne. Now, the attribute *nocturnal* is typical of the latter. But Sylvie's identity is problematized with "A Voyage to Cythèra" where Nerval continues his narrative of memories about Sylvie.

> Some years had gone by. The time when I had met Adrienne in front of the château was already only a memory from childhood. I was at Loisy again, at the time of the annual festival.

> [Quelques années s'étaient écoulées: l'epoque où j'avais rencontré Adrienne devant le château n'était plus déjà qu'un souvenir d'enfance. Je me retrouvai à Loisy au moment de la fête patronale.]

Skipping several years, Nerval comes to another festival which, if not the same as the other, closely resembles it. It is this resemblance which will lead to a progressive transformation of the different into the same.

The festival culminates in a meal given on a shady island in the middle of a pond. The island contains an oval-shaped temple built at the end of the eighteenth century, originally dedicated to Urania. This modern renovated ruin was to serve as the banqueting hall, as such conceived in the image of a painting, for "perhaps the crossing of the lake had been devised in order to recall Watteau's *Voyage à Cythère*." It is this resemblance which begins the blurring between the same and the other, between Sylvie and Adrienne.

Let me first recall that, in the coach which takes him to Loisy, Nerval, on Flanders road, remembers "a path lined with apple trees whose blossoms (he has) often seen burst in the night like stars of the earth." These stars of earth correspond, in fact, to those which, occurring in the dream cut from chapter V, designated Sylvie. The celestial star was Adrienne. These two stars can be superimposed on the two Venuses, the Venus Urania and the Venus Pandemos which, as Poulet has shown, structure our narrative. If there is a connection between Sylvie, the star of the earth, and Aphrodite Pandemos, what is she doing in a temple dedicated to Urania, to the celestial star, to Adrienne, and in addition placed in the atmosphere of a painting perhaps conceived from *Poliphilos' Dream* by Francesco Colonna and evoking the voyage to the Orient? Why would she be in this temple if not to be transformed into the other, and to be marked with celestial attributes?

> All the boats reached land. The flower basket, ceremoniously carried, occupied the center of the table and everybody sat down, the most favored men next to the girls. . . . That was why I found myself next to Sylvie. . . .
>
> A surprise had been arranged by those who had organized the festival. At the end of the meal we saw a wild swan which had been held captive under the flowers until then fly up from the depths of the huge basket. With its strong wings it lifted up a tangle of garlands and crowns of flowers, finally dispersing them on all sides. While the bird flew joyfully into the last gleams of the sun, we caught the flower-crowns at random and each man instantly decorated the brow of the girl beside him. I was lucky enough to get one of the finest and, smiling, Sylvie this time allowed me to kiss her more tenderly than before. I understood that I had erased the memory of another occasion.
>
> [Toutes les barques abordèrent en peu de temps. La corbeille portée en cérémonie occupa le centre de la table, et chacun prit place, les plus favorisés auprès des jeunes filles. . . . Ce fut la cause qui fit que je me retrouvai près de Sylvie. . . .

Une surprise avait été arrangée par les ordonnateurs de la fête. A la fin du repas, on vit s'envoler du fond de la vaste corbeille un cygne sauvage, jusque-là captif sous les fleurs, qui, de ses fortes ailes, soulevant le lacis de guirlandes et de couronnes, finit par les disperser de tous côtés. Pendant qu'il s'élançait joyeux vers les dernières lueurs du soleil, nous rattrapions au hasard les couronnes dont chacun parait aussitôt le front de sa voisine. J'eus le bonheur de saisir une des plus belles, et Sylvie, souriante, se laissa embrasser cette fois plus tendrement que l'autre. Je compris que j'effaçais ainsi le souvenir d'un autre temps.]

Captive under the flowers of the earth up to that point, Sylvie, in this temple consecrated to the celestial Venus, like the swan, bounds off toward the last gleams of the setting sun. The crown on Sylvie's head achieves her renaissance as a celestial star. Thus transformed into the other, into Adrienne, she evidently appears completely different to Nerval:

My admiration for her at this moment was undivided, she had become so beautiful! She was no longer the little village girl I had scorned for someone older and more schooled in the graces of society. Everything about her had improved . . . her smile had something Athenian about it as it suddenly illumined her irregular and placid features. I admired this countenance, worthy of antique art in the midst of the irregular baby-faces of her companions. Her delicately tapering hands, her arms which had grown whiter as they rounded, her lithe figure, all made her quite another creature from the girl I had seen before. I could not resist telling her how different from herself I found her.

[Je l'admirai cette fois sans partage, elle était devenue si belle! Ce n'était plus cette petite fille de village que j'avais dédaignée pour une plus grande et plus faite aux grâces du monde. Tout en elle avait gagné . . . son sourire, éclairant tout à coup des traits réguliers et placides, avait quelque chose d'athénien. J'admirais cette physiognomie de l'art antique au milieu des minois chiffonées de ses compagnes. Ses mains délicatement allongées, ses bras qui avaient blanchi en s'arrondissant, sa taille dégagée, la faisaient tout autre que je ne l'avais vue. Je ne pus m'empêcher de lui dire combien je la trouvais différente d'elle-même.]

Crowned as Adrienne had been before, reborn after having forgotten her celestial features, the star of the earth, different from herself, starts to resemble the celestial star. Transformed into an ancient ideal, and thus belonging, like Adrienne, to ancient families, the indescribable Athenian qualities which characterized her brings Sylvie even closer to that urban quality which Aurélia represents; it completes the process which separated her socially from her companions. Thus, in order to be reborn from forgetfulness, Sylvie will have to die one more time in order to become another, different from herself. Different from herself she is the same, the same as the other.

IV

But Sylvie is not only *not* herself, she differs as well from herself in that she is *no longer* the same.

Nerval escapes this dreamlike world which had thrust him into the world of memories representing this ancient mystery play at the Abbey of Châalis. Upon reaching Loisy "on unfrequented roads," he again finds Sylvie at the ball, Sylvie whom he had not seen for years. Driving her back at the dawn of a gloomy day, he learns that she has changed, that she is *no longer* the same person. That, evidently, abruptly halts all repetition.

> Do you remember the day we put on my aunt's wedding clothes?
> . . . The illustrations in the book (*La Nouvelle Héloïse*, R. G.) also showed lovers in old prints of yesteryear, so that for me you were Saint-Preux, and I saw myself in Julie. Ah! Why didn't you come back to me then?

> [Vous souvenez-vous du jour où nous avons revêtu les habits de noces de la tante? . . . Les gravures du livre présentaient aussi les amoureux sous de vieux estampes du temps passé, de sorte que pour moi vous étiez Saint-Preux, et je me retrouvais dans Julie. Ah, que n'êtes-vous revenue alors!]

The image which Sylvie once had of herself as well as of her little Parisian no longer coincides with the present. In reproaching Sylvie for not realizing she is an ancient nymph, Nerval thus recognizes that she is no longer the same as his memory had retained her. If and only if she had resembled this other would she have remained the same. Now, the thing which kept Sylvie from coinciding with that other was precisely the "empty image" of this "fatal spectre" which misled Nerval. One side of the *double image* hinders the other from coinciding with itself. One part of this image always contaminates the process of identity with the other.

Here is the moment to discuss what Poulet (and others) have understood to be the "essential identity" of these two images, of the *double image*. Nerval, in the last chapter of *Sylvie*, announces:

> Ermononville! . . . You have lost your love stars which shone for me with a double light. Now blue, now rose-colored like the deceptive star of Aldebaran, it was Adrienne or Sylvie—two halves of a single love. One was the sublime ideal, the other the sweet reality.

> [Ermononville! . . . tu as perdu ta seule étoile, qui chatoyait pour moi d'un double éclat. Tout à tour bleue et rose comme l'astre

trompeur d'Aldébaran, c'était Adrienne ou Sylvie,—c'étaient les deux moitiés d'un seul amour. L'une était l'idéal sublime, l'autre la douce réalité.]

One would of course be tempted to apply Freud's development concerning love life to this double image of one love. But how could this simulacrum of antiquity, this place of doubling and repetition which for Nerval is Valois—"land where the ancient Idylls still flower,—translated once again from Gessner!"—how could it still be under the sign of one star's resistance to splitting? Or rather, how could this *double image*, in this place of repetition, ever have been *one*? All the more so since this double image is not symmetrical? One image, that of Adrienne, always prevails over the other. One image of this *double image* is in fact eccentric with respect to the structure of doubling representative of the two halves of the same love. The image of Adrienne, as we have seen, is at the origin of *the* difference, and consequently, of the *double image* itself. It is this image which sets off the entire play on the same and the other, on identity and its loss which we just saw. In other words, the scenic mechanism tied only to Adrienne's name is in excess with relationship to the specular totality of the same and the other which it engenders and which at the same time makes it impossible.

Let us return again to Nerval's attempts to get Sylvie to accept the image he has of her:

"Save me!" I concluded, "I am coming back to you for ever."

She looked at me tenderly . . .

At that moment our conversation was interrupted by violent shouts of laughter.

["Sauvez-moi!" ajoutai-je, "je reviens à vous pour toujours."

Elle tourna vers moi ses regards attendris . . .

En ce moment, notre entretien fut interrompu par de violents éclats de rire.]

If this attempt fails (and notice that Nerval will not have the same chance again), it is because of the violent laughter of Sylvie's brother (is it the Sylvain of chapter XIII, i.e. Sylvie's other?). It is he who brings the gallant to the ball, this latter being none other, we learn later, than Nerval's foster brother, his double, in short, the other. The other (but which other, then?) interrupts, through the violence of a laugh, any assimilation of Sylvie to her own image, which is that of the other. Just as Sylvie will interrupt through her outburst of laughter any possible identity between Adrienne and Aurélia, between the other and *herself*, this outburst closes all repetition, all return. This has multiple consequences. For them, let us read chapter XI entitled "Return."

The preceding chapter, "Big Curly," had already insisted on the fact that Sylvie was no longer the same. Her room has changed, she has become a glove maker, etc. The chapter "Return" continues this problematic by showing that Sylvie no longer reads Rousseau (she reads Walter Scott now), and does not read the landscape as a function of the past and of her childhood. Thus, the landscape is no longer the same. Upon reaching the ruins of Châalis, Nerval leads Sylvie into the room of the château where he had heard Adrienne sing:

> "Oh, do let me hear you!" I said to her, "Let your dear voice echo beneath these roofs and drive away the spirit that torments me, whether it be from heaven or from hell!"
> She repeated the words and the song after me . . .
> "It's very sad," she said.

> ["Oh! que je vous entende!" lui dis-je; "que votre voix chérie résonne sous ces voûtes et en chasse l'esprit qui me tourmente, fût-il divin ou bien fatal!—" Elle répéta les paroles et le chant après moi . . . "—C'est bien triste!" me dit-elle.]

Without echo, this repetition reveals that the return to the place of the fantasm is but the very impossibility of return. In fact, the ruins, as memory traces of the landscape, have stopped signifying, and Nerval meets only empty signs, ruins of signs, or what I have called the ruin of allegory. The crisis in question dates at least from the visit to the uncle's house at Montagny. It begins with the chapter entitled "Ermononville."

> Everything seemed to be in the same state as of old; only, I had to go to the farmer's house to get the key of the front door.

> [Tout semblait dans le même état qu'autrefois; seulement il fallut aller chez le fermier pour avoir la clef de la porte.]

Once he has finished the visit to the house, a house whose interior now only points to a past without power over the present, Nerval feels the need "to see Sylvie again, the only living and still youthful face that linked me to the district." Sylvie, however, since she is no longer the same, is not able to give a supplemental meaning to these ruins of the past.

This impossibility of giving the past meaning, of making it signify, will set off a crisis of recognition. (Chapter XII, "Father Dodu," is especially significant here, for it shows us that not only is the tomb of Rousseau empty, but even his memory is deformed. The only thing which remains of Rousseau in this countryside is his double, Father Dodu, who ends up transforming Rousseau into Socrates.) The crisis becomes unavoidable with the erasure of nature's signs:

> For a moment I was nearly lost, for the sign-posts marking the different roads in various places had lost their lettering.

> [Un instant je risquai de me perdre, car les poteaux dont les palettes annoncent diverses routes n'offrent plus, par endroits, que des caractères effacés.]

In broad daylight, this once familiar countryside becomes unrecognizable. Returning, because of the disappearance of the marks and characters of writing, to this former unsocial nature, Nerval runs the risk of losing himself in this landscape. What is upsetting here is that the loss of the possibility of repeating an identical trace leads not only to the ruin of any possible meaning, but even to the ruin of any possible recognition.

> Finally, leaving the "Desert" to my left, I arrived at the dancing-ring, . . . All the memories of philosophical antiquity, revived by the former owner of the estate, crowded back on me at the sight of this picturesque realization of *Anarcharsis* and *Emile*.
>
> When I saw the water of the lake glittering . . . I . . . recognized . . . the "Temple of Philosophy" which its originator had not been fortunate enough to finish. . . . This unfinished building is already no more than a ruin, with ivy gracefully festooning it, and the brambles invading its broken steps. As a child I had seen there those festivals at which girls dressed in white came to receive prizes for study and good conduct . . . Fortunately the privet of Virgil still flourishes, as if to support the master's words inscribed above the door: *Rerum cognoscere causas!* . . . Here are the island poplars and the tomb of Rousseau, empty of his ashes. Oh wise man! You gave us the milk of the strong and we were too weak to profit from it. We have forgotten your lessons, which our fathers knew, and we have lost the meaning of your words, the last echo of the ancient wisdom. But do not let us despair and, as you did in your last moment, let us turn our eyes to the sun.

> [Enfin, laissant le "Désert" à gauche, j'arrivai au rond-point de la danse, . . . Tous les souvenirs de l'antiquité philosophique, ressuscités par l'ancien possesseur du domaine, me revenaient en foule devant cette réalisation pittoresque de l'*Anarcharsis* et de l'*Emile*.
>
> Lorsque je vis briller les eaux du lac . . . je reconnus . . . le *Temple de la philosophie*, que son fondateur n'a pas eu le bonheur de terminer. . . . Cet édifice inachevé n'est déjà plus qu'une ruine, le lierre le festonne avec grâce, la ronce envahit les marches disjointes. Là, tout enfant, j'ai vu des fêtes ou les jeunes filles vêtues de blanc venaient recevoir des prix d'étude et de sagesse . . . Heureusement le troème de Virgile fleurit encore, comme pour appuyer la parole du maître inscrite au-dessus de la porte: *Rerum cognoscere causas!* . . .
>
> Voici les peupliers de l'île, et la tombe de Rousseau, vide de ses cendres. O sage! tu nous avais donné le lait des forts et nous étions trop faibles pour qu'il pût nous profiter. Nous avons oublié les leçons que savaient nos pères, et nous avons perdu le sens de ta parole, dernier écho des sagesses antiques. Pourtant ne déses-

pérons pas, et, comme tu fis à ton suprême instant, tournons nos
yeux vers le soleil.]

Before showing that this glance at the sun, instead of insuring truth,
unleashes madness, I would first note that these ruins of ruins once (allegorically) signified wisdom. But now, all that they signify is the ruin of
philosophy, ruined thought and the loss of thought. Of course this loss is
that of its allegorical signification, but also that of all thought. This is what
Nerval perceives, what he painfully undergoes. He realizes that the erasure
of difference coincides with the collapse of the same, and not with its return.
The interruption of the repetition of the same brought about through the
disappearance of differential marks causes the mnemonic landscape, of
allegorical signification, to return to "a savage unsocial state," indeed, even
to in-difference, to an undifferentiated state. Thus, a tomb without ashes
is left, just as the convent of Saint-S . . . no longer contained the living
Adrienne: an empty sign. However, the collapse of distinctions, and consequently a collapse of the same, of recognition and of consciousness, *is*
madness.

Madness *in* this particular text is in fact reliant on this apparently
abyssal play between the same and the other, the abortion of which we
have been able to witness. This play, what seems to be the very condition
of all identity, and consequently all consciousness as recognition, causes
an emptying of the sign, a halt of return and repetition, the contrary of all
thought. But the play between the same and the other, its almost abyssal
specularity, is *already* madness. Nerval writes:

> To love a nun in the form of an actress! . . . but what if they were
> one and the same!—It was enough to drive you mad! That fasci-
> nation is fatal in which the unknown leads you on like a will-o'-
> the-wisp hovering over the reeds in still water.

> [Aimer une religieuse sous la forme d'une actrice! . . . et si c'était
> la même!—Il y a de quoi devenir fou! C'est un entraînement fatal
> où l'inconnu vous attire comme le feu follet fuyant sur les joncs
> d'une eau morte.]

In this way the identical image reflected by all women, the image which
allows for the identification of the same from the different and which un-
derlies all cognizance of the other as recognition (of the same), already
brings on madness. It brings it on all the more so because this cognizance
of the other through the same always turns into its specular contrary: the
appearance of nonidentity, absence of recognition and cognition. Thus, the
double image, and all its possible implication as "essential identity," turn
into a total absence of identity. In fact, the celestial star and the star of the
earth (even idealized) gradually turn into a water star. In the chapter "The
Ball of Loisy," where we learn that Sylvie is no longer the same, we read:

I offered to take her home. It was now broad daylight but the sky was overcast. The Thève murmured on our left, leaving pools of still water at each winding in its course, and here white and yellow water lilies bloomed and the frail embroidery of the water flowers spread out like daisies.

[Je lui offris de l'accompagner chez elle. Il faisait grand jour, mais le temps était sombre. La Thève bruissait à notre gauche, laissant à ses coudes des remous d'eau stagnante où s'épanouissaient les nénuphars jaunes et blancs, où éclatait comme des pâquerettes la frêle broderie des étoiles d'eau.]

Sparkling like a will-o'-the-wisp on still water, the water star has affected Nerval, even if it hasn't yet fatally intoxicated him:

The fields were covered with stooks and hayricks whose odor went to my head without inebriation, as had at other times the fresh scent of the woods and thorn thickets.

[Les plaines étaient couvertes de javelles et de meules de foin, dont l'odeur me portait à la tête sans m'enivrer, comme faisait autrefois la fraîche senteur des bois et des halliers d'épines fleuries.]

But the pull of the water flowers can no longer be doubted with the chapter "Ermononville," where, as we saw, the unhinging of the faculty of thought through the disappearance of identical signs occurs.

I saw the château again, the peaceful waters surrounding it, the waterfall murmuring among the rocks, and that raised walk connecting the two parts of the village marked with four dovecoats at its corners, and the lawn that stretches out beyond like a savannah overlooked by shady slopes; Gabrielle's tower is reflected from afar in the waters of an artificial lake starry with ephemeral flowers; the water foams, the insects hum . . . You must shun the treacherous air it exhales and gain the dusty rocks of the "Desert" and then the moors where the purple broom relieves the green of the ferns.

[J'ai revu le château, les eaux paisibles qui le bordent, la cascade qui gémit dans les roches, et cette chaussées réunissant les deux parties du village, dont quatre colombiers marquent les angles, la pelouse qui s'étend au-delà comme une savane, dominée par des coteaux ombreux; la tour de Gabrielle se reflète de loin sur les eaux d'un lac factice étoilé de fleurs éphémères! l'écume bouillonne, l'insecte bruit . . . Il faut échapper à l'air perfide qui s'exhale en gagnant les grès poudreux du désert et les landes où la bruyère rose relève le vert des fougères.]

The abolition of Gabrielle's tower, its reflection and fall into the calm waters of the lake, convert the celestial star (to which Nerval's soul aspired) into an ephemeral water star which, like a will-o'-the-wisp, runs along the surface of the water to lead the solitary stroller astray. Just as in the following chapter where, later visiting the now remodeled room that belonged to Sylvie, Nerval is "anxious to leave the room, for it contained nothing of the past," he tries to escape from the treacherous air, from the will-o'-the-wisp (*feu follet*), from madness (*folie*).

In "Last Leaves" Nerval notes down that "the ponds, dug at such great expense, are expanses of stagnant water disdained by the swan." This remark follows the evocation of sadness caused by the memory of the "fugitive traces of a time when the natural was affected." Madness is thus not only the erasure of writing, it is also the mutation of the swan (*cygne*) into an empty sign (*signe*), into roving signs, just like the will-o'-the-wisp upon the stagnant water of a countryside where Adrienne has died in her convent, where Rousseau's tomb has been emptied of its ashes, and where Sylvie is missing from her rightful place because she is no longer the same.

> How solitary it all is and how sad! Sylvie's enchanting gaze, her wild running, her happy cries, once gave such charm to the places I have just been through.
>
> [Que tout cela est solitaire et triste! Le regard enchanté de Sylvie, ses courses folles, ses cris joyeux, donnaient autrefois tant de charme aux lieux que je viens de parcourir!]

Sylvie, the daughter of fire (*fille du feu*), once a lively young girl (*fille follette*), is henceforth a will-o'-the-wisp (*feu follet*). The madness (*folie*) here is double. There is the madness of the origin, the good madness, the good wildness, on the one hand, and on the other, there is the loss of the origin, the will-o'-the-wisp, savagery, the violence of an undifferentiated nature. There is the good madness of full signs and mastered difference of the same, and empty vagabond signs which subvert repetition. Don't these empty and hollow signs, however, represent the finalization of the idealizing movement which characterizes good madness? And doesn't the privilege of repetition without difference fall on them? The empty signs which appear in *Sylvie* as a result of the loss of the only star which sparkled with a double shine, like the deceitful star of Aldebaran, are in fact *the* condition of possibility of good madness, of the madness of identity. Only an empty sign is a discontinuous unity capable of being repeated identically. *Sylvie*, consequently, can be read as a tale about the cyclical logic whereby the sign becoming arbitrary is the condition of possibility of symbolic and allegorical signification; or also as a tale about the erasure of natural writing as artificial writing, and the natural violence of the established sign. But that must not concern us here. Of utmost importance, however, is the perfect symmetry and specular relationship between the logic of the same and its collapse.

Of course I have not exhausted all the reflexive categories. Such a categorization is theoretically possible, the specularity being infinite, and not abyssal. Nor have I exhausted the relationships between the same and the other, between the madness of plenitude and that of absence, to be allowed rigorously to postulate the specularity of the text of *Sylvie*. Remember, however, that this tale is constructed formally so that its chapters echo each other, sometimes like a circle. Thematically, on the other hand, one has simply to recall the reflection of the tower of Gabrielle in the lake, the magic mirror on the stage, the double shining of the star, etc., but especially the calculated circularity of "A Voyage to Cythèra." Perhaps imagined to echo Watteau's painting, the crossing of the lake, through its reflection in the water, again doubles the model. "This graceful *theoria*, a revival from the days of antiquity, was reflected in the calm waters of the pool separating it from the banks of the island. . . . [Cette gracieuse *théorie* renouvelée des jours antiques se reflétait dans les eaux calmes de l'étang qui la séparait du bord de l'île]." This infinite specularity, this ensemble of reflexive determinations, that is what I have called the madness *of* the text. "Last Leaves" does not escape from this madness. Instead of interrupting the reflexive logic of the preceding thirteen chapters, it *reflects* exactly as last leaf the pages facing it. But what is this last chapter about? Nerval describes the loss of illusions, the teachings of experience and sad homecomings. Now, this chapter also reports the activity of writing, and represents the place where the text reflects its own production. The "Last Leaves" begin this way:

> Such are the delusions which charm and beguile us in the morning of life. I have tried to set them down without too much order, but many hearts will understand mine.

> [Telles sont les chimères qui charment et égarent au matin de la vie. J'ai essayé de les fixer sans beaucoup d'ordre, mais bien des coeurs me comprendront.]

For this double madness, for the loss of natural writing through the erasure of identical marks, Nerval here substitutes the signs of a writing which will be capable of mastery. Reflexive, controlling writing which will master itself adds to and completes the mirror-like structure of the text. In other words, the madness *of* writing comes to complete the madness *of* the text. It is its truth.

> Illusions fall, like the husks of a fruit, one after another, and what is left is experience. It has a bitter taste, but there is something tonic in its sharpness.

[Les illusions tombent l'une après l'autre, comme les écorces d'un fruit, et le fruit, c'est l'expérience. Sa saveur est amère; elle a pourtant quelque chose d'âcre qui fortifie.]

V

Such is this text's unity. It is a specular totality which is held together by the whole of its reflexive determinations. Such a textual totality, where the reflection is continually brought to a higher power and multiplies in an infinite series of mirrors (to quote from fragment 116 of the *Athenaeum*), is the product of a chemical mixture of genres and styles, of the passage from literature to Literature, to literality, to the textual, etc. If one must trace the history of the mixture of genres back to the Greek Cynics and to the Roman *satura*, I would suggest nonetheless another origin here, the mixture of prose and of tragedy in the Scriptures. Religious history, and consequently secular, clearly impeded the formation of literary genres from its inception. In fact, everything in the Scriptures which can still be separated into genres first belongs to a global order. In accordance with the Auerbachian interpretation, the radical mixing of styles and of genres (Auerbach calls it the "levels of style") that nineteenth-century realism brought about is not only the completion and fulfillment of Romanticism, but even more the fulfillment of the figural representation of the Middle Ages, where the mixture of genres and styles had already culminated in a tragic realism. Although Auerbach uses in *Mimesis* and in his article "Figura" the notion of *figura* solely for analysing the representation of reality in late antiquity and during the Middle Ages, his analysis of realism in the nineteenth century does not in the least narrow the scope of figural interpretation. On the contrary, it increases its effectiveness to a maximum. One would simply have to compare the two types of analysis to prove it. It is true for Auerbach that figural interpretation is the characteristic mark of aging cultures. Thus its distinguishing feature is something extremely old through which these cultures return to their origin. I would emphasize however the following point, the most important for our problematic: the difference between *figura* and both symbol and allegory. The *figura* is a function of both a representation and a vertical and religious construction of the world (*religiös vertikalen Aufbaus*). It differs from the symbol and from allegory because these animate a purely spiritual, ahistorical interpretation. The *figura*, on the contrary, is always necessarily historical in the following way:

> Figural prophecy implies the interpretation of one worldly event through another; the first signifies the second, the second fulfills the first. Both remain historical events; yet both, looked at in this way, have something provisional and incomplete about them; they point to one another and both point to something in the future, something still to come, which will be the actual, real, and defin-

itive event. This is true not only of Old Testament prefiguration, which points forward to the incarnation and the proclamation of the gospel, but also of these latter events, for they too are not the ultimate fulfillment, but themselves a promise of the end of time and the true kingdom of God.

But what is this coming event, on which the fullness of meaning of those intra-historical events depends. Auerbach defines it in the following passage with relation to the *figura*:

> Thus the figures are not only tentative; they are also the tentative form of something eternal and timeless; they point not only to the concrete future, but also to something that always has been and always will be; they point to something which is in need of interpretation, which will indeed be fulfilled in the concrete future, but which is at all times present, fulfilled in God's providence, which knows no difference of time. This eternal thing is already figured in them and thus they are both tentative fragmentary reality, and veiled eternal reality.

The following question should thus concern us here: how does the *figura* provide unity for the mixture of genres and styles? Without touching on the delicate problem of its relationship to the Hegelian *Gestalt* as the living incarnation of the concept in a history, the *figura* confers unity to the mixture of genres in being their transgression toward that which founds them beyond their separation. What founds them as their common essence is a figure whose *figura* takes place until the immutable and always already prefigured Eternal is accomplished at the end of history. Without being the unity to come, but based upon it, and replacing it, the unity that the *figura* confers on the mixture of genres and styles thus necessarily remains disproportionate to itself. Now, the Romanticism of Iena had already conceived chemical mixing (which Novalis has affirmed destroyed all figures) as producing the religious. It is true that it was to be the result of the mixing of philosophy and poetry. But for the Romantics, for Schelling in particular, the exemplary historical figure of such a mixture is, as for Auerbach, the *Divine Comedy* of Dante. The difference between Auerbach's figural interpretation and the religious synthesis performed by the Romantic *menstrum universale* is however only a function of the double notion of religion which characterized Romanticism itself. On the one hand, there is the religion of F. Schlegel and of Schelling, on the other the Christianity of Novalis. Now, this double conception of the religious, its two Romantic sides, is also found in Nerval.

In fact, the specular reflection constitutive of *Sylvie*'s unity, a specularity which the Romantics aimed for through the mixing of genres, is related to the religious such as Schelling intended it, i.e., to art thought of as the absolute representation of truth. And, as Lacoue-Labarthe and Nancy have shown, it is "the becoming-artist of the work or absolute self-pro-duction itself," the question of the subject of the Work as Subject of the work, of the work-subject, that speculative metaphysics aims for on the level of art and of form, and not on the level of the concept as in Hegel. This question of the work-subject is, in fact, *the* religious question. (The madness *of* writing in *Sylvie*, seen autobiographically, must then be viewed in the perspective of the creation of such a self-reflexive and self-engen-dering work. The Nervalian practice of self-plagiarism must also be under-stood in this sense.) The specular unity of *Sylvie*, an apparently faultless unity, sustaining itself, seems then to exclude any question of figurality. But is it really so, for doesn't it also go hand in hand precisely with what has been named the "syncretism" of Nerval? "Nerval," writes Jean Richer, is he "who refuses to choose, who wants to reconcile contraries: mysticism and sensualism, paganism and Christianity." This syncretism is very close to the other side of Romanticism's religious concept. Although what has been called the theomaniacal delirium of Nerval and which, as the texts show (*Aurélia* in particular), is rather a spiritual alchemy or an aspiration to become pure spirit through the reconciliation or reintegration (to use Martines de Pasqualy's term) of all religions, this religious syncretism is not without relation to the specular unity produced from genre mixing. The mixing of religions is theoretically tied to the mixing of genres. That is what fragment 327 of the *Athenaeum* proves:

> Wanting to reunite into one all genres of religions is a very natural and almost inevitable desire. Its realization, however, is palpably called the mixture of poetic genres.

> [Es ist ein sehr natürlicher, ja fast unvermeidlicher Wunsch, alle Gattungen der Religion in sich vereinigen zu wollen. In der Aus-führung ists damit aber ungefähr, wie mit der Vermischung der Dichtarten.]

Now this reconciliation of religions within Nerval's syncretism, a mix-ture parallel to the mixture of genres and of styles, if it doesn't necessarily represent a return to Christian faith as Richer seems to suggest, it is none-theless brought about under the auspices of Christianity, despite all avowed paganism. Thus the mixture in question will not escape from figural unity. Only the *figura* can allow for some sort of mixture of religions. Doesn't Nerval write in *Diorama*: "Indicating the ruins of a world being born is a poetic idea [C'est une idée poétique que d'avoir indiqué les ruines d'un monde naissant]"? Nerval's use of figural representation, of the *figura*, is thus allegorical, but allegorical in the sense that it ruins that which it prom-ises. So being, the figural unity would coincide with the specular unity, and thus with the totality that the madness *of* the text confers upon it. But doesn't he also use it in the sense that Auerbach intends it, that is, a unity imposed upon the mixture from the outside? Nerval's religious experience, in fact, coincides with a spiritual madness, but it is also the madness of *religion*. This is certainly more obvious for *Aurélia* (especially the ending) than for *Sylvie*. But if such is the case, the figure then opens out into religious delirium and can, as figure, be founded on the promise of a unity yet to come and not yet realized. The real unity will remain incomplete.

How do we then deal with these two, or even three, religions: the madness *of* the text, the madness *of* religion and the madness of *religion*; or again, the question of the relationship between the specular, religious and figural unity? In formulating the two problems which were to guide my reading of *Sylvie*, I first raised the question of the particular figure that the mixture of genres and styles in Nerval takes. The unity of *Sylvie* which relies on the madness *of* the text as well as on the madness *of* religion and which takes the form of a specular and religious unity is not independent, it seems to me, of the figural unity and the religious madness on which this latter is based. Now, that would mean that the specular unity would be wanting, would hold to a unity always incomplete with relation to itself. It would be wanting, and would also hold to, an experience as particular as the madness of *religion*. To say it again in another way: an experience and a particular figure must come to the aid of a specular and religious unity of the text that against all appearance is found lacking.

That brings me to reformulate the second question I raised in reference to *Sylvie*, namely, where is the scenic- or stage-work in this relationship of the text with itself? First, it should be noted that for romanticism, the *menstrum universale*, the producer of the religious, is clearly poetry. This role of mediator (or *relève*) which poetry assumes is not free of problems. It is not, as Paul de Man suggests in "The Rhetoric of Temporality," that the artwork-becoming-subject is problematized under the figure of secular allegory or even that of irony. On the contrary, as the case of *Sylvie* has clearly shown, instead of subverting the work's organic totality, allegory's (or irony's) negative function contributes to this end essentially in that this organic quality relies on an infinite specularity, that is *unendlich* and not *endlos*. If the reflexive totality encounters mishaps, if the mixture of genres, and consequently of religions, creates problems, the reason is due rather to what Antonio, in *Gespräch über die Poesie*, calls *diction*, namely, the "center of every letter"; in other words, it is due to what, concerning the specific mode of composition of a genre, is of the order of writing. Romanticism, as has been seen in Nerval's *Sylvie*, masters writing by inscribing it into the reflexive weaving of its text. Thus, it is not a question of the writing I mentioned earlier: the madness *of* writing. That which, on the other hand, will not allow itself to be inscribed without remainder in the play of mirrors of the specular and religious text, that which always exists as supplementary with relation to that textual totality, and that which always overflows into what it cannot take into account is precisely that very thing which organizes the multiple self-relationships of the text. What is always in excess in the mixture of genres and of styles regarding the self-engendering and autonomy of the work is the theatrical. In fact, the specular mirage can only take place under the *direction* of writing. But simultaneously, this same scenic-work never stops disappropriating the self-mirroring of the text. Just as the theatrical space, Nerval's purgatory, already upsets the symmetrical and specular play of the same and of the other, so also the theatrical space opened up by writing is the always excessive discontinuous space upon which the representation of a continuous universe becomes possible. But, as such, this space fatally interrupts any direct relationship between spaces and times. Nerval writes: "Today there is no direct road to Ermononville. Sometimes I go there by way of Creil and Senlis, sometimes by Dammartin. [Pour se rendre à Ermononville, on ne trouve plus aujourd'hui de route directe. Quelquefois j'y vais par Creil et Senlis, d'autres fois par Dammartin]."

Let me try to bring this paper to a close, a paper which no doubt has raised more questions than it has answered, by recalling Nerval's remarks during the visit to the home of the uncle who had passed away. He notices "two Flemish paintings said to be the work of an ancient painter, an ancestor of ours." But that is not all:

> On the table was a stuffed dog which I had known alive as the old friend of my wanderings through the woods, the last King Charles (*carlin*) perhaps, because it belonged to that lost breed.
> "Let's go and see the parrot," I said . . . The parrot asked for food as it had done in its happiest days.
>
> [Sur la table, [je perçus] un chien empaillé que j'avais connu vivant, ancien compagnon de mes courses dans les bois, le dernier carlin peut-être, car il appartenait à cette race perdue.
> "Allons voir le perroquet," dis-je au fermier. Le perroquet demandait à déjeuner comme en ses plus beaux jours.]

Thus, at the beginning, a painter, a tableaux-maker, a scenemaker, perhaps even a thaumaturgist. But also a race of actors, the *carlin* named from the Italian actor Carlo Bertinazzi. What is left is the foolish, senseless and sterile repetition of a word stretching towards the past. All, within the *mise en scène* of the text.

Musset

Georges Poulet

Let us suppose you are returning from a journey . . . *Does not your heart beat faster as you turn the street corner, approach, and finally arrive?* Well! This natural but vulgar pleasure, this impatience for bed and table which you feel for all that is known and familiar to you, suppose now that you experience it for everything that exists, noble or coarse, known or brand new; suppose that your life is a continuous journey, . . . that every inn is your own house, that, on every threshold, your children await you, that there in each bed is your wife; . . . thus it is with the poet; thus it was with me when I was twenty!

The starting point with Musset is this beating of the heart at all the turnings of existence, this bounding from one moment toward another:

> Tell us
> How a heart twenty years old bounds to the rendezvous.

Life is at first a summons and a dawn. Before it springs forth, there is nothing and no one, except a kind of negative being incapable of doing anything, even of imagining its future pleasures: "Thus I do nothing, and I feel that the greatest unhappiness that could come to a man of intense passions would be to experience nothing at all . . . I need to see a woman; I need a pretty foot and a fine figure; I need to love." A need to love, a need to live. Life, love are outside one, in the future, in a world in which there are lovers, in a time when one will be able to love them. But that world is remote, that time has not come; nothing happens, and one veg-

From *The Interior Distance*, translated by Elliott Coleman. © 1959 by The Johns Hopkins University Press, Baltimore/London.

etates, till all of a sudden an occasion for loving, for living presents itself, and then, in the feeling of this lightning proximity, a human being suddenly awakens, becomes animate, feels the beating of its heart, takes cognizance of itself in the quickening and prodigious stirring of its desire:

> —Oh! how at this instant the heart of a woman leaps!
> When the single thought in which her soul is engulfed
> Ceaselessly flies and grows, and before her desire
> Recoils like a wave, impossible to seize!
> Then, memory exciting hope,
> The waiting for happiness turns into suffering;
> And the eye probes only a dazzling gulf,
> Like those which in dream Alighieri descends.

Just beyond the instant in which one is, where one is alone, where one is empty, where solitude and vacuity are conjoined to form that kind of interior gulf which one calls suffering, there is another moment, so near one thinks he can touch it, so desirable that it makes the whole fragile bodily armature vibrate with impatience, a moment which, one is certain, is immediately going to be filled to the brim with joy and with love:

> To the right, to the left, over there, at the horizon, everywhere voices call to him. All is desire, all is reverie . . . If one had a hundred arms, one would not hesitate to open them in the void; one has only to clasp there his mistress, *and the void is filled*.

The earliest of Musset's poetry is therefore the presentiment of a plenitude, the feeling of an imminence; it is a poetry of youthfulness and of youth, a poetry of pleasure or rather of the flight toward pleasure, which singularly recalls that of the true masters of Musset, that is to say, the petty masters of the eighteenth century. But whereas these, a Voltaire, a Bertin, a Boufflers, are fully confident of instantaneously capturing that instantaneous thing called happiness, the poetry of Musset cannot be resigned to awaiting the moment which is going to present him his object. It mounts up, it bursts forth in a kind of smarting realization of not yet being what it is going to be; it is the feeling of mad impatience and of extreme thirst which one experiences at the instant when the cup has not quite yet touched the lips, when one is tortured by the anguish to know if it be certain that desire will be transformed into pleasure. Thus all the thought of Musset is condensed into a sort of temporal interval in which it is possible that the duration will change and the moment transmute itself into another; and it is this anticipation, this piercing hope which gives him a life that is like the beating of a heart, like a leaping forth of being, a rapid and precipitate capturing of the consciousness of self between the time when one was not, or when one had nothing, and the time when occasion and love can bestow everything:

—Twenty times I have tried to accost her; twenty times I have felt my knees melt at her approach. When I see her, my throat tightens and I choke, as if my heart had heaved up into my mouth.

—I have experienced that. It is thus when in the depths of the forest a doe patters with short steps over the dry leaves and the hunter hears the bushes slip by her restless flanks, like the rustle of a thin gown, the beatings of his heart seize him in spite of himself; he lifts his gun in silence, without taking a step, without breathing.

The first movement of thought with Musset is thus a passionate dedication of the whole being to a future that is on the point of becoming present. Like the poetry of Vigny, that of Musset is the thought of a human being "always ready to become transfigured." But in contrast to Vignian poetry, it is by no means a pure anticipation of itself, in which one apprehends oneself as one dreams of being, as solitarily one foresees oneself. Here, on the contrary, the future is an imminent pleasure, dependent upon a precise object which has already entered the field of desire and regard. All existence feels itself dependent upon an immediate future which it must seize in flight. And the heart palpitates at the idea that its beating marks the exact instant which precedes that of happiness.

II

Love! divine torrent of the infinite source! . . .

Drunkenness of the senses, O delight! yes, like God, thou art immortal! Sublime flight of the creature, universal communion of beings, delight thrice sanctified, what have they said of thee, those who have praised thee? they have called thee passer-by, O creatress!

In the drunkenness of the senses, the human being thus attains to a creative moment. Each preceding moment existed only as an imperfect entity, which had no other use than immediately to carry thought forward toward another moment more worthy of being lived. Each preceding moment existed only in the painful feeling of a moment that is *other*, toward which it let itself move in a torrential springing forth, that of duration. But the moment of erotic drunkenness is of an entirely different kind. It is not *in* the torrent, it is the torrent itself; it is not that which eternally hurls itself beyond and elsewhere; it is that which eternally lives of itself and within itself, that which engenders its own existence. The being that succeeds in living in it abandons itself to an enveloping presence, before and after which there is nothing to cause regret or foreboding, for there is nothing any longer there except a circuit of feelings and sensations within which one is enclosed with another human being. And in this sense, therefore, love is indeed a movement, but no longer the temporal movement by which man, beyond the moment, searches for a perfection of which he cannot bear to feel himself deprived. An eternal moment, since in it source and end coincide; the moment of love surges up out of time as a pure activity. It asks nothing, it regrets nothing; it has neither past nor future. It is a present that *forgets* time and suspends the course of it:

> Oh! how, absorbed in their profound love,
> They forgot the day, life, and the world!

> I thought I felt time stop in my heart!

Thus, in Musset's eyes, the moment of love takes on an importance beyond any other, and that by reason of its "eternity." This doesn't mean, of course, that it continues forever, identical to itself, replacing the transitory duration of man by a permanent duration, like that of God; though, it is true, Musset will never explain to himself, except by the intervention of infidelity and falsehood, the abrupt termination of the lover's ecstasy and his dropping back into time. But the thing of which Musset will never entertain a doubt—save in the darkest hours when the anguish consists precisely in asking oneself if one has not lived a lie—is the revetment of eternity which these lone hours acquire when the voice of desire is silenced, and when one can forget his temporal condition. Eternal moments, in that they repudiate and erase all others, in that they do not reintegrate common duration, but stay in isolation without being linked, before or behind, to other moments which their refulgence abolishes. Hence, despite the violence of the sensual ecstasy, what Musset essentially remembers of them is the consciousness of a *pause* in time, a resting place:

> It is a pause—a calm—an inexpressible ecstasy.
> Time—that traveler whom an invisible hand,
> From age to age, at a slow pace, leads to eternity—
> Pensive, at the side of the road, pauses and stops.

But this pause, this interior silence, this peaceful dispensation from desiring, which the being who loves enjoys at the instant he loves, if it is a part of the instant, it is no longer the center, the heart, but already the end of it. This pause is no longer an ardent, actual joy; it is a joy that has been thought and is almost over. And it is striking that the two places in which Musset chooses to describe at greatest length the realization of the happiness of loving are those each time when the lover finds himself *after* the night of love "leaving with slow steps" the house of the loved one, and thanking God, not for possessing, but for *having* possessed his happiness.

III

Inevitably, as in the same period Kierkegaard was to demonstrate, the moment in which one loves draws away from the mind which experiences it and only offers an evanescing image which is soon going to become a pure memory. No doubt, with a Musset as well as with a La Fontaine or a Keats, the contemplation of this slow gliding backward is still a kind of rapture. It even seems that in order that man might make the discovery of his happiness, it is necessary that the withdrawing of what is felt create an interior distance in the depths of which sensation becomes perception. But it is nonetheless true that the thought of one's present happiness is a parting thought, and that man dispossessed of his eternity finds himself immediately transported to the after-side of the ecstatic moment, as just before he found himself situated precisely on the fore-side of it. So that for Musset, as for all who place happiness in the erotic moment, happiness is never directly apprehended, never lived interiorly and at his center of being. It is never a present happiness, but a mysterious nonactual presence hemmed in between two moments of extraordinary distinctness: the moment in which happiness is a hope that becomes present, and the moment in which it is a present that becomes memory.

As a necessary consequence, the history of the man who wants to live in the eternal moment, becomes the history of the man who perceives himself always to be withdrawing from this moment. He is going away from his ecstatic moment but continually turning back in order to measure the growing gap that separates him from it. Time becomes a perpetual fissure:

> And I felt a shred of my life
> Slowly rent to pieces.

But the pain which Musset suffers does not consist solely in the consciousness of a moving away and a tearing apart. A past from which one feels himself torn apart is an immediate occasion of great suffering at the end of which there is a hope of healing and pacification. And a past from which one is removed is a sad farewell that one says to himself, up to the moment when the being one was is effaced in the distance in order to give place to the being one is, changed and consoled. But the particularity of the eternal moment is to continue to be eternal, even when it has ceased to be a moment, ceased to be lived. And as at the moment in which it was being lived it was forgetful of all the rest, so in departing from the moment in which it ceases to be lived, it becomes impossible to be itself forgotten:

> Those memories, after I had lost her, pursued me without
>   respite.

> All that past clamored at my ears
> Its eternal oaths of a day.

> Rid me, importunate memory,
> Rid me of these eyes I see always.

The past is not blotted out then, nor cured. Can one even say that it is past, since it continues to exist? It is there, present, though outside of the present, distant without being blurred by distance, ineffaceable memory which never ceases to attest, to aggravate by its negative splendor, the tragic deficiency of the moment which it is not. Such is the strange dividing into two of being and time which Stendhal once called the "repining grief," and which is less the division of time between past and present, than the division of the present itself between a past always present to the mind but no longer lived, and a present which it is necessary to live but which is consumed and unbearable: "The repining over an instant troubles and consumes thee." Thus, for Musset, the actualization of the past has here nothing at all of the characteristics of the affective memory. No doubt it is upon the occasion of a "recollecting sign," the integral revival of experienced sensations and lived feelings. Thus when the hero of the *Confession* casts his eyes on the Luxembourg garden in which he had so often walked in his childhood:

> The garden stretched away before my eyes.
>
> As a cork which, plunged into water, seems restless under the hand which pushed it down, and glides between the fingers in order to remount to the surface, so something became agitated in me which I could neither vanquish nor set aside. The sight of the walks of the Luxembourg made my heart leap, and every other thought vanished. How many times, playing truant on its little knolls, I stretched myself out under the shade with some good book, full of mad poetry . . . I recaptured all those far-off memories in the leafless trees, in the withered grass of the flower-beds . . . "O my childhood! There you are!" I cried out; "O my God! You are here!"

As has been said, this rising up of the memory is not without resemblance to the famous Proustian episode of the *madeleine.* Yet it differs from it on one essential point. Far from totally invading the present, or of transporting the being who remembers into the epoch which it remembers, the past remains here a distinct apparition. Raised to the same level of duration as the actual being, it remains separated from it by a whole interior distance.

That is seen more clearly still in the passage in which Rolla hears a youthful romance sung by some strolling musicians:

> Ah! how the old airs one sang at twelve years
> Strike straight to the heart in hours of suffering!
> How they consume all! How *far off one feels from them*!
> How one hangs his head finding them so old!
> Are those thy sighs, dark Spirit of ruins?
> Angel of memories, are those thy sobs?
> Ah! how they fluttered, lively fleet birds,
> O'er the gilded palace of childhood's loves!
> How skilled to reopen the flowers of times past,
> And to wrap us in a shroud, they who have lulled us!

The awakening of the past is thus not an awakening of the being. It is not even in a fugitive fashion the recommencement of a lost happiness; or if it recommences and reopens its flowers, it is all in the depths of time, in the distance; so that beholding this strange and faraway resurrection, having become witness of what he was, a being recognizes that he is as different as possibly could be and, comparing himself with his former happiness, apprehends therein the most cruel consciousness of his present unhappiness.

And so Dante was right in saying that the

> greatest grief
> Is simply a happy memory in the days of unhappiness.

A *happy* memory is a *frightful* memory:

> Shall I tell you that one evening, left alone on earth,
> Consumed, like you, by a frightful memory,
> I astounded myself with my own misery,
> And with what a child can suffer without dying?

The contemplation of the past is thus the contemplation of the interior abyss into the depths of which, step by step, one has fallen down all the way to the present. How did one pass from such a height to such a depth, from such a plenitude to such a misery? Existence appears as a progressive denudation, as a rapid ageing: "It seemed to me that all my thoughts were falling like dry leaves." And if one is carried despairingly back, on the one hand, to an anterior epoch of profusion, to a time "when Life was young," in which "Heaven walked and breathed on earth in a people of gods," on the other hand one thereby perceives, and only the more clearly, the moral and physical disgrace of the time which has now become ours. And so the phantom clothed in black, which sets about constantly to accompany Musset in existence, is neither the past nor youth, but "the ghost of youth," that is to say the image of oneself one sees appear when, in solitude, regarding oneself with the eyes of the past, one begins to understand what one has become, "a shadow of oneself" stripped of its youth, its innocence, its power, a sort of tragic caricature of the being which had once lived; "a young man with a fine past," to repeat the terrible remark of Heinrich Heine:

> Yes, I am without strength and without youth,
> A shadow of myself, a trace, a vain reflection,
> And sometimes at night my ghost appears to me.

The eternity of the moment of happiness has become the perenniality of a distant, spectral, accusing conscience, in the face of which the perenniality of unhappiness, of vice, and of misery unrolls itself as a sort of "hideous disguise" or a "Déjanire's robe":

It is too late—I have got used to my trade. For me vice was a garment, now it is glued to my hide.

For the indelibility of lost happiness there is now substituted the indelibility of the unhappiness experienced because of the waste, the wrinkles, all the blemishes and stains which the sea itself could not wash away, finally the indelibility of the senile and debased image of oneself mirrored in the puddles and gutters of the streets.

Everywhere there are to be found the same wear and tear, the same withering, the same monotony:

Look at this smoke-blackened old city . . . There is not a paving stone of it over which I have not dragged these used-up heels, not a house of which I would not know the girl or the old woman whose stupid head is forever present at the window; I cannot take a step without retracing my steps of yesterday; well! my dear friend, this town is nothing in comparison with my brain. All the innermost recesses of my mind are a hundred times better known to me; all the streets, all the pot-holes of my imagination, are a hundred times more worn . . .

Then this actual feeling of insolvency, of decrepitude, of leveling becomes distributed over the totality of existence:

I am more hollow and empty than a statue of tin-plate . . . I am older than the great grandfather of Saturn.

I have come too late into a world too old.

The Earth is as old, as degenerate,
It shakes a head as desperate
As when John appeared upon the sand of the seas
. . . .
Everything here, as then, is dead with time,
And Saturn has outlasted the blood of his children.

The world and the self, all is made uniform in the same impotence. It is too late to love again or to be anything, to turn backward or to go ahead. There is now nothing to do but to seek repose, if possible, by dint of fatigue, in the consciousness of the void in which all is resolved.

Like those mad dervishes who find ecstasy in vertigo, when thought, turning upon itself, becomes exhausted with racking itself, and weary with useless labor, it stops dismayed. It seems as if man is empty, as if by dint of descending into himself, he arrives at the last movement of a spiral. There, as on mountain tops, as in the depths of mines, the air fails, and God forbids him to go farther.

By a different road, but one whose spiral conducts him to the same places, or rather to the same absence of places, it seems that Musset, like Hugo, finally arrives at the consciousness of the fundamental and terminal gulf in which human existence is suffused. When one experiences the latter as an immediate fullness, in the taking leave of which everything comes undone, sinks and disappears into indistinctness, there remains then, in a space stripped of all forms and emptied of every object, only the sole monotonous functioning of a life that is almost dead, reduced to being a mere organic activity, continuing to indicate by the beatings of the heart, in a denuded space, the regular periods of a neuter duration.

> The beatings of the blood in the arteries are a strange clock which one feels vibrate only at night. Man, abandoned then by exterior objects, falls back on himself; he hears himself live.

In the general annulment of all desires and all objects, the world, the self seem to have become a sort of anonymous space whose parts are uselessly counted off by duration; "confused dream, succession of uniform days like the motion of the pendulum."

> Well, Spark, I am taken with a desire to sit on a parapet, to watch the river flow along, and to set myself to counting one, two, three, four, five, six, seven, and so forth until the day of my death.

IV

> Yet I shall have other mistresses, the trees get covered with verdure and the odor of lilacs arises in drifts; everything is reborn and my heart leaps in spite of myself.

So eternal, for Musset, seemed the death of the heart, so unforeseeable its rebirth, finally so nimble, so prompt is the passage from the one to the other and from the past to the future, that it is as if it were supernatural, immediately and irresistibly efficacious, and of a grace coming not from on high but from below, lifting itself up from palpable depths as the odor of lilacs rises in spring. "Love, and thou shalt be reborn," but it is indeed beyond its death that the heart is now reborn. Each of these resurrections is accompanied by a total rejuvenation of the old being, by a gay gesture of forgetfulness throwing off the shroud of the past.

> From the day when I saw thee,
> My life began; the rest was nothing;
> And my heart has ever beaten only on thine.

It seems that the being awakens to life for the first time, or rather that it discovers with rapture the independence of the moment in which it is reborn, over against all preceding moments. Old promises, old hopes, old tears, and even the lot of fallen angel to which one thought himself condemned forever, all that is found, perhaps not abolished, but dropped down, left behind, like a time unloaded on the side of the road. And behold one finds oneself afresh to be desirous, happy, loving, living, carelessly participating, as if one had never lived before, in an utterly fresh time, the adventurous time of love. Doubtless this adventure is the same one which has already more than once lived. And, one knows only too well, it can end only in suffering and death. But beyond suffering and death there are still other loves, and other deaths, and other lives; so that in this mixture of experience and heedlessness, the independence of moments becomes the independence of successive loves and lives, as if the whole ensemble of duration could be constituted by a series of absolute mutations, in which one "gives his heart to each moment" and in which "all dies tonight in order to come to life again tomorrow."

"Man is thus always new." Many times Musset dreamed of organizing his life according to this ceaselessly renewed novelty of feeling. To make of existence the continuity of a discontinuous movement. It is the essence, for example, of childhood: "There's a mad thing to try: to continue to be a child." It is also the essence of the life of Octave: "Imagine a rope-dancer . . . He continues his fleet course from the East to the West. If he looks down, his head swims; if he looks up, his foot slips. He goes quicker than the wind . . ."

But this duration, made of a rapid gliding from moment to moment, is possible only in an existence which would ceaselessly content itself with actual pleasure. Now Célio is not Octave, neither Musset or himself a Marivaux. As we have seen, love is not solely constituted by the actuality of a pleasure even momentarily eternal. It is a mysterious temporal center about which there come to group themselves hopes and memories, desires and griefs which mount up from all the historic depths of the being. The heart is a bush in which, at each step, there sing all the youth, all the different youths which in turn one has received. And if one is perpetually reborn, it is at one and the same time to forget and to remember, to regain life in death, and death in life. To love without ceasing is to be reborn without ceasing; it is also "to die more than once." At each instant it seems that the whole of life is found again, but that it is also lost again. Time "pulls away the ladder behind us as soon as we reach a halting-place; nay, it breaks it under our feet, rung by rung." Musset's existence would therefore appear to be doomed to being a series of systoles and diastoles, of dilations and contractions, if the absolute character of each one of these deaths and rebirths did not furnish an unforeseen hope. For at this point we touch on something than which there is nothing more essential for Musset, something to which he returned with the greatest insistence in his writings, and yet without ever being able to explain himself fully, since, to tell the truth, at this point one perhaps leaves the domain of the explicable. He who remembers, immediately, exclusively, links his recollections to his present situation; thus he colors them with regret, with remorse, with a virulent actuality which profoundly changes their nature, and which renders them narrowly dependent upon this new source of emotions. This is what happens in all the unsuccessful affective resurrections we have seen, in which past and present are measured as two enemy actualities, at once isolated and connected one with another by their very confrontation. But sometimes, on the contrary, memory appears as something purely retrospective, withdrawn from the influence of present existence, liberated by death, forgetfulness, and the renewal of being, representing simply a consummated past, a grief lived through, an existence drawn to a close. Then this remembrance, endowed with its own life at a distance which is no longer a harrowing separation, becomes a simple anterior presence of being to being; and then all is changed, all is saved. For *to have been* is *to be*. Not actually to be, but anteriorly and eternally to be. Each "fugitive instant which was our whole life" is eternally preserved in its own duration. And the human being who has lived each one of them in its turn is capable, while undergoing the agonies of his actual existence, of preserving and revisiting each of these moments as so many independent possessions of his interior universe. None of them can be taken away from him, or destroyed, or be in the least touched by corruption; "this memory can never be wrested from him," for every one of these possessions is independent of every other, and time is made of this very independence.

Thus it is singular that the point at which Musset finally arrives, and what appears to be his ultimate belief, is the very starting point of Descartes' philosophy. The principle of the independence of the moments of time becomes for Musset a sort of creation reiterated by love. It becomes also an affirmation of the eternity of each moment of life, an eternity at which each moment arrives when, *ceasing to be, it begins to no longer cease to have been*. Each moment enters in its turn into a particular immortality which is *its truth*. It can no longer be either disavowed or denied. It is intact forever.

Théophile Gautier: Art and the Artist

Albert B. Smith

If the pursuit of happiness and the difficulties involved in that pursuit stand out as the major themes in Gautier's fantastic works, questions of art and the artistic calling receive only slightly less attention. Certain works have as their primary concern a problem of art. Others, though dealing principally with the search for happiness, may be read also from the standpoint of art. In still others, allusions to art constitute major elements of the narrative. Four areas of interest predominate: the question of artistic production; attitudes toward art; the relation of art to society; and beauty.

I

The production of art depends, in the fantastic works as in all other considerations of aesthetics, upon the character of the artist, upon those personal traits which he must possess for the highest artistic achievement. Naturally there are dangers which he must avoid, and we find in the fantastic works a number of cautions of which he must be aware. A psychological question encountered in the preceding chapter [of *Théophile Gautier and the Fantastic*] is germane here. We have observed that certain heroes in Gautier's fantastic works run the risk of madness in unqualified recourse to the imagination. Like them, the artist must keep a solid footing in reality, recognizing that the productions of his imagination are not real in themselves. Belief in the figments conjured up in the mind poses a very real threat to sanity. We have only to recall the story of Onuphrius to recognize the validity of this idea.

Deux Acteurs pour un rôle also suggests the necessity for the artist to maintain a hold on reality and not to lose himself in the images of art. This story, too, outlines the dangers of too great involvement in the imagination. Henrich, the aspiring actor, is drawn to his vocation precisely because of the rich imaginative life which it permits him: " 'que veux-tu! c'est un ascendant invincible; le théâtre m'attire; j'en rêve le jour, j'y pense la nuit; je sens le désir de vivre dans la création des poètes, il me semble que j'ai vingt existences. Chaque rôle que je joue me fait une vie nouvelle; toutes ces passions que j'exprime, je les éprouve; je suis Hamlet, Othello, Charles Moor; quand on est tout cela, on ne peut que difficilement se résigner a l'humble condition de pasteur de village.' "

This approach to acting shows itself to be extraordinarily risky. In a role particularly attractive to him, Henrich plays Mephistopheles. If we can believe his statement above, he actually becomes the character which he is representing, experiencing all the passions of the fallen angel. That Satan in fact appears to him and attempts to destroy him suggests that in becoming such a personage, Henrich risks a kind of self-destruction, the loss of his identity in that of the devil, in a word, insanity of the worst sort. Luckily he yet has enough control over his reason to recognize his danger, so that he does not go mad. He receives wounds from Satan's claws, but these are enough to bring him back to his senses. When the narrator at the end of the tale reports that Henrich's refusal to resume an acting career is partly due to concern for his salvation, we may infer that this means fear for his mental balance.

We have already considered [elsewhere] in "La Mille et deuxième Nuit" the danger of excessive concern with one's talent in the pursuit of ideal satisfactions. Mahmoud misses one occasion to perceive the ideal, because of pride in his own art. The peri's explanation to him is applicable to all aspiring artists: if they wish to enjoy ideal pleasures, they must aim singlemindedly at them, without egotism in respect to their craft.

Art is first and foremost the attempt to express the individual's vision of that which is ideal. The artist must have an idealistic orientation and hold it at all times central in his thoughts and actions. Sensuality threatens in art as well as in the quest for happiness. By surrendering to the erotic pleasures offered him by Véronique, Albertus loses forever his chances to create. His death at the hands of Véronique and her companions may be interpreted as the death of his idealistic aspirations, without which great art is impossible.

Statements and situations suggesting the need for idealism abound in Gautier's fantastic works. These relate both to the quality of the artist's production and to the personal satisfaction which idealism promises. In "Spirite," the narrator alludes to "les sphères supérieures où le désir du poète doit être enfin satisfait." "Avatar," though not concerned immediately with the question of art, also implies that the artist's satisfaction must come through a spiritual orientation. Octave de Saville would be in an excellent position to achieve union with the Countess Labinska if he were able to see in her something other than an object to be enjoyed physically.

That her husband enjoys perfect happiness is due to the non-materialistic quality so strong in their marriage. What she misses in Octave's eyes when he poses as Count Olaf is precisely the latter's expression of a sentiment that is pure as the love of the angels. It is in large part a spiritual orientation that brings Olaf satisfaction.

Throughout the fantastic works are suggestions that the greatest art is spiritual in nature. The music of Palestrina, Gluck, and Cimarosa, for example, has this quality. According to "Le Nid de rossignols," two young girls who have devoted their lives to music, train three nightingales to sing. The girls' music is extraordinarily beautiful and has an incomparable spiritual character. Their last song is characterized thus: "leur chant était plus beau que jamais; il avait quelque chose qui n'était pas de ce monde." When the girls die, the nightingales bear their song to Heaven. God keeps the birds near Him to perform their celestial music, and He later makes of them the souls of the three composers.

The ghost of the painter Raphael makes plain in "La Comédie de la mort" that creative genius is essentially a matter of spirituality. Later generations of painters will be unable to equal the master, he says, because they will not possess the necessary spiritual virtues:

> "Vos peintres auront beau, pour voir comme elle est faite,
> Tourner entre leurs mains et retourner ma tête,
>   Mon secret est à moi.
> Ils copieront mes tons, ils copieront mes poses,
> Mais il leur manquera ce que j'avais, deux choses,
>   L'amour avec la foi!"

It is no surprise that "Spirite," also, emphasizes the importance of the spiritual in art. According to this late work, great art, by its very nature, seeks to express the ideal. When Spirite plays the piano for Malivert, Gautier's narrator characterizes the composition thus: "Le morceau qu'elle joua était l'œuvre d'un grand maître, une de ces inspirations où le génie humain semble pressentir l'infini, et qui formulent avec puissance tantôt les secrètes postulations de l'âme, tantôt lui rappellent le souvenir des cieux et des paradis d'où elle a été chassée." A poem by Malivert to which she adds a musical accompaniment has a similar character: "C'était une inspiration dans laquelle, dédaigneux des joies vulgaires, il s'élançait d'un essor désespéré vers les sphères supérieures."

Human talent alone, however, is insufficient to permit the artist to reach his goal. Spirite emphasizes that even the greatest genius—the most confirmed idealist—is prevented by his materiality from achieving the fullest spiritual expression: "Non seulement Spirite rendait toutes les intentions du maître, mais elle exprimait l'idéal qu'il rêvait et auquel l'infirmité humaine ne lui avait pas toujours permis d'atteindre." Because she has achieved spiritual perfection, Spirite is able to express the master's ideal perfectly. As Malivert approaches full spirituality, he also gains in artistic capacity: "Le lendemain il voulut travailler; sa verve éteinte depuis long-temps, se ranimait, et les idées se pressaient tumultueusement dans son cerveau. . . . Jamais il ne s'éleva à une pareille hauteur, et les plus grands poètes eussent signé ce qu'il écrivit ce jour-là." The lesson is clear: the more profoundly spiritual the artist's orientation, the greater his art will be.

Allusions also recur in Gautier's fantastic works to the question of composition, the actual production of the art work. Statements not only from *Spirite* but from other works as well, if collected, would constitute a full art of poetry—or in a broader context, an art of art. Such statements appear from the earliest works. In "Albertus," for example, the narrator intrudes to assert the validity of freedom of expression, two years before the famous preface to *Mademoiselle de Maupin*. In reading the lines below, one has the impression of reading Gautier's preface before the fact:

> —Mes vers
> Sont des vers de jeune homme et non un catéchisme.
> —Je ne les châtre pas,—dans leur décent cynisme
>   Ils s'en vont droit ou de travers,
>
> Peu m'importe, selon que dame Poésie,
> Leur maîtresse absolue, en a la fantaisie,
> Et, chastes comme Adam avant d'avoir péché,
> Ils marchent librement dans leur nudité sainte,
> Enfants purs de tout vice et laissant voir sans crainte
> Ce qu'un monde hypocrite avec soin tient caché.
> —Je ne suis pas de ceux dont une gorge nue,
> Un jupon un peu court, font détourner la vue.—
> Mon œil plutôt qu'ailleurs ne s'arrête pas là.
> —Pourquoi donc tant crier sur l'œuvre des artistes?
> Ce qu'ils font est sacré! —Messieurs les rigoristes,
>   N'y verriez-vous donc que cela?

Likewise, certain works recall Gautier's famous poem, "L'Art," in their allusions to the durability which the artistic work gives to things, subject as they are to decay. Octavien, in "Arria Marcella," is able to perceive, 1800 years after the destruction of Pompeii and its people, the form of a beautiful woman shaped in the hardened ash of Vesuvius. The narrator likens the piece of stone to a sculptor's mold: "on eût dit un fragment de moule de statue, brisé par la fonte. . . . Grâce au caprice de l'éruption qui a détruit quatre villes, cette noble forme, tombée en poussière depuis deux mille ans bientôt, est parvenue jusqu'à nous; la rondeur d'une gorge a traversé les siècles lorsque tant d'empires disparus n'ont pas laissé de trace!" "Le Pied de momie" also emphasizes the ability of art to confer durability. The Egyptians whom the narrator encounters in a burial temple appear as robust as in life because of the ancient embalming techniques. Without the benefit of this "art" they would have long since decayed. A major preoccupation in the story is the Egyptian quest for permanence. Thanks to art, Princess Hermonthis' foot preserves its original form. The princess stresses her father's desire to keep her body intact until the day of judgment: " 'Ah! comme mon père va être content, lui qui était si désolé de ma mutilation, et qui avait, dès le jour de ma naissance, mis un peuple tout entier à l'ouvrage pour me creuser un tombeau si profond qu'il pût me conserver intacte jusqu'au jour suprême.' " The old pharaoh points with scorn to the shortcomings of later attempts at preservation, implying that the fault lies in the failure of more recent art to seek durability. The story ends on an ironic note which again emphasizes that art must aim at preserving that which it represents. When the narrator awakens from his dream of ancient Egypt, a friend reminds him that they are late for a visit to see the Spanish paintings of the collector Aguado. Coming immediately after the interview with King Xixouthros, this allusion can only be read as a sign suggesting that modern art scarcely has the qualities to endure.

One would gather from reading certain works by Gautier that inspiration was not a factor which concerned him. "L'Art," for example, usually cited as his definitive statement on artistic practice, gives inspiration at best a secondary position. In this poem, the favor which Gautier grants to the labor of the file is paramount. Yet in "Spirite" there is evident concern with inspiration and a strong suggestion of its desirability. We have already observed that the novelette places a high value on the spiritual orientation. Contact with a spiritual reality impels Malivert to produce his outstanding work. After Spirite's musical rendition of his poem, she leaves him for a time: "Malivert se retrouva seul, dans un état d'exaltation facile à comprendre. Mais peu à peu le calme lui revint et une langueur délicieuse succéda à cette excitation fébrile. Il sentait cette satisfaction qu'éprouvent si rarement les poètes et, dit-on, les philosophes, d'être compris dans toutes les délicatesses et les profondeurs de son génie." It is with this feeling that the desire to compose more verse returns to him. He experiences a rush of new ideas: "les idées se pressaient tumultueusement dans son cerveau. Des horizons illimités, des perspectives sans fin s'ouvraient devant ses yeux. Un monde de sentiments nouveaux fermentait dans sa poitrine." There is no question here of thoughtful composition, or of *limae labor*. Yet the poem which Malivert writes under the influence of this spiritual inspiration is superior to anything he has ever composed—and at least equal to the verse of the greatest poets. Inspiration, dependent upon contact with the spiritual ideal, fills the artist with such a sense of exaltation that he loses rational control. It is as if the spirit were speaking directly through his soul. In this ecstasy he composes his greatest work.

A question which recurs frequently in Gautier's works is that of artistic rendering. The difficulty of depicting beauty is a major element in *Mademoiselle de Maupin*. When Madelaine first appears to d'Albert without her male disguise, he is fairly dazzled by her loveliness. He complains later to his friend Silvio that he cannot fully describe her: " '—S'il y avait des mots pour rendre ce que je sens, je te ferais une description de cinquante pages, mais les langues ont été faites par je ne sais quels goujats qui n'avaient jamais regardé avec attention le dos ou le sein d'une femme, et l'on n'a pas la moitié des termes les plus indispensables.' '' His frustration is painful: '' 'avoir vu une telle beauté et ne pouvoir la rendre d'une manière ou de l'autre, il y a de quoi devenir fou et enragé.' ''

Thus the problem poses itself also in the fantastic works: the inability of any artistic medium to equal the reality which the artist wishes to render. It constitutes a second aspect of Henrich's abandonment of acting in *Deux Acteurs pour un rôle*. When the mysterious stranger publicly casts doubt on Henrich's acting ability, he specifically suggests that the young man will fail in playing Mephistopheles, because he does not know the devil, which is indispensable for truth in portraying the personage. Indeed, no matter how well Henrich acts, he can never equal the character whom he is playing. One of his reasons for giving up the theater is his recognition of this fact.

The artist's inability to render his subject adequately occurs in all mediums. No painter could render the delicate coloration of Prascovie Labinska's complexion. The narrator of ''Albertus'' exclaims that even the most talented painters cannot equal Véronique's beauty:

> —*O nature! nature!*
> Devant ton œuvre, à toi, qu'est-ce que la peinture?
> Qu'est-ce que Raphaël, ce roi de la beauté?
> Qu'est-ce que le Corrège et le Guide et Giorgione,
> Titien, et tous ces noms qu'un siècle à l'autre prône?
> O Raphaël! crois-moi, jette là tes crayons;
> Ta palette, ô Titien! Dieu seul est le grand maître,
> Il garde son secret et nul ne la pénètre,
> Et vainement nous l'essayons.

If painting is inadequate, poetry can do no better. In referring to Clarimonde, Romuald states that neither art nor poetry could give an idea of her great beauty. And, when these mediums are inapt to describe physical objects, they are certainly uncongenial for the depiction of certain feelings and thoughts. The happiness experienced by Count Olaf and Prascovie on being reunited after his return from a military campaign is literally indescribable: ''Comment peindre ces deux âmes fondues en une seule et pareilles à deux larmes de rosée qui, glissant sur un pétale de lis, se rencontrent, se mêlent, s'absorbent l'une l'autre et ne font plus qu'une perle unique? Le bonheur est une chose si rare en ce monde, que l'homme n'a pas songé à inventer des paroles pour le rendre, tandis que le vocabulaire des souffrances morales et physiques remplit d'innombrables colonnes dans le dictionnaire de toutes les langues.''

The major problem in poetic expression, then, is language itself, and language is naturally impotent when it becomes a question of expressing the ineffable. ''Spirite'' poses this crucial problem unequivocally. When the narrator attempts to describe the ethereal beauty of Spirite, he is forced to apologize: "Cette faible esquisse, faite nécessairement avec des paroles créés pour rendre les choses de notre monde, ne saurait donner qu'une idée bien vague de l'apparition que Guy de Malivert contemplait dans le miroir de Venise." Spirite herself can describe the immaterial beauties of Heaven only in physical terms, and these, she realizes, are utterly inadequate. Language simply does not have the resources to perform the tasks which she sets for it. Malivert's dreams of Heavenly union with Spirite can in no way be described so as to give even a hint of their character.

The inspiration which Malivert receives from contact with Spirite demands infinitely more than language is capable of giving. In attempting to express himself fully, he taxes language well beyond its limits: "Les vieilles formes, les vieux moules éclataient et quelquefois la phrase en fusion jaillissait et débordait mais en éclaboussures superbes, semblables à des rayons d'étoiles brisées." Yet, as we have seen, despite the distortions and irregularities of his expression, Malivert achieves a power given only to the greatest poets.

Considering the limitations of language, how can the poet reach maximum expressivity? The fantastic works respond that a particularly rich source lies in music. When language fails, music comes into play to enhance expression. The ghost in "La Pipe d'opium" speaks in marvelously beautiful verse, but at times even poetry is insufficient to convey her thoughts: "et quand le vers ne suffisait plus pour rendre sa pensée, elle lui ajoutait les ailes de la musique, et c'était des roulades, des colliers de notes plus pures que des perles parfaites, des tenues de voix, des sons filés bien au-dessus des limites humaines, tout ce que l'âme et l'esprit peuvent rêver de plus tendre, de plus ineffable." Spirite, though she already enjoys the ability to express the ideal fully, utilizes music to augment for Malivert the expressive power of his verse. Her musical rendition gives to his poem a dimension which words alone could never bestow: "—Spirite, avec une intuition merveilleuse, rendait l'au-delà des mots, le non-sorti du verbe humain, ce qui reste d'inédit dans la phrase la mieux faite, le mystérieux, l'intime et le profond des choses, la secrète aspiration qu'on s'avoue à peine à soi-même, l'indicible et l'inexprimable, le *desideratum* de la pensée au bout de ses efforts, et tout le flottant, le flou, le suave qui déborde du contour trop sec de la parole."

II

One also finds in Gautier's fantastic works expressions of general attitudes toward art. The power which the artistic work may exert over the individual receives particularly frequent attention. Music, for instance, has as if a magic virtue in its capacity to change the hearer's mood. The light, sprightly music which Alicia Ward and Paul d'Aspremont perform in duet in "Jettatura" relieves the young man of the gloom brought on by suspicions that his influence may be fatal to his fiancée. The narrator comments on the role of the music in d'Aspremont's change: "La musique a le pouvoir de chasser les mauvais esprits: au bout de quelques phrases, Paul ne pensait plus aux doigts conjurateurs, aux cornes magiques, aux amulettes de corail; il avait oublié le terrible bouquin du signor Valetta [on the evil eye] et toutes les rêveries de la jettatura. Son âme montait gaiement, avec la voix d'Alicia, dans un air pur et lumineux." In "Le Club des hachichins," the express function of the *voyant,* the musician who plays for the hashish eaters, is to control by his music the emotions of the hallucinating guests. He performs his role successfully. When the early, extraordinarily mirthful phase of the drugged state becomes intolerable, the *voyant* is able, by his choice of composition, not only to calm the guests but to lead them to entirely different feelings. Later, with another kind of music, he moves the guests from a state of terror into a mood of gaiety in which their nightmarish hallucinations are dissipated.

There is no question of the great affective power of art. Instances are frequent in the fantastic works where the influence of a piece of art is shown to be extraordinarily strong. A masterpiece, whatever its medium, can so grip the spectator that he loses all consciousness of his environment. The speaker in "Veillée," a poem containing a number of fantastic motifs, finds a sense of liberation in reading medieval legends:

> Lais, virelais, ballades,
> Légendes de béats guérissant les malades,
> Les possédés du diable, et les pauvres lépreux,
> Par un signe de croix; chroniques d'anciens preux,
> Mes yeux dévorent tout; c'est en vain que l'horloge
> Tinte par douze fois, que le hibou déloge
> En glapissant, blessé des rayons du flambeau
> Qui m'éclaire; je lis: sur la table à tombeau,
> Le long du chandelier, cependant la bougie
> En larges nappes coule, et la vitre rougie
> Laisse voir dans le ciel, au bord de l'orient
> Le soleil qui se lève avec un front riant.

The music of Mozart affects Albertus even more strongly. When he first appears in the poem, he is attending a performance of *Don Giovanni.* While all others in the theater have their eyes on the lovely Véronique, Albertus is overpowered by the music, which catches him up and transports him out of the real world:

> Seul un homme
>
> . . . .
>
> Dans une extase sainte enivre ses oreilles
> De ces accords profonds, de ces hautes merveilles
> Qui font luire ton nom entre tous,—ô Mozart!—

Ton génie avait pris le sien, et de ses ailes
Le poussait par delà les sphères éternelles.
L'heure, le lieu, le monde, il ne savait plus rien,
Il s'était fait musique, et son cœur en mesure
Palpitait et chantait avec une voix pure,
　　　Et lui seul te comprenait bien.

Art—especially music—can actually magnetize, hypnotize. The music of the mastersinger works a powerful effect on Countess Edwige in "Le Chevalier double": "il chantait d'étranges poésies qui troublaient le cœur et donnaient des idées furieuses . . . Edwige rougissait, rougissait comme des roses de l'aurore, et se laissait aller en arrière dans son fauteuil, languissante, à demi-morte, enivrée comme si elle avait respiré le parfum fatal de ces fleurs qui font mourir."

In the projected ballet, *Le Preneur de rats de Hameln*, Gautier also emphasizes the hypnotic power of music. The story of the ratcatcher's ability to magnetize the rats of Hamlin and rid the town of its scourge is familiar. So is his success in attracting the children of Hamlin away from their parents into a lovely world of fantasy. Gautier gives different details to the story, underscoring an essential point, that music has an extraordinary influence over the hearer: "le PRENEUR DE RATS commence un air à la Paganini, impérieux et sauvage, et cependant d'une douceur extrême, mêlé de *pizzicati*, de *staccati* et de tous les tours de force que peut exécuter sur le violon un virtuose accompli. Il se met en marche sur la place, entrant dans les maisons dont il fait tenir les portes ouvertes, puis se plaçant au milieu, le dos tourné à la cathédrale, il joue son grand air magique. De tous les côtés surgissent les rats, des caves, des gouttières, des soupiraux, des portes, des fenêtres, de toutes les issues, qui s'attroupent par légions aux pieds du personnage fantastique." Later, the scenario represents the ratcatcher playing an irresistible melody which draws the virgins of the town, against their will, into the underworld where the musician resides.

We do not need to detail again the effects of music on Guy de Malivert; we have already learned how Spirite's musical performance alters his entire frame of mind. Nor do we need to make a special point that music is only representative of all artistic mediums in its affective power. Painting, sculpture, and poetry—all forms of art—have the capacity to change those who live the aesthetic experience. As the narrator suggests in "La Mille et deuxième Nuit," art can—and does—temper our crudeness, making us sensitive to the spectacle of nature and compassionate for the suffering of our fellow men.

The matter of effect relates naturally to the public, to those who receive the work of art; and the fantastic works are not without direct statements on the members of this public. Their character naturally has importance in the encounter with the product of the artist's craft. According to "Spirite," if the artist must be deeply spiritual in order to produce the greatest art, then the public must be equally so in order to take the fullest advantage of that art. Spirite, because of her new essence, is able to understand perfectly the unexpressed—and inexpressible—sense both in the musical piece which she plays and in Malivert's poem. Malivert, too, as he gains in spirituality, also gains a greater sensitivity to art and its masterpieces. Arriving at Piraeus and viewing the Acropolis in the morning sun, he feels an irresistible thrill: "Malivert eut le frémissement que donne la sensation du beau, et il comprit ce qui jusqu'alors lui avait semblé obscur. Tout l'art grec se révélait à lui, romantique, dans cette rapide vision, c'est-à-dire la parfaite proportion de l'ensemble, la pureté absolue des lignes, la suavité incomparable de la couleur faite de blancheur, d'azur et de lumière."

Not only is comprehension total with spirituality; perception is correct. In addition to understanding Greek art, Malivert is able now mentally to reconstruct the Parthenon, to fill in the gaps created by the ravages of time and man. According to the story, he owes this marvellous perception directly to his spiritual orientation: "Malivert monta les degrés et s'approcha de Spirite, qui tendit la main vers lui. Alors, dans un éblouissement rapide, il vit le Parthénon comme il était aux jours de sa splendeur. Les colonnes tombées avaient repris leur place; les figures du fronton arrachées par lord Elgin, ou brisées par les bombes vénitiennes, s'étaient groupées sur les frontons, pures, intactes, dans leurs attitudes humainement divines. Par la porte de la cella, Malivert entrevit, remontée sur son piédestal, la statue d'or et d'ivoire de Phidias, la céleste, la vierge, l'immaculée Pallas-Athéné."

This capacity to perceive what is implicit in the art work must be a fundamental quality in the proper audience. Because Lavinia, even before her death, possessed it, she was able to understand Malivert's literary production perhaps better than he. Her statement concerning her reaction to his writings, together with the representation of Malivert's heightened perceptiveness cited above, underscores that the public, to understand fully, must read between the lines: " 'Il ne faut pas toujours prendre au pied de la lettre ce que dit un auteur: on doit faire la part des systèmes philosophiques ou littéraires, des affections à la mode de ce moment-là, des réticences exigées, du style voulu ou commandé, des imitations admiratives et de tout ce qui peut modifier les formes extérieures d'un écrivain. Mais, sous tous ces déguisements, la vraie attitude de l'âme finit par se révéler pour qui sait lire; la sincère pensée est souvent entre les lignes, et le secret du poète, qu'il ne veut pas toujours livrer à la foule, se devine à la longue; l'un après l'autre les voiles tombent et les mots des énigmes se découvrent.' "

As members of the literary and art public, Gautier's heroes and narrators frequently pass judgment on particular artists and artistic epochs. Their assessments are of interest, because they contribute to our understanding of the question of art not only in the fantastic works but elsewhere in Gautier's production.

We should expect, from what is already clear about matters of art and from what we know about the quest for happiness and obstacles to its success, that artistic preferences would go to earlier periods. Such is the case. Modern art and artists in the fantastic works run a wretched second. Modern art, first of all, lacks vigor. It is implicit in "Le Pied de momie" that it will not endure as have the products of the ancient Egyptian spirit. The ghost of Raphael in "La Comédie de la mort" makes a wholesale condemnation of modern artists. Not only does the great painter have no hope for the moderns because they lack love and faith; because they are products of a materialistic age, they lack especially the spiritual qualities necessary to produce great paintings:

> "Dites qui d'entre vous, fils de ce siècle infâme,
> Peut rendre saintement la beauté de la femme?
>   Aucun, hélas! aucun.
> Pour vos petits boudoirs il faut des priapées;
> Qui vous jette un regard, ô mes vierges drapées,
>   O mes saintes? Pas un."

Modern art—along with other aspects of modern culture—is inferior, according to pronouncements in the fantastic works, because it is a product of the Christian spirit. There is no contradiction between this idea and the speech above attributed to Raphael. Gautier's works make a sharp distinction between the attractive—if vain—sensuousness of some heroes and the priapism which Raphael sees as characteristic of modern artists. Gautier's hero d'Albert, of *Mademoiselle de Maupin,* contrasts clearly his personal materialistic concept of happiness and that of other men, whom he sees as depraved sensualists, all too easily satisfied by the crudest sexual pleasures. Raphael, despite his references to the Christian subject matter of his work and to saintliness and faith, does not in Gautier's works seem to belong among those morose, ascetic Christians so unsympathetic in "La Morte amoureuse" and in "Arria Marcella." These are Christians and Christians, just as there are materialists and materialists. We must take care to distinguish.

The Christian outlook has been deleterious for art precisely because of a refusal in many of its followers to grant validity to beauty and to the love of life. As we have seen, certain Christians take a gloomy view of existence, while the pagans painted even death with the bright colors of life. In "La Statue amoureuse," the priest seeks to prevent the artist Konrad from pursuing happiness in pagan materialism. The representative of the Church implicitly rejects the life-loving character of the pagan mentality. Because modern art is an element of a culture influenced by an ascetic brand of Christianity, much of it will be inferior. Inevitably tyrannized by a gloomy disposition, it will be unable to express that joy in living which makes pagan art attractive.

It is therefore easy to guess which earlier periods of art find favor in Gautier's works. Certainly antiquity, especially that of the Greeks, is admirable. The comparison between Prascovie Labinska and a graceful figure on a Greek vase is characteristic of any number of statements on antique art: "elle rappelait ces sveltes figures de toilettes grecques qui ornent les vases antiques et dont aucun artiste n'a pu retrouver le pur et suave contour, la beauté jeune et légère." Guy de Malivert speaks sympathetically of the aesthetic revolution caused in a friend by a trip to Greece: " 'Il était parti romantique enragé; il a reçu sa métope sur la tête et ne veut plus entendre parler de cathédrales. C'est un classique rigide maintenant. Il prétend que, depuis les Grecs, l'humanité est retombée à l'état barbare, et que nos prétendues civilisations ne sont que des variétés de décadence.' " Malivert's own reaction to Greece is not radically different from that of his friend. His feeling on seeing the Acropolis is typical of that expressed by other heroes toward earlier golden ages: "Il franchit les Propylées de Mnésiclès, chef-d'œuvre digne de servir de porte au chef-d'œuvre d'Ictinus et de Phidias, avec un sentiment d'admiration religieuse; il avait presque honte, lui barbare d'Occident de marcher avec des bottes sur ce sol sacré."

This is not to say that more recent times do not have isolated cases of superior artistic ability. The admiration which the narrator of "Le Club des hachichins" shows for the artistic and architectural genius of the age of Louis XIV is familiar. He, too, feels shame, like Malivert on the Acropolis, as he enters the magnificent Hôtel Pimodan. Certain individual artists have risen above their inferior age. In addition to Cimarosa, Gluck, Palestrina, Mozart, and Raphael, particular attention goes to Wagner, the only contemporary of Gautier who stands out for open praise in the fantastic works. It is clear that we are to see Wagner as a great artist, for the character who praises him in "Spirite" is none other than the Baron de Féroë. Given the context of "Spirite," it is easy to understand why Wagner is respected: he represents that spiritual orientation which alone is capable of fostering the greatest art. Indeed, all of the artists mentioned here have this disposition. On the other hand, we can also appreciate why most modern art, according to the fantastic works, is inferior: it lacks that spiritual quality which is the essential ingredient of greatness.

III

Unlike the works of a number of Romantics—those of Hugo and Vigny, for example—Gautier's fantastic works offer no clear-cut idea on the function of art. It is not certain whether the suggestion in "Albertus" that art is a consolation, the assertion in "L'Ame de la maison" that art may preserve the memory of happy times, and the concept of art as a means of escape from reality, ("Veillée"), are meant to be read as formalizations regarding function. Certainly they are not representative of a unified view. Nor, for that matter, is Spirite's idea that art, if approached in the right way, provides an insight into the artist's deepest personality, though occasional parallels to this view are evident elsewhere in Gautier's works.

One would not expect—and one does not find—a strong emphasis on the social function of art. Even the suggestion in "Le Preneur de rats de Hameln," that art may serve to purge society of its baser instincts, is not expressed without ambiguity. Though the ratcatcher succeeds in saving Hamlin from its rats, we learn later that it was he himself who inflicted the scourge. He therefore cannot stand as an unequivocal symbol of the artist whose work serves a beneficial social function.

This does not mean, however, that Gautier's fantastic works do not have something to say regarding the relations between artist and public. From what we have already seen [elsewhere] of the individual's problems in seeking happiness, it is not surprising that we find an antagonism between the artist and the social reality in which he lives. A number of works suggest that the public does not understand the artist and his aspirations. This is a lesson of "La Mille et deuxième Nuit." The peri will appear as a fairy only to Mahmoud because, as she says, people would not pardon him for enjoying a felicity superior to their own. In *La Péri*, others attempt to prevent Achmet's union with the fairy queen. They are wholly without sensitivity to the artist's idealism. Convinced that their rationalism is the only correct outlook, they make every effort to impose it upon the idealist, to his regret. Such an antagonism also characterizes "Spirite." Malivert is, after all, a man of letters and a poet. When we view the novelette from the standpoint of the social implications of art, we see the endeavor of Mme d'Ymbercourt to involve Malivert as the action of society to reduce the artist to its level of vulgarity.

The materialism of society may also take the form of profiteering, of exploiting beauty for gain. In the ballet *Gemma*, Santa-Croce, the antagonist, seeks to gain power over the rich and beautiful countess in order to restore his lost fortune: "[c'est] un débauché et un dissipateur cherchant à réparer par l'alchimie et les sciences occultes les brèches faites à sa fortune; il a, dans ses travaux hermétiques, retrouvé le secret du magnétisme connu autrefois des adeptes, et dont Mesmer sera plus tard le grand prêtre; de cette force inconnue il se sert pour satisfaire ses passions; il a résolu de dominer Gemma et de la contraindre à l'épouser; mariage qui lui donnerait plus d'or que ses alambics et ses creusets." The artist Massimo, on the other hand, loves Gemma for herself. The conflict in the ballet turns on the struggle between Santa-Croce and Massimo. The artist almost loses her, but in the end he overcomes the evil profiteer and is reunited with his beloved.

No matter how luxuriously members of society may be accommodated, if they are materialistic and vulgar, their wealth cannot hide their character. They remain fundamentally bourgeois ("Spirite"). (In a *feuilleton* of 1855, Gautier defines "bourgeois" thus: "Bourgeois ne veut nullement dire un citoyen ayant droit de bourgeoisie. Un duc peut être un bourgeois dans le sens détourné où s'accepte ce vocable depuis une trentaine d'années. *Bourgeois*, en France, a la même valeur à peu près que *philistin* en Allemagne, et désigne tout être, quelle que soit sa position, qui n'est pas initié aux arts, ou ne les comprend pas. Celui qui passe devant Raphaël et se mire aux casseroles de Drolling, est un bourgeois. Vous préférez Paul de Kock à lord Byron,—bourgeois; les flons-flons du Vaudeville aux symphonies de Beethoven,—bourgeois.—Vous décorez votre cheminée de chiens en verre filé,—bourgeois.") This means that they not only fail to comprehend art but frequently hold art and artists in the lowest esteem. Though Henrich's contemporaries praise his talent, his fiancée's parents refuse to let the two young people marry, because Henrich is an actor. How shabbily the public treats the artist is evident in "Le Preneur de rats de Hameln." After their town has been cleared of its rats, the burghers refuse to pay the strange musician the full sum agreed upon to deliver them from the scourge. Indeed, they are doubly shameless in their treatment of him. At the end of the scenario, we learn that the ratcatcher is none other than Prince Udolph, earlier banished by these same burghers. While we should not take every detail of "Le Preneur" too literally, we may see in the projected ballet a complaint regarding a specific public attitude toward artists—a complaint expressed by more than one French author in the nineteenth century.

What shall the artist do, then, given the antagonism which separates him and the bourgeois public? If we may take as an answer to this question indications from the fantastic works, he will maintain a position of aloofness. Inevitably separated, he will take advantage of his isolation. As some of the works imply, he will enjoy beauty privately. This is the lesson of "La Mille et deuxième Nuit," as it is the suggestion of *Gemma* and "Spirite."

Other works represent the pleasures afforded the artist by retreat into the imagination. While the imagination cannot bring full happiness, it can give the artist a measure of consolation. The recluse in "L'Ame de la maison" is not an entirely happy individual, but the life which he leads in his mind is substantially preferable to intercourse with the society around him. Prince Udolph's occupation of the Pays Vert, the realm of the kobolds, in "Le Preneur de rats de Hameln" is nothing other than a symbolic representation of withdrawal into the imagination. The prince has literally gone "underground" in the context of the scenario. The kingdom in which he resides is hidden from ordinary men, a place of great wealth, for the principal activity of the kobolds is the mining of precious stones. By the particular form which he gives to his story, Gautier suggests that the artist may, in his social isolation, find satisfactions superior to those offered in society, satisfactions in the imagination, that other world, remote yet abundantly rich. "Le Preneur" suggests that this is also the realm of absolute reality. Alongside the ratcatcher and his kobolds stands the figure of Truth in all her nudity. The realities of the Pays Vert are more real than those of the surface.

Nevertheless, as we now know, the fullest satisfaction for the artist lies in the fullest spiritualization. It is unequivocal in "Spirite": only in the higher spheres, in the world of transcendent realities, will the poet's desires be satisfied. Here, too, the artist will stand aloof from society. There is no place for him alongside other men; but when he has unconditionally chosen the way of the spirit, society counts for very little.

IV

Since beauty has a close relationship to art and the artist in Gautier's work, it is not out of place in the present study. In fact, consideration of beauty in the fantastic works promises to shed light on our understanding of beauty throughout Gautier's production. A large number of scholars allude to his preoccupation with beauty, but few if any attempt to get at its specific character. Paul Bernard sees Gautier's concept of beauty as based upon harmony, that is, formal equilibrium. Henriette E. A. Velthuis speaks of beauty of form, especially as revealed in the female body. Though Joanna Richardson frequently mentions Gautier's "religion of beauty," she fails to specify beyond suggesting with Velthuis that it is beauty of form that appealed to him.

The problem of beauty in Gautier is central in the recent studies by Cecilia Rizza, *Théophile Gautier critico letterario*, and Michael Spencer, *The Art Criticism of Théophile Gautier*. Both scholars are interested in the question as to whether Gautier saw beauty as objective or subjective, that is, as an eternal archetype or as an individual conception. Professor Rizza believes that Gautier saw it as an absolute, though he never clarified the metaphysical bases of this view or the relationship between beauty and reality. Spencer points out that in *Mademoiselle de Maupin* Gautier is ambivalent about beauty, seeing it now in one way, now in the other. The problem becomes even more difficult when one considers the aesthetic bases of *Les Grotesques*, with its "opposition of *irregularity* and even eccentricity to the solemnity of classicism, imprisoned in impossible rules." Then Gautier adds a further complication with his "microcosm" theory, which suggests that all great artists create according to a personal optic that gives to their work a particular cachet, inimitable and all its own.

For consideration of beauty in Gautier's fantastic works, the question of whether it is objective or subjective is a natural point of departure. With one exception, beauty is represented in these works as something subjectively conceived. In "La Morte amoureuse," Romuald suggests the existence of an eternal archetype when he says of Clarimonde: "Oh! comme elle était belle! Les plus grands peintres, lorsque, *poursuivant dans le ciel la beauté idéale*, ils ont rapporté sur la terre le divin portrait de la Madone, n'approchent même pas de cette fabuleuse réalité" (italics mine). But in "Arria Marcella," *La Péri*, and even "Spirite," beauty is the private conception of the individual. Though Octavien may love women famous in art and history, his conception of beauty is his own. It is his personal revery that has created the form which he will find concretized in Arria Marcella. Similarly, the peri who appears to Achmet is not the reflection of an archetype existing objectively in an ideal universe, but the answer to a mental creation evolved by the young Egyptian himself. Beauty in "Spirite" is unquestionably subjective. Spirite herself was once a real being. Now, with the ability to resume a small measure of density, she appears as a sort of reflection of her former self. She partakes in no way of an archetype. Certainly the ideal of Greek art mentioned by the narrator is not archetypal. It is a thought somehow related to a spiritual entity rather than to a formal abstraction.

That beauty is not conceived in objective terms does not mean that idealism has no part in its conception. Beauty in the fantastic works is divided into two general categories: terrestrial and celestial, or ideal. In opposition to Véronique, the narrator of "Albertus" alludes to the Venetian woman, "la plus et mieux aimée." Now dead, she remains with Albertus only in memory and in a portrait. Everything that is said of her implies a celestial character. She is

> Belle à ne savoir pas de quel nom l'appeler,
> Péri, fée ou sylphide, être charmant et frêle;
> Ange du ciel à qui l'on aurait coupé l'aile
>   Pour l'empêcher de s'envoler.
>
> On aurait dit, à voir cette tête inclinée,
> Une *Mater Dei* d'après Masaccio.

The same division of beauty is evident in *Spirite* when Malivert contemplates the pleasures of spiritual love: "la passion qu'il éprouvait n'était-elle pas plus noble, plus poétique, plus éthérée, plus rapprochée de l'éternel amour, dégagé ainsi de toute contingence terrestre, ayant pour objet une beauté idéalisée par la mort? L'union humaine la plus parfaite n'a-t-elle pas ses lassitudes, ses satiétés et ses ennuis? L'œil le plus ébloui voit au bout de quelques années, les charmes adorés pâlir; l'âme se fait moins visible à travers la chair flétrie, et l'amour étonné cherche son idole disparue."

The specific character of physical beauty in the fantastic tales is diverse. The varieties go far beyond the type studied by Poulet, "la blonde aux yeux noirs." Though Clarimonde and Prascovie may be blonds, Princess Hermonthis, Arria Marcella, and Alicia Ward are brunettes. While a majority are fair, Hermonthis, typically Egyptian, has a dark complexion. The eyes of beautiful women run a gamut of colors, from green, to blue-green, to dark, to midnight blue. The mouth is generally the same, with a voluptuous tone of red, while the nose is usually thin and delicate. Even in the same woman, features which might seem disparate sometimes co-exist: Arria Marcella is a brunette, but her complexion is pale, with a mat tone. Alicia Ward's skin is exceptionally fair, yet her hair is jet black. The elements common to all have little to do with coloration. What appears important in the representations of physical beauty is delicateness and an air of nobility, impossible to define.

The fantastic works do not limit themselves to female beauty. In certain works Gautier also emphasizes the beauty of the male. In these cases, too, there is variety. Albertus is dark, while Count Olaf Labinska has a light complexion, though he is tanned by his outdoor life as a military officer. Albertus' hair is dark; Olaf is a blond; Paul d'Aspremont's hair is auburn. D'Aspremont has gray eyes, while Olaf's dark eyes contrast with his fair complexion.

Particularly striking in the narrators' respective portraits of Albertus and d'Aspremont is the suggestion that, despite the beauty of the individual elements, something in the general aspect is unbecoming. The narrator of "Albertus" says, for example:

> Cependant il avait quelque chose
> Qui déplaisait à voir, et, quoique sans défaut,
> On l'aurait souhaité différént.—L'ironie,
> Le sarcasme y brillait plutôt que le génie;
> Les bas semblait railler le haut.
>
> Cet ensemble faisait l'effet le plus étrange;
> C'était comme un démon se tordant sous un ange,
> Un enfer sous un ciel. Quoiqu'il eût de beaux yeux,
> De longs sourcils d'ébène effilés vers la tempe,
> Se glissant sur la peau comme un serpent qui rampe,
> Une frange de cils palpitants et soyeux,
> Son regard de lion et la fauve étincelle
> Qui jaillissait parfois du fond de sa prunelle
> Vous faisaient frissonner et pâlir malgré vous.
> —Les plus hardis auraient abaissé la paupière
> Devant cet œil Méduse à vous changer en pierre
> Qu'il s'efforçait de rendre doux.

Similarly, the narrator of "Jettatura" says of Paul d'Aspremont: "tous ces traits, beaux en eux-mêmes, ne composaient point un ensemble agréable. Il leur manquait cette mystérieuse harmonie qui adoucit les contours et les fond les uns dans les autres. La légende parle d'un peintre italien qui, voulant représenter l'archange rebelle, lui composa un masque de beautés disparates, et arriva ainsi à un effet de terreur bien plus grand qu'au moyen des cornes, des sourcils circonflexes et de la bouche en rictus. Le visage de [Paul] produisait une impression de ce genre."

Thus, while a particular *type* of beauty—or even specific elements in physical make-up—is not constant in the fantastic works, the important question would appear to be that of the harmony of the parts. This is not, as Paul Bernard wishes, a matter of equilibrium in the strict sense of the word, but of *consonance* of the parts that go to make up the beautiful whole. The narrator of "Jettatura" underscores this preference for consonance in his description of Alicia Ward: "Miss Alicia Ward appartenait à cette variété d'Anglaises brunes qui réalisent un idéal dont les conditions semblent se contrarier: c'est-à-dire une peau d'une blancheur éblouissante à rendre jaune le lait, la neige, le lis, l'albâtre, la cire vierge, et tout ce qui sert aux poëtes à faire des comparaisons blanches; des lèvres de cerise, et des cheveux aussi noirs que la nuit sur les ailes du corbeau. L'effet de cette opposition est irrésistible et produit une beauté à part dont on ne saurait trouver l'équivalent ailleurs. . . . Alicia était assurément le type le plus parfait de ce genre de beauté." Though Paul d'Aspremont is handsome in the different elements of his physiognomy, the whole lacks harmony. Alicia, on the other hand, is beautiful precisely because of the harmonious union of elements which would normally oppose one another. It is clear that harmony, consonance, whether of form or coloration, is the essential element of physical beauty as conceived in the fantastic works.

Despite the place occupied by tangible beauty in Gautier's fantastic writings, it is evident, when we consider them in chronological order, that beauty comes more and more to be conceived in idealistic terms. Even in the earliest works physical charms are recognized to be transitory, even dangerous, since capitulation to their attractions may lead to personal grief and ruin. Preference for the enjoyment of ideal beauty—though perception of it yet requires that it assume physical form—becomes clear in "La Mille et deuxième Nuit" and in *La Péri*. A major reason for the favor given to idealism is a recognition that physical beauty is ephemeral. When the peri appears to Achmet in prison, her principal argument in urging him to follow her is that love founded on physical charms is impermanent: " 'Si tu restes, un supplice épouvantable, et pour qui? pour une femme, pour une simple mortelle, dont la beauté ne doit durer qu'un jour, et qui ne sera bientôt qu'une pincée de poussière.' "

It is thus ideal beauty that characterizes the fantastic works of the late 1850's. Prascovie, Alicia—we might add Sacountalâ—have a fundamental spiritual character. "Spirite" reveals unequivocally that such spiritual beauty is to be preferred to all other kinds. It far surpasses the greatest physical charms. When Spirite first appears to Malivert in the Venetian mirror, the narrator describes her image as "une tête de jeune femme, ou plutôt de jeune fille, d'une beauté dont la beauté mortelle n'est que l'ombre." Malivert immediately recognizes that the impalpable image is infinitely more attractive than anything created by nature or by art. His reaction to it is as strong as that of materialistic heroes to the real beauties whom they love. He experiences an ineffable delight; and his love for this spirit is instantaneous: "ce qu'il comprit tout de suite, c'est qu'il était éperdument, désespérément et irrévocablement amoureux et envahi tout d'un coup d'une passion que l'éternité n'assouvirait pas." This "celestial" beauty, as we know, offers infinite pleasures to the individual with the appropriate orientation. It opens to the spiritually minded idealist a sure path to those "sphères supérieures où le désir du poète doit être enfin satisfait."

Baudelaire: Anthropomorphism and Trope in the Lyric

Paul de Man

The gesture that links epistemology with rhetoric in general, and not only with the mimetic tropes of representation, recurs in many philosophical and poetic texts of the nineteenth century, from Keats's "Beauty is truth, truth beauty" to Nietzsche's perhaps better known than understood definition of truth as tropological displacement: "Was ist also Wahrheit? Ein bewegliches Heer von Metaphern, Metonymien, Anthropomorphismen [What then is truth? A mobile army of metaphors, metonomies, and anthropomorphisms]" ("On Truth and Lie in an Extra-Moral Sense"). Even when thus truncated before it has been allowed to run one third of its course, Nietzsche's sentence considerably complicates the assimilation of truth to trope that it proclaims. Later in the essay, the homology between concept and figure as symmetrical structures and aberrant repressions of differences is dramatized in the specular destinies of the artist and the scientist-philosopher. Like the Third Critique, this late Kantian text demonstrates, albeit in the mode of parody, the continuity of aesthetic with rational judgment that is the main tenet and the major crux of all critical philosophies and "Romantic" literatures. The considerable difference in tone between Nietzsche and Kant cannot conceal the congruity of the two projects, their common stake in the recovery of controlled discourse on the far side of even the sharpest denials of intuitive sense-certainties. What interests us primarily in the poetic and philosophical versions of this transaction, in this give-and-take between reason and imagination, is not, at this point, the critical schemes that deny certainty considered in themselves, but their disruption by patterns that cannot be reassimilated to these schemes, but that are nevertheless, if not produced, then at least brought into focus by the distortions the disruption inflicts upon them.

From *The Rhetoric of Romanticism.* © 1984 by Columbia University Press.

Thus, in the Nietzsche sentence, the recovery of knowledge by ways of its devalorization in the deviance of the tropes is challenged, even at this moment of triumph for a critical reason which dares to ask and to reply to the question: what is truth? First of all, the listing of particular tropes is odd, all the more so since it is technically more precise than is often the case in such arguments: only under the pen of a classical philologist such as Nietzsche is one likely to find combined, in 1872, what Gérard Genette has since wittily referred to as the two "chiens de faience" of contemporary rhetoric— metaphor and metonymy. But the third term in the enumeration, anthropomorphism, is no longer a philological and neutral term, neither does it complement the two former ones: anthropomorphisms can contain a metaphorical as well as a metonymic moment—as in an Ovidian metamorphosis in which one can start out from the contiguity of the flower's name to that of the mythological figure in the story, or from the resemblance between a natural scene and a state of soul.

The term "anthropomorphism" therefore adds little to the two previous ones in the enumeration, nor does it constitute a synthesis between them, since neither metaphor nor metonymy have to be necessarily anthropomorphic. Perhaps Nietzsche, in the Voltairean conte philosophique "On Truth and Lie" is just being casual in his terminology—but then, opportunities to encounter technical tropological terms are so sparse in literary and philosophical writings that one can be excused for making the most of it when they occur. The definition of truth as a collection ("army" being, aside from other connotations, at any rate a collective term) of tropes is a purely structural definition, devoid of any normative emphasis; it implies that truth is relational, that it is an articulation of a subject (for example "truth") and a predicate (for example "an army of tropes") allowing for an answer to a definitional question (such as "what is truth?") that is not purely tautological. At this point, to say that truth is a trope is to say that truth is the possibility of stating a proposition; to say that truth is a collection of varied tropes is to say that it is the possibility of stating several propositions about a single subject, of relating several predicates to a subject according to principles of articulation that are not necessarily identical: truth is the possibility of definition by means of infinitely varied sets of propositions. This assertion is purely descriptive of an unchallenged grammatical possibility and, as such, it has no critical thrust, nor does it claim to have one: there is nothing inherently disruptive in the assertion that truth is a trope.

But "anthropomorphism" is not just a trope but an identification on the level of substance. It takes one entity for another and thus implies the constitution of specific entities prior to their confusion, the *taking* of something for something else that can then be assumed to be *given*. Anthropomorphism freezes the infinite chain of tropological transformations and propositions into one single assertion or essence which, as such, excludes all others. It is no longer a proposition but a proper name, as when the metamorphosis in Ovid's stories culminates and halts in the singleness of a proper name, Narcissus or Daphne or whatever. Far from being the same, tropes such as metaphor (or metonymy) and anthropomorphisms are mutually exclusive. The apparent enumeration is in fact a foreclosure which acquires, by the same token, considerable critical power.

Truth is now defined by two incompatible assertions: either truth is a set of propositions or truth is a proper name. Yet, on the other hand, it is clear that the tendency to move from tropes to systems of interpretations such as anthropomorphisms is built into the very notion of trope. One reads Nietzsche's sentence without any sense of disruption, for although a trope is in no way the same as an anthropomorphism, it is nevertheless the case that an anthropomorphism is structured like a trope: it is easy enough to cross the barrier that leads from trope to name but impossible, once this barrier has been crossed, to return from it to the starting-point in "truth." Truth is a trope; a trope generates a norm or value; this value (or ideology) is no longer true. It is true that tropes are the producers of ideologies that are no longer true.

Hence the "army" metaphor. Truth, says Nietzsche, is a mobile *army* of tropes. Mobility is coextensive with any trope, but the connotations introduced by "army" are not so obvious, for to say that truth is an army (of tropes) is again to say something odd and possibly misleading. It can certainly not imply, in "On Truth and Lie" that truth is a kind of commander who enlists tropes in the battle against error. No such dichotomy exists in any critical philosophy, let alone Nietzsche's, in which truth is always at the very least dialectical, the negative knowledge of error. Whatever truth may be fighting, it is not error but stupidity, the belief that one is right when one is in fact in the wrong. To assert, as we just did, that the assimilation of truth to tropes is not a disruption of epistemology, is not to assert that tropes are therefore true or on the side, so to speak, of truth. Tropes are neither true nor false and are both at once. To call them an army is however to imply that their effect and their effectiveness is not a matter of judgment but of power. What characterizes a good army, as distinct for instance from a good cause, is that its success has little to do with immanent justice and a great deal with the proper economic use of its power. One willingly admits that truth has power, including the power to occur, but to say that its power is like that of an army and to say this within the definitional context of the question: what is therefore truth? is truly disruptive. It not only asserts that truth (which was already complicated by having to be a proposition as well as a proper name) is also power, but a power that exists independently of epistemological determinations, although these determinations are far from being nonexistent: calling truth an army *of tropes* reaffirms its epistemological *as well as* its strategic power. How the two modes of power could exist side by side certainly baffles the mind, if not the grammar of Nietzsche's tale. The sentence that asserts the complicity of epistemology and rhetoric, of truth and trope, also turns this alliance into a battle made all the more dubious by the fact that the adversaries may not even have the opportunity ever to encounter each other. Less schematically compressed, more elaborated and dramatized instances of similar disjunctions can be found in the texts of lyrical poets, such as, for example, Baudelaire.

The canonical and programmatic sonnet "Correspondances" contains not a single sentence that is not simply declarative. Not a single negation, interrogation, or exclamation, not a single verb that is not in the present indicative, nothing but straightforward affirmation: "la Nature *est* un temple . . . Il *est* des parfums frais comme des chairs d'enfants." The least assertive word in the text is the innocuous "parfois" in line 2, hardly a dramatic temporal break. Nor is there (a rare case in *Les Fleurs du mal*) any pronominal agitation: no *je-tu* apostrophes or dialogues, only the most objective descriptions of third persons. The only personal pronoun to appear is the impersonal "il" of "il est (des parfums) . . ."

The choice of "Correspondances" to explicate the quandaries of language as truth, as name, and as power may therefore appear paradoxical and forced. The ironies and the narrative frame of "On Truth and Lie" make it difficult to take the apparent good cheer of its tone at face value, but the serenity of "Correspondances" reaches deep enough to eliminate any disturbance of the syntactical surface. This serenity is prevalent enough to make even the question superfluous. Nietzsche still has to dramatize the summation of his story in an eye-catching paragraph that begins with the question of questions: *Was ist also Wahrheit*? But Baudelaire's text is all assurance and all answer. One has to make an effort to perceive the opening line as an answer to an implicit question, "La Nature est un temple . . . " as the answer to "Qu' est-ce que la nature?" The title is not "La Nature," which would signal a need for definition; in "Correspondances," among many other connotations, one hears "response," the dialogical exchange that takes place in mutual proximity to a shared entity called nature. The *response* to the sonnet, among its numerous readers and commentators, has been equally responsive. Like the oracle of Delphi, it has been made to answer a considerable number and variety of questions put to it by various readers. Some of these questions are urgent (such as: how can one be innocent and corrupt at the same time?), some more casually historical (such as: when can modern French lyric poetry, from Baudelaire to surrealism and beyond, be said to begin?). In all cases, the poem has never failed to answer to the satisfaction of its questioner.

The serenity of the diction celebrates the powers of tropes or "symboles" that can reduce any conceivable difference to a set of polarities and combine them in an endless play of substitution and amalgamation, extending from the level of signification to that of the signifier. Here, as in Nietzsche's text, the telos of the substitutions is the unified system "esprit/sens" (l. 14), the seamless articulation, by ways of language, of sensory and aesthetic experience with the intellectual assurance of affirmation. Both echo each other in the controlled compression of a brief and highly formalized sonnet which can combine the enigmatic depth of doctrine—sending commentators astray in search of esoteric authority—with the utmost banality of a phrase such as "verts comme les prairies."

On the thematic level, the success of the project can be measured by the unquestioned acceptance of a paradox such as "Vaste comme la nuit et comme la clarté," in which a conjunctive *et* can dare to substitute for what should be the *ou* of an either/or structure. For the vastness of the night is one of confusion in which distinctions disappear, Hegel's night in which $A = A$ because no such thing as A can be discerned, and in which infinity is homogeneity. Whereas the vastness of light is like the capacity of the mind to make endless analytical distinctions, or the power of calculus to integrate by ways of infinitesimal differentiation. The juxtaposition of these incompatible meanings is condensed in the semantic ambiguity of "se confondent," which can designate the bad infinity of confusion as well as the fusion of opposites into synthetic judgments. That "echoes," which are originally the disjunction of a single sensory unit or word by the alien obstacle of a reflection, themselves re-fuse into a single sound ("Comme de longs échos qui de loin se confondent") again acts out the dialectic of identity and difference, of sensory diffuseness and intellectual precision.

The process is self-consciously verbal or mediated by language, as is clear from the couple "se confondent/se répondent," which dramatizes events of discourse and in which, as was already pointed out, "se répondent" should be read as "se correspondent" rather than as a pattern of question and answer. As in "confuses paroles" and "symboles" in the opening lines, the stress on language as the stage of disjunction is unmistakable. Language can be the chain of metaphors in a synethesia, as well as the oxymoronic polysemy of a single word, such as "se confondent" (or "transports" in l. 14) or even, on the level of the signifier, the play of the syllable or the letter. For the title, "Correspondances," is like the anagrammatic condensation of the text's entire program: "corps" and "esprit" brought together and harmonized by the *ance* of assonance that pervades the concluding tercets: from *ayant, ambre, chantent* to *expansion, sens, transport*, finally redoubled and reechoed in *enc-ens/sens*.

The assertion, or representation, of verbality in "se répondent" (or in "Laissent parfois sortir de confuses *paroles*") also coincides, as in Nietzsche's text, with the passage from tropes—here the substitution of one sense experience by another—to anthropomorphisms. Or so, at least, it seems to a perhaps overhasty reading that would at once oppose "nature" to "homme" as in a polarity of art ("temple") and nature, and endow natural forests and trees with eyes ("regards") and voices. The tradition of interpretation for this poem, which stresses the importance of Chateaubriand and of Gérard de Nerval as sources, almost unanimously moves in that direction.

The opening lines allow but certainly do not impose such a reading.

"La Nature est un temple" is enigmatic enough to constitute the burden of any attempt at understanding and cannot simply be reduced to a pattern of binary substitution, but what follows is hardly less obscure. "Vivants piliers," as we first meet it, certainly suggests the erect shape of human bodies naturally enough endowed with speech, a scene from the paintings of Paul Delvaux rather than from the poems of Victor Hugo. "L'homme," in line 3, then becomes a simple apposition to "vivants piliers." The notion of nature as a wood and, consequently, of "piliers" as anthropomorphic columns and trees, is suggested only by "des *forêts* de symboles" in which, especially in combination with "symboles," a natural and descriptive reading of "forêt" is by no means compelling. Nor is nature, in Baudelaire, necessarily a sylvan world. We cannot be certain whether we have ever left the world of humans and whether it is therefore relevant or necessary to speak of anthropomorphism at all in order to account for the figuration of the text. "Des forêts," a plural of what is already, in the singular, a collective plural (forêt) can be read as equivalent to "une foule de symboles," a figure of amplification that designates a large number, the crowd of humanity in which it is well known that Baudelaire took a constant poetic, rather than humanitarian, interest.

Perhaps we are not in the country at all but have never left the city, the "rue assourdissante" of the poem entitled "A une passante," for example. "Symboles" in "des forêts de symboles" could then designate the verbal, the rhetorical dimension within which we constantly dwell and which we therefore meet as passively as we meet the glance of the other in the street. That the possibility of this reading seems farfetched and, in my experience, never fails to elicit resistance, or that the forest/temple cliché should have forced itself so emphatically upon the attention of the commentators is one of the cruxes of "Correspondances."

It has been enough of a crux for Baudelaire himself to have generated at least one other text, the poem "Obsession," to which we will have to turn later. For the possibility of anthropomorphic (mis)reading is part of the text and part of what is at stake in it. Anthropomorphism seems to be the illusionary resuscitation of the natural breath of language, frozen into stone by the semantic power of the trope. It is a figural affirmation that claims to overcome the deadly negative power invested in the figure. In Baudelaire's, as in Nietzsche's text, the icon of this central trope is that of the architectural construct, temple, beehive, or columbarium.

This verbal building, which has to celebrate at the same time funeral and rebirth, is built by the infinite multiplication of numbers raising each other to ever higher arithmetic power. The property which privileges "parfums" as the sensory analogon for the joint powers of mind and body (ll. 9–14) is its ability to grow from the infinitely small to endless expansion, "ce grain d'encens qui remplit une église"—a quotation from *Les Fleurs du mal* that made it into Littré. The religious connotation of "temple" and "encens" suggests, as in the immediately anterior poem in the volume,

"Elévation,"a transcendental circulation, as ascent or descent, between the spirit and the senses, a borderline between two distinct realms that can be crossed.

Yet this movement is not unambiguously sustained by all the articulations of the text. Thus in the line "L'homme y passe à travers des forêts de symboles," "passer à travers" can have two very different spatial meanings. It can be read as "traverser la forêt"; one can *cross* the woods, as Narcissus goes through the looking-glass, or as the acrobat, in Banville's poem that echoes in Mallarmé's "Le Pitre châtié," goes through the roof of the circus tent, or as Vergil, for that matter, takes Dante beyond the woods in which he lost his way. But "passer à travers" can also mean to remain enclosed in the wood, to wander and err around in it as the speaker of "A une passante" wanders around in the crowd. The latter reading in fact suits the represented scene better than the former, although it is incompatible with the transcendental claims usually made for the sonnet. The transcendence of substitutive, analogical tropes linked by the recurrent "comme," a transcendence which occurs in the declarative assurance of the first quatrain, states the totalizing power of metaphor as it moves from analogy to identity, from simile to symbol and to a higher order of truth. Ambivalences such as those noted in "passer à travers," as well as the theoretical ambivalence of anthropomorphism in relation to tropes, complicate this expectation perhaps more forcefully than its outright negation. The complication is forceful enough to contaminate the key word that carries out the substitutions which constitute the main structure of the text: the word "comme."

When it is said that "Les parfums, les couleurs et les sons se répondent . . . *comme* de longs échos," then the preposition of resemblance, "comme,"the most frequently counted word in the canon of Baudelaire's poetry, does its work properly and clearly, without upsetting the balance between difference and identity that it is assigned to maintain. It achieves a figure of speech, for it is not actually the case that an answer is an echo; no echo has ever answered a question except by a "delusion" of the signifier—but it is certainly the case that an echo sounds like an answer, and that this similarity is endlessly suggestive. And the catachresis "se répondent" to designate the association between the various senses duly raises the process to the desired higher power. "Des parfums . . . / Doux comme les hautbois, verts comme les prairies" is already somewhat more complex, for although it is possible in referential and semantic terms to think of oboes and of certain scents as primarily "soft," it makes less sense to think of scents as green; "green scents" have less compelling connotations than "green thoughts" or "green shades." The relaying "comme" travels by ways of "hautbois," solidly tied to "parfums" by ways of "doux" and altogether compatible with "vert," through the pastoral association of the reedy sound still reinforced by the "(haut)*bois,* verts" that would be lost in English or German translation. The greenness of the fields can be guided back from color to scent with any "unsweet" connotation carefully filtered out.

All this is playing at metaphor according to the rules of the game. But the same is not true of the final "comme" in the poem: "Il est des parfums frais comme . . . / Doux comme . . . / —Et d'autres . . . / Ayant l'expansion des choses infinies / *Comme* l'ambre, le musc, le benjoin et l'encens." Ce comme n'est pas un comme comme les autres. It does not cross from one sense experience to another, as "frais" crosses from scent to touch or "doux" from scent to sound, nor does it cross from the common sensorium back to the single sense of hearing (as in "Les parfums, les couleurs et les sons se répondent" "Comme de longs échos . . . ") or from the sensory to the intellectual realm, as in the double register of "se confondent." In each of these cases, the "comme" is what avoids tautology by linking the subject to a predicate that is not the same: scents are said to be like oboes, or like fields, or like echoes. But here "comme" relates to the subject "parfums" in two different ways or, rather, it has two distinct subjects. If "comme" is related to "l'expansion des choses infinies," which is grammatically as well as tonally possible, then it still functions, like the other "commes," as a comparative simile: a common property ("l'expansion") links the finite senses to an experience of infinity. But "comme" also relates to "parfums": "Il est des parfums frais . . . / —Et d'autres . . . / Comme l'ambre, le musc, le benjoin et l'encens"; the somewhat enigmatic hyphen can be said to mark that hesitation (as well as rule it out). "Comme" then means as much as "such as, for example" and enumerates scents which contrast with "chairs d'enfants" as innocence contrasts with experience or nature with artifice. This working out by exemplification is quite different from the analogical function assigned to the other uses of "comme."

Considered from the perspective of the "thesis" or of the symbolist ideology of the the text, such a use of "comme" is aberrant. For although the burden of totalizing expansion seems to be attributed to these particular scents rather than the others, the logic of "comme" restricts the semantic field of "parfums" and confines it to a tautology: "Il est des parfums . . . / Comme (des parfums)." Instead of analogy, we have enumeration, and an enumeration which never moves beyond the confines of a set of particulars: "forêt" synthesizes but does not enumerate a set of trees, but "ambre," "musc," "benjoin," and "encens," whatever differences or gradations one wishes to establish between them, are refrained by "comme" ever to lead beyond themselves; the enumeration could be continued at will without ceasing to be a repetition, without ceasing to be an obsession rather than a metamorphosis, let alone a rebirth. One wonders if the evil connotations of these corrupt scents do not stem from the syntax rather than from the Turkish bath or black mass atmosphere one would otherwise have to conjure up. For what could be more perverse or corruptive for a metaphor aspiring to transcendental totality than remaining stuck in an enumeration that never goes anywhere? If number can only be conquered by another number, if identity becomes enumeration, then there is no conquest at all, since the stated purpose of the passage to infinity was, like in Pascal, to restore the one, to escape the tyranny of number by dint of infinite multiplication. Enumerative repetition disrupts the chain of tropological substitution at the crucial moment when the poem promises, by way of these very substitutions, to reconcile the pleasures of the mind with those of the senses and to unite aesthetics with epistemology. That the very word on which these substitutions depend would just then lose its syntactical and semantic univocity is too striking a coincidence not to be, like pure chance, beyond the control of author and reader.

It allows, at any rate, for a sobering literalization of the word "transport" in the final line "Qui chantent les transports de l'esprit et des sens." "Transport" here means, of course, to be carried away beyond thought and sensation in a common transcendental realm; it evokes loss of control and ecstatic unreason. But all attentive readers of Baudelaire have always felt that this claim at self-loss is not easily compatible with a colder, analytic self-consciousness that moves in a very different direction. In the words of our text, "les transports de l'esprit" and "Les transports des sens" are not at all the same "transports." We have learned to recognize, of late, in "transports" the spatial displacement implied by the verbal ending of meta-*phorein*. One is reminded that, in the French-speaking cities of our century, "correspondance" meant, on the trolley-cars, the equivalence of what is called in English a "transfer"—the privilege, automatically granted on the Paris Métro, of connecting from one line to another without having to buy a new ticket.

The prosaic transposition of ecstasy to the economic codes of public transportation is entirely in the spirit of Baudelaire and not by itself disruptive with regard to the claim for transcendental unity. For the transfer indeed merges two different displacements into one single system of motion and circulation, with corresponding economic and metaphysical profits. The problem is not so much centered on *phorein* as on *meta* (trans . . .), for does "beyond" here mean a movement beyond some particular place or does it mean a state that is beyond movement entirely? And how can "beyond," which posits and names movement, ever take us away from what it posits? The question haunts the text in all its ambiguities, be it "passer à travers" or the discrepancy between the "comme" of homogeneity and the "comme" of enumeration. The apparent rest and tranquility of "Correspondances" within the corpus of *Les Fleurs du mal* lies indeed beyond tension and beyond motion. If Nature is truly a temple, it is not a means of transportation or a railroad station, Victorian architects who loved to build railroad stations in the shape of cathedrals notwithstanding. Nature in this poem is not a road toward a temple, a sequence of motions that take us there. Its travels, whatever they are, lie far behind us; there is no striving here, no questing for an absence or a presence. And if man (l'homme) is at home among "regards familiers" within that Nature, then his language of tropes and analogies is of little use to them. In this realm, transfer tickets are of no avail. Within the confines of a system of transportation—or of language as a system of communication—one can transfer from one vehicle to another, but one cannot transfer from being like a vehicle to being like a temple, or a ground.

The epistemological, aesthetic, and poetic language of transports or of tropes, which is the theme though not singly the rhetoric of this poem, can never say nor, for that matter, sing or understand the opening statement: "la Nature est un temple." But the poem offers no explicit alternative to this language which, like the perfumes enumerated by "comme," remains condemned to the repetition of its superfluity. Few poems in *Les Fleurs du mal* state this in a manner that is both so obvious yet, by necessity, so oblique. The poem most remote from stating it is also the one closest to "Correspondances," its "echo" as it were, with which it is indeed very easy to confuse it. Little clarity can be gained from "Correspondances" except for the knowledge that disavows its deeper affinity with "Obsession."

Written presumably in February 1860, at least five years after "Correspondances" (of which the date is uncertain but anterior to 1855), "Obsession" alludes to many poems in *Les Fleurs du mal*, such as "L'Homme et la mer" (1852) and "De profundis clamavi" (1851). But it more than alludes to "Correspondances"; it can be called a *reading* of the earlier text, with all the complications that are inherent in this term. The relationship between the two poems can indeed be seen as the construction and the undoing of the mirrorlike, specular structure that is always involved in a reading. On both the thematic and the rhetorical level, the reverted symmetries between the two texts establish their correspondence along a positive/negative axis. Here again, our problem is centered on the possibility of reinscribing into the system elements, in either text, that do not belong to this pattern. The same question can be asked in historical or in generic terms but, in so doing, the significance of this terminology risks being unsettled.

One can, for instance, state the obvious difference in theme and in diction between the two poems in terms derived from the canonical history of French nineteenth-century lyric poetry. With its portal of Greek columns, its carefully balanced symmetries, and its decorous absence of any displayed emotion, "Correspondances" has all the characteristics of a Parnassian poem, closer to Heredia than to Hugo. The "romantic" exaltation of "Obsession" 's apostrophes and exclamations, on the other hand, is self-evident. If nature is a "transport" in "Obsession," it is a temple in "Correspondances." However, by putting the two texts side by side in this manner, their complementarity is equally manifest. What is lost in personal expressiveness from the first poem is gained in the symbolic "depth" that has prompted comparisons of "Correspondances" with the poetry of that other neo-classicist, Gérard de Nerval, or supported the claim of its being the forerunner of symbolism. Such a historicizing pattern, a commonplace of aesthetic theory, is a function of the aesthetic ideologization of linguistic structures rather than an empirical historical event. The dialectical interaction of "classical" with "romantic" conceptions, as summarized in the contrastive symmetries between these two sonnets, ultimately reveals the symbolic character of poetic language, the linguistic structure in which it is rooted. "Symbolist" art is considered archaic when it is supposed to be spontaneous, modern when it is self-conscious, and this terminology has a certain crude wisdom about it that is anything but historical, however, in its content. Such a combination of linguistic with pseudo-historical terms, of "symbolic" with "classic" (or *parnassien*) or with "romantic" (or *symboliste*), a combination familiar at least since Hegel's *Lectures on Aesthetics*, is a necessary feature of systems that combine tropes with aesthetic and epistemological norms. In this perspective, the relationship between the neoclassical "Correspondances" and the post-romantic "Obsession" is itself structured like symbol: the two sonnets complement each other like the two halves of a *symbolon*. Historicizing them into a diachrony or into a valorized qualitative hierarchy is more convenient than it is legitimate. The terminology of traditional literary history, as a succession of periods or literary movements, remains useful only if the terms are seen for what they are: rather crude metaphors for figural patterns rather than historical events or acts.

Stated in generic rather than historical terms, the relationship between "Correspondances" and "Obsession" touches upon the uncertain status of the lyric as a term for poetic discourse in general. The lyric's claim of being song is made explicitly in "Correspondances" ("qui *chantent* les transports . . ."), whereas "Obsession" howls, laughs, and speaks but does not pretend to sing. Yet the *je-tu* structure of the syntax makes it much closer to the representation of a vocal utterance than the engraved, marmorean gnomic wisdom of "Correspondances." The reading however disclosed a discrepancy that affects the verb "chanter" in the concluding line: the suggestive identification of "parfum" with song, based on common resonance and expansion, is possible only within a system of relays and transfers that, in the syntax if not in the stated meaning of the poem, becomes threatened by the stutter, the *piétinement* of aimless enumeration. This eventuality, inherent in the structure of the tropes on which the claim to lyricism depends, conflicts with the monumental stability of a completed entity that exists independently of its principle of constitution and destruction. Song is not compatible with aphasia and a stuttering Amphion is an absurd figure indeed. No lyric can be read lyrically nor can the object of a lyrical reading be itself a lyric—which implies least of all that it is epical or dramatic. Baudelaire's own lyrical reading of "Correspondances," however, produced at least a text, the sonnet entitled "Obsession."

The opening of "Obsession" reads the first quatrain of "Correspondances" as if it were indeed a sylvan scene. It naturalizes the surreal speech of live columns into the frightening, but natural, roar of the wind among the trees:

> Grands bois, vous m'effrayez comme des cathédrales;
> Vous hurlez comme l'orgue;

The benefits of naturalization—as we can call the reversal of anthropomorphism—are at once apparent. None of the uncertainties that obscure the opening lines of "Correspondances" are maintained. No "comme" could be more orthodox than the two "commes" in these two lines. The analogism is so perfect that the implied anthropomorphism becomes fully motivated.

In this case, the unifying element is the wind as it is heard in whistling keyholes, roaring trees, and wind instruments such as church organs. Neither is there any need to invoke hallucination to account for the fear inspired by stormy forests and huge cathedrals: both are versions of the same dizziness of vast spaces. The adjustment of the elements involved (wood, wind, fear, cathedral, and organ) is perfectly self-enclosed, since all the pieces in the structure fit each other: wood and cathedral share a common shape, but wood also fits organ by way of the noise of the roaring wind; organ and cathedral, moreover, are linked by metonymy, etc. Everything can be substituted for everything else without distorting the most natural experience. Except, of course, for the "vous" of address in the apostrophe "Grands bois," which is, of course, absurd from a representational point of view; we are all frightened by windy woods but do not generally make a spectacle of ourselves talking to trees.

Yet the power of the analogy, much more immediately compelling than that of synesthesia in "Correspondances," naturalizes even this most conventional trope of lyric address: when it is said, in line 4, that the terror of the wind corresponds to the subjective fear of death

> et dans nos coeurs maudits,
>
> . . . .
> Répondent les échos de vos *De profundis,*

then the analogy between outer event and inner feeling is again so close that the figural distance between noise (wind) and speech or even music almost vanishes, all the more so since wind as well as death are designated by associated sounds: the howling of the wind and the penitential prayer, aural metonymy for death. As a result, the final attribution of speech to the woods (*vos* De profundis) appears so natural that it takes an effort to notice that anthropomorphism is involved. The claim to verbality in the equivalent line from "Correspondances," "Les parfums, les couleurs et les sons se répondent" seems fantastic by comparison. The omnipresent metaphor of interiorization, of which this is a striking example, here travels initially by ways of the ear alone.

The gain in pathos is such as to make the depth of *De profundis* the

explicit theme of the poem. Instead of being the infinite expanse, the openness of "Vaste comme la nuit et comme la clarté," depth is now the enclosed
space that, like the sound chamber of a violin, produces the inner vibration
of emotion. We retrieve what was conspicuously absent from "Correspondances," the recurrent image of the subject's presence to itself as a spatial
enclosure, room, tomb, or crypt in which the voice echoes as in a cave.
The image draws its verisimilitude from its own "mise en abîme" in the
shape of the body as the *container* of the voice (or soul, heart, breath,
consciousness, spirit, etc.) that it exhales. At the cost of much represented
agony ("Chambres d'éternel deuil où vibrent de vieux râles), "Obsession"
asserts its right to say "I" with full authority. The canon of romantic and
post-romantic lyric poetry offers innumerable versions and variations of
this inside/outside pattern of exchange that founds the metaphor of the
lyrical voice as subject. In a parallel movement, reading interiorizes the
meaning of the text by its understanding. The union of aesthetic with
epistemological properties is carried out by the mediation of the metaphor
of the self as consciousness of itself, which implies its negation.

The specular symmetry of the two texts is such that any instance one
wishes to select at once involves the entire system with flawless consistency.
The hellenic "temple" of "Correspondances," for example, becomes the
Christian "cathédrale" of "Obsession," just as the denominative, impersonal third person discourse of the earlier poem becomes the first person
discourse of the later one. The law of this figural and chiastic transformation
is negation. "Obsession" self-consciously denies and rejects the sensory
wealth of "Correspondances." The landscape of denial from "De profundis
clamavi":

> C'est un pays plus nu que la terre polaire;
> —Ni bêtes, ni ruisseaux, ni verdure, ni bois!

reappears as the desire of "Obsession":

> Car je cherche le vide, et le noir, et le nu!

in sharp denial of

> Doux comme les hautbois, verts comme les prairies

from "Correspondances." Similar negations pervade the texts, be it in terms
of affects, moods, or grammar.

The negation, however, is indeed a figure of chiasmus, for the positive
and negative valorizations can be distributed on both sides. We read "Obsession" thematically as an interiorization of "Correspondances," and as a
negation of the positivity of an outside reality. But it is just as plausible to
consider "Obsession" as the making manifest, as the exteriorization of the
subject that remains hidden in "Correspondances." Naturalization, which
appears to be a movement from inside to outside, allows for affective verisimilitude which moves in the opposite direction. In terms of figuration

also, it can be said that "Correspondances" is the negation of "Obsession": the figural stability of "Obsession" is denied in "Correspondances." Such patterns constantly recur in nineteenth- and twentieth-century lyric poetry and create a great deal of critical confusion, symptomatic of further-reaching complexities.

The recuperative power of the subject metaphor in "Obsession" becomes particularly evident, in all its implications, in the tercets. As soon as the sounds of words are allowed, as in the opening stanza, to enter into analogical combinations with the sounds of nature, they necessarily turn into the light imagery of representation and of knowledge. If the sounds of nature are akin to those of speech, then nature also speaks by ways of light, the light of the senses as well as of the mind. The philosophical phantasm that has concerned us throughout this reading, the reconciliation of knowledge with phenomenal, aesthetic experience, is summarized in the figure of speaking light which, as is to be expected in the dialectical mode of negation, is both denied and asserted:

> Comme tu me plairais, ô nuit! sans ces étoiles
> Dont *la lumière parle* un langage connu!

Light implies space which, in turn, implies the possibility of spatial differentiation, the play of distance and proximity that organizes perception as the foreground-background juxtaposition that links it to the aesthetics of painting. Whether the light emanates from outside us before it is interiorized by the eye, as is the case here in the perception of a star, or whether the light emanates from inside and projects the entity, as in hallucination or in certain dreams, makes little difference in this context. The metamorphic crossing between perception and hallucination

> Mais les ténèbres sont elles-mêmes des toiles
> Où vivent, jaillissant de mon oeil par milliers,
> Des êtres disparus aux regards familiers

occurs by means of the paraphernalia of painting, which is also that of recollection and of re-cognition, as the recovery, to the senses, of what seemed to be forever beyond experience. In an earlier outline, Baudelaire had written

> Mais les ténèbres sont elles-mêmes des toiles
> Où [peint] . . . (presumably for "se peignent")

"Peint" confirms the reading of "toiles" as the device by means of which painters or dramatists project the space or the stage of representation, by enframing the interiorized expanse of the skies. The possibility of representation asserts itself at its most efficacious at the moment when the sensory plenitude of "Correspondances" is most forcefully denied. The lyric depends entirely for its existence on the denial of phenomenality as the surest means to recover what it denies. This motion is not dependent, in its failure or in its illusion of success, on the good or the bad faith of the subject it constitutes.

The same intelligibility enlightens the text when the enigma of consciousness as eternal mourning ("Chambres d'éternel deuil où vibrent de vieux râles") is understood as the hallucinatory obsession of recollection, certainly easier to comprehend by shared experience than by esoteric *correspondances*. "Obsession" translates "Correspondances" into intelligibility, the least one can hope for in a successful reading. The resulting couple or pair of texts indeed becomes a model for the uneasy combination of funereal monumentality with paranoid fear that characterizes the hermeneutics and the pedagogy of lyric poetry.

Yet, this very title, "Obsession," also suggests a movement that may threaten the far-reaching symmetry between the two texts. For the temporal pattern of obsessive thought is directly reminiscent of the tautological, enumerative stutter we encountered in the double semantic function of "comme," which disrupted the totalizing claim of metaphor in "Correspondances." It suggests a psychological and therefore intelligible equivalent of what there appeared as a purely grammatical distinction, for there is no compelling thematic suggestion, in "comme l'ambre, le musc, le benjoin et l'encens," that allows one to think of this list as compulsively haunting. The title "Obsession," or the last line of the poem, which names the ghostly memory of mourned absences, does therefore not correspond to the tension, deemed essential, between the expansiveness of "des choses infinies" and the restrictive catalogue of certain kinds of scents introduced by "comme." Yet, if the symmetry between the two texts is to be truly recuperative, it is essential that the disarticulation that threatens the first text should find its counterpart in the second: mere naturalization of a grammatical structure, which is how the relationship between enumeration and obsession can be understood, will not suffice, since it is precisely the tension between an experienced and a purely linguistic disruption that is at issue. There ought to be a place, in "Obsession," where a similar contrast between infinite totalization and endless repetition of the same could be pointed out. No such place exists. At the precise point where one would expect it, at the moment when obsession is stressed in terms of number, "Obsession" resorts to synthesis by losing itself in the vagueness of the infinite

> Où vivent, jaillissant de mon oeil *par milliers,*
> Des êtres disparus aux regards familiers.

There could be no more decisive contrast, in *Les Fleurs du mal*, than between the reassuring indeterminacy of these infinite thousands—as one had, in "Correspondances," "des forêts"—and the numerical precision with which, in "Les Sept Vieillards," it is the passage from one altogether finite to another altogether finite number that produces genuine terror:

Aurais-je, sans mourir, contemplé le huitième,
Sosie inexorable, ironique et fatal,
Dégoûtant Phénix, fils et père de lui-même?
—Mais je tournai le dos au cortège infernal.

Exaspéré comme un ivrogne qui voit double,
Je rentrai, je fermai ma porte, épouvanté,
Malade et morfondu, l'esprit fiévreux et trouble,
Blessé par le mystère et par l'absurdité!

Unlike "Obsession," "Les Sept Vieillards" can however in no respect be called a reading of "Correspondances," to which it in no way corresponds.

The conclusion is written into the argument which is itself written into the reading, a process of translation or "transport" that incessantly circulates between the two texts. There always are at least two texts, regardless of whether they are actually written out or not; the relationship between the two sonnets, obligingly provided by Baudelaire for the benefit, no doubt, of future teachers invited to speak on the nature of the lyric, is an inherent characteristic of any text. Any text, as text, compels reading as its understanding. What we call the lyric, the instance of represented voice, conveniently spells out the rhetorical and thematic characteristics that make it the paradigm of a complementary relationship between grammar, trope, and theme. The set of characteristics includes the various structures and moments we encountered along the way: specular symmetry along an axis of assertion and negation (to which correspond the generic mirror-images of the ode, as celebration, and the elegy, as mourning), the grammatical transformation of the declarative into the vocative modes of question, exclamation, address, hypothesis, etc., the tropological transformation of analogy into apostrophe or the equivalent, more general transformation which, with Nietzche's assistance, we took as our point of departure: the transformation of trope into anthropomorphism. The lyric is not a genre, but one name among several to designate the defensive motion of understanding, the possibility of a future hermeneutics. From this point of view, there is no significant difference between one generic term and another: all have the same apparently intentional and temporal function.

We all perfectly and quickly understand "Obsession," and better still the motion that takes us from the earlier to the later text. But no symmetrical reversal of this lyrical reading-motion is conceivable; if Baudelaire, as is eminently possible, were to have written, in empirical time, "Correspondances" after "Obsession," this would change nothing. "Obsession" derives from "Correspondances" but the reverse is not the case. Neither does it account for it as its origin or cause. "Correspondances" implies and explains "Obsession" but "Obsession" leaves "Correspondances" as thoroughly incomprehensible as it always was. In the paraphernalia of literary terminology, there is no term available to tell us what "Correspondances" might be. All we know is that it is, emphatically, *not* a lyric. Yet it, and it alone, contains, implies, produces, generates, permits (or whatever aberrant verbal metaphor one wishes to choose) the entire possibility of the lyric. Whenever we encounter a text such as "Obsession"—that is, whenever we read—there always is an infra-text, a hypogram like "Correspondances" underneath. Stating this relationship, as we just did, in phenomenal, spatial terms or in phenomenal, temporal terms—"Obsession," a text of recollection and elegiac mourning, *adds* remembrance to the flat surface of time in "Correspondances"—produces at once a hermeneutic, fallacious lyrical reading of the unintelligible. The power that takes one from one text to the other is not just a power of displacement, be it understood as recollection or interiorization or any other "transport," but the sheer blind violence that Nietzsche, concerned with the same enigma, domesticated by calling it, metaphorically, an *army* of tropes.

Generic terms such as "lyric" (or its various sub-species, "ode," "idyll," or "elegy") as well as pseudo-historical period terms such as "Romanticism" or "classicism" are always terms of resistance and nostalgia, at the furthest remove from the materiality of actual history. If mourning is called a "chambre d'éternel deuil où vibrent de vieux râles," then this pathos of terror states in fact the desired consciousness of eternity and of temporal harmony as voice and as song. True "mourning" is less deluded. The most *it* can do is to allow for non-comprehension and enumerate non-anthropomorphic, non-elegiac, non-celebratory, non-lyrical, non-poetic, that is to say, prosaic, or, better, *historical* modes of language power.

Baudelaire as Modernist and Postmodernist: The Dissolution of the Referent and the Artificial "Sublime"

Fredric Jameson

The inaugural, the classical, status of Baudelaire in Western poetry can be argued in a number of different ways: a privileged theory of poetic value as it has been developed and transmitted by the modernist tradition is, however, a historicizing one, in which, for each successive period or moment—each successive new *present*—some new ghostly emanation or afterimage of the poet peels off the inexhaustible text. There are therefore many Baudelaires, of most unequal value indeed. There is, for instance, a second-rate post-Romantic Baudelaire, the Baudelaire of diabolism and of cheap *frisson,* the poet of blasphemy and of a creaking and musty religious machinery which was no more interesting in the mid-nineteenth century than it is today. This is the Baudelaire of Pound and of Henry James, who observed, "Les Fleurs du *Mal?* Non, vous vous faites trop d'honneur. What you call *evil* is nothing more than a bit of rotting cabbage lying on a satin sofa." *This* Baudelaire will no doubt linger on residually into the *fin de siècle.*

Then there is the hardest of all Baudelaires to grasp: the Baudelaire contemporary of himself (and of Flaubert), the Baudelaire of the "break," of 1857, the Baudelaire the eternal freshness of whose language is bought by reification, by its strange transformation into alien speech. Of this Baudelaire we will speak no further here.

Instead, I propose two more Baudelaire-simulacra—each identical with the last, and yet each slightly, oddly, distinct: these are the Baudelaire inaugural poet of high modernism (of a today extinct high modernism, I would want to add), and the Baudelaire of post-modernism, of our own immediate age, of consumer society, the Baudelaire of the society of the spectacle or the image. As my title suggests, I will attempt a reading of

From *Lyric Poetry: Beyond New Criticism,* edited by Chaviva Hosek and Patricia Parker. © 1985 by Cornell University. Cornell University Press, 1985.

this society in our present (and of the Baudelaire it deserves) in terms of the machine and the simulacrum, of the return of something like the "sublime." This will then be a speculative and prophetic exercise. I feel on more solid ground with that older period about which we are gradually reaching some general consensus, namely the long life and destiny of high modernism, about which it is safe to assert that one of its fundamental events concerned what we now call the "referent." It is therefore in terms of the disappearance of this last, its eclipse or abolition—better still, its gradual waning and extinction—that we will make our first approach to the poetic text.

CHANT D'AUTOMNE, PART 1.

Bientôt nous plongerons dans les froides ténèbres;
Adieu, vive clarté de nos étés trop courts!
J'entends déjà tomber avec des chocs funèbres
Le bois retentissant sur le pavé des cours.

Tout l'hiver va rentrer dans mon être: colère,
Haine, frissons, horreur, labeur dur et forcé,
Et, comme le soleil dans son enfer polaire,
Mon coeur ne sera plus qu'un bloc rouge et glacé.

J'écoute en frémissant chaque bûche qui tombe;
L'échafaud qu'on bâtit n'a pas d'écho plus sourd.
Mon esprit est pareil à la tour qui succombe
Sous les coups du bélier infatigable et lourd.

Il me semble, bercé par ce choc monotone,
Qu'on cloue en grande hâte un cercueil quelque part.
Pour qui?—C'était hier l'été; voici l'automne!
Ce bruit mystérieux sonne comme un départ.

[AUTUMNAL]

[Soon cold shadows will close over us
and summer's transitory gold be gone;
I hear them chopping firewood in our court—
the dreary thud of logs on cobblestone.

Winter will come to repossess my soul
with rage and outrage, horror, drudgery,
and like the sun in its polar holocaust
my heart will be a block of blood-red ice.

I listen trembling to that grim tattoo—
build a gallows, it would sound the same.
My mind becomes a tower giving way
under the impact of a battering-ram.

Stunned by the strokes, I seem to hear, somewhere,
a coffin hurriedly hammered shut—for whom?
Summer was yesterday; autumn is here!
Strange how that sound rings out like a farewell.]

Three experiences (to begin modestly, with the common sense language of everyday life)—three experiences come together in this text: one is a feeling of some kind, strong and articulated, yet necessarily nameless (is it to be described as "anxiety" or that very different thing, "sadness," and in that case what do we do with that other curious component of eagerness, anticipation, curiosity, which begins to interfere with those two other affective tones as we reach the so characteristic final motif of the "départ"—voyage and adventure, as well as death?). I will have little to say about this affective content of the poem, since, virtually by definition, the Baudelaire that interests us here is no longer the Baudelaire of an aesthetic of *expression*: an aesthetic in which some pre-given and identifiable psychological event is then, in a second moment, laid out and expressed in poetic language. It seems to me at least conceivable that the poetic producer may have thought of his work here in terms of some residual category of expression and expressiveness. If so, he has triumphantly (if even against his own will) undermined and subverted that now archaic category: I will only observe that as the putative "feeling" or "emotion" becomes slowly laid out in words and phrases, in verses and stanzas, it is transformed beyond all recognition, becomes lost to the older psychological lexicon (full of names for states of mind we *recognize* in advance), or, to put it in our own contemporary jargon, as it becomes transmuted into a verbal text, it ceases to be psychological or affective in any sense of the word, and now exists as *something else*.

So with this mention we will now leave psychology behind us. But I have suggested that two more "experiences" lend their raw material to this text, and we must now register their banal, informing presence: these are, evidently, a season—fall, the approach of a dreary winter which is also and even more strongly the death of summer itself; and alongside that, a physical perception, an auditory event or experience, the hollow sound of logs and firewood being delivered in the inner courtyard of the Parisian dwelling. Nature on the one hand, the city, the Urban, on the other, and a moment in the interrelationship of these two great contraries in which the first, the archaic cyclical time of an older agriculture and an older countryside, is still capable of being transmitted through what negates it, namely the social institutions of the City itself, the triumphantly un- or anti-natural.

One is tempted, faced with this supreme antithesis between country and city, with this inner contradiction in the raw material of Baudelaire's text between precapitalist society and the new industrial metropolis of nascent capital, to evoke one of the great aesthetic models of modern times, that of Heidegger, in the "Origins of the Work of Art." Heidegger there describes the effect and function of the "authentic" work of art as the inauguration of a "rift" between what he calls World and Earth: what I will rewrite in terms of the dimensions of History and the social project on the one hand, and of Nature or matter on the other—ranging from geographical or ecological constraint all the way to the individual body. The force of Heidegger's description lies in the way in which the gap between these two incommensurable dimensions is maintained and held open: the implication is that we all live in both dimensions at once, in some irreconcilable simultaneity which subsumes older ideological oppositions like those of body and spirit, or that of private and public. We are at all moments in History and in matter; at one and the same time historical beings and "natural" ones, living in the meaning-endowment of the historical project as well as in the meaninglessness of organic life. No synthesis—either conceptual or experiential, let alone symbolic—is conceivable between these two disjoined realms; or rather, the production of such conceptual synthesis (in which, say, History would be passed off as "natural," or Nature obliterated in the face of History) is very properly the production of ideology, or of "metaphysics" as it is often called. The work of art can therefore never "heal" this rift: nothing can do that. What is misconceived is, however, the idea that it ought to be healed: we have here indeed three positions and not two. It is not a question of tension versus resolution, but rather of repression and forgetfulness, of the sham resolution of metaphysics, and then of that third possibility, a divided consciousness that strongly holds together what it separates, a moment of awareness in which difference relates. This is then, for Heidegger, the vocation of the work of art: to stage this irreconcilable tension between History and Nature in such a way that we live *within* it and affirm its reality *as* tension, gap, rift, distance. Heidegger goes on to assimilate this inaugural "poetic" act with the comparable acts of philosophy (the deconcealment of being) and of political revolution (the inauguration of a new society, the invention of new social relations).

It is an attractive and powerful account, and one can read "Chant d'automne" in this way, as staging the fateful gap between organic death, the natural cycle, and the urban, which here greatly expands beyond the city, to include the repressive institutions of society generally, capital execution, war, ceremonial burial, and finally, most mysterious, the faint suggestion of the nomadic, of the "voyage" which seems to mark the interface between nature and human society. One can read the poem in that way, but at what price?

This is the moment to say that the limits of Heidegger's grand conception are less to be found in its account of the poetic act than in its voluntaristic implications for that other act, the act of reception or of reading. Let us assume that the poet—or the artist generally—is always in a position to open World and Earth in this fashion (it is not a difficult assumption to make, since "real" poetry does this by definition, for Heidegger, and art which does not do so is therefore not "really" art in the first place). The problem arises when the reader's turn comes, and in a fallen, secular or reified society is called upon (not least by Heidegger himself) to reinvent this inaugural and well-nigh ritualistic act. Is this always possible? Or must we take into account specific historical conditions of possibility which open or close such a reading? I pass over Heidegger's own sense of historical possibility in the fateful and unnameable moment in which he elaborated this meditation (1935). What is clear is that even this meditation must now return us to the historical in the drearier humdrum sense of the constraints, the situation, which limits possibility and traces the outer boundary even of that more transcendent vision of History as World.

So we now return to the narrower historical situation of this particular Baudelaire, which is the situation of nascent high modernism. Conventional wisdom already defines this for us in a certain number of ways: it is the moment, the Barthes of *Writing Degree Zero* tells us, of the passage from rhetoric to style, from a shared collective speech to the uniqueness and privacy of the isolated monad and the isolated body. It is also the moment, as we know, of the break-up of the older social groups, and not least those relatively homogeneous reading publics to whom, in the writer's contract, certain relatively stable signals can be sent. Both of these descriptions then underscore a process of social fragmentation, the atomization of groups and neighborhoods, the slow and stealthy dissolution of a host of different and coexisting collective formations by a process unique to the logic of capital which my tradition calls reification: the market equivalency in which little by little units are produced, and in the very act by which they are made equivalent to one another are thereby irrevocably separated as well, like so many identical squares on a spatial grid.

I would like to describe this situation, the situation of the poet—the situation this particular Baudelaire must resolve, in obedience to its constraints and contradictions—in a somewhat different, yet related way, as the simultaneous production and effacement of the referent itself. The latter can only be grasped as what is outside language, what language or a certain configuration of language seems to designate, and yet, in the very moment of indication, to project beyond its own reach, as something transcendental to it.

The referent in "Chant d'automne" is not particularly mysterious or difficult of access: it is simply the body itself, or better still, the bodily sensorium. Better yet, it is the bodily perception—better still, even more neutral a term, the *sensation*—which mobilizes the body as its instrument of perception and brings the latter into being over against it. The referent here is then simply a familiar sound, the hollow reverberation of logs striking the courtyard paving. Yet familiar for whom? Everything, and the very mysteries of modernism itself, turn on this word, about which we must admit, in a first moment, that it no longer applies to any contemporary readership. But in a second moment, I will be less concerned to suggest ways in which, even for Baudelaire's contemporaries, such a reference might have been in the process of becoming exotic or obscure, than rather to pose as a principle of social fragmentation the withdrawal of the private or the individual body from social discourse.

We might sharpen the problem of reference by prolonging positivist psychology itself—rigorously coeval with high modernism—and imagining the visual and graphic registration of this unique sound, whose "real nature"—that is to say, whose *name*—we could never guess from looking at its complex spatial pattern. Such registrations perpetuate the old positivist myth of something like a pure atomic sensation in the then nascent pseudo-science of psychology—a myth which in the present context I prefer to read as a symptom of what is happening to the body itself.

For this once "familiar" sound is now driven back inside the body of Baudelaire: a unique event taking place there and utterly alien to anything whose "experience" we might ourselves remember, something which has lost its name, and which has no equivalents: as anonymous and indescribable as a vague pain, as a peculiar residual taste in the mouth, as a limb falling asleep. The semioticians know well this strange seam between the body and language, as when they study the most proximate naming systems—the terms for wine-tasting, say—or examine the ways in which a physician *translates* his patients' fumbling expressions into the technical code of nosology.

But it is *this* that must now be historicized. I would like to make an outrageous (or at least, as they say, unverifiable) generalization, namely that before Baudelaire and Flaubert there are no physical sensations in literature. This does not quite mean advancing a proposition so sweeping as the one which might be expressed, parodying Lionel Trilling, namely, that on or around 1857 we must presume a fundamental mutation in human nature. It does mean, more modestly, and on the side of the object (or the literary raw material), that free-floating bodily perception was not, until now, felt to be a proper content for literary language (you will get a larger historical sense of this by expanding such data to include experiences like that of anxiety—Kierkegaard is after all the contemporary of these writers). And it means, on the side of the subject, or of literary language itself, that the older rhetoric was somehow fundamentally nonperceptual, and had not yet "produced" the referent in our current sense: this is to say that even where we are confronted with what look like masses of sense data— the most convenient example will be, perhaps, Balzac, with his elaborate descriptions, that include the very smell of his rooms—those apparently perceptual notations, on closer examination, prove to be so many *signs*. In the older rhetorical apparatus, in other words, "physical sensation" does not meet the opacity of the body, but is secretly transparent, and always *means* something else—moral qualities, financial or social status, and so forth. Perceptual language only emerges in the ruins of that older system of signs, that older assimilation of contingent bodily experience to the transparency of meaning. The problem, however, and what complicates the description enormously, is that language never ceases to attempt to reabsorb and recontain contingency; that in spite of itself, it always seeks to transform that scandalous and irreducible content back into something like meaning. Modernism will then be a renewed effort to do just that, but one which, faced with the collapse of the older system of rhetorical language and traditional literary meaning, will set itself a new type of literary meaning, which I will term symbolic reunification.

But now we must observe this process at work in our poetic exhibit. The irreducible, the sonorous vibration, with its peculiar hollowness and muffled impact, is here a pure positivity which must be handled or managed in some fashion. This will first be attempted metonymically, by tracing the association of this positive yet somehow ominous sound with something else, which is defined as absence, loss, death—namely the ending of summer. For reasons I will develop later on, it seems useful to formulate this particular axis—positivity/negativity—as one of the two principal operative grids of the poem, the other being the obvious and well-known movement between metonymy and metaphor. The latter will then be the second option of the poetic process: the pure sensation will now be classed metaphorically, by way of analogies and similarities: it is (like) the building of a scaffold, the sound of the battering ram, the nailing up of a coffin. What must be noted here is that this alternate route, whereby the sensation is processed metaphorically rather than metonymically, also ends up in negativity, as though the poetic imagination met some barrier or loop which fatally prevents it from reaching relief or salvation.

This is of course not altogether true: and a complete reading of the poem (not my purpose here) would want to underscore the wondrous reappearance of the place of the subject in the next line—the naive and miraculous, "Pour qui?" and the utter restructuration of the temporal system, in which the past is now abandoned, the new present—now defined, not negatively as the end of summer, but positively, as autumn—reaffirmed to the point at which the very sense datum of the sound itself becomes a promise rather than a fatality.

Let me now rapidly try to theorize the two principal strands of the argument, the one having to do with the production of the "referent," the other with the emergence of modernism. In "Chant d'automne" at least—and I don't want to generalize the model in any unduly dogmatic way—the high modernist strategy can be detected in the move from the metonymic reading of the sense datum to the attempt to reabsorb it in some new symbolic or metaphorical meaning—a symbolic meaning of a type very different from the older transparencies of the rhetorical sign to which I have already referred. What I have not yet sufficiently stressed is the way in which this high modernist or symbolic move is determined by the crisis of the reading public and by the social fragmentation from which the latter springs. Given that crisis, and the already tendential privatization and monadization of the isolated individuals who used to make up the traditional publics, there can no longer be any confidence in some shared common *recognition* of the mysterious sense datum, the hollow sound, which is the "referent" of the poetic text: the multiplication of metaphorical analogies is therefore a response to such fragmentation, and seeks to throw out a range of scattered frameworks in which the various isolated readers can be expected to find their bearings. Two processes are therefore here at work simultaneously: the sound is being endowed with a multiplicity of possible receptions, but as that new multifaceted attack on a fragmented readership is being projected (something whose ultimate stage will be described in Umberto Eco's *Open Work*), something else is taking place as well, namely the emergence of a new type of symbolic meaning, symbolic recuperation, which will at length substitute itself for an older common language and shared rhetoric of what it might be too complicated to describe as a "re-alistic" kind.

This crisis in readership then returns us to our other theme, namely the production of the referent: a paradoxical way of putting it, you will say, since my ostensible topic was rather the "eclipse" or the "waning," the "disappearance" of the referent. I don't want to be overly subtle about all this, but it seems to me very important to understand that these two things are the same. The "production" of the referent—that is, the sense of some new unnameable ungeneralizable private bodily sensation—some-thing that must necessarily resist all language but which language lives by designating—is the same as the "bracketing" of that referent, its positioning as the "outside" of the text or the "other" of language. The whole drama of modernism will lie here indeed, in the way in which its own peculiar life and logic depend on the reduction of reference to an absolute minimum and on the elaboration, in the former place of reference, of complex symbolic and often mythical frameworks and scaffolding: yet the latter depend on preserving a final tension between text and referent, on keeping alive one last shrunken point of reference, like a dwarf sun still glowing feebly on the horizon of the modernist text.

When that ultimate final point of reference vanishes altogether, along with the final desperate ideology—existentialism—which will attempt to theorize "reference" and "contingency"—then we are in post-modernism, in a now wholly textual world from which all the pathos of the high mod-ernist experience has vanished away—the world of the image, of textual free-play, the world of consumer society and its simulacra.

To this new aesthetic we must now turn, for as I suggested it also knows remarkable anticipations in the work of Baudelaire. There would of course be many ways of approaching post-modernism, of which we have not even time enough to make a provisional inventory. In the case of Baudelaire, one is rather tempted to proceed as follows, by recalling the great dictum of the Philosopher already mentioned, "Language is the house of being." The problem then posed by post-modernism, or more narrowly by the post-modernist elements in Baudelaire, could then be conveyed by the question of what happens when Language is only the *apartment* of Being; when the great urban fact and anti-nature, spreads and abolishes the "path through the field" and the very space and coordinates of some Heideggerian ontological poetry are radically called into question.

Consider the following lines, for example, from "Alchimie de la douleur":

> Et sur les célestes rivages
> Je bâtis de grands sarcophages.

> [to shroud my cherished dead,
> and on celestial shores I build
> enormous sepulchres.]

The entire poem amounts to a staging of or meditation on the curious dialectic of Baudelaire's poetic process, and the way in which its inner logic subverts itself and inverts its own priorities, something these concluding lines suggest rather well. It is as though the imagination, on its way toward opening, or toward the gratifications of some positive and well-nigh infinite wish-fulfillment, encountered something like a reality principle of the imagination or of fantasy itself. Not the transfigured nature of the wish-fulfillments of paradise, but rather the ornate, stubborn, material reality of the coffin: the poetic imagination here explicitly criticizes itself, and systematically, rigorously, undermines its first impulse, then in a second moment substituting a different kind of gratification, that of artisanal or handicraft skill, the pleasures of the construction of material artifacts. The role of the essentially nostalgic ideal of handicraft labor in Flaubert and Baudelaire has often been rehearsed; as has Baudelaire's fascination for un- or anti-natural materials, most notably glass, which Sartre has plausibly read as part of a whole nineteenth-century middle-class ideology of "distinction," of the repression of the organic and the constriction of the natural body. But this essentially subjective symbolic act, in which human craft manufacture is mobilized in a repression of the body, the natural, the organic itself, ought not to exclude a more "objective" analysis of the social history of those materials, particularly in nineteenth-century building and furnishings, a perspective which will be appropriate for our second exhibit:

> LA MORT DES AMANTS
> Nous aurons des lits pleins d'odeurs légères,
> Des divans profonds comme des tombeaux,
> Et d'étranges fleurs sur des étagères,
> Ecloses pour nous sous des cieux plus beaux.

> Usant à l'envi leurs chaleurs dernières,
> Nos deux cœurs seront deux vastes flambeaux,
> Qui réfléchiront leurs doubles lumières
> Dans nos deux esprits, ces miroirs jumeaux.

Un soir fait de rose et de bleu mystique,
Nous échangerons un éclair unique,
Comme un long sanglot, tout chargé d'adieux;

Et plus tard un Ange, entr'ouvrant les portes,
Viendra ranimer, fidèle et joyeux,
Les miroirs ternis et les flammes mortes.

[THE DEATH OF LOVERS]

[We shall have richly scented beds—
couches deep as graves, and rare
flowers on the shelves will bloom
for us beneath a lovelier sky.

Emulously spending their last
warmth, our hearts will be as two
torches reflecting their double fires
in the twin mirrors of our minds.

One evening, rose and mystic blue,
we shall exchange a single glance,
a long sigh heavy with farewells;

and then an Angel, unlocking doors,
will come, loyal and gay, to bring
the tarnished mirrors back to life.]

 I am tempted to be brutally anachronistic, and to underscore the affinities between this curious interior scene and the procedures of contemporary photorealism, one of whose privileged subjects is not merely the artificial—in the form of gleaming luxury streets of automobiles (battered or mint)—but above all, interior scenes, furnishings without people, and most notably bathrooms, notoriously of all the rooms in the house the least supplied with anthropomorphic objects.

 Baudelaire's sonnet is also void of human beings: the first person plural is explicitly displaced from the entombed chamber by the future tense of the verbs; and even where that displacement weakens, and as the future comes residually to fill up the scene in spite of itself, the twin protagonists are swiftly transformed into furnishings in their own right—candelabra and mirrors, whose complex four-way interplay is worthy of the most complicated visual illustrations of Jacques Lacan.

 But I am tempted to go even further than this and to underscore the evident paradox—even more, the formal scandal—of the conclusion of this poem, whose affective euphoria (and its literal meaning) conveys the resurrection of the lovers, while its textual elements in effect produce exactly the opposite, the reawakening of an empty room from which the lovers are henceforth rigorously absent. It is as though the text had profited from

the surface or manifest movement of its narrative toward the wish-fulfillment of resurrection, to secure a very different unconscious solution,
namely extinction, by means of assimilation to the dead (albeit refurbished)
boudoir. Here "interior" knows its apotheosis, in very much the spirit of
Adorno's pages on Kierkegaard where the passion for Biedermeier furnishings and enclosed space becomes the symbolic enactment of that new
realm of the private, the personal, of subjective or inner life.

Yet Baudelaire goes a good deal further than Kierkegaard in this historical respect, and we will not do proper justice to this glorious poem
without registering the properly dreadful nature of its contents: what is
tactfully conveyed here is indeed to be identified as the worst Victorian
kitsch already on its way to the modulation of fin de siècle decadence, as
most notably in the proto-Mallarméan flowers, of which we can at least
minimally be sure that "in real life" they are as garish as anything Des
Esseintes might have surrounded himself with. Even the "soir fait de rose
et de bleu mystique" is mediated by the most doubtful pre-Raphaelite taste,
if I may use so moralizing a word.

Now this presents us with an interesting axiological problem, as the
philosophers would say: in our engrained Cartesianism, it is always difficult
to imagine how a whole might possess value whose individual parts are
all worthless; meanwhile, our critical and aesthetic traditions systematically
encourage us in a kind of slavish habit of apologia in which, faced with a
text of great value, we find ourselves rationalizing all of its more question-
able elements and inventing ingenious reasons why these too are of value.
But culture is often more complicated and interesting than this; and I must
here briefly invoke one of the most brilliant pages in what remains I think
Jean-Paul Sartre's greatest single book, *Saint Genet*, whose riches, remarkably, have still been little explored: most notably the section in which he
reveals the inner hollowness of Genet's sumptuous style. The principal
category of Sartre's analysis is the concept of "le toc"—the phony, the
garish, that which is in and of itself and in its very essence in bad taste,
all the way from religious emblems and the Opéra of Paris, to the cheapest
excesses of horrific popular thrillers, porn ads, and the junk adornments
and heavy makeup of drag queens. In Genet, as Sartre shows us, the
acquired mental habits of Bossuet's style and classical rhetorical periods
reorder and stamp these tawdry materials with the tarnished aura of the
sublime, in an operation whose deepest inner logic is that of *ressentiment*
and of the imperceptible subversion of the bourgeois reader's most cher-
ished values.

Baudelaire, of course, represents a very different order of elegance; his
mastery of the raw material of bad taste will be more tactful and allusive,
more refined; nor do I wish to follow Sartre along the lines of an analysis
of individual or biographical impulses in this writer. Nonetheless, there
are curious analogies between the Sartrean analysis and this extraordinary
apotheosis of what should otherwise be an oppressively sumptuous inte-

rior, whose very blossoms are as asphyxiating as a funeral parlor, and whose space is as properly funereal as the worst Victorian art photographs. These characterizations are not, clearly, chosen at random: the logic of the image here conveys death and the funereal through its very tawdriness, at the same moment in which the words of the narrative affirm euphoria and the elation of hope.

We have a contemporary equivalent for this kind of stylistic operation, which must be set in place here: and this is the whole properly poststructural language which Susan Sontag was the first to identify as "camp," the "hysterical sublime," from Cocteau and Hart Crane to Jack Spicer and David Bowie, a kind of peculiar exhilaration of the individual subject unaccountably generated by the trash and junk materials of a fallen and unredeemable commodity culture. Camp is indeed our way of living within the junkyard of consumer society and positively flourishing there: it is to be seen in the very gleam and glitter of the automobile wrecks of photorealist paintings, in the extraordinary capacity of our own cultural language to redeem an object world and a cultural space by holding firmly to their surfaces (in mechanisms which Christopher Lasch and others would no doubt identify as "narcissistic"). Camp, better than anything else, underscores one of the most fateful differences between high modernism and post-modernism, and one which is also, I believe, operative in this strange poem of Baudelaire: namely what I will call the disappearance of *affect*, the utter extinction of that pathos or even tragic spirit with which the high moderns lived their torn and divided condition, the repression even of anxiety itself—supreme psychic experience of high modernism—and its unaccountable reversal and replacement by a new dominant feeling tone: the high, the intensity, exhilaration, euphoria, a final form of the Nietzschean Dionysiac intoxication which has become as banal and institutionalized as your local disco or the thrill with which you buy a new-model car.

This strange new—historically new—feeling or affective tone of late capitalism may now be seen as something like a return of the "sublime" in the sense in which Edmund Burke first perceived and theorized it at the dawn of capital. Like the "sublime" (and the "anxiety"), the exhilaration of which we are speaking is not exactly an emotion or a feeling, not a way of living an object, but rather somehow detached from its contents—something like a disposition of the subject which takes a particular object as a mere occasion: this is the sense in which the Deleuze-Guattari account of the emergence, the momentary and fitful sunburst of the individual psychological subject has always seemed exceedingly relevant:

> Something on the order of a subject can be discerned on the recording surface: a strange subject, with no fixed identity, wandering about over the body without organs, yet always remaining peripheral to the desiring-machines, being defined by the share of the product it takes for itself, garnering here, there, and everywhere a reward, in the form of a becoming or an avatar, being

born of the states that it consumes and being reborn with each new state: "c'est donc moi, c'est donc à moi!" . . . The subject is produced as a mere residue alongside the desiring machines: a conjunctive synthesis of consumption in the form of a wonder-struck: "c'était donc ça!"

(*The Anti-Oedipus: Criticism and Schizophrenia*)

Such an account has the additional merit of linking up with the great Lacanian theme of "second death," and of suggesting why death and resurrection should have been so stimulating a fantasy-material for a poet intent on capturing the highs and the "elevations" of an intermittent experience of subjectivity. If the subject exists always and only in the moment of rebirth, then the poetic fantasy or narrative process must necessarily first work its way along the path of death, in order to merit this unique "bonus of pleasure" whose place is carefully prepared in advance for it in the empty, dusted, polished, flower-laden chamber. And the latter is of course, for us, as readers, the poem itself: the chamber of the sonnet, Donne's "pretty room," waiting to be the faithful (and joyous) occasion of our own brief, fitful, punctual exhilaration as subjects: "c'est donc moi, c'est donc à moi!"

Burke's problem, as he confronted an analogous and historically equally new form of affect—the sublime—was to find some explanation—not for our aesthetic pleasure in the pleasurable, in "beauty," in what could plausibly gratify the human organism on its own scale, but rather for our aesthetic delight in spectacles which would seem symbolically to crush human life and to dramatize everything which reduces the individual human being and the individual subject to powerlessness and nothingness. Burke's solution was to detect, within this peculiar aesthetic experience, a relationship to being that might as well have been described as epistemological or even ontological (and incidentally a logic which is rigorously un- or a-symmetrical to that of his other term, "beauty"): astonishment, stupor, terror—these are some of the ways in which the individual glimpses a force which largely transcends human life and which Burke can only identify with the Godhead or the divine. The aesthetic reception of the sublime is then something like a pleasure in pain, in the tightening of the muscles and the adrenaline rush of the instinct of self-preservation, with which we greet such frightening and indeed devastating spectacles.

What can be retained from this description is the notion of the sublime as a relationship of the individual subject to some fitfully or only intermittently visible force which, enormous and systematized, reduces the individual to helplessness or to that ontological marginalization which structuralism and poststructuralism have described as a "decentering" where the ego becomes little more than an "effect of structure." But it is no longer necessary to evoke the deity to grasp what such a transindividual system might be.

What has happened to the sublime since the time of Burke—although he judiciously makes a place of a concept which can be most useful to us in the present context, namely the "artificial infinite"—is that it has been transferred from nature to culture, or the urban. The visible expression of the suprapersonal mode of production in which we live is the mechanical, the artificial, the machine; and we have only to remember the "sublime" of yesterday, the exhilaration of the futurists before the machine proper— the motorcar, the steamship liner, the machine gun, the airplane—to find some initial contemporary equivalent of the phenomenon Burke first described. One may take his point about self-preservation, and nonetheless wish to formulate this affective mechanism a little more sharply: I would have said myself that in the face of the horror of what systemically diminishes human life it becomes possible simply to change the valence on one's emotion, to replace the minus sign with a plus sign, by a Nietzschean effort of the will to convert anxiety into that experience physiologically virtually identical with it which is eagerness, anticipation, anxious affirmation. And indeed, in a situation of radical impotence, there is really little else to do than that, to affirm what crushes you and to develop one's capacity for gratification in an environment which increasingly makes gratification impossible.

But futurism was an experiment in what Reyner Banham has called the "first machine age": we now live in another, whose machines are not the glorious and streamlined visible vehicles and silhouettes which so exhilarated Le Corbusier, but rather computers, whose outer shell has no emblematic or visual power. Our own machines are those of reproduction; and an exhilaration which would attach itself to them can no longer be the relatively representational idolatry of the older engines and turbines, but must open some access, beyond representation, to processes themselves, and above all the processes of reproduction—movie cameras, videos, tape recorders, the whole world of the production and reproduction of the image and of the simulacrum, and of which the smeared light and multireflective glass of the most elegant post-contemporary films or buildings is an adequate *analogon*. I cannot, of course, pursue this theory of post-modernism in any more detail here; but returning one last time to "La Mort des amants" it is appropriate to see in the play of mirrors and lights of the funereal chamber some striking and mysterious anticipation of a logic of the future, a logic far more consonant with our own social moment than with that of Baudelaire. In that then, as in so much else, he is, perhaps unfortunately for him, our contemporary.

Les Fleurs du mal armé: Some Reflections on Intertextuality

Barbara Johnson

> *Oui, le suspens de la Danse, crainte contradictoire ou souhait de voir trop et pas assez, exige un prolongement transparent.*
>
> —MALLARMÉ

Contemporary discussions of intertextuality can be distinguished from "source" studies in that the latter speak in terms of a transfer of property ("borrowing") while the former tend to speak in terms of misreading or infiltration, that is, of violations of property. (The title, "Les Fleurs du mal armé," is designed to be read as a paradigm for the questions of intertextuality under discussion here. On the one hand, it appears to posit a linear, developmental, slightly overlapping relation between a precursor text ["Les Fleurs du mal"] and a disciple [Mallarmé] engendered out of it. On the other hand, the double function of the word "mal" renders Baudelaire's title and Mallarmé's name both inseparable from each other and different from themselves, creating new dividing lines not *between* the two oeuvres but *within* each of them. The proper names thereby lose their properness, and their free-floating parts can combine into new signifying possibilities.) Whether such violations occur in the oedipal rivalry between a specific text and its precursor (Bloom's anxieties of influence) or whether they inhere in the immersion of any text in the history of its language and literature (Kristeva's paragrams, Riffaterre's hypograms), "intertextuality" designates the multitude of ways a text has of not being self-contained, of being traversed by otherness. Such a conception of textuality arises out of two main theoretical currents: (a) Freud's discovery of the unconscious as an "other scene" that intrudes on conscious life in the form of dreams, slips of the tongue, parapraxes, etc., and (b) Saussure's discovery of the haunting presence of proper names anagrammatically dispersed in the writings of certain late Latin poets. These two discoveries have been combined by Jacques Lacan into a conception of the "signifying chain" that "insists" in

---

From *Lyric Poetry: Beyond New Criticism,* edited by Chaviva Hosek and Patricia Parker. © 1985 by Cornell University. Cornell University Press. 1985.

the human subject in such a way that "the unconscious is structured like a language." One might say by analogy that for modern theorists of intertextuality, the language of poetry is structured like an unconscious. The integrity and intentional self-identity of the individual text are put in question in ways that have nothing to do with the concepts of originality and derivativeness, since the very notion of a self-contained literary "property" is shown to be an illusion. When read in its dynamic intertextuality, the text becomes differently energized, traversed by forces and desires that are invisible or unreadable to those who see it as an independent, homogeneous message unit, a totalizable collection of signifieds.

What happens, though, when a poet decides to transform the seemingly unconscious "anxiety of influence" into an explicit theme in his writing? Can the seepage and rivalry between texts somehow thereby be mastered and reappropriated? In an early piece of poetic prose entitled "Symphonie littéraire," Mallarmé prefaces his homage to his three "masters" (Gautier, Baudelaire, and Banville) with the following invocation:

> Muse moderne de l'Impuissance, qui m'interdis depuis longtemps le trésor familier des Rythmes, et me condamnes (aimable supplice) à ne faire plus que relire,—jusqu'au jour où tu m'auras enveloppé dans ton irrémédiable filet, l'ennui, et tout sera fini alors,—les maîtres inaccessibles dont la beauté me désespère; mon ennemie, et cependant mon enchanteresse aux breuvages perfides et aux melancoliques ivresses, je te dédie, comme une raillerie ou,—le sais-je?—comme un gage d'amour, ces quelques lignes de ma vie où tu ne m'inspiras pas la haine de la création et le stérile amour du néant. Tu y découvriras les jouissances d'une âme purement passive qui n'est que femme encore, et qui demain peut-être sera bête.

> [O modern Muse of Impotence, you who have long forbidden me the familiar treasury of Rhythms, and who condemn me (pleasurable torture) to do nothing but reread—until the day you will envelop me in your irremediable net, ennui, and all will then be over—those inaccessible masters whose beauty drives me to despair; my enemy, yet my enchantress, with your perfidious potions and your melancholy intoxications, I dedicate to you, in jest or—can I know?—as a token of love, these few lines of my life written in the clement hours when you did not inspire in me a hatred of creation and a sterile love of nothingness. You will discover in them the pleasures of a purely passive soul who is yet but a woman and who tomorrow perhaps will be a dumb animal.]

It would seem that this text is quite explicitly describing the castrating effect of poetic fathers upon poetic sons. The precursors' beauty drives the ephebe to despair: he is impotent, passive, feminized, *mal armé*. Yet this state of castration is being invoked as a Muse: the lack of inspiration has become the source of inspiration. Mallarmé, as has often been noted, has transformed the incapacity to write into the very subject of his writing. In the act of thematizing an oedipal defeat, Mallarmé's writing thus maps out the terms of an escape from simple oedipal polarities: it is no longer possible to distinguish easily between defeat and success, impotence and potency, reading and writing, passivity and activity.

Before pursuing further the Mallarméan relation between impotence and writing, let us glance for a moment at the father's side of the story. At a time when Baudelaire would have had ample occasion to read Mallarmé's "Literary Symphony" along with the prose poems Mallarmé had dedicated to him, the older poet wrote the following remarks in a letter to his mother in which he had enclosed an article about himself written by Verlaine:

> Il y a du talent chez ces jeunes gens; mais que de folies! quelles exagérations et quelle infatuation de jeunesse! Depuis quelques années je surprenais, ça et là, des imitations et des tendances qui m'alarmaient. Je ne connais rien de plus compromettant que les imitateurs et je n'aime rien tant que d'être seul. Mais ce n'est pas possible; et il paraît que l'*école Baudelaire* existe.

> [These young people do have talent, but there is such madness! such exaggeration and such youthful infatuation! For several years now I have here and there come across imitations and tendencies that alarm me. I know of nothing more compromising than imitators and I like nothing so well as being alone. But it is not possible; and it seems that the *Baudelaire school* exists.]

The "father" here is "alarmed" not by the hostility but by the imitative devotion of his "sons," whose writing lacks the measure and maturity that he, Baudelaire, by implication attributes to his own. To be imitated is to be repeated, multiplied, distorted, "compromised." To be alone is at least to be unique, to be secure in the boundaries of one's self. And to have the luxury of rejecting one's imitators is both to profit from the compliment and to remain uncontaminated by the distortions. Yet even in Baudelaire's expression of alarm and self-containment, otherness surreptitiously intrudes. For while Baudelaire is ambivalently but emphatically imprinting his own name on the writing of his admirers, another proper name is manifesting itself in the very writing of his letter: in speaking of "des tendances qui M'ALARMAIENT," Baudelaire has unwittingly inscribed the name of one of the sources of his alarm. The almost perfect homophony between "m'alarmaient" and "Mallarmé" reveals a play of intertextuality in which the text, while seeming to decry the dangers of imitation, is actually *acting out*, against the express purposes of its author, the far graver dangers of usurpation. And what is usurped is not only Baudelaire's claims to authority over the work of his disciples, but also and more significantly the claims of his conscious intentions to authority over the workings of his own writing. The suppressed name of Mallarmé shows through.

Both of these thematizations of the oedipal dynamics of intertextuality are thus more complex than they at first appear. In both cases, the ongoingness of literary history is acted out by the text despite an apparent attempt to arrest it. Mallarmé carves new territory for poetry out of what looks like a writing block; Baudelaire's writing, in the act of blocking out the successors, inscribes the inevitability of their usurpation.

But what are the effects of this Muse of Impotence not on Mallarmé's critical prose but on his poetry itself? In a poem entitled "L'Azur," written the same year as the "Symphonie littéraire," Mallarmé dramatizes the predicament of the poet who seeks *forgetfulness* as a cure for impotence (thus implying that what the impotent poet is suffering from is too much memory). The poem begins:

> De l'éternel azur la sereine ironie
> Accable, belle indolemment comme les fleurs,
> Le poète impuissant qui maudit son génie
> A travers un désert stérile de Douleurs.
>
> [The eternal azure's serene irony
> Staggers, with the indolent grace of flowers,
> The impotent poet who damns his genius
> Across a sterile desert of sorrows.]

The poet tries to flee this oppressive azure, throwing night, smoke, and fog across it, until he reaches a moment of illusory victory, followed by a recognition of defeat:

> —Le Ciel est mort.—Vers toi, j'accours! donne, ô matière,
> L'oubli de l'Idéal cruel et du Péché
> A ce martyr qui vient partager la litière
> Où le bétail heureux des hommes est couché,
>
> Car j'y veux, puisque enfin ma cervelle, vidée
> Comme le pot de fard gisant au pied du mur,
> N'a plus l'art d'attifer la sanglotante idée,
> Lugubrement bâiller vers un trépas obscur . . .
>
> En vain! l'Azur triomphe, et je l'entends qui chante
> Dans les cloches. Mon âme, il se fait voix pour plus
> Nous faire peur avec sa victoire méchante,
> Et du métal vivant sort en bleus angélus!
>
> Il roule par la brume, ancien et traverse
> Ta native agonie ainsi qu'un glaive sûr;
> Où fuir dans la révolte inutile et perverse?
> *Je suis hanté.* L'Azur! l'Azur! l'Azur! l'Azur!

[—The sky is dead.—To you I run! give, o matter,
Forgetfulness of the cruel Ideal and Sin
To this martyr who comes to share the straw
Where the happy herd of men is stabled,

For I wish—since my brain no longer, emptied
Like the grease paint pot that lies against the wall,
Has the art to prettify the sobbing idea—
To yawn lugubriously toward an obscure death . . .

In vain! The Azure triumphs, I can hear it sing
In the bells. My soul, it becomes voice,
The better to scare us with its mean success,
And from the living metal bluely rings the angelus.

It rolls through the mist of old and pierces
Like a skillful sword your native agony;
Where is there to flee, in useless and perverse revolt?
I am haunted. Azure! Azure! Azure! Azure!]

This text has always been read—even by Mallarmé himself—as a description of the struggle between the desire to reach a poetic or metaphysical ideal and the attempt to escape that desire for fear of failing. As Guy Michaud puts it, "Even if the poet is freed neither of his dream nor of his impotence, he has at least affirmed the originality of his poetry. He has achieved the *general effect* he was seeking: the obsessive concern with the eternal, which the azure symbolizes." (*Mallarmé*) But should this "azure" be understood only in a *symbolic* sense? The fact that the word is repeated four times at the end of the poem would seem to indicate that what haunts Mallarmé is not simply some ideal symbolized by azure but the very word "azure" itself. Even a casual glance at nineteenth-century French poetry reveals that the word "azure" is par excellence a "poetic" word—a sign that what one is reading is a poem. The repetition of this word can thus be read as the return of stereotyped poetic language as a *reflex*, a moment when initiative is being taken by the words *of others*, which is one of the things Mallarmé will later call "chance." Azure, says Mallarmé, "becomes voice." The text ends: "I am haunted: cliché! cliché! cliché! cliché!" (Interestingly enough, there is a sentence in a letter from Mallarmé to Cazalis that seems unexpectedly to confirm this reading. In discussing the composition of "L'Azur," Mallarmé writes, "I had a lot of trouble with it because, banishing a thousand lyrical turns and beautiful lines that incessantly *haunted* my brain, I wanted to stick implacably to my subject" [January 1864, in *Correspondance 1862–1871* (Paris, 1959); italics mine].)

Impotence is thus not a simple inability to write, but an inability to write *differently*. The agony experienced before the blank page arises out of the fact that the page is in fact never quite blank enough.

To write thus becomes for Mallarmé a constant effort to silence the automatisms of poetry, to "conquer chance word by word," to perceive words "independent of their ordinary sequence." But if the blankness of the page is in a sense the place from which literary history speaks, Mallarmé ends up writing *not* by covering the white page with the blackness of his own originality but rather by including *within* his writing the very *spaces* where poetic echoes and reflexes have been suppressed. "Leaving the initiative to words" is a complex operation in which the linguistic work of poetic calculation must substitute for the banalities of poetic inspiration. And the blanks figure as a major ingredient in that calculation. As Mallarmé puts it in a note on the *Coup de dés,* his symphony in white: "The 'blanks' indeed take on importance. . . . The paper intervenes each time an image, of its own accord, ceases or dies back, accepting the succession of others. . . ." And as for prose, Mallarmé explains that his blanks take the place of empty transitions: "The reason for these intervals, or blanks . . . —why not confine the subject to those fragments in which it shines and then replace, by the ingenuousness of the paper, those ordinary, nondescript transitions?" The act of reading Mallarmé, of sounding that "transparency of allusions," becomes—in his own words—a "desperate practice" precisely because "to read" means "to rely, depending on the page, on the blank," to take cognizance of the text as a "stilled poem, in the blanks." Through the breaks and the blanks in his texts, Mallarmé internalizes intertextual heterogeneity and puts it to work not as a relation *between* texts but as a play of intervals and interruptions *within* texts. Mallarmé's intertextuality then becomes an explicit version of the ways in which a text is never its own contemporary, cannot constitute a self-contained whole, conveys only its non-coincidence with itself. While the desire to escape banality seemed to situate the challenge of poetry in the impossibility of saying something *different,* Mallarmé here reveals through the text's own self-difference an equal impossibility inherent in the attempt to say something *same.* Indeed, his notion of the Book ("the world is made to end up as a Book") is a correlative to this: if for Mallarmé all poets have unwittingly yet unsuccessfully attempted to write THE Book, and if at the same time "all books contain the fusion of a small number of repeated sayings," then difference can only arise out of the process of repetition, and the "defect of languages" that verse is supposed to make up for resides in the fact that it is just as impossible to say the *same* thing as to say something different.

It is perhaps this paradox of intertextual relations, this "unanimous blank conflict between one garland and the same," that is staged by the famous "Swan" sonnet:

> Le vierge, le vivace et le bel aujourd'hui
> Va-t-il nous déchirer avec un coup d'aile ivre
> Ce lac dur oublié que hante sous le givre
> Le transparent glacier des vols qui n'ont pas fui!

Un cygne d'autrefois se souvient que c'est lui
Magnifique mais qui sans espoir se délivre
Pour n'avoir pas chanté la région où vivre
Quand du stérile hiver a resplendi l'ennui.

Tout son col secouera cette blanche agonie
Par l'espace infligé à l'oiseau qui le nie,
Mais non l'horreur du sol où le plumage est pris.

Fantôme qu'à ce lieu son pur éclat assigne,
Il s'immobilise au songe froid de mépris
Que vêt parmi l'exil inutile le Cygne.

[The virgin, vivacious, and lovely today—
Will it rend with a blow of its dizzying wing
This hard lake forgotten yet haunted beneath
By the transparent glacier of unreleased flights!

A bygone day's swan now remembers it's he
Who, magnificent yet in despair struggles free
For not having sung of the regions of life
When the ennui of winter's sterility gleamed.

All his neck will shake off this white agony space
Has inflicted upon the white bird who denied it,
But not the ground's horror, his plumage inside it.

A phantom assigned by his gloss to this place,
Immobile he stands, in the cold dream of scorn
That surrounds, in his profitless exile, the Swan.]

The poetry of "today" would thus constitute the rendering of something that is both forgotten and haunted—haunted by the way in which a "bygone day's swan" *did not sing*. The choice of a swan as a figure for the precursor is both appropriate and paradoxical. On the one hand, if the swan sings only at the moment of death, then the poet who says he is haunted by the precursor-swan's song would in reality be marking the *death* of the father. But on the other hand, to seek to silence the father, to speak of his *not* having sung, is to run the risk of bringing the father back to life, since if he does not sing, there is no proof that he is dead. In other words, the survival of the father is in a sense guaranteed by the way in which the son does *not* hear him.

It is interesting to note that this sonnet about a bygone day's swan actually itself refers to the swan of a bygone day—a poem entitled "The Swan," written by Baudelaire and dedicated to *his* poetic precursor, Victor Hugo. It would seem that the swan comes to designate the precursor as such, and it is doubtless no accident that the predecessor-figure in Proust's *Remembrance of Things Past* should also be called by the name of Swann.

But in each of these cases, what is striking about the precursor figure, what in a sense seals his paternity, is the way in which he himself is already divided, rent, different from himself. In Proust's novel, Swann is the model of a man who is never the contemporary of his own desires. Baudelaire's "Swan" poem tells of being divided between the loss of what can never be recovered and the memory of what can never be forgotten, so that irreparable loss becomes the incapacity to let anything go. To return to Mallarmé's sonnet, we can see that the very division between "aujourd'hui" (today) and "autrefois" (bygone day) names the temporality of intertextuality as such. And this division in itself constitutes a textual allusion—to the division of Hugo's *Contemplations* into two volumes entitled precisely "Autrefois" and "Aujourd'hui." "They are separated by an abyss," writes Hugo: "the tomb."

In his preface to *Contemplations*, Hugo suggests that his book should be read "as one reads the work of the dead." In reflecting on this quotation, one can begin to see a supplementary twist to the traditional oedipal situation. For if the father survives precisely through his way of affirming himself dead, then the son will always arrive too late to kill him. What the son suffers from, then, is not the simple desire to kill the father, but the impotence to kill him whose potency resides in his ability to recount his own death.

It is perhaps for this reason that the so-called "fathers of modern thought"—Mallarmé, Freud, Marx, Nietzsche—maintain such a tremendous authority for contemporary theory. In writing of the subversion of the author, the father, God, privilege, knowledge, property, and consciousness, these thinkers have subverted in advance any grounds on which one might undertake to kill off an authority that theorizes the death of all authority. This is perhaps the way in which contemporary theory in its turn has *lived* the problematics of intertextuality.

From the foregoing it would appear that intertextuality is a struggle between fathers and sons, and that literary history is exclusively a male affair. This has certainly been the presumption of literary historians in the past, for whom gender becomes an issue only when the writer is female. In the remainder of this essay, I would like to glance briefly at the ways in which questions of gender might enrich, complicate, and even subvert the underlying paradigms of intertextual theory. What, for example, does one make of Mallarmé's experience of the "pleasures of a purely passive soul who is yet but a woman"? Is Mallarmé's femininity a mere figure for castration? Or is the Muse of Impotence also a means of access to the experience of femininity? Or, to approach it another way, how might we factor into these intertextual relations the fact that Baudelaire's protestations of solitude and paternity are written to his *mother*, and that the tomb that separates "autrefois" and "aujourd'hui" for Hugo is that of his *daughter*? What, in other words, are the poetic uses to which women—both inside and outside the text—have been put by these male poets?

It is interesting that the only text by Mallarmé on which Baudelaire is known to have commented is a prose poem in which a beautiful, naked woman stands as a figure for the poetry of the past. Mallarmé's poem, "Le Phénomène futur," describes a degenerating world in which a "Displayer of Things Past" is touting the beauties of a "woman of Bygone Days." Drooping poets-to-be are suddenly revived, "haunted by rhythm and forgetting that theirs is an era that has outlived beauty." Baudelaire, in his notes on Belgium, has this to say about Mallarmé's vision of the future: "A young writer has recently come up with an ingenious but not entirely accurate conception. The world is about to end. Humanity is decrepit. A future Barnam is showing the degraded men of his day a beautiful woman artificially preserved from ancient times. 'What?' they exclaim, 'could humanity once have been as beautiful as that?' I say that this is not true. Degenerate man would admire himself and call beauty ugliness." This encounter between the two poets is a perfect figuration of the progress of literary history from one generation to another. But the disagreement on which Baudelaire insists is less profound than it appears. While the elder poet fears that people will admire something he no longer recognizes as beautiful and the younger poet fears that beauty may no longer be recognizable in his work, Baudelaire and Mallarmé actually agree on two things: beauty is a function of the past, and beauty is a woman.

Nothing could be more traditional than this conception of Beauty as a female body: naked, immobile, and mute. Indeed, the beauty of female muteness and reification reaches its highest pitch when the woman in question is dead (cf. Poe's statement that the most poetic subject is the death of a beautiful woman) or at least—as here—artificially preserved and statufied. The flawless whiteness of the female body is the very image of the blank page, to be shaped and appropriated by the male creative pen. As Susan Gubar remarks in a recent article entitled " 'The Blank Page' and Female Creativity":

> When the metaphors of literary creativity are filtered through a sexual lens, female sexuality is often identified with textuality. . . . This model of the pen-penis writing on the virgin page participates in a long tradition identifying the author as a male who is primary and the female as his passive creation—a secondary object lacking autonomy, endowed with often contradictory meaning but denied intentionality.

In Mallarmé's work, the correlation between Poetry and Femininity is pervasive from the very beginning. The great unfinished poem, *Hérodiade,* begun in 1864 and still lying uncompleted on Mallarmé's desk at the time of his death in 1898, provides a telling record of the shifting importance and complexity of his attempt to make poetry speak as a female Narcissus, self-reflexive and self-contained. The failure of Mallarmé's attempt to *dramatize* his poetics under the guise of female psychology is certainly as instructive as the centrality of that project, and deserves more extensive treatment than is possible here. But in Mallarmé's later writing, the identification of femininity with textuality, which becomes both more explicit and more complex, becomes as well completely de-psychologized:

> A déduire le point philosophique auquel est située l'impersonnalité de la danseuse, entre sa féminine apparence et un objet mimé, pour quel hymen: elle le pique d'une sûre pointe, le pose; puis déroule notre conviction en le chiffre de pirouettes prolongé vers un autre motif, attendu que tout, dans l'évolution par où elle illustre le sens de nos extases et triomphes entonnés à l'orchestre, est, comme le veut l'art même, au théatre, *fictif ou momentané.*

> [To deduce the philosophical point at which the dancer's impersonality is located, between her feminine appearance and a mimed object, for what Hymen: she pricks it with a confident point and poses it; then unrolls our conviction in the cipher of pirouettes prolonged toward another motif, presuming that everything, in the evolution through which she illustrates the sense of our ecstasies and triumphs intoned in the orchestra, is, as art itself requires it, in theatre, *fictive or momentary.*]

> A savoir que la danseuse *n'est pas une femme qui danse,* pour ces motifs juxtaposés qu'elle *n'est pas une femme,* mais une métaphore résumant un des aspects élémentaires de notre forme, glaive, coupe, fleur, etc., et *qu'elle ne danse pas,* suggérant, par le prodige de raccourcis ou d'élans, avec une écriture corporelle ce qu'il faudrait des paragraphes en prose dialoguée autant que descriptive, pour exprimer, dans la rédaction: poème dégagé de tout appareil du scribe.

> [That is, that the dancer *is not a woman dancing,* for the juxtaposed motives that she *is not a woman,* but a metaphor epitomizing one of the elementary aspects of our form, sword, goblet, flower, etc., and that *she is not dancing,* suggesting, through the prodigy of short cuts and leaps, with a corporal writing what it would take paragraphs of dialogue and descriptive prose to express, if written out: a poem freed from all scribal apparatus.]

This would certainly seem to be an example of the denial of female interiority and subjectivity and the transformation of the woman's body into an art object. Textuality becomes woman, but woman becomes poet only unconsciously and corporally. But is it different for a man? The question of autonomy and intentionality becomes sticky indeed when one recalls that for Mallarmé it is precisely the intentionality of the poet as such that must disappear in order for initiative to be left to words: "L'oeuvre pure implique la disparition élocutoire du poète, qui cède l'initiative aux mots."

Therefore, the fact that the dancer here is objectified and denied interiority is not in itself a function of her gender. That state of "scribelessness," of "impersonality," is, rather, the ideal Mallarmé sets up for poetry. But the fact remains that the poet is consistently male and the poem female:

L'Unique entraînement imaginatif consiste, aux heures ordinaires de fréquentation dans les lieux de Danse sans visée quelconque préalable, patiemment et passivement à se demander devant tout pas, chaque attitude si étranges, ces pointes et taquetés, allongés ou ballons, "Que peut signifier ceci" ou mieux, d'inspiration, le lire. A coup sûr on opérera en pleine rêverie, mais adéquate: vaporeuse, nette et ample, ou restreinte, telle seulement que l'enferme en ses circuits ou la transporte par une fugue la ballerine illettrée se livrant aux jeux de sa profession. Oui, celle-là (serais-tu perdu en une salle, spectator très étranger, Ami) pour peu que tu déposes avec soumission à ses pieds d'inconsciente révélatrice ainsi que les roses qu'enlève et jette en la visibilité de régions supérieures un jeu de ses chaussons de satin pâle vertigineux, la Fleur d'abord *de ton poétique instinct*, n'attendant de rien autre la mise en évidence et sous le vrai jour des mille imaginations latentes: alors, par un commerce dont paraît son sourire verser le secret, sans tarder elle te livre à travers le voile dernier qui toujours reste, la nudité de tes concepts et silencieusement écrira ta vision à la façon d'un Signe, qu'elle est.

[The sole imaginative training consists, in the ordinary hours of frequenting Dance with no preconceived aim, patiently and passively, of wondering at every step, each attitude, so strange, those points and *taquetés, allongés* or *ballons,* "What can this signify?" or, better, by inspiration, of reading it. One will definitely operate in full reverie, but adequate: vaporous, crisp, and ample, or restrained, such only as it is enclosed in circlings or transported in a figure by the illiterate ballerina engaging in the play of her profession. Yes, that one (be you lost in the hall, most foreign spectator, Friend) if you but set at the feet of this unconscious revealer, submissively—like the roses lifted and tossed into the visibility of the upper regions by a flounce of her dizzying pale satin slippers— the Flower at first *of your poetic instinct*, expecting nothing but the evidencing and in the true light of a thousand latent imaginations: then, through a commerce whose secret her smile appears to pour out, without delay she delivers up to you, through the ultimate veil that always remains, the nudity of your concepts, and silently begins to write your vision in the manner of a Sign, which she is.]

What the woman is a sign of, what she *unconsciously* reveals, is the nudity of "your" concepts and the flower of "your" poetic instinct. The woman, dancing, is the necessary but unintentional medium through which something fundamental to the male poetic self can be manifested. But this state of unconsciousness, which would seemingly establish the possibility of a female poet, turns out to be valuable only when reappropriated by the male poet. This becomes clear in Mallarmé's discussion of women and jewels.

Precious stones figure often in Mallarmé's descriptions of poetry:

> L'oeuvre pure implique la disparition élocutoire du poète, qui cède l'initiative aux mots, par le heurt de leur inégalité mobilisés; *ils s'allument de reflets réciproques comme une virtuelle traînée de feux sur des pierreries,* remplaçant la respiration perceptible en l'ancien souffle lyrique ou la direction personnelle enthousiaste de la phrase [italics mine].

> [The pure work implies the elocutionary disappearance of the poet, who leaves the initiative to words, through the shock of their mobilized inequality; *they light up with reciprocal reflections like a virtual trail of fire over precious stones,* replacing the breath perceptible in the old lyric inspiration or the passionate personal direction of the sentence.]

In an interview with Jules Huret, Mallarmé expands upon the image of jewelry in the following terms:

> —*Que pensez-vous de la fin du naturalisme?*
> —L'enfantillage de la littérature jusqu'ici a été de croire, par exemple, que de choisir un certain nombre de pierres précieuses et en mettre les noms sur le papier, même très bien, c'était *faire* des pierres précieuses. Eh bien! non! La poésie consistant à *créer,* il faut prendre dans l'âme humaine des états, des lueurs d'une pureté si absolue que, bien chantés et bien mis en lumière, cela constitute en effet les joyaux de l'homme: là, il y a symbole, il y a création, et le mot poésie a ici son sens: c'est, en somme, la seule création humaine possible. Et si, véritablement, les pierres précieuses dont on se pare ne manifestent pas un état d'âme, c'est indûment qu'on s'en pare. . . . La femme, par exemple, cette éternelle voleuse . . .
> Et tenez, *ajoute mon interlocuteur en riant à moitié,* ce qu'il y a d'admirable dans les magasins de nouveautés, c'est, quelquefois, de nous avoir révélé, par le commissaire de police, que la femme se parait indûment de ce dont elle ne savait pas le sens caché, et qui ne lui appartient par conséquent pas.

> [—*What do you think of the end of naturalism?*
> —The childishness of literature up to now has been to think, for example, that to choose a certain number of precious stones and to put their names down on paper, even superbly well, was

to *make* precious stones. Not at all! Since poetry consists of creating, one must take from the human soul certain states, certain glimmerings of such absolute purity that, skillfully sung and brought to light, they constitute indeed the jewels of man: there, there is symbol, there is creation, and the word poetry takes on its meaning: that, in sum, is the only human creation possible. And if, truly, the precious stones one dresses in do not manifest a state of mind or mood, then one has no right to wear them. . . . Woman, for example, that eternal thief . . .

And think, *adds my interlocutor half laughing:* what is admirable about those high fashion stores is that they have sometimes revealed to us, through the chief of police, that women have been illegitimately wearing what they didn't know the hidden meaning of, and which consequently does not belong to them.]

Women's unconsciousness of meaning—that which makes them capable of *standing for* the male poetic instinct—is what denies the legitimacy of their ever occupying the role of poetic subject. Men know what they are doing when they leave initiative to words or jewels; women don't. It is interesting to recall that Mallarmé almost singlehandedly produced a fashion journal, *La Dernière Mode*, which dealt in great detail with jewelry, clothing, and other items of female decoration, and which he often signed with a feminine pseudonym. It is as though Mallarmé's interest in writing like a woman about fashion was to steal back for consciousness that women had stolen by unconsciousness, to write *consciously* from out of the female unconscious, which is somehow more intimately but illegitimately connected to the stuff of poetry. Intertextuality here becomes intersexuality.

Mallarmé's instatement of the impersonal or unconscious poetic subject thus somehow exposes rather than conceals a question that haunts him from the very beginning: is writing a gendered act? It is this question that informs a poem entitled "Don du poème," which serves as a dedicatory poem to *Hérodiade*. The fact that Hérodiade and Mallarmé's daughter Genevieve were "born" at the same time serves as the background for Mallarmé's reflection on gender differences:

> Je t'apporte l'enfant d'une nuit d'Idumée!
> Noire, à l'aile saignante et pâle, déplumée,
> Par le verre brûlé d'aromates et d'or,
> Par les carreaux glacés, hélas! mornes encor,
> L'aurore se jeta sur la lampe angélique.
> Palmes! et quand elle a montré cette relique
> A ce père essayant un sourire ennemi,
> La solitude bleue et stérile a frémi.
> O la berceuse, avec ta fille et l'innocence
> De vos pieds froids, accueille une horrible naissance:
> Et ta voix rappelant viole et clavecin,

Avec le doigt fané presseras-tu le sein
Par qui coule en blancheur sibylline la femme
Pour les lèvres que l'air du vierge azur affame?

[I bring you the child of a night spent in Edom!
Black, with pale and bleeding wing, quilless,
Through the glass burned with spices and gold,
Through the icy panes, alas! mournful still,
The dawn flew down on the angelic lamp.
Palms! and when it had shown this relic
To this father attempting an enemy smile,
The blue and sterile solitude was stirred.
O cradler, with your daughter and the innocence
Of your cold feet, welcome a horrible birth:
And your voice recalling viol and harpsichord,
With faded finger will you press the breast
Through which in sibylline whiteness woman flows
For lips half starved by virgin azure air?]

The question of gender is raised immediately in two very different ways
in the first line. The word "enfant" is one of the few words in French that
can be either masculine or feminine without modification. And the name
"Idumée" refers to ancient Edom, the land of the outcast Esau, or, according
to the Kabbalah, the land of pre-Adamic man, where sexless beings reproduced without women, or where sexual difference did not exist. The poem
thus begins on a note of denial of sexual difference, only to end with a
plea that the woman agree to nurture the fruit of such a denial. The means
of such nourishment is "blancheur sibylline": white textuality, the blankness that challenges interpretation. The woman, then, is to provide the
nourishing blanks without which the newborn poem might die of "azure,"
which, as we have seen, represents the weight of poetic history. "Idumée"
and "Palmes" can be found in Boileau's Satire IX in passage in which he
lists a string of Malherbian poetic commonplaces. (It is curious to note that
the word with which "Idumée" rhymes in Boileau is "alarmée," and that
"alarmes" is the first rhyme in the overture to *Hérodiade*, which follows and
imagistically grows out of "Don du Poème." Mallarmé's anagrammatical
signature seems to lurk just behind these citations of poetic history.)

It would seem at first sight that Mallarmé in this poem draws a contrast
between the fecundity of natural reproduction and the sterility of poetic
creation, and that this poem stands as a typical example of the male pen
expressing its womb envy. Yet the masculine here is equated with sex-
lessness, while the woman functions not as a womb but as a source of
music and sibylline whiteness. The opposition between male and female
is an opposition between half-dead language and nourishing non-language.
But while many writers have valued the woman as something extra-textual,
such non-language is valued in Mallarmé's system not because it is outside,

but because it is *within*, the poetic text. Both music and whiteness are extraordinarily privileged in Mallarmé's poetics precisely because they function as articulations *without* content. Mallarmé's insistence that what the word "flower" evokes is what is *absent* from any bouquet, that the text is a structure of relations and not a collection of signifieds, that there is no given commensurability between language and reality, functions polemically in the late nineteenth century debates over realism and naturalism. His emphasis on music as a "system of relations" and on blankness as a structured but "stilled" poem functions precisely as a *critique* of the pretensions to representationalism and realism in the literary text. By thus opposing naive referentiality and privileging blankness and silence, Mallarmé also, however, implicitly shifts the gender values traditionally assigned to such questions. If the figure of woman has been repressed and objectified by being equated with the blank page, then Mallarmé, by *activating* those blanks, comes close to writing from the place of the silenced female voice. In his ways of throwing his voice as a woman, of figuring textuality as a dancing ballerina, and of questioning simplistic pretensions to expressivity, potency, and (masculine) authority, Mallarmé's critique of logocentrism opens up a space for a critique of phallocentrism as well. Intertextuality can no longer be seen simply as a relation between fathers and sons. But although Mallarmé's many feminine incarnations make it impossible to read him as "simply" masculine, the revaluation of the *figure* of the woman by a male author cannot substitute for the actual participation of women in the critical conversation. Mallarmé may be able to speak from the place of the silenced woman, but as long as *he* is occupying it, the silence that is broken in theory is maintained in reality. And while there is no guarantee that when a "real" woman speaks, she is truly breaking that silence, at least she makes it difficult to avoid facing the fact that literal "women" and figurative "women" do not meet on the same rhetorical level of discourse. Indeed, in this essay we have barely begun to explore the true intertextualities of intersexuality.

Reading as Explication:
Mallarmé's "Toast funèbre"

James Lawler

Explication, Michael Riffaterre has observed, is "a machine to tame the literary work, to take away its virtue by returning it to customary paths" (*La Production* 8; trans. mine). His comment is not easy to dismiss: the traditional French method with its claims to scientific exactness has often appeared synonymous with facile demonstration. But one may consider that its procedures are not wholly misguided. It places primary emphasis on the text itself; it strives for an orderly analysis; it seeks to be answerable to the linear experience of reading; above all, it bears witness to the diverse levels of style and thought that are not reducible to a simple equation. Theoretically at least, it is as multiple as the text will allow. And if explanation suggests a naive program of critical inquiry, one can recall that explication is etymologically an unfolding—"pli selon pli," as Mallarmé writes with a view to his orphic explication of the earth—revealing patterns of significance that are substantial texture. In this perspective, I wish to apply it to a key poem of symbolism, the subtlety of which may best serve to justify such a study.

TOAST FUNÈBRE

O DE NOTRE BONHEUR, toi, le fatal emblème!

Salut de la démence et libation blême,
Ne crois pas qu'au magique espoir du corridor
J'offre ma coupe vide où souffre un monstre d'or!
Ton apparition ne va pas me suffire:
Car je t'ai mis, moi-même, en un lieu de porphyre.
Le rite est pour les mains d'éteindre le flambeau

Contre le fer épais des portes du tombeau:
Et l'on ignore mal, élu pour notre fête
Très simple de chanter l'absence du poëte,
Que ce beau monument l'enferme tout entier:
Si ce n'est que la gloire ardente du métier,
Jusqu'à l'heure commune et vile de la cendre,
Par le carreau qu'allume un soir fier d'y descendre,
Retourne vers les feux du pur soleil mortel!

Magnifique, total et solitaire, tel
Tremble de s'exhaler le faux orgueil des hommes.
Cette foule hagarde! elle annonce: Nous sommes
La triste opacité de nos spectres futurs.
Mais le blason des deuils épars sur de vains murs
J'ai méprisé l'horreur lucide d'une larme,
Quand, sourd même à mon vers sacré qui ne l'alarme,
Quelqu'un de ces passants, fier, aveugle et muet,
Hôte de son linceul vague, se transmuait
En le vierge héros de l'attente posthume.
Vaste gouffre apporté dans l'amas de la brume
Par l'irascible vent des mots qu'il n'a pas dits,
Le néant à cet Homme aboli de jadis:
"Souvenirs d'horizons, qu'est-ce, ô toi, que la Terre?"
Hurle ce songe; et, voix dont la clarté s'altère,
L'espace a pour jouet le cri: "Je ne sais pas!"

Le Maître, par un œil profond, a, sur ses pas,
Apaisé de l'éden l'inquiète merveille
Dont le frisson final, dans sa voix seule, éveille
Pour la Rose et le Lys le mystère d'un nom.
Est-il de ce destin rien qui demeure, non?
O vous tous, oubliez une croyance sombre.
Le splendide génie éternel n'a pas d'ombre.
Moi, de votre désir soucieux, je veux voir,
A qui s'évanouit, hier, dans le devoir
Idéal que nous font les jardins de cet astre,
Survivre pour l'honneur du tranquille désastre
Une agitation solennelle par l'air
De paroles, pourpre ivre et grand calice clair,
Que, pluie et diamant, le regard diaphane
Resté là sur ces fleurs dont nulle ne se fane,
Isole parmi l'heure et le rayon du jour!

C'est de nos vrais bosquets déjà tout le séjour,
Où le poëte pur a pour geste humble et large
De l'interdire au rêve, ennemi de sa charge:

Afin que le matin de son repos altier,
Quand la mort ancienne est comme pour Gautier
De n'ouvrir pas les yeux sacrés et de se taire,
Surgisse, de l'allée ornement tributaire,
Le sépulcre solide où gît tout ce qui luit,
Et l'avare silence et la massive nuit.

[Oh you, fatal emblem of our happiness! Greeting of madness and pale libation, do not think that I offer to the corridor's magical hope my empty cup in which a golden monster is suffering. Your appearance will not satisfy me, for I myself put you in a place of porphyry. The ritual is for the hands to extinguish the torch against the thick iron of the gates of the tomb, and having been chosen for our very simple feast of singing the poet's absence, one cannot fail to recognize that this fine monument contains him entire. And yet the ardent glory of the craft, until the common vile hour of ashes, returns, through the windowpane lit by an evening proud to descend there, toward the fires of the pure mortal sun!

Magnificent, total and solitary, in such a way does men's false pride tremble to express itself. That haggard crowd! It announces: we are the sad opaqueness of our future specters. But, with the heraldry of mournings spread out on vain walls, I scorned the lucid horror of a tear when, deaf even to my sacred verse that does not stir him, one of the passers-by, proud, blind and mute, the host of his vague shroud, changed into the virgin hero of posthumous waiting. Vast gulf brought into the misty mass by the angry wind of the words he did not utter, Nothingness to this man abolished of yore: "O you, memories of horizons, what is Earth?" So howls this dream; and space, a voice whose clarity wanes, has this cry for plaything: "I do not know!"

The Master, by a profound eye, as he passed, has quieted the troubled marvel of Eden whose final shiver, in his voice alone, awakens for the Rose and the Lily the mystery of a name. Is there nothing that remains of this destiny? Oh all of you, forget a dark belief. Splendid eternal genius has no shadow. Solicitous of your desire, I wish to see, in honor of the tranquil disaster, a solemn aerial agitation of words survive him who vanished yesterday in the ideal duty prescribed to us by the gardens of this planet—drunken purple and great clear chalice that, rain and diamond, the diaphanous glance, as it remains there on those unfading flowers, isolates amid the hour and the radiance of day!

It is already the whole place of our true groves where the pure poet's broad and humble gesture wards off dream, enemy of his ordination: so that, on the morning of his high repose, when as for Gautier ancient death consists of not opening sacred eyes and

remaining silent, there shall rise up, as tributary ornament of the
pathway, the solid sepulchre where lies all that harms, and mean
silence, and massive night.]

(trans. mine)

"Toast funèbre" is not a neglected work; on the contrary, it has received
searching attention since a first critique by Thibaudet in 1912. The readings,
for the most part, have been line-by-line exegeses, useful in discussing
particular images and parallel texts from other writings of Mallarmé. (Lloyd
J. Austin refers to more than twenty-five detailed discussions of the poem.)
Though the best commentaries are meticulous, they tend to treat the poem
as a puzzle to be solved and to leave its form and worth undetermined.
One may, however, turn to the latest approach, which posits the "undecidability" of the text. The meaning is held to be equivocal, and this very
equivocalness becomes the central value: " 'Toast funèbre,' " Leo Bersani
writes, "is perhaps most interesting as an extremely oblique dismissal of
the poet to whom it pays a tribute"; again: "In 'Toast funèbre' Gautier's
apparent gift for seeing the world is implicitly treated as an anti-poetic
illusion"; again: "The obscurity of 'Toast funèbre' may have less to do with
the difficulty of specific verses than with the ultimately undecidable nature
of Mallarmé's tribute to Gautier" (28, 31, 32). Bersani's analysis has the
merit of bringing traditional readings into question, of suggesting a subversive intention, of facing the problem of evaluation. The following remarks are a response that seeks to read the poem in largely different terms
and with particular reference to its formal aspects—genre, versification,
language—which have, I think, been neglected.

One may begin with the circumstances of the writing. "Toast funèbre"
was composed in 1873, in the disorder of post-Commune Paris. Mallarmé
had recently returned to the capital after eight years in the provinces, which
included the crisis of his Tournon years when he undertook to invent a
radical poetics. He laid out in detail the plans of his future work, but "Toast
funèbre," to be sure, was not yet among them. Gautier died on 22 October
1872, and within a few days his son-in-law Catulle Mendès proposed a
collective volume to honor the dead poet. The pretext would be a wake
during which each poet would rise to salute a facet of the dead master's
talent—"l'un des côtés du talent de leur maître mort [one of the aspects of
their dead master's talent]." Each would address an image of Gautier, using
the *tu* form, at least in the beginning; each poem would be approximately
sixty lines in length, arranged in stanzas; and the initial rhyme would be
feminine, the last masculine, to conform to a single pattern. Mallarmé had
known Mendès for several years so that, not surprisingly, he was invited
to submit a poem; but whereas some of the forty-two other authors were
allotted specific themes—thus, Mendès asked François Coppée to develop
Gautier's "tendresse"—Mallarmé chose to celebrate the seer:

> Commençant par *O toi qui* . . . et finissant par une rime masculine,
> je veux chanter en rimes plates une des qualités glorieuses de

Gautier; le don mystérieux de voir avec les yeux (ôtez mystérieux).
Je chanterai le *voyant*, qui, placé dans ce monde, l'a regardé, ce
que l'on ne fait pas.

[Starting with "Oh you who . . . " and ending on a masculine
rhyme, I want to praise, in couplets, one of Gautier's glorious
qualities: the mysterious gift of seeing with his eyes (delete mysterious). I shall celebrate the seer who, set down in this world,
has looked at it, which is something that people do not do.]

These lines have an elliptic vagueness, as Bersani has pointed out; but is
he right to find an implicit discrepancy in Mallarmé's references to Gautier
as artist of the real and artist of mystery? "Voyant" tells us otherwise: it
echoes Gautier's use of the word in his 1868 preface to the posthumous
edition of *Les Fleurs du mal*, which singles out the visionary element in
Baudelaire for praise, just as in his essay of 1859 Baudelaire had hailed
Gautier's visionary genius. Gautier writes:

il ne faut pas oublier que Baudelaire, bien qu'on l'ait souvent ac-
cusé de matérialisme, reproche que la sottise ne manque pas de
jeter au talent est, au contraire, doué à un degré éminent du don
de *spiritualité*, comme dirait Swedenborg.

[One must not forget that Baudelaire, although he has often been
taxed with materialism, which is a reproach that fools never fail
to level at talent, is on the contrary eminently endowed with the
gift of *spirituality*, as Swedenborg would say.]

And he pursues, making use of the biblical and gnostic term:

Il possède aussi le don de *correspondance*, pour employer le même
idiome mystique, c'est-à-dire qu'il sait découvrir par une intuition
secrète des rapports invisibles à d'autres et rapprocher ainsi, par
des analogies inattendues que seul le *voyant* peut saisir, les objets
les plus éloignés et les plus opposés en apparence. Tout vrai poète
est doué de cette qualité plus ou moins développée, qui est l'essence même de son art.

[He also has the gift of *correspondences*, to use the same mystical
language; that is to say he can by a secret intuition discover relations invisible to other men and bring together, by unexpected
analogies that only the *seer* can grasp, the most distant and most
apparently disparate objects. Every true poet has this quality in
more or less developed form, and it is the very essence of his art.]

Rimbaud read Gautier's preface and, in his 1871 letter to Demeny, used
voyant to describe what was for him the supreme poetic quality. Mallarmé
adopts it in a similar sense: whereas Coppée would show the warmth of
Gautier's reputedly cool art, Mallarmé would treat its insightfulness, not
its reputed objectivity. The theme is, then, a tribute to the talent that Gautier

shares with genuine poets. The master, who described himself as "un homme *pour qui le monde visible existe* [a man *for whom the visible world exists*]" (Goncourt and Goncourt 103), saw things as others do not, in relation to an ideal; going beyond the surface, he captured mysteriously, necessarily, the sign and sense of the visible world.

Nevertheless, given this theme, one must wonder how Mallarmé came to find the distinctive diction and form of "Toast funèbre." His art in this case does not derive from Baudelaire, although Baudelaire played a decisive role in his growth; nor does it come from Gautier, nor from Banville, nor yet from Poe, despite fugitive echoes of each of these authors. The crucial text, I believe, was Hugo's "A Théophile Gautier," which, though it appeared in 1873 in the same volume as "Toast funèbre,"was written before Mallarmé's poem. Hugo dated his manuscript 2 November 1872, which was All Souls' Day, and sent a copy to Catulle Mendès from Guernsey two days later. It is thus clear that, from an early stage in the preparation of the commemorative volume, Mendès had Hugo's text in hand, and nothing could be more natural than to share it with his collaborators at one of their meetings. However this may be—and certainly we have no documentary proof—the Hugo and Mallarmé poems have much in common: both are written in rhyming couplets; both are divided into five parts; both describe a pagan ritual—"la porte funéraire" of Hugo, "le fer épais des portes du tombeau" of Mallarmé—that reverses Christian imagery of personal survival; both use paradox as the central rhetorical figure (life is darkness, death is glory); both bring together certain key words such as the rhyme "Gautier"-"altier"; both identify the destiny of the dead poet with that of the self in an un-Parnassian, characteristically Hugoesque manner. But above all, a combined gravity and warmth of tone link the two poems. We remember the lines in Hugo: "Je te salue au seuil sévère du tombeau . . . "; "Car entrer dans la mort c'est entrer dans le temple . . . "; "Passons; car c'est la loi; nul ne peut s'y soustraire . . . " (105–6)—and a similar accent resonates in "Toast funèbre." Mallarmé adopts the register and develops the elevation and awe that in one or two lines of his poem— "Vaste gouffre apporté dans l'amas de la brume / Par l'irascible vent des mots qu'il n'a pas dits . . . "—can seem at first reading like pastiche.

Yet "Toast funèbre" escapes the shadow of Hugo. The vision is not one of poignant decline as Mallarmé asserts happiness, recovery, resurrection by the artwork itself. One detail may serve to point up the reversal of values: at the end of the fourth part of "A Théophile Gautier" we find an admirable line: "J'écoute ce grand vent sublime évanoui." The words have exceptional strength because of the rhythmic and semantic insistence of "grand vent," the effacement of the caesura, the positional balance and semantic contrast of "écoute" and "évanoui." The sense is one of universal pathos. But this line is also Mallarméan in that emptiness (Hugo's "évanoui") receives a positive value, not as the audible depth of silence but as the form in which the image of beauty will reveal itself (Mallarmé's "coupe vide," "*vains* murs," "s'évanouit"). To Hugo's lament for a dead friend and a vanishing age, Mallarmé responds by a poem of mortality overcome in death.

He writes in the formal tradition of the epitaph or threnody. He obeys Mendès's recommendations, conforms to the desiderata of length and arrangement of rhymes, but orients the mode along personal lines as "The Raven" had taught him—speaking of death, inhabiting the space of "Nevermore." A tension is created that takes the genre beyond dirge and panegyric to the dramatic exorcism of death by beauty, night by dawn, chaos by language, reality by mystery. A series of oppositions—turns and counterturns—sets the action in the poetic texture itself, beyond any anecdotal representation, as measure and timbre assert a visionary confidence. The funeral ode inscribes a salute to death that frees the work from the degradations of time. The alexandrine is the meter—"notre instrument si parfait . . . ," Mallarmé said—of public solemnity. But the pattern is modified in ways that have been learnt from Hugo and that assume Hugo's liberties: for example, the displacement of the caesura. The mold is not broken, but in a quarter of the cases—that is, fourteen lines out of fifty-six—the accent is thrown forward in the line by an energetic thrust as dramatic rhythm contends with symmetry. (When speaking of Mallarmé's prose Claudel used an expression wholly suited to "Toast funèbre": "Le dessein en projection de votre phrase . . . [the forward thrust of your sentence pattern].") Mallarmé's line is not that of "L'Après-midi d'un faune," composed of brusque transitions and unexpected breaks; where the soliloquy is bathed in summer intoxication, "Toast funèbre" moves with deliberate impetus.

One must however speak not only of the shape of individual lines but also of the voice that Mallarmé forges for his poem. Valéry was no doubt referring to the late works when he said of Mallarmé that it is "la faculté de parler qui parle [the faculty of speech that speaks]," for what is true of "Une Dentelle s'abolit" does not apply to "Toast funèbre," in which the self strikes an apostrophic note from the start and maintains vocal timbre by repeatedly echoing the vowel of the first invocation, which is also that of the title word "Toast" ("au," "beau," "flambeau," "tombeau," "carreau," "faux," "nos," "hôte," "héros," "mots," "ô," "Rose," "nos," "repos," "au," "Gautier"). The apostrophe imposes itself as a prime phonetic means of amplifying the sonority, of creating a presence. Yet this technique is not isolated; it is reinforced by multiple orchestration. The density of the first line—its solemn vocative, the positional symmetries of "O" and "toi" and of "de" and "le" in each hemistich, the alliteration—gives way to the comparatively discursive manner of the second part, which depends on the introductory sibilance of "salut" (s signifies for Mallarmé "incitation"), the force of "démence" (d: "une action suivie et sans éclat, profonde"), the liquidity of "libation" (l: "tout son pouvoir d'aspiration"), the plosive strength of "blème" (b: "les sens . . . de production ou enfantement, de fécondité, d'amplitude, de bouffissure et de courbure . . . ") (*Les Mots anglais*).

But after this consonantal energy and its mimological suggestions for

phonetic and semantic development, besides the continuity of nasals juxtaposed to the sharp vowels, a syntactical articulation commands the vocal
line, which is that of a lesson deduced from the initial imperative: "Ne crois
pas . . . Car . . . Le rite est . . . Et l'on ignore mal. . . . " However, the
argument turns on itself with the adversative "Si ce n'est que . . . ," which
is the saving insight. The intonation falls until line 12, when the change
occurs that carries the section to its lapidary resolution. The third part is
introduced by three adjectives that have a superlative denotation; while
the inversion is recalled structurally by the answering adjectives of line 23
("fier, aveugle et muet"). The syntax traces thereby a concave parabola
similar to that of the previous lines, although the adversative comes much
earlier: "[le faux orgueil des hommes] tremble . . . Cette foule . . . annonce
. . . Mais . . . j'ai méprisé. . . . " Nevertheless a second parabola occurs in
the last six lines as the question put by the gulf ("qu'est-ce, ô toi, que la
Terre?") is answered by the man's denial ("Je ne sais pas!"), so strong
indeed that it will modify the echo of the abyss ("voix dont la clarté s'altère"). We note in this stanza the use of repeated prelusive appositions
("Hôte de son linceul vague . . . ," "Vaste gouffre apporté dans l'amas de
la brume . . . ," "Souvenirs d'horizons . . . ") and of an ablative absolute
in line 20, both of which throw forward the weight of the phrase and at
the same time highlight the metaphoricity. In the fourth section, which
begins in apparently anecdotal manner, a new pattern of affirmation and
counteraffirmation governs thought and voice: "Le Maître . . . a . . . apaisé
. . . Est-il de ce destin . . . O vous tous, oubliez . . . Le splendide génie
éternel n'a pas . . . Moi, je veux voir. . . . " The apostrophe of line 37
initiates a reversal that translates the *passé composé* of the opening into the
present tense and anticipated future of the last lines. The work of the master
is taken up by the disciple, and the syntax projects the center of the lines
(by displaced caesuras, adverbial and adjectival phrases, appositions) and
the center of the sentences (by a series of inversions, the most surprising
of which, "A qui s'évanouit" in line 40, precedes the semantically contrasting infinitive, "survivre," that commands it). Finally, the fifth stanza
is written as a universal truth introduced by an impersonal construction:
"C'est de nos vrais bosquets . . . Où le poète . . . a pour geste . . . De
l'interdire . . . Afin que . . . [le sépulcre] surgisse. . . . " These nine lines,
like the nine lines of the second half of the fourth section, are a single
sentence in which "surgisse" recalls the parallel articulatory force of "survivre" in line 42. As in the three previous stanzas, the syntax inscribes a
concave parabola: intonation turns on the subjunctive of line 54, which,
thrust at us by the intervening adverbial phrase and clause, leads the poem
to its brief exultant climax.

Meter, sound, and syntax reveal much, then, of this ode to the absent
poet, which is Mallarmé's attempt to create a presence in absence. The
language, similarly, goes beyond normal poetic usage in order to establish
a domain of its own. Whereas the poignancy of "A Théophile Gautier"

comes in large measure from its intermixture of the familiar and the mythological, Mallarmé has recourse to an art of abstraction. Thus he develops the phonetic series of "bonheur," "horreur," "honneur," "heure"; of "espoir," "gloire," "devoir"; of "démence," "absence," "croyance," "silence"—a mutually reinforcing incantation that succeeds in personifying abstraction. We may look at lines 16 and 17: "Magnifique, total et solitaire, tel / Tremble de s'exhaler le faux orgueil des hommes." The abstract subject is treated with a dramatic power unlike that of any allegory. The three epithets designate an ambition that contrasts with the sham of "faux orgueil"; "tremble" and the unusual reflexive "s'exhaler," uniting "s'exprimer," "exhaler," and "expirer" in the multiple senses of an ultimate expression, provide a context of physical and emotional effort; at the same time, "orgueil" will lead to "blason des deuils" in line 20, which ironically points to an ambition that sees no further than death. One could cite many such cases, which are a prime mark of "Toast funèbre"—the idea being apprehended as an active image that is defined in relation to the whole. And this applies not only to words in phonetically allied groups but also, for instance, to the cluster of abstract terms ("néant," "souvenir," "songe," "clarté") at the end of the third stanza:

> Le néant à cet Homme aboli de jadis:
> "Souvenirs d'horizons, qu'est-ce, ô toi, que la Terre?"
> Hurle ce songe; et, voix dont la clarté s'altère,
> L'espace a pour jouet le cri: "Je ne sais pas!"

Nothingness becomes a shrieking dream, space a voice that can maintain its brightness no more, and the dead Gautier—"Souvenirs d'horizons"—an image of the creative self in whom objects recede so that their truth can be apprehended in the far depths of memory. Mallarmé has fled immediacy, and his use of periphrasis invents a linguistic space that allows thought to be envisioned in theatrical terms.

Proceeding from these initial remarks on Mallarmé's language, we find an imaginative coherence of unique intensity. For the title proposes the antithesis that embraces the text in its details, as grief is contradicted by a ritual salute. This opposition is the matrix that will be transposed by consistently subtle permutations. Thus "bonheur" and "fatal emblème" take up the preliminary contrast of the title by applying it to Gautier, who becomes the image that combines regret with rejoicing; similarly, "Salut de la démence" and "libation blême" vary the terms that serve both as vocative (Gautier is this sacred offering who has gone to the ends of unreason) and prelusive apposition (the words being spoken are themselves this solemn offering that is answerable only to an ideal). The same primary antithesis is brought to focus in the third and fourth lines: "Ne crois pas qu'au magique espoir du corridor / J'offre ma coupe vide où souffre un monstre d'or!" The language is not purely ornamental but projects the tension of festive death. The empty glass contains a golden form: poetry offers the writhing image of beauty that is written on the void. Mallarmé's method is not a more or less simple variation of terms but a concerted harmonics, a drama of ideas, a language intellectual and daring. In similar fashion, "coupe vide" and "monstre d'or" will be recalled in line 20 by the "vains murs" on which beauty emblazons a proud image; by the "linceul vague" of line 24 that clothes the poet, who, in death, heroically conquers death; by the "éden" of poetic contemplation in line 33, which like the last rays of the sun captures the world in its essence:

> Le Maître, par un œil profond, a sur ses pas,
> Apaisé de l'éden l'inquiète merveille
> Dont le frisson final, dans sa voix seule, éveille
> Pour la Rose et le Lys le mystère d'un nom.

The golden monster has become this "inquiète merveille" in its supreme moment. Instead of qualifying the dead poet, or his poetry, or the present poem, or the curtains hung on the walls of death like the tapestry of *Igitur*, the metaphorical structure tropes the workings of poetic creation, whose end is immaterial language. No less vigorously, glass and monster will echo in "pour l'honneur du tranquille désastre" of line 42, which is the muted pathos and implicit glory of Gautier's life, and in "pourpre ivre et grand calice clair" of line 44, purple being the color of royal mourning, "ivre" the inspired and agitated form, and "calice" the ritual chalice that holds this poem in which Mallarmé continues the art of Gautier.

Finally, in the last stanza, the tomb—not only Gautier's but that of all poets—conforms to the same funeral salute:

> Afin que le matin de son repos altier,
> Quand la mort ancienne est comme pour Gautier
> De n'ouvrir pas les yeux sacrés et de se taire,
> Surgisse, de l'allée ornement tributaire,
> Le sépulcre solide où gît tout ce qui luit,
> Et l'avare silence et la massive nuit.

The appositive "ornement tributaire" points up the continuity of the idea: here the champagne glass is a sepulcher that takes to itself the elements hostile to poetry and contains them, the scheme showing yet again the image of beauty and the void.

The language of "Toast funèbre" is, then, this acutely self-conscious modulation that illustrates the art it praises. Structuring form and language, the five parts compose the theme, not in any declamatory way—as in the case of Hugo—but with a severe logic. (1) The first line provocatively sets the paradox, postulating the atemporal significance of Gautier's death—"notre bonheur." (2) A series of negations ends on a strong affirmation: Gautier is indeed dead, but his art shines like the daily sacrifice of the sun. (3) Inversely, a series of affirmations ends on a negation: all humans would wish to triumph over death, but their pride is false, and they come to recognize their "triste opacité"; yet Gautier's death is of another kind that brings the speaker to new awareness: not only can he look death in the face without seeking a "magic corridor" of resurrection, but he can scorn sorrow itself ("J'ai méprisé l'horreur lucide d'une larme"). Gautier's future is assured for he has overcome the abyss of chaos and old night; his "Je ne sais pas!" is the cry of the *voyant* who sees with his imagination. (4) Poetic vision is inseparable from the art of naming: Gautier found a true language in the fateful struggle of death and beauty ("frisson final"); in complementary manner, Mallarmé celebrates Gautier in his own poem, his words a sumptuous funereal offering ("pourpre ivre et grand calice clair"), his vision the combined transparency of rain and diamond ("pluie et dia-mant"), at once stylized nature and art. (5) In his work, Gautier, like all true poets, continues to ward off the antagonistic dream ("rêve" echoes the vertiginous "songe" of the third section), creating an ideal garden for all to know, but the chronological progression of "un soir" (l. 14), "amas de la brume" (l. 27), and "hier" (l. 40) leads to "le matin" (l. 51) in accordance with the myth of Orpheus; at the same time the "hôte de son linceul vague" (l. 24) becomes, like the Christ, the universal work of poetry, free of mortal coils. The dream will no longer be outside but within the tomb, encom-passed and thereby held in check: the sepulchre, or book ("le Livre . . . tenté à son insu par quiconque a écrit, même les Génies . . . [the Book . . . attempted unawares by whoever has written, even writers of Genius]."), will subsume the human imagination, since Gautier's efforts converge with those of his fellow poets past and future whose vision is that of the inner eye.

The argument in its bare outline enables us to grasp the imaginative and conceptual mastery of the text. Against the claim of undecidability and the supposed equivocalness of the poet's intention, I have tried to show an exceptionally achieved piece in which Gautier is held to exemplify *voy-ance*. Going beyond the Hugoesque and romantic lament for lost time, Mallarmé enunciates a theory of poetry that is also a theory of identity: his invocation of the seer is the poetry of the seer, both oracular and didactic. He does not dismiss Gautier in however oblique a fashion, nor does he offer a left-handed tribute: here, at the end of his crisis of faith, which coincides with the crisis of faith of his age (since, as Valéry observed, "Hugo demands Mallarmé"), he establishes his homage on a sequence of peri-phrases, of interconnected—indeed, concentric—tensions: the poet and personality, the poet and language, the poet and the world. His resolution is proposed in the name of a visionary art that owes its fervor, its sustained gravity, to the presence of death. Before the octosyllabic lightness of his late sonnets, "Toast funèbre" is his plurivalent sign, and high expression, of the poem as mortal struggle and impersonal accomplishment.

Familiar and Unfamiliar:
Verlaine's Poetic Diction

Carol de Dobay Rifelj

In order for a figure to exist, a comparison must be possible between one form of expression and another which could have been used instead. As Gérard Genette notes, "l'existence et le caractère de la figure sont absolument déterminés par l'existence et le caractère des signes réels en posant leur équivalence sémantique" (*Figures*). This is the case not only with conventional tropes, but also with diction: only if another signifier is possible: *je m'ennuie* for *je m'emmerde, catin* for *putain*, does there come into existence a different kind of figure, a figure of register. On the next level of signification, *coursier* for horse carries the message "I am poetry" just as much as does *voile* for ship. But it stands only for a certain kind of poetry. In Verlaine's time, such usage was the norm: French poetry had a highly restricted set of conventions for poetic diction, distinguishing between high or "elevated" and low diction; between the sublime and the *médiocre* or *burlesque;* between noble and common, or "roturier." The first terms of these sets are obviously highly valorized. Those nineteenth century poets, including Hugo, Rimbaud, Corbière, and Verlaine, who breached this code—using colloquial or familiar words and even vulgar and slang expressions—were clearly setting their poetry against the accepted, almost sacred canon. In doing so, they implicitly recognized that the language of this canon was now too familiar, in the sense of commonplace, and they were led to new delimitations of acceptable diction.

Theoreticians from Aristotle on have linked a specialized vocabulary like that of French neoclassical verse to the use of metaphor. But in Verlaine, the use of familiar diction does not lead to a lessening of the importance of figure; in a sense, it allows for even greater, or at least different, possibilities of figural language. If conventionally "poetic" words and their

From *Kentucky Romance Quarterly* 29, no. 4 (1982). © 1982 by the University Press of Kentucky.

opposite can be shown to be marked registers in poetic texts, it is because their existence permits a kind of movement that can be called tropological; the use of familiar diction calls attention to the surface of the work, preventing its language from being simply referential. Its very "earthiness" prevents it from being "down-to-earth" in the sense of being stabilized or giving the reader a more direct link to the outside world. Rather, it plays on the estrangement implied by its identification as an element of a specific register. As metaphor has been considered the breaking of the semantic rules of a language, register-shifts constitute a breaching of its pragmatic rules. And this breach is one aspect of the figural dimension of language.

Whether the gap between such terms and their conventional counterparts is called parody or humor or opposition to poetic tradition, the reader must attempt to integrate it into some kind of structure. By examining the role of informal or colloquial diction in the figural structure of Verlaine's poems, we can see the different ways in which they exploit its possible stylistic motivations. Incorporating such language into coherent interpretations of the texts does not prove to be simple, however, and such an analysis reveals the complexity of a poet whose works have often been seen as direct, univocal, and even simplistic.

Given the entrenchment of neo-classical diction, it is not surprising that Verlaine's use of familiar language has had a varied critical response, ranging from hailing him as a revolutionary to condemning his later works (in which such language is more prevalent) as vulgar or "prosaic." One critic tries to excuse his use of low language by referring to his low life:

> Avec Verlaine, nous avons affaire à un pauvre brave type, qui sort du bistrot ou de l'hôpital, trainant la patte, et qui nous raconte des choses très simples, ou très délicates, ou très élevées, dans la langue de tous les jours. Alors que les Parnassiens, en redingote et haut de forme, sont juchés tout en haut d'un trépied, Verlaine est sur l'asphalte du trottoir parisien.
>
> (Charles Bruneau, *Verlaine: Choix de poésies*)

But Claude Cuénot, in his study of Verlaine's style, is much less indulgent: "Une étude complète du vocabulaire argotique de Verlaine aurait une importance lexicographique, mais ne comporterait guère d'intérêt esthétique, puis-que la poésie est absente" (*Le Style de Verlaine*). "Unpoetic" words, then, cannot constitute a poem. Verlaine himself seems to support this view when he writes:

> Tu n'es plus bon à rien de propre, ta parole
> Est morte de l'argot et du ricanement,
> Et d'avoir rabâché les bourdes du moment.
> Ta mémoire, de tant d'obscénités bondée,
> Ne saurait accueillir la plus petite idée . . .
>
> (*Sagesse* I, iv)

Verlaine said that he wrote these lines about Rimbaud, but added, "Après coup je me suis aperçu que cela pourrait s'appliquer à 'poor myself.' " He had introduced language of varying degrees of familiarity during the whole of his poetic career, and especially so after *Sagesse*, where these lines appear. And indeed, he does so in this very passage: *tu n'es plus bon à . . . , la plus petite idée* and *rabâché* are certainly casual, familiar expressions. His word, then, rather than being destroyed by slang, receives a new impulse forward.

In order to make sense of such discourse, in order to make poetry of it rather than rejecting it out of hand, the reader must try to "naturalize" it, that is, to justify its use within the context of the poem. This naturalization can operate in various ways, on various levels. First, familiar language can be integrated by assigning the text to a "low" genre, where such diction would be the norm rather than an intrusion. On another level, it can be naturalized as appropriate to the poem's subject-matter: the signified might be "low" life (i.e., a popular subject) or "modern life," calling forth signifiers which mirror the level of the signified. Many examples of such motivation can be found in Verlaine. In texts which escape such categorizations, familiar diction must be incorporated at another level. "Art poétique" provides an example of a text whose self-referentiality leads to taking its unconventional language as signifying a rejection of conventional poetry. Other texts seem unmotivated even at this level and present a challenge to readability itself. In all these texts we must examine to what extent Verlaine's work justifies the naturalizations imposed on it by the urge to legibility and to what extent it defies any such analysis.

"Monsieur Prudhomme" is an example of a poem whose satirical quality helps to motivate the use of "low" language, satire being a genre characterized by the low style.

> Il est grave: il est maire et père de famille
> Son faux col engloutit son oreille. Ses yeux
> Dans un rêve sans fin flottent, insoucieux,
> Et le printemps en fleur sur ses pantoufles brille.
>
> Que lui fait l'astre d'or, que lui fait la charmille
> Où l'oiseau chante à l'ombre, et que lui font les cieux,
> Et les prés verts et les gazons silencieux?
> Monsieur Prudhomme songe à marier sa fille
>
> Avec monsieur Machin, un jeune homme cossu.
> Il est juste-milieu, botaniste et pansu.
> Quant aux faiseurs de vers, ces vauriens, ces maroufles,
>
> Ces fainéants barbus, mal peignés, il les a
> Plus en horreur que son éternel coryza,
> Et le printemps en fleur brille sur ses pantoufles.

The title already makes its status clear: Joseph Prudhomme, the main character in Henri Monnier's novels, was the archetypical bourgeois. The lampoon begins with the very first line, with the words "il est grave" and the stock expression "père de famille" heightened by the homonym *maire/mère*. M. Prudhomme is deaf, his ears "engulfed" in his collar (the word *faux* is also relevant here), as well as blind to the beauties of nature—spring is reduced to the level of his slippers. The rest of the poem confirms this description of his anti-esthetic, anti-poetic sentiments. Even the insults he addresses to poets are consummately bourgeois in the attitude they reveal (poets are unshaven, unkempt, and lazy), and in diction—*maroufles* or *vauriens* are perfectly acceptable terms. It is curious to note, however, that in order to form a contrast with his insensitivity, a conventionally poetic diction is used: not only is the subject nature and flowers, but the periphrase *l'astre d'or* for the sun is eminently neo-classical. It seems that when Verlaine wants to signal "poetry," he needs the easily recognizable "poetic" expression to do so.

Features of other registers conflict with this diction, like *coryza* and *cossu*. *Machin* is "très trivial" (Littré) and doubly comical here, recalling the word *machine* and indicating that the prospective fiancé is so conventionally bourgeois as to have lost all identity. The succession of adjectives in line 10 is funny, too, the physical epithet *pansu* following two nouns used as adjectives. *Botaniste* in this series indicates the only interest nature might have for him.

If the use of a conventionally poetic signifier is itself a sign, whose message is "I am poetry," then slang expressions, used here to ridicule the de-humanized characters should be a sign of opposition to this language, and often they do have this role. But, in this text, where poets are referred to explicitly, and a traditionally "poetic" subject, the flowered spring, appears twice and ends the poem, where *rêve sans fin* is contrasted with M. Prudhomme's thoughts of a profitable marriage for his daughter, the traditional diction is valorized and paradoxically opposed to the characters who would be likely to approve only such language, who would surely say of this text: that isn't poetry.

Even in a text that would be considered more conventionally lyrical, one might consider "low" diction to be motivated by subject-matter. An example of such a poem is "L'Auberge."

> Murs blancs, toit rouge, c'est l'Auberge fraîche au bord
> Du grand chemin poudreux où le pied brûle et saigne,
> L'auberge gaie avec le *Bonheur* pour enseigne.
> Vin bleu, pain tendre, et pas besoin de passe-port.
>
> Ici l'on fume, ici l'on chante, ici l'on dort.
> L'hôte est un vieux soldat, et l'hôtesse, qui peigne
> Et lave dix marmots roses et pleins de teigne,
> Parle d'amour, de joie et d'aise, et n'a pas tort!

La salle au noir plafond de poutres, aux images
Violentes, *Maleck Adel et les Rois Mages,*
Vous accueille d'un bon parfum de soupe aux choux.

Entendez-vous? C'est la marmite qu'accompagne
L'horloge du tic-tac allègre de son pouls.
Et la fenêtre s'ouvre au loin sur la campagne.

Here the popular milieu calls forth many elements usually excluded from poetry: *vin bleu* (cheap wine), cabbage soup, and so on. The pictures of the wise men and Maleck Adel, the hero of a popular novel, would be typical in such an inn. In its homely and banal elements, the text resembles the poetry of Coppée or the Parnassian poets who treated rural subjects or even the descriptive poetry of Delille; and it is analogous to the realist/naturalist novel and its portrayal of lower-class life.

Since everything about this milieu is valorized and opposed to the dusty, painful road, familiar words in reported speech should be neither pejorative nor startling: the casual tone they create is in harmony with the place described, where one can obviously be at ease. But what differs in Verlaine's treatment of the subject is, in fact, the intrusion of familiar diction in the language of the poem. It contains elements from the speech one might expect to hear in a country inn: shortened forms like the elliptical first and fourth lines, including "pas besoin de passe-port" and familiar expressions—*n'a pas tort, entendez-vous, marmots* ("kids"), and *teigne* ("scabby").

These expressions play a role in the figural structure of the text as well, which is built on a correspondence between inside and outside. It is a poem concerned with signs, or language. "Ici l'on fume" and so forth, of course, imitate the messages on signs in shop windows, i.e. linked with the life inside the inn. Thus they recall the sign in the first stanza: "Happiness" is or should be the inn's name, since that is what is to be found within. And of what does this happiness consist? Of *talking* about happiness and comfort and love. So it is removed to yet another level, as the designatum of the inhabitants' conversation. The images or prints on the other hand are metaphors for the life outside; and they are called violent to underline the contrast. Thus, in the last line, the opening window is yet another "image" of the exterior world, framed by the window sill. The language of the poem functions as an imitation (another metaphor) or as another sign of the language of the environment.

In such a context, the speaker is placed in an ambivalent position: he is allowed, even invited within, but an inn is only a temporary lodging, a contingency of his travels. His link with it is an arbitrary one, as the phrase "pas besoin de passe-port" shows; he is just an observer. The poem has been compared to a genre painting; and indeed, it is like a print hung on the wall of a city person's apartment, with a title like "The Pleasures of the

Simple Life." But the "simple life" has turned out to be another signifier, or another metaphor; and the language of the text, rather than grounding it in a correspondence between subject and register-level, serves to destabilize the depiction of a world that seemed attractive in its stability.

In other poems, the link between the signified and the "low" register level of the signifier can be naturalized in different ways, serving a variety of stylistic functions. In the sixteenth poem of *La Bonne Chanson*, "low" language is linked with imagery of lowness and contrasted with "paradise," the presence of the loved one. In *Sagesse* III, xix ("Parisien, mon frère"), it is the countryside which is opposed to the city. The two speakers in "Qu'en dis-tu, voyageur" (I, iii) are distinguished by the levels of language they use. "Sonnet boiteux," from *Jadis et naguère*, uses low diction to denigrate the city it describes; and in conjunction with repetitions, unfamiliar sounds and unusually long verses, it creates an effect of irritation and frustration. In "Nocturne parisien" *(Poèmes saturniens)*, familiar diction sets modern Paris apart from the conventional subjects of Romantic and Parnassian poetry, as well as from the diction characteristic of such verse.

In a letter to Delahaye, Verlaine himself spoke of "ma poétique de plus en plus moderniste" (26 October 1872). There is an element of "modernism" in much of his poetry, from the *Poèmes saturniens* onward, in the sense of portraying nineteenth-century life as Baudelaire did, especially in his *Tableaux parisiens*, where the latter had himself introduced a certain amount of familiar discourse. Much of Verlaine's verse, and particularly "Croquis parisien," which echoes Baudelaire's title, recalls this section of *Les Fleurs du mal*. Dedicated to François Coppée, whose sentimental verse treated emotional moments in ordinary banal lives, usually in Parisian settings, it thematizes the opposition between the contemporary and the past:

> La lune plaquait ses teintes de zinc
>   Par angles obtus
> Des bouts de fumée en forme de cinq
> Sortaient drus et noirs des hauts toits pointus.
>
> Le ciel était gris. La bise pleurait
>   Ainsi qu'un basson.
> Au loin, un matou frileux et discret
> Miaulait d'étrange et grêle façon.
>
> [Le long des maisons, escarpe et putain
>   Se coulaient sans bruit,
> Guettant le joueur au pas argentin
> Et l'adolescent qui mord à tout fruit.]
>
> Moi, j'allais, rêvant du divin Platon
>   Et de Phidias,
> Et de Salamine et de Marathon,
> Sout l'oeil clignotant des bleus becs de gaz.

Although the third stanza was omitted in *Poèmes saturniens*, this poem was the target of several critical attacks. It was said to be "impressionistic," cacophonous, its images supposedly impossible to understand. Jules Lemaître wrote, "Il y a dans tout cela bien des mots mis au hasard.—Justement. Ils ont le sens qu'a voulu le poète, et ils ne l'ont que pour lui." He criticized especially the first stanza, which contains elements like *zinc* and *par angles obtus* which Robichez calls "inédits." Indeed, the use of artistic terminology, unusual images, elements from modern life, and familiar expressions, in their novelty, constitute a metaphor for modern life itself. In other words, new forms of expression are to traditional poetry as the new age is to the old.

Like the artist's vocabulary, *angles obtus* is an unexpected lexical item, an intrusion from mathematical terminology. Elements normally considered low are included in the poem—gas jets, the meowing tomcat. Colloquial expressions like *bouts de fumée* and *moi, j'allais* also stand out in this manner, while giving the impression of a casual, conversational style. In the eliminated stanza, *escarpe*, a slang word for thief, and *putain*, which Littré calls a "terme grossier et malhonnête" are even stronger and are surely at least part of the reason for the stanza's suppression. The poem's rhythm contributes to its conversational tone: the five-syllable second line of each stanza throws off its regularity. And the short, declarative sentences, without the inverted syntax characteristic of traditional poetry, tend to negate their division into verses. The rhymes are all masculine, another unusual procedure; and the false rhymes—*zinc/cinq* and *Phidias/gaz*—reinforce this effect. These devices heighten the contrast set up between nineteenth-century Paris and ancient Greece. The sculptor Phidias is opposed to the aquafortists and sketchers of modern times, the battles of Salamis and Marathon to those between the prostitute and her clients, the thief and his victims; and, by implication, Plato's city state to the modern city of Paris. The winking gas-jets are the guiding lights of a new age; and their mention in the last line of the poem brings us back to the everyday world.

The familiar expressions in such a poem, then, can be naturalized as appropriate to their subject, Parisian street-life, a subject or field that is itself unusual. But also, the thematization of the modern, explicitly in opposition to the classical world, is paralleled in its language: the "divine" Plato is no more as the word *divin* is no longer in everyday use. And the poem's protagonist does not ponder his philosophy; he is dreaming as he travels through the city. A conversational language and tone, then, are doubly appropriate to the text.

It is interesting to note that the artistic vocabulary employed here refers primarily to etching, as the title of the section in which it appears, "Eaux-fortes," would lead one to expect. *Plaquer*, *teintes*, *angles*, and *en forme de* refer to art work in general, while *zinc* and even *argentin* recall the metal engraving plates, and *mordre* is the expression used for the corrosive action of the acid's inscription in the metal. The line "Des bouts de fumée en forme de cinq" makes explicit the link between such inscription and writing: written figures are analogous to engraved figures (or shapes); and this analogy is itself a figure, in yet another sense of the word. It is not the city which the poem describes (or which is inscribed in the poem), but rather, a sketch, an etching of the city. The text, then, is the representation of a representation. The scene is similarly presented as a series of unrelated impressions; and the line "Moi, j'allais . . . " underlines the speaker's detachment from what he sees. In his preoccupation with ancient Greece, he makes no attempt to comprehend what he sees and hears around him. But the final line makes clear the specular relation between him and his surroundings: he is himself observed by the gas jets: he is part of the picture. This integration by means of the eye incorporates the world of Greece as well, as the analogies between it and modern Paris show. And yet, the final line does not accomplish altogether a metaphoric totalization of the disparate images in the text. Plato and the famous Greek battles are known to the speaker and to us only through books, or, as here, through his dreams. The scene is that of a sketch; and even the rain is likened to music, rather than being a natural sound. So this written text cannot be said to describe the real world, but only another text; it is the metaphor of a metaphor, opening on to the possibility of a limitless play of relations characteristic of figural language.

As poems like "Monsieur Prudhomme," "L'Auberge," and "Croquis parisien" show, even texts whose familiar diction would seem to be motivated by genre or subject-matter can be seen to resist the totalization imposed upon them by the process of naturalization. Such resistance can be seen even more clearly in "Art poétique," which calls for analysis at another level: as a metalinguistic text, it has often been taken as a description of Verlaine's poetics. It exhibits a characteristic trait of the *ars poetica* genre: the tending toward the limit of performative, toward what Austin in *How to Do Things with Words* called the coincidence of action and utterance. Of course, there is no explicit performative "I hereby poeticize correctly" but the poem itself comes to represent such an utterance, and its theory/illustration model can bring into play a certain amount of self-referential discourse.

In this text, there are moments of theoretical statement simply followed by illustration. The second stanza, for instance, can be taken as a reading of the third, where the juxtaposition of the "indécis" and the precise is demonstrated. The reference to beautiful eyes, presumably clear and bright (on the level of the signified), is followed by *derrière des voiles*, which blurs the effect of the first part of the line as veils might do eyes. The word *tremblant* annuls the effect of *grand jour* (broad daylight) in the same way, as does *attiédi* for *ciels d'automne*. Similarly, the last line incorporates the contrast between *fouillis* and *clair*, while *bleu* gives the impression of their fusion, since it contradicts the whiteness of *claires étoiles*.

There are several examples of what could be called "méprises" in the text as well. *Soluble en l'air* contradicts the meaning of soluble, which refers to a liquid; *assassine* is used as an adjective; and not only is the jewel said to be forged, but it conflicts with "d'un sou." *Vent crispé* is another example: *crispé* means "dont la surface est un peu crispée par le souffle de quelque vent" (Littré); and there is an added resonance of the English "crisp air." But there are always instances of "méprises" in the choice of words; for the confusion of words, the taking of one for the other, is just another way of designating figural language. *Bijou d'un sou,* for example, can be called an oxymoron; *vent crispé* a kind of hypallage.

The last two stanzas present themselves as a summa of the precepts set forth in the poem. It incorporates vague expressions like *la chose, d'autres,* and plural nouns. There is a "méprise" in *la bonne aventure,* which here has the sense of "adventure" as well as its usual meaning of "fortune" (telling); it can also be taken as a metonymy for "fortune teller" or gypsy. That its epithet is *éparse* is another instance of a turning away from normal usage. Only *aventure/littérature* is a rich rhyme. But there are moments where precept and illustration coincide more directly. First, with reference to the rhythm: "préfère l'Impair" is part of a nine-syllable line. Second, there is an instance of onomatopoeia in which the coincidence of sound and sense parallels the precept enunciated: "sans rien en *lui qui pèse* ou *qui pose.*" The stanza on rhyme, a critique of Parnassian verse and its extremely rich and rare rhymes and the funny, tricky rhyme of Banville, incorporates a mixture of internal rhyme and alliteration in *f* and *s* to a degree that has been called cacophonous. The two interior lines—where *ou* is repeated six times and echoes the rhyme in the preceding stanza—are difficult to read aloud, and their exaggerated rhyme has a comic effect. And the phrase "sans *quelque* méprise" itself illustrates imprecision.

But perhaps the clearest example of self-referentiality is the line "Prends l'éloquence et tords-lui son cou": the expression is itself the antithesis of eloquence, both as signified and as signifier, since the use of *tords-lui* and *son* rather than *le* are markers of a more casual style. This "neck-wringing" takes place throughout the poem in the conversational rhythm and the use of familiar expressions. *Fouillis* is a colloquial expression, and this status underlines its contrast with *claires étoiles. Grise,* while obviously representing the indécis/précis distinction, carries with it a resonance of its familiar meaning, "tipsy." Other elements from conversational speech include the *tutoiement;* "c'est des beaux yeux," *tu feras bien,* and *elle ira jusqu'où,* where the omission of the interrogative inversion is reinforced by its position as the rhyming word. Elements from situational registers usually avoided in poetry can be found here, too: *assagie* carries a connotation of childishness; and *ail de basse cuisine* is highly unusual in poetry. The use of familiar speech and elements from everyday life serve to create a contrast with the title, which would have led one to expect an elevated style like that of Boileau. And in this contrast itself resides the "message" of the *art poétique.* There is a reversal of the hierarchy: "la pointe" or eloquence, which should have been "elevated" is "basse" here. And it is music, which is "before everything else," which lets verse fly away and the soul go off to "other skies."

But, curiously enough, there are parts in the poem which are self-contradictory rather than self-referential. *Cou/jusqu'où* is an example of the exaggerated rhyme censured. Though impure laughter is to be avoided, "cet ail de basse cuisine" is used to refer to it. And the most curious instance of this procedure occurs in the fourth stanza, where *nuance* is repeated three times, contrasted with color to render it even clearer and creating an internal rhyme like that decried in the seventh stanza. The harping tone created by all this is reinforced by the demanding "nous voulons"; and *pas, rien que* and *seul* are also pleonastic. All this thwarts the nuance so expressly called for. This circumventing of the theory/illustration model can be seen again in the relation of the lyrical last two stanzas to the rest of the poem. The didactic tone—though at times a comic one—of the first section is absent here; the imperatives have become much more gentle subjunctives; there are no traces of familiar vocabulary (in fact, *vont fleurant* is an obsolete, literary construction); the garlic has been transmuted into much more delicate seasonings. This poem, then, might seem to repeat the pattern of a text like Hugo's "Réponse à un acte d'accusation": polemical passages using familiar discourse followed by a relapse into the elevated style. In that case the last two stanzas would represent ideal poetry, while the preceding explanations could be dismissed as didactic theorizing. But this poem cannot be called a simple statement of Verlaine's poetics—nor a "simple statement" at all. Verlaine himself said of it: "Puis—car n'allez pas prendre au pied de la lettre *L'Art poétique* de *Jadis et naguère*, qui n'est qu'une chanson, après tout, JE N'AURAI PAS FAIT DE THEORIE" (Préface aux *Poèmes saturniens*).

The last line, relapsing into the casual mode, forestalls an interpretation which would divide the poem into a theoretical first part followed by a contradictory application. The *Petit Robert* gives as one meaning of the word *littérature:* "ce qui est artificiel, peu sincère," and uses this line as the example. But there was no such meaning of the word at the time: it is this poem itself which turns *littérature* into a pejorative word. The use of familiar discourse in this poem, then, because it is a "song" and in its deviation from conventional diction constitutes a sign denoting a rejection of traditional "literature." Verlaine has taken Boileau's title for a poem that, in its shiftings of style and tone, is distinctly anti-classical. The text's awareness of itself as language, as indicated by the title, leads to its disruption as simple assertion. Each time it seems to refer to something outside itself, beautiful eyes, for instance, it refers instead to its own language: here, the words "beaux yeux" and what follows. The signs become the referents; and the poem itself refers to this referring, or deferring. This *va-et-vient* between the surface of the text and its referent puts into action the figural movement of the text, a circular motion indicated by the imagery of joining and the figure of the sun. It seems to be a text about poetry; but it can only be "about," and turning about, itself.

Other texts likewise play on the reader's recognition of the stylistic incongruity of familiar language and invite interpretations which can take it into account. "Paysage," from the section called "A la manière de plusieurs," parodies the dixains of Coppée, turning around the familiar Romantic topos of a day in the country with a lover and using familiar expressions and constructions to push Coppée's platitude to the extreme. Poems like "Charleroi," "Jean de Nivelle" (*Romances sans paroles*), and "Images d'un sou" (*Jadis et naguère*), combine elements from different milieux and several registers to produce a humorous tone or the disorienting effects prized so greatly later on by the decadents. Another text in which familiar language is at odds with rather than justified by its context is "Un Pouacre," where insults, slang, and repugnant details produce a comic effect in their juxtaposition with the cliché of seeing the spectre of one's past, the figure of remorse.

Sometimes it seems that such contradictions in tone and level are impossible to incorporate at any level whatever. An example of such an instance is "Nouvelles Variations sur le Point du Jour" (*Parallèlement*) where a description of Paris calls up familiar language with no contrasting elevated moments.

> Le Point du Jour, le Point blanc de Paris,
> Le seul point blanc, grâce à tant de bâtisse
> Et neuve et laide et que je t'en ratisse,
> Le point du Jour, aurore des paris!
>
> Le bonneteau fleurit "dessur" la berge,
> La bonne tôt s'y déprave, tant pis
> Pour elle et tant mieux pour le birbe gris
> Qui lui du moins la croit encore vierge.
>
> Il a raison, le vieux, car voyez donc
> Comme est joli toujours le paysage:
> Paris au loin, triste et gai, fol et sage,
> Et le Trocadéro, ce cas, au fond . . .
>
> Puis la verdure et le ciel et les types
> Et la rivière obscène et molle, avec
> Des gens trop beaux, leur cigare à leur bec:
> Epatants ces metteurs-au-vent de tripes!

The diction ranges from casual ("Il a raison le vieux," *voyez donc*) to slang (*birbe*, "old man," *type, bec épatants, je t'en ratisse*) to vulgar expressions like *metteurs-au-vent de tripes* (murderers, who disembowel their victims), and especially *ce cas*. This last word has two slang senses: "excrement" and "penis" and whichever applies in this case is highly improper in poetry.

This poem appears in the section of *Parallèlement* called "Lunes," which has the same slang meaning as *mooning* does in English. Robichez finds such usage an "aveulissement du langage." Since there is no opposition of such language to a different milieu, it cannot be naturalized in the same way as in the earlier poems. It seems that the language of the poem is taking over, responding to the impulses of sound and figure rather than logic. Word play is evident, as in the phrase "Sur le point de" in the title. "Point du Jour de Paris" calls forth "aurore de paris!" and it is related to the gambling imagery in the text, *paris, bonneteau,* and *je t'en ratisse,* meaning to "take" someone in a card game. As in a card game, the relations between the words are purely arbitrary or metonymic; they have only their sound in common. Thus *le bonneteau* becomes "la bonne tôt . . ."; *Paris* calls up *paris; tant, t'en.* The name of the quarter, "Point du Jour" has no relation to its referent either, since it is situated at the west of Paris. Verlaine had noted this fact earlier in the poem "Aube à l'envers," evidently referred to indirectly in the title "Nouvelles Variations." The manuscript of the later poem shows an alternative title, "Couchants," which makes this explicit and which contains another twist because of the meaning of *coucher,* "to sleep with." *Grâce à* rather than *par la faute de* is another shift from what would be expected; as *épatants* seems an unlikely epithet for "metteurs-au-vent de tripes." *Car* has lost its function of drawing a conclusion from evidence: the countryside has no obvious connection with the maid's virginity. Besides, we have already been told she is corrupted and that the old man is in fact wrong. The poem seems carried along by its words as by the river it describes: the accumulation of disparate nouns and contradictory adjectives joined by *et*'s, *puis,* and *avec,* the repetitions of the first stanza, all seem purely gratuitous. There is no consciousness ordering experience, no totalizing power. Attempts to link the white color of the dawn to the virginity of the maid or to her apron in a metaphoric process are futile: only metonymic relations of sound and contiguity seem to apply. The use of vulgar diction contributes to this contravention of the traditional mode of poetry, indeed of language in general. The only element joining this fragmented assemblage together is the poem's rhythmic structure, its rhyme, and its disposition into stanzas on a printed page. "Variations" could lead one to expect a theme in which the variations would be grounded. But the point of "Le Point du Jour" is its pointlessness: that where there should be a theme there is a hole or rather, a river, carrying the unordered detritus of the life in the city.

"Nouvelles Variations" is only an extreme example of a process seen in the poems discussed earlier: familiar discourse can play an important role in the texts where it appears, but it is an intrusion into conventional poetry and it does not let itself be dismissed with easy generalizations. It reminds us of its otherness, and as such, improper language becomes *impropre,* figural, standing for a message not carried by its surface signification. In taking its place in the figural structure of the text, it escapes our attempts to account for it fully. The texts in which Verlaine uses familiar discourse, then, are far from lacking "poetry"; they are not to be excused by referring to his low life: from *Les Poèmes saturniens* on, they exploit important stylistic resources and take their place among the innovations in poetic language during the course of the nineteenth century. It is through the practice of such poets as Verlaine that the use of familiar language, slang, technical words, and so on have come to be more predictable in poetry. Because of the resistance these texts oppose to the reader's efforts to incorporate them into seamless, totalizing interpretations, they show Verlaine to be a much more complex, innovative, and interesting poet than the "naïf" versifier he is often taken to be.

Corbière, Hélas!: A Case of *Antirayonnement*

Robert L. Mitchell

Few would deny that Victor Hugo—by both presence and *parole*—exerted some positive influence on almost every important poet in nineteenth-century France, from the early romantics to Mallarmé (who, in "Crise de vers," remarked that Hugo "était le vers personnellement"). Perhaps the most prominent among his admirers was Baudelaire, who, despite sporadic derogations in his correspondence (to his mother and *Le Figaro*) and in *Fusées*, still dedicated two essays in *L'Art romantique* and three major pieces of *Tableaux parisiens* to his elder. And who can forget the unabashedly (and appropriately) hyperbolic opening quatrain of the sonnet Verlaine affixed to the copy of *Sagesse* he sent to Hugo?

> Nul parmi vos flatteurs d'aujourd'hui n'a connu
> Mieux que moi la fierté d'admirer votre gloire:
> Votre nom m'enivrait comme un nom de victoire,
> Votre œuvre, je l'aimais d'un amour ingénu.

Even Rimbaud, that ruffian *maudit*, despite some reservations, bestowed on "Olympio" a near-ultimate compliment, in the celebrated 1871 letter to Demeny: "Hugo, *trop cabochard*, a bien du vu dans les derniers volumes: *Les Misérables* sont un vrai *poème*." A rare, but significant exception to this *rayonnement* is the case of Tristan Corbière, whose esthetics and "aberrant" method of writing poetry, besides rejecting, even mocking the verse of many of the Romantics (e.g., Lamartine in "Le Fils de Lamartine et de Graziella" and Musset, Lamartine, and Byron, among others, in "Un Jeune qui s'en va") and of all the Parnassians (e.g., in "I Sonnet, avec la manière de s'en servir"), compelled him to select Hugo as one of his favorite parodic targets.

From *The French Review* 51, no. 3 (February 1978). © 1978 by *The French Review*.

It would be difficult to imagine two more diametrically opposed contemporaneous literary figures, and, indeed, Hugo represented everything that Corbière was not. A series of antitheses, explaining in part the genesis of the phenomenon of *antirayonnement*, might include the following: universality ("je vous parle de vous," from the preface of *Les Contemplations*) vs. a certain solipsism; the cosmic vs. the comic; the poet of France vs. the provincial (Corbière hailed from, and wrote of, Brittany); a politically-motivated exile of one-quarter of a lifetime vs. a self-imposed exile of an entire lifetime; physical strength and vitality vs. the chronic invalid; a life of eighty-three years vs. one of twenty-nine; hyperbole vs. often-understated irony; the "écho sonore" vs. the *sourd*; the "bonnet rouge" vs. the "couv'-tifs bariolé" (my neologism); the *voyant* vs. the *aveugle*; the family-man vs. the pariah; the optimist vs. the contumacious poet; the Poet vs. the Non-poet (one of Tristan's favorite poses: "Poète en dépit de ses vers," "Artiste sans art,—à l'envers," etc.).

In the light of these antithetical characteristics, then, it is not surprising that Corbière reacted so negatively (by resentment *and* conviction) to various aspects of Hugo's poetic manner. The explicit manifestations of this antagonism are several in the former's sole *recueil*, *Les Amours jaunes*. In "A l'éternel madame," for instance, Tristan pokes fun at the assonance of "Les Djinns": "Quand le poète brame en *Ame, en Lame, en Flamme*." "Un Jeune qui s'en va" caricatures the "apocalyptic" Hugo:

> —Hugo: l'Homme apocalyptique,
> L'Homme-Ceci-tûra-cela,
> Meurt, gardenational épique;
> Il n'en reste qu'un—celui-là!

And Corbière is particularly acerbic in his taking to task of Hugo's poetic method and conception (i.e., a rhetorical, "literary" transmutation of reality which results in what may be called a "vicarious intimacy") in "La Fin," a parodic reply to "Oceano Nox."

If "La Fin" (nine stanzas) is an explicit attack by Corbière on Hugo's method, an elusive (and generally neglected) little poem, "A une demoiselle," is a more subtle illustration of the manner in which Corbière both posits his own oblique esthetics and deconstructs a "false" practice of emoting and of poetic discourse of the "Romantic" Hugo. (Here, the target is partially implicit—although there are several specifically parodic textual hints—in the context of other more blatantly facetious pieces in the *recueil*.) In the creative act of writing the sonnet, Corbière performs a pair of "substitutions," namely, of spontaneity for artificiality and elegiac hyperbole; and of discord for lyrical harmony:

> A UNE DEMOISELLE
> *Pour Piano et Chant.*
> La dent de ton Erard, râtelier osanore,
> Et scie et broie à cru, sous son tic-tac nerveux,

La gamme de tes dents, autre clavier sonore . . .
Touches qui ne vont pas aux cordes des cheveux!

—Cauchemar de meunier, ta: *Rêverie agile*!
—Grattage, ton: *Premier amour à quatre mains*!
O femme transposée en *Morceau difficile*,
Tes croches sans douleur n'ont pas d'accents humains!

Déchiffre au clavecin cet accord de ma lyre;
Télégraphe à musique, il pourra le traduire:
Cris d'os, dur, sec, qui plaque et casse—Plangorer . . .

Jamais!—La *clef-de-Sol* n'est pas la clef de l'âme,
La *clef-de-Fa* n'est pas la syllabe de *Femme*,
Et deux *demi-soupirs* . . . ce n'est pas soupirer.

Tristan attempts to throw us off our guard from the very outset. The unassuming title and evocative subtitle set the scene of love and music to follow, suggesting tenderness and lyricism appropriately accompanied by a musical background. This is short-lived, however, despite the opening words ("La dent de ton . . . "), which seem to be announcing some kind of *blason* in honor of the damsel of the title. Just as in Rimbaud's "Le Cœur volé," however, where the melancholy opening hemistich ("Mon triste cœur") is brutally undermined by the second ("bave à la poupe"), here an ironic note intrudes: our poet is speaking not of his lady's tooth, but of the "fake" keys of her piano, which plays nothing but artificial notes. From this point on, both the lady and her instrument are under constant attack; and, as we shall discover, the title and subtitle accrue an irony not immediately apparent to the reader.

In the first stanza, Tristan deftly presents us with a pair of "reciprocal" metaphors: not only is the lady's piano described as dentures, but her teeth are transformed into a "clavier sonore." Next, the tunes played by both transformed metaphors are described as scratchings, lacking the human touch. The lady has become an automaton, playing (and thus emoting) by rote the same monotonous song. The tone shifts in the tercets to pleading, and although there are interpretative difficulties in the first tercet, a contrast between Corbière's lyre and the lady's harpsichord is clearly drawn. He asks her to decipher, or translate, on *her* instrument (that is, metaphorically, in her own emotive way) *this* harmony of *his* lyre. A curious ellipsis follows, at the conclusion of verse 11. One means of translating the "accord" would be "plangorer," a neologism meaning "to bemoan." This "Romantic" solution is rejected—and Corbière surely has the early Hugo in mind as well, not only because the term, borrowed from the Latin, may well recall Hugo's title, "Oceano Nox," but also because of his critical attitude toward Hugo's tone of lamentation in the same poem. In the final tercet, Corbière explains that neither type of music offered by the lady (plaintive, monotonous) is adequate to express what is the essence of "Woman," what is love. The entire poem, on a second reading, is, then, metaphorical: Tristan is speaking not of bridgework and keyboards, but of means of expression, and it is significant that the "rejected" means correspond precisely to two methods of contemporary *poetic* expression: Romantic and Parnassian. The key to poetry is to express the soul of things; this cannot be accomplished by standard musical (or poetic) means, but by the unorthodox techniques utilized by Corbière himself.

The essential statement of "correct" manner of self-expression appears not directly (although verse 11 is rather explicit), but in Corbière's poetic performance. The fundamental aspects of the lady's music which keep her from the Truth are *artificiality* (seen in "râtelier osanore"; the "keys" which do not correspond to the "strings" elsewhere, i.e., teeth and hair lack a sensual unity in the lady; the "practiced" musical pieces she plays in the second stanza; and the inadequate "logic" of musical notation in the final tercet) and *lyricism or harmony* (seen in the subtitle; the ironic "sonore," yet another possible oblique attack on Hugo's "écho sonore"; and "plangorer"). Against these elements, Corbière opposes his own—*spontaneity* and *discord*—which attempt to capture the quintessence of affective experience.

What appears to be simply an attack is, more subtly, a "defense" of methodology. For one thing, the apparent spontaneity of the sonnet itself removes the barriers represented by the artifice of the damsel's music. Punctuation appears, as it does so often with Corbière, quite unexpectedly, as suspension points (3), exclamation marks (5), dashes (4), and colons (3) intrude whenever they are called upon to express his thought at the moment (for instance, the excessive punctuation in verses 11–12, reflecting the poet's internal monologue). The *jeu de mots*, typifying the "essential" Tristan, also abounds, eminently representing the "accent humain" resonating from his lyre and absent from the automated, artificial scratchings of his lady's piano. What, for example, is a "dent de piano"? Apparently nothing, according to the best dictionaries. "Dent de scie" does exist, however; what Corbière has done is to manufacture the expression "dent de piano" and then to justify the new usage by the subsequent verb, *scier*, "to bore" or "to fatigue." This is the verb's familiar meaning; its literal meaning, "to saw," imparts to the word "dent" the dual possibility of being a saw's tooth moving monotonously back and forth, or a real tooth (indeed, Erard is metaphorically transformed into a set of dentures) crunching ("broie à cru") in a regular rhythm. In transforming the lady into a piano, into a "difficult piece," Corbière also alters the "first piece for four hands" to "first love for four hands," thus contaminating the musical allusion with a "romantic" notion (the same kind of contamination occurs in the previous verse, where the "*Rêverie agile*" is in apposition to the "Cauchemar de meunier," or the monotony of the grinding of the mill). Words are also happily manipulated in each of the final three verses of the sonnet. Let us proceed backwards in order to justify the claim of trickery in verse 12. In music, two eighth-rests do, of course, make a quarter-rest (two *demi-soupirs* mathematically, logically, equal one *soupir*). But the expected substantive *soupir* is replaced by the verb *soupirer* (the lover's sigh), and the equation of musical notation and affective experience cannot, of course, be tolerated. Similarly, the key of "F" cannot embody Womanhood: the resemblance in sound—[fa]—is purely coincidental. It is only natural that the twelfth verse join in the fun, . . . but how? Since there are no semantic or phonetic links between *Sol* and *âme*, the only possibility is the English homonym for *Sol*, "soul," which also happens to be the translation for "âme"! This is not as incredible as it sounds, since there are a good number of examples of this type of borrowing in *Les Amours jaunes*. In fact, in verse 11 of *this* poem, "Cris d'os," a rather strange conjoining of words, may have been conceived with another play on words in mind: can it not refer to the English homonym, "Credo"? After all, "cet accord de ma lyre" (the "Cris d'os") was one of the few entities in which Corbière had any *belief*. There are even more subtle possibilities for *jeux de mots* in the poem's title and subtitle, which suggest that here, as so often elsewhere in his verse, Tristan was more interested in "ludic" than in "lyric" poetry. After we have seen the lady metamorphosed into a piano, we can now substitute her for the "Piano" in the subtitle, which leaves a rather ridiculous redundancy: "A une demoiselle Pour demoiselle. . . ." We may even wonder why he is dedicating the poem to her in the first place; in fact, if we look carefully at Corbière's *recueil*, we find well-documented precedence for his referring to his Muse as a "demoiselle" or variations thereof. Indeed, Corbière looked upon his Muse as a kind of *courtisane*, with no attachments (least of all to him) and no possessive preoc-cupations. With this in mind, we can now reconsider the title, not as a song dedicated to his fair lady (he had none save the unrequiting "Mar-celle," and the "demoiselle" is significantly preceded by an indefinite ar-ticle, not a possessive adjective), but to the only woman who asked (and was given) nothing in return, his Muse. In this light, again, the metaphoric value of the sonnet is clear: the *real* subject is poetry, his own in particular, and if the poem is dedicated *for* Tristan's Muse, the irony might also be extended to the subtitle, where "contre" may be substituted for "pour" with impunity.

After the substitution of spontaneity for artifice, Corbière's replacement of discord for harmony (including Hugo's brand of lyrical harmony, at least the Hugo of *Les Rayons et les ombres*, of whom we know Corbière disap-proved) is apparent in the way in which the poem is structured. Unlike March, the poem comes in like a lamb and goes out like a lion. The quatrains are almost entirely composed of nearly-classical alexandrines, and they are structured in a parallel manner: in each case, the first three verses present a series of separate negative statements, resolved (the term is to be inter-preted in its musical sense as well) in the stanza's final verse, which extracts the essence of the preceding verses (in both cases, the "inhuman" aspects of the lady's playing). Once Corbière begins to wander to thoughts of his *own* poetry, however, the balance is destroyed, its harmony replaced by the chaos and discord of the tercets. Two of the explicitly stated qualities of his poetry—"qui plaque et casse"—are implicit in his practice. First, the final three verses are neither "resolved" harmoniously nor are they "scratchings": Corbière bangs out his message loud and clear ("dur," "sec"). More importantly, the tercets break ("casse"), or dislocate, what has preceded. What was balance is now chaos, seen in the unpredictability of punctuation, rhythm, and even syntax: verses 9–10 must be read with more care, and the ellipsis in verses 11–12 interrupts the dialogue between the poet and his damsel simply by eliminating the latter and turning the poet's thoughts inward. The key phrase in the poem is surely "cet accord de ma lyre." The irony implicit in it is that what is traditionally seen as "harmony" is rejected by Corbière in his pejorative treatment of expressions which connote this very quality: "piano," "gamme," "clavier," "touches," "cordes," "croches," "clavecin," "musique," "clef," and, certainly not least of all, the faintly Hugolian "sonore." In contrast, true harmony (only possible from *his* poetic instrument) resides in what is traditionally perceived as discordant ("Cris d'os, dur, sec, qui plaque et casse"); for Tristan, there is at least nothing phony or mechanical about these sounds which he creates.

This "musical" disparity between Corbière's discord and more conventional lyricism is only one in a series of conflicts between the Breton poet and his contemporaries. The abyss separating his perspective and that of his peers is apparent in the expressions "déchiffre" and "il pourra le traduire" (the verb "pourra" is wishful thinking on the part of the harpsichord, which will never be in tune with the Corbièrian lyre). For so many poets of nineteenth-century France, and Hugo's "écho" in particular, the homologous relationship between poetry and song was an essential ingredient of self-expression. But for Corbière, the adherence to traditional concepts of harmony or lyricism resulted inexorably in an intolerable lie perpetrated by the Musician, the Poet, or, in "A une demoiselle," the Lady.

The value of this type of brief analysis is that it reveals not only to what degree Corbière, as an isolated instance, rejected the poetics of certainly the most imposing writer of his century, but also in what manner he utilized this very rejection in order to fortify, even reflect (that is, by its "negative," in both the critical and photographic senses) his *own* poetic method. (This "rejection" may well be a marginal case of what Harold Bloom terms "reductiveness" in *The Anxiety of Influence*: "By 'reductiveness' I mean a kind of misprision that is a radical misinterpretation in which the precursor is regarded as an over-idealizer.") What is perhaps most significant about this divergence of the poetic methods of Hugo and Corbière is the latter's emergence as a kind of "écho muet" of the century to follow, of a poetry of the future—we see him touching responsive chords in Eliot, Pound, and Breton, among others—based not on harmony, rhetoric, and cosmic motifs, but rather on the just-discussed elements of discord, spontaneity, and introspection.

Surviving Lautréamont: The Reader in *Les Chants de Maldoror*

Robin Lydenberg

Much of contemporary criticism has turned from analyses of the novel's relation to reality or society to analyses of the more immediate relationship between the literary work and its reader. The recent revival of critical interest in the works of Isidore Ducasse may be attributed in part to this nineteenth-century writer's systematic exploration of the nature of the reading process. In his article "Une Lecture compromettante" (*L'Arc*, no. 33), Roger Borderie presents Ducasse's *Les Chants de Maldoror,* published in 1869 under the flamboyant pseudonym and persona of le comte de Lautréamont, as a unique representation of the phenomenology of reading, as an exercise in supreme compromise. Never before, he claims, have the reader and what he reads been so completely joined; never before has a book been written so exclusively to be read.

While Borderie acknowledges that a concentration on the reader's activity is a latent characteristic of all literary discourse, he fails to credit an entire tradition of narratives preceding *Les Chants* in which the narrator/reader relationship is the major content of the fiction. A concern with the activity of the reader *as* reader is certainly a central focus in a novel like Laurence Sterne's *Tristram Shandy,* and Sterne himself recognizes his debt to a tradition of novels about the writing and reading of fiction, particularly to the works of Rabelais and Cervantes. In order to assess properly the uniqueness of *Les Chants,* it is necessary to understand Ducasse's assimilation and transformation of the techniques or reader involvement already developed by his predecessors.

In *La Révolution du langage poétique,* Julia Kristeva also presents Ducasse's work as a radical literary breakthrough, but her study clarifies in some detail the ways in which *Les Chants* both continue and deviate from

From *L'Esprit Créateur* 17, no. 3 (Fall 1977). © 1977 by *L'Esprit Créateur.*

conventional discourse. Linguistic traditionalism is defined by a structural opposition of the narrative "je" (*narrateur*) with a "tu" (*narrataire*) who is the receiver of the discourse, the other, the reader. Any play or interplay of the "figurants du texte"—"je" "tu" and "il"—is camouflaged in the conventional narrative, logically justified by plot structures and a traditional use of fictional personae. Kristeva contrasts this conventional model with the modern revolutionary texts of Ducasse and Mallarmé. The radical discourse of these poets defies the legality of the separate functions of the "figurants du texte," producing instead a kaleidoscopic confusion between and within each of the textual pronouns. As innovative and self-conscious as their works may be, Ducasse's predecessors in the classical narrative never fully abandon the logical security of individual identity. It is precisely in the uncertainty of all identity in *Les Chants* that Ducasse's reader finds himself most exposed and endangered.

When the dividing line which differentiates *narrateur* and *narrataire* is blurred, the reader loses the security of his distance from the narrative. Confused and manipulated by arbitrary shifts in the discourse, he finds himself gradually assimilated into the text and implicated in its production. The process of *Les Chants* is a redefinition of the function and identity of the reader.

Ducasse elaborates theoretical guidelines for this new science of reading in *Poésies I* and *Poésies II*, a series of aphorisms published one year after *Les Chants*. Ducasse demonstrates his theories by reproducing in this later work his own activity as a reader. In what he calls reading "appréciation," Ducasse substitutes his own formulations within the most well known quotations from Pascal, Vauvenargues and others, often completely reversing their original meaning. His continual metamorphoses of these classical texts replace the conventional passive receptivity of the reader with a more aggressive and creative involvement in the making of a text. Reproducing the same confusion he imposes on his own reader in *Les Chants*, Ducasse will repeatedly "serre de près la phrase d'un auteur" until it becomes his own, *narrateur* and *narrataire* converging in the corrected text. In this new poetry authorial identity becomes communal ("La poésie doit être faite par tous. Non par un.") and all meaning is thrown into a flux of continual correction and reversal. Thus both content and identity are obscured and undermined, leaving only the "fil indestructible de la poésie impersonnelle"—Ducasse's rigorous and convoluted rhetoric.

Each reader's assumptions about the relationship between narrator and reader and the responsibilities of the narrative to meaning and structure are laid bare and contradicted in *Les Chants* and *Poésies*. Beyond the conventional activity of creating or inventing an audience, the narrator of *Les Chants* practices what he calls the cretinising of each individual reader and the tradition embodied in that reader's expectations. *Les Chants* cannot be dismissed as the wild flailings of adolescent anarchy, for Ducasse's radicalism is carefully and dialectically structured. Rather than simply denying or circumventing the narrative tradition which precedes him, Ducasse attempts to encompass the movement of literary history itself, assimilating the very conventions he seeks to overthrow by absorbing and manipulating his audience. Ducasse achieves this gradual assimilation by a series of rhetorical devices which progress from fictional analogies for the reader's situation to his direct involvement and even imprisonment in the discourse. Through the contradictions, the illogicalities, the verbal accumulations and convoluted digressions which characterize his style, Ducasse transforms the conventions of an artificial rhetoric into a rhetoric come alive as the immediate and disturbing experience of the reader. I propose to trace in the narrative of *Les Chants* the progressive stages leading up to a major shift in the status of the reader in literary discourse which has ushered us into an age of modern revolutionary poetics.

THE READER FICTIONALIZED

Let us begin by examining the vestiges in *Les Chants* of one of the more conservative devices of the self-conscious fictional narrative: the use of consistent and identifiable "personnages" whose experiences within the fiction suggest analogies with the reader's situation in the discourse. The danger of confusing literature with life, of misunderstanding the relationship between fiction and reality, are pointedly dramatized in the novel from Cervantes' Don Quixote to that character's more tragic descendant Emma Bovary. While the classical novel may indirectly warn the reader not to expect reality to conform to fiction, Ducasse is more concerned with asserting his autonomy as an author warning his readers to abandon any expectation that *Les Chants* will conform to the conventions of reality.

After five *chants* of poetic chaos Ducasse introduces (although in his own stylistically unorthodox manner) a highly conventional novelistic framework supported by an elaborate network of "bourgeois" clichés. It is within the security of this familiar genre of the family novella that Ducasse indirectly asserts some of his most violent threats against the reader. The hero of this little drama is one Mervyn, an ingenuous adolescent whom we first encounter dutifully returning home from his fencing lesson. The narrator is irritated by Mervyn's expectation that he will, in fact, reach home safely; and omnisciently aware of the dangerous Maldoror lurking nearby, he concludes somewhat sadly, somewhat maliciously, "Que ne fuyait-il donc? C'était si facile . . . cependant, il lui est impossible de deviner la réalité. Il n'est pas prophète." It is Mervyn's expectation of happiness and normalcy which must be punished, and as we shall see Maldoror carries out that punishment rigorously.

The history of Mervyn and Maldoror demonstrates most clearly the danger of retaining any expectations of the written word. Maldoror first approaches his prey in writing, and it is Mervyn's romantic and naive reading of Maldoror's letter which eventually causes his demise. Always hoping for the best, Mervyn accepts on faith the vow of mutual confidence and trust which Maldoror offers him. In what Lautréamont hails as a "scène unique qu'aucun romancier ne retrouvera," Mervyn is made to suffer for this expectation of sincerity. A meeting is arranged between the two, but instead of the brotherly embrace Mervyn awaits anxiously, the young man is quite unceremoniously stuffed in a sack and smashed against the parapet of the Pont du Carrousel. The reader has been forewarned by analogy against any similar misinterpretation of the respectful formality and concern which often characterize Lautréamont's direct addresses to *his* audience. The reader's relationship to *Les Chants* is thus hopelessly paradoxical. Confronted with an arbitrary and unpredictable fictional world, the reader is totally dependent on the guidance of the narrator, but he is also repeatedly advised to distrust the poses and promises of that persona.

The perverse self-contradictions of the narrator of *Les Chants* are further complicated by Ducasse's stance in *Poésies*, where he adopts a highly conventional moral voice in total opposition to the amorality of the reckless comte de Lautréamont. The narrator of *Poésies* anticipates and discourages any critical objections to this polar reversal by asserting forcefully, "Je ne permets à personne, pas même à Elohim, de douter de ma sincérité." This aphorism should not be read as a claim to sincerity—for in this "poésie impersonnelle" sincerity is only one pose among many—but as Ducasse's exercizing of the absolute authorial will which establishes the narrative voice above question, like all other first principles and absolute truths, "à ne pas discuter."

The narrator of the conventional self-conscious novel often mobilizes his resistance to the interference of readers and critics, asserting an absolute control over fictional events and the order of their revelation. Sterne's Tristram, for example, declares he would tear out the next page of his book if he thought the reader could guess its contents. Like his predecessors, the narrator of *Les Chants* will not tolerate any assumption on the reader's part which would question his arbitrary autonomy. Lautréamont's tyrannical domination, however, extends beyond the aesthetics of storytelling to annex the territory of logic itself. Mervyn may be denied his expectations of the future, but the reader of *Les Chants* is even denied any certainty as to the apparent reality of the present of the discourse. The original version of the final stanza of Chant I, "Ce premier chant finit ici," reads more tauntingly in a later variant, "S'il est quelquefois logique de s'en rapporter à l'apparence des phénomènes, ce premier chant finit ici." The confusion and uncertainty which dominate the fictional world of *Les Chants* are reproduced here not by analogy but in the immediate experience of the reader, in his perception of the material structure of the written text.

While the reader may gradually learn to protect himself against the unexpected and the illogical by abandoning all assumptions in his reading of *Les Chants*, he is still forced to witness acts of violence perpetrated against more naïve and innocent victims in the course of the fiction. In Chant II, stanza 4, the narrator relates the story of a helpless child chasing after an omnibus in the hopes that it may carry him to safety. The passengers are all indifferent to the fate of the child and even annoyed at his continual cries. There is only one spectator who reacts indignantly to this injustice: "L'adolescent se lève, dans un mouvement d'indignation, et veut se retirer, pour ne pas participer, même involontairement, à une mauvaise action. Je lui fais un signe, et il se remet à mon côté." Maldoror's coercion of the adolescent, who is not allowed to disassociate himself from the inhumanity of his fellow men, mirrors Ducasse's insidious corruption of an audience committed to the ingestion of his terrible fictions.

While the reader may learn from such fictional analogies to distance himself from the fiction, he cannot so easily escape his function within the discourse as the consciousness through which the narrative is realized. As Ducasse insists in *Poésies*, the reader always "makes" what he reads.

In addition to peopling his fictional world with characters who are essentially writers and readers, Ducasse also practices the convention of addressing his readers directly in several fictionalized incarnations: the intimidated adolescent, the sceptical philosopher or the courageous but imprudent explorer of the text. Lucienne Rochon has described the prolif- eration of such reader figures in *Les Chants* as a powerful weapon of the discourse in which "c'est toujours son histoire que lit le lecteur." I would argue that as long as his complicitous responsibility for the fiction is rep- resented by analogy within the text—through fictional characters like the indignant adolescent on the omnibus or fictionalized readers like the "âme timide" addressed in Lautréamont's initial invitation to his audience—the actual reader retains his identity and independence outside the discourse. Critics who identify so literally the actual reader with the fictionalized *nar- rataires* in the text, while generously lending themselves to the spirit of the narrative, are undermining Ducasse's attempt to demonstrate the rhetorical artificiality of such fixed roles within the discourse. The author of *Les Chants* has plotted a far more aggressive program of assimilation of the audience, creating techniques radical enough to force the reader to *live*, not just to read, his history as coproducer of the text.

THE READER COMPROMISED

Against the opposition *narrateur/narrataire* which establishes the reader's distance from the text, Ducasse practices in *Les Chants* an intermittent and unpredictable confusion of the "je" and "tu" of the discourse, creating a free and unlimited fictional space in which fixed identity and function may be temporarily dissolved. Once again asserting his arbitrary autonomy within the narrative, Ducasse challenges the laws of a consistent grammar which would assume the identification and differentiation of "person- nages." The effect of this confusion of pronouns is that the reader may become, beyond analogy and artificial rhetoric, an actual participant in the fiction.

One clear example of this technique of assimilation appears early in *Les Chants* in the torture scene in Chant I, stanza 6. The stanza begins with an impersonal structure using "on" and the extratemporal verb form: "On doit laisser pousser ses ongles pendant quinze jours. Oh! comme il est doux d'arracher brutalement de son lit un enfant . . . de faire semblant de passer suavement la main sur son front . . . d'enfoncer les ongles longs dans sa poitrine molle." The narrative continues with a similarly hypothetical and impersonal description of the drinking of the child's blood and tears, but the impersonal "on" is replaced by a communal persona rendered specific and individual as the object of the narrator's direct address: "Homme, n'as-tu jamais goûté de ton sang, quand par hasard tu t'es coupé le doigt?" Having initiated the reader's involvement on these as yet inoffensive grounds, the narrator increases his assumptions by implying that he shares with the reader a certain predilection for the taste of blood. Assumption becomes intimacy as the narrative presumes to conjure the reader's memories and "réflexions lugubres": "ne te souviens-tu pas d'avoir un jour . . . porté la main, creusée au fond sur la figure maladive mouillée par ce qui tombait des yeux; laquelle main ensuite se dirigeait fatalement vers la bouche, qui puisait à longs traits, dans cette coupe, tremblante comme les dents de l'élève qui regarde obliquement celui qui est né pour l'oppresser, les larmes?" Surely not every reader will recognize himself in this romantic misanthrope, but in his deciphering of the text the details of these actions are embedded in the reader's memory and become part of his past (poetic) experience.

From the first innocent admission that he may have on occasion tasted his own blood and tears, the reader soon finds himself portrayed in somewhat more compromising circumstances. The narrator accomplishes this transition through the parenthetical analogy, "comme les dents de l'élève," which associates the reader's hypothetical private preoccupations with the sado-masochistic scene about to be described in the fiction. From this analogy the narrator's reasoning follows logically:

> Donc, puisque ton sang et tes larmes ne te dégoûtent pas, nourris-toi, nourris-toi avec confiance des larmes et du sang de l'adolescent. Bande-lui les yeux, pendant que tu déchireras ses chairs palpitantes; et, après avoir entendu de longues heures ses cris sublimes, semblables aux râles perçants que poussent dans une bataille les gosiers des blessés agonisants, alors, t'ayant écarté comme une avalanche, tu te précipiteras de la chambre voisine, et tu feras semblant d'arriver à son secours. . . . Comme le cœur déborde de pouvoir consoler l'innocent à qui l'on a fait du mal: "Adolescent . . . pardonne-moi."

The narrative has progressed from an impersonal third person to a series of hypothetical actions addressed to an abstract and rhetorical "tu" and finally to an imperative address which seems to button-hole the actual reader and designate to him very specific words which, in his reading, he does in fact pronounce. There is an imperceptible shift of the discourse into an immediate present tense in which the adolescent is consoled and begged for forgiveness in the voice of the reader. Because this shift takes place in a subtle grammatical slippage within the discourse rather than in an overt characterization of some particular reader/"personnage" the reader has not foreseen the necessity of disassociating himself from the "tu" of the text. Thus at this very early point in *Les Chants* Ducasse has implicated his audience in one of Maldoror's most terrible deeds, as each reader discovers himself mouthing the hypocritical words of the evil torturer.

The territorial overlapping in *Les Chants* of the arena of the fictional adventures and the interaction of narrator and reader in the discourse have a disorienting effect on the reader's conception of his place in the textual structure. Just as the critic who continues to read the chronicles of Gargantua and Pantagruel after the narrator has dismissed all "grabeleurs de correction" becomes by definition part of Rabelais' accepting audience, any reader who fails to turn back at the warning on the first page of *Les Chants* has established his complicity throughout the rest of the text. "Il n'est pas bon," we are told, "que tout le monde lise les pages qui vont suivre; quelques-uns seuls savoureront ce fruit amer sans danger. Par conséquent, âme timide, avant de pénétrer plus loin dans de pareilles landes inexplorées, dirige tes talons en arrière et non en avant. Ecoute bien ce que je te dis: dirige tes talons en arrière et non en avant." Merely by proceeding in the text the reader has sanctioned any "fruit amer" Ducasse may offer in the course of *Les Chants,* and from the outset the reader shares with the narrator the complicity of all fallen men. While the reader may still disassociate himself from the specific "personnages" of Rabelais' drinking companions or hypocritical censors, from the pompous Sir or Madam of *Tristram Shandy,* Ducasse's text is far more threatening because it addresses us all ultimately in our most basic function as readers, continually calling into question our understanding of the limits and responsibilities of that function.

THE READER EDUCATED

Despite the complicity generated between narrator and reader by Ducasse's confusion of the "figurants du texte," no reader could experience in *Les Chants* a communion with the author. It is precisely this sentimental conceit of the discourse as a meeting of souls, as an intimate interaction between "je" and "tu" which Ducasse has set out to undermine. The theory of an impersonal poetry which Ducasse develops in *Poésies* frequently defines itself in opposition to the abuses of a romanticism which indulges itself in the display of sentimentality. Ducasse's directives against such behavior are severe: "Si vous êtes malheureux, il ne faut pas le dire au lecteur. Gardez cela pour vous." Ducasse is particularly impatient with the passive role the sentimental poet adopts with his readers: "Il existe une convention peu tacite entre l'auteur et le lecteur, par laquelle le premier s'intitule malade, et accepte le second comme garde-malade. C'est le poète qui console l'humanité! Les rôles sont intervertis arbitrairement." In *Les Chants* Ducasse attempts to correct this error, and by reversing in his turn the roles of author and reader once again he returns his discourse to one of the earliest novelistic metaphors: literature as a cure.

The narratives of Rabelais and Sterne set out to cure the reader's spleen and to extend his life through laughter. To take the cure of Pantagruelism or Shandyism a reader need only understand the text in the proper spirit of the author's intentions, "de bon, franc, et loyal couraige." Relaxing his critical spleen-producing faculties, the ideal reader will duplicate the author's wit and become the "dear Friend" or drinking companion addressed in the text. Ducasse sees his contemporaries ("nos époques phtisiques"), infected by the morbid self-indulgence of their ailing authors, as particularly in need of the curative powers of a literature which establishes the author as doctor, the reader as patient and the text as beneficial medication. He appropriates and applies this convention in *Les Chants* to his own radical purposes, and his offers to cure the reader are as ambiguously hostile as his aggressive gestures of friendship. Ducasse's text, in fact, operates as a cure only in that the reader is gradually less repulsed by what he encounters there.

In the voice of a patient but conservative school master, Lautréamont insists on the necessity of practice and discipline to conquer our instinctive repulsion to his words. He is hopeful that the reader's continual "application à la lecture" will increase his tolerance for *Les Chants*, carrying him from convalescence to complete deliverance. The numbing of the reader's sensibilities caused by his reading of the text must be followed up by a regimen which also demands complicitous actions. Again we find that the narrative shifts from hypothesis and analogy into imperative and concrete action. With no change in the tone of his bedside manner, the narrator prescribes the following "substances médicamenteuses": "Comme nourriture astringente et tonique, tu arracheras d'abord les bras de ta mère (si elle existe encore), tu les dépèceras en petits morceaux, et tu les mangeras ensuite, en un seul jour, sans qu'aucun trait de ta figure ne trahisse ton émotion. Si ta mère était trop vieille, choisis un autre sujet chirurgique, plus jeune et plus frais . . . ta sœur, par exemple." The dutiful patient will be rewarded with the open embrace of the text, likened to the vampire-kiss of the louse at the hair root. There is no sentimental elective affinity in the treatment offered by the narrator of *Les Chants*, for his cure threatens to be more of an infection. While we hardly feel constrained to obey Lautréamont's detailed instructions for our future conduct, the insinuating device of the reader's hypothetical crime draws the audience more deeply into the text than all of Rabelais' rhetoric of conviviality.

Although Ducasse's version of the curative powers of literature operates only negatively and destructively, one might argue that his motive is the same as that of the classical author: to remake the audience in the image of the narrator. The success and even the survival of the reader of *Les Chants* depends on his ability to become as ferocious as the text and as vigilant as its narrator. Like the speaker who introduces Baudelaire's *Les Fleurs du mal*, Lautréamont ultimately addresses himself to an ideal reader— a double or brother. Because of his hyperbolic nature, this search often leads Lautréamont to posit impossible prerequisites for his audience: "Celui qui, pendant un jour, a poursuivi l'autruche à travers le désert, sans pouvoir l'atteindre, n'a pas eu le temps de prendre de la nourriture et de fermer les yeux. Si c'est lui qui me lit, il est capable de deviner, à la rigueur, quel sommeil s'appesantit sur moi." These descriptions of a hypothetical ideal reader often grow into extended metaphorical fictions within what begins as a digression from the fictional content of the narrative. Thus Lautréamont's simple assertion that he is tired spins into the following convoluted elaboration:

> Mais, quand la tempête a poussé verticalement un vaisseau, avec la paume de sa main, jusqu'au fond de la mer; si, sur le radeau, il ne reste plus de tout l'équipage qu'un seul homme, rompu par les fatigues et les privations de toute espèce; si la lame le ballotte, comme une épave, pendant des heures plus prolongées que la vie d'homme; et, si, une frégate, qui sillonne plus tard ces parages de désolation d'une carène fendue, aperçoit le malheureux qui promène sur l'océan sa carcasse décharnée, et lui porte un secours qui a failli être tardif, je crois que ce naufragé devinera mieux encore à quel degré fut porté l'assoupissement de mes sens.

For those of us who have not lived through such an experience Ducasse conveniently provides an identical storm in Chant II, stanza 13.

An experience accessible only in the fiction itself becomes the necessary training for a proper reading of the narrative. The world of *Les Chants* once again begins to feel uncomfortably claustrophobic. Reality and fiction no longer present a dual structure, for fiction has replaced reality by establishing itself as the primary existential experience. Lautréamont equates the reader's witnessing of his fictional storm with an understanding of life: "Celui qui n'a pas vu un vaisseau sombrer au milieu de l'ouragan, de l'intermittence des éclairs et de l'obscurité la plus profonde, pendant que ceux qu'il contient sont accablés de ce désespoir que vous savez, celui-là ne connaît pas les accidents de la vie." Only the imaginative reader who has successfully absorbed the shipwreck scene already described in this stanza has the proper knowledge of "les accidents de la vie" demanded by the narrative.

This particular scene, however, does not portray the vicissitudes of life but the arbitrary control of the narrator/hero who explicitly states his intention to destroy all the passengers on the ship. The "accidents de la vie" must be understood in the literary context of the author's autonomy. What the reader actually witnesses is the destruction of fictional content as embodied in the ship and its passengers. After a slow and detailed account of the drownings and wreckage, the scene is finally literally consumed by sharks, leaving only the narrator and the triumphant survivor of the shipwreck feast, "la femelle du requin," sinking to the bottom of the sea in a hideous embrace.

The shipwreck episode begins, in fact, with the narrator's fruitless search for a "semblable," for "quelqu'un qui eût les mêmes idées que moi," and here ends with the recognition of the shark as his very image. This shark may be Ducasse's ideal reader who devours the text and survives, who braves the poisonous cure, traverses the "marécages désolés" and emerges not only as part of the fiction but in the image of its maker.

No reader will ever achieve this ideal assimilation into the fiction of *Les Chants* or the image of its narrator, for Ducasse's discourse depends on the continuing process of confrontation, confusion and correction which is the reader's education and the life of the text. Ducasse introduces *Poésies I* with the following declaration: "Je remplace la mélancolie par le courage, le doute par la certitude, le désespoir par l'espoir, la méchanceté par le bien, les plaintes par le devoir, le scepticisme par la foi, les sophismes par la froideur du calme et l'orgueil par la modestie." In this arbitrary reversal of the pose he cultivated in *Les Chants*, Ducasse discredits the entire system of moral dualism within which his earlier work was misinterpreted. In its denunciation of the dark romanticism of *Les Chants, Poésies* continue the education of the reader, warning him that any conventional assumptions about the sincerity or consistency of a writer's work may be met with such hostile contradiction. Ironically, critical assessments which respond to *Poésies* as Ducasse's renunciation of his previous work, as a chronological development of his personal morality, merely corroborate the necessity of an infinite ducassian pedagogy.

If the reader could become the ideal *narrataire*, the impossible double of the narrator, the perpetual struggle within the discourse of *Les Chants* would be reduced to the sterility of a shallow mirror reflection. The terror and temptation of Ducasse's narrator to be his own reader, to merge completely with the "other" who stands outside the text, is a dilemma he shares with many radical poets. The total autonomy of the narrator who would become his own reader, however, threatens to produce a frightening isolation. As technician the narrator would play the master ventriloquist, framing and manipulating the audience's responses; but his powers can only be realized within the dialogue of the discourse, against the continued resistance of some "other" who is the reader.

THE READER IMMOBILIZED

Despite repeated warnings to the reader not to trust the narrator's apparent intentions to educate his audience, to illuminate for them the mysteries of heaven and earth, *Les Chants* have been hailed by critics as a guide to the complexities of the reading process. If the reader looks to this narrative for direction, however, he must be prepared to adjust to a circuitous methodology, for Ducasse's only pedagogical aim is to provide the reader with a lesson in endless contradiction. Ducasse promises, for example, to set down in his poetic aphorisms the laws and the source of a new poetic science: "Le phénomène passe. Je cherche les lois," "Je ne chante pas [la science distincte de la poésie]. Je m'efforce de découvrir sa source." He punctuates those promises with tyrannical demands for his reader's blind faith in the laws and sources which must remain unspoken and unexamined.

The ultimate aim of the new poetry, Ducasse also insists in *Poésies*, must be a practical and not a mystical truth. Thus the reader's education in *Les Chants* and *Poésies* consists of direct experience in the assertive and manipulative powers of language. The reader learns to match the aggressiveness of Ducasse's philosophical pronouncements or extravagant fictions with an equivalent resistance. Ducasse's works overcome the contradiction of their content in the common battle of wills which is generated by Ducasse's hostile and assimilative brand of discourse.

In the pedagogy of the more conventional narratives of Rabelais and Sterne the reader is instructed in the proper approach to the text, but he is expected to apply these novelistic lessons to his extraliterary life. Ducasse's instruction leads us only from *Les Chants* to *Poésies*, and from *Poésies* to an infinite network of other texts, past and future, conventional and apocryphal. The fierce rhetoric of *Les Chants* threatens to imprison the reader permanently within his function in the literary discourse, leaving him no private space, cutting off his extraliterary afterlife. The infinite pedagogy of *Les Chants* and *Poésies* threatens the complete assimilation of the reader and his immobilization under the hypnotic spell of Ducasse's style.

The narrator's warnings that the reader assimilate with caution and skepticism the "âcre sérosité suppurative qui se dégage avec lenteur de l'agacement que causent [ses] intéressantes élucubrations" may be seen as merely an ominous variation on the convention in which Cervantes or Fielding warn their readers against the literal identification of fiction and reality. *Les Chants*, however, asserts the literalness of fiction, and the metaphorical dangers of the narrative are disturbingly immediate. Instead of the intellectual intimacy of narrator and reader which the conventional discourse often assumes, Lautréamont threatens his reader with an aggressive intimacy which is more physical than rhetorical: "Que ne puis-je regarder à travers ces pages séraphiques le visage de celui qui me lit. S'il n'a pas dépassé la puberté, qu'il s'approche. Serre-moi contre toi, et ne crains pas de me faire du mal; rétrécissons progressivement les liens de nos muscles. Davantage." The dramatic immediacy of this confrontation escapes the realm of fiction and becomes concrete: "Je sens qu'il est inutile d'insister; l'opacité remarquable à plus d'un titre, de cette feuille de papier, est un empêchement des plus considérables à l'opération de notre complète jonction." By inserting the materiality of the page between *narrateur* and *narrataire* Ducasse reminds his reader of the literal confines of the discourse. While the reader is protected by the page from the advances of the narrator (who is, after all, only part of this literary construct), his immediate experience as a reader has been petrified within the narrative. Finding himself simultaneously on the far side of the printed page and within the content of the text, the reader is obliged to collect himself, like Sterne's fragmented Tristram, before he can continue his progress through the narrative.

In another attempt to fix his audience in its function, Lautréamont assigns to the reader an obedient posture: silent, hands humbly folded over his breast and eyes lowered—an attitude which mimics the posture of reading. "O vous," he continues, "qui que vous soyez, quand vous serez à côté de moi, que les cordes de votre glotte ne laissent échapper aucune intonation . . . n'essayez nullement de me faire connaître votre âme à l'aide du langage." As fierce as the narrator's impositions of silence and servility on the reader may be, such directives remain pure rhetorical bravado which the actual reader may still resist by terminating or interrupting his reading. Behind the artificial conventions of such direct addresses to the reader, however, Ducasse is operating a far more devious and powerful weapon which will assure the helpless immobility of his audience: the hypnotic power of his intimidating and convoluted style.

While earlier novels treated the problem of the reader's involvement in a fiction as a general numbing of his consciousness which endangers his ability to distinguish literature from reality, Ducasse is perhaps the first author to deal explicitly with the phenomenology of reading. The narrator of *Les Chants* describes the immobility and estrangement caused by the reading process in which the reader is taken by surprise, uncertain of where he is being led. Ducasse has made every effort to take advantage of the "remarquable stupéfaction" to which readers of fiction are particularly susceptible. The stupefaction that results from reading *Les Chants* is not the conventional magnetism of an ideal or adventurous fictional world which replaces the reader's banal reality, but rather the stupefaction of confusion. The real hypnotic and assimilative power of Ducasse's work lies in his use of language, for the audience's concentration is riveted to the text in an effort to follow the mere syntactic progress of a sentence.

Ducasse's syntax mirrors his narrative style: both are infinitely digressive. The stylistic arabesques of his digressions leave content further behind with each parenthetical elaboration. One of the first laws of the poetic science of manipulation which Ducasse practices is revealed in *Poésies I*: "Il faut que la critique attaque la forme, jamais le fond de vos idées, de vos phrases. Arrangez vous." Ducasse has arranged his defense against conventional critics by obscuring the meaning of his own phrases through the reversals and contradictions within and between *Les Chants* and *Poésies*. The logical and metaphorical spirals of Ducasse's digressions and "corrections" continually disorient the reader who loses his way, as he has lost his independent identity, in the stylistic maze of the discourse.

The following digression, for example, prepares the return to Lautréamont's interrupted description of a hanging with this single sentence:

> Pour clore ce petit incident, qui s'est lui-même dépouillé de sa gangue par une légèreté aussi irrémédiablement déplorable que fatalement pleine d'intérêt (ce que chacun n'aura pas manqué de vérifier, à la condition qu'il ait ausculté ses souvenirs les plus récents), il est bon, si l'on possède des facultés en équilibre parfait, ou mieux, si la balance de l'idiotisme ne l'importe pas de beaucoup sur le plateau dans lequel reposent les nobles et magnifiques attributs de la raison, c'est-à-dire, afin d'être plus clair (car, jusqu'ici je n'ai été que concis, ce que même plusieurs n'admettront pas, à cause de mes longueurs, qui ne sont qu'imaginaires, puisqu'elles remplissent leur but, de traquer, avec le scalpel de l'analyse, les fugitives apparitions de la vérité, jusqu'en leurs derniers retranchements), si l'intelligence prédomine suffisamment sur les défauts sous le poids desquels l'ont étouffée en partie l'habitude, la nature, et l'éducation, il est bon, répété-je pour la deuxième et la dernière fois, car, à force de répéter, on finirait, le plus souvent ce n'est pas faux, par ne plus s'entendre, de revenir la queue basse (si, même, il est vrai que j'aie une queue) au sujet dramatique cimenté dans cette strophe.

In traditional rhetoric this single sentence merely constitutes an extended digression. In Ducasse's living rhetoric, however, we may discern his aggressive attempt to intimidate and manipulate the reader, who must follow the narrative's tortuous path if he is ever to find his way back to the fictional content.

This single digression resumes and demonstrates the process of Ducasse's education and assimilation of the reader. Insinuating his way through the digression to unearth what he calls the fugitive apparitions of truth, Lautréamont is also attempting to unearth the reader, to raise him, despite the weight of defects ingrained in him by habit, nature and education, to the higher level of the "nobles et magnifiques attributs de la raison," to the contemplation of those absolute and indiscussible laws of poetic science. For Ducasse the truth is only to be found in these digressive flights which realize the ideal poetry he describes in *Poésies*. Leaving behind the "accidents" and "phénomènes" of the fiction, the dialogue of *narrateur* and *narrataire* proceeds unencumbered by content, liberated from the limits of time, space and identity.

The laws of gravity, however, defeat the narrator's digression, bringing him back down to earth to the content "cimenté dans cette strophe." The reader—whom the narrator has threatened by turns to absorb, to destroy, to carry away with him into the thinner air of pure reason—returns with some relief to more solid ground. While Lautréamont seems to extend his control by dictating his own epitaph to be delivered by the humbled reader,

"Il faut lui rendre justice. Il m'a beaucoup crétinisé," he is also acknowledging that the reader *will* outlive him.

Lautréamont's impossible program of destruction, his struggle against the "Grand Objet Extérieur," his attempts to violate convention, to confound content, and to absorb and annihilate his readers, leave behind material traces: the text of *Les Chants de Maldoror*. Instead of the culminating execution with which both reader and text have been threatened from the beginning of the narrative, the final gesture of *Les Chants* points to survival, to the perpetuation of the struggle between *narrateur* and *narrataire*.

The narrative ends where it began, with an invitation to the reader. The infinite pedagogy of Ducasse's prose will practice on the inexhaustible generations of students he summons to try their will and intellect against the hypnotic power of *Les Chants*. As he suggests in *Poésies*, the corrective activity of reading merely develops the latent content of a text, and so in the end as in the beginning the reader serves the discourse, realizing and revitalizing its exploration of the immediate experience of reading. Perhaps a more appropriate epitaph for the narrator of *Les Chants* may be found in Francis Ponge's celebration of the latent power which awaits every reader of this perpetually revolutionary text: "Ouvrez Lautréamont! Et voilà tout la littérature retournée comme une parapluie! Fermez Lautréamont! Et tout aussitôt, se remet en place."

Poetic Doctrine in Three
of Rimbaud's Verse Poems

Marshall Lindsay

Each of the three poems considered constitutes, among its other possible meanings, a statement about the nature of poetry which this paper attempts to isolate. "Le Coeur supplicié" is an example of what Rimbaud called "objective" poetry in his letter to Izambard and contains an explicit rejection of "subjective" poetry by subverting the traditional poetic notion of the heart. The last four stanzas of "Le Bateau ivre" illustrate, by the rigorous use of Rimbaud's temporality, voyance in its sense of prophecy. In the final two sections of "Mémoire" Rimbaud sees in the opposition river/woman/past vs. sun/man/future the options for poetic inspiration; he rejects the former.

The poems considered in the following pages—"Le Coeur supplicié," the end of "Le Bateau ivre," and the two final sections of "Mémoire"—are poems in their own right; they are also, in my view, poems about poetry. That is to say that each makes a statement of some sort about the nature, the inspiration, the writing, etc., of poetry and constitutes an aspect or fragment of an *art poétique*. The analyses that follow make no claim to completeness; they merely represent an attempt to single out the reflective meanings of poems from among the other intentions that govern them. They provide new interpretations of three texts on the sense of which critics are far from unanimous. They further suggest either additions to or modifications of what we already infer about Rimbaud's poetic doctrine from the standard sources: the "Lettre du Voyant," the "Alchimie du verbe," and elsewhere in his work and correspondence.

Rather than a strict methodology, I have followed principles that are appropriate to the kind of inquiry proposed. Reference to the poet's life—experiences and attitudes he is known to have had—are avoided as a key to the meaning of the texts in question. Interpretation, wherever possible, has been based on clues found within the text, on the possibilities in certain verbal signs of referring to poetic doctrine, and, of course, on the critic's intuition. Special emphasis has been placed in these analyses on time, an important yet not completely understood element in Rimbaud's theory and in the fabric of his verse.

"LE COEUR SUPPLICIÉ"

Before one can think clearly about this poem, it is essential to realize that its tone, attitude, and diction clearly make it a humorous work. This point

From *Orbis Litterarum* 38 (1983). © 1983 by Munksgaard International Publishers Ltd.

has surprisingly been missed by most critics, and that, in turn, has not surprisingly led them astray in their understanding of the text, inducing them to see it as fundamentally tragic, as a confession.

It is also necessary to reject the whole tradition of criticism which considers the poem in relation to Rimbaud's so-called fourth *fugue* to Paris, between April 18 and the first days of May, 1871, when he supposedly participated in the Commune and possibly observed or was subjected to a brutal and probably homosexual experience in a military barracks. Neither the trip to Paris nor the barracks experience can be proved or disproved. While some critics hold to the theory of the homosexual ordeal, others see the poem as dealing in a broader, less explicit, sense with feelings Rimbaud might have had: disillusionment regarding the Commune, the failure of his own involvement in it, or a general sense of discouragement. In either case, it is assumed that the poem refers to an experience that Rimbaud had or could have had; if his biography does not provide such an event, critics have had to invent one.

In reading "Le Coeur supplicié," as in most of Rimbaud's texts, we confront the problem that except for *Une Saison en enfer* we have no idea of the order in which he intended his poems to be arranged, if any. This deprives us of the opportunity of studying the poem in relation to other poems that surround it in a printed collection, as we are able to do when we read Shakespeare's sonnets, for instance, or *Les Fleurs du mal*. Interpreting Rimbaud's difficult poems in the absence of a meaningful context, where the signs within the text often point to no specific or interrelated objects, becomes a matter of identifying meanings within the text.

The closest thing to a context for "Le Coeur supplicié" is found in the letters to Georges Izambard (May 13, 1871) and to Paul Demeny (June 10, 1871), in which it first appeared. Both letters include interesting, if ambiguous, comments on the intention of the poem, to which I shall return later, and different titles for it. "Le Coeur supplicié" was sent to Izambard, "Le Coeur du pitre" to Demeny. Another title, "Le Coeur volé," taken from a line in the poem, heads Verlaine's copy. The constant element in all these titles is *coeur,* and since the same word dominates the three stanzas of the text, it is central to any reading of the poem. *Supplicié* is a semantic intensive for words generally associated with the heart in conventional poetry: *triste, malheureux,* or *brisé.* In the title sent to Demeny, *pitre* is the clown who habitually provokes laughter or jeering. That we do not know what Rimbaud intended to call the poem, has not helped critics to interpret it. However, any one of the three titles does seem a suitable, if not perhaps perfect, introduction to the text itself.

> Mon triste coeur bave à la poupe,
> Mon coeur couvert de caporal:
> Ils y lancent des jets de soupe,
> Mon triste coeur bave à la poupe:

> Sous les quolibets de la troupe
> Qui pousse un rire général,
> Mon triste coeur bave à la poupe,
> Mon coeur couvert de caporal.

The caesura in the first line separates two opposing *énoncés*, which are nevertheless related syntactically:

> Mon triste coeur bave à la poupe

The first three words are undermined by the following four which complete the sentence but subvert the meaning. *Mon triste coeur* is a conventional and sentimental poetic clause; in *bave à la poupe* the sound and sense of both the verb and the prepositional group cast doubt on the assumptions expressed at the beginning: that the heart is the seat of true emotions, that it can be sad, and even that it can be considered "mine." The second line uses the same device, repeating *mon coeur* and then modifying it with unexpected and brutal words that apply neither physically nor metaphorically to the notion of the heart. The subversion of the modifying group is rendered more radical by the alliteration of hard *c* and the suppression of the normal caesura:

> Mon coeur couvert de caporal.

The double sense of *caporal*, which suggests a military rank as well as chewed or spit tobacco, brings to the poem a series of words denoting or connoting soldiery: *troupe, général, pioupiesque,* the function of which becomes clear in the third line:

> Ils y lancent des jets de soupe,

That which is opposed to *mon triste coeur*, which is now reduced to a simple *y*, comes to focus in the pronoun without antecedent *ils*, and signifies the others, the *non-moi*, or more precisely for the context, the *anti-coeur*. And *ils* is in opposition to the heart at different levels. The disdain of *ils* for the heart and all it is supposed to stand for is expressed in the violent verb and burlesque object group. If *poupe* and *caporal* (as tobacco) are destructive to the heart physically, as it is evident in the propositions that relate each in a material way to it, the military terms are opposed on the level of feelings. *Les quolibets* and *un rire* of soliders contest the adjective *triste* and its modification of the metaphorical heart. The repetition, required by the *triolet* form, of the first two lines at the end of the stanza, where they stand as an exclamation, puts in relief the opposing sets of *énoncés*. In its third use modifying *coeur*, the word *triste* itself becomes ironic, annulling, by the insistence of its repetition, the notion of the heart's sadness. The next stanza adds precision:

> Ithyphalliques et pioupiesques
> Leurs quolibets l'ont dépravé!
> Au gouvernail on voit des fresques

> Ithyphalliques et pioupiesques.
> O flots abracadabrantesques,
> Prenez mon coeur, qu'il soit lavé!
> Ithyphalliques et pioupiesques
> Leurs quolibets l'ont dépravé!

Thus it is the obscenities, vulgar humor, and salacious drawings associated with the military, strictly male, and active world that threaten the notion of the heart and its sadness. But here a new dimension is added: the opposition purity/corruption, which suggests that the poem has gone beyond the physical and sentimental levels and is now concerned with a moral question. The speaker's heart has been depraved by its availability to others; it has lost its original purity through contact with the exterior and hostile world. For the desired repurification of the heart, the marine image already present in *poupe* and *gouvernail* is brought back into play, with the added precisions of seasickness and vomiting, bringing us back momentarily to the physical and emotional planes. But the corruption has involved the heart; therefore, according to the ethical code implied by the notion of *mon triste coeur*, it has been profound, and ordinary cleansing will not be sufficient. The purifying element must be endowed with magical powers; thus the *flots abracadabrantesques*.

There has been a temporal progression from the first stanza, where the verbs are in the present tense, signifying the speaker's predicament at the time of speaking. The *passés composés* in the second and last lines of the second stanza indicate that the acts of subversion of the first stanza have been accomplished, while the present tense of the third line implies that they are nevertheless not at an end. What recourse is left to the speaker is in the imperative (*prenez*) and the optative of *qu'il soit lavé* in the sixth line; this introduces the future which will be central to the last stanza.

> Quand ils auront tari leurs chiques,
> Comment agir, ô coeur volé?
> Ce seront des hoquets bachiques
> Quand ils auront tari leurs chiques:
> J'aurai des sursauts stomachiques,
> Moi, si mon coeur est ravalé;
> Quand ils auront tari leurs chiques
> Comment agir, ô coeur volé?

The future is a matter of hypothesis and of interrogation. Exposing one's heart and its sadness has led to mockery, corruption, and ultimately to theft, loss of the heart to those to whom it has never belonged. The *anti-coeur* has alienated the inner feelings of the speaker to the point of paralysis. But as physiological organ, the heart is still attached, and if it can be vomited, as in seasickness, it may also be swallowed back. When the orgy of jeering and obscenities is over and the others have ceased spitting on the speaker's heart, he will experience drunken hiccups, and (emphasized at this point by the disjunctive *moi*) will suffer from something more violent, what in English might be called the "heaves." There follows a feeling of utter weakness (the poem is stunningly effective in expressing and implying the gamut of sensations associated with throwing up), which prompts the speaker to ask how he can act after such an experience.

It is the notion of action that recuperates that of the heart's sadness and provides an alternative for the speaker. Action is impossible so long as one's heart is in the possession of others; thus the necessity for its reintegration, for it to become once again truly "mine." If the poem concludes by asking if action is possible, this final interrogation also expresses a wish.

"Cela ne veut pas rien dire," Rimbaud wrote immediately after the text of "Le Coeur supplicié" in his letter of May 13, 1871, to Izambard, who, despite this urgent appeal that the poem be taken seriously, was to ridicule it. Just before the text, Rimbaud had written: "Je vous donne ceci: est-ce de la satire, comme vous diriez? Est-ce de la poésie? C'est de la fantaisie toujours." Satirical poetry it certainly is, in the tradition of Horace and Boileau, in the manner of many of Rimbaud's own poems written in 1871. Perhaps it is the *fantaisie* that sets it apart from the other satires like "Les Assis" or "Les Mains de Jeanne-Marie." In satirizing the conventions of sentimental poetry—one thinks of Musset's "Chanson" ("J'ai dit à mon coeur, à mon faible coeur") as a prototype—Rimbaud is mocking not sentiment as such but the practice in some poets of taking their emotions too seriously, of exposing them to general ridicule, thus rendering them incapable of provoking action, which, as the "Lettre du Voyant" claims, is to be now the true goal of the poetic art. He seems to say that for poetry to be *en avant de l'action* the poet must remain united with his heart, not opposed to it in a dualistic relationship.

It is not certain what Rimbaud meant, in the letter to Izambard, by the distinction he drew between *poésie subjective* and *poésie objective*. Yet could it not be argued that "Le Coeur supplicié," the only poem included in that letter, is an example of the latter? In that case, the type of poetry implied in the words "Mon triste coeur" is subjective. The opposition of the two kinds of poetry, as we have found it in this poem, is in accord with the general trend of poetic theory at the time, from the *doctrine d'impassibilité* of the Parnassians to the refusal of personal lyricism found at various stages in the work of Gautier, Baudelaire, Verlaine, and Mallarmé. And it corresponds in intention to the parody of romantic sentimentality found in Lautréamont and Corbière. Although Rimbaud's poetry is never impassive, his rejection of the kind of pathetic mode associated with Musset is complete.

"LE BATEAU IVRE": THE LAST FOUR STANZAS

No one who has studied the critical literature devoted to this poem can fail to recognize, along with general agreement as to the sense of the first twenty-one stanzas, an almost complete divergence of opinion concerning the poem's conclusion. And what is astounding to see is the lack of acknowledgement, in most cases, that the interpretation being promoted by one critic conflicts with nearly all other interpretations on record. It seems, furthermore, that most explicators, after they have accounted for the internal play of motifs and images and explained the grammatical and lexicographic difficulties found in the body of the poem abandon such concerns when they arrive at the end and shift their focus to Rimbaud's biography, his general intentions, or the sentiments he may be presumed to have wished to express.

The difficulties encountered in the final stanzas are real, and their origin lies in the fact that the poem does not make the following points clear:

1. the relationship of the concluding section to the line that precedes it: "Je regrette l'Europe aux anciens parapets!"
2. the sense of the image of *future Vigueur*
3. the sequence of ideas or statements in the final three stanzas
4. the sense of the conditional sentence in the second last stanza.

Before confronting these difficulties, one should recall the preceding sections of the poem. It begins with the departure and liberation of a boat which refers to itself as *je* and floats downstream, crewless and without rudder, to the ocean. There the elements of an allegory are clearly established as the boat begins in total freedom to enjoy a series of fantastic sea adventures.

> Et dés lors, je me suis baigné dans le Poème
> De la Mer . . .

What had begun as the conventional joining *life:sea* becomes explicitly in "poème de la mer" *life:sea:poetry*. In the symbol of the sea, Rimbaud relates life and poetry and claims their perfect identity.

The next twelve stanzas can be understood in the light of this relationship. *Je sais, j'ai vu, j'ai rêvé, j'ai suivi*, etc.; the boat experiences a series of extraordinary visions that are given as images in a poem but which go beyond the poetic since they are "plus vastes que nos lyres." Rimbaud's theory of voyance, which first appeared to him in the form of an *art poétique*, becomes here an *art de vivre*. His boat has lived its visions, and, in a sense, has become united with them.

> Et j'ai vu quelquefois ce que l'homme a cru voir.

The speaker opposes not only *je* (i.e. *bateau*) and *l'homme*, but more essentially *voir* and *croire voir*. The first hemistich belongs to the realm of truth, while the second refers to poetry and dream. But in the context of Rimbaud's allegory, this means that poetry itself has abandoned the domain of dream and entered that of *le vécu*, and it is all the more fantastic and beautiful for its shift of habitat. Poetry has become more fabulous for its adherence to the real.

A new section begins with the statement: "Or moi, bateau perdu . . ."
The boat now considers itself lost, and at the end of a long sentence relating
adventures of a most awesome kind, it finally admits defeat:

> Fileur éternel des immobilités bleues,
> Je regrette l'Europe aux anciens parapets!

What ultimately forces the boat to express this sudden nostalgia for a past
both personal and historical, which stands in direct opposition to the boat's
previous liberation, is not terror. The emotional reactions to its experiences
have been singularly subdued: it feels wonder, reverence, only once does
it tremble. Nor is it bothered by its physical disintegration. The cause is
rather the sameness that the boat encounters, the feeling that its goal is
infinitely receding before it. It has become *fileur éternel*, where the first word
can be taken both as that which spins and as that which goes or passes.
It creates ceaselessly its own immobility as well as the immobility which
surrounds it. Blue is usually an affirmative concept for Rimbaud, as in
"Voyelles," and its use here can accommodate the notion of the ideal realm,
an incarnation of the absolute. But it is immobile and the boat follows it
eternally. The regret is for another temporality, for the heavy, opaque time
of history that has already spun its destiny into the old walls of Europe,
for a time that has reached its goal.

> J'ai vu des archipels sidéraux! et des îles
> Dont les cieux délirants sont ouverts au vogueur:
> —Est-ce en ces nuits sans fonds que tu dors et t'exiles,
> Million d'oiseaux d'or, ô future Vigueur?

Here we return to the boat's wandering, but only to realize its endlessness.
For the journey in the sea of life and poetry has not led to the future *Vigueur*,
which we now understand to be the goal of the boat's quest and to lie
beyond freedom. It has only led to the deterioration of the boat as material
object (stanzas 17 & 18). Now the boat sees before it a new, even more
fantastic voyage into space; the delirious skies of the *archipels sidéraux* are
open to a boat or at least what is left of it: that part which is spiritual: thus
vogueur. And the boat addresses its goal asking if it is *virtual* ("dors et
t'exiles"), although infinitely distant, like the stars, the million golden birds
that fly away whenever they are approached. The similarity of "ces nuits
sans fond" to Lamartine's Platonic heaven is striking, and the boat suspects
that it must die *qua* boat before it can ascend to the skies. The Poem, as
long as it is identical with the sea and with life, is earthbound, for the
future as future cannot be possessed within human time.

> Mais, vrai, j'ai trop pleuré! Les Aubes sont navrantes.
> Toute lune est atroce et tout soleil amer:
> L'âcre amour m'a gonflé de torpeurs enivrantes.
> O que ma quille éclate! O que j'aille à la mer!

Mais signifies that the question was rhetorical, that the boat expects the *future Vigueur*'s answer to be yes. But the boat's response to the sky's invitation is no. Because the *aubes*, the *soleil*, the *lune*, all elements associated with the sky, have ceased to inspire joy as they had earlier; they have become bitter. And the love that the sea has always provided as an immediate environment to the boat's drunken existence ("Plus fortes que l'alcool . . . / Fermentent les rousseurs amères de l'amour!") has become unbearable. Caught in a dilemma between the sky which it cannot yet or perhaps ever reach, and the sea which it can no longer bear, the boat admits defeat, asks for total destruction, to be engulfed by the ocean. The last two stanzas explain why.

> Si je désire une eau d'Europe, c'est la flache
> Noire et froide où vers le crépuscule embaumé
> Un enfant accroupi plein de tristesses, lâche
> Un bâteau frêle comme un papillon de mai.
>
> Je ne puis plus, baigné de vos langueurs, ô lames,
> Enlever leur sillage aux porteurs de cotons,
> Ni traverser l'orgueil des drapeaux et des flammes,
> Ni nager sous les yeux horribles des pontons.

The penultimate stanza has been rightly admired for its sudden quiet lyricism, but I believe it has generally been misunderstood. Every element in the image contrasts with the rest of the poem: the restriction in space, the darkness, the cold, the sweet odor, the sadness, the toy boat. But in its context, the image provides an answer to the regret for Europe expressed earlier. Europe, with its comfort, its security, its quiet melancholy, would constitute imprisonment in a past; the toy boat is frail because it is but the dream of a real boat, and all childish dreams ultimately fly away. The *si* clause introduces a definition: the only desirable *eau d'Europe* is the dark, cold puddle, etc. The final stanza explains why the boat cannot desire *une eau d'Europe*: the ships depicted there provide another, more sobering, image of it: it is the vision of an adult boat, so to speak, one in which the boat must compete with commercial and military ships, one in which it cannot escape the threat of prison boats. It is the rivers, ports, and waterways of bourgeois Europe, the unpleasant reality of the present moment. When the drunken boat states that the only water of Europe it can desire is the toy boat's puddle, it knows that this is a dream-past that cannot be realized because it is outside the realm of possibility in the becoming of time. The real water of Europe, the *sillage* of the last stanza, is the only European water available to a boat which has outgrown its puddle, and it is unacceptable. That "je ne désire pas une eau d'Europe" is signified by the telescoping of two notions in "Je ne puis plus." The boat is no longer able to accept a water of Europe because it is "baigné de vos langeurs, ô lames": once it has had a *vision* of the infinite variety and beauty of the adventures the ocean holds open to it, no domestic waterway can satisfy the boat in its thirst for the unknown.

Thus "Le Bateau ivre" does not relate a voyage that has taken place and ended in disaster; *it foretells that same voyage.* The *eau d'Europe* is not a place the boat may return to but the place in which it must remain if it does not set out on its fabulous adventure. Hence the cyclical structure of the poem: it ends literally at its beginning; it concludes with the choice that provokes its opening lines. Up to the twenty-first stanza the verbs are in the imperfect and *passé composé*, standard tenses for a narrative poem. This is disconcerting only because in Rimbaud's time scheme they are used to narrate not what has happened or what is imagined to have happened but what is to come. The present tense dominates the last four stanzas, and the last verb (*je ne puis plus*) points to a future. The boat rejects any *eau d'Europe* in order to choose a destiny it knows will ultimately destroy it. Thus the structure of "Le Bateau ivre" permits the poem to recommence infinitely.

J.-P. Richard has written eloquently of the "heure indicible, l'heure rimbaldienne par excellence, l'heure du commencement absolu, de la naissance (*Poésie et profondeur*). Indeed, the particular quality of the present moment for Rimbaud is that it transcends itself toward the future. His poetic theory is similarly oriented in the direction of the future; the "Lettre du Voyant" is "de la prose sur l'avenir de la poésie" and stresses that "La Poésie ne rhythmera plus l'action; elle sera *en avant*." I should like to suggest, in concluding this analysis, that the notion of *voyant* in Rimbaud's doctrine be understood not only as "visionary" but also in its ordinary sense, that of "prophet." Had not Rimbaud, as early as the age of fourteen, claimed that he would become a *Vates*, poet-prophet in the ancient sense?

SECTIONS IV AND V OF "MÉMOIRE"

One of the most subtle and complex of Rimbaud's verse poems, "Mémoire" has received recently the attention of critics like Nathaniel Wing whose methods and insight permit them to come to grips with and resolve the poem's difficulties in a manner commensurate with its delicately nuanced composition. I have no occasion to argue with Professor Wing's expert description of the general movement of the poem's imagery ("Metaphor and Ambiguity in Rimbaud's 'Mémoire' "), his analysis of Rimbaud's freedom in reversing the terms of metaphors, his understanding of the poem as a whole, or the way in which he relates "Mémoire" to the rest of Rimbaud's writing. Yet there is one point in his analysis that in my opinion should be modified in order to give a simpler, more unified view of the poet's intentions. Although my reading of "Mémoire" owes much to Professor Wing's perceptions and although I agree in general with his conclusions, I question the distinction he makes between the emotions of the woman and those of the speaker, or to put it another way, his assumption that the woman's voice is present at all, as such, in the text. This leads him to fragment section IV into two opposing stanzas and, finally, to refuse to identify the "vieux, dragueur," at the end of that section, with the *je* of section V. The poem's unity, in my view, demands that these separations be integrated.

The speaker's voice is the constant source of the poem's imagery, which leads from *l'eau claire* to *à quelle boue*, from purity of the water element to its opposite, mud. The principal image is a river which, as it flows and expands, undergoes metamorphoses in the constant shift of analogies and metaphors describing it or substituting for it. Dominant among the metaphors are those associated with women, and they progress from projections of a child's sexual reveries to the reality of bourgeois adult womanhood ("Madame se tient trop debout dans la prairie"). The tension of the poem derives in part from the implied conflict between the river/woman and what turns out to be, in section III, the sun/man, the two of which were united in the first lines, and whose separation becomes definitive at the end of III:

> Elle, toute
> froide, et noire, court! après le départ de l'homme!

This is of course a vast oversimplification of the texture of the first three sections of a highly complex poem. But it does account for the principal elements without interpreting them. The presence of the speaker's voice is manifest throughout by exclamations such as *Non* (5), *Eh!* (9), *ô l'Épouse!* (14), *Hélas!* (21), and so forth. These signify not only affective reactions to the events presented, and some of these reactions are certainly ironic, but also stages in a temporal/spatial plane. The *Non* of line 5 is not so much a negation of fact as it is an indication of change in time and place. Along with words like *prairie prochaine* (17/18), *après* (24), *à présent* (29), and *puis* (31), these exclamations give the poem a strong sense of linear direction.

If the relation river/woman was dominant in Section 3, it is only incidental in 4;

> Regret des bras épais et jeunes d'herbe pure!
> Or des lunes d'avril au coeur du saint lit! Joie
> des chantiers riverains à l'abandon, en proie
> aux soirs d'août qui faisait germer ces pourritures!
>
> Qu'elle pleure à présent sous les remparts! l'haleine
> des peupliers d'en haut est pour la seule brise.
> Puis, c'est la nappe, sans reflets, sans source, grise:
> un vieux, dragueur, dans sa barque immobile, peine.

Here the speaker states or recalls emotions and visions associated with various stages of the river's progress. The stages are identifiable not only in the landscape images but also in the parallel syntactical elements which further stress the river's linear development:

> Regret   des bras épais
> Or   des lunes d'avril
> Joie   des chantiers riverains

Each noun—*regret, or, joie*—is an independent entity and represents a different moment of emotion. The first two refer to earlier moments of the poem: *bras, herbe, lit,* and even *or* repeat fragments of preceding images; but they are separated from the earlier moments by the very act of referring. *Regret* is an emotion concerning the past, but it is felt absolutely in the present. The gold of moonlight may be at the same time a reminiscence and a sensation, linking present and past. *Joie* is present both in experiencing and in the object of experience. But the sequence *avril-août-à présent* shows that each of these moments is past. The real temporal perspective, that of the speaker in his own present, comes to light when we read the imperfect tense of *qui faisait germer ces pourritures.* Each moment of emotion was experienced as a present; the whole series has become past.

The river proceeds to another stage. The unmodified *elle* has already stood for the river in lines 6 and 23. That it can also be understood as a woman is part of the basic strategy of the poem, which permits the constant interplay of river and woman. The sadness of these lines and the sense of deprival in *pleure, est pour la seule brise,* and *sans* are part of the general direction of the poem and prepare the final image. *Puis c'est la nappe* constitutes another moment of the river, but this is a final moment of the past and becomes present in the verb *peine.* In the meeting of past and present, the speaker discovers his present self, and the *vieux, dragueur* becomes *je* in section V.

> Jouet de cet oeil d'eau morne, je n'y puis prendre,
> ô canot immobile! oh! bras trop courts! ni l'une
> ni l'autre fleur: ni la jaune qui m'importune,
> là, ni la bleue, amie à l'eau couleur de cendre.
>
> Ah! la poudre des saules qu'une aile secoue!
> Les roses des roseaux dès longtemps dévorées!
> Mon canot, toujours fixe; et sa chaîne tirée
> Au fond de cet oeil d'eau sans bords,—à quelle boue?

At this point the images that have accumulated begin to make a kind of sense that can be articulated. In a poem entitled "Mémoire" the past and memory have been dissociated, and the ambiguity of their relationship is felt throughout the development of the imagery. To convey a sense of the past as "stream of life," Rimbaud has chosen the conventional metaphor of the river. But memory, the only means of capturing the past, is a phenomenon of the present, and does not appear until these two stanzas of section V which give a sense of the present. Instead of capturing the past, memory imprisons consciousness in the present in such a way that time ceases to become, and the self is caught up in introspection. What is left of the past? Only fragments of images: the dust of the willows (which had once been little girls), the thought of long dead roses (which owe their memory to a pun), and finally, at the bottom of the now formless river, silt. It is to this that consciousness is chained by memory, and the poet-dredger searches in it to find some impurity from the past still hidden in the opaque depths of this present self. The flowers also grow in the mud of the past, and they are reminders of the once beautiful, limpid stream. Whatever else they may symbolize, they are the flowers of conventional poetic inspiration so often associated with the past. In the poet's quest to explore the past for its dynamism toward poetic creation, he has found that memory so enwraps him in his present self that he is unable to reach even those most common sources of inspiration.

"Mémoire," at another level, is an exploration of the infinite possibilities in poetic language that can be drawn from the image of the river. One of these possibilities, as we have seen, is the linking of the river and the stages of womanhood. In this sense, the river is bound and constant. It could be said to represent Rimbaud's *anima,* a cluster of feelings that include the need for security, a feeling of weakness, a fondness for nostalgia, all hateful in his system of values; yet the *anima* is an integral part of life. His *animus,* the sun and masculine principle, periodic and free in nature, was once united with water at the source of life. But subsequently in the poem it frees itself of the feminine principle; it is always escaping, always ahead. When the river-anima becomes an adult, strict, and oppressive woman, the sun-animus is by contrast angelic:

> Hélas, Lui, comme
> mille anges blancs qui se séparent sur la route,
> s'éloigne par delà la montagne!

In terms of time, the sun is that which is *en avant,* which proposes a poetry quite different from that of meditating on things past, which is more suitable to the river. Ideally, the principles represented by the sun and by water and the two temporalities associated here with them should be fused as they are in "Eternité," where, significantly, eternity must be found again, not in the past, but in the joining of past and future:

> Elle est retrouvée.
> Quoi?—L'Eternité.
> C'est la mer allée
> Avec le soleil.

But the poet of "Mémoire," at the meeting place not of past and future but of past and present, finds only a present tinged with the past. Absorbed in his own plight, he is prisoner of the present, restricted to the wide river that no longer changes, and deprived of the sun. Memory cannot recreate the past, and its attempt to do so imprisons consciousness in a present of pure duration where it can only search for vestiges of a nonexistent time hidden within the present. True poetry is found in another temporal dimension, and, only after the past has been totally dismissed in *Une Saison en enfer*, can it flourish in the light of *Illuminations*.

Lettre I: The Subject Questioned

Karin J. Dillman

The two most important letters of Rimbaud's correspondence are those to Georges Izambard on May 13, 1871, and to Paul Demeny on May 15 of the same year. (As the text of the letters for this study I have taken the edition of Gérald Schaeffer, *Lettres du voyant* [Genève: Droz, 1975], which is to my knowledge the only printed text to follow the organization of the written words of the manuscript and to maintain the orthography and punctuation of the original.) These letters, written within two days of one another, are Rimbaud's only known formulation of a theory of poetry. The letters have been dealt with very unevenly by the critics. The first letter is more often than not disregarded as only a draft for the second one which is longer and provides a more detailed presentation of Rimbaud's view of the history of poetry. Another reason for the focus of attention on the second letter lies in its definition of Rimbaud's theory as the poetics of the *voyant*. The term *voyant*, used only once in the first letter, is mentioned several times in the second, which is therefore generally referred to as "La Lettre du voyant."

The definition of the poetic theory in terms of *voyance* often leads to a discussion of that concept as part of a long orphic tradition, and to an evaluation of the originality of the concept in Rimbaud's work. Moreover, the focus on the originality of the term *voyant* emphasizes a historical continuity and tends to overlook the definition of the term within the text itself. This approach is very different from the reading I shall propose, which will consider the text as generating its own definitions and its own logic.

In more recent studies the historical approach is abandoned for a re-valuation of the importance of the letters and of the theory they present. The letters are considered as a single statement of Rimbaud's poetic theory,

From *The Subject in Rimbaud: From Self to "Je."* © 1984 by Peter Lang Publishing Co.

or each letter is given equal importance. This revaluation of both letters is illustrated in the way the letters are referred to as "Les Lettres du voyant."

The renewed interest in both letters has brought to light some important differences between them other than their comparative lengths. Some of these differences have been overlooked, partly as a result of the way the letters are reproduced in most editions. The text of both letters consists in part of prose, in part of poetry in verse. The first letter contains one poem in verse which more or less closes the letter, while the text of the second letter is interrupted three times with a poem. In most editions of Rimbaud's works the prose text is included under the heading "correspondence" while the poems appear in the section "poésies." This division obscures some important insights into an understanding not only of each letter and the link between the text in prose and the text in verse, but also of a distinction between the first and second letter. The separation of the text in prose from the text in verse hides the fact that the poems are framed differently in each letter. In the second letter the poems (all three of them) are accompanied by marginalia provided by Rimbaud, "Quelles rimes, ô! quelles rimes!" which create a critical distance and function as a mediating factor. The absence of such commentary in the first letter makes the link between the statement of the letter and of the poem less self-explanatory. Another distinguishing feature between both letters which seems similar to the one just mentioned is the humoristic fashion in which the second letter is presented. Rimbaud introduces the humoristic element by stating in the opening sentence, "J'ai résolu de vous donner une heure de littérature nouvelle [I have decided to give you an hour's worth of new literature]," and by assuming the role of the professor. The first letter is furthermore different in its use of *je* which becomes "poete" in a similar context in the second letter. (The words "poete" and "poesie" are never with an accent in Rimbaud's work.)

The absence of obvious mediating devices such as humor and marginalia, and the use of *je* instead of "poete," make the first letter seem more personal and sincere than the second one. The reason for this sincerity lies undoubtedly in the special relationship between Rimbaud and Izambard, the addressee of the letter. The first letter is therefore often used, as [Mario] Richter points out, as a "vérification d'un épisode biographique," rather than as a literary text (*La Crise du logos et la quête du mythe*). This is especially true for the poem "Le Coeur supplicié" included in the letter which is almost always seen as an expression of a traumatic and biographical experience. My interest in the letter lies in its formulation of a poetic theory. I recognize the emotional and personal aspect of the letter and I will emphasize these aspects because they are crucial to an understanding of the theory as it is stated in the first letter.

Charleville, 13 mai 1871
   Cher Monsieur!

Vous revoilà professeur. On se doit à la Société, m'avez-vous dit; vous faites partie des corps enseignants: vous roulez dans la bonne ornière.—Moi aussi, je suis le principe; je me fais cyniquement *entretenir*; je déterre d'anciens imbéciles de collège: tout ce que je puis inventer de bête, de sale, de mauvais, en action et en parole, je le leur livre: on me paie en bocks et en filles.—*Stat mater dolorosa, dum pendet filius.*—Je me dois à la Société, c'est juste,—et j'ai raison.—Vous aussi, vous avez raison, pour aujourd'hui. Au fond, vous ne voyez en votre principe que poésie subjective: votre obstination à regagner le ratelier universitaire,—pardon!— le prouve! Mais vous finirez toujours comme un satisfait qui n'a rien fait, n'ayant rien voulu faire. Sans compter que votre poesie subjective sera toujours horriblement fadasse. Un jour, j'espère,— bien d'autres espèrent la même chose,—je varrai dans votre principe la poesie objective, je la verrai plus sincèrement que vous ne le feriez!—Je serai un travailleur: c'est l'idée qui me retient, quand les colères folles me poussent vers la bataille de Paris—où tant de travailleurs meurent pourtant encore tandis que je vous écris! Travailler maintenant, jamais, jamais; je suis en grève.

Maintenant je m'encrapule le plus possible. Pourquoi? je veux être poete, et je travaille à me rendre *voyant*: vous ne comprendrez pas du tout, et je ne saurais presque vous expliquer. Il s'agit d'arriver à l'inconnu par le dérèglement de *tous les sens*. Les souffrances sont énormes, mais il faut être fort, être né poete, et je me suis reconnu poete. Ce n'est pas du tout ma faute. C'est faux de dire: Je pense: on devrait dire: On me pense.—Pardon du jeu de mots.—

Je est un autre. Tant pis pour le bois qui se trouve violon, et Nargue aux inconscients, qui ergotent sur ce qu'ils ignorent tout à fait!

Vous n'êtes pas Enseignant pour moi. Je vous donne ceci: est-ce de la satire, comme vous diriez? Est-ce de la poesie? C'est de la fantaisie, toujours.—Mais, je vous en supplie, ne soulignez ni du crayon, ni—trop—de la pensée:

                    Le Coeur supplicié

                    . . . .

Ça ne veut pas rien dire.—REPONDEZ-MOI: chez M Deverrière, pour A.R..

                              Bonjour de coeur,
                                   Art. Rimbaud.

[Charleville, 13 May 1871
Dear Sir!
    There you are, a teacher again. One must pay one's debt to Society, you told me; you are a Member of the Teaching Profession: you're rolling in the right rut. I'm following your principle too: I

am getting myself cynically *kept*. I dig up old idiots from school: the stupidest, dirtiest, nastiest things I can think of I dish up for them; I get paid in beers and bottles. *Stat mater dolorosa, dum pendet filius*. I'm paying my debt to Society. Precisely. And I'm right. You're right too, for today. Basically, you see in your principle only a kind of subjective poetry; your obstinacy in getting back to the University trough—sorry—proves it. But you'll always wind up satisfied without having done anything, since you don't want to do anything. Which is not to mention the fact that your subjective poetry will always be horribly wishy-washy. One day, I hope—many others hope the same thing—I will see objective poetry in your principle, and see it more sincerely than you! I will be a worker: That's what holds me back when a wild fury drives me toward the battle in Paris, where so many workers are still dying while I am writing to you! Work, now? Never, never. I'm on strike.

Right now, I'm depraving myself as much as I can. Why? I want to be a poet, and I am working at making myself a *visionary*: you won't understand at all, and I'm not even sure I can explain it to you. The problem is to attain the unknown by disorganizing *all the senses*. The suffering is immense, but you have to be strong, and to have been born a poet. And I have realized that I am a poet. It's not my doing at all. It's wrong to say: I think. Better to say: I am thought. Pardon the pun.

I is somebody else. So what if a piece of wood discovers it's a violin, and the hell with those who can't realize, who quibble over something they know nothing at all about!

You are no *teacher* for me. I give you the following: is it satire, as you would say? Is it poetry? It's fantasy, anyway. But I beg you, don't underline in pencil, nor too much in thought:

The Stolen Heart

. . . .

That does not mean nothing.
Write me an answer care of M. Deverrière, for A.R.

Very, Very best,
Arth. Rimbaud]

The letter is addressed to Izambard and can be divided in three parts. The first part, lines 1–30, seems to be an imaginary dialogue between Rimbaud and Izambard. The second part, lines 31–46, is an explanation of what it means to be a poet and how to become one. The third part consists mainly of the poem "Le Coeur supplicié," introduced by a short paragraph which suggests certain interpretations, rejects Izambard's role as "Enseignant," but which ends by asking for his judgment and that it be gentle. The poem is followed by a comment, "Ça ne veut pas rien dire," which closes the letter.

In the first part Rimbaud establishes an opposition between himself and Izambard by way of a distinction between *je* as the source of the discourse and *vous* as the addressee. The opposition proceeds resembling an imaginary dialogue in which Rimbaud talks to Izambard about Izambard, and in which he talks to Izambard about himself. The two parts are separated by dashes which are repeatedly used in the first part. Rimbaud is in complete control of this little drama in which he plays both roles, the *je* as well as the *vous*, and manipulates Izambard's imagined responses and objections.

The opposition between Rimbaud and Izambard proceeds in the form of an apparent resemblance: "Moi aussi. . . . Vous aussi. . . ." The resemblance is that both act according to the same principle: "On se doit à la Société." Izambard follows the principle by joining the ranks of the "corps enseignants": he can thus combine his idealism with his livelihood by working within an institutionalized system. Rimbaud ends this description of Izambard's occupation with the remark, "vous roulez dans la bonne ornière," which, all by itself, is already a negative judgment rather than encouragement. The extent of the negative judgment becomes known only after the statement "moi aussi . . . ," which seemingly establishes a strong similarity between the two.

> je me fais cyniquement *entretenir*; je déterre d'anciens imbéciles de collège: tout ce que je puis inventer de bête, de sale, de mauvais, en action et en parole, je le leur livre: on me paie en bocks et en filles.
>
> (ll. 6–11)

Rimbaud also plays the role of a professor who is paid for his teaching. His occupation, however, seems very different from and diametrically opposed to Izambard's. Whereas the latter's are legitimate and even honorable, Rimbaud's teachings undermine and corrupt the ideals of Izambard. The key word of this passage is "cyniquement"; for if Rimbaud is doing the same, he does it cynically, that is, he makes a conscious attempt at being unscrupulous. The conscious and voluntary aspect of his action is the important difference between Izambard and Rimbaud. Izambard is portrayed as a follower ("vous faites partie . . . vous roulez dans la bonne ornière"), whereas the passage describing Rimbaud's occupation is dominated by *je*: "je suis," "je me fais," "je déterre," "je puis inventer." The entire scene, even its subjugation in "je me fais" and in "on me paie," is set up by that *je*.

The similarity between the occupation of Izambard and of Rimbaud exists not only because the latter plays a role that resembles, in form, that of a professor; the resemblance goes much deeper. While Rimbaud's activity is a usurpation of the role of teacher and an undermining of the ideals of Izambard, the description of his activity is also an expression of what is already implied in the description of Izambard's work. Izambard, by becoming a professor again, contributes to the corruption of the principle that he himself once explained to Rimbaud, but he does so unconsciously and unwillingly.

The relation between the two statements, the first one to Izambard about Izambard, "On se doit à la Société . . . vous faites partie des corps enseignants," and the second one to Izambard about Rimbaud, "Moi aussi, je suis le principe," is thus very complex. They form a sharp contrast and place Izambard and Rimbaud in opposition to one another with respect to "le principe." What Rimbaud does is word for word the opposite of what Izambard does and intends to do. The latter wants to educate and to put the ideal into practice, whereas Rimbaud contributes to the corruption of his listeners. There is, however, also a strong similarity between the two and their occupations. What Rimbaud does is modeled on Izambard's role: he teaches *them* what *they* want and is paid for his work. Rimbaud is in that respect doing exactly what he thinks Izambard does, and the description of his occupation is therefore a critical comment on and a rejection of Izambard's work as a professor. The important difference is that Rimbaud, "cyniquement," is aware of what he does; he gives them what they want, having no illusions of changing them or communicating his own interests to them. Rimbaud is thus, as opposed to Izambard, in control of the situation he has himself created. The consequence of his position is that he remains an outsider, the *je* as opposed to the *ils* ("d'anciens imbéciles de collège"); he can only be cynical and has to hide his own interests, otherwise he falls into the same trap as Izambard. Rimbaud's "cyniquement" is opposed to the naïve idealism of Izambard who believes he can teach *his* principle to *them* in *their* system, but who ends up joining their system and taking on their restricted view of the principle.

The opposition as well as the similarity hinge upon "Moi aussi, je suis le principe. . . . " "*Le* principe," I stress the definite article as different from "votre principe" later on in the text (ll. 15 and 23). The definite article presents the principle as a general rule, "*on* se doit . . . ," and attaches it neither to Rimbaud nor to Izambard. It is a rule that they shared and that later, because of Izambard's interpretation, becomes his, "*votre* principe," which is very different from Rimbaud's.

When "principe" is mentioned again it is accompanied by a possessive adjective and linked to a particular form of expression: "Au fond, vous ne voyez en votre principe que poesie subjective . . . " (ll. 13–14). At the same time when "principe" is linked to Izambard, subjective poetry is introduced in a restricted sense ("ne . . . que"), as only one of the possible ways to put the principle into practice. Both restrictions, "votre principe" and "poesie subjective" as the only kind of poetry the subject *vous* is capable of seeing, are the direct result of Izambard's rejoining the "ratelier universitaire." The word "ratelier," translated in Varèse and in Fowlie as "trough," also has the meaning of a rack to store things in, tool-rack or pipe-rack, and of dentures. The word "trough" in French has the negative meaning of living off someone, which recalls "vous faites partie des corps enseignants," and most of all of "entretenir." The meaning of "rack" suggests a rigid line and a repetition of a uniform pattern, which recalls "vous roulez dans la bonne ornière."

The university and everything related to it is thus defined in negative terms: it is uniform, rigid, it restricts the view of the person associated with it and corrupts his ideals. Subjective poetry, the only form of expression that can exist in the system, is therefore defined in similar terms: it is and will always be "horriblement fadasse" (l. 21). The definition of subjective poetry is thus derived from the personal opposition between Izambard and Rimbaud. The reasons why the latter rejects and rebels against his former teacher are the same as his reasons for rejecting subjective poetry. And both Izambard and subjective poetry are shaped by the system of tradition and convention that is upheld by the university.

Rimbaud's response, after his rejection of Izambard and after his criticism of the university and of subjective poetry, is the announcement of a new poetry: "Un jour, j'espère,—bien d'autres espèrent la même chose— je verrai dans votre principe la poesie objective" (ll. 22–23). If subjective poetry is defined in terms of Izambard and his work, one can assume that the definition of objective poetry is in direct opposition to subjective poetry and related to Rimbaud's personal rejection of Izambard. Izambard is rejected, it appears, because he cannot see. He is accused of *seeing* in *his* principle only subjective poetry (l. 15), whereas Rimbaud will see *in that same* principle objective poetry. Both subjective and objective poetry are posited as already existing, even though both are not practiced at the same moment; objective poetry is announced for the future. The choice does not depend on the principle either, because subjective poetry will be seen in Izambard's principle. The choice between the two depends only on the subject and its way of seeing. Izambard does not see, not consciously; his view is determined by his position. He follows the easy road of tradition which does not require any effort and creates a false feeling of satisfaction: "Mais vous finirez toujours comme un satisfait qui n'a rien fait, n'ayant rien voulu faire." Being able to see objective poetry, on the other hand, is a learning process that requires hard work and suffering.

The poet dedicated to objective poetry has to be *voyant*: "Je veux être poete et je travaille à me rendre *voyant*" (in italics in the manuscript; ll. 32–33). This statement expresses some important differences between Izambard and Rimbaud, and between subjective and objective poetry. It outlines a method of seeing and arriving at objective poetry that takes the subject away from the now and the known. The fact of being born a poet is not sufficient, it is only the beginning and the precondition for becoming an objective poet. The method of becoming *voyant* is thus most of all a process; it is, as the present participle indicates, a *being in process*, which forms a sharp contrast to the method of subjective poetry which does not require any effort at all. Subjective poetry is therefore the poetry of the now, " . . . vous avez raison pour aujourd'hui" (l. 14), while objective poetry has the future.

The idea of poetic creation as action and as a process is present from the very beginning of the letter, and is derived from the description between Izambard's work and Rimbaud's: "je me fais cyniquement *entretenir*." It is the conscious and deliberate aspect of Rimbaud's subversive behavior which is repeated several times, "je suis en grève" (l. 30) and "je m'encrapule" (l. 31). Each one of these instances is negative and passive according to the logic of Izambard. In comparison to Rimbaud's description of Izambard, however, it is active and an expression of a conscious choice of the subject *je* to break with tradition. *En* thus indicates a reaction against everything that is upheld by the university, and it is an active process that requires work. Thus, the sentence, "Travailler maintenant, jamais, jamais; je suis en grève" (ll. 29–30), is contradictory only within the logic of Izambard; for Rimbaud, the very act of being on strike is work and suffering. It is the necessary step to arrive at *voyance*.

The method of subversion and of becoming *voyant*, as expressed by *en* and -*ant*, is both work and suffering. While the aspect of suffering is expressed only explicitly toward the end of the text, "les souffrances sont énormes" (l. 37), it is implied from the very beginning of the letter in the very way in which Rimbaud opposes himself to Izambard. Rimbaud imitates Izambard by doing exactly the opposite. He refers to himself as following the principle like his former professor: "Moi aussi, je suis le principe" (ll. 5–6). This phrase can also be read as "je suis [am] le principe," in which "principe" is a definition of *je* itself. (The French "principe" is derived from the Latin *principium* which means beginning or origin. The theme of the origin or the new beginning is present everywhere in Rimbaud's work.) As "le principe," both as principle and as origin, Rimbaud consciously and willingly prostitutes himself in an act which is both a subversion of the old and the affirmation of the new. Rimbaud's defiance is thus also suffering: it is, in this case, a sacrifice of himself for the cause of the new. These two aspects cannot be separated, which is clearly emphasized by the sentence which follows Rimbaud's description of his own debauchery, *Stat mater dolorosa, dum pendet filius* (ll. 11–12). This sentence can be either a variation of St. John 19:25, as pointed out by Schaeffer, or a quotation transposed in the present from a medieval chant. In either case the reference to the sacred juxtaposed to the café scene functions both as a defiance and as a comparison.

The theme of suffering, even though it is presented in the guise of irony, is what distinguishes Rimbaud from Izambard most of all. When, in the last paragraph, Rimbaud rejects Izambard as a teacher in "Vous n'êtes pas Enseignant pour moi" (l. 47), this rejection is based on Izambard's refusal to work and to suffer: he is neither "en-seignant" nor "en-saignant," but takes the easy road of "la bonne ornière."

Subjective poetry is the product of a subject with a limited view; it is defined by the restrictive ("ne . . . que") and by the possessive ("votre"). "Je travaille à me rendre *voyant*" is thus to be taken literally as wanting to see and to break out of the restricted mode of the subjective. Objective poetry, on the other hand, is preceded by a definite article which suggests that it is impersonal and general, "je verrai dans votre principe la poesie objective" (ll. 21–22). It is not related to one particular subject. Moreover, if the term "subjective" is to be understood, following the text's suggestion, as related to a subject, "objective" poetry, following the same reasoning, would then be related to an object. This conclusion is, however, contradicted by the theme of suffering which distinguishes Rimbaud from Izambard. The latter is depicted as a follower who acts unconsciously as opposed to Rimbaud who "cyniquement" stages the drama of his own suffering. Thus, while the logic of the argument suggests an opposition between subjective and objective poetry based on the presence or absence of a subject, the subversion of subjective poetry is initiated by a conscious subject which is highly visible in the strong repetition of a *je*. To resolve this contradiction (real or apparent), I should like to turn to an analysis of the nature and the function of the subject as presented in the text's definition of subjective and objective poetry.

One of the key phrases in the second part of the letter in which Rimbaud presents his view on how to be and to become a poet is the sentence, "C'est faux de dire: Je pense: on devrait dire: On me pense" (ll. 40–41). The opposition between "Je pense" and "On me pense" is analogous to the personal opposition between Izambard and Rimbaud. The former teacher, as stated earlier, is rejected because he acts unconsciously (as opposed to "cyniquement"), and because he rejoins the university. He is thus one of the "inconscients, qui ergotent sur ce qu'ils ignorent tout à fait" (ll. 45–46). The academic debate is depicted as quibbling and as hairsplitting, because the important subjects remain hidden for those who belong to the university; they are both "inconscients" and "ignorants." This quibbling passes, however, for thinking. Both the phrase "Je pense" and the word "ergoter" evoke the Cartesian "cogito," "cogito ergo sum" ("ergoter" from the Latin "ergo" literally meaning "dire donc" [Shoshana Felman, "Tu as bien fait de partir, Arthur Rimbaud," *Littérature* 11 (1973)]). The method is rejected as a linear and mindless procedure characteristic of the university which is described earlier in the letter as "la bonne ornière" and as "le ratelier." The subject of subjective poetry is thus defined as a thinking and a reasoning subject.

In the second part of the formula, "On me pense," the grammatical subject *je* becomes *me*, and the personal subject form is replaced with an impersonal one, *on*. In the change from *je* to *me* the subject becomes an object "subissant et non pas agissant, agi et non pas agent, tandis que le véritable sujet est 'on' [submitting and not acting, acted and not agent, whereas the real subject is *on*]" (Felman). The subject loses its position as initiator and origin of the thinking process, a role that is taken over by *on*. The nature of that *on* is different from the *on* in the short phrase which precedes it, in "on devrait me dire." In that sentence it acts as a fixed expression which has a kind of proverbial quality that is completely impersonal. It is not opposed to any other term which could emphasize its impersonal character, and it thus remains neutral. The use of *on* in "On me pense" is very different, it presents an important force in relation to *me*; it takes the place of *je* in "Je pense," which suggests a resemblance between the two. However, *je* in "Je pense," as defined in the letter, points to a determined and a personalized subject; that is, it is the sign of a subject (modeled after Izambard), that thinks it knows itself and what it is doing, while, in fact, its perspective is limited; it is not *voyant*. And it is the sign of a subject that exists because it *thinks* it thinks: it posits its own existence through an act that the letter defines as "ergoter," as quibbling and hair-splitting. To translate this in linguistic terms, one could say that the *je* is accepted as the sign for a speaking subject that says "Je pense." In pronouncing *je* the speaking subject appropriates the grammatical category of the first person and posits its own presence. *On*, on the other hand, is an impersonal pronoun; it is undetermined and invariable. Its meaning does not move or shift and does not take on the form of a specific subject at a particular moment. Moreover, as a sign of a third person it is, as Benveniste states, excluded from the "corrélation de personnalité" which characterizes the first two pronouns (I and you). *On* is never personalized, and it acts as an omnipresence; it is the unknown, "l'autre," in relation to *me*.

The verb "pense" is closely linked to the subject *je* and the substitution of that subject by *on* questions not only the nature of *on* but of "pense" as well. The letter proposes an answer to both questions in the remark, "Pardon du jeu de mots" (ll. 42–43). The presence of this remark at this particular point in the text is significant. Whether the remark refers to a word play on "pense/panse" as suggested by some critics, or whether it is a comment on "Je pense" as a reference to the Cartesian "cogito," is of less importance than the fact that it introduces "jeu de mots" as a concept which is directly related to the role of *on*. It represents the presence and the role of *on* and points to its imprint on the text which takes the form of a visible proliferation of *on*: "*on* devrait . . . On me pense . . . pard*on* . . . viol*on*" (Felman). The visible presence of *on* reinforces the impression mentioned earlier, that objective poetry is generated by *on* and speaks through the subject as *me* which becomes a kind of medium only. This reading of "On me pense" only reiterates the contradiction between the implied disappearance of *je* in objective poetry and the visible presence of *je* in the letter.

To conclude that in objective poetry *je* is absent poses several problems. While the opposition between "Je pense" and "On me pense" seems to invite this conclusion, the letter also emphasizes the *je*. Its presence distinguishes the description of Izambard and of Rimbaud in the first paragraph and it appears again as a significant sign of distinction in the paragraph introduced by "Je est un autre" (ll. 43–46). This phrase immediately follows the opposition between "Je pense" and "On me pense" and is followed by a long sentence, "Tant pis pour le bois qui se trouve violon, et Nargue aux inconscients, qui ergotent sur ce qu'ils ignorent tout à fait." The second part of this sentence is more problematic. It can be read as a reference to the new as opposed to the subjective poet. Wood is made into a violin, an instrument that has to be played in order to produce sound. The passive construction ("se trouve") recalls that of *on* in "On me pense" and suggests a similarity between both sentences. The subject, presented as violin in one case and as *me* in the other, is objectified; it serves as an object through which someone or something expresses itself. The subject is thus literally and in every sense *violon:* the perfect image of the poet as described in the letter: poet by birth and through suffering, and acted upon by *on:* "violon/ violé/viol-on."

The ease with which "violon" can be read as the sign of the new poet, both suffering and objectified and as similar to "On me pense," is problematic for several reasons. In the first place because the entire sentence beginning with "Tant pis," and followed by the rejection of those who "ergotent," is in opposition to "Je est un autre." This phrase following the opposition between Izambard and Rimbaud, and subsequently between subjective and objective poetry, is an expression of the new poetic theory. The image of the poet as "violon," on the other hand, seems, in this paragraph, to be presented as the image of the subjective poet and as such is rejected: "tant pis." The opposition between "Je est un autre" and the poet as violin seems to contradict the opposition in the preceding paragraph between "Je pense" and "On me pense." Moreover, the description of a creative process in which the subject serves as a medium, as *me* or as *violon,* for an undetermined other, an *on,* is contrasted by a description in which a *je* is present: " . . . il faut être fort, être né poete, et je me suis reconnu poete. Ce n'est pas du tout de ma faute" (ll. 38–49). The *je* in this statement is however, as in most other instances in the letter ("je me fais" and "je m'encrapule"), accompanied by a reflexive verb which makes the subject both the active and the passive agent of the action. The reflexive construction occurs also frequently in the second letter and is particularly strong in a passage that resembles the paragraph in the first letter introduced by "Je est un autre":

> Car Je est un autre. Si le cuivre s'éveille clairon, il n'y a rien de sa faute. Cela m'est évident: j'assiste à l'éclosion de ma pensée: je la regarde, je l'écoute: je lance un coup d'archet: la symphonie fait son remuement dans les profondeurs, ou vient d'un bond sur la scène.

> [For I is somebody else. If brass wakes as a bugle, it is not its fault at all. That is quite clear to me: I am spectator at the flowering of my thought: I watch it, I listen to it: I draw a bow across a string: a symphony stirs in the depths, or surges onto the stage.]

In this paragraph, as opposed to the one in the first letter, there is no opposition but an extended explanation instead. "Si le cuivre s'éveille clairon, ill n'y a rien de sa faute" is presented as similar to the statement "Car Je est un autre," whereas in the first letter there is a relationship of opposition between "Je est un autre" and "Tant pis pour le bois qui se trouve violon." The similarity between "bois-violon" and "cuivre-clairon," both raw material forged into an instrument, is striking and extends to *on* inscribed in both "viol-on" and "clair-on." The similarity between the two sentences tends to hide their difference which lies precisely in the role of the *je*. Whereas the presence of *je* in the form of an extended reflexive comparison seems firmly grounded in this passage of the second letter, the first letter seems less consistent in its presentation of *je*. It at once announces the disappearance of the *je* and reaffirms its presence. The first letter and the new theory it proposes create an ambiguity which is situated in the role and the nature of the subject. Related to this ambiguity of the subject is the contrast between Izambard's poetry which is rejected as subjective, and a new poetry which the letter calls objective. The difference between the two is not always clear, especially not in so far as the role of the subject is concerned. While "le bois qui se trouve violon " is thematically consistent with the role of the poet (the transformation of raw material into an instrument, the objectification and the suffering), and with the reflexive self-activated character of the creative process (*se* and *on*), it is also presented with enough ambivalence that it can instead be taken as a statement about the objective poet. Both problems depend on a definition of the subject: on its nature and on its function in the creative process.

Because of an apparent inconsistency in the opposition between subjective and objective poetry in the letter, I turn to a text which defines its poetic theory in less ambiguous terms and which can, when compared to Rimbaud's text, provide a better understanding of the role and the nature of the subject in the new poetic theory in Rimbaud's text. This text is the Preface to the *Méditations* of the 1849 edition in which Lamartine provides the theoretical basis of his work. He proposes a break with traditional form in order to establish a new kind of poetry in a spirit that is very similar to Rimbaud's letter. The tradition established by Lamartine's poetry becomes in turn the tradition against which Rimbaud reacts. This is not to say that the letter is a rejection of Lamartine's poetry in particular. On the contrary, Rimbaud credits Lamartine with having been "quelquefois voyant. . . . " Lamartine is, however, the main theoretician of the dominant poetic tradition of the first half of the nineteenth century, and that tradition is characterized by the importance of the personal—of the role of the subject. Rimbaud's rejection of Izambard and of subjective poetry focuses precisely on these two aspects: poetry as part of a systemized tradition in the university, and the restricted view of the subject. Moreover, the theme of suffering and of the poet as an instrument in the first letter closely resemble the theory of poetic creation of the romantic tradition. Because the letter is problematic precisely in those matters, a comparison with the old can shed light on the new. I have also pointed out earlier, in the discussion of the first paragraph of the letter, that Rimbaud's behavior is a rejection of Izambard's role as a professor, but that it remains patterned after it. It is therefore of importance to see whether and how the poetic theory which is based on the personal opposition is different or whether it remains within the same theoretical model.

Lamartine defines the break with traditional form and the new role of the poet as follows:

> Je suis le premier qui ait fait descendre la poésie du Parnasse, et qui ait donné à ce qu'on nommait la muse, au lieu d'une lyre de sept cordes de convention, les fibres mêmes du coeur de l'homme, touchées et émues par les innombrables frissons de l'âme et de la nature.

> [I am the first to have made poetry come down from Parnassus, and to have given to what used to be called the muse, instead of a conventional seven-string lyre, man's heart's very fibers, touched and moved by the innumerable shivers of the soul and of nature.]

The exact source of poetry is and remains the muse. The muse, i.e., "inspiration," will act on the poet's own "âme" rather than on an instrument of convention external to him. The presentation of the muse with a small rather than a capital letter is significant in this respect and in accordance with the intent to make the creative act a more human rather than a divine process. Furthermore, the role of the human factor is stressed because the locus of what will transform inspiration into poetry is within rather than without. There are two aspects to the poet's outside, "l'âme et la nature," which have an effect on the inside, the "coeur." The "coeur" will reverberate with the outside through the "frissons," a cliché which translates as an emotional relation to the outside. The fibers of the heart are thus not exactly played and not directly touched, but they are more subtly "touchées et émues par les innombrables frissons de l'âme et de la nature." The fibers of the heart tremble in accordance with the poet's outside. The creative process is thus presented as a perfect communication between inside and outside.

Lamartine's definition provides a detailed account of all aspects of the creative process. It defines the different aspects that are active in the process: "coeur" as the physical and the emotional inside, and "l'âme et la nature," which represent the poet's general sensitivity and the physical outside. The communication between inside and outside takes place by way of "frissons," a term which is already an expression of emotion. Each and every aspect of the self that is involved in the creative process is a carrier or a container of emotions and feelings. The product of the communication between inside and outside, the poem, is thus an expression of emotion in which both inside and outside are in harmony. The poem is, as Lamartine states elsewhere in the same Preface, "un soulagement de mon propre coeur" or "un cri de l'âme [my own heart's sigh . . . a cry of the soul]."

To summarize, Lamartine represents the creative process as a human and as a personal endeavor. Both the origin and the locus of the expression are situated within the poet's own self and all aspects and stages of the process are described in detail. The entire process consists of a transformation of feelings and emotions into poetry without any mediation of a reasoning subject. Lamartine's definition of the creative process thus seems to prove wrong Rimbaud's remark "Je pense" as a definition of subjective poetry, and my reading of the remark as a reference to the French romantic tradition as defined in Lamartine's Preface. There is no visible presence of a *je* as a thinking and a reasoning subject in the creative process itself. It is, on the contrary, defined in terms of emotion and feeling. Neither is there an *on* as an unknown: the creative process takes place within the poet's own self and the entire process is described in detail. Nor is there an *on* as an active agent: the process takes place in a determined individual which is an active rather than a passive subject.

The absence of *on* is particularly clear when Lamartine's definition of the poetic creation is compared to Rimbaud's "Tant pis pour le bois qui se trouve violon." In Lamartine the instrument is played by the muse, i.e., inspiration, which is humanized and presented as one of the several aspects of the poet himself that is involved in the creative process. If Rimbaud's image of the "violon" can be seen as a reference to romantic poetry, it is very different from Lamartine's definition. The poet as "violon" is acted upon by *on*; it is "violon/violé/violon" (Felman). There is a passive and an unknown in "violon," both of which are absent from Lamartine's definition.

Another difference between the two descriptions which is of importance to the present discussion is that Lamartine is more concerned with the process itself and does not address the nature or the function of the subject of the process. Rimbaud's description, on the other hand, presents both the creative subject, the violin as "sujet violé/violon," and it presents the process of becoming a poet in the transformation of raw material into an instrument. The relation between "bois" and "violon" and the reflexive nature of "se trouve" (which is a repetition of the other reflexive and passive constructions in the text) express an objectification and a suffering which are both sincerely and passively suffered, and at the same time willingly and consciously staged. The sentence "Tant pis pour le bois . . . " thus resembles closely Rimbaud's debauchery described in the first paragraph of the letter in which the suffering is at least in part staged by the subject itself. The sentence "Tant pis pour le bois . . . " is thus on the one hand a representation of the role and the function of the poet and similar to the phrase "On me pense," and it presents in "tant pis" a mocking distance which mitigates the seriousness of the statement. This ambivalence characterizes the first letter from the beginning until the end. (See especially the sentences that introduce the poem, "Vous n'êtes pas Enseignant pour moi" [ll. 47–48] and "Mais, je vous en supplie, ne soulignez ni du crayon, ni—trop—de la pensée" [ll. 50–52]. In the first sentence Izambard's role is rejected while the last sentence begs for his judgment and for it to be gentle.) This kind of ambivalence distinguishes the first from the second letter where *on* is less and *je* is more visibly present. While there is indeed a strong similarity between "Tant pis pour le bois qui se trouve violon" in the first, and "Si le cuivre s'éveille clairon" in the second letter, there is also a strong difference. *On* inscribed in both sentences is in the second letter clearly a part of the creative process and of the creative subject: " . . . j'assiste à l'éclosion de ma pensée: je la regarde, je l'écoute . . . " (ll. 62–63). The objectification is not, as it is in the first letter, imposed by an outside and an unknown *on*.

While the presence of *on* is firmly established in the first letter, its role and origin are not consistent. It is presented as an outside force that objectifies the subject *je* and transforms it into *me*, and it is, in "violon," more closely integrated into the creative process and the creative subject. The reason for this plurality of *on* lies in the personal relationship which forms the basis of the first letter. The way in which Rimbaud imitates and subverts the role of his former teacher is at once an active usurpation and a staging of his own suffering. To analyze this problem further I should like to focus on the subject *je* which is opposed to *on* and rejected in "Je pense." Moreover, *je* appears later on in the letter (and it dominates the passage of the second letter quoted above), in an apparently similar initial position in "Je est un autre" which also contains a reference to *on* in "un autre."

The discussion of Lamartine's definition of the creative process and its comparison with Rimbaud's has revealed that there is indeed a consistent presence of *on* and of a passive element in the letter, both of which are absent from Lamartine's statement. However, "Je pense" as a definition of subjective, and thus of romantic, poetry seems inaccurate. There is no reasoning or thinking *je* in Lamartine's description which defines poetry instead in terms of emotion. I have shown earlier that "Je pense" and its reference to the Cartesian "cogito" is rejected as "ergoter." This pejorative term reflects not only on the meaning of the verb but on the entire phrase as a performative act; the *je* does not think, it cannot say "I think" and it therefore cannot posit its own existence through an appropriation of the linguistic discourse. In "On me pense" the *je* is removed from its initial position from where it could (thought it could) posit its own existence. Turning once again to Lamartine's description we see that, beginning with "je suis le premier," the position and the role of the *je* are well established. The *je* places itself at the beginning of a new tradition as its first participant and even as the creator of the tradition. This tradition, which is based on a process of creation that is very personal and individual, is presented with the use of the definite article and as "le coeur de *l'homme*" (emphasis is mine), as the general and the universal. This presentation is similar to the linguistic reading of "Je pense" in which a *je* asserts its presence by appropriating (without questioning and without doubt) discourse as its own. The *je* in Lamartine's description proposes itself as the model of the creative subject and of poetic creation. Moreover, the creative process itself, as a communication between inside and outside, depends on the presence and the point of view of a *je* which analyzes this personal process from a distance. The *je* contemplates its own self as a third person, as an object. This otherness is neither perceived nor presented as a problem. It serves instead to establish the process as a general rule and to provide a theoretical basis for the new tradition. The *je* is thus in command, *thinks* itself in command, of the poetic tradition as well as of the linguistic representation of that tradition.

The answer in Rimbaud's letter to the *je* of "Je pense" and to the *je* of the subjective/romantic tradition, which presents itself as both the origin and the locus of the poetic discourse, is "On me pense." This phrase shows the *je* as a de-centered subject. The subject *je* is objectified, its place as initiator of the action and as origin of the discourse is taken over by *on*, and its function is reduced to that of a medium through which *on* is expressed, or expresses itself (*on* is the subject of an active verb). While *on* takes over the place where the poetic discourse originates, the origin or identity of *on* itself remains ambiguous, and this ambiguity is related to the definition of the subject *je* itself. Whereas in "On me pense" the *je* is reduced to the role of an object and is thus completely passive, the comparison with "Tant pis pour le bois qui se trouve violon" has revealed that the role of the subject *je* is more complex. The relationship between *on* and *me* is based on Rimbaud's imitation and usurpation of Izambard's role as professor, and the way in which the acting out of that role is at once an act of defiance and aggression toward an outside other is a personal defense toward that other, and is a staging of the subject's own suffering. I have also pointed out that Rimbaud's debauchery as an imitation of opposition remains determined by and within the limits of the tradition it seeks to destroy. The same model of opposition within the tradition itself is apparent in the phrase "On me pense" where the potential meaning of *on* and the role of the subject *je* remain locked within the grammatical and rhetorical logic of "Je pense."

The problem of *on* and of *je* and their relation to the grammatical and rhetorical tradition of "Je pense" brings me to a discussion of the sentence "Je est un autre" which contains both a *je* and a reference to its otherness or to its objectification by *on*. The sentence can be read as similar to "On me pense"; that is, as an expression of *je* which, as a medium for *on*, defines itself as "un autre." This reading applies to "Je est un autre" the method of reading according to "Je pense": *je* is the actualization of the subject in discourse, the origin and locus of its expression. "Un autre" is thus, following that reading, a definition of *je* and by *je* in the same way as Lamartine's description defines the *je* of its creative process; "un autre" is thus read as a definition of the *je* rather than as a failure to define it or than as a questioning of its identity. The problem with this reading is that it fails to see the grammatical break between *je* and the verb form *est*. This reading is based on the assumption that *je* is a first person and the sign of the speaker of the text. It gives more attention to the *je* as a figure than to grammatical and textual logic.

The *je* in "Je est un autre" is accompanied by *est*, a third person verb form, rather than the first person form *suis*. The *je* as the figure for the first person speaker has thus no *raison d'être*; it fails to impose its imprint on the verb which is, besides the pronoun, "la seule espèce de mots qui soit soumise à la catégorie de la personne [the only kind of words subordinated to the category of person]." (E. Benveniste, *Problèmes de linguistique générale*). The *je* is thus without a proper verb according to this logic of reading, and the sentence can only be understood as the expression of a fundamental break between the subject and its form of expression. The sentence can also be read as an introduction to a new form of reading: not as discontinuous, as a break between *je* as the sign of a person and its verb, but as continuous and radically different. This reading proposes a complete redefinition of the subject *je*. It exposes the *je* as a third person, as an *il* literally and textually: *je* is the personal pronoun *je*. It literally is "un autre" from the subject, it is a textual subject: *"Je est un autre je."* This reading constitutes a break with the tradition that the letter defines as subjective and it solves the ambiguity of "On me pense" according to which the sentence would read, "Je est un autre = *on*." Seeing "un autre" as the equivalent does not touch the logic upon which the *je* as a figure and as a referent for discourse is based. The subject *je* is objectified by and through *on* but its presence as referent continues to exist. "Je est un autre *je*," on the other hand, expresses the objectification of *je* not in rhetorical, thematic, or psychological terms, but in purely grammatical and textual ones. *Je* is not a figure and not *the* referent, but a third person pronoun, a *je* as *"un autre"* before it can be read as a figure or a referent. The definition of *je* as "un autre" rather than "l'autre" eliminates the inherent referential character of the *je*, or, rhetorically speaking, it eliminates its status and its meaning outside of and independent from the text. As "un autre" the definition of the *je* depends on its context, rather than on a rhetorical logic which is established by tradition.

The reading of "Je est un autre" as a redefinition of the subject in grammatical or textual rather than in rhetorical terms, sheds a new light on the opposition between subjective and objective. The letter gives the impression by way of "Je pense" versus "On me pense" that the opposition is based on the presence or absence of a subject and is thus part of the debate pursued throughout the nineteenth century between subjective as "l'esprit conscient [conscious mind]" and objective as "ce qui appartient à l'objet de la pensée, au non-moi [what belongs to the object of thought, to the non-self]." (Schaeffer). "Je est un autre" breaks away from the traditional opposition by defining the *je* as a grammatical object. In doing so the formula eliminates the ambiguity that characterizes "On me pense" and most of the first letter. Both formulas are part of the same theory and thus closely related. However, the differences between the two are important and establish a sequential relationship between the two: "Je est un autre" follows "On me pense," and translates the discovery of otherness in grammatical terms. It thus constitutes a radical break with the preceding tradition, while "On me pense" is a reaction to the tradition, yet determined by its laws.

The opposition between subjective and objective, as between "Je pense" and "Je est un autre," is to be understood as between two different methods of reading. "Je pense" suggests a method of reading as "ergoter" and as following "la bonne ornière." "Je est un autre," as a rejection of *je* as the referent and as rhetorical figure for the speaking voice, proposes a method of reading as "arriver à l'inconnu par le dérèglement de *tous les sens*" (11. 36–37). The meaning of the *je* cannot be assumed anymore and it cannot be found by following a linear logic, but it has to be defined in relation to the context and its poetic inscription in the text takes many different forms. Even though the formula "Je est un autre" is an important part of this text, it still functions largely according to the formula "On me pense" as does the poem "Le Coeur supplicié." . . . The poetic application of "Je est un autre" as the theory of a textual subject and of a method of reading becomes evident in later texts.

The presence and the function of the *je* in this theory is largely a reaction against the *je* as *the* speaking subject; and this aspect requires further discussion. "Je est un autre" problematizes the subject in the form of the *je* which is the very sign or figure of the traditional subject as speaker of the text. The formula exposes this concept as a grammatical category, that is, as an impersonal pronoun, and it shows that this inherent figurative character is part of a particular poetic tradition. While the formula thus constitutes a break with that poetic tradition to which the letter refers as "subjective," that term is, in its turn, still applicable to the new poetry proposed by the formula. However, the term "subjective," just as the term *je*, takes on a very different meaning. Rather than defining a relationship between the text and its origin or its creator, "subjective" implies a relationship between the text and the new, impersonal subject. This can best be explained in relation to Felman's analysis of Rimbaud's sentence, "Il faut être absolument moderne." This sentence, as Felman contends, seems to present a general rule without any trace of a personal subject: "*il*, sujet neutre, grammatical, est un signe vide qui annonce simplement un verbe à la troisième personne [*il*, neutral, grammatical subject, is an empty sign that simply announces a verb at the third person]." (Felman). While the verbal structure is without an imprint of a personal subject, there is an implied personal subject in "moderne." The meaning of "moderne" as "qui est de *son* temps" and "qui est du temps de *celui qui parle*" ["who is of *his* time" and "who is of the time of *the one who speaks*"] (emphasis is mine) introduces the place of a speaking subject. It is only in relation to a subject that "être de son temps" fully makes sense. The word "moderne" is thus a perfect example of a term that makes sense in context only; it is what Jakobson calls a shifter.

To say "moderne" is thus also, and at the same time, to say *je:* " . . . l'appel à la modernité . . . dépend avant tout de la voix locutrice: qui dit *moderne* dit *je* [. . . the call to modernity . . . depends before all else upon the locutionary voice: who says *modern* says *I*]." Without the *je* as speaking voice, "moderne" remains an empty term. Both terms depend on the moment of speech to be fully defined. What Felman says about "modern" applies as well for *je:* " . . . le 'moderne,' de par sa définition, implique un rapport fatalement *subjectif* entre temps et langage, entre temps de l'énoncé et l'acte même de l'énonciation [. . . the 'modern,' by definition, implies an inevitably *subjective* relation between the time of the enunciation and the act of enunciation itself]." The term "subjectif" has the full meaning of relative, depending on a point of view, and on a particular moment; it is relative as opposed to fixed, determined and objective. It does not and cannot, as the word "fatalement" so dramatically expresses, constitute or refer to a subject as an objective entity ("ne renvoie pas à la réalité spatiale-temporelle 'objective' "), but creates meaning only at the moment of speech ("à la réalité du discours, à l'instance de l'énonciation").

The term "subjectif" as used by Felman in the analysis of the sentence "Il faut être absolument moderne" opposes objective and subjective in a new and different way which reverses the apparent opposition between these terms in the letter. "Subjective" expresses the nature of *je* and of key terms of the text (e.g., "moderne") as shifters, and the fact that the subject(ivity) can be expressed in terms other than *je.* The term "objective," then, refers to the traditional subject that posits itself as the fixed referent of the text. Defined in these terms the opposition between both terms is free of any trace of personal or psychological subject and object relationships. "Subjective" emerges instead as a definition that implies a new poetry and a new method of reading—textual subjectivity which depends on the grammatical function of the text rather than on inherent or traditional rhetorical ones.

The difference between the old and the new tradition and the old and the new subject is most clearly expressed by opposing "Je pense" to "Je est un autre" rather than to "On me pense," which serves as an intermediate phase in the discovery of the subject *je* as an other. The *je* is in both phrases in the initial position and in both is the grammatical subject, but the similarity ends there. In "Je pense," the *je* is the figure for the narrator and the speaking voice and as such it initiates and posits its own being. The *je*, as the comparison with Lamartine's description of the creative process has shown, is the origin as well as the locus of the poetic discourse. This power of the subject *je* over language and over its own discourse is radically disrupted by "Je est un autre" which eliminates the figural character of the *je* and thus removes its role as reference and origin of discourse. The *je* in "Je est un autre" is in every sense an impersonal, an *il*. However, it is important to notice that the *je* continues to be present. As the grammatical category of the first person, the *je* serves as the very *locus* of the problematization of the subject and . . . as the locus of the transformation of poetic form as well. The new poetic theory proposed by the letter remains linked to a *je*, even though the function and the nature of the *je* have changed. It no longer performs the dual function of origin *and* locus, but serves only as the locus of the new poetic discourse.

Jules Laforgue: The Ironic Equilibrium

Warren Ramsey

Today . . . the European Hamlet stares at millions of ghosts. But he is an intellectual Hamlet. He meditates on the life and death of truths. For phantoms he has all the subjects of our controversies; for regrets he has all our titles to glory; he bows under the weight of discoveries and learning, unable to renounce and unable to resume this limitless activity. He reflects on the boredom of recommencing the past, on the folly of always striving to be original. He wavers between one abyss and the other, for two dangers still threaten the world: order and disorder.

—PAUL VALÉRY

The first of January 1886, Laforgue, still reader to the Empress [Augusta of Germany] but growing more and more restless in that post, visited Elsinore. "The whole heartbreaking irony," he wrote to Kahn, "of being in these rockbound, windswept islands on the first day of '86 (the year when we'll check out, perhaps)." He erred by only a few months in his prediction, and he was entirely right and true to his own vein when he went on to say, "in any case we shall have spoken into the wind a respectable number of relatively immortal words."

He mentions, among other events of that wind-tormented day, the composition of some "literature." By this he did not mean "Hamlet, ou les conséquences de la piété filiale," though he was then in the process of writing that tale, and it was certainly on its account that he had ventured beyond the picture galleries of Copenhagen and exposed himself to the seven-hour boat trip between Kiel and Korsör. Nor did he mean his little sketch "A propos de Hamlet," which eventually appeared in the magazine *Le Symboliste.* He was referring to a poem that apparently surprised him on the journey, the spare and confessional "Avertissement," in which many of the emotions of "Hamlet" are brought to a poetic point. "Avertissement" is interesting throughout, with its nine unsettled syllables to the line and the colloquial slurrings by which that number is often obtained; with its incisive details—"My father, a timid man, hence hard, Died with a stiff and frowning air"; with its establishment of this Hamlet as a literary man.

> Alors, j'ai fait d'la littérature,
> Mais le Démon de la Vérité
> Sifflotait tout l'temps à mes côtés:
> "Pauvre! as-tu fini tes écritures? . . . "

So then I determined to be a writer,
But the Demon of Truth at my elbow
Had a way of murmuring soft and low,
"Well, lad, have you spoiled enough paper?"

The poem ends:

C'est pourquoi je vivotte, vivotte,
Bonne girouette aux trent'-six saisons,
Trop nombreux pour dire oui ou non . . .
—Jeunes gens! que je vous serv' d'Ilote!

And that is why I struggle and veer
Like a weathercock with the winds that blow,
Too various to say yes or no.
Young men! There's a moral here!

Of course, "Avertissement" might never have been written without Verlaine's poem on Gaspard Hauser. But whereas "Je suis venu, calme orphelin" was a sort of happy accident ("travail de manoeuvre," as Baudelaire might have called it), Laforgue realizes Baudelaire's desire that the poet be thoroughly aware of what he is doing. Undoubtedly Laforgue had read Corbière's autobiographical "Bâtard de créole et Breton," and perhaps taken suggestions from it. But if we compare Corbière's quatrains with Laforgue's we see that the latter are distinguished by more complexity, more salutary irony. "Avertissement" is conspicuously ironical. It was unexpected that a poet should make such deprecations with such intonations. And beneath the irony of expression lie profounder ironies of situation. This Hamlet is the first to notice the disparity between what he is able to do and all that ought to come out of what he should be doing. He is like Marlow in Conrad's *Lord Jim*, the observer wise to the world's ways, who cannot help the victim; and he is also like Jim, the actor who cannot act. He is the slayer and the slain. To present this kind of irony not many words are necessary, only enough to cover the given segment of the human situation. In *Des Fleurs de bonne volonté* and in *Derniers Vers*, Laforgue's last two collections, we have come a long way from the verbal self-indulgences of the young poet exulting in his instrument and in his newly discovered manner of using it—the "logopoetic" ironies of some of the lesser Complaintes.

Having looked at some of the themes and images that are treated straightforwardly in Laforgue's early work, we might do well to indicate what is meant by irony susceptible to "equilibrium." We must proceed warily, of course, for irony is like Syrinx, the nymph restored to life in the most purely delightful of Laforgue's tales—a figure that flees before the pursuer and vanishes when pressed, leaving only the syrinx, a somewhat pathetic reed instrument, in overanxious hands. We are grateful for every indirect, light-footed approach to the subject of irony. Ezra Pound wrote, out of his enthusiasm for Laforgue, that "the ironist is one who suggests that the reader should think," and "this process being unnatural to the majority of mankind, the way of the ironist is beset by snares and furze-bushes" (*Make It New*). This, while it does not define, illumines. So does another critic's description of Laforgue's irony as a magnesium spark struck out between the halves of a divided personality. Even a definition of irony as "the fragile inheritance of ancient French wisdom" has its tenuous element of truth. François Ruchon characterizes Laforgue's irony as an attitude of detachment from emotions, ideas, life itself. Irony does involve detachment. None of the pursuits of the evanescent essential quality of Laforgue's work has been quite fruitless.

The essence of ironic utterance is oppositeness. Not the expected, but the unexpected, and even the contrary of the expected thing, is said. Of course, unexpectedness in some degree is characteristic of most witty remarks, of wit in general. Laforgue's irony is always verging on the melancholy pleasantry, as when he writes in a love poem wordily entitled "Autre Complainte de Lord Pierrot,"

> Celle qui doit me mettre au courant de la Femme!
> Nous lui dirons d'abord, de mon air le moins froid:
> "La somme des angles d'un triangle, chère âme,
>   Est égale à deux droits."

> She who on womankind must be my mentor,
> We shall tell her at once, in my least chilling tones,
> "The angles of a triangle, my dear,
>   Equal, all told, two right ones."

The reader is surprised by such lines in a poem of putatively amorous intent. He is probably taken aback by the contrast, within the lines, between the theorem and the ceremonious "chère âme." " Celle qui doit me mettre au courant de la femme" is not exactly a Romantic formula for the beloved, and the plural "nous" is more in the style of the prefect of a French département than that of a proper poet. Within the title itself there is a collision between the terms "Lord" and "Pierrot." The surprise occasioned by these and other differences between the reader's expectation and the poet's statement is evidence of the irony. If the early I. A. Richards was right, if the differences between reader and poet are slight, if the poet is only a person somewhat more proficient than the reader at channeling his impulses, the poet himself must be astonished by the contrarieties proceeding from the divided "individual," by the chorus of mixed voices arising from that "compagnie un peu bien mêlée" within the self.

In matter-of-fact discourse, the understanding of the ironic remark as the opposite of the expected one is sufficient. But in the further reaches of connotative language it becomes clear that what is opposite on one level of signification may be apposite on another. In a poem a word or group of words may have more than one meaning. In the quatrain just quoted, for example, the remark that contrasts so sharply with the expected Romantic protestation is also, on another plane of meaning, in dead earnest: this geometrical theorem is one of the symbols of Laforgue's sense of fatality. The speaker of the poem is, among other things, telling the lady that what will be is bound to be. In poetry, oppositeness between expectation and fulfillment can exist only along with other relationships between the thing said and the thing anticipated. But the fact that this irony, this oppositeness, exists on one level is at once a revelation and a safeguard of the multifariousness of experience. The flash of irony illumines for an instant, if not the chaos, at least the complexity of the reader's mind—"the equilibrium of opposed impulses," as I. A. Richards calls it, existing there. That equilibrium, says Richards, "which we suspect to be the ground-plan of the most valuable aesthetic responses brings into play far more of our personality than is possible in experiences of a more defined emotion. We cease to be oriented in one definite direction; more facets of the mind are exposed" (*Principles of Literary Criticism*). A flash born of ironic utterance illuminates the complexity, the "equilibrium" within the reader's mind, which he then surmises to exist within the poet's. In any case, ironic poetry, a poetry of inclusion rather than exclusion, which puts several kinds of poetic force to work upon the page, satisfies that need for light on his own mind which the reader learns to expect from poetry.

A procedure of Laforgue's wit closely related to the ironic consists in the unexpected confrontation of ideas in mixed words. Sometimes the invention is as amusing as that of Heine's poor lottery agent, who bragged that the great Baron Rothschild had treated him as an equal, quite "familillionaire." In the "Complainte des nostalgies préhistoriques," the cry of someone "violupté à vif" is heard from the bushes. Elsewhere "volupté" is wedded to "nuptial" in "voluptial." We read of the "spleenuosités" instead of the "sinuosités" of cities. The prelude to the *Complaintes* has one of the most ambitious of these combinations:

> Mondes vivotant, vaguement étiquetés
> De livres, sous la céleste Eternullité.

> Worlds jogging along, identified obscurely
> By books, beneath the celestial Eternullity.

"Sangsuelles" is untranslatable, since there is no way of fitting "blood" into a word sounding exactly like "sensual."

> Mais, fausse soeur, fausse humaine, fausse mortelle,
> Nous t'écartèlerons de hontes sangsuelles . . .
> ("Complainte des voix sous le figuier bouddhique")

> But, false sister, false human, false mortal,
> We will draw and quarter you with disgrace *sangsuelles*. . . .

Nor can we do much with "crucifiger," where the word ends in the equivalent for "clot." But no reader familiar with Baudelaire's "Harmonie du soir," where "Le soleil s'est noyé dans son sang qui se fige," could fail to be struck by

> Soleil qui, saignant son quadrige,
> Cabre, s'y crucifige!

Not all of these combinations are instantly plausible. "Omnivers" and "omniversel," for instance, fall rather flat. But the passion for verbal invention, sometimes successful, sometimes not, was enduring. "Love me over a slow fire, inventory me, massacre me, massacrilege me," Elsa appeals to Lohengrin in the tale bearing that hero's name. And we read of "elephantastic" jokes in "The Two Pigeons," one of the last stories.

Like the examples of Laforgue's irony, these mixed words are unexpected. But whereas the ironic utterance depends on the degree of difference between what is expected and what is said, here success seems to be in proportion to the closeness with which the new invention fits an anticipated syllable-pattern, the nearness with which it misses a mark.

The Latinisms that Laforgue relished—"alacre" from "alacer," "albe" from "alba," "errabundes" from "errabundus"—are regularly pressed into ironic service, and clash with colloquial vocables in the same or proximate lines. Words lifted or derived from the rich and fine sixteenth-century language—"arbrillon" meaning "little tree," "pigrite" for "idleness"—are ironically erudite. Equally so are the scientific terms. We read in "Lohengrin": "The golden valves of the Tabernacle dehisce,"—the verb ordinarily being reserved for ripe pods that open to release their seeds. When Lohengrin appears in the nick of time to save Elsa from the executioners, the latter inquire, "Who is this fine knight advancing over the seas, melodious with gallantry, his forehead carunculated with fidelity?" "Carunculated," like "aptère" (wingless) and "fongosité," is a biological term. So is the adjective in the description of Pierrot, "hydrocephalic asparagus." Naturally, in poetry with strong popular ties, the colloquial word is likely to let down the lyric mood. "C'est le printemps qui s'amène," we read in the "Complainte des printemps," and the word "s'amener" is one with which a workingman might urge along his laggard wife on a Sunday outing. Puns such as "dies irraemissibles" and "s'in-Pan-filtrer" reflect the same satiric intent.

Rimbaud had already made free use of scientific and popular words in poetry. Romantic verse, especially Hugo's, had enriched the poetic vocabulary on a massive scale. The Decadents of the Left Bank coteries into which Laforgue had ventured as a very young man were addicted to neologisms, and the Symbolists who followed them coined rare and mysterious vocables for musical effect. It is, however, accurate to state that no young writer of the last hundred years has experimented with a more varied vocabulary than Laforgue's. In none has the "life of words" been more ebullient. No other nineteenth-century writer anticipates so clearly the intense word-consciousness, the linguistic innovations of Léon-Paul Fargue and James Joyce.

After the uneven *Complaintes,* where the verbal inventions are not uniformly happy, and where the arrangement of lines of varied length in novel stanza-forms is often arbitrary, Laforgue moved toward delicately balanced poetic discourse in two quite different collections. The first is the volume of forty-one poems, most of them brief, which appeared early in 1886, dedicated "to Gustave Kahn and also to the memory of little Salammbô, priestess of Tanit": *L'Imitation de Notre-Dame la Lune.*

The most limited tonally of Laforgue's collections, this is the one in which he most consistently attains that *suraigu* for which he strove during his years in Germany. The moon is exalted at the expense of the sun: the elaborate anti-solar invective opening the book shows a poetry of praise yielding to one of recrimination. The poet who now calls the sun "old trooper plastered all over with decorations and crosses," and who fills another line with miscellaneous abuse —"fop, pimp, ruffian, low adventurer"—had once invoked the "picturesque star," like any docile disciple of the Romantics, and had written the conventional sunset passages of *Stéphane Vassiliew.*

There have been a number of attempts to seize the symbolic significance of Our Lady the Moon. Jean Pérès remarked on the sterility, the death-like attributes of the planet in his friend's verse. François Ruchon finds the Laforguian moon to be "queen of Silence and of Sterility." Marc Eigeldinger sees in it a symbol of Buddhistic renunciation: "the moon is raised to the dignity of a symbol, representing a world empty of all intellectual content, escape into nirvana, aspiration to death in nothingness." This applies at least as well to Laforgue's aquarium symbol as to Our Lady of the Evenings. Associating the moon with an irrational Unconscious and pointing to its non-temporal connections, Anna Balakian considers it a symbol of dehumanization. But what Mallarmé's symbols illustrate very well, Laforgue's hardly exemplify. Our Lady the Moon should have a meaning that would not rob a notoriously human poet of his humanity. Of Kant's *History of Nature and Theory of the Heavens* Laforgue knew at least the passage in which the philosopher makes the fineness of bodies and faculties in his series of inhabited worlds depend on distance from the sun. For Laforgue as for Kant, the sun was a source of grossness; it is a short step to make the moon source and symbol of the opposite quality. Of course, Our Lady the Moon has a perfect right to change her meaning, and she does, standing, like any frequently recurring poetic image, for a number of things: for sterility, for evasion by suicide, for unrealizable Romantic aspiration. She also represents, frequently and simply, finesse.

Framed by half a dozen prefatory poems and a dozen concluding ones, twenty-three poems presenting Pierrot or expounding his ideas form the lunar center of the volume. For Pierrot is first and last the creature of Our

Lady the Moon, despite a family tree springing directly from the *commedia dell' arte.* Before the first Pierrot (or Pedrolino) there had been Pagliacco, who differed from other buffoons of Italian farce in that he wore no mask but had his face whitened with flour. He was a butt, an unsuccessful lover, a lackey. At the end of the sixteenth century came Pedrolino (or Piero). Slightly more complex than his predecessor, he rather resembled the butts in Molière's farces; he was a vainglorious coward, a cuckold on occasion, but not invariably victimized, and was endowed with a rough, comforting common sense. The give and take between comic characters was such, moreover, that for a while Piero lost his identity to his hated rival, Arlecchino, who had a fanciful twist to his humor; and Harlequin was the first Pierrot-type to appear in France, when companies of Italian players began to perform for Paris audiences about the beginning of the seventeenth century. He speedily became naturalized, assuming the sentiments along with the accents of popular songs, hesitating delicately between comic and pathetic, for Harlequin-Pierrot—and this is his distinguishing quality—lost his buffoon-like traits to take on the profounder nature of the clown.

Laforgue and some of his elders were devoted to eighteenth-century prints and paintings, among them Watteau's picture of Gilles, a close cousin of Pierrot. But it remained for an actor at the celebrated Théâtre des Funambules to give Pierrot the costume that we recognize in Laforgue's word-portraits, the black silk skullcap and ample blouse. At the Théâtre des Funambules, Pierrot earned the right to say things that people would tolerate from no one otherwise attired, because what he had to say was too much like their shamefast thoughts. Thanks to the genius of a mime named Deburau he became once for all a clown rather than a figure of farce. Baudelaire remarked that what distinguished the French from the English Pierrot was his melancholy, moonpale air.

French writers who flourished a decade or two before Laforgue thus had a familiar clown-like figure at hand, and they interpreted him according to individual lights. Gautier wrote enthusiastically about Deburau and composed *L'Esquisse d'un Pierrot posthume.* Théodore de Banville was concerned for the most part with lighter aspects of the figure; but he also wrote the "Saut du Tremplin," in which the circus clown prays for a loftier spring, a mightier bound, and vaults into eternity. And his *Promendade galante* has wraith-like figures surprisingly like those that Verlaine fitted into his better known *Fêtes galantes.* Verlaine, in a later sonnet, reflected a change that had been wrought in the character of Pierrot, while others, including Joris-Karl Huysmans and Léon Hennique, authors of that *Pierrot sceptique* which Laforgue urged upon Charles Henry in 1881, were exploiting Pierrot's appeal to theater audiences.

Once we have traced Pierrot's long lineage and glanced at treatments that attracted Laforgue's attention, we are struck more than ever by the originality of this young poet's clown, by the vibrancy of the life Laforgue is able to instill in a figure that another might have regarded as quite literally played out. He was without rival when he turned the venerable flour-faced creature into one subject to all the hesitations and interior debate characterizing an impressionable man of the time.

His Pierrots (for Laforgue often used the plural, thereby gaining a greater degree of ironic detachment) are white-faced, in obedience to tradition. In fact, everything about them is white except the black skullcap and the scarlet mouth.

> C'est, sur un cou qui, raide, émerge
> D'une fraise empesée *idem*
> Une face imberbe au cold-cream,
> Un air d'hydrocéphale asperge.
>
> Les yeux sont noyés de l'opium
> De l'indulgence universelle,
> La bouche clownesque ensorcèle
> Comme un singulier géranium.
>
> Bouche qui va du trou sans bonde
> Glacialement désopilé,
> Au transcendental en-allé
> Du souris vain de la Joconde.
>
> ("Pierrots")

You see a neck that, stiff, emerges
From a ruff starched tight as a drum,
A beardless face smeared with cold cream
Like a hydrocephalic asparagus.

The eyes are blurred with the opium
Of universal tolerance,
The scarlet clown-like mouth enchants
Like a singular geranium.

Mouth supremely flexible,
From the hole gaping glacially
To the transcendental fadeaway
Of Mona Lisa's futile smile.

When they dine as Laforgue dined in his Paris days, their food is white, or at least appropriate to pilgrims of the Absolute.

> Ils vont, se sustentant d'azur,
> Et parfois aussi de légumes,
> De riz plus blanc que leur costume,
> De mandarines et d'oeufs durs.
>
> Ils sont de la secte du Blême . . .
>
> ("Pierrots")

They dine upon the absolute
And occasionally on vegetables,
On rice bleached whiter than their dress,
On hard-boiled eggs and a little fruit.

They are of the pallid sect . . .

They have

Le coeur blanc tatoué
De sentences lunaires,

Their white hearts tattooed
With lunar sentences,

these "blancs parias," these "purs pierrots," for they are as white inside
as they are out, abstaining archly from such consolations as other men
seek. The Pierrots

. . . n'ont personne
Chez eux, qui les frictionne
D'un conjugal onguent.

. . . have nobody at home,
No one to rub them down
With conjugal balm.

But then they do not want anyone, or profess not to.

Of course, it is all a joke, given away in the fifth and sixth of this set
of "Pierrots" and in nearly all the "Locutions des Pierrots" that follow.
Laforgue really believes in this world and

Qu'il faut pas le traiter d'hôtel
Garni vers un plus immortel,
Car nous sommes faits l'un pour l'autre.

That it shouldn't be treated like a hotel
Toward some less mortal lodging place,
For we're by nature complementary.

Some of his finest verse is to be found in these poems in which the human
fragility pierces through the irony. And yet, paradoxically, Laforgue was
possessed by an ideal of intactness, of purity. It is, to say the least, ironical
that Pierrot, for centuries the disappointed or deceived lover, should become the disappointer and gay deceiver, the ostentatiously chilly creature
of the poems and the little play, *Pierrot fumiste*, who subjects his lawful
wife Columbine to the harshest kind of indignity before overwhelming her
with affection one night and then abandoning her utterly. We think of
Lohengrin, an extension of the Pierrot figure, hard pressed by Elsa on the
marriage bed, gripping his pillow so hard, so imploringly that it turns into

the swan that lifts him safely away from the Will to Live. We think of Andromeda and Salomé, furiously self-possessed in their different ways, and of Syrinx, who ran away. Never was there a Pierrot, or a gallery of Pierrotic characters, like this. Even Verlaine's Pierrot allowed Columbine to lead him by the nose. But if the Swiss Amiel, another witness to the hesitations of the late nineteenth-century intellectual, had written smilingly ironic verse instead of tormented diaries, it might have been something like Laforgue's.

If the voice of the Pierrots is sharper, keener than that of any speakers in Laforgue's early verse, that of his feminine interlocutor (the human one, not the Moon) is correspondingly graver and more ingenuous. Out of this calculated dramatic opposition the poet drew one of his best brief dialogues, ''Pierrot: on a des principes,'' compactly plotted, melodious, with two final quatrains abstaining nicely on the point of eloquence:

> Mais voici qu'un beau soir, infortunée à point,
> Elle meurt!—Oh! là, là; bon, changement de thème!
> On sait que tu dois ressusciter le troisième
>   Jour, sinon en personne, du moins
>
> Dans l'odeur, les verdures, les eaux des beaux mois!
> Et tu iras, levant encore bien plus de dupes
> Vers la Zaïmph de la Joconde, vers la Jupe!
>   Il se pourra même que j'en sois.

> But now suppose that some fine evening
> She died! aha! Now there's a change of tune!
> You will, needless to say, be resurrecting
>   On the third day, if not in person, then
>
> In summer's fragrance, in the leaves and waters.
> And you'll go on collecting innocents
> Toward Mona Lisa's veil, toward the skirt!
>   I do not say I won't be one of them.

This clear definition of the parties to the dialogue was accompanied by a general whetting of tools. The *Imitation* contains Laforgue's most polished verse. Getting away from the involved stanza divisions of the *Complaintes,* so often artificial and confusing, he makes excellent use of alexandrines rhyming in couplets, of octosyllables in quatrains with the usual *abab* or *abba* schemes, and writes some of the most vigorous decasyllables since the sixteenth century.

> Voilà le Néant dans sa pâle gangue,
> Voilà notre Hostie et sa Sainte-Table,
> Le seul bras d'ami par l'Inconnaissable,
> Le seul mot solvable en nos folles langues!

Au delà des cris choisis des époques,
Au delà des sens, des larmes, des vierges,
Voilà quel astre indiscutable émerge,
Voilà l'immortel et seul soliloque!

There is the ore of Nothing unrefined,
There is our sacrament and its holy board,
The only arm outstretched through the Unknown,
In our mad tongues the single solvent word.

Beyond the senses, beyond tears and virgins,
Beyond the chosen utterances of history,
There the unchallengeable star emerges,
There the immortal lone soliloquy.

The metaphors stand for the moon in its whiteness; and the originality of three of them, together with the ironic "solvable" and "discutable," lends the quality of Laforgue's later verse to lines possessing the rhythmic vitality of his earlier. Such metrical and rhythmical experimentation as there is succeeds. The first of the "Locutions des Pierrots" has an unprecedented combination of ten- and seven-syllable lines. There is an interesting pattern of sevens and threes in "Stérilités." The tenth of the "Locutions" is in those five-syllable lines that have more movement than any other verse in French; and the fourteenth poem of the same group, which by a certain heartiness of manner recalls Corbière, also has five-syllable lines. "Jeux" is a skillful exercise in nines. Altogether, the uneven, the *impair* recommended by Verlaine, receives its share of attention.

As far as rhyming is concerned, Laforgue is not quite so perversely intent as before on upsetting the Malherbian applecart. But the *rimes riches* are decidedly in the minority (about one in seven), and often these rhymes are far from "unexpected," as sound tradition prescribed, but associate too obviously similar words. No attempt is made to satisfy the capricious rules "for the eye": singulars rhyme regularly with plurals. In the absence of rhyme, words are linked by assonance or by similar consonants. What might have been rich or sufficient rhymes or true assonances are often rendered "false" by differing vowel quality.

From Laforgue's production up to and including *L'Imitation* we might conclude that he wrote verse either appreciably less free than that of the Decadents or perceptibly more so; he is not at ease with a Verlainian technique of guarded liberties. He can write strong-membered Parnassian alexandrines having neither more nor less musical timbre than the traditional French measure usually has in capable hands. It is as though he sometimes consented that his verse should sing, and sing bravely, using the firmest accentual patterns the language afforded. This means, fundamentally, the binary alexandrine:

Sache que les Pierrots, phalènes des dolmens
Et des nymphéas blancs des lacs où dort Gomorrhe,

> Et tous les bienheureux qui pâturent l'Eden
> Toujours printanier des renoncements,—t'abhorrent.

It means, incidentally, the ringing decasyllables of "Au Large," with their pauses after the fourth syllable. In this lyrical verse there are no innovations to speak of. Meanwhile the other and principal current, the conversational monologue, is straining the dikes and dams of traditional versification.

In the third and fourth lines of "Pierrot: on a des principes" cited above, for instance, the overflow of "jour" is awkward. Line three was crying to be written thus:

> On sait que tu dois ressusciter le troisième jour

except that the poet would then have had a line of at least fourteen syllables, fifteen if "siè" were counted as two, as it should have been all the time.

L'Imitation offers many examples of ill-poised conventional measures. The most striking examples of lines dragging their anchors, however, are to be found in *Des Fleurs de bonne volonté*, a collection on which Laforgue worked at intervals between 1883 and 1886:

> Un Soir, je crus en Moi! J'en faillis me fiancer!
> Est-ce possible . . . Où donc tout ça est-il passé! . . .
> Chez moi, c'est Galathée aveuglant Pygmalion!
> Ah! faudrait modifier cette situation. . . .

Laforgue had good reasons to abandon these lines except as raw material for the fine passage in *Dernier Vers:*

> Bref, j'allais me donner d'un "Je vous aime"
> Quand je m'avisai non sans peine
> Que d'abord je ne me possédais pas bien moi-même.
>
> (Mon Moi, c'est Galathée aveuglant Pygmalion!
> Impossible de modifier cette situation.)

The earlier lines are manageable as alexandrines only by difficult synaereses, and even so are unconscionably broken up. The same ideas and images find inevitable form in five verses of uneven length. The following passage is likewise subject to transformation:

> Oh! qu'une, d'Elle-même, un beau soir, sût venir,
> Ne voyant que boire à Mes Lèvres! ou mourir . . .
>
> Je m'enlève rien que d'y penser! Quel baptême
> De gloire intrinsèque, attirer un "Je vous aime"!
>
> L'attirer à travers la société, de loin,
> Comme l'aimant la foudre; un', deux! ni plus, ni moins.
>
> Je t'aime! comprend-on? Pour moi tu n'es pas comme
> Les autres; jusqu'ici c'etait des messieurs, l'Homme . . .

This becomes:

> Oh! qu'une, d'Elle-même, un beau soir, sût venir
> Ne voyant plus que boire à mes lèvres, ou mourir! . . .

> Oh! Baptême!
> Oh! baptême de ma Raison d'être!
> Faire naître un "Je t'aime!"
> Et qu'il vienne à travers les hommes et les dieux,
> Sous ma fenêtre,
> Baissant les yeux!

> Qu'il vienne, comme à l'aimant la foudre,
> Et dans mon ciel d'orage qui craque et qui s'ouvre . . .

The ejaculations obviously gain vividness with brevity, and the contrasting sixth line has its hint of grandeur, albeit ironic. Why should not the ideas, "under my windows" and "lowering his eyes," be expressed in four syllables each?

Sometimes the poet deliberately adds a word that disrupts the neat rhythmic pattern of an earlier effort:

> Nous nous aimions comme deux fous;
> On s'est quittés sans en parler.
> (Un spleen me tenait exilé
> Et ce spleen me venait de tout.)

remains the same except for the loss of the 's' on 'quittés' and the last line, which becomes

> Et ce spleen me venait de tout. Bon.

These are examples of the free verse that Laforgue began to compose early in 1886—ten poems published in *La Vogue* between August and December of that year, which his editors eventually assembled in the volume they called *Derniers Vers*. There have been numerous attempts to say what free verse is; there have even been some denials that it ever was, on the not wholly unreasonable grounds that verse is never free but always has its own laws. However, to deny the existence of free verse is to assume a superbly paradoxical, unhistorical position. For there is no doubt whatever that Rimbaud included in his *Illuminations* two poems free as poetry had never been before; that Gustave Kahn theorized at length on the nature of free verse and did what he could toward providing examples to fit his theories; that Jules Laforgue theorized very little but wrote a substantial volume of a kind of verse that represents a logical final step in the evolution of nineteenth-century poetry. Critics of the time perceived that a new form had developed and felt called upon to define it. "True free verse," said Rémy de Gourmont, "is conceived as such, that is to say as a fragment designed on the model of its emotive idea and no longer determined by the law of number" (*Esthetique de la langue française*). A line of free verse is ordinarily a unit unto itself, obedient to a law of its own, what Gourmont called its "emotive idea." There is no overflow; the line finds its own length, longer or shorter, and a stanza usually forms a sentence.

The question of who first used it (after Rimbaud) has been much vexed, and none too profitably. One claimant for the honor was a certain Marie Krysinska, familiarly known in literary circles of the time as "The Queen of Poland." After reading "L'Oiseau crucifié," which verges on *vers libre*, Laforgue commented [in a letter], "Marie Krysinska does have an original artistic sensibility, but one pretty well submerged in fashionable rhetoric." The judgment is a fair one and could be applied to most other free versifiers writing in France during the nineteenth century, Rimbaud and Laforgue excepted. However fine the artistic sensibilities of the other *vers-libristes*, however praiseworthy their attempts to parcel the poem into portions corresponding to the broken lines of Impressionist painting, their gifts were not up to their aspirations. Gustave Kahn, theorist of the movement, prescribed better than he was able to perform. As Jules Supervielle, himself a *vers-libriste* at one time, has written: "There has been much conjecture as to whether Laforgue or Gustave Kahn was the first to use free verse in France. For me the question does not arise. I don't know whether Kahn is a poet so far as other people are concerned; for me he is not. Consequently his verse does not interest me, it is non-existent, whereas Laforgue is always with us, a poet even when he errs." Rimbaud's efforts in this direction having consisted of two brief poems only, Laforgue is preeminently the poet of free verse in France during the nineteenth century, and it is of particular interest to the American reader that his earliest ventures were translations from Walt Whitman.

In this as in many other domains, Laforgue was *avant-gardiste.* No one of consequence has translated Whitman into French. The enthusiasm of André Gide and the Naturist poets for *Leaves of Grass* was all to come; even in Germany, where fervor for the American poet was one day to approach the proportions of a cult, he was known only to the few.

One experiences a certain mild surprise, coming upon Laforgue's translations in that highly artistic periodical which was the first *Vogue.* Walt seems to be keeping queer company with the last of the Decadents, the first of the Symbolists, and the barbaric yawp of several "Inscriptions" and "A Woman Waits for Me" somehow jars with the usual tone of the retiring reader to the Empress of Germany.

> It is I, you women, I make my way,
> I am stern, acrid, large, undissuadable, but I love you,
> I do not hurt you any more than is necessary for you,
> I pour the stuff to start sons and daughters fit for these
>   States,
>   I press with slow rude muscle . . .

This Laforgue translates manfully:

> C'est moi, femme, je vois mon chemin;
> Je suis austère, âpre, immense, inébranlable, mais je t'aime;
> Allons, je ne te blesse pas plus qu'il ne faut,
> Je verse l'essence qui engendrera des garçons et des filles
>   dignes
>   de ces Etats-Unis; j'y vais d'un muscle rude et
>   attentionné.

The differences between the two poets, however, are not as great as they appear at first. Whitman was a Byronic dandy, although an inverted one. Laforgue was a Baudelairian dandy. Whitman saw in nature a vague automatic impulse resembling the Hartmannian Unconscious. And Whitman's verse is as strongly impregnated throughout by the ideas of nineteenth-century science as Laforgue's was at the beginning. Whitman also wrote about the nebular hypothesis and universal evolution, about planets and suns biologically conceived. Thus, in one of the poems that Laforgue translated:

> Star crucified—by traitors sold,
> Star panting o'er a land of death, heroic land . . .
>
> Sure as the ship of all, the Earth itself,
> Product of deathly fire and turbulent chaos,
> Forth from its spasms of fury and its poisons . . .

> Etoile crucifiée, vendue, par des traîtres,
> Etoile palpitante sur un pays de mort, héroïque pays . . .
>
> Aussi sûrement que le vaisseau de tout, la Terre elle-même,
> Produit d'un incendie de mort et du tumultueux chaos,
> Se dégageant de ses spasmes de rage et de ses déjections . . .

The lines of this free verse are rhythmic units tending to compose a stanza-sentence:

> O star of France,
> The brightness of thy hope and strength and fame,
> Like some proud ship that led the fleet so long,
> Beseems today a wreck driven by the gale, a mastless hulk,
> And 'mid its teeming maddened half-drowned crowds,
> Nor helm nor helmsman.

> O Etoile de France,
> Le rayonnement de ta foi, de ta puissance, de ta gloire,
> Comme quelque orgueilleux vaisseau qui si longtemps mena
>   toute l'escadre,

> Tu es aujourd'hui, désastre poussé par la tourmente, une
>   carcasse démâtée;
> Et au milieu de ton équipage affolé, demi-submergé,
> Ni timon, ni timonier.

At critical points these rhythms are strengthened both by alliteration and by assonance, though there is less need for either in English than in French:

> O star! O ship of France, beat back and baffled long!
> Bear up O smitten orb! O ship continue on . . .

Words are reiterated at points of different stress in the rhythmic units:

> Star crucified—by traitors sold,
> Star panting o'er a land of death, heroic land,
> Strange, passionate, mocking, frivolous land.

Here, in short, are all the main characteristics of free verse. It would be unprofitable to argue that Laforgue learned to write *vers libre* from Whitman. Suffice it to say that at a critical stage in his development as a poet he was studying Whitman with the translator's concentrated attention.

The *Derniers Vers* have a rough kind of plot. "L'Hiver qui vient," the opening section, treats autumn for the most part in pastoral terms but has one stanza full of urban images. The motif of the horn call makes its appearance, preparing the next section, "Le Mystère des trois cors," a little allegory on the fortunes of introverts and extroverts. Poems III and IV, both entitled "Dimanches," work out Laforguian themes in a kind of Sunday-imagery now familiar. Singly or in groups the young ladies go off to church, while the "Polar Bear," the "Lord High Chancellor of Analysis," observes them from afar. "Pétition," poem V, is a meditation on young girls, how they are

> Jamais franches,
> Ou le poing sur la hanche . . .

and a firm statement of opinion on how they ought to be—comradely—somewhat in the fashion of Whitman's Woman who Waits. In poem VI, "Simple Agonie," we seem to have weathered "les années mortes," the dying and dead part of the year, "et revoici les sympathies de mai." A phrase of this sixth poem introduces the next section, "Solo de lune," in which the speaker is shown taking a long, heart-rending journey away from the beloved. "Légende," poem VIII, is a dream-like respite. For after these "clots of memories," after strangely poignant evocation of loss,

> Ah! ce n'est plus l'automne, alors,
> Ce n'est plus l'exil.
> C'est la douceur des légendes, de l'âge d'or,
> Des légendes des Antigones,
> Douceur qui fait qu'on se demande:
> "Quand donc cela se passait-il?"

> Ah! it is no longer autumn then,
> Nor any longer exile.
> Rather a legendary mildness, an age of gold
> Befitting legends of Antigones,
> Such gentleness as makes one ask,
> "When did all this come to pass?"

After two more dreamlike interludes (or only one, for sections IX and X were published by the author as one poem, "Les Amours," later divided by the editors) in a different vein—ironic visions of love satisfied—autumn closes down again in the final sections:

> Noire bise, averse glapissante,
> Et fleuve noir, et maisons closes,
> Et quartiers sinistres comme des Morgues,
> Et l'Attardé qui à la remorque traîne
> Toute la misère du coeur et des choses,
> Et la souillure des innocentes qui traînent,
> Et crie à l'averse. "Oh? arrose, arrose
> Mon coeur si brûlant, ma chair si intéressante!"

> Bitter blast and howling rain,
> Somber river, and houses shut,
> And quarters sinister as morgues,
> And the belated Soul who drags behind him
> His heart's misery and all creation's,
> And the defilement of strayed innocents,
> Who cries to the torrent, "Oh, assuage, refresh
> My burning heart, my so exceptional flesh!"

The concluding lines are a fair example of the poet's latest manner of turning upon himself, averting the peril of overstatement.

Structure has seldom been as flexibly bent to materials. Thus, among many instances, these lines from the opening section:

> Soleils plénipotentiaires des travaux en blonds Pactoles
> Des spectacles agricoles,
> Où êtes-vous ensevelis?

> Plenipotentiary suns of labors in gold-bearing torrents
> Of agricultural landscapes,
> Where have you vanished to?

The broad burst of sixteen syllables stands for the energy of the summer sun and the works carried on beneath it; this energy dwindles visibly to the seven ironic syllables of the second line and the query of the third. Immediately afterward the "picturesque star" of the poet's early writings—

a star that is still personified—is treated offhandedly in lines tapering off a syllable at a time from the thirteen of the first:

> Ce soir un soleil fichu gît au haut du coteau,
> Gît sur le flanc, dans les genêts, sur son manteau.
> Un soleil blanc comme un crachat d'estaminet
> Sur une litière de jaunes genêts . . .

Again the diminution is communicated by the shape of the verses. We are better able to see the sun fading, declining on the hilltop, because the poet presents the scene in verses of thirteen, twelve, twelve, and eleven syllables. Thirteen- and eleven-syllable lines are especially hard to bring off because they are so likely to give the effect of alexandrines that have missed fire. Poetic success has come with the surmounting of two obstacles; and indeed the variants of these later poems, which Dujardin and Fénéon included in their edition of 1890, show the poet overcoming many and diverse difficulties. He rejected, picked, chose, happened on a more vivid word by the way and finally fitted it into the rhythmic frame that had first occurred to him, almost as though he had not been a poet writing by direct dictation of the Unconscious. Here, for instance, are the stages of one of the concluding lines of "Avertissement," the poem conceived at Elsinore, in which the poet sees his Hamletic hesitations in the guise of a weathercock's waverings:

> Bonne girouette aux quatre saisons
>
> Ivre girouette aux quatre saisons
>
> Bonne girouette aux quatre saisons
>
> Bonne girouette aux trent' six saisons
>
> Girouette peinte aux trent' six saisons
>
> Bonne girouette aux trent'-six saisons

In the extraordinarily plastic verse of the *Derniers Vers* the major Laforguian themes reappear, assuming the forms most peculiarly their own. Poems on autumn open and close a cycle; and with the death of the year is associated the death of the individual. Most often the death implied is tubercular. In "Le Mystère des trois cors," on the other hand, it is by suicide. Then there are the less radical forms of denial of life: the sense of separation from society, the sense of incapacity for life in society, the theme of exile.

These are the great Romantic subjects with which Laforgue deals in verse that contrives never to be portentous, since the theme is nothing without its embodiment. The expansive description of a season is purposely made overexpansive, grandiose, and we are shortly told of some quotidian consequence for human beings. Death, by whatever cause, is suggested in the barest of terms. The appreciation of the difference between Shaun the

Postman and Shem the Penman, Fortinbras and Hamlet, extrovert and introvert, is profound, but is expressed by *ironic* manipulation of an image dear to the Romantic mind, the call of the hunting horn. And the life from which the speaker of these poems—a prolongation of Pierrot and an anticipation of Hamlet—sees himself cut off is most often represented by the girls' boarding school, the detachment being felt with certain reserves. "Forever astonished" and astonishing, tempestuous, continually bursting free of the immediate design to which their author would subordinate them, the *jeunes filles* of Laforgue are the most vivid in French literature until we come to those of Jean Giraudoux. Without neglecting the Balzacian Woman of Thirty—an "aging sinner" appears in both "Légende" and "Solo de lune"—Laforgue succeeds in turning attention to a woman of half that age.

The life of the world from which the poet sees himself divided finds other symbols, and memorable ones, including the casinos of "Légende." But Laforgue, who had pointed so knowingly to the spoiled children in Baudelaire and Corbière, understands perfectly well that his exile is self-inflicted.

> Je suis la Gondole enfant chérie
> Qui arrive à la fin de la fête,
> Par je ne sais quoi, par bouderie,
> (Un soir trop beau me monte à la tête!)
>
> Me voici déjà près de la digue;
> Mais la foule sotte et pavoisée,
> Ah! n'accourt pas à l'Enfant Prodigue!
> Et danse, sans perdre une fusée . . .
>
> Ah! c'est comme ça, femmes volages!
> C'est bien. Je m'exile en ma gondole
> (Si frêle!) aux mouettes, aux orages,
> Vers les malheurs qu'on voit au Pôle!
>
> —Et puis, j'attends sous une arche noire . . .
> Mais nul ne vient; les lampions s'éteignent;
> Et je maudis la nuit et la gloire!
> Et ce coeur qui veut qu'on me dédaigne!

> I am the favorite child canoe
> That arrives toward the party's end,
> I couldn't say why, but sullenly,
> (Too fine an evening goes to my head!)
>
> Here I am almost at the water-wall,
> But the foolish crowd in its finery
> Doesn't rush out to welcome the Prodigal
> And dances on giddily.

So that's the way of it, flighty females!
All right, I'll just take my frail vessel
(My fragile canoe!) toward the gulls and the gales
And the perils that lurk at the Pole.

Then I pause beneath a somber archway . . .
But nobody comes. The lanterns are dead.
And I execrate nighttime and glory,
And this heart that desires to be scorned!

The last line was a second or third thought. It had been:

Et tout ce qui fait qu'on me dédaigne!

Mon coeur qui veut qu'on me dédaigne!

Ce coeur qui veut qu'on me dédaigne!

As it stands it is probably the weightiest one-line demonstration of Laforgue's ability to see around his own position, that clairvoyance that made him the greatest of French Romantic ironists.

Among the unpublished papers of Laforgue is the following note, inspired no doubt by his own and his brother's art studies: "In the great glassed-in hall of ancient art, especially about midday, when he was alone sketching among the white and calm statues. The room was deserted. It was the great silence of noon. There were echoes of footsteps on the tiles as the pupils of the school went to lunch—But he stayed on, forgetting his hunger—A near-by bell (St.-Sulpice or St.-Germain-des-Prés) tolled, adding a further note of solemnity to the vast noonday calm under the full daylight falling from above, on the tranquillity of those white and motionless statues. Solemn thoughts came to him. He was in an ideal life far from the narrow and muddy streets of the clamorous left bank, far from garrets, far from greasy pub-keepers, tailors, tradesmen, he was there transported to other ages, far from our feverish democracy, delighting in a calm and noble life.— The bourgeois who stare you down in the street, casting glances at your shoes—a Jack of poverty on his arrival in Paris—dinners at fifty centimes— shoes down at heel—his health threatened—theadbare cuffs from which one snips the threads." At the end of the passage, in the handwriting of a later period, is the comment: "Hello, dear Jack! Still your little cosmic cares?"

There could be no more graphic demonstration of the difference between the Laforgue of 1880 and the writer of 1885–6, when the bulk of the *Moralités légendaires* were composed. And we do not approach the later man and his works without certain misgivings. Was there something to the opinion of that doughty defender of good prose, H. L. Mencken, that no one can possess a prose style before the age of thirty? So much mysterious tissue, incarnate experience, enters into authentic prose. Its absence is less palpable so long as objectives are limited, models evident, as in the passage just quoted; it is only too apparent in a work such as the earliest *Moralité*,

"Le Miracle des roses." The tales, however, are progressively better. "Lohengrin" and "Salomé," dating from 1885, are inferior to "Hamlet," finished in 1886. "Persée et Andromède" and "Pan et la Syrinx," the last written of these works, prove that Mencken, who applied quantitative measurements to the wrong kind of subject matter, was mistaken.

Half-realistic, "Le Miracle des roses" is remarkable for its broadsides against Baden-Baden, that resort of valetudinarians and vacationers, and for its record of a bullfight witnessed at San Sebastian in 1883. There is a gossamer veil of plot. Ruth, a victim of advanced tuberculosis, spreads an even more baneful Romantic affliction about her: her path is strewn with suicides, from the Paris art amateur and the *presidente* of the bullfight to a young man of the Corpus Christi procession who works the final wry miracle permitting her to see roses rather than blood. Laforgue conveys the impression that Ruth is averse to none of the gore, or to the disembowelment of the horses either. Sound observations reminiscent of Mérimée and Maupassant are couched in an exasperatingly parenthetical style: "Patrick s'assied au chevet de sa soeur: il tient son mouchoir diaphane comme un parfum, sa bonbonnière de cachou à l'orange, son éventail (un éventail, ô ironie et triste caprice de la dernière heure!) son flacon de musc naturel (le dernier réconfort des mourants). Such a sentence merely shows that the style of *Stéphane Vassiliew* has disintegrated, and that nothing has arisen in its place.

"Lohengrin, fils de Parsifal" has good touches: Elsa's apparent indifference to everything but her own image in a mirror as she awaits the knight whose defection would bring about her blinding; the transformation of the lordly executioners into shuffling yokels when Lohengrin flies in on his swan ("How rich and refined his family must be! Oh! in what magic groves must they be taking ices, at this very hour!"). There are more dated details, such as Lohengrin's introduction of himself to the dazzled company: "No, I am not Endymion. I come directly from the Holy Grail. I am Lohengrin, Knight Errant, the lily of future crusades for the emancipation of woman. In the meantime, however, I was simply too bored in my father's offices (I am a trifle hypochondriac by nature)." The suspense in the nuptial villa is well managed, as Elsa impatiently invites the objectification of the Unconscious and Lohengrin resists until his swan-pillow bears him away, as he says, "toward the Holy Grail where my father Parsifal is preparing a blueprint for the redemption of our little sister, so human and so down to earth . . . toward those glacier mirrors that no young girl will ever tarnish with her breath in order to trace her name and the date." The dialogue of this piece is properly pointed, and the Laforguian word-mine is by this time in full production, turning out such high-grade ore as Elsa's "Massacrilege me!" and her inquiry, "Child, child, are you familiar with the voluptial rites?" A prose prolongation of themes and images of *L'Imitation de Notre-Dame la Lune*, "Lohengrin" is weakened by a certain fundamental lack of control.

The satire of "Salomé" is too obvious. This is the only Moralité that would justify an uncharitable description of the collection as the "Parodies artificielles." Style, characters, major and minor episodes of Flaubert's "Hérodias" are aped in a manner verging dangerously on that of the class yearbook. Here, for instance, in a style meant to suggest Flaubert's packed sentences, is Laforgue's notion of an old Palestinian pleasantry: "The followers of the Northern Princes could be heard laughing hugely, in the court where the gutters converged, laughing without understanding one another, playing at quoits, swapping tobaccos. The Tetrarch's followers were showing their foreign colleagues how white elephants prefer to be curried. 'But back home we don't have any white elephants,' the visitors gave to understand. And they saw these stablemen cross themselves, as though to conjure impious thoughts."

A clever sophomore turns "Hérodias" upside down, changing Herod Antipas to Emeraude-Archetypas of the Esoteric White Isles, a weary aesthete; Vitellius to an emissary of the Prussian militarized state; John the Baptist to a deported socialist agitator, his spectacles tied up with bits of string; Salomé into yet another etiolated dilettante who exacts John's head after having trifled with his affections. It is all quite witty and it is all, considering the model, a little disappointing. Yet the most adverse critics of Laforgue could hardly deny the interest of the elements held in suspension by this none too limpid prose. At the fatal feast are the clowns of the Idea, the Will, and the Unconscious, characterizing clearly if summarily the Absolute according to the Hegelian, Schopenhauerian, and Hartmannian philosophies: "Idea chattered about everything, Will knocked his head against the scenery, and Unconscious made the large mysterious gestures of someone who knows more than he is yet permitted to reveal. This trinity had, moreover, a single refrain:

> O promised land
> Of utter void!
>
> O void, a pox
> On all your books . . ."
>
> O Chanaan
> Du bon Néant!
>
> Néant, la Mecque
> Des bibliothèques . . .

This comes from *L'Imitation de Notre-Dame la Lune.* After the chorus of the clowns, Salomé, dressed in jonquil yellow chiffon with black dots, chants to the music of her little black lyre an ample discourse on the Unconscious. Here, too, inserted willy-nilly in the tale is a revised version of the prose poem "L'Aquarium," Laforgue's most sustained sequence of imagery treating of the unconscious mind. Here is satire on authority in the shape of those Princes of the North who have ejected Iaokanaan from their territories, who gloat over him in his dungeon. One of them cannot refrain from observing: "Ah ha! There you are, ideologist, scribbler, ex-conscript, bastard of Jean-Jacques Rousseau. So this is where you came to get yourself hanged, you broken-down pamphleteer, you! And how nice your un-washed top-piece is going to look in some guillotine basket." It appears that the revolution Iaokanaan had engineered in the North has failed, and the organizer, who for a moment imagined that this was a conciliatory mission sent by the royal family, dies thoroughly disillusioned. Like other community leaders of the period, the Princes of the North are Darwinians, convinced positivists, meliorists:

> Et tout honnête homme, d'ailleurs, professe
> Le perfectionnement de l'Espèce.

> Every gentleman, of course, believes
> In the perfecting of the species.

If "Salomé" is a heterogeneous effort, "Persée et Andromède" is as skillfully unified as so original a work could be. From the beginning we are struck by the symbolic value of the sea. Young, red-haired, nubile, Andromeda is surrounded, along with her guardian dragon, by a sea as profoundly monotonous as her life, a sea that is, in fact, the objective equivalent for a life. When, unspeakably bored and restless, she rushes out into the unfurling waves, she is returing to the mother and matrix of her being. The amiable dragon, who before the end of the story manages to identify himself with most of the dragons of antiquity, cherishes Andromeda with unrequited affection, until the day when a daintily elegant Perseus wings in on his hippogriff. Andromeda all but goes off with him instanter. But the dragon shows a little fight, and is not turned to stone because the Gorgon, at the critical moment, closes her eyes: "The good Gorgon recognized our Monster. She recalled that rich and spacious time when she and her two sisters lived next door to this Dragon, at that time keeper of the Garden of the Hesperides, the marvelous Garden of the Hesperides located in the neighborhood of the Columns of Hercules. No, no, a thousand times no, she would not petrify her old friend!" Enraged because of his ill success and Andromeda's first skeptical smile, Perseus runs the dragon through, mutilating him unnecessarily—so much so that Andromeda realizes that he had been a fairly good dragon after all, had gratified all her caprices (within the limits of his income, of course), col-lecting and polishing a whole heap of precious stones for her sake. In the pinch she refuses to go off with the interloper, who flies away indignant and abusive. Andromeda weeps over her slain guardian. "She recalls that he had been a good friend to her, an accomplished gentleman, an indus-trious scholar, an eloquent poet. And her little heart bursts with sobbing." She even asks, in words that sound very much like Philoctetes on Lemnos, "With what lamentations can I now make these stony shores resound?" Then, after opening one eye and telling his story, the Monster is trans-formed into a personable young man. "Leaning against the entrance of the cave, his human skin inundated with the enchantment of moonlight, he speaks of the future."

Penetrating thus deeply toward the mythical foundations, appropriating as much as he needed of the story of Perseus and Andromeda to tell the story of Beauty and the Beast (the Monster had hinted to his uncomprehending ward that he could not be changed into himself until she loved him, that he was imprisoned within a vicious circle), Laforgue is at his best and his most rewardingly complex. "Pan et la Syrinx" is an equally graceful story, dealing with love and the artist's self-discovery in loss; but it does not alter the main lines of the myth. There is no fusion of legends as in "Persée," nor is the prose quite so prophetic. As unmistakably as the rhythms of Rimbaud's *Illuminations,* of Lautréamont's *Chants de Maldoror,* cadences of "Persée et Andromède" are echoed by later writers. "And then there came those strange Argonauts, whose likes we shall not see again," the dragon reminisces. "Splendid epochs! Jason was their leader, Hercules followed, and his friend Theseus, and Orpheus who undertook to charm me with his lyre (and who was later to come to such a tragic end!) and also the twins: Castor, tamer of horses, and Pollux, clever at fisticuffs. Vanished epochs! Oh, their bivouacs, and the fires they kindled in the evenings!" Some of the grandeur and none of the bourdon of Saint-John Perse are in these lines. Glimmering throughout is the fantasy, the irony of the greatest of Fargue, the best of Supervielle. And more important even than intonations so distinct that they could not but be caught and repeated is the step taken beyond realism, toward mythic structure.

The importance of the *Moralités légendaires* is due partly to their chronological place. Laforgue's inventive power, increasing steadily throughout his career, found its freest play in his last-written works. In his verse, too, he had been in search of the fundamental though changeful figure. His hero, "un Philippe de Champaigne / Mais né Pierrot," belonged to "L'école des cromlechs / Et des tuyaux d'usine," and fished in troubled waters for her who is at once "Eve, Joconde, et Dalilla." The Romantic pair escaped together toward an isle that was simultaneously Eden, the Pole, and Eldorado. The evolution of a passage in *Derniers Vers* shows Laforgue accumulating fables. He begins by thinking of "un cimetière plein d'Antigones," adds a reference to a gravedigger suggesting *Hamlet,* then a mention of Philomela, and finally the words "Alas, poor Yorick!" to clinch matters. He ends with:

> C'est l'automne, l'automne, l'automne,
> Le grand vent et toute sa séquelle
> De représailles! Et de musiques! . . .
> Rideaux tirés, clôture annuelle,
> Chute des feuilles, des Antigones, des Philomèles:
> Mon fossoyeur, *Alas poor Yorick!*
> Les remue à la pelle! . . .

> Now it is autumn, autumn, autumn,
> The wind in earnest and all its crew
> Of reprisals and concertos! . . .
> Drawn curtains, yearly closing-down,
> Fall of leaves, Antigones, and Philomelas:
> My gravedigger, *Alas poor Yorick!*
> Turns them by shovelsful!

Figures from three tragedies combine with the falling leaves, high wind, drawn curtains, to yield one universal, the falling away of everything. It is primarily the last written of the prose tales, however, which convince us that Laforgue would, time allowing, have employed on a larger scale a dramatic technique based on the fluid shift of personage into related dramatic personage: this Monster who is at once nearly all the dragons of antiquity and the Beast transformed by Beauty's liberating love; this Andromeda who is also Beauty, who comforts and resurrects—the female principle.

"Hamlet, ou les suites de la piété filiale" cannot be discussed in quite the same way as the author's other works can. Laforgue wrote "Persée" in a short time during the spring of 1886. "Pan" was composed with dispatch, despite physical handicaps, in Paris the following winter. Though "Hamlet" was put down on paper in 1885–86 it had, in an important sense, been a work in progress for at least seven years, ever since Laforgue's first mention of the Shakespearian hero in an early poem. Jean-Aubry said with considerable justice that Hamlet was for Laforgue what Saint Anthony was for Flaubert. The story whereby Laforgue sought to lay one of his oldest ghosts is not his best; it was too close to him, as another *Hamlet* may have been to its author; but there is no doubt about its fascination.

This Hamlet is, if not a clown, at least the brother of a clown: one of the gravediggers in the little cemetery reveals that the prince and Yorick were sons of the late king by the same gypsy mother. Since poor Yorick's remains are now being disinterred to make room for Ophelia's, Hamlet strays over to the open grave, picks up his brother's cranium, and soliloquizes in words that are like an ironic echo to Laforgue's Pascalian apostrophe of some years before. As far as content is concerned, the two speeches to a skull are not very different: the underlying attitudes are equally pessimistic; there is a similar lack of confidence in religion; and in both the earth is dismissed as one of an overwhelming number of planets. What is new is the tone, the defensive irony, the twist at the end: "As for me, with my genius, I could have been what is commonly called a Messiah, but here I am, too, too spoiled, a veritable benjamin of Nature. I understand everything, I adore everything, I want to fecundate everything. That's why, as I have observed in a limping distich carved in my bed:

> My rare faculty of assimilation
> Cannot but thwart the course of my vocation."

Ma rare faculté d'assimilation
Contrariera le cours de ma vocation.

Hamlet is also, if not a writer, at least one who aspires to be a writer, and even before he spies the band of strolling players across the stagnant bay we know that the play's the thing. What Hamlet would really like would be to unshoulder the few responsibilities he has not already disclaimed and be off to Paris, where a group of neo-Alexandrians is flourishing around Mount Sainte-Geneviève. Since that appears to be impossible, he has tackled the theme of his play in earnest; and the longer he has spent with this work designed, on one level, to ferret out the murderers' guilt, the more he has become convinced that he has got hold of a really first-rate subject. The arrival of William and Kate and their fellow players, his enthusiastic reading of his work, its performance and alarming repercussions, even his increasingly friendly feelings for the actress, are purely subordinate to his literary ambition, and toward the end we find him heading for Paris after all, with Kate. But on the way he stops off at the cemetery for just a moment, as an act of filial piety, is stabbed by a Laertes who does not seem too persuaded of the importance of what he is doing, and dies murmuring, *"Qualis . . . artifex . . . pereo!"*

If the rare faculty of assimilation displayed in "Hamlet" works against its unity, if its somewhat haphazard ending makes it inferior to both "Persée" and "Pan," it nonetheless encompasses more characteristically Laforguian themes and images, more ironic oppositions springing from inner contradictions, than any other tale. Hamlet speaks of his "dear Philoctetes," and has had, he says, his "moment of apostolic madness." He is endowed with a "sixth sense, a sense of the infinite," and cherishes the "immemorial sadness of a tiny chord struck on the piano." His tower room, like his spirit, is invaded by "an insoluble, an incurable autumn"—even in July, for "today is the fourteenth of July 1601, a Saturday; tomorrow is Sunday and all over the world girls will go artlessly to church." He had been fond of Ophelia, and yet—"She would never have understood me. Whenever I stop to think of that! No doubt she was adorable and mortally sensitive, but scratch the surface and you would have found the Englishwoman tainted from birth by the egotistical philosophy of Hobbes: 'Nothing is more agreeable about the possession of our own property than the thought that it is superior to other people's.' That was the way Ophelia loved me, as a piece of property." "Method, method," he exclaims, "what have you to do with me? You know very well that I have eaten of the fruit of the Unconscious." Yet he remains in spite of that, as Gustave Kahn said, a reasoner, a methodical doubter, a searcher. Over Hamlet, this final embodiment of Laforgue's irony exposed to all the winds of doubt, veers the metaphorical weathercock of "Avertissement," the poem he wrote the day he visited Elsinore:

Bonne girouette aux trent'-six saisons,
Trop nombreux pour dire oui ou non . . .

On Time and Poetry:
A Reading of Apollinaire

Dennis G. Sullivan

We would like to interrogate the prose and poetry of Apollinaire, and develop an aspect of their thematic unity, by posing the question of his intuition of the nature of poetry. We should like to initiate our meditation on the sense of poetry for the poet by considering certain definitions he poses in his theoretical writings on poetry itself. "L'Esprit nouveau et les poètes," in the fundamental categories it presents, in its heterogeneity of vocabulary and structure and its general ellipses and contradictions, may be considered representative of all of Apollinaire's aesthetic writings. He describes poetry here, and "l'esprit nouveau" in general, as an ontological, and not simply an aesthetic category. It is presented as the adequation of a subject and a real, described alternatively as "la vérité" and an existent defined by historical change. Poetry is one with the perception of the poet who desires "des vues d'ensemble sur l'univers." Manifest as "le désir du poète d'habituer son esprit à la réalité," it permits an absolute continuity of subject and object. The poet's perception is actualized in an image considered identical to this perception itself, and in no way secondary to it, or dependent upon a mediating process. The poet produces a representation which totalizes a plurality of phenomena existing beyond itself, while maintaining its own identity and unicity. A constant obsession of Apollinaire, identical in its formal structure to the ideal of painting of *Les Peintres cubistes*, this figure would constitute a ground in which an existent defined as discontinuous and multiple might exist simultaneously and spatially. Poetry requests the "liberté . . . d'un journal quotidien qui traite dans une seule feuille des matières les plus diverses, parcourt des pays les plus éloignés. On se demande pourquoi le poète n'aurait pas une liberté au

From *MLN* (French Issue) 88, no. 4 (May 1973). © 1973 by The Johns Hopkins University Press, Baltimore/London.

419

moins égale et serait tenu, à une époque de téléphone, de télégraphie sans fil et d'aviation à plus de circonspection vis à vis des espaces." The poet would effect an inherence in the real by means of a totalizing synthesis:

> La rapidité et la simplicité avec lesquelles les esprits se sont ac-coutumés à désigner d'un seul mot des êtres aussi complexes qu'une foule, qu'une nation, que l'univers n'avaient pas leur pen-dant dans la poésie. Les poètes comblent cette lacune et leurs poèmes synthétiques créent de nouvelles entités qui ont une valeur plastique aussi composée que des termes collectifs.

Apollinaire cannot define these terms more fully in his theoretical writ-ings. The "poème synthétique" is inaccessible to systematic elaboration of contextual situation. And it is not directly accorded a specificity within the global dimensions of this concept of representation itself. Poetry, more significantly, may not even be situated coherently within this conception of representation. It receives its only rudiments of specific definition from the contradictions which appear in Apollinaire's discourse. For Apollinaire says, on the one hand, that totalization and synthesis define "l'esprit nou-veau" in general, and that poetry is but one of the modes of representation which exist beneath its aegis. But he assumes, simultaneously, that poetry is the sole mode of representation which must be different from "l'esprit nouveau" and related to it as a potentiality unactualized. Poetry exists, in the theoretical writings of Apollinaire, as a mode of representation *left behind:*

> Les mathématiciens ont le droit de dire que leurs rêves, leurs préoccupations dépassent de cent coudées les imaginations ram-pantes des poètes. C'est aux poètes à decider s'il ne veulent point entrer résolument dans l'esprit nouveau.

Only poetry has been left behind. Behind mathematics, the newspaper, and "le langage scientific"; behind even that "rapidité et simplicité" by which perceptual consciousness defines its historical actuality. Poetry, Apollinaire implies, functions according to the model of a perceptual con-sciousness itself. It poses an immediate relationship between the subject and real, and an absolute continuity between his representation and its referent. But poetry, he simultaneously implies, permits an adequation of the poet and the real which no way functions analogically. Apollinaire cannot elaborate a process by which the "poème synthétique" might be produced, but he does say how it must *not* be produced. Poetry must never employ a "harmonie imitative," or become a "trompe-oreilles auquel la réalité sera toujours supérieure." It desires a referential immediacy, yet it has no mimetic pretensions. Poetry desires the magical immediacy of "l'es-prit nouveau" but rejects the conditions of possibility of such immediacy. Poetry aspires to what is simply, beneath the impressionism of Apollinaire's theoretical vocabulary, and beyond the conceptual limitations of his maxims, the classical status of immediate perception. Yet poetry is always some-how *behind* this.

We would like to afford Apollinaire's definition of poetry a greater precision by means of a systematic elaboration of its identity with, and its difference from, the ideal of representation of "l'esprit nouveau." We should like to seek the rationality of this identity and difference, or what is left *unsaid* in his theoretical writings, by transporting the structural categories of "l'esprit nouveau" to those texts in which his meditation is more profound—his prose and poetry themselves. For this conception of representation may be held to govern the entire content of Apollinaire's poetical discourse and to determine all its images, themes and functions. And the figure of the poet in the poems, or rather Apollinaire's quest to determine such a specific mode of subjectivity, could be considered the dynamic component of these texts. Such a quest for definition is necessary because the poet, in the poetry of Apollinaire, is never immediately defined in relation to perception. And if the categories of totalization and synthesis appear here, the spatial totality is never given to "existe inéluctablement." This conception is rather presented as highly problematic and functions as the source of other problematics. If Apollinaire's theoretical discourse is marked by contradiction, it is because his poetry says that this discourse is *wrong*.

The conception of totality exists in the poetry of Apollinaire, but is never accorded a positive status. Rather than the continuity of sign and referent assumed in "L'Esprit nouveau et les poètes," rather than the *presence* of a plurality in any image, there is a structure of discontinuity between any totality and existence, and the absence of the presence of the referent. No totality is presented as a plenitude, but rather in terms of absolute negativity. We may refer, as an emblem of a totality whose parts are condemned to exist without individuation, to the perception of Justin Couchot in the story, "D'Infirme Divinisé." We may refer, as an analogue of the "journal"—associated, like any "synthèse" in Apollinaire's poetry, with the themes of memory, absence and death:

> Souvenirs de mes compagnons morts à la guerre
> L'olive du temps
> Souvenirs qui ne faites plus qu'un
> Comme cent fourrures ne font qu'un manteau
> Comme ces milliers de blessures ne font qu'un
>   article de journal
>   ("Ombres," in *Calligrammes*)

—to that character called "L'Eternel." Justin Couchot is the poet's fullest example of his ideal of a perceptual consciousness and he is presented as a radically problematic figure. Exempt from "la notion du temps," we are told, his perception is analogous to that of "Dieu, auquel il ressemblait mentalement" (*Le Poète assassiné*). He apprehends always the spatial totality of "L'Esprit nouveau et les poètes," but this conception is now given certain qualifications. The parts of this totality will be without individuality; this whole will never have the function of a natural object. It will appear always as an image without origin, without analogy with a specific object in the world. Justin Couchot *perceives*, but immediate apprehension is deprived of its classical predicates. To that woman who asks, "Que pensez-vous de moi?", Justin can only reply, in a statement emblematic of this dialectic of totality and absence:

> Millions d'êtres que tu es, de toute taille, et de tant de visages: d'enfant, de jeune fille, de femme et de vieille, vous vivez et tu es morte, vous riez et vous pleurez, vous aimez et vous haissez et tu n'es rien et vous êtes tout.
>
> (*Le Poète assassiné*)

He must reply that she is simultaneously everything and nothing, because she never existed as a *specific* thing. She is an image which is preceded by no object, a totality intuited as lacking substance, and she becomes a function of the death of Justin in the text. She illustrates the constants of every expression of totality in the prose and poetry of Apollinaire. For whether the conception of totality is expressed directly, or manifested through those metaphors whose articulations it governs, it always presents a configuration of identity without difference and an object deprived of interiority. Any passing evocation of a figure which assembles the multiple will receive a negative characterization: "Le monde entier et toutes les époques étaient les fournisseurs de cette boutique où bijoux, robes, tableaux, bronzes, bibelots, livres voisinaient comme les morts voisinent au cimetière" (*Le Poète assassiné*); every random expression of the category of resemblance will be qualified thusly:

> Usines manufactures fabriques mains
> Où les ouvriers nus semblables à nos doigts
> Fabriquent du réel à tant par heure
>
> . . . .
> Visages de la chair de l'onde de tout
> Vous n'êtes que des masques sur des
>   faces masquées
>
> ("Vendémiaire," in *Alcools*)

Any totality will be marked, to refer to one constant antithesis of the poet's imagination, by the characteristics of "la silhouette impressioniste" and never by those of "le profil égyptien." Every totality functions as a phantasm and it *must* function always as a phantasm. It can never effectively synthesize a plurality of objects which exist exterior and prior to a process of totalization because there is no function of the *presence* of the object in the creative texts of Apollinaire. His prose and poetry are peopled by corpses, by mannequins, and by beings without faces—they are peopled by beings who have never had faces. Figures of a manifold whose parts are without differentiation, these beings exhaust the metaphorical articulation of the perceptual object in his work. The object is always experienced as an absence, and within the total field of its figured manifestation, one image assumes a quantitative predominance. An object which appears without specificity, all beings and no being at once; a totality in virtue of this qualification, yet a totality without substance or presence—the mode of perception posed as the ideal of "l'esprit nouveau" takes as its correlative object in the poetry itself, the ubiquitous figure of the *ombre*.

The shadow, the crowd, the phantasm . . . the object as totality may have no presence, in turn, because it maintains a real presence in no *space*. It derives a presence from no ontological ground, it remains always a phenomenon without genetic origin, because there is no conception, in Apollinaire, of a domain of substance which *endures*. There is rather an intuition of time as the absence of such an origin and support of the object, of time as a principle of absolute discontinuity. If Apollinaire poses the question of Being as Becoming—"si on fait le progrès consister dans un éternel devenir . . . " (*L'Esprit nouveau et les poètes*)—this question is answered categorically in the structure of his texts. It is answered by the thematization of a universe where the shadow or its analogue, the machine—equally a being without substance, neither present to itself, nor present elsewhere— is opposed to no natural object and thus exhausts the definition of the existent. It is answered more radically in that intuition which leads Apollinaire to stage himself in his poems as "Le Guetteur mélancholique," ubiquitous spectator for whom exteriority is thematized or which leads him to state, concerning Justin Couchot, that "le monde entier et toutes les époques étaient pour lui un instrument bien accordé que son unique main touchait avec justesse" (*Le Poète assassiné*). It is answered by the assignment, in this universe where no matrix may actually *be*, of a perceptual subject to the function of a center without efficacy. The problem of representation in Apollinaire, and its analogue, the problem of temporality, are initially thematized through that subject who, functioning as the sole origin and ground of the existent, must experience the existent as only a simulacrum. These problems are articulated by a voice which plaintively repeats, assuming the paternity of the negative totality:

> Mais si le temps venait où l'ombre enfin solide
> Se multipliait en réalisant la diversité formelle
>   de mon amour
> J'admirais mon ouvrage
>
> > (*Alcools*)

This time will never come. No totality will ever exist substantially; none will achieve a continuity with the plurality of the real existent. In his writings on painting, and most centrally in *Les Peintres cubistes*, Apollinaire poses the categories of simultaneity and succession as terms through which this problem might be elaborated. He describes duration as a linear series of moments, and poses the totalization of these moments, in a spatial panorama for a spectator, as a process which the subject must effect. This reified conception of temporality, which restates the problem of totalization in the guise of offering a solution, will have neither structural effect nor anecdotal predication in his properly creative writings. For if Apollinaire, in his poetry, must stage the temporal passage of phenomena as a spectacle to which a subject is always exterior, if he must conclude "Le Pont Mirabeau" with the words "je demeure," and thematize even his themes of Past and Future in terms of distance and proximity to a perceiving subject, the possibility of spatial perception will never itself be in question. If he must present phenomena in his endless "cortèges" not, as elsewhere, in a polyrhythmic plurality, but as a succession in a scene ordered by a spectator, he may *assume* the identity of the instant and the spatial totality. For this temporal succession is bounded by the subject, and this linearity exists within a circle: the present of any object is never more than a moment of a predetermined totality, and that totality is never more than the entelechy of the full presents assumed to constitute the successive series. There is never an exigency of a transcendence of an inherence in time because the subject is never initially defined as temporal. The position of absolute subject has no antecedents, Justin Couchot is always already there. The problem of time and the subject lies elsewhere. It lies first in the necessity of Apollinaire's adding, whenever and however he expresses this original integrity of the subject, say—"Ma voix fidèle comme l'ombre"—that this integrity is marked by a lack—"veut être enfin l'ombre de la vie" ("La Victoire," in *Calligrammes*). It lies in the fact that if Apollinaire says, having elaborated the position of the absolute subject of perception:

> Quelques cris de flamme annoncent sans cesse ma présence
> J'ai creusé le lit où je coule en me ramifiant en mille
>   petits fleuves qui vont partout
> Je suis dans la tranchée de première ligne et cependant
>   je suis partout ou plutôt je commence à être partout

he must add that this subject lacks the ratification of a coincidence with an object that exists in the real:

> Et ce serait sans doute bien plus beau
> Si je pouvais supposer que toutes ces choses
>   dans lesquelles je suis partout
> Pouvaient m'occuper aussi
> Mais dans ce sens il n'y a rien de fait
> Car si je suis partout à cette heure
>   il n'y a cependant que moi qui suis en moi
>   ("Merveille de la guerre," in
>   *Calligrammes*)

It lies in the contradiction, implicit in "L'Esprit nouveau et les poètes", by which Apollinaire can only conceive of the object according to a classical configuration of perception, yet is unable to accord this configuration the slightest degree of ontological efficacy. He assumes that subject and object are discrete and substantial entities, capable of maintaining a relationship of analogical continuity in the perceptual event because each maintains an autonomous presence in the real. Yet he experiences each term as temporal, ineluctably absent from itself, and beyond the possibility of a relationship of analogy. Unable to renounce the perceptual proposition of an absolute subject, he accounts for its lack of actualization by thematizing a distance of the object and a deficiency of the perceptual event. He stages the lack of plenitude and presence of the object as its lack of presence to the perception of the subject; he then places the category of presence *beyond* the apprehension of the subject and any object accessible to his perception. The object perceived as a phantasm is thus accorded the status of a representation which simultaneously poses, and assumes the absence of, its referent. It defines the referent globally as the real presence of the existent—in lexicon of Apollinaire, "la vie"—and locates the subject within a metaphysics of separation. It maintains the configuration of the perceptual subject only by thematizing this subject as problematic. If the object apprehended exists, yet originates in no natural ground, if this image is continuous with the subject, but discontinuous with that which functions as the real, it exists exclusively in reference to the subject and the subject is its sole ontological ground. The object is experienced as the creation of the subject, or rather the fabrication of the subject; the totality is defined as the constitution of subjectivity, and subjectivity is thus defined as negation.

This structure of perceptual discontinuity will govern that domain of poetic expression in which Apollinaire as spectator is always *voyeur*: origin and source of an object, intact and integral as subject, yet excluded ineluctably from the real, and never experiencing his subjectivity as a plenitude. It will cast him as "L'Ermite" of *Alcools*, as the spectator of "La Maison des morts," and "cet employé pour qui seul rien n'existe" of "La Porte." It will govern his themes of human solitude and exclusion, initiate his thematics of death, and form the first moment of his erotic dialectics. The woman *given* to the apprehension of the subject will be shadow, memory-image or ideal; but never first a presence exterior to the subject, thus never effecting a modification of the subject, she may be experienced only as an absence.

This structure will govern Apollinaire's poetic identity as *voyageur*, determining the rationality of doubles like "Le Juif errant," and defining the emigrant of Landor Road as an "ombre aveugle." Defined by his temporal discontinuity with the presence of any object in the world, the subject never abided, and never will abide, in a space. Thus consecutive with the experience of a phantom stasis is experience of the absolute motion of desire. This journey without origin towards the real, offering no possibility of return, contains no term which might permit a positive resolution. Its only terminus, thematically, will be those doors which exist in perpetual closure, barring the traveller from the proximity to the real. The refrains of Apollinaire the *voyageur*:

> Ouvrez-moi cette porte où je frappe en pleurant
> > ("Le Voyageur," in *Alcools*)

> J'ai cherché longtemps sur les routes
> Tant d'yeux sont clos au bord des routes
> Le vent fait pleurer les saussaies
> Ouvre ouvre ouvre ouvre
> > ("A travers l'Europe," in
> > *Calligrammes*)

will be answered only by their own plaintive repetition.

A structure of subjectivity is defined which posits an imaginary to which no real is opposed, a circle of representation to which no presentation was ever opposed. Or to which a real may be posed only rhetorically. For the Apollinaire who experiences representation as the failure of perception, who suffers as *voyeur* and searches as *voyageur*, desires always a universe governed by the principle of identity. And the Apollinaire whose discourse is governed by the equation of subjectivity and totalization seeks always a term upon which this equation might be validated. Thus he will say—in passing—of Pierre Albert Birot:

> Et cependant comme j'aime avant tout la réalité
> > L'avenir m'importe peu
> Mais lui Pierre Albert-Birot il est
> > Avec vous
> > Avec moi
> > Le présent
> > > ("Poèmepréface prophétie II," in *Poèmes*
> > > *Retrouvés*)

And he attempts to thematize, most specifically when desire is expressed as sexual desire, sensation as a means of attenuating the discontinuity between subject and object. He proposes an object which maintains its historical existence while apprehended as immanent to the subject, and he poses the sensual plenitude of an intuition as the means of this apprehension. If his ontology does not permit an objectively constituted ground to sustain each term, rendering a full totality in an instant, it will permit, as we have said, the illusion of adequation within a punctual present. It permits the proposition of an object which maintains an extraneousness to the subject even though it may not endure as such, a present which was, and will be negated within a linear flow of time, and a momentary analogy of subject and object within this moment. He proposes that absence is but the contingent absence of this present, the image a deficit of the object, and that representation is a deviation of sensation. But he discovers always that this immediacy is illusory: it assumes no normativity within his work, and it is inaccessible to presentation as an actuality. Whenever Apollinaire attempts to actualize such a punctual present in an erotic configuration—

> Je t'ai prise contre ma poitrine comme une colombe
>   qu'une petite fille étouffe sans le savoir
> Je t'ai prise avec toute ta beauté ta beauté plus riche
>   qu tous les placers de la Californie ne le furent au
>   temps de la fièvre de l'or

—he discovers that the object was absent even from this present itself. Temporal succession cannot negate the original plenitude of this moment because the moment was *never* experienced as a plenitude. The object was never present as a totality to the subject because it maintained always a dimension of inaccessible interiority; "le corps" itself was never wholly accessible to the subject because it never functioned as an integral object:

> J'ai bien cru prendre toute ta beauté et je n'ai eu que ton
>   corps
> Le corps hélas n'a pas l'éternité
> Le corps a la fonction de jouir mais il n'a pas l'amour
> Et c'est en vain maintenant que j'essaie d'étreindre ton esprit
> Il fuit il me fuit de toutes parts comme un nœud de
>   couleuvres qui se dénouent
> . . . .
> Le corps ne va pas sans l'âme
> Et comment pourrais-je espérer rejoindre ton corps de
>   naguère puisque ton âme était si éloignée de moi
> Et que le corps a rejoint l'âme
> Comme font tous les corps vivants
> O toi que je n'ai possedée que morte
>   ("L'Amour le dédain et l'espérence" in *Poèmesà lou*)

The subject, in turn, "semblable à Ixion après qu'il eut fait l'amour avec le fantôme de nuées fait à la semblance de celle qu'on appelle Héra ou bien Junon l'invisible," returns to a state of solipsism. When Apollinaire attempts to describe the successful apprehension of a spatial totality itself, rather than this humble analogue, his failure is even more radical. He situates the moment of perception in that metaphorical space beneath the earth, that "domaine idéal" of his thematics, where all contradictions are momentarily suspended. If Apollinaire, for one example, stages himself as a *voyageur* before whom doors finally open; if, in "Le Roi-Lune," he enters a "cavern très spacieuse," he may, in virtue of this privileged context, propose the apprehension of an object in the present and the experience of the self as an absolute presence. Choosing a sexual motif for the expression of this representational configuration, his *voyageur* comes upon an "orgie anachronique" whose visible participants at first, as always, articulate the auto-referentiality of a perceptual consciousness: "il me parût," he says, "qu'il devaient tous ressembler à Ixion, lorsqu'il caressait le Fantôme des Nuées, l'invisible Junon . . . Bientôt ils devinrent plus lascifs et, pétulants, se marierent avec le vide" (*Le Poète assassiné*). But he soon discovers that the participants possess magic machines which attenuate the imaginary character of their objects, rendering visible these "cadavres amoureuses." "Cette machine avait pour fonction," we are told, "d'une part, d'abstraire du temps une certaine portion de l'espace et de s'y fixer à un certain moment et pour quelques minutes seulement, car l'appareil n'était pas très puissant; d'autre part, de rendre visible et tangible à qui ceignait la courroie la portion du temps ressuscitée." The machine accords the existent a physical presence which is total and exhaustive, as a guarantee of its exteriority to the subject. Apollinaire adds, with the humor of Bataille, "J'ai eu le même soir le même/Jolie Tyrolienne du XVIII siècle/A ses ages de 16, 21, et 33/." Yet it permits the accessibility of this object to a subject who, unseen by the object he apprehends, maintains an absolute autonomy: "C'est ainsi que je pouvais regarder, palper, besogner en un mot (non sans quelque difficulté) le corps qui se trouvait à ma portée, tandis que ce corps n'avait aucune idée de ma présence . . . " (*Le Poète assassiné*). Only in virtue of this machine may the synthesis of perception be realized. Only beneath the earth may the apprehension of a totality be staged as a positivity. And these circumstances, in turn, receive a qualification in the narrative. The traveler who may finally *perceive* is staged as a stranger to the domain of le Roi-Lune. The possibility of perception itself has the condition that the stranger is not discovered as such. But he is immediately discovered and threatened with castration and death by the king. Rather than receiving a normative function for the texts as a whole, perception is given as dependent upon an impossible condition. The absolute presence of the subject is ironically equated with his absence, and perception retains its function of negation. The traveler flees the kingdom in terror and the kingdom itself disappears. The proposition of an absolute subject disappears and the traveler resumes his search. The search he assumes will be, and may only be, a repetition of the search he has already undertaken. For the conception of a spatial totality with substance has *no* possibility of positive realization. Thus poetry and the poet, for Apollinaire, to escape this negative status themselves, will seek definition on the *far* side of perception.

II

If Apollinaire cannot thematize perception as a positive term, he has no absolute need to do so. For there is another movement in his poetry to which our anterior considerations might stand as a preface. There is a second dimension of his meditation which both encompasses and redefines the first.

There is the categorization of the proposition of perception, of the immediate totalization of the existent, by a subject himself exterior to the existent, beneath the aegis of the temporal category of the *past*. There is a relegation of the totality lacking substance, and all its metaphorical articulations—the image, the shadow, the corpse; the *voyeur*, the *voyageur*, the spectator; the swan, silence, *stérilité*—to the governance of the signifier *souvenir*. The past and memory do not derive this generic function from any authentic thematic precedence: they exist simply, for the text as a whole, as *other* signifiers of an imaginary which originates in no real. They may be accorded no positive definition in terms of the poet's biographical obsessions, and Apollinaire's inability to effectively thematize a linear conception of time precludes any attempt to situate them in relation to the psychological and philosophical categories of his day. He will never stage a past as a deviation from a present and he never produces a configuration in which negativity is the residue of an event. The past will function exclusively as the index of an horizon in which presence is, and always was distant from the subject; it describes the locus of a subject who is absent to himself. Thus the theme of the past for Apollinaire, no less than for Proust, will possess no specificity prior to its manifestation in the metaphorical systems of his texts; it never functions as the *source* of its analogues. The theme of the *souvenir*, in its turn, never articulates the configuration of the absence, in one punctual present, of an object that was actual in another punctual present. An analogue, simply, of the shadow, another metaphor of an originary image, it figures, for Apollinaire as for Proust, any object that was never present.

Existing as unmotivated metaphors, these terms derive their significance from their purely transitional function in the texts. Unable to enter into opposition with a present, the past will seek a function in a duality of a different order. It will be opposed to the substance fire, it will be antinomous to the signifier *avenir*. It permits Apollinaire to structure his poetic universe, with the refrain of an "Avenir sans souvenir," in virtue of a configuration of unmediated contraries. It introduces a duality into his thematic discourse which is not predicated upon two perceptual moments of a subject, but rather upon two radically divergent propositions of the subjectivity and representation. It will introduce a movement into the texts of Apollinaire which responds to the contradictions of "L'Esprit nouveau," and permits poetry to be defined in a differential context.

Apollinaire opposes to the subject who *perceives*, demanding an impossible continuity with the real, a subject who claims that he *creates*, and yet assumes an immediate discontinuity with the existent. The poet thematizes through the signifier *avenir*, and its thematic adjunct *fécondité*, a real which is definitively without center, in opposition to this real with a simulacrum of a center. There is a subject who, in virtue of "La Victoire," assumes willfully the role of a demiurge:

> Certains hommes sont des collines
> Qui s'élèvent d'entre les hommes
> Et voient au loin tout l'avenir
> Mieux que s'il était le présent
> Plus net que s'il était passé
> ("Les Collines," in
> *Calligrammes*)

Yet this is a demiurge who constantly stresses, choosing "Le Brasier" as his major textual locus, and saying "Flamme je fais ce que tu veux," his lack of integrity as subject. There is a subject who thematizes "la volonté" as his mode of inherence in the real, rejecting the perceptual nexus of vision. Yet this is a subject who functionally defines the will, as he stages the demiurge as Icarus, as an emblem of his own ontological inefficacy. There is a subject who, dwelling beneath the aegis of the theme of *l'avenir*, opposes himself to the proposition of a natural consciousness and rejects the possibility of an unmediated apprehension of the existent. This being, by means of his rejection of the category of identity, and of the mode of representation derivative of its subject, assumes the identity of the poet. The poet Apollinaire attempts to define in "L'Esprit nouveau" will be actualized in his prose and poetry itself, upon the basis of his authentic conditions of possibility.

The figure of the poet, in these texts, emerges neither magically nor autonomously. And this poet's proposition of a creative subjectivity, in the words of J.P. Richard, his "rêve d'une créativité absolue," will never function, as that critic would have it, within the dimensions of an idealist configuration. It cannot properly be qualified as "le projet d'une annexion totale des choses par l'esprit" ("Etoiles chez Apollinaire," in *De Ronsard à Breton, Hommages à M. Raymond*), for it lies beyond all propositions of immediacy and identity. The figure of the poet is thematized, it is true, within the limits of the problem of perception: he will be defined as poet by the structure of his relation to the existent, and no explicit precedence is given to the mediation of a system or code. But he never transcends the givens of our initial perceptual configuration in a positive manner, and he never succeeds in rendering substance to the shadow. The proposition of a continuity with the object, to be manifest as a substantial totality, will be accorded no more positive solution by the will than it was by vision. It may be, as many critics have maintained, that the *calligramme* itself is the realization of this totality. It may be that a product of language can fulfill such an ontological function, but if this is so Apollinaire, for one, is unaware of it. For when Apollinaire speaks of poetry in his poetry itself, the proposition of totality will never function as its analogue. Whenever and wherever *avenir* appears in these texts, the conception of totality is *rejected*, and that is the condition upon which poetry may be spoken of.

Apollinaire never presents the theme of *avenir* autonomously—it functions only in opposition to the theme of *souvenir*. The accession of the subject to the figure of the poet, the transition between our propositions of the subjectivity, is thematized initially as a psychological choice. As in "Le Brasier," the subject will renounce the thematic dimension of the past:

> J'ai jété dans le noble feu
> Que je transporte et que j'adore
> De vives mains et meme feu
> Ce passé ces têtes de mort
> Flamme je fais ce que tu veux

He will then emerge in a different mode of being, beneath the sign of the "directeur de feu et des poètes." He will never do so, however, without stressing the anteriority of his immediate domain of his origination. Left behind, typically, will be the attempt of memory to constitute the unmediated coincidence of subject and object, homosexuality as a metaphor of an analogical identity with the existent, the swan as a figure of a phantom stasis, and silence as the subject's lack of nexus with the real:

> O Mémoire Combien de races qui forlignent
> Des Tyndarides aux vipères ardentes de mon bonheur
> Et les serpents ne sont-ils que les cous de cygnes
> Qui étaient immortels et n'étaient pas chanteurs
> Voici ma vie renouvelée

He will never emerge in a different mode of being without differentiating his present from his anterior state:

> Voici le paquebot et ma vie renouvelée
> Ses flammes sont immenses
> Il n'y a plus rien de commun entre moi
> Et ceux qui craignent les brûlures

Avenir and *souvenir* are given as absolutely complementary terms. For the poet who states that "Je me suis enfin detaché/de toutes choses naturelles" ("Les Collines"), and the figure of an immediate consciousness which he is *no longer*, exist only in relation to one another. The poet exists only in relation to his other and he must be defined in relation to our initial perceptual configuration. His condition of possibility *must* be defined, initially, by the negative moment of this opposition, the radical rejection of any proposition of identity. For when Apollinaire renounces the thematic dimension of the past, when he renounces the negativity of perception and the attempt to reduce the Other to the Same, he offers no replacement for these terms. He renounces *any* proposition of a subject who might totalize the existent and any possibility of a positive solution to the problem of perception. The necessity of this configuration of renunciation, in asserting both the originarity and the finality of the temporal discontinuity between subject and object, permits no term which might effect a synthesis between perception and creation, and creation will never signify, in Apollinaire, the analogue of an existent ideally perceived. There is no condition upon which the failure of an immediate consciousness to apprehend the presence of an object in the real might be transcended by the creation of a natural object, present simultaneously to the subject and to itself. There is no possibility of the dialectical continuity with such an object which would render actual the proposition of an absolute subject. The subject designated *poet* does not achieve such an absolute adequation with the object, he states rather that such an adequation is impossible. But the renunciation of presence is *chosen* by this subject and as such receives an equivocal positivity. The poet transcends the duplicity of perceptual representation by explicitly refusing to effect its mechanisms. He refuses to represent, yet he accepts representativity as the essence of the existent, and this conjunction liberates the existent from representation. His renunciation of the pretentions of perceptual totalization, his acceptance of the existent as always already totalized, posits the *function* of a real beyond totalization, defined as that which may never be totalized. He posits a real beyond representation, yet secondary to representation, a real which never is or never was accessible to a subject, and thus is defined as the inaccessible. He places the poet in the *presence* of this real by virtue of the act by which he produces it. Every figure of the poet in the poetry of Apollinaire, and his elliptical intuitions of the nature of poetry, correspond systemically to the structure of this negative process. Every thematic manifestation of poetry in his creative texts will begin with the negation of the configuration of perception and end with the residue of this negation: the presence of the poet to the existent, and to an existent defined as temporal.

Whenever Apollinaire stages the poet in his poems, he casts him metaphorically as a spectator. The poet's demiurgic project, like that of his thematic predecessor, is expressed as an exigency of totalization and accompanied by a visual imagery. "La Victoire," we know, "avant tout sera/ De bien voir au loin/De tout voir/De près"; "Le poète," we are told "est cet observateur de la vie et il invente des lueurs innombrables qu'il faut repérer . . . " ("Lueurs," in *Poèmes à Madeleine*). But the similarity of the poet and the figure of a natural consciousness serves only to permit an articulation of their differences. A difference first in their relationship to the proposition of totalization itself. Apollinaire never gives the poet the illusion of power he gave Justin Couchot, of whom he said: "Et il s'accordait si bien avec la nature qu'elle lui était un effet de sa volonté, à qui l'evénément répondait sans cesse avant qu'il pût connaître le regret ou le désir. . . . Le monde entier et toutes les époques étaient ainsi pour lui un instrument bien accordé que son unique main touchait avec justesse" (*Le Poète assassiné*). He does not present totalization as an actuality for the poet, but rather as a pure prospectivity. "La Victoire" is a potentiality never actualized and this prospectivity, in turn, must be defined as its essential characteristic. The poet is that being given to dwell in a moment which precedes totalization, a moment which, in itself, articulates the absence of any process implying synthesis. The category of totalization may never be separated from the correlative category of negation, but both terms may be simultaneously suspended. The subject, in this moment, the subject who emerges from the flames of "Le Brasier," no longer experiences the failure of the proposition of identity, but experiences *himself* as the failure of this proposition. He no longer experiences the object as phantasm, but experiences rather the *sense* of the phantasm. The poet actualizes a perceptual structure in which the category of the object is no longer manifest as an illusory image, but rather articulated by the term this image defines as its absent referent. The object is manifested as a plurality whose components are distinct, like the "bêtes nouvelles" of "Le Brasier," figures of an inassimilable alterity:

> Et voici le spectacle
> Et pour toujours je suis assis dans un fauteuil
> Ma tête mes genoux mes coudes vain pentacle
> Les flammes ont poussé sur moi comme des feuilles
>
> Des acteurs inhumains claires bêtes nouvelles
> Donnent des ordres aux hommes apprivoisés

The poet, existing only in and *as* this moment in which representation is suspended, does not apprehend a visible which is illusory, but rather apprehends the visible as the Other of the real. He no longer inhabits the simulacrum of an essential space, but experiences immediately his inherence in that non-space articulated as time. He no longer apprehends an image whose immediacy masks the distance of "la vie"; he apprehends immediately "la vie," with its essential characteristic of distance:

> Moi j'ai ce soir une âme qui s'est creusée
>   qui est vide
> On dirait qu'on y tombe sans cesse
>   et sans trouver de fond
> Et qu'il n'y a rien pour se raccrocher
> Ce qui y tombe et qui y vit
>   c'est une sorte d'êtres laids
>   qui me font mal et qui viennent
>   de je ne sais où
> Oui je crois qu'ils viennent de la vie
>   d'une sorte de vie qui est dans l'avenir
>   dans l'avenir brut qu'on n'a pu encore
>   cultiver ou élever ou humaniser
>   ("Dans l'abri-caverne," in
>   *Calligrammes*)

He dwells now in the proximity of the real, defined for the poet, no less than for the figure of a natural consciousness, as that which is exempt from the assimilation of subjectivity. He dwells now in the presence of an exteriority which, liberated from the negativity of the image, is experienced immediately as alterity and distance.

This exteriority originates globally with the subject himself, because the existent is not substantially grounded. If the inaccessible were accorded a natural status, if it were deprived of its temporal foundation, it could not maintain the function of an ineluctable alterity. In spite of his statements concerning an Eternal return, there is no function of the sacred in Apollinaire. There is rather the category of History and the proposition of the wholly cultural constitution of the real. Thus Apollinaire must assign the poet an origin, having him say: "Je sentais en moi des êtres neufs plein de dextérité/Bâtir et aussi agencer un univers nouveau" ("La Petite Auto," in *Calligrammes*). He must also describe the poet as demiurge, assuming the burden of the production of the existent, and possessed of the instrument of this production, "La volonté qui mène à tout." But this will maintains its secondary to representation, and functions only to negate the illusion of presence—it is in fact a will which leads nowhere. For between the functions of origin and producer, between subjectivity as the origin of the existent, and the regulative power of the individual subject, a contradiction, rather than a continuity is assumed. The existent produced within time, never possessing an essential status, may never permit a subject whose action, in immediate continuity with the real, is possessed of ontological efficacy. The existent produced by history, never possessing the stability of an essence, does not permit a subject structured according to such a dimension of stability, situated exterior to time and the real, and principle rather than function of history itself. When Apollinaire attempts to actualize his intuitions of *volonté* and creation, when he attempts to predicate the dependent theme of *fecondité*, he may have recourse to but one obsessional motif. He refers, in *Les Mamelles de Tirésias* as elsewhere, to the image of men giving birth to children. Image *par excellence* of the non-genetic origin of phenomena, graphic metaphor of the cultural production of the phenomenon, these are described as beings born to immediately die. As beings wholly subordinate to time, they exist within a metaphysics of difference and appear as discontinuous, rather than continuous with their producer. When he attempts to predicate his figure of this producer himself, he must have recourse, in virtue of this discontinuity, to his passive themes of *l'espoir* and *l'intelligence*, rather than to a romantic mythology of the demiurge. The theme of hope, presented always in opposition to metaphors of power— "Pas de glaive/Mais l'espoir" (14 Juin 1915," in *Calligrammes*)—will articulate the absolute inefficacy of the subject, and his lack of regulative power. *L'intelligence*, posing as nexus between the subject and the real an interrogation whose finality is to be definitively without answer, is the ultimate rejection of perceptual adequation. These themes, complements rather than contradictions of that *volonté* which itself places the existent in the horizon of time, form the basis of that intuition of subjectivity presented always by the figure of the poet. One must, we are repeatedly told, "perdre la vie/ pour trouver la victoire" ("Photographie," in *Calligrammes*). One must renounce, to accede to the position of the poet, the proposition of the full and integral subject of perception.

Every figure of the poet in Apollinaire's poetry, and his every elliptical statement about the nature of poetry, may be situated within the limits of this configuration. But it is only when he speaks most directly of poetry, it is only *where* he attempts to meditate the genesis and odyssey of the poet, that he himself presents this configuration, in its entirety, with its functions sequentially aligned as a process. Only in *Le Poète assassiné* does he attempt an integral portrait of the poet and present the context which defines his specificity.

Croniamantal, respecting the necessity of a negative origin, is not accorded the identity of the poet immediately in this text. He is first tutored by, and identified with, Janssen, figure of a perceptual consciousness. Janssen assumes that the real is essentially constituted "car peut-être il n'y a rien de nouveau et la création a cessé"; he assumes that he is master of the existent, possessing "le destin secret des astres." Exempt from the discontinuity of time—"j'ai la conscience des vies précedentes de mon âme"—when the existent is grounded in time, he pays the inevitable penalty—"elle n'a jamais animé que les corps stériles des savants." Croniamantal becomes the poet only upon, and only *as*, the death of Janssen. Yet when Croniamantal enters the atelier of *L'Oiseau du Bénin* after Janssen's death, this role is momentarily withheld from him. The being to whom the narrator still ascribes a function of totalization: "Ses yeux dévoraient tout ce qu'ils regardaient et quand ses paupières se approchaient rapidement comme des mâchoires, elles engloutissaient l'univers qui se renouveait sans cesse . . . il se réfugia dans sa mémoire, et allait de l'avant, tandis que toutes les forces de sa destinée et de sa conscience écartaient le temps pour qu'apparût la vérité de ce qui est, de ce qui fut et de ce qui sera," may not yet be given the identity of the poet. Apollinaire presents him as a being without identity, simply "un jeune homme mal habillé." This character becomes the poet, he may state, "c'est moi Cronimantal," only when he is properly situated: "Puis soudain il eut de nouveau la notion du temps dont les seconds martelées par une horloge qu'il entendit alors tombaient comme des morceaux de verre et la vie le reprit tandis que de nouveau le temps passait." He becomes the poet only when *L'Oiseau du Bénin* designates that term, Tristouse Ballerinette, in relation to which this subject may define his being as temporal. As the metaphor of the temporal multiplicity of the object, "l'illimité et l'avenir" of "La Jolie Rousse"; as the agent of the absolute discontinuity of the subject and the existent, through the ubiquitous "éternités différentes de l'homme et de la femme," woman functions always as this figure for Apollinaire.

Croniamantal assumes the identity of the poet when he defines himself in relation to Tristouse. He assumes his position as subject through his desire for a possession of, and a continuity with, the existent. Accepting the originative status of representation, he experiences the exigency of totalization. Yet Croniamantal, as poet, knows both that this desire cannot be satisfied and that it appears too easily satisfied. He accepts both the impossibility of absolute presence and the necessity of the illusion of presence; he knows that this illusion defines the immediate and that the negation of perception must be willed. Thus when Tristouse appears to him in the forest, he refuses the offer of her proximity: "Sans regarder Tristouse, Croniamantal se pencha vers la source." To maintain his status as subject, he affirms his desire for a transcendence of time and opposes this to the existent defined as temporal:

> J'aime les sources, elles sont un beau symbole d'immortalité, quand elles ne tarissent point. Celle-ci n'a jamais tari. Et je cherche une divinité, mais je veux qu'elle me paraisse éternelle. Et ma source n'a jamais tari. Il se mit à genoux et pria devant la source, tandis que Tristouse, éplorée, se lamentait.

Yet the existent rejected in virtue of its temporality exhausts the definition of the real, and the object placed at a distance by the subject functions to define subjectivity as negativity. For the "source" without Tristouse does not render present the desired divinity, but evokes only the world of the phantasm. Paponat, the rival, will immediately tell Cronimantal: "Je suis heureux de vivre, et toi tu te meures auprès de la source." And Cronimantal, with neither Tristouse nor the *divinité* desired in her place, is not deceived by the fiction of an absolute object, and he has no illusions of functioning as absolute subject. He describes himself now as a "voyageur sans baton, pèlerin sans bourdon et poète sans écritoire, je suis moins puissant que tout autre homme, je n'ai plus rien et je ne sais rien. . . . " Cronimantal, like the traveller in "Le Roi-Lune," is deprived of an inherence in the real and thus experiences an impossible desire for the *presence* of the object. But unlike that previous traveller, he is not deceived by the illusion of preception and he does not assume that the object *is* present. Rather than assuming an immediate continuity between the totality posed by the subject and the real presence of the object, between the image produced by the source and the historical woman herself, he himself places these terms in contradiction. Accepting his condemnation to a position from which the real is forever distant, he himself places the real at a distance. And he does so again, later in the text, when taking Tristouse as the subject of poetry he renders her desirable to others and assures her loss to himself. Through the ironic function of this dialectic, Cronimantal simultaneously asserts the priority of subjectivity and representation and their hopeless inadequation with the real. He accepts the necessity of the subject's desire for an absolute continuity with the object, but refuses to attempt to *effect* such an impossible possession. Thus Croniamantal, as poet, is not condemned to an alteration of illusion of presence and the experience of absence, an alteration of the desire for totality and the totalization, only, of the shadow. In refusing the illusion of the total possession of the historical Tristouse, in rejecting the duplicity of perception, he liberates the object from negation and permits it to retain its historical status. In affirming the deficiency of representation he simultaneously affirms, and his immediacy is now one with, that real in relation to which they are deficient. A nexus, then, becomes possible between the real and that subject called the poet. A structure is articulated by the figure of poetry in which subject and object may exist simultaneously within the *ground* of their temporal discontinuity, performing what we might call, after Bataille, "la danse autour du temps" (*Sur Nietzsche*). The Same and Other may effect a simultaneity which rejects any proposition of identity and lies beyond the constraints of spatiality. A modality of apprehension is presented as the essence of poetry in which representation and reference may maintain an interrelationship upon the basis of an equivocal continuity. A sign is produced by the poet through which the object is both presented and *is*. As the manifestation of a desire which intends exteriority rather than absence, and thus transcends both irony and dialectics, Croniamantal's quest involves a third and final stage. The moment after he rejects Tristouse for "la source," and experiences the insufficiency of the self, he rejects the "source" for Tristouse, now defined as the object of an infinite search. He is related within the dimensions of this search to an epiphany of "Junon l'invisible," an object *produced* by the action of the poet and staged as the *presence* of an absence. The poet is that being who may state, before an object he contended was *never* present, and thus never absent as a presence, "J'ai hâte de rejoindre quelqu'un que j'ai perdu et dont je suis la trace." The rejection of perception produces a "trace," a phenomenon which originates authentically in the real, and not, like the shadow, with the subject; an object accessible as the fragment of no absent totality, but as the sign of a multiplicity beyond totalization. The poet produces this object which, never claiming an analogical relation with its referent, and thus never negating its plenitude, functions only as the witness of its incommeasurability.

Or rather the poet, as presented by Apollinaire himself, is that being who apprehends the *woman* as a "trace." This configuration exhausts his consideration of the nature of poetry and its specific terms define the limits of his meditation. He is unable, or perhaps too wise, to assign either a more specifically literary definition to the poetic term, or to afford it a greater technical predication. He would not be so naive as to seek the essence of poetic representation, given the dimension of history he respects, in any but the global dimensions of the category of representation itself. And he would not speak, even *within* his meditation of Being, reduced by history, to representation, of poetry as poetry more autonomously, without reference to the category of sexuality. The identity of poetry and sexuality may be considered more positive than allegorical, and there is a necessity in

Apollinaire's saying: "C'est en courant après Tristouse que Croniamantal continua son éducation littéraire." For he situates poetic representation within the limits of a desire which is free from the exigency of a return, and thus intends exteriority and not absence. And he grounds this desire in a subject who intends a real exceeding any symbolic order given as originary, and a real which may never be totalized. As the access of the subject to the real, this mode of representation is neither referential, nor self-referential, but both: it functions within an authentic ontology of plurality. There are fragments in the poetry of Apollinaire which might permit this configuration to be thematized in relation to the category of language. Poets, he sometimes says, "fondés en poésie," have "des droits sur les paroles qui forment et défont l'univers" ("Poème lu au marriage d'André Salmon," in *Alcools*), and poets are "Epris des mêmes paroles dont il faudra changer le sens." "La Victoire," we know, requires that "tout ait un nom nouveau." The conception of poetic nomination implied, the specific way in which the sense of words might be changed, is most fully elaborated at the beginning of *Le Poète assassiné*. Poetic language is actualized in the creation of puns and neologisms. The *parole* of the poet is rendered possible, a subject is only possible, through syntactical deformation and the exploitation of the semantic plurality of individual words. In the most common function of this complex, the poetic act would afford a word an independence from the linguistic system in which it originated by rendering it discontinuous from the significations constituted as referents by that system. Janssen's "Chateau," we are told, "n'avait de seigneurial que le nom et n'était qu'une vaste demeure à laquelle tenaient une laiterie et une écurie. . . ." And that is *all* we are told. The word "Chateau" is deprived of its conventional referent, yet existing only in relation to the referent negated, and not in relation to other words, it posits the *function* of an unspecified real beyond itself. "La Victoire," we might say, consists in things having names which are *wrong*, and establishing a presence in virtue of this dissonance. The poetic word would establish a discontinuity which permits representation and reference to exist simultaneously, and poetic language would imply an ontological plurality in which phenomena coexist without synthesis or reduction. Yet Apollinaire will not say this explicitly, nor will he thematize poetry in reference to the category of linguistic representation. He *refuses* to do this in *Le Poète assassiné*, but refers instead to the category of sexuality, to which he always accords a priority:

> O paroles
> Elles suivent dans la myrtaie
> L'Eros et L'Antéros en larmes

For if languge might permit a thematization of this plural structure, it is a category whose definitions permit too many *other* possibilities. The category of plurality itself, and an order of relationships irreducible to totality, presents a configuration to which sexuality has more exclusive rights to serve as a model.

Apollinaire may only speak of poetry more specifically by differentiating it from other modes of representation. In staging Croniamantal as the central figure of a trilogy, situated between Paponat and Tograth, *Le Poète assassiné* presents a contextual delimitation of poetry, defining it in reference to what it is *not*. Apollinaire stages Paponat as his hero's rival, having him state: "J'ai versifié pour m'amuser, mais je ne suis pas poète." Paponat desires Tristouse, but demands an immediate continuity with the object. He has faith in the visibility of forms, and in spatial proximity to Tristouse he assumes an access to her absolute presence. But as the figure of the illusion of immediacy, and the negativity of a perceptual consciousness, he must hear Tristouse announce: "J'adore passer pour ce que je ne suis pas." She appears to him only in travesty, "habillé en garçon," deprived of the femininity which functions as the index of the alterity of the object, and constitutes its authentic exteriority to the subject. Paponat possesses only a phantasm and Apollinaire says, in conclusion:

> L'homme heureux a la même odeur que le mort.

Tograth, on the other hand, rejects any pretence of an originative continuity with the real. In distinction to Paponat's proposition of immanence, he poses the solution of transcendence: in Tograth we have thematized, for the only time in Apollinaire's creative texts, a positive conception of the demiurge. The Australian "chimiste-agronome" claims a desire possessing absolute finality, uninhibited by the negativity of its origins—he is capable of changing the world. "Savant et thaumaturge," a figure of technological representation, he performs miracles which are visible to all, curing the sick and controlling the weather. Addressing the "besoin de conservation que connaissent tous les êtres," he effects a continuity with the real, and presents the model of an absolute subject, by means of a will which is ontologically efficacious. Yet if Tograth presents the will as a positivity, he has neither a positive nor an autonomous function in the text. He exists exclusively in relation to Croniamantal and functions only to present a contrast to poetry. The thesis of the efficacity of will is staged as the *other* of poetic production, and Tograth's realization of the will in history defines him as the enemy of poets:

> Si les républiques et les rois, si les nations n'y prennent garde, la race des poètes, trop privilégiée, croîtra dans de telles proportions et si rapidement qu'avant peu de temps personne ne voudra plus travailler, inventer, apprendre, raisonner, faire des choses dangereuses, remédier aux malheurs des hommes et améliorer leur sort.
>
> Sans tarder, donc, il faut aviser et nous guérir de cette plaie poétique qui ronge l'humanité.

The demiurge is not the poet, nor even an alternative to the poet. For Tograth is not given to desire Tristouse, but rather an undifferentiated mass of women "prêtes à faire sa volonté." This will whose action encompasses the totality of the existent, by destroying any ground upon which an object might be *present*, produces only the phantasm which perception encounters, and which poetry itself would demolish. Rather than presenting an alternative to poetry, Tograth functions as the assassin of the poet: "Monde, choisis entre ta vie et la poésie; si l'on ne prend pas de mesures sérieuses contre elle, c'en est fait de la civilization. . . . On massacra les poètes."

Technology functions as the other of poetry and the analogue, in its pretensions, of perception. Any representation which assumes an immediate continuity with the real is opposed to poetry. Yet poetry may only be defined in relation to these. For *they* determine the actual historical status of the existent and *they* prescribe the historical effacement of the category of the real. As the sole mode of representation which states the negativity of representation itself, as a representation which assumes this effacement as the constitutive definition of the real to which it refers, poetry is a revelation of their duplicity. In claiming no ontological efficacity for itself, and in revealing the consequences of *any* such claim, poetry alone permits an exteriority to representation and the function of a subject within this category. In a universe defined by technological production, the exteriority to representation which poetry establishes becomes the *only* definition of the real.

Biographical Notes

François Villon (François de Montcorbier) was born in 1431, the year that Joan of Arc was burned at the stake. He attended the Sorbonne from 1449 through 1452, receiving three degrees. He spent the next several years with adventurers and thieves, murdered a priest, burgled, exiled himself, and was finally pardoned in 1460. His long poem, *Testament* (1461), chronicles his misdeeds. Villon continued to live outside the law and in 1462 was sentenced to be "hanged and strangled." This prompted him to write his "Ballade des pendus," which was so popular that his sentence was commuted to a ten-year banishment. Little is known about Villon's subsequent life. The first dated edition of his poetry appeared in 1489.

Marguerite de Navarre was born duchesse d'Angoulême in 1492. The daughter of Louise de Savoie and Charles d'Orléans, she was the elder sister of Francis I. Her first husband, the duc d'Alençon, died in 1525. In 1527 she married Henri d'Albret, Count of Bearn and King of Navarre, thereby becoming an ancestress of the line of Bourbon kings. She bore a daughter in 1528. She received a particularly extensive education for her times, learning Latin, Greek, Italian, Spanish, and Hebrew. She protected followers of the Reformation who were persecuted, such as Lefèvre d'Etaples, Marot, and Calvin, at her court of Navarre. Her correspondance with Guillaume Briçonnet, Bishop of Meaux, led her to mystic preoccupations and the philosophy of Plato and Platonic love later associated with her writings. In 1531, she published *Dialogue* and *Miroir de l'âme pécheresse* and, in 1533, a reedition of the latter with some new poems. In 1547, she collected under the title *Marguerites de la Marguerite des princesses* many spiritual songs, allegorical comedies, and poems. She died in 1549. Her best known work, *L'Hemptaméron*, a collection of stories, was published posthumously. *Les Prisons*, a long poem, was not discovered until this century.

Maurice Scève was born in Lyon sometime between 1500 and 1510, the son of a city magistrate. In 1533, while studying in Avignon, he claimed to have discovered the tomb of Petrarch's Laure de Noues. After returning to Lyon the following year he published *Deplourable Fin de Flamente*, a translation from a Spanish novel by Juan de Flores. In 1536 he met and fell in love with Pernette du Guillet. His most famous work, *Délie* (1544), is widely supposed to chronicle their platonic love affair. After du Guillet's death in 1545, Scève withdrew to the country. The facts of his life after 1550 are disputed. Some biographers conjecture that he became a protestant and moved to Germany; others maintain that he died of the plague in 1563. His final work, the epic *Microcosme*, was published in 1562.

441

Louise Labé was born sometime between 1516 and 1523 in Lyon, the daughter of a rope-maker. In 1542, she dressed as a man and took part in the tournament of Perpignan. Sometime within the next year she married Ennemond Perrin, also a ropemaker. In 1548 she began to compose *Le Débat de Folie et d'Amour*. Four years later, in 1552, she began to write sonnets. The recipient of poetic dedications from her close friend Olivier de Magny, Louise Labé was well enough known in her own lifetime to be cited by Calvin as a "plebia meretrix," a vulgar harlot. In 1555, Labé petitioned the king and received permission to publish her works. Her first book, *Oeuvres*, was published that year. Sometime between 1555 and 1557, her husband died. In 1565, Labé became ill and died early the following year, probably of the plague.

Pernette du Guillet was born sometime around 1520 to a noble family in Lyon. Considered a "perfect woman of the Renaissance," both beautiful and talented, she knew some Greek, was fluent in both Spanish and Italian, and was skilled on the lute. In 1536 she met Maurice Scève and became a member of his Lyon poetic circle, which included Louise Labé. Although she and Scève were in love, Pernette was forced to marry du Guillet in 1537 or 1538. She died quite prematurely, on July 17, 1545, perhaps a victim of the plague. After her death, her husband sent her poems to Antoine du Moulin, who published them under the title *Rymes*.

Joachim Du Bellay was probably born in 1522 in the Loire Valley to a noble family. He studied law and the humanities in Poitiers and Paris, publishing his first sonnets sometime between 1540 and 1550. A member of the Pléiade group with Ronsard, he published *La Défense et illustration de la langue française* in 1549, arguing that the French were capable of producing literary works equal to those of the Italians. Du Bellay's *Antiquités de Rome*, an account of the wonders of the ancient world, was published in 1558. Plagued by poor health and periodic deafness, Du Bellay died on Janurary 1, 1560, in Paris.

Pierre de Ronsard was born on September 11, 1524, the son of a noble family. Deafness kept him from a military career and led him into the church, where he was tonsured in 1543. Ronsard studied classics for five years with the humanist Jean Dorat at the Collège Coqueret. With his fellow students, Ronsard formed the group which came to be known as the Pléiade; they were poets who wrote, not in Latin, but in French, in the classical style. Ronsard's first poetic work, *Odes*, was published in two parts, in 1550 and 1552. In his preface to this work, he claimed to be the first French lyric poet. *Les Amours* appeared in 1552 and *Hymnes* in 1556. Two years later he became the official court poet to King Charles IX and began to publish an edition of his collected works. Following this appointment, much of his writing was political. In 1572 Ronsard began writing an epic of the French nation, the *Franciade*. Though somewhat critical, he sided with the Catholic church in the religious struggles following the Council of Trent. *Sonnets pour Hélène* appeared in 1578, followed by various panegyrics for the new king, Henry III. In 1584, suffering from gout, Ronsard made a last collection of his works. He died on December 27, 1585, at the Priory of Saint Cosme near Tours.

Jean de La Fontaine was born in Château-Thierry on July 8, 1621. The oldest son of a forest ranger and chief huntsman in the royal service, the young La Fontaine attended grammar school in Reims and perhaps even studied law. He married for wealth, and he and his wife were quickly estranged. In 1658 he went to Paris, where he began to write light verse and plays and won noble favor. After gaining support from various members of the aristocracy, La Fontaine was adopted by Mme. Marguerite de la Sablière, with whom he lived for twenty years until her death. His first volume, *Contes*, was published in 1664, followed by a second series in 1666. In 1669 he published two short novels, *Les Amours de Psyché et Cupidon* and

Adonis, as well as several plays. His most famous works, his fables, were published over a period of sixteen years. The first volume, 124 fables in six books, appeared in 1668, followed by second and third installments in 1678 and 1679. The twelfth and final book, bringing the total to 238 fables, was published in 1694. La Fontaine died on April 13, 1695, two years after the death of his benefactress.

Alphonse de Lamartine was born in 1790 to an aristocratic family in Mâcon, Burgundy. His first book of poetry, *Méditations* (1820), was a huge success. It was followed in 1823 by *Les Nouvelles Méditations,* also a very popular book. In 1820 he married an Englishwoman, Marianne Eliza Birch, and divided his time between diplomatic duties in Italy and poetry writing. In 1830, Lamartine was successfully elected to the Académie Française and published *Harmonies poétiques et religieuses.* This was followed by two epic works, *Jocelyn* (1836) and *La Chute d'un ange* (1838). In the 1830s and 1840s Lamartine's political interests and duties increased. He was elected to office, began to write political histories and analyses, and ran a biweekly paper in Mâcon called *Le Bien public.* During the February Revolution of 1848, Lamartine became provisional head of the French government. His popularity was brief, however: fearing him to be too radical, the bourgeoisie voted him out of the Office of the Presidency in December. Following his defeat, Lamartine began a ten-year career as a hack, writing furiously in an attempt to pay the debts he had contracted while in office. He died in 1867, in poverty and after a long illness.

Alfred de Vigny was born into a military family in Loches in 1797. He, too, entered the military—the year before the Battle of Waterloo—but was invalided out at age thirty. He married an Englishwoman, Lydia Jane Bunbury and, after she became ill, spent the next thirty years caring for her. His *Cinq-Mars,* a novel, and *Poèmes antiques et modernes* were published in 1826. De Vigny translated several of Shakespeare's plays into French, as well as writing plays of his own. At least one of these, *Chatterton,* was a theatrical success, in 1835. In January 1846, de Vigny was elected to the French Academy. He continued to write and publish poetry in journals and periodicals until his death in September 1863. A posthumous collection of his poetry, *Les Destinées,* was published in 1864.

Victor-Marie Hugo was born on February 26, 1802. He began writing when a child and in 1819 founded *Le Conservateur littéraire* with his brothers. In 1822 he married his childhood sweetheart, Adèle Foucher, and published *Les Odes et poésies diverses,* for which he received a 1,000-franc pension from the king. *Notre-Dame de Paris* appeared in 1831, followed by a collection of poems, *Les Chants du crépuscule,* in 1835. In 1841 he was elected to the French Academy. A supporter of Louis Napoleon Bonaparte in 1848, Hugo founded *L'Evénement* and used its pages to call for universal suffrage and freedom of the press. When *L'Evénement* was banned in 1850, he began a second journal called *Avènement du peuple.* A third collection of poems, *Les Contemplations,* appeared in 1856, *Les Misérables* in 1862, and *Quatre-vingt treize* in 1874. A very popular national figure, Hugo was elected a Senator of Paris in 1876. When he died on May 22, 1885, the city of Paris held a national funeral. His works are today still widely published.

Aloysius (Louis Jacques Napoléon) Bertrand was born on April 20, 1807, in Italy, but his family settled in Dijon in 1815. When he grew up, Bertrand attempted to support himself by journalism. The manager of a newspaper in Dijon, his contributions caught the attention and praise of Hugo and Saint-Beuve. His most famous work, *Gaspard de la nuit,* about medieval Dijon, introduced the prose poem to France. It was not published during Bertrand's lifetime, however. Bertrand died of tuberculosis and starvation in 1840. *Gaspard de la nuit* was first published in 1842.

Gérard de Nerval (Gerard Labrunie) was born in Paris on May 22, 1808, the son of a physician.

He began to write poetry at the age of thirteen and his first book, *Elégies nationales*, was published in 1826. Labrunie quickly became known for his excellent translations of German poets and, according to one account, his work on *Faust* earned praise from Goethe himself. Between 1828 and 1830 he invented and patented a printing machine. After a long battle with his father over his choice of writing as a career, Gérard broke with his family in 1831 and took the name de Nerval. A year later, he entered medical school, but dropped out in 1834 when he received an inheritance from his grandfather. The 1836 failure of a journal he had started, *Monde dramatique*, put Nerval in debt for the rest of his life. Throughout the 1830s and 1840s, he made his living as a journalist. In 1839 he revised the play *Leo Burckhart*, initially a collaborative effort with Alexandre Dumas, and it had a run of twenty-six performances. Nerval's first breakdown, in February 1841 led to eight months in an asylum. His friends, believing that he could not be cured, published an "obituary" to his genius. He recovered, however, and in December traveled through the East, gathering material for his *Voyage en Orient* (1851). From 1849 on, Nerval's periodic breakdowns became more frequent, but when he was well he wrote feverishly. His later works include *Les Illuminés*, *Lorely: Souvenirs d'Allemagne*, and *La Bohème Galante* (1852), *Sylvie* (1853), and *Les Filles du feu* and *Les Chimères* (1854). On January 26, 1854, Nerval hung himself in the rue de la Vieille Lanterne.

Louis Charles Alfred de Musset was born in Paris on December 11, 1810. His first volume of poetry, *Contes d'Espagne et d'Italie*, was published when he was nineteen, followed the next year by *Poésies*. *Le Spectacle dans un fauteuil* appeared in 1833. A love affair with Georges Sand in the winter of 1833–34 inspired *Nuits*, other love poems, and *La Confession d'un enfant du siècle*, published in 1836. De Musset went on to write popular comedies and songs and was elected to the Académie Française in 1852. He died in Paris on May 2, 1857.

Pierre-Jules Théophile Gautier was born in Tarbes in 1811, to Adélaïde and Pierre Gautier, the latter a minor government official. In 1814, the family moved to Paris. In 1822, Gautier entered the Collège Charlemagne, where he befriended Gérard de Nerval. In 1829, he studied painting at the Rioult studio. That same year he met Victor Hugo and became a member of the "Cénacle," the literary group which met in the salon of Charles Nodier. In 1830, the year of the battle of *Hernani*, he published his first volume of poetry, *Poésies*. A prolific writer, Gautier wrote in many different genres. Besides volumes of poetry (*La Comédie de la mort* [1838], *Espagna* [1845], *Emaux et Camées* [1852]) he wrote novels (*Mademoiselle de Maupin* [1835], *Le Capitaine Fracasse* [1863]), fantastic short stories (*Le Club des hachichins* [1843], *Le Roman de la momie* [1857], *Spirite* [1865]), plays (*Une Larme du diable* [1839], *Pierrot Posthume* [1847]), ballets (*Giselle* [1841], *La Péri* [1843]), travel accounts (*Voyage en Espagne* [1843], *Constantinople* [1853]), as well as art and literary criticism (*L'Art moderne* [1856], *Histoire de l'art dramatique depuis vingt-cinq ans* [1858], *Histoire du romantisme* [1872]). A lifelong proponent of art for art's sake, he expounded his aesthetic theory in the preface to *Emaux et Camées*, whose poem "L'Art" was read as its manifesto. Gautier died in 1872 of a heart condition.

Charles Pierre Baudelaire was born on April 9, 1821, in Paris. On his twenty-first birthday Baudelaire received a small inheritance from his father which enabled him to devote his attention to writing. He made his literary debut in 1843 with a collection entitled *Vers* and joined Théophile Gautier at Madame Sabatière's for the Club des Hachichins. Baudelaire continued to write and to publish in small journals. He also began to translate Poe and to write prose poems. In 1851 the first part of *Paradis artificiels* appeared, and in 1855 eighteen poems under the title *Les Fleurs du mal* were published in *La Revue des Deux Mondes*. The complete *Fleurs de mal* was published on June 25, 1857. Denounced in July, the publisher's stock of the book was confiscated and *Les Fleurs du mal* was brought to trial on August 20. Six poems were suppressed and a new, amended version of the book was brought out in

1860. In September 1862, twenty prose poems were published in *La Presse*, followed the next year by other prose poems in *Le Figaro* and *La Revue de Paris* under the title *Le Spleen de Paris*. Frequently in ill health, Baudelaire was hospitalized in 1866 and died on August 31, 1867.

Etienne (Stéphane) Mallarmé was born on March 18, 1842, in Paris, the son of a clerk in the Registry and Public Property Office. His mother died when he was five and his younger sister when he was fifteen. He wrote his first poems, strongly influenced by Baudelaire, in 1861. In 1862, Mallarmé's first poems were published and he traveled to England with Maria-Christina Gerhard, later his wife, to learn English. The following year, after the death of his father, Mallarmé married Maria and took a job teaching English at Tournon. He published his first prose poems in 1864, the year his daughter, Geneviève, was born. In 1866 he published ten poems in *Le Parnasse contemporain*. *Hérodiade* appeared in the next issue, in 1871, the same year his son, Anatole, was born and Mallarmé received a teaching appointment in Paris at the Lycée Fontanes. He began his "Tuesday evening" poetry sessions in 1872 and published a number of prose poems and translations of Poe. In 1874, he published eight issues of *La Dernière Mode*, a fashion magazine, and in 1878 and 1880 two textbooks: *Les Mots anglais* and *Les Dieux antiques*. His son died in 1879, inspiring the never-completed *Un Tombeau pour Anatole*. *Les Poésies de Stéphane Mallarmé* and *Album de vers et de prose*, Mallarmé's first book-length collections, were published in 1887. Elected Prince of Poets in 1896, Mallarmé died on September 9, 1898, at Valvins, his summer home.

Paul (Marie) Verlaine was born in Metz on March 30, 1844, and brought to Paris when he was seven years old. Verlaine wrote his first known poem, "La Mort," when he was fourteen and sent it to Victor Hugo. Initially employed in an insurance firm, Verlaine spent his afterhours with artists and writers. His first published work, an article on Baudelaire, appeared in *L'Art* in 1865. The following year, seven of his poems appeared in the series *Le Parnasse contemporain*, and *Poèmes saturniens* was published. *Fêtes galantes* appeared in 1869. Married in 1870, Verlaine met Rimbaud in 1871 and began to separate himself from his wife and son. In 1872–73 Rimbaud and Verlaine lived and traveled together in England and Belgium. This liason ended in July 1873, in Brussels, when Verlaine shot Rimbaud in the wrist in an attempt to prevent him from leaving. Verlaine was imprisoned for two years, during which he continued to write, published *Romances sans paroles* (1874), and converted to Catholicism. In 1875 he left prison, was expelled from Belgium, and began to teach in France. Although his health, finances, and familial circumstances declined considerably, he continued to write and publish books through the remainder of his life. Among them were: *Sagesse* (1880), *Poètes maudits* (1885), *Jadis et naguère* (1885), *Amour* (1888), *Dédicaces* and *Femmes* (1890), *Choix de poésies* (1891), *Liturgies intimes* (1892), *Elégies, Odes en son honneur*, and *Mes Prisons* (1893), and *Confessions* (1895). Verlaine died, ill and proverty-stricken, on January 8, 1896, in Paris.

Tristan Corbière was born on July 18, 1845, in Morlaix, Brittany, the son of a writer. Extremely shy, he lived in Morlaix for all but the three years he spent in Paris. His first and only work, *Les Amours jaunes*, appeared in 1873. Corbière died on March 1, 1875, in Morlaix. He remained virtually unknown until Verlaine included some of his work in *Les Poètes maudits*, published in 1884.

Comte de Lautréamont (Isidore Lucien Ducasse) was born on April 4, 1846, in Montevideo, Uruguay, where his father was in the foreign service. At age sixteen, the young Ducasse went to France to study in Tarbes. He traveled to Paris in 1867, where he completed *Les Chants de Maldoror*, lyrical prose fragments published between 1868 and 1869 as the work of "Comte Lautréamont." The book remained uncirculated and unsold until its republication in 1890. *Poésies* appeared in June 1870, the year also of Lautréamont's death, in Paris, on November 24.

Jean-Nicolas-Arthur Rimbaud was born on October 20, 1854, in Charleville to Vitalie Cuif and Frédéric Rimbaud, an infantry captain. In 1869 he published three Latin verse compositions in *Le Moniteur de l'enseignement secondaire*. The third composition, "Jugartha," received first prize in the Concours Académique. That same year Rimbaud also composed his first French verse, "Les Étrennes des orphelins," published in *La Revue pour tous* on January 2, 1870. Rimbaud wrote twenty-two poems in 1870, and befriended the young teacher Georges Izambard. He wrote the "voyant" letters the following year and received an invitation from Verlaine to come to Paris. Rimbaud spent much of the next two years with Verlaine in Paris, London, and Brussels. Attempting to leave Verlaine in 1873, Rimbaud was shot in the wrist. He returned home to Charleville and wrote and published *Une Saison en enfer*. In 1874, Rimbaud renounced literature and began an intensive program of language aquisition so that he could become an explorer. In 1876 he signed up with the Dutch Colonial Army, but after three weeks deserted, joined a British crew on a sailing ship, and returned home. In 1878–79 Rimbaud traveled to Alexandria and Cyprus, but caught typhus and had to go home. In 1880 he returned to Cyprus and then went to Egypt, where he began to work for a firm which traded hides and coffee. Under the auspices of this firm, he explored Somalia and northeast Africa and sent reports back to la Société de Géographie. He began gun running in 1887, and then from 1888 through 1891 he ran a trading post in Harar. In 1891 Rimbaud became ill, returned to France, and died on November 10.

Jules Laforgue was born in Montevideo, Uruguay, on August 16, 1860. In 1866, he sailed to Tarbes, France, with most of his family. Ten years later, the entire family moved to Paris. Laforgue's first poems were published in 1879 in small magazines in Tarbes and Toulouse. A part-time assistant in 1881 to Charles Ephrussi, an art historian and collector, Laforgue was appointed to the Court at Coblenz as a French reader to Empress Augusta of Germany. His first book of poetry, *Les Complaintes de Jules Laforgue*, was published on July 25, 1885, followed later in the year by *L'Imitation de Notre-Dame*. Laforgue began to learn English in 1886 and translated some poems of Walt Whitman. He gave up his appointment in the German court that same year and married his tutor, Leah Lee. The following year, on August 20, Laforgue died. *Moralités légendaires* (1887), *Les Derniers Vers de Jules Laforgue* (1890), and *Berlin, la cour et la ville* (1922) were published posthumously.

Guillaume Apollinaire (Wilhelm Apollinaris de Kostrowitzky), the son of a Polish emigrée and an Italian officer, was born on August 26, 1880, perhaps in Rome. He went to Paris at age twenty and managed an avant-garde review, *Les Festins d'Esope*. His first work, *L'Enchanteur pourissant*, appeared in 1909, followed by *L'Hérésiarque et Cie* (1910), *Le Bestiaire* (1911), and *Alcools* (1913). A friend of numerous painters, including Picasso, Apollinaire attempted to elaborate a cubist aesthetic in literature, in *Peintures cubistes* (1913). In 1914, he enlisted as a second lieutenant in the infantry. Two years later, he received a wound in the head and was discharged. *Le Poète assassiné* followed in 1916. *Les Mamelles de Tirésias*, a play which Apollinaire, in perhaps the first use of the word, called "surrealist," was staged in 1917. *Calligrammes* was published in 1918. Apollinaire died later that year on November 9.

Contributors

Harold Bloom, Sterling Professor of the Humanities at Yale University, is the author of *The Anxiety of Influence, Poetry and Repression*, and many other volumes of literary criticism. His forthcoming study, *Freud: Transference and Authority*, attempts a full-scale reading of all of Freud's major writings. A MacArthur Prize Fellow, he is general editor of five series of literary criticism published by Chelsea House. During 1987–88, he served as Charles Eliot Norton Professor of Poetry at Harvard University.

Jefferson Humphries is Assistant Professor of French and Italian at Louisiana State University and A & M College in Baton Rouge. He is the author of *The Otherness Within: Gnostic Reading in Marcel Proust, Flannery O'Connor, and François Villon*, and *Losing the Text: Readings in Literary Desire*.

Robert D. Cottrell is Professor of French at Ohio State University. He is the author of *Colette, Simone de Beauvoir, Sexuality-Textuality: A Study of the Fabric of Montaigne's* Essais, and *The Grammar of Silence: A Reading of Marguerite de Navarre's Poetry*.

Elisabeth Guild teaches French at Robinson College, Cambridge.

Ann Rosalind Jones is Associate Professor of Comparative Literature at Smith College. She has written on Maurice Scève, French feminism, theories of the novel, and Renaissance women poets.

Daniel Russell is Professor and Chairman of the French and Italian Department at the University of Pittsburg. He is the author of *The Emblem and Device in France*.

Terence C. Cave is a Tutor in Modern Languages and a Lecturer in French at St. Johns College, Oxford. He has written *Devotional Poetry in France* and

447

The Cornucopian Text: Problems of Writing in the French Renaissance, and edited *Ronsard the Poet.*

Ross Chambers is Professor of French at the University of Michigan. He is the author of *Story and Situation: Narrative Seduction and the Power of Fiction.*

Georges Poulet was a member of the Institut de France in Nice, and formerly, in the United States, he was Chairman of the Department of Romance Languages at the Johns Hopkins University. His books which have appeared in English include *The Metamorphoses of the Circle, Studies in Human Time, The Interior Distance,* and *Exploding Poetry: Baudelaire/Rimbaud.*

Martha Noel Evans is Associate Professor of French at Mary Baldwin College in Staunton, Virginia.

Joan C. Kessler is Assistant Professor of French at the State University of New York, New Paltz. She has written articles on *Le Roman de la Rose* and Victor Hugo.

Margery Sabin is Associate Professor of English at Wellesley College. She has written on the avant-garde, and is the author of *English Romanticism and the French Tradition.*

Richard Sieburth is Associate Professor of French at New York University. He has translated works by Hölderlin and Benjamin, and is the author of *Instigations: Ezra Pound and Remy de Gourmont.*

Shoshana Felman is Professor of French at Yale University. She is the editor of *Literature and Psychoanalysis: The Question of Reading—Otherwise,* and the author of *La "Folie" dans l'oeuvre romanesque de Stendhal, The Literary Speech Act: Don Juan with J. L. Austin, or Seduction in Two Languages, Writing and Madness (Literature/Philosophy/Psychoanalysis),* and a forthcoming collection of essays on Jacques Lacan.

Rodolphe Gasché is Professor of Comparative Literature at the State University of New York, Buffalo. His works include *System und Metaphorik in der Philosophie von Georges Bataille* and *The Tain of the Mirror: Derrida and the Philosophy of Reflection.*

Albert B. Smith teaches in the Department of Romance Languages at the University of Florida, Gainesville. He is the author of *Ideal and Reality in the Fictional Narrative of Théophile Gautier* and *Théophile Gautier and the Fantastic.*

Paul de Man taught Comparative Literature and French at Yale University, where he was Sterling Professor in the Humanities. He taught previously at the universities of Zurich, Harvard, Cornell, and Johns Hopkins. He published two books during his lifetime—as well as numerous articles. They have been and are being collected in posthumous volumes: *The Rhetoric of Romanticism, The Resistance to Theory, Aesthetic Ideology,* and *Fugitive Essays.*

Fredric Jameson is the William A. Lane Professor of Comparative Literature at Duke University. He is the author of *Marxism and Form, The Prison-House of Language,* and *The Political Unconscious.*

Barbara Johnson is Professor of Romance Languages and Literatures at Harvard University. She is the author of *Défigurations du langage poétique, The Critical Difference,* and *A World of Difference.*

James Lawler is Professor of French at the University of Chicago. He is the founding editor of *Dalhousie French Studies,* the editor of a Valéry anthology, and the author of *The Language of French Symbolism, The Poet as Analyst: Essays on Paul Valéry,* and *René Char: The Myth and the Poem.*

Carol de Dobay Rifelj, Professor of French and Dean of the French School at Middlebury College, is the author of *Word and Figure: The Language of Nineteenth-Century French Poetry.*

Robert L. Mitchell teaches at Ohio State University. He is the author of *Tristan Corbière* and the editor of *Corbière, Mallarmé, Valéry: Preservations and Commentary* and *Pretext, Text, Context,* a collection of essays on nineteenth-century French authors.

Robin Lydenberg teaches in the Department of English at Boston College.

Marshall Lindsay is Professor of French at the University of California at Davis. He has published articles on nineteenth- and twentieth-century poetry and novels, and is the author of *Le Temps jaune: Essais sur Corbière.*

Karin Dillman teaches French at the University of Washington in Seattle. She has written on nineteenth- and twentieth-century poetry and poetic theory, and is the author of *The Subject in Rimbaud: From Self to "Je."*

Warren Ramsey is the author of *Jules Laforgue and the Ironic Inheritance* and the editor of *Jules Laforgue: Essays on a Poet's Life and Work.*

Dennis G. Sullivan was Professor of French at The Johns Hopkins University. He has recently published articles on Proust and on poetic language.

Bibliography

GENERAL

Borowitz, Helen O. *The Impact of Art on French Literature: From de Scudéry to Proust.* Newark: University of Delaware Press, 1985.

Bowen, Barbara C. *Words and the Men in French Renaissance Literature.* Lexington, Ky.: French Forum, 1983.

Brereton, Geoffrey. *An Introduction to the French Poets: Villon to the Present Day.* London: Methuen, 1973.

Caws, Mary Ann, and Hermine Riffaterre, eds. *The Prose Poem in France: Theory and Practice.* New York: Columbia University Press, 1983.

Charlton, D. G., ed. *The French Romantics.* Cambridge: Cambridge University Press, 1984.

De Ley, Herbert. *The Movement of Thought: An Essay on Intellect in Seventeenth-Century France.* Urbana: University of Illinois Press, 1985.

Engelberg, Karsten, ed. *The Romantic Heritage: A Collection of Critical Essays.* Copenhagen: University of Copenhagen Press, 1983.

Hartman, Geoffrey. "Reflections on Romanticism in France." *Studies in Romanticism* 9 (1970): 233–48.

Hornik, Henry. *Studies on the French Renaissance: Theory and Idealism.* Geneva: Slatkine, 1985.

Hošek, Chaviva and Patricia Parker, eds. *Lyric Poetry: Beyond New Criticism.* Ithaca: Cornell University Press, 1985.

Knapp, Bettina L. *Dream and Image.* Troy, N.Y.: Whitston, 1977.

La Charité, Raymond C., ed. *Kentucky Romance Quarterly* 19, suppl. 1 (1972).

Leiner, Wolfgang, ed. *Onze Nouvelles Etudes sur l'image de la femme dans la littérature française du dix-septième siècle.* Paris: Eds. Jean-Michel Place, 1984.

Mitchell, Robert L., ed. *Pretext Text Context.* Columbus: Ohio State University Press, 1980.

Nash, Jerry C., ed. *Pre-Pléiade Poetry.* French Forum Monographs 57. Lexington, Ky.: French Forum, 1985.

Prescott, Anne Lake. *French Poets and the English Renaissance: Studies in Fame and Transformation.* New Haven: Yale University Press, 1973.

Riffaterre, Michael. *Semiotics of Poetry.* Bloomington: Indiana University Press, 1978.

────. *Text Production*. New York: Columbia University Press, 1983.

Rousset, Jean. *La Littérature de l'âge baroque en France*. Paris: Corti, 1953.

Sabin, Margery. *English Romanticism and the French Tradition*. Cambridge, Mass.: Harvard University Press, 1976.

Spitzer, Leo. *Essays on Seventeenth-Century French Literature*. Translated and edited by David Bellos. Cambridge: Cambridge University Press, 1983.

Stade, George, ed. *European Writers: The Age of Reason and the Enlightenment: Voltaire to André Chénier*. New York: Scribner's, 1984.

Weber, Henri. *La Création poétique au XVIᵉ siècle en France*. Paris: Nizet, 1956.

FRANÇOIS VILLON

Burger, André. *Lexique de la langue de Villon*. Geneva: Droz, 1957.

Dragonetti, Roger. " 'La Balade de fortune.' " *Revue des Langues Romans* 86 (1982): 177–89.

DuBruck, Edelgard. "Villon's Two Pleas for Absolution." *L'Esprit Créateur* 7 (1967): 188–96.

Fein, David A. "The Povre Villon and Other Martyred Loves of the *Testament*." *Neophiloloqus* 64 (1980): 347–57.

────. "The Conclusion of Villon's *Testament*: An Image in the Shroud?" *Fifteenth-Century Studies* 5 (1982): 61–66.

────. *A Reading of Villon's* Testament. Birmingham, Ala.: Summa, 1984.

Fox, John. *The Poetry of Villon*. London: Thomas Nelson & Sons, 1962.

Guiraud, Pierre. *Le Jargon de Villon, ou le gai savoir de la Coquille*. Paris: Gallimard, 1968.

Kinnell, Galway. *Introduction to the Poems of François Villon*. Boston: Houghton Mifflin, 1977.

Kuhu, David. *La Poétique de François Villon*. Paris: A. Cohn, 1967.

Lacy, Norris J. "Villon in His Work: The *Testament* and the Problem of Personal Poetry." *L'Esprit Créateur* 18, no. 1 (Spring 1978): 60–69.

────. "The Voices of Villon's *Testament*." *Dalhousie French Studies* 4 (October 1982): 3–12.

Rice, Winthrop H. *The European Ancestry of Villon's Satirical Testaments*. New York: Corporate Press (Syracuse University Monographs), 1941.

Vitz, Evelyn Birge. *The Crossroad of Intentions: A Study of Symbolic Expression in the Poetry of François Villon*. The Hague: Mouton, 1974.

────. "Symbolic 'Contamination' in the *Testament* of François Villon." *MLN* 86 (1971): 456–95.

MARGUERITE DE NAVARRE

Auld, Louis E. "Music as Dramatic Device in the Secular Theatre of Marguerite de Navarre." *Renaissance Drama* 7 (1976): 192–217.

Baker, M. J. "The Role of the Moral Lesson in Heptaméron No. 30." *French Studies* 31 (1977): 18–25.

Benson, Edward. "Marriage Ancestral and Conjugal in the *Heptaméron*." *Journal of Medieval and Renaissance Studies* 9 (1979): 261–75.

Clements, Robert J. "Marguerite de Navarre and Dante." In *Peregrine Muse: Studies in Comparative Renaissance Literature*. Chapel Hill: University of North Carolina Press, 1969.

Clive, H. P. *Marguerite de Navarre: An Annotated Bibliography*. London: Grant & Cutler, 1983.

Costa, Jean. "Sentiment et humanisme dans les *Chansons spirituelles* de Marguerite de Navarre." *Revue de l'Université de Laval* 2 (1966): 767–74.

Cottrell, Robert D. *The Grammar of Silence: A Reading of Marguerite de Navarre's Poetry.* Washington, D.C.: Catholic University Press, 1986.

Davis, Betty J. *The Storytellers in Marguerite de Navarre.* Lexington, Ky.: French Forum, 1978.

Ely, Gladys. "The Limits of Realism in the *Heptaméron* de Marguerite de Navarre." *Romanic Review* 43 (1952): 3–11.

Gelernt, Jules. *World of Many Loves: The* Heptaméron *of Marguerite de Navarre.* Chapel Hill: University of North Carolina Press, 1966.

Heller, Henry. "Marguerite de Navarre and the Reformers of Meaux." *Bibliothèque d'Humanisme et Renaissance* 33 (1971): 271–310.

Krailsheimer, A. J. "The *Heptaméron* Reconsidered." In *The French Renaissance and Its Heritage: Essays Presented to Alan M. Boase by Colleagues, Pupils, and Friends.* London: Methuen, 1968, pp. 75–92.

Leckman, Hannah Hone. "Mysticism in the Poetry of Marguerite de Navarre." Ph.D. diss.: Catholic University of America, 1982.

Masters, G. Mallary. "Structured Prisons, Imprisoned Structures: Marguerite de Navarre's *Prisons.*" *Renaissance Papers* 30 (1973): 11–22.

Meijer, Marianne. "The *Heptaméron:* Feminism with a Smile." *Regionalism and the Female Imagination* 3 (1977–78): 1–10.

Norton, Glyn P. "The Emilio Ferretti Letter: A Critical Preface for Marguerite de Navarre." *Journal of Medieval and Renaissance Studies* 4 (1974): 287–300.

———. "Narrative Function in the *Heptaméron* Frame-Story." In *La Nouvelle française à la Renaissance*, edited by Lionello Sozzi and V. L. Saulnier. Geneva: Slatkine, 1981.

Stone, Donald. "Narrative Technique in *L'Heptaméron.*" *Studi Francesi* 11 (1967): 473–76.

Tetel, Marcel. "Marguerite de Navarre et Montaigne: relativisme et paradoxe." *Kentucky Romance Quarterly* 19, suppl. 1 (1972): 125–35.

———. *Marguerite de Navarre's* Heptaméron: *Themes, Language, and Structure.* Durham, N.C.: Duke University Press, 1973.

Wiley, William L. "The Complexities of Marguerite de Navarre's Secular Theatre." *Kentucky Romance Quarterly* 21, suppl. 2 (1974): 319–30.

Winandy, André. "Piety and Humanistic Symbolism in the Work of Marguerite d'Angoulême, Queen of Navarre." *Yale French Studies* no. 47 (1972): 145–69.

Zamparelli, Thomas L. "Duality in the *Comédies profanes* of Marguerite de Navarre." *South Central Bulletin* 38 (1978): 166–69.

MAURICE SCÈVE

Coleman, Dorothy G. "Les Emblesmes dans la *Délie* de Maurice Scève." *Studi Francesi* 8 (1964): 1–15.

———. *Maurice Scève: Poet of Love—Tradition and Originality.* Cambridge: Cambridge University Press, 1975.

———. "Scève: A Virile Intellect Aerated by Sensibility." In *The Equilibrium of Wit: Essays for Odette de Mourgues*, edited by P. J. Bayley and D. G. Coleman. French Forum Monographs 36. Lexington, Ky.: French Forum, 1982.

Cool, Kenneth E. "Scève's Agony of Expression and Petrarchan Discourse." *Stanford French Review* 3 (1979): 193–210.

Dellaneva, Joann. *Song and Counter-Song: Scève's Délie and Petrarch's "Rime."* Lexington, Ky.: French Forum, 1983.

Duval, E. M. "Articulation of the *Délie:* Emblems, Numbers, and the Book." *Modern Language Review* 75 (1980): 65–75.

Garlic, Barbara. "As Much Modesty as Cunning: Maurice Scève's Use of a Renaissance Commonplace in the Escort Sonnets to *Microcosme.*" *Parergon* 2 (1984): 205–14.

Giordano, Michael J. "Reading *Délie*: Dialectic and Sequence." *Symposium* 34 (1980): 155–67.

Graff, M. "Nombres et emblèmes dans *Délie.*" *RHR* 6 (December 1980): 5–12.

Greene, Thomas M. "Styles of Experience in Scève's *Délie.*" *Yale French Studies* no. 47 (1972): 57–75.

———. "Rescue from the Abyss: Scève's Dizain 378." In *Textual Analysis: Some Readers Reading,* edited by Mary Ann Caws. New York: Modern Language Association of America, 1986.

Hallyn, F. "Les Emblèmes de *Délie*: Propositions interprétatives et méthodologiques." *Revue des Sciences Humaines* 179 (July–September 1980): 61–75.

Klein, Richard. "Straight Lines and Arabesques: Metaphors of Metaphor." *Yale French Studies* no. 45 (1970): 64–86.

McFarlane, I. D., ed. *The* Délie *of Maurice Scève.* Cambridge: Cambridge University Press, 1966.

Melançon, C. "Les Décimales de *Délie.*" *Les Etudes Françaises* 11 (February 1975): 33–53.

Nash, Jerry C. "The Notion and Meaning of Art in the *Délie.*" *Romanic Review* 71 (1980): 28–46.

———. "Logic and Lyric: Poetic Closure in Scève's *Délie.*" *French Studies* 38 (1984): 385–96.

Pivato, Joseph. "Maurice Scève's *Délie:* Unpetrarchan and Hermetic." *Studi Francesi* 27 (1979): 14–28.

Quignard, Pascal. *La Parole de la* Délie. Paris: Mercure de France, 1974.

Rigolot, François. "Paronymie et sémantique nominale chez Pétrarque et Scève." In *Poétique et onomastique: L'Exemple de la Renaissance.* Geneva: Droz, 1977.

Risset, Jacqueline. *L'Anagramme du désir: Essai sur la* Délie *de Maurice Scève.* Rome: Mario Bulzoni, 1971.

Runyon, Randolph. "Scève's 'Autre Troye': Placement and Other Tie(r)s in *Délie.*" *MLN* 90 (1975): 535–47.

Saulnier, V.-L. *Maurice Scève.* Paris: Klinksieck, 1948.

———. "Aspects de Maurice Scève: La Voix et le silence dans *Délie.*" In *L'Humanisme lyonnais au XVIᵉ siècle.* Grenoble: Presses Universitaires de Grenoble, 1974.

LOUISE LABÉ AND PERNETTE DU GUILLET

Ardouin, Paul. *Maurice Scève, Pernette du Guillet, Louise Labé: L'Amour à Lyons au temps de la Renaissance.* Paris: Nizet, 1981.

Baker, M. W. "The Sonnets of Louise Labé: A Reappraisal." *Neophilologus* 60 (1976): 20–30.

Benkov, Edith J. "The Pantheon Revisited: Myth and Metaphor in Louise Labé." *Classical and Modern Literature* 5 (1984): 23–31.

Champdor, Albert. *Louise Labé, son oeuvre et son temps.* [Trévoux]: Editions de Trévoux, 1981.

Harvey, Lawrence E. *The Aesthetic of the Renaissance Love Sonnet: An Essay on the Art of the Sonnet in the Poetry of Louise Labé.* Geneva: Droz, 1962.

Jondorf, Gillian. "Petrarchan Variations in Pernette du Guillet and Louise Labé." *Modern Language Review* 71 (1976): 766–78.

Perry, T. A. "Pernette du Guillet's Poetry of Love and Desire." *Bibliothèque d'Humanisme et Renaissance* 35 (1973): 259–71.

Poliner, Sharlene M. "*Signes d'amante* and the Dispossessed Lover: Louise Labé's Poetics of Inheritance." *Bibliothèque d'Humanisme et Renaissance* 46 (1984): 323–42.

Rigolot, François. "Quel genre d'amour pour Louise Labé?" *Poétique* 55 (1983): 303–17.

Sharratt, Peter. "Introduction" and "Commentaries." In *Louise Labé, Sonnets*. Edinburgh: Edinburgh University Press, 1970.

Wiley, Karen F. "Louise Labé Deceptive Petrarchism." *Modern Language Studies* 11 (1981): 51–60.

Zamaron, Fernand. *Louise Labé: Dame de franchise*. Paris: Nizet, 1968.

JOACHIM DU BELLAY

Castan, Felix. "The Realm of the Imaginary in Du Bellay/Ronsard and Du Bartas/La Ceppède." *Yale French Studies* no. 47 (1972): 110–23.

Deguy, Michel. *Tombeau de Du Bellay*. Paris: Gallimard, 1973.

Dickinson, Gladys. *Du Bellay in Rome*. Leiden: Brill, 1960.

L'Esprit Créateur 19, no. 3 (1979). Special Du Bellay issue.

Ferguson, Margaret W. "Joachim Du Bellay: The Exile's Defense of His Native Language." In *Trials of Desire: Renaissance Defenses of Poetry*. New Haven: Yale University Press, 1983.

Griffin, Robert. *Coronation of the Poet: Joachim Du Bellay's Debt to the Trivium*. Berkeley: University of California Press, 1969.

Katz, Richard A. *The Ordered Text: The Sonnet Sequences of Du Bellay*. New York: Lang, 1985.

Riffaterre, Michael. "Intertextual Semiosis: Du Bellay's 'Songe VII.' " In *Text Production*. New York: Columbia University Press, 1983.

Satterthwaite, A. W. *Spenser, Ronsard and Du Bellay: A Renaissance Comparison*. Princeton: Princeton University Press, 1960.

Saulnier, V.-L. *Du Bellay, l'homme et l'oeuvre*. Paris: 1951.

Smith, Malcolm. *Joachim Du Bellay's Veiled Victim, with an Edition of the Xenia*. Geneva: Droz, 1974.

PIERRE DE RONSARD

Barbier, Jean Paul. *Bibliographie des discours politiques de Ronsard*. Geneva: Droz, 1985.

Cave, Terrence. *The Cornucopian Text: Problems of Writing in the French Renaissance*. Oxford: Clarendon Press, 1979.

———. "Ronsard's Bacchic Poetry: From the *Bacchanales* to the *Hymne de l'automne*." *L'Esprit Créateur* 10 (1970): 104–16.

———. "The Triumph of Bacchus and Its Interpretation in the French Renaissance: Ronsard's 'Hinne de Bacus.' " In *Humanism in France at the End of the Middle Ages and in the Early Renaissance*, edited by A. H. T. Levi. Manchester: Manchester University Press, 1970, pp. 249–70.

———. ed. *Ronsard the Poet*. London: Methuen, 1973.

L'Esprit Créateur 10, no. 2 (1970). Special Ronsard issue.

L'Esprit Créateur 12, no. 3 (1972). Special Ronsard issue.

Humiston, Christon C. *A Comparative Study of the Metrical Technique of Ronsard and Malherbe*. Berkeley: University of California Press, 1941.

Langer, Ullrich. "Gunpowder as Transgressive Invention in Ronsard." In *Literary Theory/Renaissance Texts*, edited by Patricia Parker and David Quint. Baltimore: The Johns Hopkins University Press, 1986.

Lapp, John C. "The Potter and His Clay: Mythological Imagery in Ronsard." *Yale French Studies* no. 38 (1967): 89–108.

Ortali, Ray. "Ronsard: From *Chevelure* to *Rond parfait*." *Yale French Studies* no. 47 (1972): 90–97.

Stone, D. *Ronsard's Sonnet Cycles: A Study in Tone and Vision*. New Haven: Yale University Press, 1966.

Wilson, D. *Ronsard, Poet of Nature*. Manchester: Manchester University Press, 1961.

JEAN DE LA FONTAINE

Biard, J. D. *The Style of La Fontaine in His Fables*. Oxford: Basil Blackwell, 1967.

Chambers, Ross. "Narrative in Opposition: Reflections on a La Fontaine Fable." *French Forum* 8 (1983): 216–31.

Danner, Richard. "La Fontaine's *Fables*, Book X: The Labyrinth Hypothesis." *L'Esprit Créateur* 21, no. 4 (Winter 1981): 90–98.

———. *Patterns of Irony in the Fables of La Fontaine*. Athens: Ohio University Press, 1984.

DeJean, Joan. "La Fontaine's *Psyché*: The Reflecting Pool of Classicism." *L'Esprit Créateur* 21, no. 4 (Winter 1981): 99–109.

Gross, Nathan. "Strategy and Meaning in La Fontaine's 'Adonis.' " *MLN* 84 (1969): 605–26.

Guiton, Margaret. *La Fontaine: Poet and Counterpoet*. New Brunswick, N.J.: Rutgers University Press, 1961.

Lapp, John. *The Esthetics of Negligence*. Cambridge: Cambridge University Press, 1971.

———. "Ronsard and La Fontaine: Two Versions of 'Adonis.' " *L'Esprit Créateur* 10 (1970): 125–44.

Nancy, Jean-Luc. "*Mundus est Fabula*." *MLN* 93 (1978): 635–53.

Nicolich, Robert N. "The Triumph of Language: The Sister Arts and Creative Activity in La Fontaine's *Songe de vaux*." *L'Esprit Créateur* 21, no. 4 (Winter 1981): 10–21.

Ridgely, Beverly S. " 'Disciple de Lucrèce une seconde fois': A Study of La Fontaine's *Poème du Quinquina*." *L'Esprit Créateur* 11, no. 2 (Summer 1971): 92–122.

Tiefenbrun, Susan. "The Art and Artistry of Teaching in the Fables of La Fontaine." *L'Esprit Créateur* 21, no. 4 (Winter 1981): 50–65.

Vincent, Michael. "Naming Names in La Fontaine's 'Le Chat, La Belette et le petit Lapin.' " *Romanic Review* 73 (1982): 292–302.

Wadsworth, Philip A. "Ovid and La Fontaine." *Yale French Studies* no. 38 (1967): 151–55.

ALPHONSE DE LAMARTINE

Araujo, Norman. *In Search of Eden: Lamartine's Symbols of Despair and Deliverance*. Brookline, Mass.: Classical Folia Editions, 1976.

Birkett, Mary Ellen. *Lamartine and the Poetics of Landscape*. Lexington, Ky.: French Forum Publishers, 1982.

Fortescue, William. *Alphonse de Lamartine: A Political Biography*. New York: St. Martin's Press, 1983.

George, Albert J. *Lamartine and Romantic Unanimism.* New York: Columbia University Press, 1940.

Godfrey, Sima. "Foules Rush in . . . Lamartine, Baudelaire and the Crowd." *Romance Notes* 24 (1983): 33–42.

Hamlet-Metz, Mario. *La Critique littéraire de Lamartine.* The Hague: Mouton, 1974.

Iknayan, Marguerite. "*La Chute d'un ange:* Heaven and Hell on Earth." *Nineteenth-Century French Studies* 13 (1985): 191–99.

Ireson, J. C. *Lamartine: A Revaluation.* Hull, Yorkshire: University of Hull, 1969.

Lombard, Charles M. *Lamartine.* New York: Twayne, 1973.

Main, Alexander. "Liszt after Lamartine: *Les Préludes.*" *Modern Languages* 60 (1979): 133–48.

Tosca, Maurice. *Lamartine ou l'amour de la vie.* Paris: Albin Michel, 1983.

ALFRED DE VIGNY

Doolittle, James. *Alfred de Vigny.* New York: Twayne, 1967.

Fabry, Anne Srabian de. *Vigny, le rayon intérieur ou, la permanence de* Stello. Paris: La Pensée Universelle, 1978.

Houston, John Porter. "Vigny's Demonic World." In *The Demonic Imagination: Style and Theme in French Romantic Poetry.* Baton Rouge: Louisiana State University Press, 1969, pp. 70–84.

Jarry, André. "Les Lieux de l'écriture chez Alfred de Vigny: Etude de quelques manuscrits." *Littérature* 52 (December 1983): 81–111.

Majewski, Henry F. "Alfred de Vigny and the Poetic Experience: From Alienation to Renascence." *Romanic Review* 67 (1976): 268–89.

McGoldrick, J. M. "Vigny's Unorthodox Christ." *MLN* 85 (1970): 510–14.

Porter, Lawrence M. *The Renaissance of the Lyric in French Romanticism: Elegy, "Poème", and Ode.* Lexington, Ky.: French Forum, 1978.

Saint-Géraud, Jacques P. *Les Destinées d'un style: Essai sur les poèmes philosophiques de Vigny.* Paris: Minard, 1979.

Smith, Albert B. "Vigny's 'Le Cor': The Tragedy of Service." *Studies in Romanticism* 7 (1968): 159–65.

VICTOR HUGO

Ahearn, Edward J. "Confrontation with the City: Social Criticism, Apocalypse and the Reader's Responsibility in City Poems by Blake, Hugo and Baudelaire." *University of Hartford Studies in Literature* 10 (1982): 1–22.

Bloom, Harold, ed. *Modern Critical Views: Victor Hugo.* New Haven: Chelsea House, 1988.

Brody, Jules. " 'Let There Be Night': Intertextuality in a Poem of Victor Hugo." *Romanic Review* 75 (1984): 216–29.

Brombert, Victor. "*Les Travailleurs de la mer:* Hugo's Poem of Effacement." *New Literary History* 9 (1978): 581–90.

———. "Sartre, Hugo, a Grandfather." *Yale French Studies* no. 68 (1985): 73–81.

de Man, Paul. "Hypogram and Inscription." In *The Resistance to Theory.* Minneapolis: University of Minnesota Press, 1986, pp. 27–53.

Denommé, Robert T. "The Palimpsest of the Poet's Remembrance in Hugo's 'Tristesse d'Olympio.' " *Kentucky Romance Quarterly* 29 (1982): 15–24.

L'Esprit Créateur 16, no. 3 (1976). Special Hugo issue.

Greenberg, Wendy. "Structure and Function of Hugo's Condensed Metaphor." *French Review* 56 (1982): 257–66.

————. *The Power of Rhetoric: Hugo's Metaphor and Poetics.* New York: Lang, 1985.

————. "Symbolization and Metonymic Chains in Hugo." *Nineteenth-Century French Studies* 13 (1985): 224–37.

Houston, John Porter. "Design in *Les Contemplations.*" *French Forum* 5 (1980): 122–40.

————. *Victor Hugo.* New York: Twayne, 1974.

Mitchell, Robert L. "Poetry of Religion to Religion of Poetry: Hugo, Mallarmé, and the Problematics of 'Preservation.' " *French Review* 55 (1982): 478–88.

Nash, Suzanne. Les Contemplations *of Victor Hugo: An Allegory of the Creative Process.* Princeton: Princeton University Press, 1976.

Patty, James S. "Hugo's Miniature Pyramid ('Lettre,' *Les Contemplations,* II, VI)." *Romance Notes* 26 (1985): 27–30.

Peyre, Henri. *Victor Hugo: Philosophy and Poetry.* Translated by Roda P. Roberts. University: University of Alabama Press, 1980.

Poulet, Georges. "Hugo." In *The Interior Distance.* Translated by Elliott Coleman. Baltimore: Johns Hopkins University Press, 1959, pp. 153–81.

Riffaterre, Michael. *Text Production.* New York: Columbia University Press, 1979.

Sabin, Margery. "Victor Hugo and the Wordsworthian Perception." In *English Romanticism and the French Tradition.* Cambridge, Mass.: Harvard University Press, 1976.

Ward, Patricia. *The Medievalism of Victor Hugo.* University Park: Pennsylvania State University Press, 1975.

ALOYSIUS BERTRAND

Beaujour, Michel. "Some Paradoxes of Description." *Yale French Studies* no. 61 (1981): 27–59.

Goldsmith, H. H. "Art and Artifact: Pictorialization in *Gaspard de la nuit.*" *French Review* 44 (1971): 129–39.

Hubert, Renée R. "The Cult of the Visible in *Gaspard de la nuit.*" *Modern Language Quarterly* 25 (1964): 76–85.

Riffaterre, Hermine. "Reading Constants." In *The Prose Poem in France: Theory and Practice,* edited by Mary Ann Caws and Hermine Riffaterre. New York: Columbia University Press, 1983.

Slott, Kathryn. "Le Texte e(s)t son double: *Gaspard de la nuit.*" *French Forum* 6 (1981): 28–35.

————. "Bertrand's *Gaspard de la nuit:* The French Prose Poem as a Parody of Romantic Conventions." *Francofonia* 5 (Spring 1985): 69–92.

GÉRARD DE NERVAL

Blackman, Maurice. "Byron and the First Poems of Gérard de Nerval: Psychocriticism and 'Literary Influence.' " *Nineteenth-Century French Studies* 15 (1986–87): 94–107.

Dragonetti, Roger. "Portes d'ivoire ou de corne dans *Aurélia* de Gérard de Nerval, tradition et modernité." In *Mélanges offerts à Rita Lejeune.* Gembleaux: J. Duculot, 1969.

DuBruck, Alfred. *Gérard de Nerval and the German Heritage.* The Hague: Mouton, 1965.

Felman, Shoshana. "Gérard de Nerval: Folie du lyrisme." In *La Folie et la chose littéraire.* Paris: Editions du Seuil, 1978.

Houston, John Porter. "Nerval and *Les Chimères.*" In *The Demonic Imagination: Style and Theme in French Romantic Poetry.* Baton Rouge: Louisiana State University Press, 1969, pp. 125–39.

Knapp, Bettina. *Gérard de Nerval: The Mystic's Dilemma.* University: University of Alabama Press, 1980.

Kofman, Sarah. *Nerval, le charme de la répétition.* Lausanne: Editions de l'Age d'Homme, 1979.

Poulet, Georges. "*Sylvie* ou la pensée de Nerval." In *Trois Essais de mythologie romantique.* Paris: Corti, 1966.

Richer, Jean. *Gérard de Nerval et les doctrines ésotériques.* Neuchâtel: Griffon d'Or, 1947.

Sieburth, Richard. "Nerval's *Lorely,* or the Lure of Origin." *Studies in Romanticism* 22 (1983): 199–239.

Tristsmans, Bruno. "Nerval et l'indétermination textuelle." *Poétique* 60 (1984): 423–36.

ALFRED DE MUSSET

Affron, Charles. *A Stage for Poets: Studies in the Theatre of Hugo and Musset.* Princeton: Princeton University Press, 1971.

Bishop, Lloyd. "Musset's First Sonnet: A Semiotic Analysis." *Romanic Review* 74 (1983): 455–60.

———. Musset's 'Souvenir' and the Greater Romantic Lyric." *Nineteenth-Century French Studies* 12/13, nos. 4/1 (Summer–Fall 1984): 119–30.

King, Russel. "Indecision in Musset's *Contes d'Espagne et d'Italie.*" *Nottingham French Studies* 8, no. 2 (October 1969): 57–68.

———. "Musset: The Poet of Dionysus." *Studies in Romanticism* 13 (1974): 323–32.

Odoul, Pierre. *Le Drame intime d'Alfred de Musset: Etude psychanalytique de l'oeuvre et de la vie.* Paris: Presses Universitaires de France, 1976.

Padgett, Graham. "Bad Faith in Alfred de Musset: A Problem of Interpretation." *Dalhousie French Studies* 3 (October 1981): 65–82.

Rees, Margaret A. *Alfred de Musset.* New York: Twayne, 1971.

Siegel, Patricia J. *Alfred de Musset: A Reference Guide.* Boston: Hall, 1982.

Zielonka, Anthony. "Images of the Poet in Musset's *Le Poète déchu.*" *Nineteenth-Century French Studies* 15, nos. 1/2 (Fall–Winter 1986–87): 87–93.

THÉOPHILE GAUTIER

Dillingham, Louise B. *The Creative Imagination of Théophile Gautier: A Study in Literary Psychology.* Princeton: Princeton University Press, 1927.

Du Camp, Maxime. *Théophile Gautier.* Translated by J. E. Gordon. London: T. Fisher Unwin, 1893.

Gould, Cecil H. M. *Delaroche and Gautier: Gautier's Views on the Execution of Lady Jane Grey and on Other Compositions by Delaroche.* London: National Gallery, 1975.

Grant, Richard B. *Théophile Gautier.* New York: Twayne, 1975.

Killick, Rachel. "Gautier and the Sonnet." *Essays in French Literature* 16 (November 1979): 1–16.

Palache, John G. *Gautier and the Romantics.* New York: Viking, 1926.

Richardson, Joanna. *Théophile Gautier: His Life and Times.* London: M. Reinhardt, 1958.

Richer, Jean. *Etudes et recherches sur Théophile Gautier prosateur.* Paris: Nizet, 1981.

Savalle, Joseph. *Travestis, métamorphoses, dédoublements: Essai sur l'oeuvre romanesque de Théophile Gautier.* Paris: Librairie Minard, 1981.

Smith, Albert B. *Ideal and Reality in the Fictional Narratives of Théophile Gautier.* Gainesville: University of Florida Press, 1969.

————. *Théophile Gautier and the Fantastic.* University, Miss.: Romance Monographs, 1977.

Spencer, Michael C. *The Art Criticism of Théophile Gautier.* Geneva: Droz, 1969.

Tennant, Philip E. *Théophile Gautier.* London: Athlone Press, 1975.

Voisin, Marcel. *Le Soleil et la nuit: L'Imaginaire dans l'oeuvre de Théophile Gautier.* Bruxelles: Editions de l'Université de Bruxelles, 1981.

CHARLES BAUDELAIRE

Auerbach, Erich. "The Aesthetic Dignity of the *Fleurs du mal*." In *Scenes from the Drama of European Literature.* Minneapolis: University of Minnesota Press, 1984, pp. 201–26.

Bataille, Georges. "Baudelaire." In *Literature and Evil.* Translated by Alistair Hamilton. London: Calder & Boyers, 1973.

Benjamin, Walter. *Charles Baudelaire: A Lyric Poet in the Era of High Capitalism.* Translated by Harry Zohn. London: New Left Books, 1973.

————. "Central Park." Translated by Lloyd Spencer. *New German Critique* 34 (Winter 1985): 32–58.

Bersani, Leo. *Baudelaire and Freud.* Berkeley: University of California Press, 1977.

Bloom, Harold, ed. *Modern Critical Views: Charles Baudelaire.* New Haven: Chelsea House, 1987.

Brombert, Victor. "The Will to Ecstasy: The Example of Baudelaire's 'La Chevalure.' " *Yale French Studies* no. 50 (1974): 55–63.

Chase, Cynthia. "Paragon, Parergon: Baudelaire Translates Rousseau." *Diacritics* 11, no. 2 (Summer 1981): 42–51.

————. "Getting Versed: Reading Hegel with Baudelaire." *Studies in Romanticism* 22 (1983): 241–66.

Eliot, T. S. "Baudelaire." In *Selected Essays.* Rev. ed. New York: Harcourt, Brace, 1950.

L'Esprit Créateur 13, no. 2 (1973). Special Baudelaire issue.

Jakobson, Roman S., and Claude Lévi-Strauss. "Charles Baudelaire's 'Les Chats.' " In *The Structuralists*, edited by Richard and Fernande De George. Garden City, N.Y.: Doubleday, 1972.

Jauss, Hans Robert. "The Poetic Text within the Change of Horizons of Reading: The Example of Baudelaire's 'Spleen.' " In *Toward an Aesthetic of Reception.* Minneapolis: University of Minnesota Press, 1982.

Johnson, Barbara. "Poetry and Its Double: Two 'Invitations au voyage.' " In *The Critical Difference.* Baltimore: Johns Hopkins University Press, 1980, pp. 23–51.

Klein, Richard. " 'Bénédiction'/'Perte d'Auréole': Parable of Interpretation." *MLN* 85 (1970): 515–28.

Poulet, Georges. "Baudelaire." In *Exploding Poetry: Baudelaire/Rimbaud.* Translated by Françoise Melzer. Chicago: University of Chicago Press, 1984, pp. 1–72.

Reed, Arden. "Abysmal Influence: Baudelaire, Coleridge, De Quincey, Piranesi, Wordsworth." *Glyph* 4 (1978): 189–206.

————. "Baudelaire's 'La Pipe': 'De la vaporisation du *Moi*.' " *Romanic Review* 72 (1981): 274–84.

Riffaterre, Michael. "Describing Poetic Structures: Two Approaches to Baudelaire's 'Les Chats.' " In *Structuralism*, edited by Jacques Ehrmann. Garden City, N.Y.: Doubleday, 1970, pp. 188–230.

Sartre, Jean-Paul. *Baudelaire.* Translated by Martin Turnell. New York: New Directions, 1950.

Stamelman, Richard. "The Shroud of Allegory: Death, Mourning, and Melancholy in Baudelaire's Work." *Texas Studies in Literature and Language* 25 (1983): 390–409.

Swain, Virginia E. "The Legitimation Crisis: Event and Meaning in Baudelaire's 'Le Vieux Saltimbanque' and 'Une Mort héroique.' " *Romanic Review* 73 (1982): 452–62.

Welch, Cyril and Liliane. *Emergence: Baudelaire, Mallarmé, and Rimbaud.* State College, Pa.: Bald Eagle Press, 1973.

Wohlfarth, Irving. " 'Perte d'Auréole': The Emergence of the Dandy." *MLN* 85 (1970): 529–71.

STÉPHANE MALLARMÉ

Austin, Lloyd J. "Mallarmé and Gautier: New Light on 'Toast Funèbre.' " In *Balzac and the Nineteenth Century,* edited by D. G. Charlton, J. Gaudon, and A. R. Pugh. Leicester: Leicester University Press, 1972.

Bersani, Leo. *The Death of Stéphane Mallarmé.* Cambridge: Cambridge University Press, 1982.

Blanchot, Maurice. *The Space of Literature.* Translated by Ann Smock. Lincoln: University of Nebraska Press, 1982.

Bloom, Harold, ed. *Modern Critical Views: Mallarmé.* New Haven: Chelsea House, 1987.

Chambers, Ross. "An Address in the Country: Mallarmé and the Kinds of Literary Contest." *French Forum* 11 (1986): 199–216.

Cohn, Robert Greer. *Toward the Poems of Mallarmé.* Berkeley: University of California Press, 1965.

de Man, Paul. "Criticism and Crisis" and "Lyric and Modernity." In *Blindness and Insight.* 2d ed. Minneapolis: University of Minnesota Press, 1983.

Derrida, Jacques. "The Double Session." In *Dissemination.* Translated by Barbara Johnson. Chicago: University of Chicago Press, 1981.

Fowlie, Wallace. *Mallarmé.* Chicago: University of Chicago Press, 1953.

Isaacs, Bonnie J. " 'Du fond d'un naufrage': Notes on Michel Serres and Mallarmé's *Un Coup de dés.*" *MLN* 96 (1981): 824–38.

Johnson, Barbara. *The Critical Difference.* Baltimore: Johns Hopkins University Press, 1980.

Kristeva, Julia. *Revolution in Poetic Language.* Translated by Margaret Waller. New York: Columbia University Press, 1984.

Poulet, Georges. "Mallarmé." In *The Interior Distance.* Translated by Elliott Coleman. Baltimore: Johns Hopkins University Press, 1959.

Richard, Jean-Pierre. *L'Univers imaginaire de Mallarmé.* Paris: Editions du Seuil, 1961.

Yale French Studies no. 54 (1977). Special Mallarmé issue.

PAUL VERLAINE

Carter, Alfred E. *Verlaine: A Study in Parallels.* Toronto: University of Toronto Press, 1969.

———. *Paul Verlaine.* New York: Twayne, 1971.

Chadwick, Charles. *Verlaine.* London: Athlone Press, 1973.

Erasmo, Leiva-Merikakis. "Verlaine in German: Translation as Fulfillment." *Romance Notes* 23 (1982–83): 10–16.

Houston, John Porter. "Rimbaud, Mysticism, and Verlaine's Poetry of 1873–74." *L'Esprit Créateur* 9 (1969): 19–27.

Monkiewicz, Bronislawa. *Verlaine critique littéraire*. Geneva: Slatkine, 1983.

Porter, Laurence M. "Text versus Music in the French Art Song: Debussy, Fauré, and Verlaine's 'Mandoline.' " *Nineteenth-Century French Studies* 12, nos. 1/2 (Fall/Winter 1983–84): 138–44.

Ruwet, Nicolas. "Typography, Rhymes and Linguistic Structures in Poetry." In *The Sign in Music and Literature*, edited by Wendy Steiner. Austin: University of Texas Press, 1981.

Stephan, Philip. *Paul Verlaine and the Decadents 1882–1890*. Manchester: University of Manchester Press, 1974.

Storey, Robert. "Verlaine's Pierrots." *Romance Notes* 20 (1979–80): 223–30.

Thody, Philip. "The Analysis of Poetry: A Barthesian Approach." *Essays in French Literature* 20 (November 1983): 95–107.

TRISTAN CORBIÈRE

Dansel, Michel. *Langage et modernité chez Tristan Corbière*. Paris: Nizet, 1974.

Lindsay, Marshall. *Le Temps jaune: Essais sur Tristan Corbière*. Berkeley: University of California Press, 1972.

Macfarlane, Keith H. *Tristan Corbière dans* Les Amours jaunes. Paris: Minard, 1974.

Mitchell, Robert L. "The Muted Fiddle: Tristan Corbière's 'I Sonnet' as *Ars (Im)poetica*." *French Review* 50 (1976): 35–45.

———. *Corbière, Mallarmé, Valéry: Preservations and Commentary*. Saratoga, Calif.: Anma Libri, 1981.

———. *Tristan Corbière*. Boston: Twayne, 1979.

La Nouvelle Tour de Feu 11, 12, and 13 (Spring–Autumn 1985). Special Corbière issue.

Sonnenfeld, Albert. *L'Oeuvre poétique de Tristan Corbière*. Princeton: Princeton University Press, 1960.

———. "Tristan Corbière: The Beautific Malediction." *L'Esprit Créateur* 9 (1969): 37–45.

Warner, Val. Introduction to *The Centenary Corbière*. Chatham: Carcanet New Press, 1975.

COMTE DE LAUTRÉAMONT

Balakian, Anna. "Lautréamont's Battle with God." In *Surrealism: The Road to the Absolute*. London: Allen & Unwin, 1972, pp. 50–66.

Bersani, Leo. "Desire and Metamorphosis." In *A Future for Astyanax: Character and Desire in Literature*. New York: Columbia University Press, 1984.

Blanchot, Maurice. *Lautréamont et Sade*. Paris: Editions de Minuit, 1963.

Bouché, Claude. *Lautréamont: Du lieu commun à la parodie*. Paris: Larousse, 1974.

Derrida, Jacques. "Outwork." In *Dissemination*. Translated by B. Johnson. Chicago: University of Chicago Press, 1981.

Kristeva, Julia. *Revolution in Poetic Language*. Translated by Margaret Waller. New York: Columbia University Press, 1984.

Lawler, Patricia M. "Lautréamont, Modernism, and the Function of Mise en Abyme." *French Review* 58 (1985): 827–34.

———. "Lautréamont's Outrageous Text: Language as Weapon and Victim in the *Chants de Maldoror*." *Chimères* 17 (1984): 3–13.

Lydenberg, Robin. "Metaphor and Metamorphosis in *Les Chants de Maldoror.*" *L'Esprit Créateur* 18, no. 4 (Winter 1978): 3–14.

Ponge, Francis. "Adaptez à vos bibliothèques le dispositif *Maldoror-Poésies.*" *Cahiers du Sud* 275 (August 1946).

Riffaterre, Michael. "Generating Lautréamont's Text." In *Textual Strategies: Perspectives in Post-Structuralist Criticism*, edited by Josué Harari. Ithaca: Cornell University Press, 1979.

Rochon, Lucienne. *Quatre Lectures de Lautréamont.* Paris: Nizet, 1972.

Sollers, Philippe. "Lautréamont's Science." In *Writing and the Experience of Limits*, edited by David Hayman. New York: Columbia University Press, 1983.

Sussman, Henry. "The Anterior Tail: The Code of *Les Chants de Maldoror.*" *MLN* 89 (1974): 957–77.

ARTHUR RIMBAUD

Ahearn, Edward J. *Rimbaud: Visions and Habitations.* Berkeley: University of California Press, 1983.

Bloom, Harold, ed. *Modern Critical Views: Arthur Rimbaud.* New Haven: Chelsea House, 1988.

Bonnefoy, Yves. *Rimbaud par lui-même.* Paris: Editions du Seuil, 1961.

Chisholm, A. R. *The Art of Arthur Rimbaud.* Melbourne: Melbourne University Press, 1930.

Cohn, Robert Greer. *The Poetry of Rimbaud.* Princeton: Princeton University Press, 1973.

Etiemble, René. *Le Mythe de Rimbaud.* Paris: Gallimard, 1952–68. 4 vols.

Felman, Shoshana. "Arthur Rimbaud: Folie et modernité." In *La Folie et la chose littéraire.* Paris: Editions du Seuil, 1978, pp. 97–120.

Fowlie, Wallace. *Rimbaud.* Chicago: University of Chicago Press, 1965.

Frohock, Wilbur M. *Rimbaud's Poetic Practice: Image and Theme in the Major Poems.* Cambridge, Mass.: Harvard University Press, 1963.

Hackett, Cecil Arthur. *Rimbaud: A Critical Introduction.* Cambridge: Cambridge University Press, 1981.

Houston, John Porter. *The Design of Rimbaud's Poetry.* New Haven: Yale University Press, 1963.

Miller, Henry. *Time of the Assassins: A Study of Rimbaud.* With an introduction by Anthony Burgess. New York: Quartet Books, 1984.

Morrissette, Bruce. *The Great Rimbaud Forgery: The Affair of* La Chasse spirituelle. St. Louis: Washington University Studies, 1956.

Peschel, Enid Rhodes. *Flux and Reflux: Ambivalence in the Poems of Arthur Rimbaud.* Geneva: Droz, 1977.

Poulet, Georges. "Rimbaud." In *Exploding Poetry: Baudelaire/Rimbaud.* translated by Françoise Meltzer. Chicago: University of Chicago Press, 1984, pp. 73–141.

Starkie, Enid. *Arthur Rimbaud.* New York: New Directions, 1962.

Wing, Nathaniel. *Present Appearances: Aspects of Poetic Structure in Rimbaud's Illuminations.* University, Miss.: Romance Monographs, 1974.

JULES LAFORGUE

Arkell, David. *Looking for Laforgue: An Informal Biography.* New York: Persea Books, 1979.

Benamon, Michel. "Laforgue and Wallace Stevens." *Romanic Review* 50 (1959): 107–17.

Champigny, Robert. "Situation of Jules Laforgue." *Yale French Studies* no. 9 (1952): 63–73.

Collie, Michael. *Laforgue*. Edinburgh: Oliver & Boyd, 1963.

Eliot, T. S. "The Metaphysical Poets." In *Homage to John Dryden*. London: Hogarth Press, 1924. Reprinted in *Selected Essays*. Harcourt, Brace, 1950.

———. "Talk on Dante." *Adelphi* 27 (1951): 106–14.

Franklin, Ursula. "Laforgue and His Philosophers: The 'Paratext' in the Intertextual Maze." *Nineteenth-Century French Sudies* 14 (1986): 324–40.

Hannoosh, Michele. "The Early Laforgue: "*Tessa*." *French Forum* 8 (1983): 20–32.

Pound, Ezra. "Irony, Laforgue and Some Satire." *Poetry* 11 (November 1917): 93–98. Reprinted in *Literary Essays of Ezra Pound*. Norfolk, Conn.: New Directions, 1954.

———. "A Study of French Modern Poets." *Little Review* 4, no. 10 (February 1918): 3–61.

Ramsay, Warren. *Jules Laforgue and the Ironic Inheritance*. New York: Oxford University Press, 1953.

———, ed. *Jules Laforgue: Essays on a Poet's Life and Work*. Carbondale: Southern Illinois University Press, 1969.

Soldo, John J. "T. S. Eliot and Jules Laforgue." *American Literature* 52, (1983): 137–50.

Temple, Ruth Z. "Eliot: An English Symbolist?" In *The Symbolist Movement in the Literature of European Languages*, edited by Anna Balakian. Budapest: Akadémia Kiadó, 1982.

GUILLAUME APOLLINAIRE

Balakian, Anna. "Apollinaire and the Modern Mind." *Yale French Studies* 2 (1949): 79–90.

———. "Apollinaire and l'Esprit nouveau." In *Surrealism: The Road to the Absolute*. London: Allen & Unwin, 1972, pp. 80–99.

———. Breton in the Light of Apollinaire." In *About French Poetry from Dada to Tel Quel: Text and Theory*, edited by Mary Ann Caws. Detroit: Wayne State University Press, 1974.

Bohn, Willard. "Apollinaire's Reign in Spain." *Symposium* 35 (1981): 186–214.

———. "Metaphor and Metonymy in Apollinaire's *Calligrams*." *Romanic Review* 72 (1981): 166–81.

Breunig, LeRoy C. "The Laughter of Apollinaire." *Yale French Studies* no. 31 (1964): 66–73.

———. "From Dada to Cubism: Apollinaire's 'Arbre.' " In *About French Poetry from Dada to Tel Quel: Text and Theory*, edited by Mary Ann Caws. Detroit: Wayne State University Press, 1974.

Butor, Michel. "Monument of Nothing for Apollinaire." Translated by Richard Howard. *TriQuarterly* 4 (Summer 1965): 23–40.

Davis, Margaret. "Merveilles de la guerrre: The Evolution of Apollinaire's 'Idéogrammes lyriques.' " In *Mélanges de littérature française moderne offerts à Garnet Rees par ses collègues et amis*, edited by Cedric E. Pickford. Paris: Minard, 1980.

Edson, Laurie. "A New Aesthetic: Apollinaire's 'Les Fiançailles' and Picasso's 'Les Demoiselles d'Avignon.' " *Symposium* 36 (1982): 115–28.

L'Esprit Créateur 10, no. 4 (Winter 1970). Special Apollinaire issue.

Essays in French Literature 17 (November 1980). Special Apollinaire issue.

Forsyth, Louise Barton. "Apollinaire's Use of Arthurian Legend." *L'Esprit Créateur* 12 (1972): 26–36.

Fowlie, Wallace. "Apollinaire the Poet." In *Age of Surrealism*. Bloomington: University of Indiana Press, 1963.

Jauss, Hans Robert. "Group Interpretation of Apollinaire's 'Arbre.' " In *New Perspectives in German Literary Criticism*, edited by Richard E. Amacher and Victor Lange. Princeton: Princeton University Press, 1979.

Shattuck, Roger. "Apollinaire, Hero-Poet." In *Selected Writings of Guillaume Apollinaire*. New York: New Directions, 1950.

————. "Guillaume Apollinaire: The Impressario of the Avant-garde" and "Guillaume Apollinaire: Painter-Poet." In *The Banquet Years*. New York: Harcourt, Brace, 1955.

Steegmuller, Francis. *Apollinaire: Poet among Painters*. New York: Farrar, Straus & Giroux, 1963.

Truhn, J. Patrick. "The Wave of Wine: Revolution and Revelation in Apollinaire's 'Vendémaire.' " *Romanic Review* 72 (1981): 39–55.

Turnell, Martin. "The Poetry of Guillaume Apollinaire." *Southern Review* 5 (1969): 957–75.

Acknowledgments

"François Villon, the Misfit" by Jefferson Humphries from *The Otherness Within: Gnostic Readings in Marcel Proust, Flannery O'Connor, and François Villon* by Jefferson Humphries, © 1983 by Louisiana State University Press. Reprinted by permission of Louisiana State University Press.

"Marguerite de Navarre: The Rhetoric of Tears" (originally entitled "The Rhetoric of Tears") by Robert D. Cottrell from *The Grammar of Silence: A Reading of Marguerite de Navarre's Poetry* by Robert D. Cottrell, © 1986 by the Catholic University of America Press. Reprinted by permission of the publisher.

"Writing and Drawing in Scève's *Délie*" by Elisabeth Guild from *Paragraph* 6 (October 1985), © 1985 by the Modern Critical Theory Group. Reprinted by permission of Oxford University Press.

"Louise Labé and Pernette du Guillet: Assimilation with a Difference: Renaissance Women Poets and Literary Influence" (originally entitled "Assimilation with a Difference: Renaissance Women Poets and Literary Influence") by Ann Rosalind Jones from *Yale French Studies* no. 62 (1981), © 1981 by *Yale French Studies*. Reprinted by permission.

"Du Bellay's Emblematic Vision of Rome" by Daniel Russell from *Yale French Studies* no. 47 (1972), © 1972 by *Yale French Studies*. Reprinted by permission.

"Ronsard as Apollo: Myth, Poetry and Experience in a Renaissance Sonnet-Cycle" by Terence C. Cave from *Yale French Studies* no. 47 (1972), © 1972 by *Yale French Studies*. Reprinted by permission.

"Histoire d'oeuf: Secrets and Secrecy in a La Fontaine Fable" by Ross Cham-

467

bers from *Sub-Stance* 32 (1981), © 1981 by *Sub-Stance*. Reprinted by permission of the University of Wisconsin Press.

"Lamartine" by Georges Poulet from *The Metamorphoses of the Circle*, translated by Carley Dawson and Elliott Coleman in collaboration with the author, © 1966 by The Johns Hopkins University Press, Baltimore/London. Reprinted by permission of The Johns Hopkins University Press.

"Alfred de Vigny: Mirror Images in 'La Maison du berger' " (originally entitled "Mirror Images in 'La Maison du berger' ") by Martha Noel Evans from *The French Review* 56, no. 3 (February 1983), © 1983 by the American Association of Teachers of French. Reprinted by permission.

"Babelic Ruin, Babelic 'Ebauche': An Introduction to a Hugolian Problematic" by Joan C. Kessler from *Stanford French Review* 7, no. 3 (Winter 1983), © 1983 by ANMA Libri & Co. Reprinted by permission of ANMA Libri & Co.

"Victor Hugo: From Spectacle to Symbol" by Margery Sabin from *English Romanticism and the French Tradition* by Margery Sabin, © 1976 by the President and Fellows of Harvard College. Reprinted by permission of Harvard University Press.

"Aloysius Bertrand: *Gaspard de la nuit*: Prefacing Genre" (originally *Gaspard de la nuit*: Prefacing Genre") by Richard Sieburth from *Studies in Romanticism* 24, no. 2 (Summer 1985), © 1985 by the Trustees of Boston University. Reprinted by permission of the Trustees of Boston University.

"Gérard de Nerval: Writing Living, or Madness as Autobiography" by Shoshana Felman from *Writing and Madness* (*Literature/Philosophy/Psychoanalysis*), translated by Martha Noel Evans and the author with the assistance of Brian Massumi, © 1985 by Cornell University Press. Reprinted by permission of the publisher, Cornell University Press.

"The Mixture of Genres, the Mixture of Styles, and Figural Interpretion: *Sylvie*, by Gérard de Nerval" by Rodolphe Gasché from *Glyph: Textual Studies* 7 (1980), © 1980 by The Johns Hopkins University Press, Baltimore/London. Reprinted by permission of The Johns Hopkins University Press.

"Musset" by Georges Poulet from *The Interior Distance*, translated by Elliott Coleman, © 1959 by The Johns Hopkins University Press, Baltimore/London. Reprinted by permission of The Johns Hopkins University Press.

"Théophile Gautier: Art and the Artist" (originally entitled "Art and the Artist") by Albert B. Smith from *Théophile Gautier and the Fantastic* by

Albert B. Smith, © 1977 by Romance Monographs, Inc. Reprinted by permission.

"Baudelaire: Anthropomorphism and Trope in the Lyric" (originally entitled "Anthropomorphism and Trope in the Lyric") by Paul de Man from *The Rhetoric of Romanticism* by Paul de Man, © 1984 by Columbia University Press. Reprinted by permission of Columbia University Press. The passages from Baudelaire are from *Les Fleurs du mal* by Charles Baudelaire, translated by Richard Howard, and published in 1981 by David R. Godine, Inc., Boston. Reprinted by permission.

"Baudelaire as Modernist and Postmodernist: The Dissolution of the Referent and the Artificial 'Sublime' " by Fredric Jameson from *Lyric Poetry: Beyond New Criticism*, edited by Chaviva Hosek and Patricia Parker, © 1985 by Cornell University Press. Reprinted by permission of Cornell University Press. The passages from Baudelaire are from *Les Fleurs du mal* by Charles Baudelaire, translated by Richard Howard, and published in 1981 by David R. Godine, Inc., Boston. Reprinted by permission.

"*Les Fleurs du mal armé*: Some Reflections on Intertextuality" by Barbara Johnson from *Lyric Poetry: Beyond New Criticism*, edited by Chaviva Hosek and Patricia Parker, © 1985 by Cornell University Press. Reprinted by permission of Cornell University Press.

"Reading as Explication: Mallarmé's 'Toast funébre' " by James Lawler from *Textual Analysis: Some Readers Reading*, edited by Mary Ann Caws, © 1986 by the Modern Language Association of America. Reprinted by permission of the Modern Language Association of America.

"Familiar and Unfamiliar: Verlaine's Poetic Diction" by Carol de Dobay Rifelj from *Kentucky Romance Quarterly* 29, no. 4 (1982), © 1982 by the University Press of Kentucky. Reprinted by permission.

"Corbière, Hélas!: A Case of *Antirayonnement*" by Robert L. Mitchell from *The French Review* 51, no. 3 (February 1978), © 1978 by *The French Review*. Reprinted by permission.

"Surviving Lautréamont: The Reader in *Les Chants de Maldoror*" by Robin Lydenberg from *L'Esprit Créateur* 17, no. 3 (Fall 1977), © 1977 by *L'Esprit Créateur*. Reprinted by permission.

"Poetic Doctrine in Three of Rimbaud's Verse Poems" by Marshall Lindsay from *Orbis Litterarum* 38 (1983), © 1983 by Munksgaard International Publishers Ltd. Reprinted by permission.

"Lettre 1: The Subject Questioned" by Karin J. Dillman from *The Subject in Rimbaud: From Self to 'Je'* by Karin J. Dillman, © 1984 by Peter Lang Publishing Co. Reprinted by permission of Peter Lang Publishing Co.

"Jules Laforgue: The Ironic Equilibrium" (originally entitled "Ironic Equilibrium") by Warren Ramsey from *Jules Laforgue: Essays on a Poet's Life and Work,* edited by Warren Ramsey, © 1969 by Southern Illinois University Press. Reprinted by permission of Southern Illinois University Press.

"On Time and Poetry: A Reading of Apollinaire" by Dennis G. Sullivan from *MLN* (French Issue) 88, no. 4 (May 1973), © 1973 by The Johns Hopkins University Press, Baltimore/London. Reprinted by permission of The Johns Hopkins University Press.

Index